JULY 22
THE CIVIL WAR BATTLE OF ATLANTA

.

JULY 22

The Civil War Battle of Atlanta

EARL J. HESS

University Press of Kansas

Published by the University Press of Kansas (Lawrence, Kansas 66045), which was
organized by the Kansas Board of Regents and is operated and funded by Emporia
State University, Fort Hays State University, Kansas State University, Pittsburg State
University, the University of Kansas, and Wichita State University.

Library of Congress Cataloging-in-Publication Data

Names: Hess, Earl J., author.
Title: July 22 : the Civil War Battle of Atlanta / Earl J. Hess.
Other titles: Civil War Battle of Atlanta
Description: Lawrence, Kansas : University Press of Kansas, 2023. | Series:
    Modern war studies | Includes bibliographical references and index.
Identifiers: LCCN 2022043596 (print) | LCCN 2022043597 (ebook)
    ISBN 9780700633968 (cloth) | ISBN 9780700633975 (ebook)
    Subjects: LCSH: Atlanta, Battle of, Ga., 1864.
Classification: LCC E476.7 .H47 2023 (print) | LCC E476.7 (ebook) | DDC
    973.7/371—dc23/eng/20220909
LC record available at https://lccn.loc.gov/2022043596.
LC ebook record available at https://lccn.loc.gov/2022043597.

British Library Cataloguing-in-Publication Data is available.

Printed in the United States of America

10 9 8 7 6 5 4 3 2 1

The paper used in this publication is acid free and meets the minimum
requirements of the American National Standard for Permanence of Paper for
Printed Library Materials Z39.48–1992.

For Pratibha and Julie, with love

CONTENTS

MAPS AND ILLUSTRATIONS

In 1866, when Lurton Dunham Ingersoll wrote a book on the participation
of Iowa regiments in the Civil War, he pinpointed the engagement fought
on July 22, 1864, as a highlight of their service. "The battle of Atlanta was a
warfare of giants," he concluded.[1] Taken by surprise, the Iowans and their
comrades in the Union Army of the Tennessee fought their most desperate
battle since a similar surprise attack had struck them at Shiloh on April 6,
1862. In both cases, the surprise was accomplished by the main Confederate
army in the western theater, at Shiloh called the Army of the Mississippi but
later renamed the Army of Tennessee. On both days, the Federals fought
with dogged resistance that barely saved their position and their army.
Losses were heavy, Confederate hopes for victory were dashed, and the war
went on.

The Battle of Atlanta, also known as the Battle of July 22 (the only engagement of the Civil War widely referred to by the date of its occurrence),
was the largest and most prominent engagement of the four-month-long
campaign for control of Atlanta. It occurred soon after Gen. John Bell Hood
replaced Gen. Joseph E. Johnston as commander of the Army of Tennessee
in a controversial decision by Confederate president Jefferson Davis to infuse a more aggressive tone into the defense of the Gate City of the Deep
South. Beginning early in May, Johnston had conducted a series of defensive
battles combined with a readiness to retire from strong positions whenever
his flanks were threatened. When he fell back across the Chattahoochee
River and retired to the strong defenses of Atlanta, Davis had had enough
of his style of management. He chose Hood to replace Johnston precisely
because the young corps commander had convinced him he would attack
rather than fall back. The result was a series of three severe battles fought
around the periphery of Atlanta as Hood lashed out at the larger Union
army group that Maj. Gen. William T. Sherman had skillfully handled in its
long advance from northwest Georgia.

The Battle of Atlanta was the second engagement of this series, fought
just east of the city. It involved about 30,000 Confederates and 25,000 Federals in a massive slugfest that lasted all afternoon of that hot, bloody day.
Hood's forces flanked Sherman's line, crushed the end of it, but could go
no farther. Yet the Confederates came closer to achieving a major tactical

victory on July 22 than on any other day of the Atlanta Campaign. It had been a very close thing for the harried Unionists.

Despite its high drama and its equally high profile among students of the Civil War, the Battle of July 22 has generated surprisingly little historiography. True, it is always mentioned in survey studies of the Atlanta Campaign and of the Civil War in the West, but there is very little in the way of detailed tactical study or evaluation of its significance within the larger campaign and the larger war in the West. The first book appeared only in 1958. Written by William Key and entitled *The Battle of Atlanta and the Georgia Campaign*, the contents began as a series of newspaper articles. They collectively cover the entire campaign, with only seven of eighty-seven pages devoted to the Battle of July 22.

To date, the only other book specifically dealing with the engagement came out in 2010. Gary Ecelbarger's *The Day Dixie Died: The Battle of Atlanta* has many strong points. Based on far more research than went into Key's very slim volume, especially in personal accounts appearing in newspapers of the era, Ecelbarger took pains to estimate precise troop numbers and exact times when certain actions took place on the battlefield. This is admirable, but one must also keep in mind that Ecelbarger could only guess about this kind of data; the most elastic topics associated with Civil War battles are troop numbers and the precise times of events. The sources are too unreliable to provide solid evidence for such exact information. Ironically, Ecelbarger's analysis leads him to place the death of Confederate division commander Maj. Gen. William H. T. Walker at the wrong time and wrong place in the battle.

One key difference between Ecelbarger's book and my own is the wider and deeper research base that underwrites my study, especially in the area of archival resources. I have consulted every source of unpublished material in archival institutions that I was able to locate. Moreover, the rich resources of published primary material on this battle have been consulted as well. Most of these items are available electronically, making it very easy to accumulate a large database of published reports, diaries, letters, and memoirs. The recent publication of Richard A. Sauers's *The National Tribune Civil War Index: A Guide to the Weekly Newspaper Dedicated to Civil War Veterans, 1877–1943*, opens to the researcher thousands of veteran reminiscences published in this newspaper. Many letters to the editor of the *National Tribune* from Union veterans of July 22, privates and generals alike, clarified gray areas of the battle's story not illuminated by any other source. The same was true of some archival material that has been seldom if ever used by researchers. The postwar material in the William T. Sherman Papers at the Library of Congress consists of many letters and statements that particularly relate to the death of Army of the Tennessee commander Maj. Gen. James B. McPherson previously unused by historians. Additionally, Richard Beard, the Confederate captain whose skirmishers shot McPherson, wrote many accounts of the battle that have not been consulted by researchers. There is no substitute, in other words, for trying to track down every possible source on a subject like July 22, evaluating the item's contents, and using it judiciously to fill in the many holes that exist in the history of any battle.

Tracking down every bit of information also results in another important benefit—reliable information about unit placement in different phases of the battle. Obscure sources often contain unique information about where a particular regiment was located or how the regiments of a brigade were formed. That information is reflected in the maps of this study, which contain the most detailed knowledge about unit placement and topographical detail available. The map coverage here is more extensive, detailed, and accurate for the Battle of July 22 than is available in other books that discuss the engagement.

Another difference between Ecelbarger's book and this one is the wider coverage of my study, which seeks to shape a holistic understanding of the battle (including such topics as care of the wounded, disposal of prisoners, burial of the dead, battlefield preservation, commemoration, and memory). As with all my other Civil War battle books, I think it is important to understand an engagement from all perspectives, and I attempt to do so as much as possible within the confines of a single volume published by an academic press.

But the most important difference between Ecelbarger's study and mine lies in the assessment of July 22. Ecelbarger, a biographer of Maj. Gen. John A. Logan, supports that general's comment that the Battle of Atlanta had a vital impact on shaping the course of the Civil War. Writing in *The Volunteer Soldier of America*, published in 1887, Logan declared that July 22 was "one of the 'decisive battles of the war'—in fact, the only decisive battle in 1864. It resulted in the fall of Atlanta and enabled General Sherman to accomplish his march to the sea."[2] Logan came to this conclusion because he commanded the Army of the Tennessee during most of the engagement after McPherson, its beloved leader, was killed. As an ambitious politician both before and after the war, Logan was not shy about promoting his war record.

Ecelbarger not only supports Logan's assessment but also takes it a step further. He argues that the Battle of Atlanta was decisive within the context of both the Atlanta Campaign and the Civil War. He writes that by foiling Hood's best chance to win a battlefield victory, Logan's men not only saved Sherman's campaign for Atlanta but also reelected Abraham Lincoln for another term as president the following November. Because the fall of

Atlanta is generally credited with going a long way toward instilling public confidence in the president's handling of the war, Ecelbarger links the result of the fighting on July 22 with the fall of the city and with a key political victory that brought the war to an end within five months after Lincoln's reelection.[3]

I do not find this conclusion to be convincing. It links events with a cause-and-effect relationship that did not necessarily exist. Hood certainly tried to achieve a campaign-winning blow on July 22 but failed with heavy losses. The tactical status quo remained on July 23 as it had on July 21. Sherman was in no better condition to capture Atlanta after the battle than before it. In fact, he did not find a way to enter the city until he devised a scheme for a massive flank movement in late August, temporarily cutting away from his vital railroad link with the North. Only then could the Federals kick down the door to Atlanta and bring the campaign to a conclusion that had an impact on Northern perception of how Lincoln handled the war effort. If any battle of the campaign was decisive in winning Atlanta, it had to be the fighting associated with this final move at the town of Jonesboro.

The only possible argument in favor of July 22 as decisive is that it prevented Hood from achieving a significant battlefield victory. But what was the worst that the Confederates could have done to the Army of the Tennessee on that day? Judging by how most Civil War battles played out, this would have been inflicting heavy losses, pushing back Sherman's left wing to a more compact (and more easily defensible) position, and costing the Federals some lost prestige. Much of that had already been accomplished by the Army of the Mississippi / Army of Tennessee at Shiloh on April 6, 1862; at Perryville on October 8, 1862; at Stones River on December 31, 1862; and at Chickamauga on September 20, 1863. Yet in every one of those prior engagements, the Federals had rebounded and won either the battle or the campaign that accompanied or succeeded the engagement. In the Atlanta Campaign, Sherman still had the far-larger Army of the Cumberland and the smaller Army of the Ohio to count on even if his Army of the Tennessee had been more heavily damaged on July 22. There is little reason to assume a Confederate victory that day would have resulted in the Confederates retaining Atlanta in the long run or in the electoral defeat of Lincoln three and a half months later.

But there is no reason to ignore the Battle of July 22 simply because it did not determine the outcome of the Civil War. Federal success that day severely limited important damage to the Union war effort, even if that potential damage was unlikely to lose the war for the North. Confederate failure that day paved the way for the continuation of Sherman's ultimately successful operations to capture Atlanta. Also, as one of the larger and more vigorously fought engagements of the conflict, involving a major and successful flank march, the Battle of Atlanta stands out as an example of Civil War operational history. The combination of maneuver, unit handling, stout combat by the individual soldier, and combative spirit by both sides make July 22 one of the most interesting battles in American history. There is much for the student of military history to learn on many levels of tactics, the experience of combat, and battlefield leadership.

The engagement on July 22 was the greatest day of fighting by the Union Army of the Tennessee and one of the great days of battle by the Confederate Army of Tennessee. The planning and execution of movements prior to and during the engagement are significant of course, but what stands out in this battle is the human endurance of the common soldier and their officers on the regimental, brigade, and divisional levels. In many ways, it was the most trying day of the war for most of the men involved, whether in blue or gray. Units in both armies were bled white before the sun set that day, barely holding on to pursue their tactical missions and eventually settling their contest with a stalemate that rebounded far more to the strategic benefit of the Federals than the Confederates. Sherman's men had to hold on, and they did, against one of the most deadly threats ever presented a Union force on a Civil War battlefield. In this, they went a long way toward saving Sherman's campaign for Atlanta.

But the Confederates had to do much more than just "hold on" in this battle. Their goal was to significantly damage Sherman's left wing, if not roll it up with disastrous consequences, before they could lay claim to success. Hood's men needed a big victory, not a middling and ephemeral success. They fell considerably short of those goals, and their postbattle claims to victory ring hollow.

Deciding what to call this battle has an interesting history in itself. "As I know no name I call it the battle of the 22nd of July," wrote Capt. Thomas J. Key, artillery chief of Cleburne's Division, the day after the bloodletting. Key expressed the tendency of his fellow participants who strongly favored naming the battle after the day of its occurrence. He also expressed the basic reason—there seemed to be no landmark nearby that would better serve the purpose. Fourth Corps commander Oliver Otis Howard, who keenly witnessed the combat from the vantage of Sherman's headquarters, referred to it as the fight "upon the Augusta railroad," but that designation could have no traction with the public. Lt. Col. Hiram Hawkins, who commanded the 5th Kentucky (C.S.), called it "the battle of Intrenchment Creek July 22d," while Capt. James Iredell Hall of Company C, 9th Tennessee referred to it as "the bloody and disastrous battle of Decatur." But neither designation took root. Capt. Evan P. Howell, another Confederate artilleryman, simply referred to it as "our big fight on last Friday."[4]

For a decade afterward, veterans and civilians alike widely designated the engagement east of Atlanta as the Battle of July 22. But then, for unexplained reasons, veterans began to call it by a different name. By 1875, when Sherman published his memoirs, he stated that the "battle of July 22d is usually called the battle of Atlanta." Henry V. Boynton, a newspaper correspondent and former commander of the 35th Ohio, noted the same thing in a book published the same year as Sherman's memoirs. Logan also called it the "battle of Atlanta, fought on the 22nd of July, 1864," to cover both bases in this interesting twist on naming practices.[5]

Wilbur G. Kurtz, an Atlanta illustrator and engraver who studied the engagement in the 1930s, mimicked this trend by referring to it as "the Battle of Atlanta, fought July 22, 1864." But later historians decisively shifted to calling it simply the Battle of Atlanta, as Richard McMurry states in his book on the Atlanta Campaign published in 2000. Some historians have attempted to place a different name on the battle. In his study of the campaign published in 1992, Albert Castel has argued that the Federals and later historians tended to designate it as the Battle of Atlanta, while the Confederates called it the Battle of Decatur. I did not find evidence to support such broad statements, but Castel goes on to assert that it should be called the Battle of Bald Hill. No one has taken up his call except, in a small way, Russell S. Bonds, whose book on the campaign published in 2009, not only calls it the Battle of Bald Hill but also the Battle of Atlanta and Hood's Second Sortie.[6]

I find all this fascinating and wonder what it means within the context of American cultural history. Regardless of the shifts in naming practices, it is important to be true to the viewpoints of the generation that fought and endured the Civil War. In the immediate aftermath of the engagement, the majority of Federals and Confederates alike preferred to call it the Battle of July 22, and that is the term I generally use throughout this study. Given the tendency for the veterans to later call it the Battle of Atlanta, I will also use that term now and then in these pages.

The story of the events that led up to and included this impressive day of battle in American history unfolds in the following chapters. It begins with Sherman's crossing of the Chattahoochee River on July 17 and the day-by-day progress of his armies to July 20 (chapter 2). The short but bitterly fought battle for Bald Hill from 8 A.M. to about 10 A.M. on July 21 fills part of chapter 3. The fighting on July 22 readily divides into five phases. In the first, the combat along Sugar Creek to the rear of the Union line, took place from noon until about 3 P.M. (chapter 5). The second phase, which resulted in bitter fighting south of Bald Hill, lasted from 1 P.M. until 5 P.M. (chapter 7). Phase three was the dramatic Confederate breaking of the Fifteenth Corps line along the Georgia Railroad (chapter 8) and the effective Union counterattack that restored the line (chapter 9), the two efforts lasting from 3:15 P.M. to about 5:15 P.M. The fourth phase was the culmination of Confederate efforts to control the area south of Bald Hill and the subsequent fighting that took place east of that hill from 5 P.M. to 8 P.M. (chapter 10). The fifth and final phase of the Battle of Atlanta was the fight at Decatur from 1 P.M. to 3 P.M., discussed in chapter 11.

This study of July 22 follows in the wake of three other books I have written on Atlanta Campaign battles. The four books together constitute a step-by step study of Union and Confederate operations from the confrontation at Kennesaw Mountain in late June to the Battle of Ezra Church on July 28, arguably the key period of Sherman's long effort to seize Atlanta. The Confederates held their strongest position thus far in the campaign at Kennesaw, delaying Sherman for two weeks and compelling him to launch the most serious Union attack on Confederate earthworks, which took place on June 27. After the confrontation at Kennesaw came the pivotal crossing of the Chattahoochee River, the change of Confederate commanders, and the three heavy battles fought at Peach Tree Creek, on July 22, and at Ezra Church.

This sequence is studied in detail in *Kennesaw Mountain: Sherman, Johnston, and the Atlanta Campaign* (2013), *The Battle of Peach Tree Creek: Hood's First Effort to Save Atlanta* (2017), *July 22: The Civil War Battle of Atlanta* (2023), and *The Battle of Ezra Church and the Struggle for Atlanta* (2015). Readers interested in a detailed study of the use of field fortifications, including descriptions of their design and construction as well as how they fitted into the operational history of the entire Atlanta Campaign, can consult my *Fighting for Atlanta: Tactics, Terrain, and Trenches in the Civil War* (2018). *Fighting for Atlanta* constitutes a short general history of the campaign as well as a technical study of a key aspect of its operational history.

It is a pleasure to thank the staff members at archival institutions who aided me in accessing their rich holdings and to thank all those who have shared my interest in the Battle of July 22. I especially wish to thank Hal Jespersen for working with me on producing the maps that support the text of this book. But mostly, it is gratifying to thank my wife, Pratibha, for all her support, encouragement, and love, not only for now but for all time.

I

Atlanta Is in Sight

July 22, 1864, marked a day of high-profile drama during a campaign that had already been grinding along for nearly three months without a decisive moment. Beginning in stages during the first week of May, Maj. Gen. William T. Sherman had carefully maneuvered a large army group of some 100,000 men from the vicinity of Chattanooga, Tennessee, toward the key city of Atlanta, Georgia. His force was drawn from three different departments composing his Military Division of the Mississippi. The largest contingent was the Army of the Cumberland, under Maj. Gen. George H. Thomas, with 60,000 men. The next-largest component was Maj. Gen. James B. McPherson's Army of the Tennessee, consisting of about 30,000 men after two divisions of the Seventeenth Corps joined it in early June. Last but not least was Maj. Gen. John M. Schofield's Army of the Ohio, consisting of one corps and about 10,000 men.[1]

In opposition to Sherman's advance was Gen. Joseph E. Johnston's Army of Tennessee, the only major field force of the Confederacy in the western theater. It consisted of about 60,000 troops after the Army of Mississippi reinforced it in mid-May. Ever cautious, Johnston elected to act almost entirely on the defensive during the campaign. He established strongly fortified positions on key ground before awaiting Sherman's reaction to his tactical strength. Sherman normally avoided direct attacks on those positions, choosing instead to find and turn a flank to pry his opponent out of his trenches. While not averse to trying an attack, Sherman recognized that preserving his manpower and his tactical flexibility were imperatives if he hoped to penetrate 100 miles of Confederate-held Georgia on his way to Atlanta.

Sherman conducted the campaign with an effective blend of aggression on the operational level mixed with caution on the tactical level. He knew his men had to keep rolling toward Atlanta to fulfill the strategic vision set by Lt. Gen. Ulysses S. Grant as general in chief of all Union forces, who also was personally directing the movements of Maj. Gen. George G. Meade's Army of the Potomac in Virginia. Most importantly, Sherman had to make sure that Johnston did not detach troops to reinforce Gen. Robert E. Lee's Army of Northern Virginia in the titanic struggle raging in Virginia. Grant was pushing Lee relentlessly in part to prevent him from sending troops to help Johnston. The key difference between Sherman's and Grant's conduct that spring and summer was the former's relative caution in avoiding attacks on fortified positions and the latter's readiness to launch such assaults on many occasions. Sherman's caution left himself open to sallies by the Confederates, but fortunately for him, Johnston was so hesitant to conduct tactical offensives during the campaign that the Union commander rarely had to worry about such threats.

The contest between Sherman and Johnston was heavily influenced by the geography of northwest Georgia. Mountains, vegetation, and three major rivers were the key terrain features of the campaign. From Chattanooga south to the Oostanaula River, typical Appalachian topography offered Johnston tall, commanding ridges well suited for defensive positions. But these positions could easily be outflanked by columns of Federal troops moving along valleys shielded by similar ridges. This is how Sherman pried Johnston loose from his first position near Dalton without a major battle. Falling back to Resaca, just north of the Oostanaula, the opposing forces engaged in a slugging match on May 14–15, which featured several major assaults by Federal troops in what developed as the closest thing to a general engagement in the campaign. Sherman was unable to break the Confederate position but forced Johnston to evacuate it anyway by establishing a lodgment on the south side of the river.[2]

The Confederates found another high ridge near Cassville by May 19. But when Union artillery established an enfilading position on this line, Johnston reluctantly ordered an evacuation that night, crossing the second major river, the Etowah, in the process. South of that stream, Johnston found terrain well-suited to his defensive tastes. The landscape leveled off into a rolling piedmont topography cluttered with dense woods, few roads, and even fewer settlements. When Sherman crossed the Etowah on May 23, his

William T. Sherman. Mastermind of the Atlanta Campaign, Sherman had penetrated the defenses of northwest Georgia with his army group and carefully crossed the Chattahoochee River, the last natural barrier to the city, by mid-July 1864. His plan to cut the railroads feeding the Confederate army led to three fierce battles fought north, east, and west of Atlanta. The second of these engagements, the Battle of July 22, also called the Battle of Atlanta, was the biggest of the entire campaign and the closest the Confederates came to achieving some sort of offensive victory over the Federals. Library of Congress, LC-DIG-cwpb-07315.

rapid advance slowed dangerously in this tangled environment. Progress was measured in yards rather than miles, and daily skirmishing increased in intensity. There were small battles at New Hope Church on May 25, Pickett's Mill on May 27, and Dallas the next day, but no major engagements took place in the sprawling thicket that seemed to engulf both armies. Only by tedious movements could the Federals make slow progress until reaching more-open country near Kennesaw Mountain just outside Marietta.

Here Johnston found his strongest position yet, anchored on Kennesaw, a high mountain with two peaks that dominated the region. The Confederates stalled Union forces for two weeks, from June 19 to July 2, at their Kennesaw Line. Frustrated and worried that he was not fulfilling Grant's directives, Sherman launched the largest Federal attack of the campaign, with 15,000 troops assaulting three sectors of the Rebel position on June 27. All three were bloodily repulsed with total Union losses of 3,000 men, and Sherman returned to his cautious maneuvering. When he was on the verge of turning their left flank, the Confederates evacuated the Kennesaw Line.[3]

Johnston had given up territory north of the Etowah River at a rate that caused alarm in Richmond, but he settled down into a much more dogged resistance south of that stream. Instead of moving many miles between defensive lines, he now moved shorter distances, digging in more often and at places that were not necessarily strong positions. This meant that after giving up Kennesaw, Johnston fell back only a short distance to Smyrna Station, presenting Sherman with yet another position that had to be turned by flanking moves. He gave up the Smyrna Line on July 5 and retired a short distance to his last line north of the Chattahoochee River. This stretched across the countryside along the last good ground on that side of the stream, straddling the Western and Atlantic Railroad that linked his army with Atlanta, now only eight miles to the south.

The Chattahoochee was Johnston's Rubicon. His constant retreats had greatly stressed the government in Richmond, and a further fall back across the last natural barrier protecting Atlanta would be the final straw. The river was also a sort of Rubicon for Sherman as well. Crossing it would place his troops beyond the last natural obstacle to his prize. It would also place his army group just outside the heavily fortified city of Atlanta with barely enough room to maneuver forward or backward. Once across the Chattahoochee, Sherman had to succeed; any withdrawal to the north side would be widely viewed as a defeat in his campaign. The Chattahoochee was more than just another river in the way; it was a defining boundary in the course of the struggle for Atlanta, laden with emotional significance.[4]

The campaign had reached an important phase by the time Johnston fell back to his Chattahoochee River Line on July 5. It was the eleventh defensive

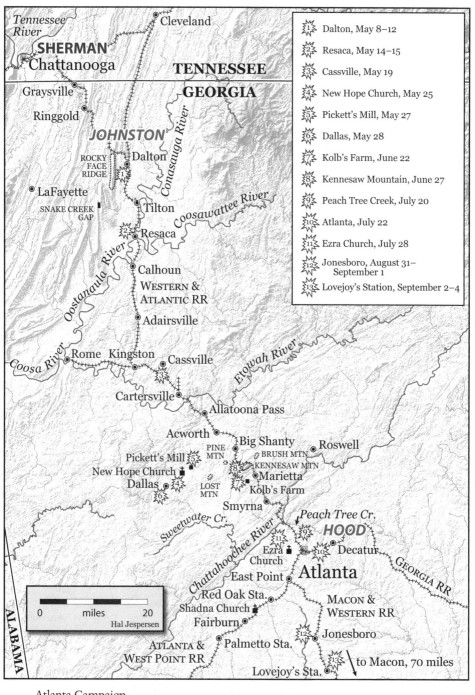

1	Dalton, May 8–12
2	Resaca, May 14–15
3	Cassville, May 19
4	New Hope Church, May 25
5	Pickett's Mill, May 27
6	Dallas, May 28
7	Kolb's Farm, June 22
8	Kennesaw Mountain, June 27
9	Peach Tree Creek, July 20
10	Atlanta, July 22
11	Ezra Church, July 28
12	Jonesboro, August 31–September 1
13	Lovejoy's Station, September 2–4

Tennessee River

SHERMAN
Chattanooga

TENNESSEE
GEORGIA

Cleveland

Graysville

Ringgold

JOHNSTON

ROCKY FACE RIDGE
Dalton

LaFayette

SNAKE CREEK GAP

Tilton

Conasauga River

Coosawattee River

Resaca

Calhoun
WESTERN & ATLANTIC RR

Oostanaula River

Adairsville

Coosa River
Rome   Kingston   Cassville

Cartersville

Etowah River

Allatoona Pass

Acworth

Big Shanty   Roswell

PINE MTN
Pickett's Mill
BRUSH MTN
KENNESAW MTN
New Hope Church
Dallas
LOST MTN
Marietta
Kolb's Farm

Smyrna

Sweetwater Cr.

Chattahoochee River

Peach Tree Cr.
HOOD

Ezra Church
Decatur

East Point
Atlanta

GEORGIA RR

Red Oak Sta.
Shadna Church
Fairburn

MACON & WESTERN RR

0   miles   20
Hal Jespersen

ALABAMA

ATLANTA & WEST POINT RR

Palmetto Sta.

Jonesboro

Lovejoy's Sta.

to Macon, 70 miles

Atlanta Campaign

position the Confederates had constructed thus far during the campaign, and it was one of the strongest. But like all the others, it was subject to being outflanked with the right kind of movement, and Sherman by now was quite adept at planning such moves. The difference here was that he also had to plan the simultaneous crossing of the Chattahoochee, for prying the Confederates out of their entrenchments went hand in hand with preparations for the most significant stream crossing of the campaign. And crossing the Chattahoochee, in turn, required Sherman to plan for his approach to the outskirts of Atlanta as well. All three operations were to be conducted in sequence because the two armies were now within a stone's throw, so to speak, of Atlanta.[5]

"I propose to study the crossings of the Chattahoochee," Sherman informed Maj. Gen. Henry W. Halleck, chief of staff of the U.S. Army, on July 6. "Instead of attacking Atlanta direct, or any of its forts, I propose to make a circuit, destroying all its railroads. This is a delicate movement and must be done with caution."[6]

With several possible crossing points from which to choose, the Federals could feint at one place and be serious at several others. To do this, Sherman would need to operate on a wide front, which his troop strength and the division of his force into three armies facilitated.

Sherman had always been partial to the Army of the Tennessee, not only because he had commanded its Fifteenth Corps during the Vicksburg operations but also because he had commanded the army after Grant took charge of the Military Division of the Mississippi in October 1863. In fact, next to Grant, Sherman was the most important man in the creation of the Army of the Tennessee. It was now the best campaigning army in the country's military forces, able to move through enemy territory with confidence and ready for a fight whenever one cropped up.

The Army of the Tennessee served a special role for Sherman during the campaign for Atlanta. It was "not allowed to be idle, I assure you," wrote division commander Walter Q. Gresham. "General Sherman calls us the 'cracker to his whip,' and uses us to touch up the enemy's flanks."[7] At the start of the campaign, it was this army that conducted the wide flanking movement aimed at Resaca that convinced Johnston to abandon his position at Dalton. Elements of this army later established a bridgehead on the south side of the Oostanaula River that, in turn, convinced the Confederates to evacuate Resaca. Sherman sent McPherson off to the far right when the army group crossed the Etowah River, the most dangerous flank of his extended and mobile formation. The Army of the Tennessee conducted one of the three attacks against the Kennesaw Line on June 27 and then was tapped to flank the left of that line on July 2, a move that led Johnston to evacuate his strong position. McPherson continued to hold Sherman's right flank during the confrontations with the Smyrna Line and then the Chattahoochee River Line, the farthest of his three armies from the vital railroad they all relied on to sustain their drive toward Atlanta.

Sherman also had full confidence in McPherson, his friend and subordinate. Born November 14, 1828, at Clyde, Ohio, McPherson impressed nearly everyone he met during his short but full life. He graduated from the U.S. Military Academy at the head of his class in 1853 and secured a coveted assignment in the Corps of Engineers. On duty in California in the spring of 1859, he met Emily Hoffman, which led to a long courtship interrupted by the outbreak of war. McPherson's talents led him to be appointed to the staff of Halleck as aide-de-camp and then to Grant as chief engineer before being commissioned brigadier general of volunteers in June 1862. Grant assigned him to run the military railroads in his department before giving McPherson field commands in October of that year. From that point, he rose from division command to lead the Seventeenth Corps during the operations against Vicksburg, then succeeded Sherman in command of the Army of the Tennessee in March 1864.[8]

Hoffman returned to her home in Baltimore during the fall of 1863, and she and McPherson tried to arrange their wedding the following March, when he obtained a leave of absence. According to his biographer, their plans were postponed when the new army commander was suddenly called back to Nashville for consultations with Sherman. His superior wrote a consoling letter to Hoffman, explaining why it was important to postpone the wedding and urging his fiancée to be patient. McPherson thereafter remained in the field; there was no possibility of marriage just yet.[9]

Everyone who came in contact with McPherson liked him. "McPherson is tall, robust, but not stout, and has an honest, good-humored, plain face with a retroussé nose," wrote Col. William J. Palmer of the 15th Pennsylvania Cavalry, who saw him briefly at Rossville, Georgia, early in the Atlanta Campaign. "His manners are very simple, easy, and cordial. As we had no whiskey he said he preferred water. This was no doubt to make us feel at ease about it."[10]

While everyone admired McPherson's personality and character, his military skills showed signs of limitations. He was a superb administrator of large organizations, which was very important in a commander of a field army, but his campaigning skills left something to be desired. McPherson himself felt that, in Georgia, he was going into a campaign that would severely test his abilities. "I have a much greater responsibility than I desire," he confided to his mother on April 4, 1864.[11]

McPherson's confidence was severely tested in the first move of the campaign. He managed to entirely flank Johnston's position on Rocky Face Ridge at Dalton by passing through Snake Creek Gap and began to move directly toward Resaca. The Confederates were caught flatfooted, but the small garrison of the town he approached showed enough resistance to intimidate McPherson. He had no idea how strongly Resaca might be held and realized he was isolated from the rest of Sherman's army group. McPherson decided to retreat instead of press home his advantage, digging in to secure Snake Creek Gap.

The move, nevertheless, compelled Johnston to evacuate Rocky Face Ridge and protect Resaca. But Sherman knew that much more could have been accomplished; he sought to severely damage the Army of Tennessee, not just force it to move south. McPherson came to realize that he had thrown away a golden opportunity. "The General evidently felt keenly disappointed with himself over his failure to press on aggressively," wrote Andrew Hickenlooper, a trusted member of McPherson's staff since the Vicksburg operations. "He was never again the cordial and genial man he had been." We can trust the first part of Hickenlooper's statement, but he exaggerated in the second part. While McPherson was "keenly disappointed" in himself, many observers noted that he retained his trademark cordiality and genial nature after mid-May.[12]

In one of the last personal letters McPherson wrote, on July 12 during Sherman's preparation for crossing the Chattahoochee River, he mused on the war generally and what lay in his immediate future. Corresponding with a lady friend from his West Point–cadet days, McPherson marveled at the crisis of the nation. "Little did we imagine then that our beloved Country would so soon be plunged into all the horrors of a Civil War. But it is upon us, and all we have got to do is to sustain the honor of our glorious old Flag and battle, earnestly, heroically, and persistently for the right and I have Faith to believe that our Country will come out of this struggle stronger and more respected than ever." When thinking of the pending crossing of the river and what awaited him near the gates of Atlanta, McPherson expressed a good deal of optimism. "We are having a rough hard campaign in this mountain region, but so far we have been successful. We have driven Johnston & his Army across the Chattahoochie & Atlanta is in sight."[13]

Sherman crafted a long, multistage process for crossing the last natural barrier before Atlanta. That process began on July 6, when he sent Brig. Gen. Kenner Garrard's cavalry division to seize Roswell, located just north of the river about seventeen miles upstream from the crossing of the Western and Atlantic Railroad and well beyond the right flank of Johnston's Chattahoochee River Line. A "few hundred rebels" contested Garrard's advance, burning the wagon bridge over the river after falling back to the south side. The Federal troopers devoted much time to destroying factories at Roswell, facilities that were making material for the Confederate army. Garrard found some 400 factory women, who Sherman later sent north.[14]

The next step to secure crossings occurred when Schofield's Army of the Ohio moved to the mouth of Soap Creek on the north side of the Chattahoochee. His engineers laid a pontoon bridge that his troops crossed to establish the first Union bridgehead south of the river by the evening of July 8. This led Johnston to evacuate his Chattahoochee River Line that night, clearing all Confederate troops from the north side of the river by dawn of July 9.[15]

Before he became aware of Johnston's withdrawal, Sherman charged Schofield with sending out patrols to learn all they could about the topography and the road system south of the river. He especially needed information about the territory "toward Stone Mountain and Decatur," the latter a major town and station on the Georgia Railroad six miles east of Atlanta. "If you can catch a few people who ought to know all about it, send them to me." On July 9, Schofield expanded his bridgehead to make it one mile deep and wide enough for two of his divisions. Sherman was pleased. He told Halleck he planned to have control of five bridges and three fords "before I put the army across the Chattahoochee."[16]

Garrard forded the river and secured one of these crossings near Roswell on July 9. He also sent a detachment six miles upstream from town in an effort to secure McAfee's Bridge. Confederate cavalry stymied that move for the time being, but at least Garrard controlled a small bridgehead opposite Roswell, the second Union position south of the Chattahoochee.[17]

Sherman now began to strengthen and enlarge both bridgeheads on the south side of the river. Maj. Gen. David S. Stanley's division of the Fourth Corps, Army of the Cumberland crossed at Isham's Ford near Schofield's command and then moved five miles northward along the bank of the river to clear the area to Powers' Ferry. There the 58th Indiana constructed another pontoon bridge on which Brig. Gen. Thomas J. Wood's division of the Fourth Corps crossed to join Stanley. These moves enlarged the Isham's Ford–Powers' Ferry bridgehead to five miles wide and less than a mile deep, and it was held by four divisions. Fourth Corps commander Maj. Gen. Oliver O. Howard sent his last division, led by Brig. Gen. John Newton, to cross the river at Roswell on July 13 and then move south to join Stanley and Wood in the Isham's Ford–Powers' Ferry bridgehead.[18]

The bridgehead at Roswell, about three miles north of Powers' Ferry, was small and isolated for a time, but Sherman soon strengthened and enlarged it. He sent Maj. Gen. Grenville M. Dodge's Left Wing, Sixteenth Corps of McPherson's army to cross the river there on July 10 and establish itself on the other side. Some of Dodge's troops crossed on a hastily thrown up footbridge, while others waded the river. The latter removed their pants, placed them and their accoutrements on musket barrels to hold them above the water, and walked across the stream. It took two hours for one brigade to prepare, cross, and dress again, but the Federals encountered no opposition. In addition to constructing earthworks to protect the perimeter of the bridgehead, Dodge superintended the reconstruction of a wagon bridge at Roswell. The older structure had been 642 feet long and 14 feet above water level, divided into six spans resting on stone piers. Dodge's infantrymen, pioneers, and engineer officers, employing one thousand men on the job, completed the bridge on July 13 by tearing down some buildings and using the timbers rather than cutting new pieces from trees.[19]

In addition to his efforts north of the railroad crossing of the Chattahoochee, Sherman also extended south of that point. He moved cavalry forces as far as Baker's Ferry, eight miles downstream from the railroad bridge, but did not authorize them to cross the river. Nevertheless, the Federals now covered a stretch of nearly twenty-five miles along the north bank of the Chattahoochee from Roswell down to Baker's Ferry, with two bridgeheads on the south side of the stream and north of the railroad crossing.[20]

Those two bridgeheads were the key to Sherman's future moves. He intended to shift all of his men across the river and strike out toward the southeast, aiming to cut the Georgia Railroad linking Atlanta with Augusta to the east. Roads from his two bridgeheads led to important road junctions north of Atlanta at Cross Keys and Buck Head. Other roads radiated from there in nearly all directions across the region north, northeast, and east of the city.

Johnston's plan to deal with Sherman's crossing mixed astute judgment with lax implementation. He massed the bulk of the Army of Tennessee northwest of Atlanta, between the heavy defenses known as the Atlanta City Line and the railroad crossing of the Chattahoochee, so it could move east or west depending on which direction the Federals approached. Given the presence of large Union forces at Isham's Ford–Powers' Ferry and opposite Roswell, he assumed they would cross entirely at those locations and then approach from the north. Therefore, Johnston positioned sizeable cavalry forces in their potential path.

Maj. Gen. Joseph Wheeler, commander of the Cavalry Corps, sent Col. George G. Dibrell's brigade of horsemen to the Cross Keys area by July 10. Williams's Brigade took position to Dibrell's left and north of Buck Head, astride the road toward Roswell. Col. Robert H. Anderson moved his brigade into place to the left of Brig. Gen. John S. Williams's command, with his left flank nearly touching the Chattahoochee close to the mouth of Long

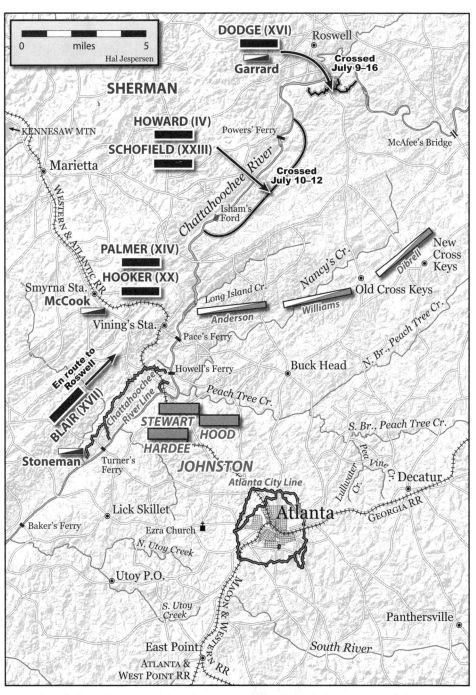

Crossing the Chattahoochee River

Island Creek. "Please watch the force you mention as on this side of the river," Johnston instructed Wheeler on July 13, "and whenever it moves forward impede its march as much as you can, destroying bridges after you. Give notice of all the roads by which they march, also."[21]

Thus far Johnston had evolved a reasonable plan for meeting the Federals after they crossed the Chattahoochee. But the deep flaw in his plan was in not taking advantage of the river itself. He failed to contest any of the crossing sites, relying on small numbers of Confederates to watch them and report when the Federals came over. Both his infantry and cavalry were positioned to meet the Unionists only after they had firmly established themselves on the south side. Sherman found the crossing of his Rubicon far easier than anticipated, as Johnston busied himself with strengthening the Atlanta City Line and awaiting developments.

Once south of the river, Sherman planned to cut three rail lines that fed Johnston's army in Atlanta. The city was located between the Chattahoochee River to the northwest and the Ocmulgee River to the southeast. To its north, most of the region actually drained first into Peach Tree Creek, which ran from east to west about four miles from Atlanta and emptied into the Chattahoochee just upstream from the railroad bridge.[22]

Sherman needed to keep in touch with his railroad supply line and thus had to plan a massive right wheel after crossing the river. McPherson would be the whip in that wheel, starting from the Roswell bridgehead and moving toward Decatur. Schofield would move to his right, in the middle of the wheeling movement, while Thomas would hold down the right wing and maintain connection with the rail life line. Thomas would have the shortest route to follow once he created a third bridgehead at Pace's Ferry, two miles north of the railroad bridge, and shifted the Fourteenth and Twentieth Corps to the south side of the Chattahoochee. As those two corps marched from there, Howard would move his Fourth Corps from the Isham's Ford–Powers' Ferry bridgehead to join Thomas. The Army of the Cumberland would cover the entire northern face of Atlanta once it closed in on the city.

Schofield and McPherson, coming out of the Isham's Ford–Powers' Ferry and Roswell bridgeheads, would act in concert with each other. Extending to Thomas's left, their two armies had the longest route to march: McPherson's move from Roswell would take him eighteen miles in a straight line to Decatur, while Schofield from Isham's Ford would have to march fifteen miles. In contrast, Buck Head was located only five miles east of Pace's Ferry and two miles north of Peach Tree Creek. Thomas's proximity to Johnston's army also meant that the Confederates would likely pay more attention to the Army of the Cumberland during the pending movement than to the Army of the Tennessee and the Army of the Ohio. The last two would be moving on the periphery of Confederate vision, with only Confederate cavalry forces reporting their movements.

By July 12, the Union stance along the Chattahoochee River was very favorable. Dodge's Left Wing, the Fourth Corps, the Twenty-Third Corps, and Garrard's cavalry division were all on the south side in two bridgeheads. They represented Sherman's left wing. In the center, Thomas's Fourteenth and Twentieth Corps were massed in the vicinity of Vining's Station on the north side of the river to be near Pace's Ferry, supported by Brig. Gen. Edward M. McCook's cavalry division. On the right wing, extending downstream from near the railroad bridge, McPherson superintended his Fifteenth and Seventeenth Corps, which were supported by Maj. Gen. George Stoneman's cavalry division. By this time, the only real purpose of this concentration on the Union right was to send Stoneman across the river and attempt to reach the railroad that entered Atlanta from the south and cut it. Sherman told McPherson to leave the Seventeenth Corps here until Stoneman returned from his mission, but he wanted the Fifteenth Corps to move to Roswell, making of that town "a kind of secondary base for operations against Atlanta and the roads east toward Augusta and Macon."[23]

Responding to Sherman's directive, Maj. Gen. John A. Logan pushed his Fifteenth Corps out on the evening of July 12 and marched east by way of Marietta. His lead division reached Roswell on the evening of July 13, with the other two divisions bivouacking a short distance west of town. The corps gathered on July 14 and began to cross the Chattahoochee at midafternoon, taking post on good ground to enlarge and strengthen the bridgehead to the left of Dodge's Sixteenth Corps troops. Logan's men finished their earthworks on July 16.[24]

Meanwhile, Stoneman's planned raid came to nothing. Maj. Gen. Frank P. Blair, Seventeenth Corps commander, assigned Brig. Gen. Mortimer D. Leggett's division to relieve the cavalry troops in picket duty along the north side of the river so they could mass for the strike. Stoneman left on the night of July 10 but, over the course of several days, could not find an uncontested crossing. By July 15, it was clear that there was no possibility of a strike south toward the railroad at this time, so Sherman made plans to shift Blair to Roswell. The corps had been picketing along fourteen miles of the river for several days now but gave up its position and marched thirty miles to reach Roswell barely in time for the move south of the Chattahoochee on July 17. Stoneman would remain near Turner's Ferry to maintain a Union presence in this area.[25]

South of the river, the Confederates remained in their static positions awaiting the next Union move, but their retreat across the Chattahoochee had created a great deal of anxiety in the city. By this time, Atlanta was home to 20,000 people, many of them refugees, and the atmosphere was tense with fear. Among many of the soldiers, there was an assumption that Johnston now had to take the offensive, and some of them believed they could drive Sherman back across the river after he crossed it. "I am getting very wearied of this eternal retiring," wrote Maj. Gen. William H. T. Walker, one of Johnston's division commanders. At army headquarters, opinion was divided as to which direction Sherman would take while crossing the Chattahoochee. Despite the bridgeheads to the north, some still believed he might cross the main bulk of his army group south of the railroad bridge.[26]

But Sherman had every intention of crossing north of that span. This move placed his troops between the enemy and his own line of supply more securely than crossing south of the railroad, and it spread his command out across the countryside in a way to divert Confederate attention. "If he neglect his right or center we get on his Augusta road," Sherman wrote of Johnston. "If he neglect Atlanta, we take it." If Stoneman could not cut the other railroads south of the city, Sherman hoped that another cavalry force under Brig. Gen. Lovell H. Rousseau, riding from Middle Tennessee, could strike one of them in central Alabama. The Federals had enough pontoon material between their three field armies to provide adequate crossing points of the Chattahoochee where fords did not exist, and Sherman extended the telegraph line to Roswell. His repair crews could not rebuild the railroad bridge over the river until the infantry had firm control of the area south of it, so his columns would take enough supplies along in wagon trains to operate for some time once across.[27]

Recognizing that it would be impossible to maintain a continuous line of battle as the army group wheeled across the countryside from the Chattahoochee south, Sherman instructed McPherson, Schofield, and Thomas to form a line with their own troops and connect their positions with neighboring units by picket lines. Each army was to help its neighbor in case of attack. "A week's work after crossing the Chattahoochee should determine the first object aimed at, viz, the possession of the Atlanta and Augusta road east of Decatur, or of Atlanta itself," he informed them.[28]

Sherman had hoped to start his move south of the river on July 15 but had to postpone it two days. Meanwhile, he pushed his army commanders to send out patrols and gather information about the roads and enemy positions in this area. Dodge sent the 9th Illinois Mounted Infantry out five miles and made a map of the road system for Sherman. Schofield also sent in a new map based on information gleaned by his patrols. "There are no people left in the country except a few ignorant women and children," he told Sherman. "Hence, it is impossible to get accurate information except by actual reconnaissance." McPherson's chief engineer and his chief signal officer personally scouted the area south of Roswell.[29]

The final preparations occurred early on the morning of July 17, as Sherman sent a newly minted map of the region to his three army commanders. "It is the best [and] will be the standard for orders." Thomas would move directly on Atlanta, Schofield would head toward Decatur, and McPherson would aim for the railroad between Decatur and Stone Mountain, the next station east. "As soon as the road is broken all the armies will close on General Thomas." The resulting general line would bend southward to straddle the Georgia Railroad as the whole moved close to the city's defenses. McPherson and Garrard were to "risk much and break the railroad" on July 18 or 19. The next important move in Sherman's conduct of the campaign for Atlanta, perhaps the most important one, was about to begin.[30]

For a few days before the move of July 17, the Army of the Tennessee occupied itself with "resting, washing, and receiving supplies." The men swam in the river whenever possible. It was obvious they would be the whip in Sherman's move south of the Chattahoochee. When McPherson went through the camps of Dodge's men, Lt. Col. Edwin A. Bowen of the 52nd Illinois knew it meant an imminent move. "I presume Gen. McFersons Army is destined to flank Atlanta on the left. Objective point I presume will be Decatur Ga." Blair's Seventeenth Corps was still several miles away but planned to be at Roswell in time to cross the river sometime on the seventeenth.[31]

"We now commence the real game for Atlanta," Sherman told Halleck, "and I expect pretty sharp practice, but I think we have the advantage, and propose to keep it." To his wife, he expressed confidence that his men could deal with anything Johnston threw at them in an open fight, "but being on the defensive he can take great advantage of Forts, field works, and the nature of the ground." To boost Sherman's confidence still higher, Halleck praised his handling of the campaign. "Your operations thus far have been the admiration of all military men; and they prove what energy and skill combined can accomplish."[32]

2

From Roswell to Bald Hill, July 17–20

Sherman had prepared carefully for his big push south of the Chattahoochee River and was ready to start early on the morning of July 17. Three infantry corps and two cavalry divisions were still on the north side of the stream that day. McCook moved his horsemen downriver from the area of Vining's Station to join Stoneman in covering the area south of the Western and Atlantic Railroad as the Fourteenth, Seventeenth, and Twentieth Corps prepared to cross the river. The Fourth and Fifteenth Corps, Left Wing of the Sixteenth Corps, and Garrard's cavalry, already on the south side, began to march into Confederate-held territory.

Logan's Fifteenth Corps led the way south from Roswell with Brig. Gen. William Harrow's division in the van, followed by Brig. Gen. Charles R. Woods's division, then Brig. Gen. Morgan L. Smith's division. The troops started at 5:30 A.M. with three days' rations and 100 rounds of ammunition per man. Heading toward Cross Keys, Harrow reached Providence Church and took a road to the left that was "sometimes called the Decatur road." The Federals encountered Confederate pickets on all the roads, but only slight skirmishing with the cavalrymen of Dibrell's Brigade took place during the day. By midafternoon, Harrow's division settled into a defensive position at Nancy's Creek about a mile short of Cross Keys. Brig. Gen. Charles C. Walcutt's brigade crossed the creek, while the other two brigades remained north of it. All erected breastworks of fence rails after moving no more than six miles during the day. The men collected blackberries from the countryside and noted that the few houses along the way were mostly deserted. The remaining civilians told them their neighbors had run away from the Yankees in droves.[1]

Logan's other two divisions closed up on Harrow. At least one of the brigades in Smith's division constructed rail breastworks and cleared the underbrush for thirty feet in front to be ready for an attack. Charles Woods, who had taken over the First Division two days before when Brig. Gen. Peter J. Osterhaus went on sick leave, brought up the rear of the Fifteenth Corps. Logan was about twelve miles from Decatur on the evening of July 17.[2]

To Logan's right, Sixteenth Corps troops encountered stiffer resistance. The 9th Illinois Mounted Infantry moved ahead of Dodge's lead division, which was commanded by Brig. Gen. John W. Fuller. The Illinois regiment encountered Confederate cavalry and a couple of pieces of artillery when it neared Nancy's Creek. Fuller reinforced it with his own infantry and artillery, which enabled the Federals to push back the elements of Dibrell's Brigade. Fuller also was new to division command, having replaced the ailing Brig. Gen. James C. Veatch only a few days before. Brig. Gen. Thomas W. Sweeny's division followed Fuller's men.[3]

Behind both Logan and Dodge moved Blair's Seventeenth Corps, which had the longest march of the day. Blair started early and moved the rest of the way to Roswell, with Brig. Gen. Mortimer D. Leggett's division in the lead, followed by Brig. Gen. Walter Q. Gresham's division. Leggett crossed the Chattahoochee during the late afternoon and bivouacked for the night two and a half miles south of the river, while parts of Gresham's division crossed at dusk and bivouacked just on the south side. Many Seventeenth Corps regiments had marched up to twenty miles by nightfall.[4]

Garrard moved his cavalry division south, maintaining a distance of one mile to the left of Logan's advancing corps. He left two regiments behind to guard McAfee's Bridge, which the Confederates had abandoned several days before, while the rest of his division kept pace with Logan's van. Garrard found out from local people that there actually were two places called Cross Keys. The one on Sherman's map was the old community, and the other was a newer town located three miles east of it.[5]

To McPherson's right, Schofield tried to cover the large gap between the Army of the Tennessee and Thomas's Army of the Cumberland with his Twenty-Third Corps. He led the advance with Brig. Gen. Jacob D. Cox's division. Like Dodge, Cox skirmished with Confederate cavalry when he neared Nancy's Creek. The Federals pushed the opposition back and established their skirmish line south of the stream while keeping the main battle

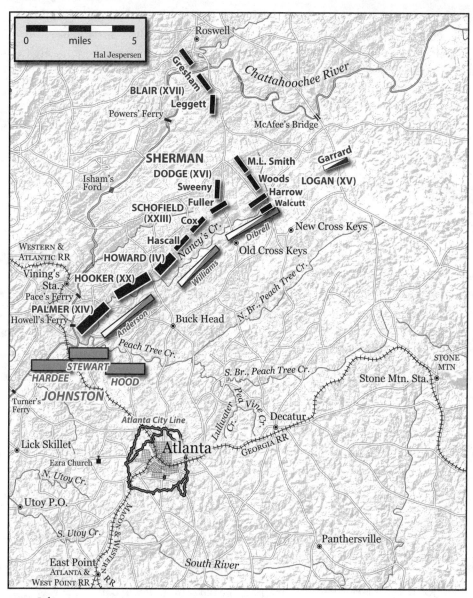

July 17

lines north of it. Even though Brig. Gen. Milo S. Hascall's division took post to Cox's right, the two divisions could not establish contact with each other. Schofield assured them not to worry about connecting their picket lines. "Make your position strong, and rely on yourself," he told Hascall.[6]

Thomas's move proceeded smoothly that day. His men erected a pontoon bridge at Pace's Ferry, allowing the Fourteenth and Twentieth Corps to cross the Chattahoochee River. Howard's Fourth Corps marched out of the Isham's Ford–Powers' Ferry bridgehead as Thomas's large army moved cautiously a few miles to a position along Nancy's Creek for the night.[7]

Sherman marched with Schofield's columns and bivouacked a couple of miles from Powers' Ferry that evening. Everything was moving well even though at a cautious pace. No significant opposition had been encountered, and despite the gaps in the Union formation, there was no danger yet of a Confederate counterstroke. Wheeler had no more than 1,600 troopers plus the cavalry brigade of Brig. Gen. Samuel W. Ferguson from Brig. Gen. William H. Jackson's Army of Mississippi division to oppose the Union move. All they could do was watch, skirmish, and burn bridges.[8]

But developments took place on July 17 that disrupted the Confederate response. Jefferson Davis was alarmed by a report that arrived at Richmond the previous day that indicated the Federals had advanced in force from the Chattahoochee River and were extending a fortified line toward the Georgia Railroad. This garbled and inaccurate report compelled him to demand of Johnston what the general planned to do about it. The army commander explained that the information was inaccurate, but he failed to assure the Confederate president that he was on top of the situation. "We must be on the defensive," Johnston told him. "My plan of operations must, therefore, depend upon that of the enemy. It is mainly to watch for an opportunity to fight to advantage."[9]

This was the final straw for Davis. It was, in fact, the same generic plan Johnston had followed ever since the start of the campaign and had led to the abandonment of northwest Georgia. According to some sources, Johnston issued an order to his troops that he intended to attack the Federals as they moved south of the river, but there is no confirmation of this claim in the official documents. Nevertheless, it came as a shock to Johnston to receive at 9 P.M. on July 17 an order relieving him of command. Written at Davis's behest by Adj. Gen. Samuel Cooper, the order was based on Johnston's constant retreating and the fact that he could "express no confidence that you can defeat or repel" the Federals.[10]

Davis replaced Johnston with one of his corps commanders, Lt. Gen. John Bell Hood, who had been writing critically of his superior for some time during the campaign. Hood, an effective brigade and division commander in Lee's Army of Northern Virginia during the first half of the war, suffered debilitating injuries to his left arm at Gettysburg and lost a leg at Chickamauga. But he had gained the good will of Gen. Braxton Bragg, longtime commander of the Army of Tennessee and now Davis's military adviser, in addition to developing a supportive friendship with Davis himself.

Because Hood positioned his image with key Confederate administrators as an aggressive general, the command of the army fell into his lap. "Be wary no less than bold," Secretary of War James A. Seddon cautioned Hood as he urged him to do something about the distressing situation outside Atlanta.[11]

Ironically, the appointment came as a shock to Hood. His first reaction was to defer or cancel it. A clash with Sherman seemed imminent, so Hood joined with his colleagues, Lt. Gen. William J. Hardee and Lt. Gen. Alexander P. Stewart, in a telegram urging Davis to rescind the order and let Johnston play out his hand. That delayed the transfer of command for many hours, but Davis flatly refused the request in a telegram received at 2 P.M. on July 18. By this time, precious hours had been wasted in the ability of the Confederates to keep track of and respond to Sherman's movements.[12]

Unaware of the developing turmoil in the Confederate camp, the Federals rose for an early start on the morning of July 18. Sherman planned to continue traveling with Schofield and instructed Thomas to reach Buck Head "and then feel down strong on Atlanta." He was eager for McPherson to hit the link between the city and Augusta. "I want that railroad as quick as possible," he told Thomas, "and the weather seems to me too good to be wasted."[13]

McPherson started at 5 A.M. but had to veer to the east, which meant widening the gap between his command and Schofield's. Logan continued to lead the Army of the Tennessee, with Wood's division in the van. The Fifteenth Corps moved by way of Widow Rainey's to Browning's Court House two and a half miles north of the Georgia Railroad. At that point, the troops paused while Garrard's cavalry advanced to the track. Logan's task was to cover the cavalry push in case the Confederates moved toward the area in force, but after a while, McPherson told him to send some infantry south to help Garrard tear up the railroad.[14]

Garrard moved two of his three brigades south, encountering one Confederate cavalry brigade soon after leaving Browning's Court House. His men pushed back light opposition until reaching the railroad between Decatur and Stone Mountain at 1 P.M. and began tearing it up. Soon after, Brig. Gen. Joseph A. J. Lightburn's brigade of Morgan L. Smith's division reached the railroad two miles from Stone Mountain and west of Garrard's location. Lightburn drove away Confederate cavalry and then set his men to tearing up the line. With the cavalry and infantry hard at work, McPherson's command destroyed several culverts in addition to "upsetting the tie, putting the iron on top, and setting fire to the pile." Logan increased the work force by sending fifty mounted men from the 8th Indiana Cavalry and his escort company to tear up a short stretch. By 5 P.M., the Federals had destroyed two

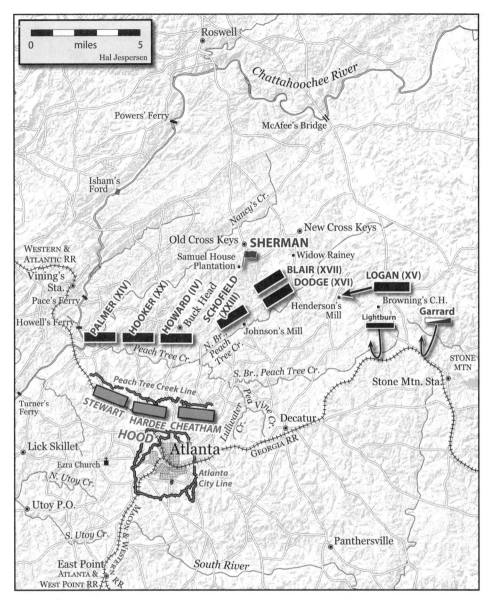

July 18

large sections of track for a total of more than three miles and burned the water tank at Stone Mountain Station.[15]

Sherman was pleased with this early strike on the Georgia Railroad. By noon, he had stopped at the plantation home of Samuel House, a brick structure near Old Cross Keys and four miles northeast of Buck Head. "A sick negro, the only human left on the premises," told him the house was eleven miles from Atlanta. A sign on the road indicated it was eleven miles from Roswell too. Sherman was in the heart of the disputed territory northeast of the city, and his men had already broken one of Johnston's lines of communications.[16]

The destruction of July 18 was but a foretaste of what would come. Logan concentrated his corps by pulling Lightburn back to the main column that evening and then moved away from Browning's Court House, which did not have enough good sources of water for his troops, reaching Henderson's Mill by dark. Meanwhile, Dodge's Sixteenth Corps troops skirmished their way south before bivouacking at the North Branch of Peach Tree Creek two miles south of Widow Rainey's. Blair's Seventeenth Corps also moved to the North Branch that evening and bivouacked. Logan's command at Henderson's Mill represented the far left of Sherman's extended front, planted six miles northwest of Stone Mountain and seven miles northeast of Decatur. Dodge and Blair near the crossing of the North Branch of Peach Tree Creek were located about two and a half miles west of Henderson's Mill.[17]

While McPherson was maneuvering on July 18, Cox's division led Schofield's advance by way of Old Cross Keys and old Peach Tree Road, passing by House's residence as it skirmished with Confederate cavalry. Schofield bivouacked near Johnson's Mill on the North Branch of Peach Tree Creek more than a mile southwest of Dodge's location and three miles east of Buck Head. Farther west, Thomas's left flank, consisting of Howard's Fourth Corps, reached Buck Head that day and turned south. The other Army of the Cumberland troops strung out in a rough line from that community back toward the Chattahoochee River, the whole line facing south and preparing to approach the main stem of Peach Tree Creek the next day.[18]

While the Federals were prepared to close in on Atlanta and had already snipped the railroad east of the city, the Confederates were preoccupied in controversy over the removal of Johnston. The center of that controversy lay at Army of Tennessee headquarters, located at the Nelson House three miles northwest of Atlanta. There, Johnston received the news that Hood's telegram to Davis, urging him to cancel the change of command, had been refused. "I cannot suspend it without making the case worse than it was before the order was issued," Davis asserted. Therefore, Hood assumed command of the army on the afternoon of July 18.[19]

When word circulated through the ranks, the news prompted an outpouring of anger, regret, and sadness. Johnston had been the most beloved commander of the army, and although some men were worried about his

John Bell Hood. Promoted above his native ability and prior command performance, Hood struggled to gain a handle on his new job when he was unexpectedly named to command the Confederate Army of Tennessee on July 18, 1864. The Battle of July 22 was his second strike in an attempt to save Atlanta and, like the first at Peach Tree Creek on July 20, was generally sound in its outline but flawed in its execution. Library of Congress, LC-DIG-cwpb-07468.

constant withdrawing, he retained the affection and confidence of most of its personnel. Hood, in contrast, was relatively unknown to them. William H. T. Walker was not surprised by Johnston's removal but remained hesitant about Hood. "He is brave, whether he has the capacity to command armies (for it requires a high order of talent) time will develop." At the very least, as Walker assured his wife, "a fight now is obliged to come off."[20]

Army of Tennessee headquarters learned that the Federals had broken the Georgia Railroad near Stone Mountain and that a Union cavalry strike from Middle Tennessee had hit the Atlanta and West Point Railroad near Opelika, Alabama. But nothing was done in response to either threat to Hood's lifelines because of the dislocation caused by the sudden transfer of command.[21]

Sherman was aware of Johnston's removal. At ten o'clock on the morning of July 18, a member of Thomas's staff brought a citizen to Sherman with newspaper reports even before the transfer of command was finalized. When he asked Schofield about Hood (they knew each other from West Point–cadet days), Sherman learned that the new Rebel commander was "bold even to rashness, and courageous in the extreme; I inferred that the change of commanders meant 'fight.'" Later that day, Blair found a newspaper at a farmhouse that contained news of Johnston's relief. He sent it to Sherman, who responded that it was "very good news, but to look out for an attack."[22]

Writing after the war, Sherman recalled being pleased but cautious when he found out about Hood's accession to command. "This was just what we wanted, viz., to fight in open ground, on any thing like equal terms, instead of being forced to run up against prepared intrenchments; but, at the same time, the enemy having Atlanta behind him, could choose the time and place of attack, and could at pleasure mass a superior force on our weakest points. Therefore, we had to be constantly ready for sallies." According to a memorandum found in an abandoned Confederate camp on July 18, Hood commanded 44,400 troops. Though outnumbered, the Army of Tennessee had enough manpower to make a determined attack.[23]

"I want a bold push for Atlanta," Sherman told Thomas of his plans for July 19. His troops had encountered so little opposition thus far that he wondered if Johnston planned to give up the city, but the news of Hood's appointment convinced him a fight was imminent. Sherman planned for McPherson to align the Army of the Tennessee to straddle the Georgia Railroad and advance toward Atlanta the next day. "I am fully aware of the necessity of making the most of time," he assured Halleck, "and shall keep things moving."[24]

Sherman instructed his subordinates to start at 5 A.M. on July 19 and converge in a coordinated drive toward Atlanta. Thomas was to move south and cross Peach Tree Creek, while Schofield would move directly toward Decatur and occupy the town. McPherson was to concentrate his army and move west along the Georgia Railroad toward Atlanta, while Garrard moved east along the line as far as prudent, destroying it as he went. All "should not lose a moment's time until night."[25]

Schofield pushed against "a heavy force of dismounted cavalry" as he moved south of the North Branch of Peach Tree Creek but made steady headway. His skirmishers reached the outskirts of Decatur by 1 P.M., allowing Sherman to establish headquarters at the Chapman Powell House on Shallowford Road (modern Claremont Avenue) one mile north of Decatur by noon. James Oliver Powell, son of Chapman, had moved there with his bride just before the war broke out and now was serving in the Georgia Militia. The house became the nerve center of the Union army group until early the next morning.[26]

After the 19th Ohio Battery shelled the Confederates in Decatur for some time, careful not to damage the town too much, Col. Peter T. Swaine's brigade of Hascall's division drove them out by 3 P.M. His men destroyed a mile of track, although they found that the retreating Confederates had already burned the depot and many army wagons. Hascall pushed the rest of his division through Decatur to establish defensive positions on its western perimeter.[27]

Cox's division had followed Hascall during the first half of the day but diverged to the west when the van of his command reached a point one and a half miles north of Decatur and headed for Pea Vine Creek. Cox established a strong defensive position along its eastern bank after skirmishing with Confederate cavalry along the way.[28]

McPherson instructed his Army of the Tennessee subordinates to move directly toward the railroad between Stone Mountain and Decatur from their respective bivouac areas and then tear up the track as they moved west. The primary task was to be undertaken by Logan and Dodge, with Blair trying to find room for his corps along the track if possible. They also were to send their empty wagons back to Roswell for another load of supplies.[29]

Dodge began the day by following in the wake of Schofield's command, but the going was slow. He halted just behind Cox's division two and a half miles south of the North Branch of Peach Tree Creek. Here, one of his scouts came in from Atlanta confirming news of Hood's replacement of Johnston. Then Dodge ordered his troops to cut a new road east of the Decatur Road, which was temporarily blocked by Cox, so his Sixteenth Corps troops could move over the South Branch of Peach Tree Creek, driving Confederate cavalry along the way. By 5 P.M., the van of Dodge's column entered

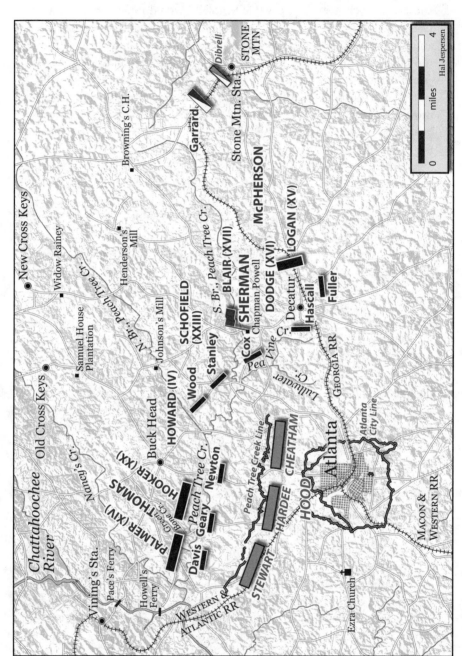

New Cross Keys

Old Cross Keys

Chattahoochee River

Vining's Sta.

Pace's Ferry

Howell's Ferry

Nancy's Cr.

Buck Head

Samuel House Plantation

Widow Rainey

Johnson's Mill

Henderson's Mill

Browning's C.H.

N. Br., Peach Tree Cr.

PALMER (XIV)

THOMAS

HOOKER (XX)

Davis

Geary

Newton

Green Cr.

Bone Cr.

Peach Tree Cr.

HOWARD (IV)

Wood

Stanley

SCHOFIELD (XXIII)

Cox

S. Br., Peach Tree Cr.

BLAIR (XVII)

SHERMAN

Chapman Powell

DODGE (XVI)

LOGAN (XV)

McPHERSON

Garrard

Dibrell

STONE MTN.

Stone Mtn. Sta.

Pea Vine Cr.

Decatur

Hascall

Fuller

GEORGIA RR

Nutwater Cr.

Peach Tree Creek Line

STEWART

HARDEE

CHEATHAM

HOOD

Atlanta

Atlanta City Line

WESTERN & ATLANTIC RR

Ezra Church

MACON & WESTERN RR

0   miles   4

Hal Jespersen

July 19

Decatur and assumed occupation duties from Swaine's brigade, which rejoined Hascall's command. He placed Fuller's division in position south of town, but Fuller received Confederate artillery fire as he crossed the railroad and lost several men, including the surgeon of the 64th Illinois. The 14th Ohio Battery returned fire and soon silenced the Rebel guns. An angry Ohio artilleryman blamed Schofield's troops for not properly securing the south perimeter of the town, claiming they spent their time plundering the abandoned houses. The citizens who remained were terrorized by the Confederate artillery fire that descended on their community.[30]

Logan moved his Fifteenth Corps troops directly to the railroad and began to destroy it west toward Decatur. They encountered only light cavalry opposition, although some units were compelled to detach skirmishers while the rest tore up track. The men of Lightburn's brigade already were "very stiff" from their railroad work of the previous day but bent to it again on July 19. The corps stopped just east of Decatur to bivouac that evening.[31]

Blair's Seventeenth Corps did not leave the previous night's bivouac on the North Branch of Peach Tree Creek until 10 A.M. With so many other units in his front, there was no clear route for his two divisions to the railroad, so Blair called a halt during the late morning, which lasted most of the afternoon. After this long break, the corps approached Decatur and bivouacked some two miles north of town for the night. It had taken no part in either the railroad destruction or the occupation.[32]

Garrard returned to the railroad that morning and pushed east toward Stone Mountain but encountered the stiffest opposition of the day. He reported two Confederate cavalry brigades in his front, one of them commanded by Dibrell, that fought dismounted. Garrard deployed two brigades of his own to push them back. When the Federals entered Stone Mountain Station, they found the Confederates had burned the depot, which contained "large amounts of quartermaster and commissary stores," and had also burned 200 bales of cotton. Garrard's command used artillery to drive the remaining Rebels out of civilian houses they were using as defenses.[33]

As the Union cavalry kept these Confederates busy, McPherson's army was concentrating east and north of Decatur. That community, one of thirteen towns named for Stephen Decatur, the only naval hero to emerge from the Tripolitan War of 1801–1805, suffered a traumatic introduction to war on July 19. In some ways, the town of 800 inhabitants impressed the Federals as "rather old, but [with] nice shade trees" and a good courthouse. About half the residents had already fled, while those who remained were "very shy, and act almost like frightened deer," fearful the Yankees would burn everything.[34]

The Federals were not shy about supplying their wants from publicly available stores in Decatur. Members of Hascall's division found enough coffee pots in a warehouse to supply all of their needs. Other Federals did not spare private houses either, especially those of the families who had fled; all empty residences had been "thoroughly ransacked" within two hours of entry into town. Some of Dodge's men brewed their coffee "on the still smoking timbers of rebel wagons" set afire by retreating Confederates. The occupiers were surprised to find 500 pikes accumulated for the use of a nearby conscript camp. The blade of each weapon was ten inches long and attached to a handle ten or twelve feet in length with a projecting iron hook to add a second piercing element. They were "terrible looking" but a curiosity as well. Many Federals took one as a souvenir, "giving the troops the appearance as though we were still in the middle ages," as an orderly on Dodge's staff put it.[35]

As Schofield and McPherson pressed forward on the Union left, Thomas struggled to close in on Atlanta from the north. At two locations his troops fought small but hard battles to secure crossings of Peach Tree Creek. Wood's division of the Fourth Corps forced its way along the Buck Head and Atlanta Road. Later that day, Newton's division relieved Wood in the large bridgehead on the south side of the creek. Farther west, Brig. Gen. Jefferson C. Davis's division of the Fourteenth Corps barely won a bitter fight to cross at the mouth of Green Bone Creek, only a short distance east of the Chattahoochee River. Part of the Twentieth Corps crossed between those two locations with relatively light opposition. Still, by the evening of July 19, Thomas had managed to get only a portion his army across Peach Tree. Moreover, he had no connection with Schofield to the east. A large gap had developed in the center of Sherman's moving formation. Howard tried to occupy that gap with Maj. Gen. David S. Stanley's and Brig. Gen. Thomas J. Wood's divisions, but they could not make firm contact with Schofield to their left or with Newton's division to their right. For the time being, this gap posed little danger because the Confederates were completely unaware of it.[36]

In the Confederate camp, July 19 was a day of desperate efforts by Hood to get a handle on his new responsibilities. As Johnston left the army for Macon, the new commander sought information about Union progress. Thomas's approach loomed as the greatest threat, not only because of the size of that force but also because of its nearness to the city. In contrast, Hood knew nothing of Schofield and McPherson's movements except by what Wheeler told him. The men at Confederate headquarters understood that the Unionists had captured Decatur in force, but there were few details. Hood moved headquarters from the Nelson House to the Luckie House on Peach Tree Road due north of Atlanta that afternoon. At 2:15 P.M. one of Hood's aides informed Wheeler that the general had received his short note indicating it seemed as if the Federal left wing was concentrating on Decatur. "It is important to get exact information of the state of affairs in that vicinity," he told the cavalry chief.[37]

But Wheeler apparently failed to do so, and exactly why is not clear. There are very few dispatches from him during the period July 17–21, and his official report of this phase of the campaign offers little in the way of useful information. Wheeler claimed to be "so heavily pressed as to be obliged to call for re-enforcements" on July 19, "but none could be sent me." Both Wheeler and W. C. Dodson, one of his soldiers who wrote a eulogizing book about him after the war, exaggerated the casualties the Cavalry Corps inflicted on the Federals in this skirmishing. The few personal accounts by his cavalrymen also are not helpful. No one can criticize the Confederates for lax resistance, but the failure to feed Hood detailed information about operations in this sector affected the course of events. Hood became focused on opposing Thomas first and then Schofield-McPherson.[38]

We do not even know with certainty which units Wheeler used in opposing the advance of Schofield and McPherson, but they were utterly inadequate to hinder the Federal advance. "I am astonished that the enemy have allowed us to get so near to Atlanta without any more opposition," wrote Capt. Edward B. Moore of the 54th Ohio in his diary. "It would seem as though our presence in this quarter unlooked for." Moore even wondered if the Confederates had sent most of their troops to Virginia and were mounting only a token defense of the city.[39]

Sherman tended to agree. His troops met "such feeble resistance" on July 19 "that I really thought the enemy intended to evacuate the place." By that evening, he was confident Schofield and McPherson could close in on the defenses of Atlanta the next day but thought it "extra hazardous" if they could not make firm connection with Thomas's army. That gap in his center worried Sherman, and he wanted to know more precisely where Thomas's men were located. "If Hood fights behind forts close to the town, I will swing in between Atlanta and the river" in order to move west of the city and hit the last two railroads feeding the Army of Tennessee. "But if he fights outside, we must accept battle." Sherman was confident of success even if he confronted the entire Army of Tennessee with only McPherson, Schofield, and Howard, "leaving you to walk into Atlanta," as he told Thomas. "But with Schofield and McPherson alone, the game will not be so certain."[40]

Sherman began what he called "the universal movement on Atlanta" at dawn of July 20. "In advancing this morning, of course we will bring on a heavy battle, and should be as fully prepared as possible." In orders issued for the movement, he charged his chief subordinates to "accept battle on anything like fair terms" but to halt and await orders if they came within range of the fortifications ringing Atlanta. If fired on, they should not hesitate to return artillery fire randomly on the city.[41]

McPherson prepared to lead his advance with Logan's corps north of the Georgia Railroad and Blair south of it, while Dodge followed behind Logan. He gathered all Army of the Tennessee trains at and north of Decatur, taking along only ordnance wagons and ambulances. "The command will move forward prepared for battle," he wrote, "divested of all useless incumbrances."[42]

Logan started at 5 A.M., passing west through Decatur and proceeding along the main Atlanta and Decatur road that paralleled the Georgia Railroad. Lightburn's brigade of Morgan L. Smith's division encountered Confederate cavalry two miles west of Decatur and skirmished forward before the cautious advance halted roughly two miles short of Atlanta by about noon. Along the way that morning, Logan sent an officer to contact Schofield and learn what progress he was making and which road the Twenty-Third Corps was using. Smith's division garnered the distinction of firing the first Union shots into Atlanta sometime that afternoon. Capt. Francis De Gress ordered his Battery H, 1st Illinois Light Artillery to fire three shells from its 20-pounder Parrotts at a range of two and a half miles. Signal officers observed as these rounds struck buildings in town. Meanwhile, Woods and Harrow followed Smith with caution. Toward evening, after part of Harrow's command aligned with Smith, the men of both divisions constructed breastworks as Woods and the rest of Harrow's division bivouacked to the rear in reserve. The Federals could see the opposing cavalrymen improving their own line of works some 800 yards to the west.[43]

Dodge did not start until 1 P.M., having allowed Logan's corps to pass his position and take the lead. His men pulled away from their bivouacs south and west of Decatur and moved behind the Fifteenth Corps at a leisurely pace. When Logan asked him to fill the gap between McPherson and Schofield, Dodge sent Sweeny's division to Logan's right, extending pickets to make contact with the Twenty-Third Corps. The men also constructed breastworks that evening. Fuller's division took position behind Sweeny to be ready to cover the gap that still existed between McPherson's and Schofield's main battle lines.[44]

Blair moved the Seventeenth Corps south through Decatur late that morning and then headed west on small roads toward Atlanta. Gresham deployed his division to link with Logan on the right. Col. Benjamin F. Potts, who had taken command of Gresham's First Brigade only three days before,

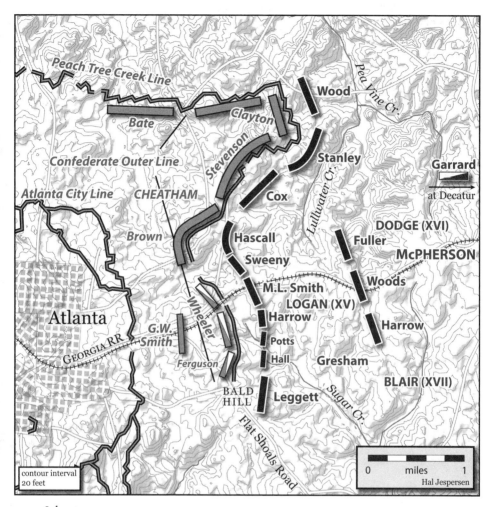

encountered Confederate pickets two miles west of Decatur. He deployed a heavy skirmish line and pushed forward with his brigade in line of battle until he came into line with the Fifteenth Corps. Col. William Hall's Third Brigade aligned to Potts's left. Gresham's division lost a total of fifty-one men in the process. As the Federals established their position, skirmishers used a house made of hewn logs to fire at the Confederates. The men also made breastworks of fence rails.[45]

With Leggett's division in reserve, Gresham's men were for the time the only Seventeenth Corps force in line. Gresham rode to the skirmish line, where Potts asked him to examine the terrain in front in preparation for a further push that evening. A politician from Indiana, Gresham had served as lieutenant colonel of the 38th Indiana from the fall of 1861 before becoming colonel of the 53rd Indiana early the next year. His solid performance in the field led to a commission as brigadier general by August 1863, and he replaced Marcellus M. Crocker on May 27, 1864, as commander of Blair's Fourth Division. He was one of the most reliable division leaders in Sherman's army group.[46]

But a Confederate soldier on what Blair later called "a high, bald hill" to the left of the Fourth Division's line soon deprived Sherman of Gresham's services. Before the division leader reached the hewn-log house, a bullet hit his left leg below the knee, shattering the bone. An Iowa soldier remembered "the look of agony upon his face" as Gresham was carried to the rear. According to one report, earlier he had been slightly injured on the finger by a shell fragment, but this leg wound was far more dangerous, the left tibia was shattered three and a half inches below the knee. Gresham refused amputation, so surgeons simply removed bone fragments that night, probably at the nearby Green B. Clay House.[47]

Immediately after Gresham's fall, Blair came forward to examine the terrain and noticed that the Confederates on Bald Hill could enfilade the Fourth Division as it moved forward. The feature, which was "so commanding," had to be taken before his corps could make more progress. Blair sent a staff officer to bring up Leggett's Third Division, taking position to the left of the Fourth Division, and assault the hill. There was just barely enough time to accomplish this move that evening if everything worked smoothly, but a foul-up occurred. The staff officer merely told Leggett to take position, "leaving out the most important part of the order," as Blair soon after learned, "which was 'to assault immediately.'" The corps leader was frustrated. "I am sure the hill would have been carried without serious loss on our part" if the order had been relayed to Leggett properly.[48]

Was this a golden opportunity lost? Perhaps Blair was right, but it is also possible that Leggett might not have been able to take the hill even if he had been instructed to do so. At any rate, his troops moved forward and settled in to the left of the Fourth Division. They fortified by piling fence rails in a line and digging a trench, covering their rails with dirt, until midnight.[49]

Col. William Hall temporarily took command of Gresham's division, but Blair had to find a permanent replacement who held the rank of a general. At 8:45 that evening, McPherson informed Sherman that Gresham was wounded and asked that Brig. Gen. Giles A. Smith replace him. Smith commanded a brigade in the Fifteenth Corps division led by his older brother, Morgan L. Smith. Sherman immediately approved, and Giles reported for duty at 2 A.M. of July 21. Described by Blair's acting assistant adjutant general as "a typical Western man" from "a fighting family," Giles Smith "had sandy

GEN. GRESHAM WOUNDED.

See page 141.

Wounding of Brig. Gen. Walter Quintin Gresham. One of the best division commanders in Sherman's army group, Gresham was severely wounded while trying to observe from the Union skirmish line late on July 20. His wounding delayed Federal efforts to organize an attack on Bald Hill, postponing it until early the next morning, by which time the Confederates had firmed up its defenses. A Rebel soldier on Bald Hill shot Gresham in the left leg below the knee. The general refused amputation and suffered greatly from the aftereffects of that gunshot wound for the rest of his life. From F. Y. Hedley, *Marching through Georgia* (Chicago: Donohue, Henneberry, 1890), 119.

hair, a bright blue eye and always a pleasant smile and a cheerful word. His negligent air was never changed in battle, and no excitement could be detected except by the enlargement and brilliancy of his eyes." Like his brother, Giles Smith was a superb brigade and division commander.[50]

Although skirmishing proved to be heavier than on any previous day, no battle developed as the Army of the Tennessee moved cautiously toward Atlanta on July 20. Decatur was for the time the nerve center of operations. William E. Titze, an orderly on Dodge's staff, observed his general interact with Logan and McPherson in the streets that afternoon. "Dodge rather nervous, McPh. cool as could be & smiling as ever & Logan silent & twisting his moustache, which is long enough to reach behind his ears." By 3 P.M., McPherson moved west to his army's new position and wrote a full report of progress to Sherman. All apprehensions about a major battle with Hood proved unnecessary, at least as events so far indicated.[51]

Schofield moved forward as cautiously as had McPherson that day. Cox's division led the way, skirmishing in advance, until coming to a fortified Confederate line three miles from Atlanta. Cox deployed three brigades in line to front this position, holding a fourth in reserve, and sent a regiment to the left to make contact with McPherson. To his right, contact was made with Stanley's and Wood's divisions of Howard's Fourth Corps. This allowed Schofield to place Hascall's division in line to Cox's left. Hascall pushed forward skirmishing until coming into line with Cox not far from the Howard House, located on top of a high hill the Confederates occupied a mile north of the Georgia Railroad. Both divisions constructed earthworks and continued skirmishing.[52]

During the day, Garrard's cavalry division moved to Decatur and covered the rear of the Army of the Tennessee, but Sherman had other plans for it. Late on July 20, he ordered Garrard to move toward Covington, thirty miles east of Decatur, the next day. The objective was to tear up a large stretch of the Georgia Railroad from Lithonia to Covington, especially destroying the rail and wagon bridge over the Yellow River between the two towns. He also was to burn the bridge over the Ulcofauchee River five miles east of Covington. Sherman allowed the cavalry two days to thoroughly wreck the track, twisting rails and burning ties, and told Garrard it would be worth the loss of a quarter of his men to accomplish the task. While this raid would strip McPherson of his cavalry screen, Sherman thought the objective was worth the risk. He planned to shift the Army of the Tennessee away from the railroad very soon and wanted to leave large sections of the line unusable.[53]

While all these developments took place on the Union left wing, unknown to Sherman, Thomas's Army of the Cumberland fought the first battle south of the Chattahoochee River that afternoon. It also was the first strike by Hood against the Federal threat to Atlanta. Hood had been scrambling since the afternoon of July 18 to manage his new command and arrange some offensive action. By that time, the Army of Tennessee was in the process of assuming a new defensive position staked out by Johnston's order along the high ground just south of Peach Tree Creek. In fact, the troops were in the process of moving from their bivouac areas northwest of Atlanta when they were informed of Johnston's removal. The Peach Tree Creek Line was just two miles north of Atlanta and covered the main roads approaching the city from near the railroad bridge east to Pea Vine Creek. As the infantry dug in, Wheeler shifted his cavalry on the evening of July 18, removing three brigades from north of the city and sending them to the east of town. Kelly's division had been in position there for some time and had provided the forces that skirmished with McPherson and Schofield on July 20.[54]

Hood prepared for a strike against Thomas on July 19, but word of McPherson's and Schofield's progress diverted some attention to the need for defenses to the east as well. The right flank of the Peach Tree Creek Line ended near Pea Vine Creek two miles north of the Georgia Railroad, with only cavalry between those two points. Hood authorized the beginning of a new line to cover the eastern approaches, but it was built in stages. To begin, Brig. Gen. John C. Brown shifted Hindman's Division of Hood's Corps, currently led by Maj. Gen. Benjamin F. Cheatham after Hood's promotion to army command. Brown moved south from the east end of the Peach Tree Creek Line until his right flank rested one and a half miles north of the railroad. The cavalry continued to cover the rest of the area to the tracks.[55]

Confederate dispositions remained so until the middle of July 20, when further word of McPherson's and Schofield's progress led Hood to extend the infantry line farther south toward the railroad. Cheatham shifted Maj. Gen. Carter L. Stevenson south, but this still was not enough to allow Brown to touch the railroad. By midafternoon, Cox's division and part of Stanley's division faced Stevenson's Division. The rest of Stanley's and all of Wood's divisions, however, approached the right wing of Clayton's Division, which faced north at the eastern end of the Peach Tree Creek Line. Maj. Gen. Henry D. Clayton's left wing and the entire division of Maj. Gen. William B. Bate were positioned opposite of what was now a gap of one and a half miles separating Wood from Newton's division. Fortunately for the Federals, the Confederates were still unaware of this gap.[56]

The shifting of Stevenson strengthened the Confederate Outer Line, as the position between the east end of the Peach Tree Creek Line and the railroad was known, but that movement also took several hours away from Hood's scheduled 1 P.M. assault on Thomas. Three hours later, the

Confederates finally launched their attack, which opened the Battle of Peach Tree Creek at about 4 P.M. Hardee's Corps and the Army of Mississippi, under Lt. Gen. Alexander P. Stewart, moved north from the Peach Tree Creek Line and caught the Federals by surprise. Despite that advantage, the Confederates were unable to deal Thomas a dangerous blow. Hardee mismanaged his assault even though heavily outnumbering Newton's division. The Federals, toughened by years of experience, held fast to their position and repelled every attack. Maj. Gen. Joseph Hooker's Twentieth Corps, which barely completed its crossing of Peach Tree Creek before the attack, also responded well and threw back the assaulting lines. Brig. Gen. Richard W. Johnson's division of the Fourteenth Corps held its position against the left end of Stewart's command. By dusk, all Confederate efforts had come to nothing because of a combination of poor management, uneven combat morale among the rank and file, and very stout Union resistance. It was a sterling accomplishment by Thomas's veterans.[57]

Hood actually employed more men in this failed assault than Thomas used in repelling it. Of 26,000 troops engaged, the Confederates lost 2,500 (9.5 percent). The Federals lost 1,900 out of 20,000 men engaged (also 9.5 percent). Ironically, Sherman remained unaware that the battle had even taken place until very late on July 20. Heavily involved in managing the fight, Thomas did not write a report until 6:15 P.M. "The enemy attacked me in full force at about 4 P.M.," he stated, and were "repulsed handsomely." That dispatch did not reach Sherman until midnight, perhaps because he had shifted his headquarters from the Chapman Powell House. Sherman accompanied Col. Silas A. Strickland's brigade of Hascall's division for a while, then rode over to Howard's headquarters with Stanley and Wood. Throughout the evening before the dispatch arrived, Sherman was thinking of shifting McPherson to the west of Atlanta but needed Thomas to close in on the city to shorten the general Union line. He also wrote his nearly daily report to Halleck at 9 P.M. before knowing of the battle that had already ended on his army group's right. The news when it arrived came as something of a surprise; Sherman had assumed Hood would hit McPherson and Schofield rather than Thomas.[58]

But the Union advance along the railroad played a significant role in the course of the fighting at Peach Tree Creek. Hood relied on Wheeler to delay McPherson and Schofield while he fought Thomas, but that was a slender reed on which to rely. The caution with which the Federals moved aided Wheeler, but still his command was able only to maintain its presence in front of Sherman's left wing while skirmishing and falling back. Sometime before 4 P.M., Ferguson's Brigade on the right gave way, and Wheeler had to personally intervene to stop its retreat. The only available troops to offer support were 700 men of the recently mobilized Georgia Militia under Maj. Gen. Gustavus W. Smith. "There is nothing to my right," Smith informed Wheeler at 4:35 that afternoon, but he was ready to help the cavalry if needed. The militiamen straddled the railroad to the rear of Wheeler's position. Cheatham worried about the security of his own line, stretched pretty thin in a vain effort to reach the railroad. Although the Outer Line was advantageously placed on high ground west of Lullwater Creek, a tributary of Pea Vine Creek, it was inadequately held and vulnerable.[59]

The pressure on Wheeler compelled Hood to call off the assaults at Peach Tree Creek earlier than planned. He sent an order to Hardee to provide a division to support the cavalry. That order reached Hardee at about 7 P.M., just minutes before his reserve division, commanded by Maj. Gen. Patrick R. Cleburne, was set to begin its advance as part of a renewal of the effort against Newton's Federal division. That renewal was immediately canceled, and Cleburne moved his men south to rest near Atlanta before moving east by dawn of July 21. Whether these troops could have crushed Newton is open to question, but there is no doubt that McPherson's and Schofield's slow advance that day paid significant dividends for Thomas's embattled army.[60]

Although not engaged, Cleburne's Division suffered some losses due to Federal artillery fire on July 20. The men left the Peach Tree Creek battlefield that evening and moved south to the heart of Atlanta, from where they headed east along the Georgia Railroad. Then the brigades formed along the imperfect works of the Outer Line from a point just north of the track down toward Bald Hill, relieving the cavalry to shift farther south in an effort to cover that modest rise of ground. There was little rest for any of Cleburne's men. It was a night of marching and deepening trenches. The members of Govan's Brigade carried poles and logs with them to use as the base for an enlarged parapet, piling dirt on them with their hands after loosening the ground with bayonets. Wheeler's cavalrymen also had no rest that night. Shifting to the south, they had to dig new works from scratch and were only half done when dawn began to peak over the eastern horizon. They could see, however, that the ground in their front was generally clear and open for a good field of fire.[61]

As if the pressure of events near Atlanta was not enough, Hood also had to worry about his supply line running through central Alabama. Word that it was being seriously damaged by a Federal cavalry raid filtered in on July 20. Maj. Gen. Lovell H. Rousseau led 2,500 Union troopers from Middle Tennessee and took Confederate forces in Alabama by surprise. From July 17 to 19, his men tore up more than thirty miles of the West Point and Montgomery Railroad at and near Opelika, encountering virtually no resistance. Rousseau then rode unopposed toward Marietta, Georgia, to join Sherman.[62]

The Federals could not know of these pressures on Hood's ability to control affairs inside the perimeter of Atlanta's defenses. Before word of the battle at Peach Tree Creek arrived, McPherson partially excused his slow progress by informing Sherman that Wheeler's cavalrymen were armed not with short range carbines, but with short versions of the Enfield infantry arm, which made it more difficult than usual to push them back. McPherson also ordered his army to dig in that evening and prepare to repel any attacks early the next morning. Even before Garrard moved out on his Covington raid, Blair warned McPherson that Confederate cavalry patrols were seen hovering around his left flank and into the rear areas. Garrard was not doing his job properly; he concentrated his troopers too much at Decatur instead of establishing a strong presence in close touch with Blair's left flank. Not only slowness but also a degree of carelessness characterized McPherson's advance that day, which did not bode well for the future.[63]

3

Battle of Bald Hill, July 21

At 1 A.M. on July 21, an hour after learning of Hood's attack on Thomas, Sherman wrote a dispatch to McPherson. "I was in hope you could have made a closer approach to Atlanta yesterday, as I was satisfied you had a less force and more inferior works than will be revealed by daylight, if, as I suppose, Hood proposes to hold Atlanta to the death." This gentle rebuke for McPherson's cautious approach on July 20 was followed by instructions about what to do if the Confederates actually evacuated Atlanta. Sherman believed that was a real possibility based on Hood's sound defeat at Peach Tree Creek and the relatively light Confederate artillery fire McPherson encountered. He was not convinced the city would be emptied, but if the Confederates abandoned it next morning, then they would go toward Macon. Should this happen, McPherson was to pass by Atlanta to the south and pursue for a couple of days at least. If they did not evacuate, Sherman believed Hood would reinforce his right to oppose McPherson and Schofield.[1]

Several hours later, dawn brought forth a beautiful, clear morning. The Confederates had not moved, so McPherson's first order of business was to take Bald Hill. This feature loomed large in the consciousness of Federal commanders, posing a danger- ous threat to a further advance. Variously called Bald Knob, Bald Hill, and Gold Hill, the bare part was a cleared field 200 yards wide north to south that had been cut to provide wood for the

Confederate government bakery in Atlanta. The only house on the hill belonged to Henry Spear, a baker before the war who had returned from service in Lee's army to superintend the timber cutting that gave his hill its distinctive appearance. His house was located about twenty-five yards in front of the Confederate line, with a strong fence about five yards farther east. The hill lay two and a quarter miles from Atlanta, and the Federals assumed its view of the city was commanding.[2]

McPherson relied on Leggett's division of about 4,000 men to take the hill while Gresham's division, now led by Giles A. Smith, would advance as a diversion to the north. Brig. Gen. Samuel W. Ferguson's cavalrymen of his brigade of Brig. Gen. William H. Jackson's Army of Mississippi division held the hill. An Alabama cavalry brigade led by Brig. Gen. William W. Allen and a Georgia cavalry brigade commanded by Brig. Gen. Alfred Iverson Jr., both belonging to the division of Maj. Gen. William T. Martin, were positioned to the left of Ferguson and fronted Giles A. Smith's command. To Iverson's left lay the right end of Cleburne's infantry position, taken up only a few minutes before the near-dawn Union assault. Brig. Gen. James A. Smith had his brigade of Texas infantry and dismounted cavalry ready to assist Iverson and Ferguson in holding the right end of the Confederate Outer Line.[3]

At 7 A.M., Leggett tapped Brig. Gen. Manning F. Force's brigade, which fronted Bald Hill, to fulfill McPherson's order. "I want you to carry that hill," he told him, and gave Force an hour to prepare. Force arranged his regiments in two lines, with the 16th Wisconsin on the left and the 12th Wisconsin on the right of the first line, while the 20th Illinois, 30th Illinois, and 31st Illinois formed the supporting line. The men deposited their knapsacks as brigade skirmishers crept forward. When his men were nearly ready, Force walked among them. "Boys, now be cool and firm," he said, "don't waver, don't falter; just make up your mind to drive the enemy from yonder hill, and you'll do it. Be cool and determined, boys, and it will be all right." To the left of Force's command, Col. Robert K. Scott's brigade was in line and would advance with it. Col. Adam G. Malloy's brigade, consisting only of the 17th Wisconsin and a battalion comprising detachments from three other regiments, formed a refused divisional line on the left of Scott to guard against an enemy flank movement.[4]

The task ahead would have been easier if McPherson had advanced quickly enough to attack Bald Hill on the evening of July 20. By the time Force was ready to assault, Cleburne's Division had bolstered the Confederate Outer Line. Wheeler was happy to see the infantry arrive but disappointed that Cleburne placed his men so closely together that only half the cavalry's original position was filled by them. Thus, troopers instead of infantrymen still confronted Leggett. Cleburne's Division arrived before dawn

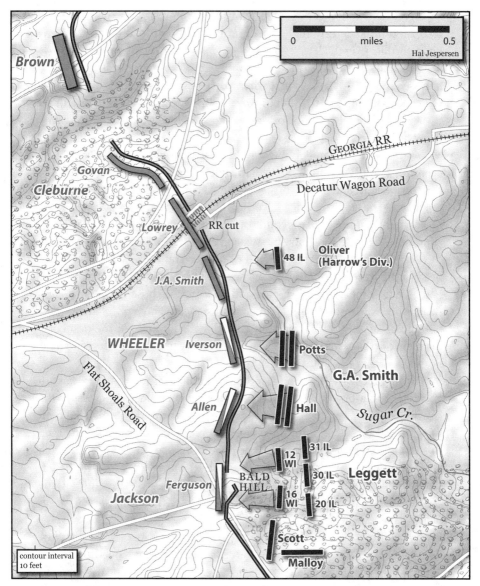

Battle of Bald Hill, July 21

and went into position quietly, with Brig. Gen. Daniel C. Govan lining up his brigade on the left, Brig. Gen. Mark P. Lowrey establishing his brigade in the center and straddling the railroad, while James A. Smith's Brigade occupied the right, extending the infantry line to a point one mile south of the track. The cavalry had thus far constructed only slight works, so Cleburne's men improved them. When dawn revealed the situation, Capt. Irving A. Buck of Cleburne's staff was disgusted with the position. It "was weak, ill protected, commanded by higher ground in front, and badly enfiladed" by Union artillery on the left.[5]

Cleburne's men had little time to prepare. They were still digging in, harassed by deadly artillery fire, when Force began his assault to the south. Officers walked along the line of Smith's Brigade and told their men that they "must drive them back or die, as the safety of Atlanta and the army depended on us."[6]

On the Federal side, Force was right—the only way his men could succeed was to push up the slope of Bald Hill without hesitation, regardless of the consequences. It was lightly held, but the killing ground before it was open and exposed. The brigade commander and one of his aides-de-camp positioned themselves just behind the first line while placing his assistant adjutant general, Capt. J. Bryant Walker, and another aide just behind the second line. Force was described as "one of those remarkable men that were produced by the war." His appearance aided his command presence. He had a "fair complexion, very pale and had one of those impressive faces which show no emotion under any circumstances. These peculiarities gave him the greatest control over his men and made him one of the best commanders of troops in the army." He and probably his staff officers rode their horses during the assault.[7]

The brigade started at 8 A.M. and moved quietly through the trees until encountering a brook with grassland skirting both sides. In crossing the stream, the line became disordered, especially in the center, which led both wings to advance a bit faster once across. Force shouted orders for the men to straighten their formation, but they had difficulty executing them. The instruction was "give off to the left!" but short movements toward the left did not solve the problem. With company officers repeatedly shouting the order, the men in the center at last turned and "fairly *ran* to the left" to finally straighten the line.[8]

By this time, Force's first line had passed through the grassland skirting this little brook and hit the edge of a cornfield that sloped up to the Confederate position. The field was filled with "green corn nearly ready to blossom," recalled a man in the 31st Illinois. On reaching the stout fence at its western edge and near Spear's house, the men were ordered to stop and lie down as the skirmishers vainly tried to tear down the bordering fence. Then Force ordered the troops to stand, fix bayonets, and advance at the double quick. Now was the time for them to heed Force's advice about steeling their nerves and not stopping until they reached the top of the hill. "They charged steadily," reported an observer in Dodge's command, "in a regular will-have-victory style, accompanying the movement with the yell and cheer peculiar to such conflicts." Many fell as they climbed the fence, but the Union line continued forward. Ferguson's cavalrymen continued to fire intensely as the Federals closed in.[9]

Soon Force's first line came onto the Federal skirmishers, who had stopped short of the enemy position to pepper the top of the hill with rifle fire. "The brigade received and enveloped them," as Capt. Gilbert D. Munson aptly phrased it, and marched on without a halt. "Our men fell in bunches," but the rest closed in and kept moving. Most of Ferguson's troops stopped firing when the first Union line was only twenty paces away and began to evacuate the works. The Federals barely hesitated when reaching the top, where they found the Confederate fortifications three feet deep with a parapet two feet high. "We carried the works, jumping right in among" those Confederates who remained, reported a man in the 16th Wisconsin. "Hardly any of them left their works until we got within two or three rods . . . , and many of the men remained in their position until we compelled them to surrender." Col. Cassius Fairchild of the 16th Wisconsin reopened a wound received at Shiloh as he jumped across the parapet.[10]

Ferguson's Brigade "gave way in some confusion," as Wheeler frankly reported. Many Federals, buoyed by adrenaline, pursued a short distance. "Our orders are to carry this hill, General," Munson reminded Force, who replied that he thought his men could do more. But then it became apparent that Giles A. Smith's division to the right had been stopped at the Confederate Outer Line and could not support a further advance. Force then sent Walker to retrieve the troops who had continued west of the hill, among them the 16th Wisconsin, which had advanced 100 yards beyond the Confederate earthworks. Then he sent Walker to inform Leggett of his success.[11]

The effect of Force's attack extended northward from Bald Hill. Judging by the very scarce Confederate reports, Ferguson's left flank probably did not extend very far north of the hill. Panic seized the cavalrymen of Allen's Alabama Brigade and Iverson's Georgia Brigade as they watched with horror while Ferguson abandoned them and moved hastily off Bald Hill. In a short while, the cavalry end of the Outer Line melted away, exposing the right flank of Cleburne's position.[12]

It was a supreme moment of opportunity for the Federals, but they could not exploit it. Giles A. Smith had waited until Force was quite near the top of Bald Hill before he ordered his men forward in a supporting move at 8:30 A.M. Potts's brigade held the right wing while Hall's brigade held the left, each arrayed in two lines. Six hundred yards separated the division from the Confederate Outer Line, the ground between open and ascending. James

A. Smith's Brigade, shifting south, opposed the Federals, delivering "a murderous fire of musketry" as they struggled up the slope. "Our men began to fall fast," admitted William F. Graham of the 53rd Illinois.[13]

The two Union brigades managed to reach a point about 50 to 100 yards from the blazing earthworks. The troops then lay on the ground and endured the punishment for thirty minutes. "Language would fail to give you any idea of the terrible conflict," wrote Lt. John J. Safely, provost marshal on Hall's brigade staff. The men had to lie with their faces close to the ground and soon grew hot as well as excited by the danger. It was "almost suffocating to lie so close to the ground," wrote Charles E. Smith of the 32nd Ohio. Some of them tried to dig a slight protection, but it was too dangerous to raise even an elbow. After some time different regiments began to fall back, often one company at a time, until gradually all of Potts's and Hall's troops gave up their demonstration and returned to the starting point of their advance.[14]

James A. Smith's Brigade saved Cleburne's line, but it was touch and go on the right flank. Its rightmost unit, the consolidated 24th and 25th Texas Cavalry (dismounted), also had given way when the troopers to the south retreated in disorder. A cavalry officer ran along the regiment's line shouting, "'Leave here; you will all be captured; the cavalry has given way and the enemy is surrounding you.'" Lt. Col. William M. Neyland of the 24th and 25th Texas Cavalry sent Maj. William A. Taylor to inform brigade leader Smith, but Taylor could not find him. The major saw the regiment leave its works and rushed back to help Neyland reform the men to the rear. The two managed to organize a regimental line at a right angle to the brigade line. Then Neyland counterattacked at quick time, swinging roughly in a left wheel to restore his original position. He then extended his line by forming one rank instead of two and was able to occupy about 200 yards of the position formerly held by the cavalry. Although a few cavalrymen helped Neyland in this counterattack, the Texans had little but contempt for the way the troopers had retreated.[15]

The firming up of Cleburne's right flank not only halted the dangerous fracturing of the Confederate Outer Line but also set up an odd tactical situation. Bald Hill was now in Union hands, while only a few hundred yards north the Confederate position held firm. Force's right flank, held by the 12th Wisconsin and 20th Illinois, now received galling enemy fire on its flank. The Federals dug in as fast as they could, which helped relieve the punishment. But Cleburne's line was punished even more by slanting Union artillery fire from the north.[16]

Leggett asserted that the Confederates "made repeated efforts to drive us from the hill," McPherson adding that the first attempt was "vigorous" while the other two were "feeble." But there is no indication that Ferguson, Allen, or Iverson reformed and counterattacked. William A. Taylor, in fact, reported that the 24th and 25th Texas Cavalry (dismounted) was forced to fall back twice because of lack of support to its right after it restored the line. Neyland was wounded in the thigh during the third withdrawal, and Taylor took command of the regiment to restore the position once and for all. But there is no indication from the Federal side of these actions. It is possible that the pressure of Union skirmishing alone caused the Texas regiment to fall back temporarily after it reestablished its original position. Two regiments from Lowrey's and Govan's Brigades arrived to support James A. Smith's command.[17]

On the Federal side, one regiment from the Fifteenth Corps advanced to offer some degree of support for Giles A. Smith's demonstration. Col. John M. Oliver sent forward the 48th Illinois from his brigade in Harrow's division. It had no support to either right or left, as the rest of Oliver's regiments continued constructing earthworks. The 48th advanced part way across the empty space between the lines, then plopped to the ground and waited an hour, accomplishing nothing, until falling back. It suffered forty-five losses and made no impression on the opposing line.[18]

Even so, Bald Hill remained in Union hands, and some Federals insisted on calling it Leggett's Hill to honor the division leader who grabbed it. But Leggett thought the rise of ground deserved to be called Force's Hill to honor the brigade leader who masterminded its capture. Leggett moved Capt. Marcus D. Elliott's Battery H, 1st Michigan Light Artillery to the hill, where its six Rodman steel guns opened fire on the Confederates manning the Atlanta City Line. He later replaced Elliott with Lt. John Sullivan's 3rd Ohio Battery so its 20-pounder Parrots could shell Atlanta itself. McPherson also received another confirmation of Hood's replacement of Johnston in command. While watching Force attack Bald Hill, a Union spy brought in yet another Atlanta paper of July 18 with the news. McPherson told a staff officer, "we must now look out for different tactics—that Hood, though he might lack in judgment, would certainly fight his army at every opportunity that offered and with desperation and . . . we must take unusual precautions to guard against surprise."[19]

The fight for Bald Hill was short but bitterly contested. Force suffered 258 casualties, the 12th Wisconsin alone losing 134 out of 600 engaged. The regiment captured forty-eight Confederates and picked up 500 small arms on the battlefield. It suffered a great deal from enfilade fire from units to the north as well. Clement Abner Boughton was hit by three bullets while carrying cartridges along the regimental line after the hill had been captured and died later of his multiple wounds. Many other men in his regiment shared similar fates that day. Totaling the losses in Seventeenth Corps units, Leggett's division posted casualties of 365 men and Giles A. Smith's division lost 363. Blair's total casualties on July 21, 728 good veterans, represented a heavy toll for the capture of one hill.[20]

Confederate losses were substantial, considering the lower troop strength engaged in the battle. There are no reports of casualties among the three cavalry brigades, but James A. Smith's Texas brigade suffered 186 losses. Lowrey's Brigade lost an additional 48 men that day, but we cannot account for losses in any of the other Confederate units.[21]

For Smith's Texans, the battle of Bald Hill was only the beginning of their worst day of the war. Union artillery fire peppered their exposed position without mercy. "Everytime a shell came over, we could hear men groan & call for the litterbearers," remembered Charles A. Leuschner, a Prussian serving in the 6th Texas. Smith blamed most of the damage to his brigade on one Union battery located only 800 yards away, the fire of which "swept my line from left to right, committing dreadful havoc in the ranks. I have never before witnessed such accurate and destructive cannonading." One round took out seventeen of eighteen men in one company of the 18th Texas Cavalry (dismounted). It struck the company on the flank and ranged along its trench. "Knocked one man in a hundred pieces," recalled Capt. Samuel T. Foster of the 24th Texas Cavalry (dismounted), "one hand and arm went over the works and his cartridge box was ten feet up in a tree."[22]

The intensity of this artillery fire waxed and waned but never entirely ceased during the day. Officers suffered as much as the rank and file. Lowrey's and Govan's men to the left were better protected and did not suffer as did Smith's Texans. It seemed to Irving Buck that "a modern Joshua had appeared and commanded the sun to stand still," for the day seemed to drag on without end. Late in the evening, an artillery round decapitated Bill Sims of Company K, 18th Texas Cavalry (dismounted). The severed head struck W. W. Royall on the chest and knocked him down. By that time of the day, as Royall recalled, "our clothes were sprinkled with blood and men's brains and the bottom of the breastworks was nearly half covered with blood."[23]

After the war, Lt. Col. William W. Belknap of the 15th Iowa spoke with Buck, Cleburne's assistant adjutant general, who thought this devastating fire had been delivered by Capt. Francis De Gress's Battery H, 1st Illinois Light Artillery, of Morgan L. Smith's Fifteenth Corps division. But that was not possible. De Gress reported no firing from his battery on July 21. On the other hand, Lt. William H. Gay reported that his 1st Iowa Battery fired "with great effect, as could be plainly seen, causing the enemy great discomfort" that day. Part of the time he placed three of his pieces forward of the Union works in an open field to obtain a better crossfire on the Confederates. Capt.

Josiah H. Burton also reported obtaining "nearly a flank fire" on the Rebels with his Battery F, 1st Illinois Light Artillery that day, but Gay's battery probably dealt out most of the punishment on Smith's Texans. Both Gay and Burton belonged to Harrow's Fifteenth Corps division.[24]

Hood arranged to bolster the Confederate Outer Line beyond Cleburne's right flank. By 9 A.M., he had begun to shift Cheatham's Division, now led by Brig. Gen. George E. Maney, toward the line east of Atlanta. After taking a heavy part in the fighting at Peach Tree Creek the previous day, Maney's men moved into the city for some rest, catching glimpses of Georgia governor Joseph E. Brown before moving east. It is unclear whether the division relieved all of Wheeler's cavalry and exactly where this relief took place. Dispatches from Hood's headquarters refer to a gap between Maney and Cleburne that was filled with cavalry. Maney probably positioned his troops somewhere between the Atlanta City Line and Bald Hill, with some cavalry units remaining to his left. His men began replacing the cavalry by 1 P.M. and started to dig trenches, although they had to give up the entrenching tools before they had finished the job.[25]

While Cleburne's men endured terrible Union artillery fire all day of July 21, Leggett's troops busily prepared the Bald Hill area for further action. They now held a salient protruding several hundred yards forward of the rest of McPherson's line and had to be concerned with defensive measures on three sides. Force placed the 12th Wisconsin and 16th Wisconsin on the northern slope, the troops extending north into the woods beyond the cleared area but facing west. The 20th Illinois was next in line, with the 31st Illinois to its left; both regiments mainly held the cleared area and the top of the hill. The 30th Illinois extended into the woods south of the cleared space; the lines of the 31st and 30th Illinois deflected a bit toward the southeast to stay on the best ground available. Scott's brigade extended Leggett's line to the left, with Battery H, 1st Michigan Light Artillery between it and Force's command. Leggett shifted Malloy's brigade from his left to his right to make connection with Giles A. Smith's division. In order to do that, Malloy had to form a refused line west to east because Smith was still part of McPherson's main line several hundred yards east and north of Bald Hill. As Leggett recognized, his was an awkward position, protruding forward and requiring protection on both flanks. "In fact, my line was a prolongation of the enemy's line," he wrote after the war. Cleburne's Division was arrayed directly to the north but facing east rather than west.[26]

Everyone in Leggett's division felt the need to dig in, and they pursued that desire all day and well into the night of July 21. The best defense against threats to the flank was to construct traverses, earthen banks extending from the trench or parapet toward the rear and facing the vulnerable flank.

Leggett's men constructed dozens of traverses, placing them in the line of every one or two companies of each regiment. The 12th Wisconsin, whose flank was exposed to Cleburne's Division, made their traverses "especially solid and strong." Leggett's men also tore down Spears's house to provide timber for revetting their works.[27]

To crown Bald Hill, the Federals constructed a small fort on the right of the 20th Illinois. They cut three embrasures on the north side and one on the west side. The configuration of the work was in the shape of a horse-shoe, no more than forty feet wide, with a short trench to the rear for infantry to support the guns. Although small and not very impressive, this fort would play a key role in the coming battle.[28]

Captain Elliott's Battery H, 1st Michigan Light Artillery had initially been placed on Bald Hill soon after Force captured the position. It was later shifted to the south and replaced by Lieutenant Sullivan's 3rd Ohio Battery. Before the end of the day, Sullivan also was moved and replaced by Capt. Edgar H. Cooper's Battery D, 1st Illinois Light Artillery. Cooper had four 24-pounder howitzers and placed some of them in the little fort.[29]

While Leggett made his salient as defensible as possible, he worried greatly about the security of his left flank. Sherman's decision to send Garrard's cavalry division to Covington to tear up track deprived McPherson's left flank of a proper screening force. Jacob D. Cox later surmised that Sherman was motivated in this by warnings from Grant that Lee may be sending reinforcements to the Army of Tennessee. A big break in the railroad forty-two miles east of Atlanta could hinder the transport of these troops. As it transpired, the Confederates never had any intention of shifting troops between East and West; even though Sherman could not know that, it was incautious of him to take away the only cavalry available to McPherson.[30]

Ironically, Garrard was only barely screening McPherson's flank even before he left for Covington. On July 21, his division was scattered about well to the rear of the Army of the Tennessee rather than concentrated near its flank. He had three regiments at Old Cross Keys, ten miles from Decatur, with pickets spread out up to four miles from that crossroads. One regiment held McAfee's Bridge, and another was stationed at Roswell on the Chattahoochee River. That left five regiments to screen the road system around Decatur, where Garrard made his headquarters and where McPherson's trains were parked. Garrard spent most of July 21 issuing orders to concentrate his scattered regiments. He had placed pickets south and east of Decatur who were "constantly exchanging shots with rebel cavalry pickets," but that did not unduly alarm anyone. It could be expected that the enemy would scout the area for information as to Union troop positions and movements. Garrard did not actually leave for his Covington raid until 7:30 on the evening of July 21.[31]

"I will simply remark," McPherson told Sherman in a dispatch written at 3 P.M. that day, "that I have no cavalry as a body of observation on my flank." He also had to worry about Decatur once Garrard was gone. To deal with the latter problem, McPherson ordered Dodge to detach a brigade of Fuller's division to the town as guard for his trains. Garrard was expected to be gone only two days.[32]

The lack of an effective screen for the army's left flank became an even more serious problem when Leggett submitted reports that large Confederate infantry forces were seen moving south from Atlanta. Sometime during the early afternoon, Force called Leggett's attention to this movement from his vantage point on Bald Hill. The two officers counted at least ten regiments, with wagons and ambulances, on the move and worried that it portended a strike against the Union left flank. Leggett sent reports to Blair, who informed McPherson before 3 P.M. It is something of a mystery as to what these officers saw, because the Confederates did not start their major flank march until about dusk that evening. Possibly they witnessed the shifting of Cheatham's divisions into the Atlanta City Line or Maney's movement of his division.[33]

McPherson authorized efforts to shore up his left. Giles A. Smith moved his division to continue the line south of Leggett's position that afternoon. His troops arrayed roughly along the Flat Shoals Road (which also was known to the Federals as Old McDonough Road) but at a slant compared to the general Union line. He also refused the end of his position so the line crossed that road. While Potts's brigade connected with Leggett, Hall's brigade held the far end of this vulnerable line. The 16th Iowa was positioned east of the road and the 11th Iowa west of it, with two Napoleons of Lt. Walter H. Powell's Battery F, 2nd Illinois Light Artillery on the road itself. The 15th Iowa settled to the rear of the 16th Iowa in a detached position, while the 13th Iowa was placed a shorter distance to the rear of the 16th. All regiments dug in that evening and cleared the brush for at least fifty yards in their front. Still, given the scattered nature of Hall's deployment, patches of brush continued to obscure the full view of one position from another. Various officers sent men out to serve as pickets on the roads south of Smith's new line.[34]

Fuller's division was called on as a source of manpower to bolster McPherson's stance. When McPherson instructed Dodge to send one of its brigades to Decatur that morning, Fuller selected Brig. Gen. John W. Sprague's command, which started on the five-mile march east. The brigade arrived by noon and established pickets on all the roads leading to town. While many of the Army of the Tennessee trains were parked near Decatur, some were on the move, bringing supplies down from Roswell.[35]

Late on July 21, in response to Leggett's report of Confederate movement southward from Atlanta, McPherson shifted the remaining brigade of Fuller's division to his vulnerable left flank. Fuller himself accompanied his old brigade, now led by Col. John Morrill, and Battery F, 2nd U.S. Artillery as they moved from behind Logan's Fifteenth Corps south of the railroad. When he reported to Blair, the Seventeenth Corps leader provided a staff officer to guide him the rest of the way. Fuller placed Morrill between a quarter to a half mile east of G. A. Smith's extreme left, facing south to overlook the valley where Sugar Creek forked. Apparently, commanders thought it important to cover this valley area as a natural approach to the rear of the Seventeenth Corps line, but the gap between Morrill's isolated brigade and Giles A. Smith's fortified division also offered the enemy an opportunity for a concealed advance. Moreover, Morrill did not dig in but bivouacked in the open. Fuller placed Battery F, 2nd U.S. Artillery in the Seventeenth Corps line between Leggett and Smith.[36]

Logan adjusted the position of his Fifteenth Corps on July 21 by moving Woods's division to the right of Morgan L. Smith's command. Dodge moved one brigade of Sweeny's Sixteenth Corps division into line to Woods's right and connected with the Twenty-Third Corps to the north while keeping the other brigade in reserve. Logan also shifted Harrow's division to Morgan L. Smith's left, replacing Giles A. Smith's division after it had moved south of Leggett. Harrow now connected with Blair's Seventeenth Corps. For the first time, McPherson and Schofield achieved a tight link between their two armies. Twenty-Third Corps men dug in and skirmished all day, some climbing trees to catch a glimpse of Atlanta. Battery F, 1st Michigan Light Artillery fired into the city. Many Federals could hear the repeated sound of train whistles drifting from the west, feeding the impression that Hood might be evacuating the city. "It's the general opinion we will take the place without much opposition," William H. Nugen of the 25th Iowa informed his family. "The next letter you receive from me will be written in the City of Atlanta."[37]

But Hood had no intention of giving up the city so easily. McPherson's approach, slow and cautious though it was, created a need for the Confederate commander to react. The fracturing of the Confederate Outer Line by Force's capture of Bald Hill signaled trouble to the east of the city. As Hood later reported, McPherson "made it necessary to abandon Atlanta or check his movements." He decided to strike back. When cavalry patrols reported the Union left flank was vulnerable, Hood planned to take advantage of it.

A devotee of Lee's bold tactics, he envisioned a major turning movement to gain the rear of the Union Army of the Tennessee and roll up Sherman's line. It would be the most ambitious tactical offensive ever launched by the Confederate Army of Tennessee.[38]

But, true to his muddled performance in these early days as the army's commander, the plan was characterized by unrealistic expectations and unclear instructions to subordinates. Hood outlined his idea in a conference held late that afternoon or early in the evening of July 21 at his new headquarters in the Austin Leyden House on Peach Tree Street in Atlanta. Hardee, Cheatham, Stewart, Wheeler, and Georgia Militia commander Gustavus W. Smith listened as Hood explained that he did not want just to turn and hit McPherson's flank, he intended to plant an entire corps of his army several miles to the rear of the Union line. He relied on Hardee, who commanded the best corps in the army, to accomplish this unusual feat, even though bad blood had long been evident between the two men. Hardee had looked upon Hood as a young upstart ever since the early days of the campaign and resented that he now had to take orders from him. Yet Hardee also was the best corps leader available. Cheatham and Stewart were too new to their elevated responsibilities to have proven whether they could be relied on for such a daunting move.[39]

Hardee's initial instructions were to march well around the Union flank and head for Decatur, with no discretion as to his ability to alter that plan. Even though his command had fought at Peach Tree Creek the day before and Cleburne's Division suffered terribly in the Confederate Outer Line all day on July 21, Hardee began the move at about dusk. But the worn condition of the troops and the prospect of an all-night march and a heavy battle the next day compelled him to request a revision of the plan. Hood called a second conference at his headquarters to discuss this. Taking place a bit after 10 P.M. and attended by Hardee, Cheatham, and Wheeler, the discussion was rather intense but ended with Hood relenting a little. He allowed Hardee to make a shorter march merely to strike McPherson's left flank. Wheeler's cavalry would now hit Decatur in a detached but complementary move.[40]

In his typically muddled way, Hood inaccurately characterized all this when filing his overdue report of the Atlanta Campaign in February 1865. According to him, there was no first and second plan, but Hardee was to move to McPherson's rear "even should it be necessary to go to or beyond Decatur." Both he and Wheeler were expected to attack at daylight "or as soon thereafter as possible." Then, when Hardee had McPherson on the run, Cheatham was to attack the front of the Army of the Tennessee. If both corps succeeded, then Stewart was poised to strike Thomas. Exactly at what time Hood developed this very ambitious plan is unclear, but he probably had decided on it before 2:30 P.M., when one of his aides instructed Wheeler to visit army headquarters that evening. Because Hood planned to wait for dusk to cloak the start of Hardee's long march, he placed a heavy burden on the troops.[41]

Those men began their ambitious flank move at dusk, a couple of hours before the conference at Hood's headquarters that allowed them a shorter route. From the center of Atlanta south on the McDonough Road to Cobb's Mill on Entrenchment Creek was a walk of nine miles. The mill, located four miles on a direct line southeast of Atlanta, was the key point. From there, a road led an additional six miles northeast to Decatur. An alternate route could take the Confederates three miles to McPherson's left flank, which rested a bit west of due north from Cobb's Mill. To reach Decatur from Atlanta along Hardee's route was a distance of fifteen miles, but to strike McPherson's left flank was only twelve. For tired men marching all night, the three-mile difference was important. Either way, it was a longer, more difficult flank march than that accomplished by Stonewall Jackson at Chancellorsville. Hardee started with up to 18,000 troops, but historian Gary Ecelbarger estimates he lost 7,000 of them through straggling along the way. Wheeler probably took 3,500 cavalrymen with the column. Despite the straggling, Hardee delivered a formidable force of manpower to surprise the Federals.[42]

The entire Army of Tennessee was in movement during the night of July 21–22. As Hardee's divisions evacuated the Peach Tree Creek Line, Stewart's divisions did the same. While Hardee's men moved into the city to regroup and prepare for the march, Stewart's filled the northern perimeter of the Atlanta City Line, the last system of earthworks protecting the place. Cheatham's divisions also evacuated what was left of the Confederate Outer Line north of Bald Hill and fell back to the eastern perimeter of the Atlanta City Line. All this was done without alerting the Federals, and few Confederates knew anything about Hood's plans for the morrow. When some of Cheatham's troops encountered Hardee's marching columns heading south through Atlanta, they were perplexed by this unusual movement.[43]

Bate's Division led Hardee's Corps in the flank march. It was in some ways "a glorious night," with a full moon shining brightly across the landscape. Some men sang their favorite songs, such as "Annie Laurie," "Enpidee," and "Anne Darling," but others found only misery with the roads ankle deep in dust and their canteens empty. Sgt. Washington Ives of the 4th Florida admitted that he "was compelled to rest as thousands did though I did not straggle as many did."[44]

Walker's Division followed Bate, but before it set out from Atlanta, the commander stopped to see Hood at the Leyden House on Peach Tree Street.

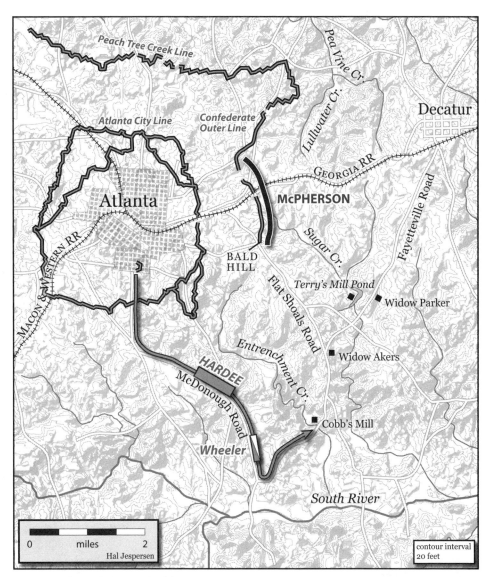

Hardee's Flank March, July 21–22

Walker came out of the meeting "full of serious enthusiasm." As he rode along, he told his assistant adjutant general, Maj. Joseph B. Cumming, "that Hood had earnestly impressed him with the conviction that a battle next day was necessary to prevent the immediate fall of Atlanta, and had rapidly unfolded his plan and the arduous nature of the undertaking." Walker "was aglow with martial fire," Cumming recalled. His men would need martial fire to endure the heavy all-night march. Even Cumming nodded off and slept in his saddle now and then. "How many better men fell literally out of the ranks having first fallen asleep!" he remembered years later.[45]

Cleburne's tired division followed Walker's. Initially, it was to begin withdrawing from the Confederate Outer Line at dusk, but delays ensued until, at 11 P.M., Hardee's headquarters told Cleburne to pull out at 1 A.M. on July 22, leaving skirmishers in position to cover the withdrawal. It already was clear that Hardee could not bring the weight of his corps to bear on the Federals at dawn. Cleburne's men could not possibly march a dozen miles in the dark with such a late start after their grueling day in the trenches.[46]

James A. Smith's Texas brigade pulled out of its position, some men forced to do so on their hands and knees to minimize exposure to Federal pickets on this moonlit night. They stopped long enough in Atlanta to refill cartridge boxes, then set out "without having the least idea of our destination or even of the direction in which we were moving," recalled William J. Oliphant of the 6th Texas Infantry. The other brigades pulled out in similar fashion, but Govan worried about his men. "The loss of another night's rest was a heavy tax upon their powers of endurance," he reported.[47]

All of Cleburne's brigades left behind heavy skirmish lines for the time being. Lowrey, for example, deployed 180 men to cover his brigade sector, James A. Smith left 5 men from each company, while Govan left an entire regiment. These skirmishers evacuated the Confederate Outer Line as soon as possible. Samuel T. Foster commanded Smith's skirmishers. When the brigade left the works he pulled his men back into the trenches, where they lit fires and made noise, talking loudly and knocking sticks on logs, to fool the Federals into thinking the line was fully manned. Then they quietly pulled out sometime before daylight. Foster's men marched quickly, taking shortcuts across country, and barely rejoined Smith's Brigade before the start of the battle.[48]

George Maney, currently commanding Cheatham's Division, was the last in Hardee's column, but no one seems to have recorded his men's experiences during this night march. The division evacuated its position between the Atlanta City Line and Bald Hill and fell back to the city before hitting the road south.[49]

Hardee stripped his artillery complement down to the minimum to facilitate the march. This happened at least in Cleburne's Division. Capt. Thomas J. Key, in charge of the three batteries assigned to that command, detached two of them to the army's artillery chief before leaving Atlanta and took only one along on the march. If that was typical, then Hardee had only four batteries when he struck McPherson later that day.[50]

Cheatham's divisions had relieved what was left of the cavalry in the works after dark on July 21, and Wheeler soon began his march. But T. B.

Roy of Hardee's staff recalled a good deal of mixing as the mounted troops shared the same road as the infantry, "making it the most tedious and harassing night march I ever experienced."[51]

Unfortunately for Atlanta, its residents had no clue as to why the Army of Tennessee was moving about and were especially alarmed to realize that Hardee's Corps was leaving their city. Not surprisingly, the rumor that Hood was evacuating spread like wildfire and created a panic. Army headquarters made some effort to allay this but failed. Hood's assistant adjutant general informed Brig. Gen. Marcus J. Wright, commander of the post of Atlanta, to be prepared to evacuate the city "should it become necessary." He was to be ready to move "without saying [anything] about it" to civilians. Even Hood's headquarters wagons were prepared to leave, and Wright informed Isham Harris, the itinerant Confederate governor of Tennessee, to evacuate by railroad.[52]

From the start of Hardee's march, frightened civilians began packing what they could and leaving Atlanta on the assumption the Yankees would soon be among them. The streets of the city and the roads leading south were thronged with refugees, and dozens of houses stood empty yet filled with household goods. The temptation was too great for Hardee's soldiers, who "plundered and robbed indiscriminately" as they passed through Atlanta. They often stole worthless objects simply because they had the opportunity to do so. "All over the army . . . can be seen fancy ornaments, brass door and porcelain bureau knobs, small bells etc. decorating the harness of the mules and horses," recalled William L. Trask, one of Hardee's couriers. Trask especially blamed Wheeler's cavalrymen, who ransacked stores, "gutted them completely; clothing of all kinds, notions of every description, cigars, tobacco, and whiskey were gobbled and carried off." Sam Richards verified that Wheeler's men, not the infantry, ransacked his stationery store. Cavalry and infantry alike assumed the army was once again retreating and meant to grab what they could before it was too late. Some civilians also took advantage of the situation and plundered as hard as the soldiers. The agent in charge of the Adams Express Company's office panicked and told everyone to help themselves with the packages entrusted to his care as the plundering became general and unrestrained.[53]

Atlanta was home to a number of staunch Unionists who had been persecuted by city authorities and the overwhelmingly pro-Confederate population of the city ever since the start of the war. Cyrena Stone lived in a house on the northeast edge of town and just behind the Atlanta City Line. A Confederate field hospital moved onto her property early on July 21, and all that day soldiers begged for food and drink. An officer made an effort to protect her as best he could, but it was a trying time for this Unionist. The hospital was moved away later that day, giving Stone some respite. She left that night to stay with a friend elsewhere in town, even though Atlanta was in a frightful uproar.[54]

A short distance east of the troubled city, the Federals settled in for the night. Leggett continued to worry about news of enemy troop movements and consulted with Giles A. Smith. Both officers thought those reports portended an attack on McPherson's left flank, but when Leggett visited Blair, the corps commander seemed to believe they portended instead a Confederate evacuation of Atlanta. All Leggett could do was ride along his division line and encourage the men to continue strengthening their earthworks. McPherson clearly was concerned. At 5:30 P.M. he wrote a dispatch to Blair encouraging him to cut brush and small trees for up to 100 yards in front of the works to make a clear field of fire for his men and an obstruction to the enemy. He further urged him to impress on his men the importance of being alert to an attack early the next morning. Blair circulated McPherson's dispatch, a copy of which reached Leggett's headquarters just before midnight. Soon after, when the division commander received a report of noise heard in front of the Federal skirmish line, he sent two scouts to investigate. They returned with a report that the Confederates definitely were moving south of Atlanta. Leggett sent this intelligence to Blair at 1:30 A.M. on July 22. Even this news prompted no unusual note of alarm or intensified any preparations on the part of high-level Federal officers.[55]

In one of his almost-daily dispatches to Halleck in Washington, Sherman briefly mentioned Force's capture of Bald Hill as well as further information about the Battle of Peach Tree Creek the day before. McPherson and Schofield were now connected and on good ground. It was possible to see the Atlanta City Line from some parts of their position, and Federal batteries had already fired on the town. He planned to open a stronger shelling the next day. "I doubt if General Hood will stand a bombardment; still he has fought hard at all points all day," Sherman concluded. He had received a dispatch from Grant at 6 P.M. that warned him Hood would defend Atlanta "at all hazards and to the last extremity," but Sherman saw little likelihood of another Confederate offensive like that at Peach Tree Creek. "I do not believe the enemy will repeat his assaults," he told Halleck, "as he had in that of yesterday his best troops and failed signally."[56]

4

Morning, July 22

For the Federals, July 22 began with a great deal of uncertainty as to whether their campaign for Atlanta was over or just entering a new phase. The first reports that the Confederates had evacuated the Outer Line began to filter in by 11 P.M. of July 21. Word from pickets indicated "unusual restlessness" in the Confederate defensive works. This could mean an evacuation, but did that mean the abandonment of the city? In an effort to find out, McPherson woke Andrew J. Alexander (Blair's assistant adjutant general) and asked him to go out and obtain more information. Alexander readied himself, then crawled out as close as possible to the Confederate position and concluded it was empty. McPherson waited, however, until closer to dawn for confirmation.[1]

At near daylight, Alexander went out again to an oak tree on high ground and saw signs that convinced him the Confederates were evacuating Atlanta. Returning, he found McPherson in consultation with Blair and Giles A. Smith. The army commander questioned him closely and then admitted, "I don't know what Hood is doing," but he intended to strengthen his left flank at any rate.[2]

Sherman also suspected Hood was giving up Atlanta. At 2 A.M. he called for one of his inspectors general, Willard Warner, and sent him to tell McPherson that the Army of the Tennessee should push forward at dawn and pursue the enemy. Warner reached McPherson's headquarters at 4 A.M. with instructions to bypass the city to the south and head for East Point, six miles south of Atlanta and Hood's probable destination, where the two railroads from Macon and Montgomery feeding the city converged. Thomas would bypass Atlanta to the west while Schofield would move through the city.[3]

When reports that the Confederates had evacuated the Outer Line were confirmed, Sherman fully believed Hood was giving up Atlanta. He issued orders for "a vigorous pursuit," as McPherson put it, and spread the word to Thomas's army. McPherson and Blair rode to Bald Hill, but Leggett could not believe the Confederates would give up the city so easily. When the generals rode toward Atlanta and drew Rebel skirmish fire, Leggett managed to talk them into going back to his position on the hill. Logan also rode impetuously toward the city on the center of his Fifteenth Corps line. "'What the h—l are you doing here?'" he yelled at Federal skirmishers. "'Don't you know the town's evacuated?'" When Logan continued to ride forward with his staff, he drew so much enemy fire that the group quickly rode back out of danger.[4]

But neither of these incidents proved that Atlanta was still held in force—the fire could have been delivered by covering forces in an attempt to delay Union pursuit. Whether Hood was gone or not remained a mystery for some time early that morning. When dawn arrived at about 5:30 A.M., the silence in the area was "phenomenal and profound," as Leggett recalled, which seemed to support the notion that the enemy had fled. The sky was mostly clear with occasional summer clouds. The temperature already was warm, and birds twittered among the pine trees.[5]

Ignoring the peaceful start of the day, McPherson continued to ride about with Blair in tow. They found a high spot from which to view the Atlanta City Line and also observed Confederate troop movement, still thinking it possible that Hood was evacuating. Regardless, the Federals prepared to move forward and occupy the abandoned Outer Line. Only Leggett's and Giles A. Smith's divisions remained in place because they already were in position at and south of Bald Hill and 1,200 yards from the Atlanta City Line.[6]

On the right of McPherson's army, Woods's division moved forward three-quarters of a mile and rested its right flank on the highest ground in the area. (After the war, this eminence was named Copenhill and became the location of the Jimmy Carter Presidential Library.) Its most prominent feature was the Howard House. Schofield advanced his Twenty-Third Corps troops and linked his left flank to Woods's right on this hill. Woods's men began to reverse the Confederate earthworks by literally moving the parapet and abatis from the east side to the west side of the trench. A gap of 250 yards, occupied by an area of swampy lowland at the foot of Copenhill and unsuitable for a line of infantry, separated Woods's left flank from Morgan L. Smith's division.[7]

Morgan L. Smith's men moved forward to extend the Union line south of the swampy lowland at 6:30 A.M. Their line straddled the Georgia Railroad as each regiment began to reverse the Confederate earthworks. Harrow's division also moved forward to Smith's left, connecting on the left with Leggett's division near Bald Hill. Harrow's men worked with the few entrenching tools available, moving the parapet from east to west, until their new earthworks were "tolerably defensible." While most men in the Fifteenth Corps improved their defenses as ordered, some of them thought the effort was wasted. The notion that Hood was giving up Atlanta had seeped down into the ranks of some units. Battery F, 1st Illinois Light Artillery initially took position without any earthworks until Harrow came along and ordered the men to dig in. Still, they only half-heartedly put their shoulders into it.[8]

On and south of Bald Hill, the men of Leggett's and Giles A. Smith's divisions were still "very much fatigued from yesterday's doings." They had not only captured the hill in a heavy fight but also had fortified it nearly all day and evening of July 21. Some of the dead from that battle still lay unburied on the morning of July 22. But the earthworks were stronger on and near the hill than anywhere else along McPherson's line. The Fifteenth Corps was now aligned with Blair's troops on and south of Bald Hill.[9]

The Federals established a strong skirmish line well in advance of their new main position. They fortified this advanced post, digging earthworks in places and piling up fence rails as breastworks in other spots. On Morgan L. Smith's sector, an especially heavy skirmish position sprang up 600 yards in front of the main line. The 111th Illinois shouldered most of the responsibility here, but it was supported by the 53rd Ohio and two pieces of Battery A, 1st Illinois Light Artillery, all under the command of Col. Wells S. Jones.[10]

On McPherson's extreme right, Sweeny's division had served as his connection to Schofield's army the previous day and evening. Skirmishers informed Sweeny of the Confederate evacuation of the Outer Line, and he relayed that news to Dodge by 4 A.M. But the concerted move forward shortened the Union line and squeezed Sweeny's command out of the formation as Woods established contact with Schofield at Copenhill. At 8 A.M. McPherson verbally ordered Dodge to shift Sweeny to the far left, where he would join Fuller's lone brigade to protect that flank. He showed Dodge on his map the high ground near the head of Sugar Creek and close to the road running west to east between Blair and Fuller. McPherson instructed Dodge to personally scout the area and select a good position for his men.[11]

Dodge set out with some staff members and found a strange atmosphere in the area. "The stillness was oppressive," he later wrote, "and I thought almost ominous." The party could see Confederates working on the Atlanta City Line. "We wondered why our presence was ignored," recalled W. H. Chamberlin, Dodge's assistant commissary of musters. But when the party left, a Rebel gun fired, the shell exploding "within a few yards of us" but hurting no one. Dodge concluded that it would be too dangerous to move Fuller and Sweeny into this area without proper entrenchments, so he gave orders for working parties to begin digging in. He also sent word to Sweeny to stop his division near Fuller's position until those earthworks were ready. Dodge then rode along the Seventeenth Corps line and consulted with Giles A. Smith, who assured him there were no cavalry patrols screening his left. Dodge also gave orders for the return of Battery F, 2nd U.S. Artillery to Fuller's command. It had been loaned to Blair earlier, but now Dodge correctly thought it should be with its assigned command.[12]

Sweeny's division started its move from the right to the left of the Army of the Tennessee at 9:30 A.M. No sense of urgency attended its slow march east along the Georgia Railroad before turning south to use a secondary road leading toward the general area where Fuller was located. Sweeny consumed most of the morning in moving his two brigades two miles. Once he was positioned near Fuller's lone brigade, the Left Wing, Sixteenth Corps waited from three-quarters to one mile behind Blair's command and about half a mile south of the Georgia Railroad on good ground overlooking Sugar Creek.[13]

Sweeny left his contribution to the skirmish line in place when his division departed McPherson's right. Those skirmishers had advanced at dawn, when it became apparent that the Outer Line was empty, and pushed three-quarters of a mile beyond before stopping. Initially, it appeared as if the enemy had evacuated Atlanta, and this news created "a half-glad, half-doubting look" on men's faces until the reality slowly sank in. Sweeny's skirmishers constituted a firm connection between the Fifteenth Corps and Twenty-Third Corps skirmish line, but it would take some time for other troops to replace them. Meanwhile, the 52nd Illinois remained behind. Half of its companies were on the skirmish line, and the other half acted as a reserve to the skirmishers. Its commander, Lt. Col. Edwin A. Bowen, had orders to rejoin the division as soon as possible.[14]

To McPherson's right, Hascall received reports at 1 A.M. that the Confederates seemed to have evacuated the Outer Line. Schofield instructed him at 3:30 A.M. to confirm those reports, and by 5 A.M. both Hascall and Cox assured Army of the Ohio headquarters that the enemy had fallen back. Hascall secured the abandoned enemy works, resting his left flank on Copenhill as his command reversed the entrenchments. From their new position, Hascall's men were "in full view of his [Hood's] works around the city and, under the fire of his artillery," as they dug in. Schofield's artillery returned the fire as the notion that Hood had evacuated Atlanta evaporated.[15]

In fact, the entire Union line was in motion on the morning of July 22 because Hood had not only evacuated the Outer Line but the Peach Tree Creek Line as well. The Army of Tennessee already was ensconced in the Atlanta City Line at dawn before the Federals realized it. But for a time, all the Unionists could do was explore forward and find out where the enemy had gone. Meanwhile, Col. Charles Ewing, Sherman's aide-de-camp, foster brother, and brother-in-law, rode to Thomas's headquarters to spread the erroneous report that Hood had evacuated Atlanta. For the moment it seemed a plausible surmise based on the available evidence, but as soon as Thomas's skirmishers neared the City Line, they were stopped cold by Confederate skirmishers and heavy artillery fire. Nevertheless, the move forward had shortened the Union line and allowed Sherman the room to transfer McPherson's army from east of the city to its west and south, a move he hoped to initiate quite soon now that the Georgia Railroad was out of commission.[16]

In fact, Sherman's desire to tear up even more of the Georgia Railroad before leaving the area east of Atlanta threatened to further endanger McPherson's army. Not only had he already sent off Garrard's cavalry division, but he also wanted to use Sweeny's two brigades to thoroughly wreck the track between the Army of the Tennessee's position and Stone Mountain. McPherson had received an order to that effect at 7 or 7:30 A.M. but refused for the time to obey it, even though written in Sherman's own hand. "I want that road absolutely and completely destroyed," read the directive, "every tie burned and every rail twisted." But McPherson instead ordered Dodge to send Sweeny to his left flank at 8 A.M., delaying the move to the left a bit to give him an opportunity to talk with Sherman about it.[17]

McPherson took his time to reach army-group headquarters. On the way he stopped at Blair's headquarters tent, where the chief surgeon reported Confederate cavalry prowling near Seventeenth Corps hospitals to the rear. McPherson also received reports of similar enemy appearances near his own headquarters on the Decatur Road. It was not so unusual for opposing cavalry patrols to be spotted in rear areas, so no immediate sense of alarm developed. But Blair and McPherson agreed that something should be done, and the former told Leggett to dispatch a regiment to protect the corps hospitals. Leggett sent the 68th Ohio from Scott's brigade.[18]

Sherman's new headquarters site became the most visible feature of the Union line. Copenhill was the highest point in the area, affording a good view of Atlanta and much of the landscape to its east. Sherman established himself in the spacious Howard House, actually owned by Augustus Hurt but used by Thomas C. Howard, who ran a whisky distillery at Clear Creek west of the Union line. Hurt, a strong Unionist, had built the residence about 1858 at a cost of more than $12,000. He left Atlanta in the fall of 1862 to stay at a family plantation in Alabama. According to Atlanta historian Wilbur G. Kurtz, a Tennessee refugee named Dr. Sehon and a Black man who took care of the house occupied the place late in 1863 and early in 1864. When they departed, Howard moved in without permission. Only three weeks before Sherman's arrival, the distiller had hosted a social gathering of Atlanta elite who insisted on their rounds of "parties, picnics and entertainments of different kinds" despite the imminent approach of the Yankees. Sherman's staff used this palatial house, with its eight major rooms, a broad veranda that ran entirely around the building, and a central hallway through the entire house twelve feet wide, as their own.[19]

Sherman was yet too busy to enjoy the spacious structure. At 10 A.M. he rode with Schofield to a point opposite Howard's distillery, where the pair attracted both artillery and small-arms fire. This finally convinced them that Hood had not abandoned Atlanta. Soon after the two returned to the Howard House, McPherson and his staff arrived at the 200-acre property sometime between 10 and 11 A.M. Sherman told McPherson that since the enemy still held Atlanta, he wanted to shift the Army of the Tennessee to the west as soon as possible; he did not want its current line to be shifted much to the left. McPherson made it clear, however, that he had to maintain his grip on Bald Hill for the time being because it was "essential to the occupation of any ground to the east and south of the Augusta railroad on account of its commanding nature." Sherman agreed.[20]

McPherson then spoke of the order to send Sweeny to tear up the Georgia Railroad. He insisted that the division be posted on his left flank instead, explaining this need due to the earlier dispatch of Garrard's cavalry. Sherman readily agreed to the change in plan. McPherson believed that if Hood meant to attack his left, it would happen by 1 P.M. that day. If nothing transpired by then, he would shift Sweeny to railroad work.[21]

Then Sherman and McPherson took a walk along the lane leading to the house from the west, where they could see the area better, and sat down at the foot of a tree. Here Sherman spread his map and explained to McPherson Thomas's new position and his plans to move the Army of the Tennessee behind the Army of the Cumberland to reach disputed areas west of Atlanta to cut all rail lines into the city. Before long, the sound of stray musket firing steadily increased to the east in the direction of Decatur and to the south in the direction of McPherson's left flank. Sherman wondered what it meant, and both men pulled out their pocket compasses to obtain accurate directions. While Sherman was more concerned about the noise coming from Decatur, McPherson worried more about the firing near his left flank. The latter felt the need to find out what it meant and prepared to leave.[22]

It was the last time they would see each other. Sherman recalled that McPherson was decked out in his finest even though on active campaign. "He had on his boots outside his pantaloons, gauntlets on his hands, had on his major-general's uniform, and wore a sword-belt, but no sword." McPherson placed some papers in a pocketbook and rode away with his staff. The time was about 11 A.M.[23]

The group rode all along the line of the Army of the Tennessee, starting with Copenhill and heading south. "We rode very rapidly but McPherson frequently stopped for a moment to speak to Division and Brigade Commanders," recalled Lt. Col. William E. Strong, his assistant inspector general.[24]

As soon as McPherson left the Howard House, Sherman sat down to inform Thomas of his plans. He wanted the Army of the Cumberland to press as close as possible to the Atlanta City Line and keep the Confederates occupied with a heavy artillery bombardment, shelling the city itself as well as the defenses. He hesitated to rely on cavalry to break the railroads to the south since Hood's cavalry seemed largely stationed in that area. The task could only be done with certainty by large infantry forces, and the Army of the Tennessee would do the job. He did not yet specify a day for McPherson's transit to the west but wanted it to take place soon. Meanwhile, Dodge would see to it that the Georgia Railroad could not be put back into operation for many months to come.[25]

McPherson's line occupied the best ground in the area, from Copenhill down to the refused left flank of Giles A. Smith's division three miles away. The terrain was typical of the surrounding piedmont region. Sherman noted that the Georgia Railroad and Decatur Road ran along the watershed that divided drainage northward toward Peach Tree Creek and the Chattahoochee River from that southward toward the Ocmulgee River. "The ridges and level ground were mostly cleared," he wrote, "and had been cultivated as corn or cotton fields." Bottomlands along the streams, however, were mostly left "in a state of nature—wooded, and full of undergrowth." Two cleared valleys fronted the Union line. On the north, opposite Schofield and Woods, Clear Creek flowed north, but on Blair's front, a branch of Entrenchment Creek that flowed south also was cleared. To Blair's rear, Sugar Creek originated near the high ground Dodge's command occupied and flowed south to South River. Artificial means of strengthening this position proved to be vital in the looming battle, but Fifteenth Corps troops had managed to reverse the Outer Line only imperfectly by noon. Seventeenth Corps troops had better, stronger earthworks, but Sixteenth Corps units had no artificial defenses of any kind.[26]

The anxious residents of Atlanta, recovering from the fright of the night before when they thought the army was abandoning the city (and ransacking it on the way out), were curious about the Federals. Union observers could see dozens of civilians crowding the streets and rooftops, straining to catch glimpses of the Yankees. Lt. Henry O. Dwight of the 20th Ohio saw a group of young ladies "waving white handkerchiefs, and had a large sheet hoisted over the building, by way of a flag of truce."[27]

Inside the city, the streets were littered with the plundering of the previous night. There was plenty of noise and bustle that morning, but instead of being oriented around business transactions, it was the noise and bustle of families packing what they could and leaving. "It is a hurried scramble to get away fleeing from the wrath to come," noted Lt. Andrew Jackson Neal, a Confederate artillerist who rode through the streets that morning.[28]

By 11 A.M., Sherman informed Thomas that it was all too clear the Confederates still held Atlanta in force. Even before that time, at 10 A.M., increasing signs that the enemy was moving toward the left began to appear. Federal signal officers established observation stations in trees on and near the new Union line and reported signs of large-scale troop movements.[29]

These reports failed to hasten preparations for battle among the Federals, despite McPherson's concern about their import. He apparently thought the pace of shoring up the left flank was proceeding fast enough. A new line was not yet ready for Sweeny or Fuller by the time McPherson and a large group of officers ate lunch around noon. They selected a shady spot in a grove of oak trees just south of the Georgia Railroad and three-fourths of a mile behind the Union line.[30]

After eating, while everyone relaxed and smoked cigars, McPherson penciled a note to Dodge. He had decided to send Fuller's lone brigade instead of Sweeny's division to wreck the railroad in the afternoon. Sprague's brigade of Fuller's division, already at Decatur, could cooperate with Morrill's brigade when it arrived to thoroughly tear up the track. Sweeny's intact division would assume the new position guarding his left flank that afternoon. McPherson gave this note to a staff member for delivery to Dodge. Not long afterward, at about 12:10 or 12:15, "a rattling volley of small arms" and artillery fire erupted to the south near the position occupied by the Sixteenth Corps. The staff officer did not have a chance to deliver McPherson's message because Dodge was too busy by then; the corps leader knew nothing about the note until after the war.[31]

It had taken longer than anticipated, but the "rattling volley" heralded the start of Hood's greatest effort to stop Sherman. Hardee's troops had struggled against exhaustion, short rations, and darkness all night, stumbling along the road system that conveyed them from Atlanta to a position where they could flank McPherson's left. The van of Hardee's column moved south from Atlanta along McDonough Road until its intersection with Fayetteville Road near the South River. It then moved northeast until reaching William Cobb's mill on Entrenchment Creek at 3 A.M. The troops rested there while Hardee consulted with Cobb about the road system in the area. Some of the men drew rations, but most took advantage of the break to rest or sleep.[32]

Three-quarters of a mile northeast of the mill, Flat Shoals Road branched off from Fayetteville Road and headed toward Bald Hill. One and three-quarters of a mile northeast of that intersection lay the head of Sugar Creek, near which (unknown to the Confederates) Fuller and Sweeny already were positioned. Hardee decided that Bate and Walker, commanding the first two divisions in his column, should proceed up Fayetteville Road, turn left, and advance across country along the valley of Sugar Creek to strike the rear of McPherson's army. Case Turner, an employee of Cobb, would guide the two divisions. Hardee directed his last two divisions, led by Cleburne and Maney, to advance north along Flat Shoals Road to strike McPherson's left flank. Cobb himself would guide them to its intersection with Fayetteville Road.[33]

For unexplained reasons, Maney agreed to loan one of his division's four brigades, his own brigade, currently led by Col. Francis M. Walker, to Bate. Maney would follow Cleburne and go into action with his remaining three brigades along Flat Shoals Road. The plan called for Bate to advance east of Sugar Creek and Walker west of it.[34]

Wheeler played a role in the conference at Cobb's Mill. His scouts brought in reports about McPherson's deployment, and Wheeler collected a handful of civilians in the area who offered bits of information. When he indicated that one of the citizens claimed there were no obstacles in Hardee's path, someone more closely questioned the man, who admitted that Terry's Mill Pond on Sugar Creek was "ten feet deep and a mile long," according to Hardee's staff member T. B. Roy. Other sources indicate the presence of this pond was revealed to Hardee by Cobb. Whoever offered the information, it is apparent that neither Hardee nor any other Confederate general took the pond seriously as an impediment to Bate's or Walker's advance.[35]

But Wheeler also brought disturbing news. His scouts confirmed reports that Garrard's cavalry division was on its way toward Covington. "Shall I pursue and break up Garrard, or shall I detach a force to follow him?"

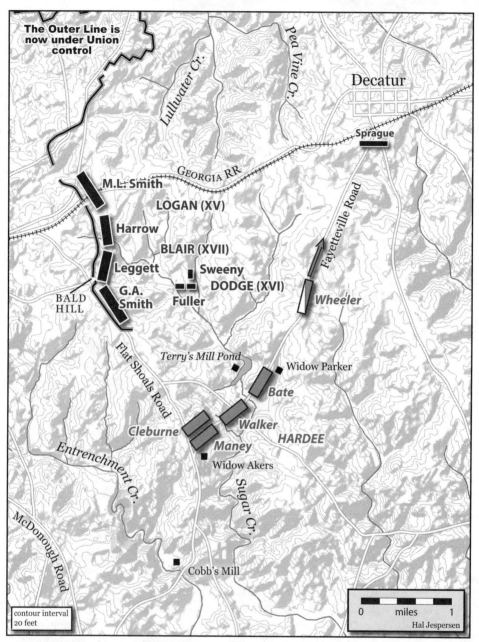

The Outer Line is now under Union control

Lullwater Cr.

Pea Vine Cr.

Decatur

Sprague

GEORGIA RR

M.L. Smith

LOGAN (XV)

Harrow

BLAIR (XVII)

Leggett

Sweeny

G.A. Smith

Fuller

DODGE (XVI)

Wheeler

Fayetteville Road

BALD HILL

Flat Shoals Road

Terry's Mill Pond

Widow Parker

Bate

Cleburne

Walker

HARDEE

Entrenchment Cr.

Maney

Widow Akers

Sugar Cr.

McDonough Road

Cobb's Mill

contour interval 20 feet

0   miles   1

Hal Jespersen

Hardee's Flank March, Morning, July 22

Wheeler asked Hardee. "I cannot spare you or any force to pursue Garrard now," the corps leader responded. "We must attack, as we arranged, with all our force. I think our attack will bring Garrard back. You had best report the facts to General Hood."[36]

As Wheeler prepared to detach his cavalry from Hardee's infantry column and head for Decatur, he knew full well that by dawn of July 22, the Confederates had essentially fulfilled Hood's directive. "We knew we were in rear of General McPherson's line," Wheeler wrote, "at least in rear of his left." This point would produce controversy later. As already noted, Hood's initial plan was for Hardee to march his entire corps to Decatur, placing it entirely in the rear of McPherson's line, before engaging the Federals. But Hardee convinced him in the 10 P.M. conference of July 21 to give him the latitude to shorten the march and strike McPherson's left flank. Unfortunately, Hood either forgot that alteration of the plan or deliberately ignored it. After the battle, he criticized Hardee for failing to fulfill his original directive, arguing that a march to Decatur would have sealed McPherson's fate and damaged Sherman's army group beyond repair.[37]

This was typical of Hood's spiteful, defensive attitude toward the failures of his tenure as commander of the Army of Tennessee, and it was completely unjustified. The truth was that he had given Hardee full authority to shorten the march and strike the Federal left, and Hardee fulfilled that directive to the letter. Moreover, moving his entire corps to Decatur would have been an extremely hazardous venture. While it would have placed thousands of Confederate infantrymen three miles to the rear of McPherson's line, it also would have placed the corps far away from the rest of Hood's army, with the Federals in between. Hardee would have been vulnerable and unsupported unless Hood could order Cheatham to attack McPherson's front at the right moment. Even as it was, with Hardee striking the Federal left flank and his progress visible to Hood in Atlanta, the army leader was unable to coordinate Cheatham's attack precisely with Hardee's advance. The march to Decatur was too ambitious, too complicated, and too risky. Hardee's alternative had better chances of success. Half of his corps actually marched beyond McPherson's left flank and took a path that enabled it to strike the Federal rear area without having to march all the way to Decatur.

These arguments would surface in the wake of the battle; for now, Hardee's Corps continued its flank march as the morning sun began to climb in the sky. The Confederate van left Cobb's Mill and moved three miles along Fayetteville Road to Widow Parker's House, three miles northeast of the mill. Here Bate stopped and prepared to face left. He was three miles short of Decatur, the target of Wheeler's advancing cavalrymen. Bate instructed his brigade leaders to form two lines west and north of Widow Parker's.[38]

Bate faced a daunting task in advancing northwest one and a half miles across country without knowing exactly where the Federals were located or how they were positioned. For his division, the attack would be an exploratory move largely in the dark. The same was true of Walker's Division to his left, which stopped to deploy just south of where Sugar Creek crossed Fayetteville Road. Cleburne and the majority of Maney's command would have a less uncertain advance of two miles along Flat Shoals Road directly to the Federal left flank. As Cleburne stopped in the area of Widow Akers's House, where Flat Shoals Road diverged from the Fayetteville Road one and a half miles from Cobb's Mill, the men were issued extra ammunition. Word spread through the ranks that the division was about to pounce upon Sherman's left flank.[39]

Hood ever after remained critical of one of the most remarkable flank movements attempted by any army during the Civil War. Hardee's march was longer, more difficult, and in some ways more successful than Stonewall Jackson's more famous flank march at Chancellorsville on May 2, 1863. Even the Federals praised Hardee's execution of the flank movement in their postwar writings. It was a "Jacksonian march," in the words of Oliver O. Howard, whose Eleventh Corps had been the target of Jackson's attack at Chancellorsville.[40]

With Hardee's and Cheatham's commands poised for action, the Confederates managed to bring more troops to battle than their opponents. The Federals later estimated that Hood committed a total of 37,000 men to the fight, while only 26,000 Unionists opposed them. Modern historians have lowered that estimate to 30,000 Confederates and 25,000 Unionists. Either way, it is clear that for once in the Atlanta Campaign, the Rebels employed more men than their opponent.[41]

Those in the know on the Confederate side waited anxiously for the result of Hood's complicated plan. "Hardee moved . . . this morning to the rear of the enemy," wrote Benedict J. Semmes, Hood's commissary of subsistence, to his wife. "If successful Atlanta is saved—if not, God knows what will become [of] this army."[42]

5

Dodge Stops Bate and Walker

The Confederates opened the Battle of July 22 with their most promising move, the advance of two divisions directly toward the rear areas of McPherson's Army of the Tennessee. These two divisions led Hardee's advance and thus were farther behind the Union line than any others. But many unexpected difficulties appeared in their path.

By late morning of July 22, the van of Hardee's Corps had formed lines of battle and began moving toward the Federals. Bate formed his division just west and north of Widow Parker's House in two lines. On the first, the Kentucky brigade of Brig. Gen. Joseph H. Lewis (also known as the Orphan Brigade) held the right. The Florida brigade commanded by Brig. Gen. Jesse J. Finley held the left. Tyler's Brigade (led by Brig. Gen. Thomas B. Smith) formed the second line. The only artillery available, Capt. Cuthbert H. Slocomb's 5th Company, Washington Artillery, took position between the two lines. Hardee gave Bate part of a cavalry regiment, which screened his division as it formed. Bate instructed the cavalry commander to precede his division during the advance but then to break away to allow his infantry to close in on the enemy. The troopers were then to screen his unprotected right flank. Hardee had promised to detach Maney's Brigade, now under Colonel Francis M. Walker, from Cheatham's Division (now led by George E. Maney) to Bate's assistance, but that unit was nowhere to be seen.[1]

Finley formed his brigade in two lines. The 6th Florida and a consolidated unit (1st Florida Cavalry, Dismounted, and 3rd Florida Infantry) composed the first line, while the 7th Florida joined another consolidated unit (1st and 4th Florida) to form the second line. The men of the 7th Florida were then treated to "a good speech in regard to going in a fight" by their commander, Lt. Col. Robert Bullock.[2]

Some confusion ensued about how the approach should be conducted. Bate assumed that the entire corps would guide by his own movement, but others thought the order was to guide left. When Bate sent a staff member to inquire about the matter, he returned with orders for every unit to guide left. That could make little difference because Sugar Creek, which separated Bate from Walker to his left, would soon offer a solid barrier to break any connection between the two divisions. To his right, Bate had no support—Wheeler's cavalry was off to Decatur more than four miles away.[3]

Bate formed his division parallel to the Fayetteville Road, which linked Cobb's Mill with Decatur. He was just east of the spot where the road crossed Sugar Creek. It was "a straight, level, dirt road, skirted by thick woods on our left," recalled artilleryman Philip D. Stephenson. The infantry faced left, formed line, and moved off into the woods. Stephenson recalled that the troops in front could be seen as "a long brown dirt colored line" and moved "deeper into the forest until swallowed up by the trees."[4]

Bate advanced blind, with no opportunity to scout the lay of the land or the Federal position ahead of his troops. The terrain was undulating and covered with patches of brush, forcing him to stop two times on his way north to either adjust the formation or allow lagging parts of the division to catch up with the rest. He urged the men on, but soon they came to an unexpected and serious obstacle to their advance. Widow Terry's large millpond was located at a pronounced bend of Sugar Creek; in fact, the stream flowed south in a nearly ninety degree turn one-fourth of the way from Fayetteville Road to the Union position. Bate's Division unwittingly approached the sharp bend of the stream in a slanting line of advance from southeast to northwest and thus hit the bend in a way that forced all three brigades to wade through at least part of the millpond. The creek bottom here was wooded and filled with undergrowth, but the millpond was wide and "filled with the *debris* and brushwood peculiar to such," according to Ed Porter Thompson of the Orphan Brigade.[5]

Another Kentuckian, L. D. Young, described the obstacle more vividly. The millpond was "filled with logs, stumps, brush and what-not in water and mire knee-deep." His comrades had to help each other over these impediments as they sloshed and struggled through the water. Not surprisingly, the experience disrupted Lewis's formation and strained his men. "Out of

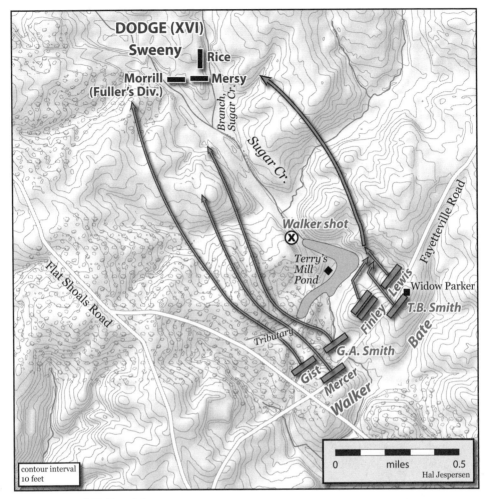

Bate and Walker Advance

dust ankle deep into water and mire knee-deep was too much for the nerves and patience of the strongest man and most patient Christian," concluded Young.[6]

Finley's Brigade, on the left of the first line, encountered the pond earlier than Lewis's, and its pace dramatically slowed as the unit tried to deal with the obstruction. After the Florida men began making headway through the water, Smith's brigade followed. The 20th Tennessee waded until the water was waist deep before the men emerged from the pond.[7]

The millpond slowed and disrupted Bate's advance considerably, forcing more effort and physical strain on the men. They had been warned by Cobb and Turner of its existence but had no idea that its location would play such a large role in their advance to battle that day. The pond was half a mile long and nearly as wide, at its south end serving a gristmill east of the creek and a sawmill on the west side. Thomas Terry, the original owner, had been murdered in Atlanta by John Wilson, aided by his son James, because of a sordid personal grudge against him held by the Wilson family. When Terry went to town on August 3, 1861, John Wilson hit him over the head with a champagne bottle and the son further injured him with a rock. Terry died a few hours later. Although John Wilson was sent to the state penitentiary, Gov. Joseph E. Brown later released all prisoners to provide manpower to resist Sherman's March to the Sea. Wilson deserted and was never heard of again. Mary Terry and her six children lived in a house on Flat Shoals Road during the battle.[8]

Unaware of this sad history and of the pond itself, Bate lost the service of his one battery on the way north. Slocomb found that the underbrush prevented him from keeping pace between the two lines and, early in the advance, veered off to the left. The battery marched around a good deal, unaware of exactly where to go, and failed to reach the scene of action until it was too late to participate in the battle.[9]

Despite its troubles, Bate's Division was heading straight toward the rear of McPherson's line, with the Federals as yet wholly unaware. But the Confederates would soon discover an impediment to their advance far more serious than a hundred millponds—the Left Wing of the Sixteenth Corps happened to be placed exactly where McPherson needed it to block not only Bate but Walker too. The two Confederate divisions were advancing on both sides of Sugar Creek, and Dodge's three brigades were located on high ground near the origin of that stream. Without realizing it, the two sides were on a collision course.

By late morning, Dodge had finished his scouting of the new position where his troops were to connect with Blair's left flank. He also heard that Seventeenth Corps hospitals had been threatened by Rebel cavalry. This news alarmed him, so much so that he ordered skirmishers sent south to screen the area. Then Dodge rode to Fuller's headquarters, where the division leader invited him to lunch. It was exactly noon, and the pair had barely sat down and lifted their forks when the pace of small-arms fire to the south picked up dramatically. Fuller thought it was "the boys shooting hogs," but Dodge disagreed. Capt. William H. Chamberlin, Dodge's commissary of musters, thought his corps commander was "an intensely active, almost nervously restless, officer," and he responded instinctively to the sound. "No; get out and put your men in," Dodge told Fuller, "it is the enemy." At 12:15 the two hastily parted as the battle began.[10]

Dodge sent orders for Sweeny to form line where his division was resting and instructed Fuller to form in connection with him. He also tried to deal with a nagging problem, the gap between Blair's corps and his own position, which invited disaster if the enemy found and exploited it. He sent an aide-de-camp, Capt. Edward Jonas, to find Giles A. Smith and ask him to refuse his division's left flank to reach the Sixteenth Corps. Smith agreed to do so, but the onset of Hardee's attack intervened and prevented him from even trying to bend his flank back such a distance.[11]

Sweeny was able to place his two brigades faster than Fuller because he already occupied the best ground in the area. A veteran of the Mexican War, where he lost his right arm because of a wound inflicted at the Battle of Churubusco, Sweeny was sitting on a log smoking his pipe when one of his scouts arrived with the news that "large bodies of the enemy were moving through the woods in front and to the left of" his position. He rode to the skirmish line to find a good deal of firing and sent word to his brigade leaders to form their men as fast as possible.[12]

Col. August Mersy's brigade formed facing south, with the 12th Illinois on the right, the 81st Ohio in the center, and the 66th Illinois on the left. Two companies of the 66th Illinois were on the skirmish line, with an additional two companies as the skirmish support. Most of the men of the 66th Illinois had purchased Henry repeating rifles for forty-three dollars each early in 1864, weapons that gave them something of an advantage in the art of skirmishing.[13]

Brig. Gen. Elliott W. Rice's brigade faced east, with its right flank connected at a right angle to Mersy's left. Rice placed the 66th Indiana on his right, the 2nd Iowa next to it, and the 7th Iowa on his left. He also sent out one company of each regiment as skirmishers but had no time to construct earthworks, nor did Mersy. Both brigades were on open, high ground that was good for observation but quite visible to the enemy as soon as Confederate lines emerged from the thick wood cover on the lowland south and east of their position. Rice noted that Fuller's lone brigade was located half a mile west and to the rear of his right flank, with Mersy in between them.[14]

Dodge had only two batteries, but they took post on the best ground available and would play key roles in the fight. Lt. Andrew T. Blodgett's Battery H, 1st Missouri Light Artillery, assigned to Sweeny's division, set up in Rice's line between the 2nd and 7th Iowa. Lt. Seth M. Laird's 14th Ohio Battery, assigned to Fuller's division, established itself at the apex of Sweeny's line on the best artillery ground of the battlefield. Battery F, 2nd U.S. Artillery, assigned to Fuller, was still on its way from the Seventeenth Corps line. Blodgett and Laird barely got into position in time. Blodgett quickly assessed the nuances of terrain and posted his sections accordingly. Five minutes later the Confederates appeared in force.[15]

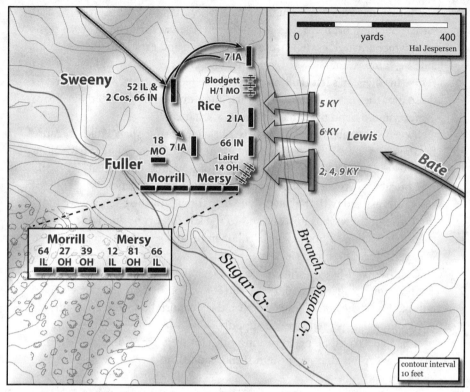

Lewis Attacks

Fuller's lone brigade, under Col. John Morrill, who had taken command when Fuller advanced to division leadership on July 17, had to double-quick half a mile to close on Sweeny's right flank. The 39th Ohio settled in position on Morrill's left, with the 27th Ohio next in line. Morrill placed the 64th Illinois to the right of the 27th Ohio and kept the 18th Missouri in reserve to the rear of his brigade. Both the 39th and 27th Ohio sent out a skirmish line just in time to meet advancing Confederate skirmishers. Fuller had selected Morrill's position because of its high, commanding ground, and it was roughly an extension of Mersy's line.[16]

Dodge could muster no more than 4,500 men in his three brigades to oppose Bate's and Walker's Divisions. "I had every man in line—no reserves," he later wrote. Opposing him, Bate probably had 1,200 men, but only one brigade of 500 troops would be actively engaged. Walker fielded 4,000 men, and all his brigades would soon be engaged. The Confederates, in short, held a numerical advantage of 5,200 compared to 4,500 troops, but the Federals were in a strong position, were ready for their adversaries, and were under tighter control than the Confederates.[17]

After dealing with Terry's Mill Pond, Lewis's Brigade now found itself projecting forward. Finley's and Smith's units had fallen far behind the Orphan Brigade because of their complicated passage through and around the water obstacle. Nevertheless, Bate tried to urge the Kentucky troops forward. He rode along their line, "hat in hand, saying, 'at em,' *at em!* at em! The enemy knows nothing of our approach."[18]

Lewis had one more watery obstacle to negotiate before closing in on Rice's brigade. A branch of Sugar Creek flowed almost due north to south directly in the Kentuckians' path. It was a small stream bordered by a miry bottomland. Once across this impediment, the Confederates completed their approach through the woods until reaching a stake-and-rider fence at the edge of the timber. "Load boys, then go over the fence & rush on them," Johnny Green of the 9th Kentucky recalled his officers' instructions. "When in close range give them a volley & then charge & give them the bayonet." In places the fence was weak and easily removed, but other sections could not be taken down. Green got hung up crossing this obstacle when his water-filled canteen, strapped around his neck, lodged on the Confederate side of the fence as he climbed across to the Federal side. A skirmisher's bullet happened to cut the canteen strap and freed him.[19]

That shot came from Rice's skirmish line, which had barely been able to advance from his main position to near the edge of the woods. The Federal skirmishers immediately saw Lewis's Brigade advancing through the trees and began to retire, firing. Rice could plainly see the Confederates pop out from the tree cover seconds after his skirmishers began to fall back. They "emerged from the woods in heavy charging column with battle-flags proudly flaunting in the breeze," He reported. "They burst forth from the woods in truly magnificent style in front of my right."[20]

It was important for the Federal main line to open fire as soon as possible, but the withdrawing skirmishers were in the way. The solution came when Sweeny told his orderly to call out in a loud voice for the skirmish line to break, the right wing retiring by the flank to the south and the left wing by the flank to the north. This opened up a clear field of fire in time for the Federals to severely punish Lewis's men. Blodgett and Laird especially did good execution from their superb positions as the 66th Indiana and 2nd Iowa opened small-arms fire. Blodgett's performance especially impressed Rice, who praised "the splendidly managed and magnificently fought battery." Lewis had no artillery support; Slocomb's guns were still floundering about in an attempt to rejoin the Confederate infantry. But Rice's "thin line stood like a fence of iron," as the Union brigade leader put it.[21]

Laird's 14th Ohio Battery was in the perfect position at the apex of Sweeny's line. Lewis's men "appeared where we expected to see them, and where we could give them the best possible reception." In fact, Dodge asserted that the guns had "a direct and point-blank range" on the Kentuckians. Laird began firing shell and switched to canister as the distance decreased. The lieutenant remained mounted as his gunners rolled up their shirt sleeves, warming to their work under the blazing noontime sun.[22]

Lewis's right wing confronted the center of Rice's line, pitting Lt. Col. Hiram Hawkins's 5th Kentucky (C.S.) against Lt. Col. Noel B. Howard's 2nd Iowa. Blodgett's guns fired salvos of canister, and when Howard's men delivered their second round of small-arms fire, the 5th Kentucky hesitated at only eighty yards from the Union line. In a "few seconds," Hawkins later wrote, one-third of his men had fallen. Half of the color company was lost as the flags fell to the ground. Hawkins himself barely escaped, as eight bullets pierced holes through his coat. Others cut his sword belt and still another struck his left hip, knocking him down. By the time Hawkins could rise again, his regiment had fallen back, so he followed.[23]

Col. Martin H. Cofer's 6th Kentucky (C.S.) experienced much the same thing. "Balls flew thicker than I ever before experienced," wrote Gervis D. Grainger. "It seemed I was among a swarm of bees." The Confederates tried to endure "a withering volley, rapidly repeated and unusually destructive," but it was no use. Half the regiment fell within a few minutes, and when the order to retire was sounded, it came as "a welcome one, and we who survived, obeyed with alacrity."[24]

Only on their left did Lewis's men cause some trouble for the Federals. Col. James W. Moss's 2nd Kentucky (C.S.), Lt. Col. Thomas W. Thompson's 4th Kentucky (C.S.), and Col. John W. Caldwell's 9th Kentucky (C.S.) advanced close to the Union position, where they threatened Lt. Col. Roger Martin's 66th Indiana. Because the 7th Iowa was not confronted by any Confederates, Rice moved Lt. Col. James C. Parrott's regiment south at the double-quick. Parrott ordered his Iowans to lay prone within supporting distance behind the 66th Indiana in case they were needed. After a while, Rice pulled the Indiana regiment out and relieved it with Parrott's fresh troops. Then the 7th Iowa fired a couple of volleys to convince the Confederates it was time to retire.[25]

The timely arrival of reinforcements sealed the fate of Lewis's attack. Earlier that day, when Woods relieved Sweeny near Copenhill, the latter had left a considerable force behind on the skirmish line, consisting of two companies of the 66th Indiana and five of Lt. Col. Edwin A. Bowen's 52nd Illinois. The rest of the 52nd Illinois acted as a skirmish reserve. It took some time for these Sixteenth Corps skirmishers to be replaced, after which they started east and south to rejoin Sweeny. Soon after they began their march, an orderly brought an urgent message from Rice. "Tell Col Bowen to move up as fast as God will let him the Enemy are in our rear and the Brigade is fighting like Hell." With news like that, Bowen had to move quickly, but he knew the heat was too great for his men to double-quick the entire distance. He ordered them "to march as fast as they could walk" until about three-quarters of a mile from the battlefield. Here another orderly from Rice told him to double-quick, and Bowen gave the order. Only half a dozen men fell out of ranks during this forced march, and even those men all caught up fifteen minutes later, but two of Bowen's troops "were so overcome by the heat" that he had to send them to the hospital in ambulances.[26]

Bowen's arrival on the field was a memorable moment for his men and for the anxious Rice. Entering the open high ground on which the brigade was fighting, Bowen was struck by a "beautiful & Grand" sight. He told his men to "give a harty cheer" and they did, yelling "a wild Huzar such as Soldiers can only give." Rice initially placed the regiment to the rear of Blodgett's Missouri gunners but later shifted it to extend his left now that the 7th Iowa no longer held that position. The arrival of Rice's last regiment gave everyone emotional comfort, but Bowen noted that his men were not directly engaged once they arrived on the field. They received scattered gunfire but never had to repel a Confederate attack.[27]

Lewis's Brigade spent its strength in an assault that was boldly repulsed by Rice's brigade line, forcing the Kentuckians to retreat. Exactly what Finley's Brigade did that day is somewhat unclear. The absence of reports from the unit along with the lack of evidence from the Federal side that a second Rebel brigade closed in leads to the conclusion that Finley was unable to bring his men to bear on the target. According to the diary of William McLeod of the 7th Florida, the brigade marched around a good deal. "We had Creeks and Branches to wade & we pitched rite in like they were not their & I never got so hot in all my life." His regimental line broke up because of heavy vegetation, and the portion he was in moved far to the right. "We done nothing" was McLeod's final word about the fighting on July 22. There is no indication of any kind that the Floridians became engaged, and the main reason lies in the obstruction posed by Terry's Mill Pond, which disrupted and diverted the brigade's movements.[28]

While Finley's Brigade is represented by a lone diary, there literally are no reports, diaries, letters, or memoirs representing the activities of T. B. Smith's brigade that day. There is no indication from the Federal side that this unit even made an appearance. Historian Gary Ecelbarger believes Smith's men failed to even leave the cover of the thick woods, but that apparently also was true of Finley.[29]

Bate's ill-starred attack on Rice lasted at least half an hour; that was the sum of the division's activities on July 22, for we hear nothing of either the major general or his brigades for the rest of the day.[30] Rice's prime defensive position and the fact that he was ready just in time to receive Lewis's assault were the main reasons for Confederate failure. But closely behind these factors is Bate's abysmal handling of his division. A politician who never really learned how to be a general, Bate was hated by most of his men and had already compiled a dismal record on the battlefield long before July 22. He had mishandled an attack at Dallas on May 28 earlier in the campaign that thereafter soured the mood of his men. The fact that only one of three brigades closed on the target on July 22 was yet another indication that Bate was woefully inadequate as a division commander. Finley and Smith also failed to handle their commands as well as Lewis had done, contributing to Bate's failure, but the division commander seems to have done nothing to correct their mistakes.

Lewis lost 135 men in this first and only attack of the day by Bate's Division. Ecelbarger assumes that Finley attacked to Lewis's left and at the same time, but there is no evidence for this conclusion nor for Ecelbarger's assumption that Finley lost 300 men on July 22.[31]

In contrast, Walker's Division brought more men to bear on the Union position and fought a harder battle than Bate had been able to do. Consisting of 4,000 men in three brigades, the van of Walker's column had halted just short of the ford where Fayetteville Road crossed Sugar Creek that morning. In forming his division, Walker placed Stevens's Brigade on the right. It was led by Col. George A. Smith since Stevens's mortal wounding two days before at Peach Tree Creek. Brig. Gen. States R. Gist positioned his brigade to Smith's left, while Brig. Gen. Hugh W. Mercer followed with his brigade in reserve. The Confederates had to advance across country, keeping Sugar Creek on their right, but had no idea that Mersy's and Morrill's brigades stood in their way more than one and a half miles ahead.[32]

Walker encountered difficulties from the start of his advance. Gist tried to maintain contact with Cleburne's Division to his left without crowding the two commands. He placed his assistant adjutant general, Maj. B. Benjamin Smith, at the junction of his left flank and Cleburne's right with instructions "to keep them apart the proper distance." But Smith soon observed that Cleburne seemed to be moving forward at an angle that slowly shifted toward Walker's Division. The major urged Gist to move his brigade by the right flank to avoid entanglement. This caused him to lag behind Brig. Gen. James A. Smith, whose brigade held the right of Cleburne's Division, and bringing his men to the Union position sometime after Smith became engaged. This shift also took Gist completely out of sight of Cleburne's command. With no possibility of a connection on the right with Bate since

Sugar Creek separated the two divisions, Walker, too, was going in alone and unsupported.[33]

Walker paid no attention to these matters. He was desperate to engage the Federals and angry over a small argument he just experienced with his corps commander. Before starting the advance from Fayetteville Road, Walker noticed "a thick tangled briar patch" in front of one of his regiments. His assistant adjutant general, Maj. Joseph B. Cumming, suggested the regiment move by the right of companies through it. For some reason, Walker felt he had to obtain Hardee's approval for such a minor tactical decision and rode to consult with him. The corps leader also was anxious to get his men on the move as soon as possible and lost his temper when the division commander began to ask permission to do what any subordinate had the perfect right to do on their own. Hardee did not even let Walker finish his plea. "No sir! This movement has been delayed too long already. Go and obey my orders!" he shouted loud enough to be heard by everyone nearby. Walker, a sensitive man, was deeply mortified. Riding back to his division, he asked Cumming if he had heard the remarks. "Yes, General Hardee forgot himself," Cumming replied. "I shall make him remember this insult," continued Walker. "If I survive this battle, he shall answer me for it."[34]

Hardee quickly cooled off and sent a staff member to offer his apologies, but Walker remained angry. Cumming had been away on an errand when the staff member delivered the apology. When the major returned and discovered what Hardee conveyed, he told Walker, "now, that makes it all right." The division commander retorted, "no, it does not. He must answer me for this." Cumming had had enough. He "ventured to remonstrate with [Walker] and to say that the occasion called for other thoughts." Walker finally cooled off enough to pay attention to his division. As he rode off on another errand for his hotheaded chief, Cumming later recalled, it was only half an hour before Walker's death.[35]

During that half hour, Case Turner ran afoul of Walker's temper. The guide warned him of Terry's Mill Pond, but because it did not appear on Walker's map, he dismissed the information. Everyone was stunned when they encountered what turned out to be an expansive lake rather than a small pond, with water backed up in a tributary of Sugar Creek that lay directly in the division's line of march. Walker became angry and threatened to shoot Turner but was dissuaded by his staff. As George A. Smith's brigade, the only one this far forward, began to negotiate the flooded tributary by moving left, Walker sent off his remaining staff members to urge his other two brigades forward—all three of them were separated from each other. Walker then personally scouted the area around the northern end of

William H. T. Walker's March. Having participated in the flank march by Hardee's Corps, Walker's Division advanced from Fayetteville Road northwest along the west side of Sugar Creek. After negotiating the huge extent of Terry's Mill Pond, Walker and his entourage rounded the northern fringes of the pond as they closed in on Dodge's Left Wing, Sixteenth Corps. This image by Wilbur G. Kurtz, an Atlanta historian with artistic talent, depicts the time just before the division commander was shot by Federal skirmishers from the 66th Illinois armed with Henry rifles. Walker died almost immediately, becoming the highest-ranking Confederate casualty of the Battle of July 22. From Wilbur G. Kurtz, "Major-General W. H. T. Walker," *Atlanta Constitution*, July 27, 1930.

the millpond in an effort to move the division farther to the right once it passed the watery impediment.[36]

With Case Turner by his side, Walker rode into the valley of Sugar Creek just north of the millpond and stopped to look through his field glasses. Just then, Mersy's skirmish line, consisting of men from the 66th Illinois with their Henry rifles, spotted him and opened fire. Walker was hit and died almost instantly. Turner fled the scene, but the general soon was attended by his men, who arranged for the removal of his body. It was placed in a wagon and driven southwest to the home of Widow Terry and later moved to Atlanta.[37]

Walker was much admired by his men, and when his death became widely known, it produced a great deal of sorrow. But a controversy arose about when and how he died. Rumor circulated that Walker fell much later in the battle while leading elements of Gist's Brigade against Fuller's command. Even Dodge, possibly influenced by these rumors, later claimed that he saw Walker fall then and there. But none of those rumors were confirmed by eyewitnesses on the Confederate side, and how Dodge could have picked out Walker, who he apparently had never met, on a crowded, smoke-engulfed battlefield from hundreds of yards away is difficult to understand. In contrast, Turner's story is much more reliable. He told it to a Confederate veteran named J. W. McWilliams of the 42nd Georgia when the latter worked for him as he managed Cobb's Mill after the war. Atlanta historian Wilbur G. Kurtz extensively interviewed McWilliams in 1930 and recorded the details in his papers and published articles. "I have never seen any reason to doubt the basic elements of Case Turner's story," Kurtz stated in 1955.[38]

At the time Walker was shot, Stevens's Brigade under George A. Smith was only a few minutes behind the division commander but considerably ahead of Gist. No one in the brigade knew of Walker's fate as they moved northward, the brigade's right flank a relatively short distance west of the general's death site. As the brigade continued north, it had to cross Sugar Creek, which ran from the northwest to the southeast toward the millpond. In crossing, the right wing moved northeast of the small stream before the left wing reached it. In its approach, George A. Smith's men confronted two Union brigades. Mersy's fronted the Confederate right wing northeast of Sugar Creek and Morrill's opposed the Confederate left wing southwest of the stream. As these Rebels emerged from the woods, Walker's struggling division finally became engaged.[39]

Dodge played a huge role in the Federal reaction to Smith's appearance. Later he claimed that Sweeny was not up to managing his men.

> When I went on to the field, he had not come to the front, although his division was in line of battle and fighting. When he did come, he came on foot and I saw that he had been drinking; therefore I stayed right in the rear of the 2nd Division all the time, on a high piece of ground just behind the batteries from which I could see the whole of my corps and the enemy's forces as they came out of the woods.

There is no corroboration for the idea that Sweeny had been drinking on July 22, and this may be Dodge's postbattle justification for his actions. But there is no doubt that Dodge upstaged him, essentially taking control of the division's units, and acted very effectively to blunt Smith's attack.[40]

Seeing the Confederates emerge from the trees in an uneven line, Dodge seized the initiative. He ignored Sweeny and told Mersy to launch

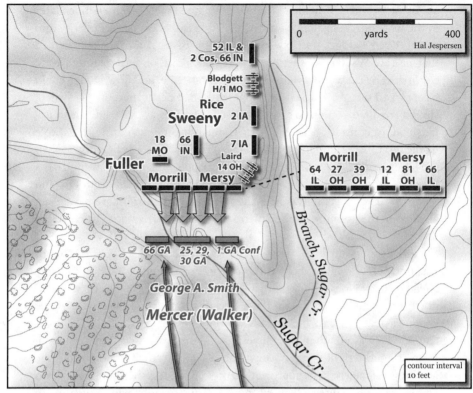

Map labels:
52 IL & 2 Cos, 66 IN

Blodgett H/1 MO

Rice
Sweeny 2 IA

18 MO 66 IN 7 IA
Fuller   Laird 14 OH

Morrill Mersy

Morrill   Mersy
64 IL 27 OH 39 OH   12 IL 81 OH 66 IL

66 GA 25, 29, 30 GA 1 GA Conf

George A. Smith

Mercer (Walker)

Branch, Sugar Cr.

Sugar Cr.

0   yards   400
Hal Jespersen

contour interval 10 feet

George A. Smith Attacks

an immediate counterattack. Lower-ranking officers gleefully reported that Dodge issued this order directly to regimental commanders, "cutting red tape all to pieces," but Dodge insisted he went through Mersy. The corps leader also gave encouragement to the 7th Iowa of Rice's brigade, which supported Laird's battery at the apex of the Union line: "Boys, . . . don't give them an inch if they come on to you." Colonel Parrott assured him "not to fear as his men were all right."[41]

Of course, Sweeny later claimed that he gave the order to counterattack himself without Dodge's help. "I made them lie down until the rebels came within 40 or 50 yards, when I gave the order to charge," he wrote in a self-serving letter to a friend. But the evidence overwhelmingly gives credit to Dodge for taking charge of the situation.[42]

Two of Mersy's regiments fulfilled Dodge's order with spirit. Tension in the ranks of Lt. Col. Robert N. Adams's 81st Ohio had been building ever since the men saw gray-uniformed troops emerge from the trees. "It'll be as hot as hell here in a few minutes," someone said. The order to move forward broke the tension, and the Ohioans yelled and surged forward. The 12th Illinois also waited impatiently until Dodge came along and shouted to Lt. Col. Henry Van Sellar, "Move your regiment forward and strike the enemy." By this time, both Blodgett and Laird on Rice's line had noticed the emerging threat and redirected their fire at the Confederates as they began to cross the open ground to the south. At least some of Smith's Georgians managed to get pretty close to the Union position, fifty yards or so, before Dodge got the 81st Ohio and 12th Illinois moving forward to confront them.[43]

With the element of surprise on their side, the Federals achieved a stunning success. The right wing of George A. Smith's command stopped and then quickly fell back. The 81st Ohio captured two Rebel flags and 226 prisoners. The 12th Illinois did not get a flag but nabbed an additional 200 prisoners. After having marched all night and struggled through the countryside only to meet a wall of charging Yankees, many captured Confederates seemed "bewildered," according to Charles Wright of the 81st Ohio. One placed his hand on Wright's shoulder and asked, "What countryman are you, sir?" Wright replied, "I am an Ohioan, and you are my prisoner." The "confused expression in his face" never left the prisoner as he was led away to the rear. Other Rebels were aware of what had happened but remained defiant. "You've had a fair fight this time, anyhow," one of them bragged. "Yes, and you see that you're badly whipped, don't you?" retorted a comrade of Wright. Some captives were downright generous. When a Federal asked a prisoner if he had tobacco, the man gave him a plug and told him to share it with his comrades. In addition, the prisoner told him where he had left his knapsack, which contained even more tobacco, behind a nearby stump.[44]

The right wing, which contained at least the 1st Georgia (Confederate) Regiment (its flag was taken by the 81st Ohio), had been quickly and bluntly repulsed northeast of Sugar Creek. At some point early in the fight, George A. Smith was wounded, but the next-ranking officer, Col. James Cooper Nisbet, remained unaware of it. Nisbet was busy managing his 66th Georgia on Smith's far left southwest of Sugar Creek. Fuller kept a watchful eye over Morrill in a cooperative arrangement between division and brigade leader, and the result was another quick repulse of the Confederates. Fuller told Lt. Col. Henry T. McDowell of the 39th Ohio and Lt. Col. Mendal Churchill of the 27th Ohio to move their regiments forward in another counterstrike. He wanted them to charge when the enemy had reached a point halfway across the open space, but the men could not wait that long. The two Ohio regiments sprang forward at the double-quick, took the Confederates by surprise, and "routed" them, as Fuller put it.[45]

After struggling through brush-entangled terrain, the troops of the 66th

The Battle of Atlanta, July 22, 1864, by James E. Taylor, featuring Grenville M. Dodge. Taylor was a well-known artist who mostly painted images of the Civil War in the East, but after the conflict he agreed to execute two paintings depicting the fight of Dodge's Left Wing, Sixteenth Corps on July 22. This image features Dodge himself at the center of the action. It is not mere hyperbole, for Dodge was deeply immersed in the heroic stand of his three brigades as they stopped two Confederate divisions in their tracks, saving the Army of the Tennessee from a devastating defeat. At one point Dodge bypassed his division and brigade commanders and issued orders directly to regimental leaders for a timely counterattack that paid huge dividends toward Federal victory. Image ID 81354, Picture Collection of Miriam and Ira D. Wallach Division of Art, Prints and Photographs, New York Public Library.

Georgia emerged into the open only to find a line of yelling Federals moving against their front. The regiment was not in order, which made it almost impossible to organize a defense, and the Confederates simply collapsed. Members of the 39th Ohio captured Nisbet, an adjutant, a captain, and thirteen men, while the 27th Ohio nabbed some more Rebels. All were escorted to the rear, where prisoners were assembled near the Georgia Railroad for the time being. The left wing of George A. Smith's command had failed to make a dent in Dodge's position, and the brigade had lost its new commander at the same time.[46]

"Our brigade was cut up bad," wrote Angus McDermid of the 29th Georgia, "more killed and wounded than I ever saw." Another member of the same regiment blamed the failure on *"bad generalship."* The men acted "gallantly," but "our Brigade was cut all to pieces" because of lack of support from the rest of the division.[47]

Gist's Brigade was too far behind to support George A. Smith's command in its attack. But it soon approached the Union position to the left of Nisbet's shattered regiment and moved past the Georgians, angling toward the northeast in search of Fuller's right flank. Gist had no support to his left, and Smith's retreating brigade offered no help to his right. Fuller saw these fresh Confederates moving north soon after the 39th and 27th Ohio repulsed Smith's left wing. "The extraordinary spectacle presented itself of our men rushing across the field in one direction, while the rebels on their right were marching steadily the opposite way." He sent orders for both regiments to retire immediately and face west to meet the new threat.[48]

That would not be easy. The two regiments already were receiving flank fire when they began to pull back. The 39th Ohio was farther from the threatening enemy and yet experienced "some disorder" in the movement. Nevertheless, the experienced troops managed to get back to higher ground and face to the right in time to confront Gist.[49]

The 27th Ohio, on the right flank and exposed to the worst of the Rebel fire, had much more difficulty obeying Fuller's instructions. "It was almost impossible to execute a change of front under such a flank fire as we were sustaining," reported Mendal Churchill. He refused his right wing to offer immediate resistance to Confederate skirmishers who, according to Churchill, were seventy-five yards away at that point. He then tried to shift the regiment by the right flank to edge it back. To move a regimental line that was bent like this by the flank was very difficult even under parade-ground conditions. "I hesitated about giving the order to fall back, well knowing the danger of never getting the Regt stopped again, at the proper time," Churchill told his wife. Nevertheless, he ordered the regiment to fall back as best it could in this awkward formation. Fuller noticed that the Ohioans "kept stopping and turning about to fire. This broke their formation" even more, so that "they were coming around in a mass," just when Churchill saw the "dirty flag" of the Rebels appear at the head of Gist's main line.[50]

Fuller correctly judged that the regiment was nearing a moment of crisis in its effort to retire and therefore acted decisively to save it. The 27th Ohio had once been his own command; he knew the men and was certain they would respond to him on a personal level. So Fuller ran as fast as he could toward the regiment, which by then had struggled close to a good spot to reform. He grabbed the flag without explanation, and in his own words moved it "a few paces toward the enemy, then turning around stuck the flag-staff in the ground, and with my sword showed where to re-form the line. With a great shout the men came forward and instantly formed."[51]

The 27th Ohio regained its formation just in the nick of time. It began pouring fire into Gist's main line and stopped the Confederate advance.

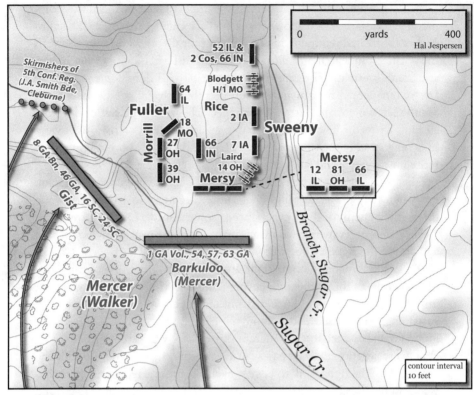

Gist and Barkuloo Attack

Churchill was struck with a ball that bruised his abdomen. "The blow bent me up & made me sick and faint," he informed his wife. He left the field for a while but realized the injury was not incapacitating and returned to his regiment. Fortunately for Fuller, the 27th and 39th Ohio reformed near enough to support each other and stopped the Confederates when the gray line was little less than 100 yards away.[52]

This was the first genuine chance for the Confederates to seriously damage Dodge's position, and Fuller had barely blocked it. Gist's formation extended beyond the front of the two Ohio regiments, bringing the 64th Illinois and 18th Missouri into the fighting. Brigade leader Morrill was on the scene and ordered Lt. Col. Michael W. Manning to change the front of his 64th Illinois to the right, "perpendicular to my then present position, in order to present my front to the woods" where many of Gist's men had appeared. Manning's right wing executed the maneuver sharply by wheeling and driving the Confederates from the woods. But his left wing, more exposed and suffering more heavily from fire, fell back behind the right wing,

Fuller's Division Rallying after Being Forced Back by the Confederates, by James E. Taylor, featuring John W. Fuller. In the second of Taylor's pictures depicting the Sixteenth Corps in action on July 22, the artist has featured Brig. Gen. John W. Fuller, the division commander who played a key role in saving Dodge's right flank from an attack by Gist's Brigade. The 27th and 39th Ohio had previously advanced to repel the right wing of Col. George A. Smith's command but were immediately threatened on their right flank by Gist's approach. In pulling back, the 27th Ohio became mixed up and was on the verge of collapse when Fuller raced to the front, grabbed the regimental colors, and planted them where he wanted the regiment (his old command) to rally. The men did so, and the Union flank held firm. Both of Taylor's paintings are magnificent examples of mid-nineteenth-century battle art, but the originals apparently have disappeared. They were reproduced in a couple of publications written by veterans, including the *Battles and Leaders* series, but today the only prints available are held by the New York Public Library. Image ID 813549, Picture Collection of Miriam and Ira D. Wallach Division of Art, Prints and Photographs, New York Public Library.

thus reducing the regimental front by half. While what was left of that front had secured its position, there now was increased danger of being flanked on the left.[53]

But then, the right wing of the 64th Illinois surged forward into the woods and produced an unexpected success. Members of the regiment captured about forty Confederates, some of them belonging to the 5th Confederate in James A. Smith's Brigade, Cleburne's Division. When searching these prisoners, Union soldiers found some papers and a pair of field glasses that apparently belonged to a Federal officer. It took a bit of time for them to understand the significance of their discovery. When they gave the items to their officers, it became apparent that the material belonged to McPherson, giving Dodge's command its first intimation that something dreadful had happened to their army commander.[54]

Before that realization could settle in, Sixteenth Corps troops were too busy contending with the enemy to worry about larger matters. Lt. Col. Charles S. Sheldon's 18th Missouri came to the aid of the 64th Illinois in shoring up Morrill's right flank. From its reserve position, Sheldon saw Gist's approach and, without orders, moved his line back a few paces, then redirected his front toward the west. His men fired three volleys, catching the enemy as Gist's men tried to cross "a high post and rail fence" only forty yards away. Sheldon heard "the commands of their mounted officers, as they encouraged their men to go forward." But the volleys were too much for them, and the Confederates retired. Ben Sweet of the 18th Missouri believed that the volleys caused "a perfect stampede" among the retreating Rebels. Sheldon was slightly wounded and departed for treatment. He soon found out that the bullet had been fired from a revolver and probably was already spent, inflicting little damage, so the persistent officer returned to his Missourians half an hour after leaving them. By then, the regiment had moved to the left to form "an obtuse angle" with the right flank of the 27th Ohio. The 64th Illinois remained to its right but still with a gap between it and the 18th Missouri.[55]

Gist personally tried to rally his troops after their repulse and was wounded in the hand. Col. James McCullough of the 16th South Carolina then took command of the brigade. It is possible the wounding of Gist led to rumors that Walker had been killed while encouraging Gist's Brigade forward. More than one Federal, including Dodge, later claimed to have seen or heard that Walker fell among Gist's men. Prisoners told Fuller that Walker was killed among them. As mentioned earlier, Dodge claimed to have seen Walker fall from his horse, but that is very difficult to credit. Even Sheldon later repeated the story of Walker's fall in front of his regiment that day. As explained earlier, however, the evidence is overwhelming that Walker had been shot just before the battle near the northern end of Terry's Mill Pond.[56]

At this point, enough elements of Gist's Brigade rallied to attempt another advance. They managed to find Manning's exposed flank, and soon the 64th Illinois was peppered with small-arms fire on front, flank, and rear. Morrill told him to fall back to a clump of pine trees a quarter mile to the rear and reform. Fuller then lost the brigade leader during this brief Confederate surge. Morrill had been slightly hurt at the start of the action but continued on duty. Now the colonel was "severely wounded in two places," according to one report, forcing him to leave the field. Robert Russell, a member of the 64th Illinois, helped get him to the rear. Lt. Col. Henry T. McDowell of the 39th Ohio took over the brigade. After the 64th Illinois fell back, heavy and accurate firing by Laird's 14th Ohio Battery stopped the Confederate advance. Gist's troops threw together a breastwork of rails "from behind which they did some wicked firing," as Fuller put it. The Federals lay on the ground and responded for a time as the fighting settled down in this part of the field. At 4:30 P.M., Fuller ordered Manning to send half of the 64th Illinois out to secure as much of the contested ground as possible to bring off the dead and wounded.[57]

First George A. Smith, then Gist had tried the stout Union defenders and were repulsed, the former by impromptu counterattacks that took the Confederates by surprise at exactly the right moment to be thoroughly effective. The latter was repulsed in part by the same tactic (a counterattack by the 64th Illinois) but by defensive action as well. That work was not conducted as smoothly as Rice's brigade had rebuffed Lewis—the 27th Ohio nearly collapsed before Fuller inspired the men to reform and hold on—but it was ultimately effective as well. In all cases the fighting was in the open field without the aid of fortifications, and the Union success was greatly facilitated by the lack of coordination among the Confederates.

One more brigade was available in Walker's Division, Mercer's reserve force, which trailed behind George A. Smith and Gist. It did not go into action before Mercer was informed that he had to take over the division from the fallen Walker, and that delayed its advance even more. After Gist was wounded and his brigade fell back to regroup, B. Benjamin Smith told the fifty-five-year-old Mercer that Gist's Brigade was ready for a third assault if Mercer's Brigade would cooperate with it. Although a graduate of the U.S. Military Academy at West Point, Mercer had mostly commanded the Post of Savannah during the war and had no combat experience. "The old man (he ought to have been behind his desk in Savannah) could not make up his mind to get any of his brigade injured and hesitated," Smith recalled after the war. "His Colonels came up and urged him and he finally told me to go back and hold the brigade in readiness to move forward when his left should be in line with us." B. Benjamin Smith then went back to get Gist's shattered command in order.[58]

Smith would wait in vain because, even though Mercer's Brigade moved forward, it never made an attack. When Mercer took over the division, Col. Charles H. Olmstead of the 1st Georgia (Volunteer) took over the brigade. Before the start of the battle, the troops had marched with difficulty through the tangled land between Fayetteville Road and the head of Sugar Creek, stopping to change direction to the right in an effort to stay within the line of march taken by the other two brigades, which contributed to its late arrival at the scene of action. At some point before the order to attack arrived, Olmstead was injured by the explosion of an artillery round; a fragment hit his head and rendered him unconscious. When he recovered consciousness sometime later in the hospital, the colonel came to the conclusion that he would have been much more seriously hurt if not for the fact that he had earlier that day exchanged "the light kepi" he usually wore for "a stout felt hat with a broad brim." The hat was one of many Gov. Joseph E. Brown had recently sent to the regiment. Although it had been "literally torn to pieces," the felt hat might well have saved his life.[59]

With Olmstead down, Col. William Barkuloo of the 57th Georgia took over Mercer's Brigade. Barkuloo heard from passing officers that Gist had already attacked and had been driven back, and that George A. Smith probably had suffered the same fate. This produced a sense of caution; Barkuloo sent out scouts who reported that the Federals were three-fourths of a mile in front but that he could expect no support to either right or left if he moved to the attack.[60]

When Mercer told him to advance, Barkuloo gave the order. His brigade moved through the woods and emerged onto the open space before the Union position where George A. Smith had already been repulsed. Barkuloo stopped his men at Sugar Creek, which was here fringed with bushes, because the brigade was already receiving heavy artillery fire from Laird's 14th Ohio Battery and Blodgett's Battery H, 1st Missouri Light Artillery. Taking in the situation, Barkuloo concluded that his men would have to advance across what he estimated to be 500 yards of open space, that the Union line extended farther in both directions than his own, and that an attack would be a senseless waste of manpower. He gave the order to retreat, estimated his losses at fifteen killed and wounded, and briefly reported to Mercer what he had done.[61]

Dodge could not know it yet, but the fighting was essentially over on his sector of the battlefield. His three brigades had decisively repelled the efforts of six Confederate brigades to overrun his commanding position. Dodge still worried about the gap between the Sixteenth Corps units and Blair's Seventeenth Corps. His initial request to Giles A. Smith to swing around and connect with Fuller had been delivered and agreed to, but it soon became obvious that Smith had not done so. At some point before the repulse of Gist's Brigade, Dodge sent another message with Lt. George C. Tichenor, an aide-de-camp. Tichenor returned and told him that Giles A. Smith had orders to hold his line and already was heavily engaged. The dangerous opening would remain, a gaping invitation to Confederate advances, for most of the day.[62]

Dodge managed to obtain a handful of regiments sent to him from the Fifteenth Corps, although they did not arrive in time to take part in the repulse of Bate or Walker. At the start of the battle, he had sent his assistant commissary of musters, Capt. William H. Chamberlin, to request of McPherson a brigade to help the Sixteenth Corps. Chamberlin rode to the Seventeenth Corps just as the fighting there erupted and wisely considered it useless to ask them for help. But when he rode to the as yet unengaged Fifteenth Corps, Logan obliged him, telling Morgan L. Smith to send Col. James S. Martin's brigade. Martin decided to personally lead the regiments of his second line (106th Illinois, 127th Illinois, and 6th Missouri), leaving the 55th Illinois and 57th Ohio, under Lt. Col. Samuel R. Mott of the latter regiment, to hold his sector of the Fifteenth Corps line just south of the Georgia Railroad. Martin had to move a couple of miles across country and was delayed by negotiating the areas occupied by Army of the Tennessee wagon trains. The teamsters were nervous and assumed a retreat was underway when they saw so many troops passing by; "it required all the skill and energy of their superiors to prevent a stampede" among the drivers. Martin's men found this amusing and began "laughing and gibing them."[63]

As for the Confederates confronting Dodge, they already had a spare brigade near the scene of action but could not employ it. Hardee fulfilled his commitment to provide Maney's Brigade, commanded by Col. Francis M. Walker, from Cheatham's Division (now led by Maney). But that unit floundered across the confusing, cluttered landscape between Fayetteville Road and the head of Sugar Creek without making its presence felt where it counted. According to Capt. James Iredell Hall of the 9th Tennessee, the brigade struggled through "dense undergrowth of bushes and brambles" until stopped "by an impassable creek and millpond." Already tired from the flanking march, this struggle exhausted and overheated the men even more. Before they could catch their breath and figure out a way to proceed, an urgent order arrived for the brigade to double-quick all the way over to Hardee's left flank, where it was judged to be more crucially needed than on the right. Francis M. Walker's men failed to support Bate or W. H. T. Walker but had a chance to help Cleburne and Maney if they moved fast enough. Dodge later estimated it was between three and four in the afternoon when the Confederate brigade left his sector and moved west.[64]

The mismanagement of Francis M. Walker's command points up the severe contrast in command and control between the Confederates and the Federals in this first phase of the Battle of July 22. No one on the Rebel side was in charge of the fighting here. Hardee decided, probably for good reason, to remain with Cleburne and Maney and expected Bate and W. H. T. Walker to cooperate with each other as they saw fit. Bate, however, was incapable of controlling his own division, wasting two of his three brigades in wandering across the countryside, much less in coordinating its actions with that of his colleague to the west. For his part, Walker had no opportunity to control anything, given that he fell even before his division became engaged. Mercer, his replacement, was utterly incapable of grabbing control of the battle. As was typical of the Army of Tennessee, it all depended on the brigade commanders, and they did not do well either. Of the six brigades in the two divisions, half of them lost their commander early in the engagement (two to battle injuries and one to division command). Literally every one of the Confederate brigades that went into action did so without support from any of the others, greatly contributing to the Federals' ability to repel their advances.

In stark contrast, command and control rose to a high level on the Union side of the fighting at Sugar Creek. Dodge was tightly involved in the flow of events from the very beginning and intervened to start a counterattack at exactly the right moment to repel George A. Smith's advance. Fuller also intervened personally at a key moment to rally the 27th Ohio and thus shore up his threatened right flank. Sweeny's role in the fighting was less significant, although it is not easy to sift truth from brag in his account of the battle. While Sherman and Hood had nothing to do with the flow of events along Sugar Creek, McPherson (as discussed in the next chapter) was a keen observer of Dodge's fight. On realizing his corps leader had things well under control, he did not interfere with his work.

Dodge proudly reported that his men captured 351 Confederates from forty-nine regiments in addition to eight flags. The Federals fired so heavily that four regiments in Sweeny's division ran out of the ammunition in their cartridge boxes and had to have more brought forward. Laird's battery fired 651 rounds, playing a key role by providing artillery support. As Sherman accurately reported, "Dodge had caught and held well in check the enemy's right, and punished him severely."[65]

The losses did not necessarily reflect a Confederate rout, although the flow of action was a dismal repulse for them. Gary Ecelbarger estimates that Bate's and Walker's Divisions each suffered about 500 casualties, while Dodge lost close to 700 men. Planted on high and open ground, perfect for defense but exposed to enemy fire, the Federals paid something of a penalty. The 66th Illinois lost 44 men, and survivors counted sixty-five bullet holes in its flag after the engagement. The teamsters that Martin's regiment laughed at as they passed by had some reason for concern. Stray Confederate artillery fire sailed into the rear areas of the Union line. James M. Thurston, a hospital worker in Sweeny's division, stood next to an ambulance team when a shell ploughed through one of the horses.[66]

But relative losses were unimportant compared to the enormous significance of Dodge's achievement. His men literally saved the Army of the Tennessee from the most serious threat emerging from Hardee's flank march—a direct attack on the unprepared rear of the Union line. The battle was far from over, however, for the rest of Hardee's Corps was yet to be heard from, and Cheatham's divisions were ready to go into action. But the first round had been decisively won by the defenders.

6

McPherson's Last Ride

Dodge was aware that his commander had been watching the early phase of the important battle between his troops and the divisions led by Bate and Walker. McPherson wisely refrained from interfering with his direction of events; he did not even contact Dodge during the course of the fight but took a position from which most of the Sixteenth Corps battlefield was visible. After it became clear that the situation was in hand, McPherson rode off to meet his destiny.

McPherson's last ride began at the lunch site under the grove of oak trees just south of the Georgia Railroad and three-fourths of a mile behind the Fifteenth Corps line. At about 12:15, the party heard a sudden surge of small-arms fire to the southeast and knew it portended something serious. McPherson sent Capt. George R. Steele (aide-de-camp) to Decatur with instructions for Sprague's brigade, then sent Lt. Col. William T. Clark (assistant adjutant general), Capt. Chauncey B. Reese (chief of engineers), and Capt. David H. Buel (chief of ordnance) to conduct various errands. He took Lt. Col. William E. Strong (assistant inspector general), Capt. David H. Gile (aide-de-camp), and Capt. Andrew Hickenlooper (chief of artillery) with him as he rode from the grove toward the sound of firing.[1]

The party moved through heavy timber until reaching some open fields where wagon trains were parked. The sound of firing had made the teamsters nervous, and many wagons already were moving away. "Gile, stop those teams; they'll get up a general stampede," McPherson shouted. The rest of the group rode on until reaching a drove of beef cattle on the verge of stampeding, which McPherson sent Hickenlooper to prevent. That left only Strong and one orderly, Andrew Jackson Thompson Sr. of the 4th Independent Company of Ohio Cavalry, with the general. The three rode on another quarter of a mile but picked up a group of signal officers and enlisted men along the way. Capt. Ocran H. Howard, McPherson's chief signal officer, was bringing these three officers and ten "flagmen and orderlies" to his commander's assistance, and McPherson told them all to follow.[2]

The party reached a point at the northern edge of the open space upon which the Sixteenth Corps battle was playing out and stopped not far from the extreme right of Dodge's extended line and near his ammunition train. As the drama unfolded, McPherson sent Strong to tell Giles A. Smith to hold his position at the southern end of the Seventeenth Corps line while troops were found to block the gap between Blair and Dodge. Strong had served as a private in the 2nd Wisconsin in Sherman's brigade at the First Battle of Bull Run and later as major of the 12th Wisconsin. McPherson had recognized his abilities and assigned him to his staff in 1862. "Strong always seemed the most active, either in carrying orders or reconnoitering and selecting positions," Sherman testified, and always "displayed not only courage and industry but a high degree of military skill." Strong now faced his sternest test in this unfolding drama. He rode along the most convenient road through the woods in that area between the Sixteenth and Seventeen Corps formations to fulfill his mission. Strong found Blair consulting with Giles A. Smith, whose division was not yet engaged, and the two generals told him there were ominous signs of approaching Confederates. Then Strong returned to McPherson by the same road as quickly as possible.[3]

McPherson then sent Strong to see Logan about detaching a brigade from his Fifteenth Corps line and moving it into the gap to the best defensive position it could find. Strong once again rode along that same road and on to the center of the army's line, where Logan readily complied with McPherson's message. His corps was not yet threatened, and the necessary orders were issued.[4]

Back at McPherson's observation point, the general and Thompson saw a man riding toward them in haste. It was Capt. John B. Raymond of Leggett's staff, sent by the division commander to make contact with the army leader. Raymond asked if McPherson had any special instructions for his commander. "Tell Gen. Leggett to straighten his lines parallel with this road, just as quick as God will let you," he replied, according to Thompson.[5]

What McPherson meant, apparently, was for the Seventeenth Corps to

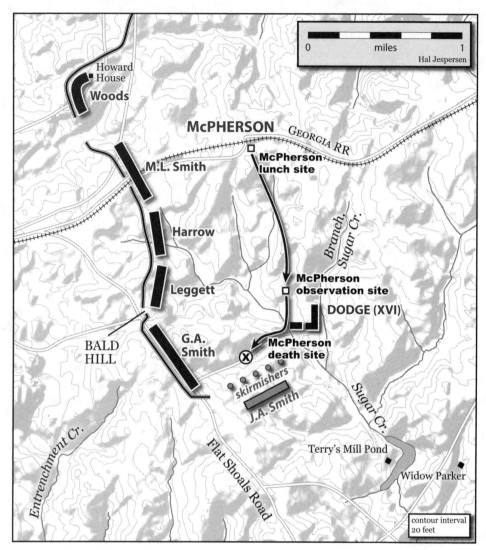

McPherson's Last Ride

refuse the Union line to close the space with Dodge. Its line already was parallel to the Flat Shoals Road, so the only road McPherson could have meant was the obscure one that ran west to east through the woods that Strong and others were using. This, of course, contradicted his earlier instruction to Giles A. Smith to hold his current position, but McPherson likely meant to change that instruction. His conception of how to defend the Union left was quickly evolving with the passage of time. Rather than filling the gap with a lone brigade, he now meant to draw back the two Seventeenth Corps divisions to connect with Dodge, which was a much more secure way to protect the exposed flank of his army.

McPherson had seen enough of Dodge's fight to know the situation was under control. Now, pushed by the desire to get Giles A. Smith's division drawn back to fill the dangerous gap between Blair and Dodge, he decided to deliver the new instruction personally. Many men had already ridden along the obscure road linking the two corps, so there was no immediate sign that it was dangerous to continue using it. Sometimes referred to as a wood path, this road "ran nearly in prolongation" of Dodge's line and was the fastest means of moving across the gap. Ironically, Blair had sent his Seventeenth Corps headquarters guard, twenty-five men, to secure the road at the start of the battle. They were there only twenty minutes before Blair recalled them to protect his headquarters once again. The men moved off at the double-quick, leaving the road again empty of Union troops except for those who hurried along it.[6]

McPherson received one warning about riding along the road but ignored it. Lt. William H. Sherfy, an acting signal officer assigned to Dodge, had been busy trying to calm teamsters and now returned to Ocran Howard's group. He passed McPherson just as the general was starting from his observation point and warned him it was dangerous to ride west. "He disregarded it though, and went on," Sherfy later reported, with Thompson the orderly riding right behind the general. Sherfy turned his horse and trailed after as well, with Howard's entire signal party thirty yards behind Sherfy.[7]

This is the grouping of Union officers and enlisted men that rode along the narrow road through the woods at about 1 P.M. Raymond led the way, riding west to give Leggett the army commander's instruction, followed 150 yards behind by McPherson and Thompson, then came Sherfy and the rest of Howard's signal men. This extended group attracted some attention. John S. Bosworth of the 15th Iowa, who was filling canteens to the rear of the Seventeenth Corps line, later claimed he saw the group riding along. Even Blair reported seeing McPherson ride into the woods along the road. He and an orderly were in the area searching for the army commander, but they were too late. McPherson had disappeared into the trees.[8]

Deadly trouble soon became apparent. Thompson saw Raymond rounding a slight bend in the road when the sound of musketry erupted and Raymond's horse fell. The captain tumbled off to the left and fell among the leaves that littered the ground next to the roadside. Within seconds, the woods to the left of the road "became alive with gray uniforms" as Confederates emerged from the brush in a long thin line only a few yards away from McPherson and Thompson.[9]

These Rebels constituted the skirmish line of James A. Smith's Brigade, advancing north directly into the gap between Blair and Dodge. Not yet engaged, the Texas skirmishers initially saw and fired at Raymond. Now they confronted McPherson and Thompson. What happened next took place within seconds but became permanently engraved on the minds of those who experienced it.

At this section of the skirmish line, the man in charge was Capt. Richard Beard. Born near Canton, Mississippi, his father later became a professor of theology at Cumberland College in Lebanon, Tennessee. The family owned fifteen slaves. Beard was a college student when the war broke out, and he enlisted in the 7th Tennessee. His first and worst battle experience took place at Seven Pines during the Peninsula Campaign in the summer of 1862. It "gave a better conception of Hell than any that I passed through afterwards," he wrote at age eighty. "Never saw men fall around me as fast as they did there." Beard was hit three times "almost before I could turn around," but he recovered from his injuries to be commissioned in Company B, 5th Confederate.[10]

Beard's skirmishers had struggled through dense undergrowth and blackjack trees before reaching the "little wagon road" used so often by the Federals that day. He was surprised to see a Union officer and orderly riding so near the spot where he emerged from the trees. Beard gave McPherson a signal to stop, and the general's horse nearly fell as McPherson reined him to a halt. "I was so near him as to see every feature of his face," Beard recalled. "I was satisfied he was a General officer." Beard raised his sword in the air as an encouragement for him to surrender, but McPherson decided against it. The general "raised his hat as if he were saluting a lady, wheeled his horse's head to the right, and dashed off to the rear in a full gallop." According to Thompson, many Confederates near Beard yelled out "halt you Damed Sons of biches."[11]

Of the several Rebels who instinctively raised their muskets to fire at McPherson, Beard was confident he knew which one of them hit the mark. Cpl. Robert F. Coleman of Company B, 5th Confederate was "as gallant a young soldier as I ever saw on the battlefield, but very excitable," Beard recalled. He had served in a Tennessee regiment that was consolidated into the 5th Confederate. In the excitement of the encounter, Coleman fired from close distance. He recalled that McPherson leaned forward both to avoid the shooting and to be clear of the overhanging limbs of the pine trees along the north side of the road. Coleman saw McPherson fall immediately after he fired. The bullet entered the general's back and traveled up through his leaning body, cutting through the lung, passing near the heart, and almost exiting from the left breast.[12]

Orderly Thompson was very near to McPherson when all this happened.

He also turned his horse's head to escape and caught a glimpse of his general falling. Rebel bullets sailed over Thompson and "fairly blistered the back of my neck," and the orderly "either struck against a tree or was dragged off by a heavy bough." Falling to the ground, he remained stunned for a few seconds. Then he stumbled to McPherson's side. His commander "was lying on his right side with his right hand pressed against his breast and every breath he drew, the blood flowed in streams between his fingers." "General, are you hurt?" Thompson asked. "Oh! Orderly, I am," McPherson moaned. "Immediately after McPherson had spoken to me he turned over on his face, straightened himself out and convulsively clutched the leaves with his hands, his body in the meantime quivering and trembling like an aspen," but the general never spoke but later turned over onto his back again.[13]

The Confederates moved quickly to the spot and began to harass Thompson as McPherson lay dying. They "caught holt [sic] of my Revolver belt and pushed and draged [sic] me away from him, and called me a yanky Son of bich, told me to go to the rear or they would Sho[o]t me." About this time, McPherson turned from his back onto his front but still made no sound.[14]

Beard, among the first Confederates to reach McPherson, recalled the general as kneeling with his face on the ground. "Even as he lay there, dressed in his Major-General's uniform, with his face in the dust, he was as magnificent a looking specimen of manhood as I ever saw." Capt. William A. Brown, Beard's friend and colleague, picked up McPherson's hat and used it as his own for the rest of the war. Beard asked Thompson who it was that Coleman had shot. "Sir, it is Gen. McPherson. You have killed the best man in our army," the orderly replied with tears in his eyes.[15]

A good deal of argument later developed over whether and how far the Confederates took items from McPherson during the next few minutes. Beard admitted that Brown appropriated the hat but insisted that none of his men took anything else, blaming other troops for anything more that was purloined. But someone stole McPherson's watch, his sword belt (he was not wearing a sword), and a pocket book with private papers. In fact, the bullet that killed the general had nearly severed the strap supporting his field glasses. Ironically, the Confederates failed to discover that McPherson carried a good deal of cash (reportedly one thousand dollars) and also overlooked a ring.[16]

Besides Raymond, McPherson, and Thompson, another man fell under a hail of Confederate bullets near and at about the same time, but it is impossible to verify exactly where and when. Col. Robert K. Scott, commander of Leggett's Second Brigade, was wounded and captured while trying to return to his command. That morning, Scott and Lt. Abram C. Urquhart of his staff had guided the 68th Ohio from the brigade's position toward

James B. McPherson. A friend and protégé of Grant and Sherman, McPherson rose from the engineers to become a good corps and generally reliable army commander. He tended to be a bit lax at times during the Atlanta Campaign—for example, taking his time to secure the left flank of the Army of the Tennessee on the morning of July 22. But his personality and character were the basis of his widespread reputation as well as the deep mourning that followed his death during the Battle of Atlanta. Everyone was impressed by his kindness, genial disposition, and good nature. Library of Congress, LC-DIG-cwpb-07051.

the east to protect Seventeenth Corps hospitals, prompted by reports of Confederate cavalry hovering nearby. According to one of its number, the regiment encountered enemy infantry instead, fired a volley, and escaped. While Lt. Col. George E. Welles guided it back toward Leggett in a three-mile detour to the north and west, Scott took the most direct route along the infamous road. He apparently rode ahead of Raymond and was felled by the skirmishers of James A. Smith's Brigade, who killed his horse and slightly injured and captured Scott. When brought to Irving Buck, one of Cleburne's staff men, Scott offered his sword (which Buck still possessed in 1908).[17]

Well to the rear of this string of Federals involved in the incident, Howard's signal party saw and heard the firing that felled McPherson. Lt. William W. Allen could hear shouts of "'Halt; halt, there; halt!'" just before the Rebel volley erupted. The firing caused the entire signal party to turn into the woods north of the road. "We were plunging wildly through the trees," recalled Allen, "a race for life, each one for himself, and lost to sight from his fellows until reaching" an open field to the north. At the start of this wild exodus, William H. Sherfy suffered an accident. "My horse dashed me against a tree, knocking me to the ground insensible." He soon recovered and made his way through the woods to the clearing, nursing a severe bruise, but lost his horse, hat, and field glasses. Allen also hurt his ankle when his horse smashed him against a tree.[18]

Sherfy contributed to efforts made to pinpoint the time of McPherson's shooting. When he had time to look at his watch, he found that it had been crushed when he smashed into the tree, and the timepiece stopped at 2:02 P.M. That has been accepted at face value by some historians, but there are several reasons to discount it. First, no one set their watches by a central timekeeper during the Civil War, and reported times varied widely when individuals looked at their pieces. Moreover, in a postwar letter to the editor of the *Indianapolis Journal*, Sherfy stated that the time on his watch was 1:02 P.M. rather than 2:02. Equally important, everyone agrees that the battle started at noon, and we have a firm understanding of McPherson's movements and the movements of the Confederate and Union formations engaged in the first hour or two of the fight. After the battle, William Strong traced the route of McPherson's last ride from the luncheon site and concluded that it would have taken at least an hour for the sequence of events to transpire. From all the evidence, the best conclusion is that McPherson was shot about 1 P.M.[19]

The signal party reassembled in the clearing after their wild ride through the woods. "Do you think the General was killed?" Howard asked Allen. The lieutenant answered that he believed he caught a glimpse of McPherson falling from his saddle before his own horse bolted into the trees. Just then, McPherson's riderless mount emerged from the woods into the clearing. It was bloody from two bullet wounds that had failed to incapacitate it while the saddle and equipment had the marks of three other bullets. Thompson's horse also appeared in the clearing. The signal officers sent word up the chain of command that the army's commander was either killed or captured. They entrusted McPherson's horse to Cpl. Robert H. Barton and Pvt. Thomas H. Burnes of Company B, 1st Ohio Cavalry, who acted as scouts for McPherson's headquarters, and to Sgt. Thomas C. Yates of the 4th Independent Company of Ohio Cavalry, McPherson's escort. Barton recalled that two pistols were still in their saddle holsters. Silver plates inscribed "To Gen. Jas. B. McPherson, by his many R. R. friends" adorned the holsters. The trio took the animal to Logan's headquarters, and it was eventually shipped to Clyde, Ohio.[20]

After the war, as McPherson's death became the most prominent aspect of the Battle of July 22, many Confederates tried to claim responsibility for it. The most vigorous contender was Pvt. Robert D. Compton of Company I, 24th Texas Cavalry (dismounted). He spread a story that mixed some real aspects of the general's death with much false detail and persisted in it for many years. For example, Compton claimed not only to have killed McPherson but also to have captured his horse. He claimed he gave it to his brigade leader, James A. Smith, to use only to have the animal killed an hour later. Lesser claims for the killing of McPherson were filed for another member of Compton's regiment, Henry H. Cowan of Company H, while a Major McPherson of the 5th Confederate was mentioned as the one who shot the general. There even were reports that someone in Francis M. Walker's brigade in Maney's command had killed McPherson. All of these claims are false; Beard's story about Robert Coleman is the only reliable account of this sad incident from the Confederate side.[21]

In fact, McPherson's death haunted Coleman for the rest of his life. Reportedly wounded at Stones River in December 1862, he also received a wound at Franklin in November 1864. After the war, Coleman wound up working on a fruit ranch in California owned by William B. Cullen, a veteran of the Army of Northern Virginia. Described as "modest and unassuming," Coleman did not tell anyone about July 22 until he reached his deathbed in 1881 or 1882. Cullen, his confidant, released the information long after Coleman's death. C. W. Frazer, a comrade in the 5th Confederate, wrote that Coleman "always regretted this shot so fatally made on the impulse of the moment."[22]

The impact of McPherson's death proved to be severe on everyone involved. But very soon after the shooting, the Confederate skirmishers

Site of McPherson's Death. Exposed by civilian photographer George N. Barnard, who worked under government contract, this was one of four scenes he took of McPherson's death site in September 1864. Someone, probably Barnard, assembled unexploded artillery shells, horse bones, artillery wheels, and some clothing and accoutrements to set the décor for this image. None of this material would have been there during the battle. Note the board nailed to the tree, which reads "Maj. Gen. J. B. McPherson July 22d, 1864." Barnard took more photographs in early November 1864 or late May 1866. His 1864 images were sold as prints by the E. and H. T. Anthony Company of New York City early in 1865, and one appeared as a woodcut engraving in *Harper's Weekly* on February 18, 1865. Barnard's photographs helped feed a growing public fascination with McPherson's tragic death. Library of Congress, LC-DIG-cwpb-03427.

continued moving forward toward the north. Thompson was roughly handled toward the rear, and John B. Raymond was taken back as well. The two met at the place in Atlanta where the Confederates were corralling their prisoners and exchanged notes about the incident. Both men survived their imprisonment, with Thompson spending more than nine months in Andersonville.[23]

After the Rebel skirmish line moved north, an eerie silence prevailed at McPherson's death site until three Union soldiers accidentally stumbled on the area. George Reynolds of Company D, 15th Iowa, a farm boy from near Ottumwa, had been detailed to headquarters work for several months. Along with five other such men, he was on his way to rejoin the regiment when the group ran into part of the skirmish line fronting James A. Smith's Brigade. Most of them were killed, but Reynolds was wounded in the arm and abdomen and was taken prisoner. His captor became careless, and very soon Reynolds managed to escape but was disoriented and wandered about in the wooded gap between Blair and Dodge. Finally, he happened upon McPherson. No one was near, but the general seemed yet to be living, although unconscious. Reynolds offered him water but received no reply. McPherson slowly moved his head as Reynolds stood and watched, unable to do anything for him, as random artillery rounds burst uncomfortably near.[24]

A Federal straggler wandered up and began to rummage through McPherson's pockets. He found a lot of cash in large bills and proposed that he and Reynolds share the loot. Reynolds was appalled and demanded the straggler return it, but despite the Iowan's efforts, the man absconded with the entire amount, probably $1,000, representing McPherson's pay received just before the campaign began. The straggler left only the empty pocketbook.[25]

Then another straggler happened by, and Reynolds believed that, by this time, McPherson had expired. Pvt. George Sherland of Company D, 64th Illinois never explained why he was wandering around in this area, but Reynolds called out when he saw him. Sherland was wary and asked "is there any danger." Only when Reynolds assured him it was safe did he approach. The two were discussing what to do when three Confederates with a stretcher appeared. The Rebels considered taking McPherson's body away, but soon decided against it because they were afraid the Federals might sweep into the area. They insisted that Reynolds and Sherland go away with them as prisoners, but because the trio were not armed, the two Unionists refused. Left alone once more, Reynolds and Sherland decided to head for where they assumed their comrades were positioned. A quarter of a mile away they found friends.[26]

McPherson's trusted staff officer George E. Strong happened to meet Reynolds and Sherland at this time and took action to retrieve the general's body. He had been sent off by the commander only minutes before the incident to ask Logan for a brigade to be placed in the gap. Logan filtered that request through Brig. Gen. Charles R. Woods's First Division, Fifteenth Corps and at 1 P.M. Woods ordered his reserve, Col. Hugo Wangelin's Third Brigade, to move out. Capt. John S. Hoover, one of Logan's aides-de-camp, guided Wangelin, and Strong rode along with him. The men moved out quickly, causing a good deal of bustle and a bit of panic among teamsters in nearby wagon trains, and assumed the double-quick. When Surgeon A. W. Reese asked Wangelin where he should move his ambulances, "that stern, old German patriot" told him "right behind the Brigade, Surgeon!" Everyone moved with a sense of urgency until reaching a point in the center of the gap. The brigade took post farther north than McPherson had intended because it was by then obvious that the area near the road where he had been shot was now impossible to occupy.[27]

The brigade established a line on a knoll and at the edge of timber with a good view of the area south. It was 2 or 2:30 P.M. when Wangelin settled into position about due east of Bald Hill. By this time. James A. Smith's Texas brigade had advanced northward to the east of Bald Hill until stopped by elements of Harrow's division in a blocking position arranged by Charles C. Walcutt (an action discussed in the next chapter). Wangelin's brigade was located to the southeast of Walcutt's blocking position but out of sight of Walcutt's men; no one in either command ever mentioned the troops in the other position. As Wangelin's men established themselves, rumors of McPherson's fall already were circulating. The colonel ordered his troops to construct breastworks of fence rails and sent a strong skirmish line toward the south. These skirmishers captured twenty Confederate stragglers. Wangelin also sent men with stretchers to search for wounded as Reese established his brigade hospital 500 yards to the rear of the line. The surgeon soon treated wounded from the Sixteenth Corps and some Confederates as well. While the brigade was entirely reliable, it also was small, no more than 700 troops, and fell far short of physically closing the gap. In fact, Wangelin was unsupported on either flank with openings of a quarter mile between his left and Dodge's command and a similar distance between his right and the Seventeenth Corps position.[28]

As Wangelin assumed his isolated post, Strong performed his best service for McPherson. Upon reaching the general area at the head of Wangelin's column, Strong quickly realized he would not be able to place the brigade where McPherson had intended, so he rode away to consult with the general. As he neared the cleared area where Ocran Howard's signal party had

William E. Strong. As lieutenant colonel and assistant inspector general on McPherson's staff, Strong played the key role in recovering the slain commander's remains from the battlefield. He had served as a private in the 2nd Wisconsin in the East and a major of the 12th Wisconsin in the West before McPherson recruited him for his staff in 1862. Strong became prominent after the war as the acknowledged expert on the death of McPherson. Library of Congress LC-DIG-cwpb-03162.

reassembled, Strong recognized McPherson's riderless horse, already secured by the group, from a distance. By the time he reached the mount,
Reynolds and Sherland appeared out of the woods. The awful truth was
quickly told. The two gave Strong some items they had taken from the
body; "an empty pocket-book, a knife, [a] bunch of keys, and a number of
other articles," as Strong recalled. They offered to guide him to the body but
warned him it would be impossible to remove it north through the woods.
They would have to reach the site along the road. So the three men went
to Wangelin's brigade to secure an ambulance. There they met Capt. David
H. Buel, McPherson's chief of ordnance, who joined the party. Wangelin
gave them an ambulance pulled by four mules. Strong and Buel each had an
orderly with them, all mounted, while Reynolds and Sherland rode in the
ambulance. With the ambulance driver, the group of seven men set out.[29]

Fortunately, the men met no opposition along the way. They found
McPherson some distance into the wooded area and about thirty yards
north of the road. As the driver turned the ambulance around, Buel and
Sherland walked along the road with revolvers to watch for any approaching Confederates as Reynolds took Strong to the body. McPherson "was
lying upon his back, quite dead, his head resting upon a blanket" Reynolds
had earlier placed there. A quick look convinced Strong that the general's
hat, watch, field glasses, sword belt, and book with memos and other papers
were gone. But his buckskin gloves and the diamond ring on his left little
finger remained. "Raising his body quickly from the ground and grasping it
firmly under the arms, I dragged it, with such assistance as Reynolds could
offer." At the ambulance, others helped them lift the body into the carriage.
Then the party rode east out of the wooded area as fast as possible, stopping
only when the men felt out of the danger zone. Here they more properly
positioned McPherson's body, straightening his limbs and folding his arms
on his chest while supporting the head on a blanket. After administering this
respect, the driver moved off toward Sherman's headquarters at the Howard
House. After depositing the general's body there, the driver went on to deliver Reynolds at the Twenty-Third Corps hospital for treatment. A number
of Union and even Confederate soldiers claimed they saw the ambulance
moving from the area of McPherson's death. It is quite possible that they
were right.[30]

Sherman had been informed of McPherson's fate before the body arrived
at the Howard House. William T. Clark of McPherson's staff brought the
news to him. "The suddenness of this terrible calamity would have overwhelmed me with grief," Sherman wrote, "but the living demanded my
whole thoughts." Still, he allowed himself some time to focus on what had

become of his friend and trusted subordinate. McPherson's body was taken into a room, the pine door wrenched off its hinges to provide a table on which to place the remains. Surgeon Henry S. Hewit, Schofield's medical director, examined McPherson and found that the bullet that traversed his body had lodged just under the skin rather than exiting. Other than this and the entrance wound, there was no disfigurement.[31]

Meanwhile, many Confederate artillery rounds blanketed the area and the Howard House was struck. In a letter written two weeks later, Sherman indicated he thought it might be necessary to burn the house in case the Federals had to evacuate Copenhill. He therefore told Gile and Steele to take McPherson's body to Marietta. When the rest of the general's personal staff asked to be part of the escort, Sherman consented. But in his memoirs, Sherman indicated that he moved the body because he feared the house might catch on fire from the artillery hits. Soon after the body reached Marietta, it was shipped by rail to Clyde, Ohio, escorted by Gile, Steele, and Lt. Col. Willard Warner. The last named officer was one of three assistant inspectors general on Sherman's staff.[32]

Many of McPherson's pilfered belongings were recovered before the battle ended. When the 64th Illinois advanced against Gist's Brigade, it helped stump the enemy movement and captured forty Confederates and a flag before retiring. One of the prisoners taken had McPherson's field glasses in his knapsack, and another prisoner had his gauntlets and some papers taken from the general. Both men belonged to James A. Smith's Texas brigade. Sometime that afternoon, the Federals delivered these items to Fuller, who examined the papers and found Sherman's last dispatch to McPherson. "That note could have been seen by nobody but the soldier who took it from McPherson's pocket, and even he could scarcely have read it." Fuller forwarded these items to Dodge on the morning of July 23, who sent them on to Strong, who now served Logan. Fuller included a note assuring Sherman that no Rebel officer could have read any of the papers recaptured from the prisoner. Sherman later admitted that he had worried about that point.[33]

Strong was grateful that the Confederates did not strip McPherson's body of clothing, something they regularly did whenever controlling a battlefield and had access to the dead. Only the general's hat and watch were never recovered. Sherland made a point of stating in print that he and Reynolds also delivered some personal items from McPherson's body to Strong, probably as a way of verifying their story.[34]

Sometime before the arrival of McPherson's body at the Howard House, Sherman had arranged for a replacement to head the Army of the Tennessee.

As soon as Clark brought him news of McPherson's death, Sherman told him to inform Logan, the next-ranking corps leader. To ensure the message got through, he also sent one of his own staff members to inform Logan to refuse the army's left wing if possible and hold on to Bald Hill at any cost. Sherman also wanted Logan to know the larger picture; that he had no intention of extending the army group farther south but would soon move the Tennessee army over to the right. Logan should concern himself with the main line of the army, while Sherman would see to the safety of Decatur and the army's rear areas. "I wanted the Army of the Tennessee to fight it out unaided," he later reported. Sherman could not recall with certainty but later thought the staff man who took this message to Logan was Maj. James C. McCoy, one of his aides-de-camp. Several other men claimed they did it; even Blair reported that he sent a man to inform Logan of McPherson's fall and that he should probably take command of the army, bypassing Sherman's headquarters.[35]

Logan had already been notified informally of "the probable death" of McPherson, only to have it confirmed a few minutes later and then to receive Sherman's instructions to succeed the fallen general a short time later. It was a verbal order but carried with it Sherman's assurance of support. Logan took command about 2 P.M., which meant that Morgan L. Smith took control of the Fifteenth Corps and Brig. Gen. Joseph A. J. Lightburn assumed command of Smith's Second Division. All of McPherson's staff except the aides-de-camp helped Logan for the rest of the day. The first thing that the new commander did was to ride along the army's line toward the left as far as he could to personally gauge conditions. He was concerned about the large, wooded gap between Blair and Dodge but saw that Wangelin now partially filled it.[36]

Dodge had received a report that McPherson probably had been wounded. But then, about 3 P.M., came confirmation of his death when Fuller told him that his men had found the general's possessions on two Confederate prisoners. Dodge sent a staff officer to inform Logan of his exposed left flank and to let him know that the gap between the Sixteenth and Seventeenth Corps was still open.[37]

Word of McPherson's death circulated fairly quickly among the Confederates as well. Hood later recalled that he heard about it that afternoon, and it "caused me sincere sorrow." McPherson had helped him a great deal at West Point. Hood had been "more wedded to boyish sports than to books," he later admitted. "Often . . . have I left barracks at night to participate in some merry-making, and early the following morning have had recourse to him to help me over the difficult portions of my studies for the day."

It is possible Hood would not have graduated in 1853 if not for McPherson's kindness toward him. "No soldier fell in the enemy's ranks, whose loss caused me equal regret."[38]

Other than Brig. Gen. Nathaniel Lyon, who fell at the head of a much smaller army at the Battle of Wilson's Creek on August 10, 1861, no other Union army commander was killed in battle during the war. For many reasons, McPherson's death on July 22, 1864, struck home far more deeply and painfully than Lyon's fall, affecting many people on both sides of the dividing line in war-torn America. But his fall did not alter the pace, intensity, or outcome of the Battle of Atlanta.

7

Desperate Struggle South of Bald Hill

As the drama attending McPherson's last ride and death played out, Cleburne's Division smashed into the Seventeenth Corps to spread the fighting westward from the scene of Dodge's battle with Bate and W. H. L. Walker. The most deadly combat of the day took place here as both sides struggled to control the area south of Bald Hill for about four hours, beginning at 1 P.M. That struggle involved some of the most dogged and costly combat of the entire war. While the three brigades of Cleburne's Division operated with little coordination, each one delivered heavy blows, and one of them, Govan's Brigade, achieved the greatest tactical success of any Confederate force that day. Maney's three brigades barely made an entry in this phase of the battle, conducting a cooperative assault that failed. The limited success of Cleburne and Maney that afternoon nevertheless set up a transition in the fighting from the area south of Bald Hill to the area east of that slight rise of ground. That shift took place at about 5 P.M. and lasted with increased fury well past the fall of night.

Deploying from marching column to battle lines near where Flat Shoals Road intersected Fayetteville Road at Widow Akers's House, Cleburne positioned the Texas brigade of James A. Smith on his right, the Arkansas brigade of Brig. Gen. Daniel C. Govan on his left, and the Alabama and Mississippi brigade of Brig. Gen. Mark P. Lowrey 500 yards to the rear as a reserve. Maney's brigades formed to Cleburne's rear. These formations moved north through a landscape covered with undergrowth and dotted with swampy sloughs; Govan guided his command along Flat Shoals Road. The terrain obstacles led to a good deal of delay until it became impossible for Cleburne to attack the Federals at the same time that Bate and Walker made contact. The terrain also played havoc with the orderly movement of the two divisions, making it impossible for the brigades to maintain contact with each other. As a result, when Cleburne's Division finally found the Union position, it closed in brigade by brigade instead of as a unified whole.[1]

Govan hit the Federals first and with devastating results. Although having only 1,000 men, Govan handled his command adroitly in its battle against Col. William Hall's larger brigade. But Hall made basic mistakes concerning the placement of his Iowa regiments that his opponent exploited with success.[2]

Govan used Flat Shoals Road as his guide, placing his left regiment west of the road and the rest of his command east of it. Cleburne told him to move forward while maintaining that relation to the road, which ran "somewhat west of north" from Fayetteville Road. He also told Govan that the rest of Hardee's Corps would guide on the movements of his brigade and that he would soon strike the Federal left flank. The Arkansans started to advance and found the terrain covered with patches of dense underbrush. Receiving a report that a large Federal wagon train lay in their path, Govan told Lt. Col. E. G. Brasher of the 2nd Arkansas, who commanded his skirmishers, to push on. Partway to the Federal flank, Govan stopped to reform his line. On continuing, he never came upon the wagons before his skirmishers met a Union skirmish line in front of the refused and fortified position created by Giles A. Smith to anchor the Union left flank. The time of contact was about 1 P.M., around the time that McPherson met his fate along the road northeast of this point.[3]

Hall had long before arrayed his Iowa brigade to protect McPherson's left flank. Lt. Col. John C. Abercrombie's 11th Iowa deployed with its left flank resting on Flat Shoals Road, which the Federals also called the Old McDonough Road. Lt. Col. Addison H. Sanders's 16th Iowa deployed east of the road in line with the 11th Iowa. Hall placed Col. William W. Belknap's 15th Iowa some distance to the rear of the 16th Iowa and facing southeast while also putting Col. John Shane's 13th Iowa to the rear of the 16th Iowa but facing south and acting as a reserve. Lt. Walter H. Powell's Battery F, 2nd Illinois Light Artillery supported Hall. Powell led one section placed on Flat Shoals Road between the 11th and 16th Iowa and facing south. Another section, led by Lt. George R. Richardson, planted itself on the west-facing line held by other brigades of Giles A. Smith's division, and the third section was held in reserve.[4]

Govan was impressed by the strength of Hall's position when his brigade stumbled on it that afternoon. He judged the length of line occupied by the 11th and 16th Iowa to be about 200 yards and noticed that the Federals occupied earthworks with "an almost impassible abatis, formed by cutting down the thick undergrowth of small oaks" in front. Powell's two Napoleons swept the area in front of the Union works. Govan's left wing, consisting of Col. J. W. Colquitt's consolidated 1st and 15th Arkansas, Col. E. Warfield's consolidated 2nd and 24th Arkansas, and half of Col. John E. Murray's consolidated 5th and 13th Arkansas, "came full upon these formidable intrenchments." Capt. Thomas J. Key, Cleburne's artillery chief, described the abatis as "formed of saplings and bushes cut off and bent over, leaving the butt or stump two feet high." Govan's assistant adjutant general later referred to this fortified position as "a curtain thrown back to protect the enemy's extreme left" and concluded that it must have been constructed well before "our attack could have been known."[5]

But the Confederates overstated the strength of these field fortifications. "We did not consider our works as strong as you describe," Belknap wrote to Govan after the war. "In many places the earth was lightly thrown over them & we had labored but little upon them." In front of the 16th Iowa, Sanders's men had cut away the brush for only forty yards to create a shallow field of fire. The main reliance for Hall was the strength and resiliency of his men, not the strength of his earthworks.[6]

Three companies of the 11th Iowa and an unknown force from the 16th Iowa were out on skirmish duty that afternoon. These men were the first to engage Govan's Brigade. The Confederates quickly drove in these skirmishers as the main line of Govan's left wing emerged from the tree cover only forty yards short of the Union trenches. Not long before this moment, Giles A. Smith had spoken with Sanders and told him that the 16th Iowa had "to hold those works to the last, as the safety of the division might depend on the delay we could occasion the enemy at that point," the colonel reported. "This was the last order that I received that day from any commanding officer."[7]

By the time they could see the Federals, Govan's troops already were within easy reach. Sanders told his Iowans to "fire low and aim well" but not to open until he gave the order, "no matter how close the enemy came." He did not keep his men waiting long. When instructed, the rear rank fired first. "There was a terrific and deadly volley, followed immediately by another" from the front rank. "Then a continuous rapid firing, fast as eager and experienced soldiers could load and discharge their guns."[8]

Govan's left wing was staggered by this initial fire and went to ground about thirty yards short of the Union position. The Confederate line

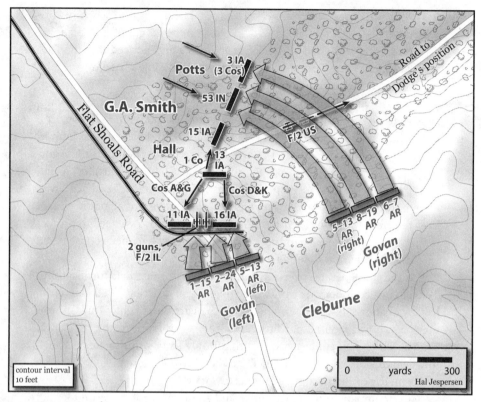

Govan Attacks

"seemed to crumble to the earth," as Sanders put it, "for even those not killed or wounded fell to the ground for protection." A static firefight now ensued for fifteen to twenty minutes, according to Govan's calculation. Some of his men crept forward and began to penetrate the abatis but not in sufficient numbers to make a difference. Govan reported that the Federals counterattacked and were repelled by Murray's 5th and 13th Arkansas troops, but there is no indication of any kind from the Union side that a counterattack took place.[9]

Unlike the brigades of Bate's or Walker's Divisions, Govan had some artillery support in his attack. Thomas J. Key had only Capt. Richard W. Goldthwaite's Alabama Battery available but selected a slightly elevated spot 600 yards from the Iowa line for one section of it; the other section took post 100 yards to the right. But Goldthwaite could offer scant help when his guns roared into action soon after Govan's left wing went to ground.[10]

About the same time, Hall felt it necessary to move help to the 11th and 16th Iowa. Giles A. Smith had cautioned him to hold his position at all costs, so Hall wanted to make sure of the developing action. He sent forward Companies A and G from the 13th Iowa to support the 11th Iowa, the latter of which contained only 200 troops because of the detachment of 100 men to fatigue duty before the onset of the fight. He also sent Companies D and K from the 13th to support the 16th Iowa. Hall sent another company from the 13th to support the 15th Iowa, leaving only half of the 13th still in reserve. Sanders was very happy to see these reinforcements when they reached his regiment. Capt. Alonzo J. Pope of Company D, 13th Iowa told Sanders that the two companies had been sent out of fear that "our ammunition as well as men must soon be exhausted." Sanders placed these reinforcements along his line, "and they went into the work like veterans."[11]

Sanders dramatically reported the heavy firing of his 16th Iowa veterans, supplemented by the equally vigorous efforts of their 13th Iowa comrades. "Officers and men worked enthusiastically; guns became so heated that they could not be handled, the powder flashing from them as the cartridge was dropped in. The officers prepared the cartridges for the men and helped them load their guns. More splendid firing, or more effectual in its results, was never witnessed in the army."[12]

Many men in Govan's left wing found themselves in a tight place. They were hardly safe from this exceedingly heavy fire at only thirty yards' distance and realized they could not advance farther because of it. Yet to retreat was almost as dangerous. After about twenty minutes, Sanders could see some white cloths raised among the Arkansas units as a token of surrender. He ordered a cease-fire, and many Confederates came into the Union works. Soon the 16th Iowa had more prisoners than it had men to take care of them. It took time to disarm the Rebels, whom Sanders sent to the rear as soon as he could. The Iowans were still in the process of collecting Confederate guns from their captives when the first inklings of trouble began to appear to the rear of the regiment's position.[13]

That trouble came in the form of Govan's right wing, which now achieved a stunning success over Hall's brigade. Consisting of half of Murray's consolidated 5th and 13th Arkansas, Col. George F. Baucum's consolidated 8th and 19th Arkansas, and Col. Samuel G. Smith's consolidated 6th and 7th Arkansas, the right wing had bypassed the fortified position of the 16th Iowa and continued to advance through the tangled countryside because the rest of Hall's brigade was positioned well to the rear of Sanders's regiment. Hearing the heavy fire confronting the left wing, Govan and his officers began to wheel the right wing in a blind effort to bring it to bear on the 11th and 16th Iowa.[14]

In the process of conducting this left-wheel maneuver, the right wing crossed the road linking Blair and Dodge's positions, but at a spot considerably west of where McPherson was killed. By sheer chance, the Confederate line hit the road exactly where Lt. Albert M. Murray's Battery F, 2nd U.S. Artillery happened to be moving east to rejoin Fuller's command. Fuller had loaned the unit to Blair the day before, but that morning Dodge authorized its return to the Sixteenth Corps. It took some time for it to disengage from the Seventeenth Corps line, and thus the battery started late. Govan's men hit it as it was moving at a trot. The Confederates captured Murray and Lt. Joseph C. Breckinridge so quickly that the other officers could not react before they were nearly engulfed as well. As a result, the battery could not unlimber or take position before the Rebels had possession of the six guns. In addition, the Arkansans killed, wounded, or captured eighteen men and 100 horses. The drivers managed to escape with most of the caissons, but the majority of the battery's equipment fell into enemy hands. Murray was wounded in the head and died of that injury in prison on August 12, 1864.[15]

Govan sent his artillery prisoners to the rear but did not take the time to collect and dispose of the captured equipment. He restarted the left wheel of his right wing as soon as possible. According to Thomas J. Key, two of Govan's regiments found a ravine not covered by Federal troops and used it to gain an advantageous position from which to deal with Belknap's 15th Iowa, which was located away from either the 13th or 16th Iowa and thus vulnerable. The second phase of Govan's fight with Hall now began.[16]

By this time, Govan would have more than Belknap to deal with, for Giles A. Smith had shifted some help to the 15th Iowa. He told Col. Benjamin F. Potts to move two of his regiments to Belknap's assistance. Potts, whose brigade was to the right of Hall's in the west-facing line, had two regiments in the works and two in reserve at this time. He sent the reserve units, Col. William Jones's 53rd Indiana and Capt. Pleasant T. Mathes's 3rd Iowa. This reinforcement was not nearly as strong as it appeared, for the 3rd Iowa only had three companies available on the field; moreover, Jones and Mathes became heavily engaged before fully taking position. Nevertheless, they temporarily stopped Govan's right wing before the Confederates discovered their left flank and turned it.[17]

The 53rd Indiana and 3rd Iowa then collapsed. In the confusion, Jones was shot through both thighs and later was hit by a shell burst in the head and killed. Sixty-five years old and described as "a brave and patriotic officer," Jones hailed from Gentryville, Indiana, where he had hired the nineteen-year-old Abraham Lincoln as a field hand for a dollar a day in 1828. Soon after Jones was killed, Maj. Warner L. Vestal took over the regiment but was soon badly wounded. The Confederates also mortally wounded Mathes and captured the flag of his 3rd Iowa.[18]

As the Indiana and Iowa men retreated, Belknap was compelled to pull his regiment back too. Apparently, the 15th Iowa was not engaged in the futile effort of Jones and Mathes to hold their position, a sure indication that the 53rd Indiana and 3rd Iowa could not reach Belknap's position before Govan hit them. Belknap moved the 15th back to the west-facing line before the Confederates could wrap around his position. At about this time, Giles A. Smith saw what was happening and ordered Hall not only to pull the 15th Iowa out of harm's way but the 13th Iowa as well.[19]

Hall's position was fast falling apart. With the pullback of both the 13th and 15th Iowa, nothing stood in Govan's way to complete the left wheel of his right wing and bear down on the rear of the 16th Iowa, whose officers and men were preoccupied with sorting out prisoners from Govan's left wing. Abercrombie's 11th Iowa was not taking in prisoners, and its men discovered their danger in time, when Govan's men were a hundred yards away. The 11th moved out of its works by the right flank and took position farther north to the rear of the west-facing line of fortifications.[20]

But this now left the 16th Iowa high and dry and without even a word of warning from its departing sister units. Samuel G. Smith's 6th and 7th Arkansas led Govan's right wing in completing the left wheel and advancing directly toward the rear of Sanders's unsuspecting regiment. The first inkling of trouble came when Sanders realized his men were receiving fire from the position of the 13th Iowa, now held by the Confederates. He ordered his troops to fix bayonets and force the prisoners from Govan's left wing to stand up to the rear of the regimental line, exposed to this fire, as a way to prompt the enemy to stop shooting. Then he was told to look at the regiment's left wing, where many Confederates with guns in their hands were moving into his works. Sanders went there and met Capt. John H. Smith of Company A, 16th Iowa, who told him "a large lot of the rebel prisoners refused to lay down their guns, and he wanted help to force them to do it." The colonel told Smith to get some men from the regiment's right wing as he went to speak to the prisoners.[21]

What followed was one of the strangest surrender episodes of the Civil War. Sanders managed to disarm two prisoners but met resistance from the rest. They surrounded and threatened him, but then offered a way out. "We won't hurt you, sir, if you surrender," they said. Sanders was "shocked at the word 'surrender'" and, upon glancing around, noticed for the first time that fresh Confederate troops had curved around his left flank, occupied the position of the 15th Iowa, and flew their colors to his left rear. His first thought was to move the 16th Iowa to the right and escape the trap. "I am not talking of surrender now," he told the prisoners and moved toward the right wing of his regiment. As he rushed off, a Confederate captain fired, the bullet passing "between my heels." But Capt. Jesse H. Lucas of Company K, 16th Iowa took a rifle from one of his men and fired back, two other Federals did the same, and between the three they killed the Rebel captain. At this turn of events, the Confederate prisoners dropped their weapons.[22]

Sanders began to put his plan into operation, pulling his troops from their works on the regimental right wing. Then he noticed that the Confederates had already occupied the earthworks once held by the 11th Iowa to his right. Taking another quick survey of his situation, it was clear that even more Rebels were closing in on his rear, and of course his left flank already was enveloped. The colonel ordered the men back into their trenches, called his officers together, and explained to them the situation. "We agreed to surrender," Sanders wrote, and then saw many of his men in the left wing already crossing the parapet unarmed, with Rebels herding them south. There was nothing to do now but follow their example on the right wing as well.[23]

Sanders personally gave up in the prescribed way. He still held the sword of a Confederate officer who had surrendered to him only fifteen minutes earlier, and now that officer confronted him. Sanders gave him back his sword and then offered his own with a request. It had been presented to him by fifty citizens of Davenport, Iowa, when the regiment had been organized in 1861. "Take it, and someday send it to Davenport, if you can, whether I am alive or not." The Rebel officer promised to do so but could not fulfill his word. Sanders survived captivity and after the war asked Govan to look into the matter about his sword. The former Confederate general found that another officer had taken it from the man who promised to return it, but Govan never learned his name or his fate.[24]

The 16th Iowa was literally engulfed by Govan's Brigade. Companies D and K of the 13th Iowa, which had so vigorously contributed to the heavy fire delivered at Govan's left wing, also were taken in. Govan rescued all the men of his left wing who had surrendered before the climax of the action except for those the Federals had already sent to the rear. As he accurately put it, "the officers of this command now received the swords of their late captors." Nearly everyone in the 16th Iowa fell captive, amounting to 225 enlisted men and thirteen officers, along with the regimental colors. Only a working party engaged in building an earthwork somewhere else escaped capture.[25]

Company A, 13th Iowa, one of the two sent to help the 11th Iowa, also became part of this disaster. Led by Orderly Sgt. Edwin R. Mason, it did not receive orders to move out with the 11th, and twenty-three of its men were captured. Mason had gone to the rear for more ammunition, and was stunned when he returned to see the works filled with Confederates. A

Rebel officer asked him "which way, Yank," and Mason replied, "for to h—l, I think." He was right, for Andersonville stared him and his comrades in the face. The hell had already begun. When one member of the company failed to drop his gun fast enough, a Rebel bayoneted him to death.[26]

Powell's section of Battery F, 2nd Illinois Light Artillery, planted on Flat Shoals Road between the 11th and 16th Iowa, also fell to the Confederates. Powell received no orders to retire and stayed where he was until too late, enduring enemy fire from all directions except the right. The lieutenant, six noncommissioned officers, and twenty-six enlisted men were captured, along with the two pieces and their limbers. Only the two caissons escaped. "It certainly looks much better that the officers and men should go with the section than be found deserting their guns," wrote Blair's artillery chief as a consolation for the disaster.[27]

Sanders struck a similar note in his report to the adjutant general of Iowa. "Why we were left alone, an isolated regiment, surrounded and help-less, while the other regiments around us were ordered from their works, as I suppose they were, I cannot realize. If the sacrifice of this noble regiment was intended to give the army in our rear time to rally, then it was well, and the sacrifice was nobly made." To have continued resistance, with am-munition virtually gone and quite literally surrounded, "would have been suicide."[28]

Govan's men acted toward their captives in a variety of ways. While some Iowans stated that the Arkansans "treated us like Gentlemen," Sand-ers frankly reported that many of his officers and men "were robbed by the rebels of almost everything as they left the ground."[29]

The Confederates made an effort to immediately use the two Napo-leons of Powell's battery on the Federals. The pieces had been captured by Colquitt's 1st and 15th Arkansas, and soon after Thomas J. Key called for volunteers to help him put the pieces into action. Enough men stepped forward, and a lieutenant from Goldthwaite's Alabama Battery also vol-unteered. Key managed to turn one piece around on the road, but in this exposed position, it drew so much Union rifle fire that he gave up the effort before firing the first round.[30]

Govan estimated that his brigade captured 700 Federals, but Gary Ecel-barger's estimate of 400 Union losses in Hall's brigade in this fight is proba-bly closer to reality. Govan could not praise his men enough for shattering the refused left flank of McPherson's line. "The whole affair was gallantly, brilliantly executed, and has never been excelled in dash and spirit by any previous action of these veteran soldiers." He could hardly believe that his left wing, grounded and giving up, eventually recovered to help capture the position by frontal attacks. Of course, that happened only because the right wing had found a way to exploit the disjointed placement of the 13th and 15th Iowa. If Hall had connected these regiments to the left wing of the 16th Iowa, covered the ravines better, and screened his extreme left flank, Govan's right wing likely would have failed to break through.[31]

But Govan's Brigade was much the worse after the fight than before. It had become scattered and had suffered heavy losses. Ecelbarger estimates casualties among the Arkansans as 300 out of the 1,000 men engaged. At least a dozen high-ranking regimental officers had been killed or wounded. The loss of Col. John E. Murray of the 5th and 13th Arkansas "cast a gloom over the whole command, where he was universally beloved." The fighting had been so deadly that all of Govan's couriers "disappeared after the first fire, and were of no assistance whatever" to him. The brigade was out of action for several hours as it put itself back together. It was an impressive victory but won at high cost.[32]

Quite a few men of Hall's brigade missed the fallout of this defeat because they were on skirmish lines or work details away from the action. Many of them eventually returned safely to Union lines, but not everyone was so fortunate. Sanders had sent off three officers and 80 men that morning to work on field fortifications. The detail had to fight its way back, losing 15 killed and wounded, around 12 captured, and about 25 missing. A detail of 125 men from the 11th Iowa suffered a similar fate. It encountered Confederate troops several times while making its way back to Union lines and became scattered. An indeterminate number of the men found refuge, while the rest were killed, wounded, or captured.[33]

Govan's attack on Hall caused Seventeenth Corps hospitals to evacuate quickly, as scattering shots pierced some tents. H. C. McArthur of the 15th Iowa, who had been wounded the day before, was carried away by attendants, but rounds fell so heavily in the area that they placed him temporarily in an open grave with a body in it. During a lull in the firing, they retrieved him only to be nearly run over by a headquarters wagon pulled by frightened horses. McArthur eventually reached a safe place and was shipped to Marietta along with many other wounded men able to travel.[34]

The other Confederate units that tried to exploit Govan's success failed to achieve anything. Hardee moved Maney's three brigades to the left in an effort to flank the Union position along Flat Shoals Road. But Maney shifted only enough so that his division straddled the road. Col. Michael Magevney Jr. positioned Vaughan's Brigade on the right, east of the roadway, and Brig. Gen. Otho F. Strahl placed his brigade on the left, west of the road. Wright's Brigade, commanded by Col. John C. Carter, trailed behind as a reserve. Maney's fourth unit, his old brigade now under Col. Francis M. Walker,

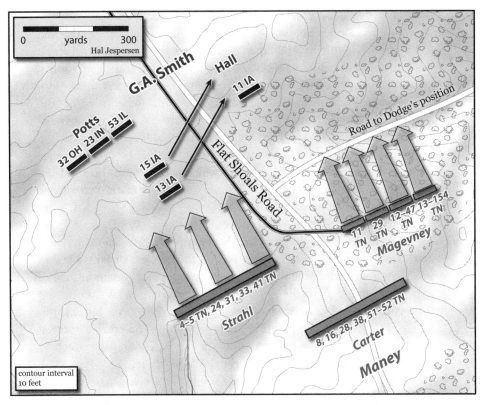

Maney Attacks

was still over on the right of Hardee's Corps vainly trying to support Bate's Division.[35]

To meet this threat, Hall placed the 13th and 15th Iowa west of the main line of works held by Giles A. Smith's division. Deployed in two lines, with the 13th in front and the 15th to the rear, both regiments faced south, with their left flank anchored on the parapet. Seventy-five yards behind Belknap's 15th Iowa, Potts formed the three regiments available in his brigade in one line. These included Lt. Col. John W. McClanahan's 53rd Illinois, Lt. Col. William P. Davis's 23rd Indiana, and Capt. William M. Morris's 32nd Ohio. The hastily organized position created by Hall and Potts barely covered the front of Strahl's Brigade, which was entirely west of the Union earthworks. The 11th Iowa remained east of the Union fortified line.[36]

When Strahl advanced to engage Hall's two regiments, a heavy firefight ensued. It lasted some minutes, as men on both sides fell. Among them was Lt. Col. John M. Hedrick of the 15th Iowa. Shot through the back, the bullet exiting at the hip, he was temporarily paralyzed. Hedrick was carried to the rear, where a second bullet hit his left forearm, but he survived all this and the war itself. Eventually, Strahl managed to flank the right end of the 15th Iowa line, and Hall ordered it to pull away to the east side of the earthworks, followed soon after by the 13th Iowa. Neither Govan nor any other Confederate brigade had been able to follow up the initial Rebel success at the refused line, so the Federals still controlled the east side of their main position along Flat Shoals Road. John Shane had some difficulty reassembling his 13th Iowa east of the line, however, because of "numerous detachments, independent commands, and stragglers which at that time thronged the road." But he managed to organize his men properly to face west against the developing threat posed by Strahl.[37]

It was now up to Potts's three regiments to stop the Confederates. Will M. McLain of the 32nd Ohio recalled that enemy rifle fire "came in *perfect sheets*" from the south. His regiment was on the far right of Potts's line at the edge of a cornfield, occupying "a little crown or hillock" without shelter except the unevenness of the ground. A lot of recruits in his Company B became nervous and were "casting furtive glances to the rear," but the officers urged them all to hug the ground for protection, and everyone stayed in place. Potts's 1,000 troops opened fire, the line extending far enough to prevent Strahl from flanking it. The firing became intense.[38]

Chaplain Russell B. Bennett of the 32nd Ohio participated in the combat. He "carried a musket throughout the entire engagement, firing rapidly and cheering and encouraging the men by both voice and example," according to one report. When Bennett became tired, he asked Pvt. William B. Mitchell of Company B to reload for him, but Mitchell "was killed by his side." Pvt. Jimmie Peters of the same company replaced Mitchell and also was killed. Bennett was not deterred by these losses. He stood on a stump to get a better view of the opposing line, at one point yelling: "Boys, I saw their flag fall again. Give it to them as fast as you can load. We are bound to lick them."[39]

The chaplain also told McLain that he saw a Rebel field officer go down under the latter's fire. "I know that I did my best," McLain explained about his firing in a letter home.

> I drew a level bead on his belt, as he waved his sword and cheered his men forward, as ever I drew on a squirrel—and I know I can cut a pigeon's head off with the same gun, at the same distance he was; and I know, too, that when my smoke blew away, his saddle was empty! Sometimes I wonder if it is right for a man to single out his mark that way; but I couldn't help it. That colonel was doing more against us

than any man I could see, and I felt that it would help us the most to drop him.[40]

Sgt. Theodore F. Fisher, color bearer of the 32nd Ohio, "a model and deserving soldier" in Potts words, exposed himself to wave the flag at the height of the firefight. He "kept his colors steadily in advance of the regiment throughout the close and bloody contest and encouraging the men by voice and example." Both Chaplain Bennett and Sergeant Fisher were later recommended for the Seventeenth Corps Medal of Honor, which was awarded by Blair's headquarters.[41]

In the ranks of Strahl's Brigade, some parts of the line advanced well to confront the Federals, while others did not. Edwin Hansford Rennolds Sr., a member of the 5th Tennessee, moved forward until realizing that only about a dozen comrades were with him; the rest had hesitated and were several yards behind. He then fell back to seek shelter behind a stump, where more men gathered nearby. The stump was not big enough for all of them, and the return fire splattered not only the stump and the ground around but some of the sheltering Confederates too.[42]

John Henry Marsh, an artilleryman detailed to Strahl's staff, found the ordeal almost too much to bear. "We were subjected to the most terrific fire I have ever seen," he wrote to a friend. "I never prayed on the battle field before; But this time I prayed to the great God; to spare me. I had no Idea I could get out with life, and limb." When Col. John A. Wilson of the 24th Tennessee was shot, he implored Henry D. Hogan, "Henry, get me away from here I will be killed." The latter enlisted three men huddled behind the trees and took out a blanket he had stolen from the Federals when being exchanged at City Point, Virginia, after his capture at Stones River. The four men used the blanket as a stretcher and carried Wilson away. Maj. Henry Hampton, commander of the consolidated 4th and 5th Tennessee, was fortunate that only his clothing suffered in the hail of bullets. It was "pierced in several places during the fight." Added to the "previous wear and tear" on it, "I am in rather a sorry plight," he wrote three days later.[43]

As these personal examples indicate, the Federal "fire was too destructive." Half an hour after engaging Potts's line, Strahl ordered his brigade to fall back. Edwin Hansford Rennolds Sr. waited until a lull in the firing before leaving his stump. Ahead he saw Lt. J. R. Crosswell walking along a path through the woods. The officer was hit in the leg and fell, but he quickly arose and limped on. When Rennolds neared that spot, he stumbled on the stump of a bush and fell down just as a bullet hit the ground near his face and "filled my eyes and mouth with dirt." At or just before this time, Strahl was wounded in the foot.[44]

Strahl's Brigade offered the most serious threat to the Federals from Maney's command, and the Unionists averted disaster by repelling it. Magevney made an effort against them, but his attack was more easily rebuffed. He arrayed his regiments east of Flat Shoals Road, with Col. George W. Gordon's 11th Tennessee on the left, then Col. Horace Rice's 29th Tennessee, Col. William M. Watkins's consolidated 12th and 47th Tennessee, and Lt. Col. John M. Dawson's consolidated 13th and 154th Tennessee on the right.[45]

While there are no reports and few personal accounts documenting the brigade's attack, the Tennesseans had to advance through the clutter surrounding Govan's victory at the refused line and up along the main Union trench that faced west. They appear to have made little headway in this effort, even though there are reports of the men receiving heavy fire, undoubtedly from the 11th Iowa. Capt. Peter Marchant of the 47th Tennessee told his wife that his Company C drove some Federals out of a trench and then used it as shelter while exchanging fire with them for some time. In Company B, 12th Tennessee, Capt. Alfred Tyler Fielder was struck in the chest, but the ball was deflected away by a hymn book and a tin box. The round nevertheless bruised him "very badly." A second bullet slightly wounded Fielder on the left wrist while several more balls penetrated his clothing. A man in the 29th Tennessee later reported severe losses in his regiment, especially among officers, "in that fearful charge," but details of Magevney's advance are too sketchy to allow a clear picture. Gary Ecelbarger's assertion that Magevney forced the Federals to retreat to Bald Hill is not supported by the evidence. His brigade apparently advanced partway through the clutter at the refused line but was stopped by heavy Union fire.[46]

The battered Union line held, even though its refused part at the very end had been smashed by Govan's command. One brigade of Cleburne's Division and two brigades of Maney's command had done their worst but with limited effect. Govan needed much more time to reorganize after his assault; Strahl and Magevney could not immediately be counted on to continue their efforts. It was now up to Cleburne's other two brigades to weigh in.

James A. Smith's Brigade had started from Fayetteville Road about the same time as and to the right of Govan's Arkansans. Maj. William A. Taylor's consolidated 24th and 25th Texas Cavalry (dismounted) was on the far left, initially connecting with Govan's right. Capt. S. E. Rice's consolidated 6th Texas Infantry and 15th Texas Cavalry (dismounted) was next in line, followed by Capt. J. William Brown's 7th Texas Infantry and Col. Roger Q. Mills's 10th Texas Infantry. Capt. George D. Manion's consolidated 17th and 18th Texas Cavalry (dismounted) was next, and the far right was held

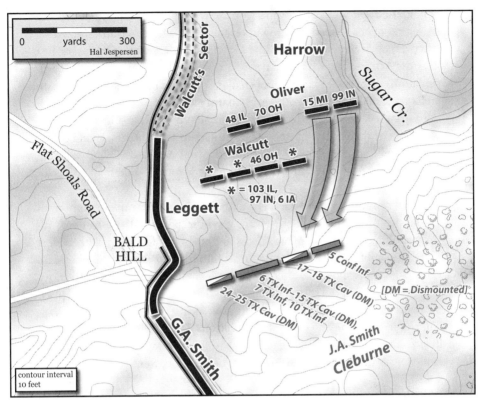

James A. Smith Attacks

by Maj. Richard Person's 5th Confederate Infantry. All of these units were small; Ecelbarger estimates the brigade had no more than 1,000 men in line. Capt. William M. Allison of the 18th Texas Cavalry commanded the brigade skirmish line, part of which encountered McPherson along the road linking Blair's and Dodge's positions.[47]

From the beginning, Smith's advance ran into difficulties. The terrain was cluttered with patches of woods and underbrush, and there were swampy marshes. All of this caused "considerable maneuvering to keep in line," starting a process of breaking up Smith's brigade formation. On the left, Taylor's 24th and 25th Texas Cavalry lost contact with Govan as the Arkansas brigade engaged Hall's Iowans. There were no Federals to Smith's front, and the Texans continued struggling forward for "several hundred yards," an effort that merely disarranged their line even more.[48]

Because the men struggled so much through the heavily cluttered landscape, their progress slowed, and the brigade line became increasingly extended. The left-most regiments began veering northwest and came in behind the right wing of Govan's Brigade without realizing it. Four of the six regiments happened to come upon the place where Govan's right wing had overrun Murray's Battery F, 2nd U.S. Artillery. They came to the site just after the Arkansas men had taken the battery and departed, giving rise to insinuations that the Texas regiments had participated in its capture. The 24th and 25th Texas Cavalry, the 6th Texas Infantry and 15th Texas Cavalry, the 7th Texas Infantry, and the 10th Texas Infantry all reported passing through the wreckage of the Federal battery. They picked up some prisoners and colors before their line pressed northward. The 17th and 18th Texas Cavalry and the 5th Confederate in the right wing of the brigade formation remained east of the captured battery.[49]

Smith would find the Federals waiting for him. From the beginning of the battle, Brig. Gen. William Harrow, whose Fourth Division, Fifteenth Corps connected with Leggett's division north of Bald Hill, had been alert to the possibility of a Confederate thrust into the rear areas of McPherson's army. Sensing trouble, he directed Brig. Gen. Charles C. Walcutt to move his Second Brigade out of the works, immediately next to Leggett, and place it perpendicular and to the rear of the line, facing south. Col. Reuben Williams's First Brigade and Col. John M. Oliver's Third Brigade extended their lines to the left in the west-facing works to fill in the space vacated by Walcutt. By the time the Second Brigade took position, Smith's men began to approach.[50]

Walcutt provided ample manpower to block the Rebels' progress. We have few details about the placement of his regiments other than that Capt. Joshua W. Heath's 46th Ohio occupied the left-center position of the four-regiment brigade line. The other units, Maj. Asias Willison's 103rd Illinois, Lt. Col. Aden G. Cavins's 97th Indiana, and Maj. Thomas J. Ennis's 6th Iowa, formed the remainder of that line. These four regiments blocked Smith's continued advance, resulting in a firefight that led to casualties. Heath was killed and replaced by Capt. Isaac N. Alexander in command of the 46th Ohio.[51]

Harrow provided help for Walcutt. He ordered Oliver to send his two reserve regiments to back up the Second Brigade line. Oliver began to shift them immediately after Walcutt began to move, sending them forward "with a cheer." He positioned Col. Alexander Fowler's 99th Indiana about 100 yards to the left rear of Walcutt's line, facing south, and Col. Lucien Greathouse's 48th Illinois about the same distance behind Walcutt's line, also facing south, but about 200 yards west of the 99th Indiana. Oliver left his other two regiments, Maj. William B. Brown's 70th Ohio and Lt. Col. Frederick S. Hutchinson's 15th Michigan, in the west-facing line of works for the time being.[52]

The Texans did not go away upon the arrival of the Union reinforcements but took cover in vegetation and behind unevenness in the ground to continue the static firefight. Smith's line had become almost unmanageable even before he encountered Walcutt, the terrain having fractured his brigade into clusters separated from and out of contact with each other. Smith sent a message to Cleburne asking for support and then pulled his men back "a short distance," as he put it, and awaited developments. Manion's 17th and 18th Texas Cavalry found itself separated from the rest of the brigade to the left by "a marshy ravine," and the only support apparent to the right was Person's small 5th Confederate. Smith later argued that all of his men were "much worn and exhausted" at this point, not only from their grueling experience on July 21 but also after struggling for two miles "through an almost impenetrable thicket of undergrowth."[53]

On the far left, Taylor reported that his 24th and 25th Texas Cavalry was so strung out as to "almost become a line of skirmishers" instead of a line of battle. But on the march north from the road where Battery F had met its fate, his men had stumbled across both the state and national flags of the 3rd Iowa. That regiment, belonging to Potts's brigade, had futilely attempted to stop Govan's right wing and had left behind both colors in its retreat.[54]

Soon after Smith began to establish his scattered brigade in this position, he was wounded and had to leave the field. Col. Roger Q. Mills of the 10th Texas took over the brigade but very quickly was wounded by a shell burst. As he left, Lt. Col. Robert B. Young of the same regiment assumed command of the brigade. Capt. John A. Formwalt then took charge of the 10th Texas.[55]

While this little drama was playing itself out, the Federals mounted a counterattack. Oliver pulled Hutchinson's 15th Michigan out of the west-facing line to add to the two regiments he already had in position behind Walcutt. The Michigan men moved on the double-quick "across the open field through the stragglers in fine order, forming on the right" of the 99th Indiana. Then Oliver pulled out the 70th Ohio to act as a reserve for his and Walcutt's brigades, leaving a gap in the west-facing works.[56]

When the 15th Michigan reached its assigned position, Hutchinson told his men to lie down and await an expected Confederate advance. When the Rebels did not move, he ordered his left four companies to advance because the nature of the ground on their front offered an opportunity to get close to the enemy without being exposed. They took Smith's men by surprise and secured a haul of prisoners and flags, which included seventeen officers and 165 men of the 17th and 18th Texas Cavalry and the 5th Confederate. All but two men of Company A, 18th Texas Cavalry were killed, wounded, or captured that day. Sgt. Maj. Andrew La Forge of the 15th Michigan captured the flag of the consolidated Texas cavalry regiment, and the flag of the 5th Confederate fell into Union hands as well. The former was given to Lt. Col. William T. Clark of McPherson's staff, whose widow returned it to Texas many years after the war, while the 5th Confederate colors resided in the State Archives of Michigan in Lansing.[57]

Among the prisoners scooped up by the 15th Michigan was Capt. Richard Beard of the 5th Confederate, a key player in the death of McPherson. He recalled seeing Andrew La Forge waving a pistol and crying out to the Rebels, "Boys, if you want to surrender now is your only chance." Beard reported that "a dozen guns were leveled on him, but the authority of cooler heads prevailed," and the men gave up. Beard offered his sword to Capt. Moses A. La Point of Company B, 15th Michigan and requested protection because just before Beard gave up, Sgt. William Nichols had pointed his musket at his head. "Yes, sir; you shall have it," said La Point. "We like to capture such men." Confederates in the 6th Texas and 10th Texas also fell into Union hands. The latter regiment reportedly lost nineteen men captured. Capt. Aaron Cox, who succeeded Person in command of what was left of the 5th Confederate, estimated the Federals suffered a "very light" loss of thirty to forty men in this countercharge.[58]

A note of controversy erupted over this splendid battlefield success. Members of the 99th Indiana not only claimed they participated in the counterattack but some of them also attempted to hog all the credit for its success. The regimental historian argued that 65 of the prisoners taken from the 17th and 18th Texas Cavalry were gathered in by the 99th Indiana while the captain of Company G claimed that only three companies captured a total of 173 Rebels. These men at best allowed the 15th Michigan only a marginal role in the operation and blamed the prominence given to that regiment on a feud existing between the Indiana officers and brigade leader Oliver. Because the Indianans had refused to sign a petition supporting Oliver's promotion to brigadier general, they asserted, he supposedly favored the 15th Michigan, his old regiment, in reports of the battle. But there is no reason to take this seriously. Sources emanating not only from the 15th Michigan but also from the Confederates confirm that this regiment rather than the 99th Indiana deserved the majority of credit for crumbling the Confederate position.[59]

Maj. Thomas Davies Maurice, artillery chief of the Fifteenth Corps, contributed to James A. Smith's repulse by assembling a number of guns to support Walcutt and Oliver. He shifted Capt. Josiah H. Burton's six Napoleons of Battery F, 1st Illinois Light Artillery, Harrow's division, along with Lt. William H. Gay's four 10-pounder Parrotts of the 1st Iowa Battery, to bear on the Texas brigade. Maurice also called on Capt. Louis Voelkner's Battery F,

2nd Missouri Light Artillery of Woods's division for two 12-pounder howitzers and attached them to Burton's battery. These twelve pieces offered needed fire support for the infantry.[60]

Soon after the conclusion of this counterattack, as the remnants of James A. Smith's Brigade fell back south, Hutchinson sent his prisoners to the rear and told his men to tear down a log house nearby. They used the timbers to construct a breastwork and settled in for the time being.[61]

All of Walcutt's and Oliver's men contributed to an important Union victory. While Walcutt mostly conducted the stop action to halt Smith's progress, Oliver's men alone executed the counterattack that drove his Texans away. If left unimpeded, Smith might have caused tremendous damage to the Army of the Tennessee despite the disjointed and uncoordinated nature of his advance. While the refused end of McPherson's line had been shattered by Govan, the rear areas of the army had been saved for the time being. Gary Ecelbarger estimates that James A. Smith's Brigade lost 250 men, about one-fourth of its strength, in this futile advance through the gap existing between Blair and Dodge.[62]

The last Confederate effort in this phase of the battle was pushed by Lowrey's Brigade, which started from Fayetteville Road 500 yards behind Smith's Brigade. Lowrey arranged his regiments with Col. John C. Wilkinson's 8th Mississippi on the far left, then Col. Harris D. Lampley's 45th Alabama, Lt. Col. J. D. Williams's 3rd Mississippi Battalion, Lt. Col. John B. Herring's 5th Mississippi, Lt. Col. Frederick A. Ashford's 16th Alabama, Col. W. H. H. Tison's 32nd Mississippi, and Lt. Col. R. F. Crittenden's 33rd Alabama on the far right.[63]

The approach to battle was difficult. Lowrey's men encountered the same terrain obstacles as all the rest of Cleburne's Division. "The whole country through which we passed was one vast densely-set thicket." The brigade had great difficulty following James A. Smith's command, to keep the 500-yard distance from it, and to maintain its own line. Most of the time Lowrey could not see more than 50 yards ahead, but he did notice that Smith moved around a great deal ahead of him. The Texas brigade seemed to shift by the right flank and then go forward, only to later move by the right flank again and then the left flank. "The difficulty of following their movements in such dense woods can scarcely be imagined," he admitted.[64]

Moreover, troops to the rear got in Lowrey's way. He understood that one of Maney's brigades, led by John C. Carter, was to advance 300 yards behind him, but due to the slow and uncertain pace of both Smith and his own command, Carter caught up with him. Part of Carter's command "passed through my line, creating great confusion, which required a considerable amount of time to repair." Meanwhile, Carter halted his brigade some distance in front of Lowrey's and waited. When Lowrey received orders from Cleburne to engage the Federals, he continued moving forward.[65]

Cleburne's order had been to "move up rapidly," but that was not possible. When Lowrey finally passed by Carter's right flank, part of the waiting brigade's line tagged along with his own. Lt. Col. Andrew D. Gwynne's 38th Tennessee accompanied him, probably thinking the advance was to be general and not realizing its parent brigade had not started. Soon after, Lowrey received an order directly from Hardee to assist Govan on the left and began to move by the left flank to comply. Soon after that, another order reached him from Cleburne "to move rapidly to the front and charge the works; that no time must be lost." Lowrey stopped his command, dressed the line, "and gave notice to each regiment what they were expected to do, and moved forward." He estimated that this took place about 500 yards from the Federal position.[66]

But that 500 yards offered continued difficulties to his movement. The right wing of the brigade crossed "a glade which was very miry." Then just after that, it came across what was left of James A. Smith's Brigade immediately after the Texans had been driven from their high tide by Oliver's two regiments. This slowed down the right wing even more. The twin obstacles of the miry glade and Smith's reorganizing troops separated Lowrey's right regiments from his left ones. By the time the brigadier realized this, in dense woods with visibility of no more than 100 yards, it was too late to do anything about it. Lowrey also reported that his troops had had little sleep for two days and nights, that the heat that afternoon was oppressive, and that many good men were "completely exhausted and could go no farther." He counted himself lucky to have any of them still in ranks, even though his fine brigade was in "great disorder" and was "scattered and thin."[67]

Despite all these varied problems, Lowrey's attack, which hit the Federals at about 4 P.M., was widely reported as being the most intense of the day thus far. He picked up not only the 38th Tennessee of Carter's command but also Lt. Thomas L. Flynt's 6th Texas Infantry and 15th Texas Cavalry. In retiring from James A. Smith's high tide, Flynt had become even more separated from the rest of his brigade. When Lowrey showed up, he attached what was left of his consolidated regiment to him. Ecelbarger's estimate that Lowrey attacked with 2,000 men is probably too high. Although Thomas J. Key had managed to get a section of Turner's Mississippi Battery in place, he was unable to use it to support Lowrey. The infantry actually "advanced between my guns and the enemy," masking his fire.[68]

Lowrey's attack was emblematic of Confederate efforts that day, disjointed, unsupported by artillery, but at times deadly in the intensity of the close-quarters infantry combat. Because of all the natural obstacles in the way and the breakdown in coordination among his brigades, Cleburne's Division struck the Federals in a piecemeal fashion that greatly aided the defenders' ability to deal with his fine command.

Lowrey approached the Union position from the southeast, heading toward the general area of Bald Hill. His left wing, by now consisting only of the 45th Alabama accompanied by the 38th Tennessee of Carter's command, would be opposed by the 11th Iowa, 13th Iowa, and 15th Iowa of Hall's brigade of Giles A. Smith's division. Lowrey's right wing, operating independently with help from the 6th Texas Infantry and 15th Texas Cavalry of James A. Smith's Brigade, by now consisted of the 16th Alabama, 32nd Mississippi, and 33rd Alabama. It approached Bald Hill directly. The rest of Lowrey's units (3rd Mississippi Battalion, 5th Mississippi, and 8th Mississippi) did not seem to participate in the attack. They probably became separated and isolated in the tangled, confusing terrain during the brigade's approach. Brig. Gen. Manning F. Force's brigade, consisting of the 20th, 30th, and 31st Illinois and the 12th and 16th Wisconsin, confronted Lowrey's right wing, supported to the rear by the 20th and 78th Ohio of Lt. Col. Greenberry F. Wiles's brigade. It is possible that the Federals could count on 3,000–4,000 men, as Ecelbarger estimates, to oppose this Confederate strike. They also had the help of at least eight supporting artillery pieces from Capt. Edgar H. Cooper's Battery D, 1st Illinois Light Artillery (four 24-pounder howitzers) and Capt. Marcus D. Elliott's Battery H, 1st Michigan Light Artillery (four 3-inch Rodman rifles).[69]

The Federals faced east when they noticed Lowrey's approach and prepared for action. The 15th Iowa, which had scarcely been engaged while fronting Govan's right wing and had been beaten by Strahl's flanking move, now had its opportunity to shine. William W. Belknap guided his men as they opened fire and stood firm to oppose Lowrey's left wing. He told the Iowans to hold their fire "until each had marked his man," then the regiment blazed away as the 45th Alabama and 38th Tennessee closed in. Many Confederates "were shot down fighting at the muzzles of our guns," Belknap reported. Some Iowans had collected abandoned rifles before the attack and used this stockpile to good effect. Poor shooters, or "timid ones," among the rank and file loaded these weapons and passed them to the good gun handlers, who now fired one round after another in quick succession. "When the Rebels came up," recalled Logan Crawford of Company H, "all we had to do was to shoot, then reach back and take another gun and shoot."[70]

The crisis of the battle seemed to be at hand, and it called out the best in many Iowans. Belknap recalled a man he had personally recruited in Keokuk, "a lazy looking" fellow who shirked duty. He had been accused of cowardice the day before, so on the morning of July 22, Belknap ordered

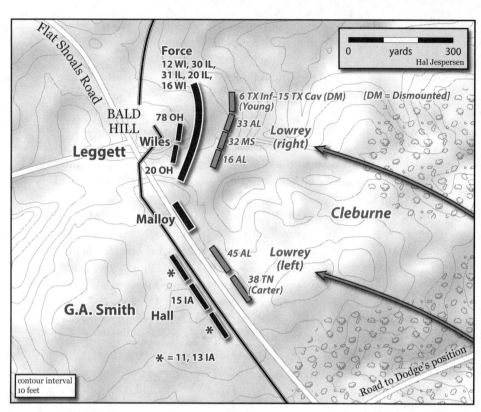

Flat Shoals Road

Force
12 WI, 30 IL,
31 IL, 20 IL,
16 WI

6 TX Inf–15 TX Cav (DM) [DM = Dismounted]
(Young)

BALD
HILL   78 OH

33 AL
Lowrey
Leggett   Wiles   32 MS   **(right)**
16 AL

20 OH

Malloy

45 AL   **Lowrey**
(left)
38 TN
(Carter)

Cleburne

G.A. Smith   15 IA
Hall

* = 11, 13 IA

Road to Dodge's position

0   yards   300
Hal Jespersen

contour interval
10 feet

Lowrey Attacks

him to wear part of a hardtack box with the word "Skulker" on it as he
marched back and forth. "He soon begged for mercy, and promised to stand
up to it in the next battle." Belknap relented when the man admitted that
"he was full of fear." An hour later, the terrible fighting of July 22 began,
and now that Lowrey's men were pressing the 15th Iowa in close combat,
the skulker rose to the occasion. "Shoot that man, John," Belknap shouted
when a tall Confederate tried to reload his gun very near him. He fired and
the Rebel fell. "Here was an illustration of what effort and discipline would
do in the face of danger, and with one who believed himself too weak to
face the fight," Belknap philosophized after the war.[71]

Belknap gained everlasting fame for a personal incident of his own in the
middle of this life-and-death struggle. "He was a man of commanding appearance, stoutly and compactly built," and "admirably proportioned," according to F. Y. Hedley, adjutant of the 32nd Illinois. Belknap also possessed
"indomitable resolution and great personal courage." All of those charac-
teristics gave him the advantage in a personal feat concerning Harris D.

Lampley, commander of the 45th Alabama. Lampley led his men forward until many of them lodged just east of the earthworks of the west-facing Seventeenth Corps line. As both sides continued the struggle so incredibly close together, Belknap was able to reach over and grab Lampley by the coat collar, pulling him bodily over the works. An unnamed corporal helped him do this.[72]

"I had the pleasure of personally hauling into our lines by his coat collar, Col. Lamply [sic] of the 45th Ala.," Belknap wrote to a friend a few days later. "A more perfect gentleman, but at the same time a more suprized [sic] individual I never saw." According to some accounts, however, Lampley spoke very ill of his men for not pushing over the Union earthworks, a comment that angered Belknap. "Look at your men!" he retorted. "They are all dead! What are you cursing them for!"[73]

There were mitigating circumstances attending this famous incident of the Battle of Atlanta. Importantly, Lampley had been shot in the right shoulder before Belknap hauled him over the earthworks and could have offered little if any resistance. It was a severe wound, and the Alabama officer was sent to the Seventeenth Corps hospital later that day and transferred to a general hospital at Marietta on August 4. Enlisting at age twenty-eight in March 1862, Lampley had risen from captain to colonel. He suffered a good deal from his wound and apparently experienced a change of heart about the cause in which he served. William Salter, a Christian Commission worker, talked with Lampley on August 1, 1864. He noted that the officer had been a merchant before the war and had done business in New York, thus he was not unaware of Northern feelings. Salter noted that Lampley "seemed dissatisfied with the Rebellion, but reticent—desirous of peace." The bullet had "entered the upper part of . . . his back, ranged down below the waist," according to the chaplain of the 12th Wisconsin, who was present when a Union surgeon probed for it. This terrible wound caused Lampley's death on August 24 in Marietta. Long before that date, on July 27, the quartermaster of the 45th Alabama arranged for Lampley's "negro boy" to take the colonel's baggage back to Huntsville.[74]

All these details of Lampley's wounding and death seem to have been hidden from most people involved in Lowrey's fight. The Confederates knew that he had died of his wounds in a Union hospital, but Irving A. Buck, one of Cleburne's staff officers, began the unfounded rumor that he was "too slightly wounded to have caused his death." Buck assumed "that depression from chagrin at his misfortune contributed largely to his sad end." This assertion led to permutations, as at least one Union veteran of the 15th Iowa proclaimed that Lampley survived his wound, was exchanged, and died "apparently of a broken heart" at home. Even some modern historians,

GEN. BELKNAP CAPTURING A REBEL COLONEL.

See page 158

Col. William W. Belknap, 15th Iowa, Captures Col. Harris D. Lampley, 45th Alabama. In this famous incident, Belknap personally captured Lampley, hauling him over the parapet by the coat collar. But Lampley had been seriously wounded in the shoulder and could have offered no resistance. The Alabama colonel died of that wound a month later, having expressed some misgivings about supporting the Confederate cause. From F. Y. Hedley, *Marching through Georgia* (Chicago: Donohue, Henneberry, 1890), 163.

including Albert Castel, have asserted that Lampley was not even wounded but died entirely of "chagrin."[75]

While one's attitude and emotion play important roles in recovery from any illness or injury, there can be no doubt that Lampley also was dangerously wounded. His emotional state was compounded by serious doubts concerning the Confederate cause, which was not unusual for one badly injured and captured in battle. The fate of so many of his men could have been on his mind, too, when he spoke so guardedly to Salter about the validity of Southern hopes for independence. As often is the case, the facts of Lampley's last few days are more important and interesting than the superficial and inaccurate stories that later circulated about him.

Lampley's capture was emblematic of an important point; the 45th Alabama was faring badly in its desperate struggle with the 15th Iowa. At about this time, Giles A. Smith rode up to Belknap's line accompanied by his assistant adjutant general, Capt. Cornelius Cadle Jr. Although assuming command of the division less than forty-eight hours before, Smith was a thoroughly experienced and capable officer who managed the reaction to Cleburne's attack well. Before Lowrey's advance, Andrew J. Alexander of

Blair's staff had visited Smith and found him "sitting in a negligent attitude on his horse." It was a studied effort to give confidence to the men. "We have had it pretty rough," Smith replied when Alexander asked him how things were going, "but I think we can hold them. I think we ought to be reinforced." Alexander assured him that was not possible, then duty called Smith away.[76]

When Smith and Cadle approached Belknap during the Iowa regiment's fierce struggle with the 45th Alabama, the colonel urged both officers to dismount as they offered too good a mark for Confederate shooters. Smith refused, and Cadle was compelled to follow his lead. It seemed important to expose themselves for the sake of inspiring the men, and maybe they were right. John S. Bosworth of Company K saw the pair sitting immobile on their horses and noticed their faces were "as white as the paper upon which this is written" when he recorded the incident after the war. Yet Bosworth could not help being impressed. "It was an exhibition of nerve and coolness that I have never seen equaled."[77]

After a few minutes of this bravado, Smith and Cadle rode away, but the division leader also had been impressed by what he saw.

> Regimental commanders, with their colors, and such men as would follow them, would not unfrequently occupy one side of the works and our men the other. The flags of two opposing regiments would meet on the opposite sides of the same works, and would be flaunted by their respective bearers in each other's faces. Men were bayoneted across the works, and officers with their swords fought hand-to-hand with men with bayonets.

Even in his long career in the Fifteenth Corps, Giles A. Smith never saw the kind of battle these Seventeenth Corps men were waging that hot afternoon east of Atlanta.[78]

While the 45th Alabama mainly confronted Belknap's regiment, the 38th Tennessee of Carter's command was also involved in the fight. It fronted part of the 15th Iowa and suffered as much as the Alabama regiment. Pvt. Lewis Crowder of Company C, 15th Iowa shot the Tennessee regiment's color bearer and secured his flag.[79]

Shane's 13th Iowa also contributed to the repulse of Lowrey's left wing. The regiment took position on the west side of the earthworks, facing the enemy with its rear rank, and delivered fire at the cheering and shouting Confederates. Its men also engaged in hand-to-hand combat when the enemy closed in on the east side of the works.[80]

Lt. John J. Safely of the 13th Iowa, who acted as provost marshal for Hall's brigade, reported that the Confederate formation "realed [*sic*] and Staggered" under his regiment's fire. He and his provost guards had been busy bringing up more ammunition for several units involved in the fight, but at one point Safely felt compelled to take direct action against the Rebels. He jumped across the works only to have a Confederate aim his musket directly at his heart. "'Don't you Shoot you Cuss,' yelled I 'or I will order twenty bullets through your Carcass [in] a moment.'" When the Rebel raised up a bit to get a better shot, the lieutenant "struck his gun to on[e] Side with one hand and grabbed him by the nape of the neck with the other, and whirled him about ten feet, head over heels, inside of our line." Safely went on to help other Federals capture Confederates in a similar manner, "though none of them offered to Shoot me."[81]

As Safely demonstrated, Belknap was not the only Federal who could capture the enemy by brute strength. Sgt. John A. Buck of Company K, 11th Iowa was credited with grabbing the major of the 45th Alabama in a similar manner. At the same time, Pvt. Edward Siberts of Company G, 11th Iowa secured the flag of the 45th Alabama and gave it to Safely to be credited to the regiment.[82]

Sgt. Maj. John G. Safely of the 11th Iowa, a cousin of Lt. John J. Safely of the 13th Iowa, also distinguished himself in the close fighting. He gathered a group of thirty to forty men and "made a dash over the works" to capture more than their number of Confederates. John G. Safely was seriously wounded in the shoulder, and his brother Louis was killed, "Shot through the neck, Arm, bowels and legs," according to John J. Safely.[83]

Union resistance to Lowrey's left wing won out in the end. After a fierce fight, the Confederates fell back. Three regiments of Hall's brigade, the 11th, 13th, and 15th Iowa, blunted the Rebel advance with devastating effectiveness, turning in the best performance of the day for those units.

Fighting a separate but related battle to the north, Lowrey's right wing also ran up against a stout Union roadblock. Those regiments aimed for the heart of the Union position, Bald Hill and Leggett's division, which had captured the site the day before. It was the opening round of battle for Leggett, whose men had thus far been within sight and sound of the fierce fighting but had not yet participated in the developing combat. Leggett, however, was keenly aware of the importance of the bare rise of ground his troops occupied. Logan had earlier sent a message: "'General, it is all-important you must hold the hill.'" According to one account, his reply was: "'Tell Logan when the hill is given up, there won't be enough left of my command to fight another battle.'"[84]

The Federals were ready when the Confederates surged from the southeast toward Bald Hill, emitting "demoniac yells," as Leggett put it. As happened with his left wing, Lowrey's right wing settled in close to the enemy as intense rifle fire, punctuated by artillery discharges from Bald Hill, erupted. Here Force's men provided the main resistance to Lowrey and began to suffer casualties. Force sent his assistant adjutant general, Capt. James Bryant Walker, to deliver an order. The son of Force's former law partner, Judge Timothy Walker, the captain walked no more than twenty yards into the open before a bullet crashed into his thigh just above the knee and shattered the bone.[85]

Force went out to tend to the captain, using a handkerchief to make a ligature in an effort to stop the bleeding. But just as he straightened up, a bullet plowed into his face, creating a serious and ugly wound. Members of Company A, 12th Wisconsin picked him up and carried him to safety as Force issued instructions for Col. George E. Bryant of the 12th Wisconsin to take over the brigade. The bullet had entered Force's left cheek and exited below the right cheek bone. The result was "very painful and aggravating" but not mortal, according to one of the general's aides. It did not affect his speech or eyesight. Still, many observers assumed the worst and thought he might die. Force, however, battled the injury with the same resolution he brought to bear when confronting the Confederates. Stopping the blood gushing from his nose and mouth, attendants transported the general to the nearest field hospital, then to Marietta, and from there on to Nashville and Louisville by July 30.[86]

Force's First Brigade stood defiantly. Color bearer Henry McDonald of Col. Warren Shedd's 30th Illinois was a big man, weighing more than 200 pounds according to his brother Granville, and parried every Confederate attempt to grab the flag. Holding the colors under his left arm, McDonald held a carbine he had acquired the day before in the fight against Confederate cavalry in his right arm and shot men at short distance. Lt. David W. Poak of Company A inspired his troops by "firing muskets rapidly at the enemy, and by his voice and gallant example," urging them to stand fast.[87]

The soldiers of Lt. Col. Robert N. Pearson's 31st Illinois initially were uncertain that the men approaching from the southeast were Confederates. Pearson's color bearer waved the Union flag, and the hail of gunfire that action brought left no doubt in anyone's mind. When the regiment adjusted its position, the Rebels yelled, "'Halt you d—d Yankee S— of a B—.'" The regiment did stop and began to deliver a raging fire at Lowrey's line. In places, the Illinoisans were crammed four to five men deep and thus could maximize the effect of their musketry. A Confederate flag fell to the ground little more than a rod in front of the regiment. Pvt. Thomas Yates of Company E protected the regimental colors, shooting a Confederate who touched the staff and knocking another one down with the butt of his musket. Pvt. George W. White of Company C was wounded in the head but refused to be taken to the rear. Shouting that "he would fight as long as he could pull a trigger," White remained with the regiment for the duration of the battle.[88]

This sort of stubbornness was the key to Union success. It was exhibited in Lt. Col. Daniel Bradley's 20th Illinois as well. The regiment's color bearer was shot, and his flag fell to the ground. Sgt. Samuel Denton of Company E rushed to save it and paid for the deed with a severe wound.[89]

In the ranks of Col. Cassius Fairchild's 16th Wisconsin, the men barely had time to get ready before Lowrey showed up. But they did not need Leggett's injunction to "hold this position at all hazards," according to a member of the regiment, for the men would have done so anyway. Fairchild told his troops to hold their fire until the Rebels were but five rods away, then "we let them have it right in the bread-baskets."[90]

The remnants of Col. Robert K. Scott's Second Brigade also participated in the fight. Scott, of course, was not present, having been captured by James A. Smith's Texans on the way back from taking his 68th Ohio to protect the Seventeenth Corps hospital. Lt. Col. Greenberry F. Wiles of the 78th Ohio had taken command of the brigade. Lt. Col. John C. Fry's 20th Ohio and the 78th Ohio, now led by Maj. John T. Rainey, were in line to support Force's brigade. Lt. Col. George E. Welles's 68th Ohio probably had managed to return to the Bald Hill area just before Lowrey appeared. The Seventeenth Corps men capitalized a good deal on the uniqueness of their fight that day, recalling with satisfaction their habit of fighting from one and then the other side of the fortified line. They called it "'Hardee's Tactics'" in a sardonic acknowledgment of the Confederate lieutenant general confronting them who had authored one of the primary tactical manuals used by Civil War soldiers.[91]

Col. Adam G. Malloy's Third Brigade consisted only of Lt. Col. Thomas McMahon's 17th Wisconsin and an improvised battalion commanded by Maj. Asa Worden. Malloy played a supporting role in the repulse of Lowrey's right wing. He found that the Confederate left flank was exposed to his command, allowing the Federals to fire obliquely into it. Malloy also called forward a section of Cooper's Battery D, 1st Illinois Light Artillery, which arrived from Bald Hill in time to add cannon fire to his musketry.[92]

Lowrey's right wing attracted the attention of many more Federal units on the battlefield. Walcutt noticed the Confederates as they surged toward Bald Hill and realized they were offering their right flank to his view. He obtained two 24-pounder howitzers, apparently from Cooper's Battery D, to pound Flynt's 6th Texas Infantry and 15th Texas Cavalry on the right end of Lowrey's line.[93]

By this time, Walcutt had two regiments available from other brigades in Harrow's division that he placed in reserve positions. The 70th Ohio had earlier been sent from Oliver's Third Brigade, and Walcutt had placed it in reserve. Soon after the repulse of James A. Smith's Brigade, Logan told Col. Reuben Williams to send a regiment of his First Brigade to Walcutt. Williams ordered his only reserve unit, Capt. Ira J. Bloomfield's 26th Illinois, to move out, leaving but two regiments to hold his brigade sector of the west-facing line. The jumbled way the Federals had dealt with Smith's advance, and the after effects of Lowrey's attack, led them to assemble more units to the rear of their line than was necessary. As a result, Harrow's sector of the west-facing line was thinly manned.[94]

Lowrey's right wing also drew the attention of Wangelin's brigade. Surgeon A. W. Reese took a break from attending wounded to look at the fight, the sound of which rose into a "tremendous and appalling roar of *musketry*" easily heard by the men in line. Reese saw the flags of Lowrey's units surge forward and then stop as the attack settled into a static firefight at close quarters. He was delighted to see that the banners did not go over the Union line.[95]

By the last half of the afternoon, Lowrey's attack had ended in failure as both wings retired from their high tide. The brigade was "cut to pieces, having lost half its number," as its commander put it, meaning losses of about 500 men. "The 45th Ala Regt wrapped itself in glory & lay down & died," Quartermaster Edward Norphlet Brown wrote to his wife. In addition, the 32nd Mississippi lost one-third of its men in the first Union volley, and two color bearers were killed "in quick succession." Belknap, who recognized that the 45th Alabama had "suffered fearfully" and had been "severely punished," proudly reported his men captured the two field officers lost by that regiment plus a captain as well as the lieutenant colonel of the 38th Tennessee. "The commanding officer of this regiment had the satisfaction of personally capturing" Lampley as well, Belknap included in his report.[96]

Lowrey tried to explain why his brigade could do nothing more than shooting down a number of opposing soldiers in a futile attempt to crack open the Union position. His attack failed "because the thing attempted was impossible for a thin line of exhausted men to accomplish." He claimed the Federals were double his number (which was an exaggeration) and the Unionists had the advantage of "strong breast-works" (also an exaggeration). "The history of this war can show no instance of success under such circumstances."[97]

By the time Lowrey's men admitted failure, the fighting on McPherson's left had lasted at least three hours. In that time, Govan's troops had captured 200–300 yards of the Union line (the refused southern end and a bit of the west-facing line). But Hardee's Corps had failed to crack the rest of the position despite Maney's and Lowrey's attempts to do so. James A. Smith's Brigade had signally failed in its attempt to range along the rear of that line as well. So far, all of the fighting had taken place in the area south of Bald Hill, with only one attack (Lowrey's right wing) aimed at the hill itself. Casualties were comparatively heavy, with 3,000 Confederates and over 2,000 Federals down so far, according to Gary Ecelbarger's estimate.[98]

Besides the fierce nature of the fighting, the other unusual feature of combat thus far was the willingness of Union regiments and brigades to shift their position as needed to meet emerging threats from any direction. Green troops usually dissolved into panic when the enemy appeared on their flanks or in their rear. But McPherson's men, hardened by years of campaigning and fighting, handled these threats with aplomb.[99]

The other key to Union success south of Bald Hill was a significant lack of command and control on the part of the Confederates, although it was not nearly as serious as that which had afflicted Bate's and Walker's Divisions at Sugar Creek. Hardee intervened at least once, to move Maney's command west to launch an attack, but seems not to have done anything more. Cleburne tried to coordinate the action of his three brigades but failed to accomplish much, which was rather unusual for one of the best division leaders in the Army of Tennessee. The terrain and its numerous obstacles to large troop movement remained the primary cause for the lack of unity in Cleburne's Division that afternoon, but that factor cannot solely explain Maney's relative lack of action. After his initial attack, in which only one brigade pressed home a vigorous advance, his division seems to have done nothing until late in the afternoon, while Cleburne's men battled fiercely. Even on the brigade level, Confederate commanders delivered a mixed record of command and control, with all three of Cleburne's brigades breaking into wings or even smaller parts while advancing and fighting. Only Govan overcame this pernicious problem to deliver a whopping tactical success, but then his command had to recover for several hours before it could resume operations.

Federal officers performed better than their Confederate counterparts in the fighting south of Bald Hill. Most of the brigade commanders maintained control of their units, although Hall's faulty placement of his Iowa regiments contributed to Govan's tactical success. Division leaders such as Giles A. Smith and William Harrow played decisive roles in moving and positioning their units to block Confederate drives. But on the corps level, Blair seems oddly out of the picture. Army-level commanders were completely disengaged in the fighting south of Bald Hill, but that is not surprising. Hood was not in a position to influence the flow of events, and Sherman could easily afford to rely on his division and brigade leaders to handle a situation they could more readily see and hear than he was able to do from Copenhill.

By about 4 or 5 P.M., a short lull developed in the battle south of Bald Hill following the repulse of Lowrey's attack. The second phase of the Battle of Atlanta had ended just as the third phase, a major Confederate attack against the front of the Fifteenth Corps line along the Georgia Railroad, was reaching a climax.

8

Breaking the Fifteenth Corps Line

Hood had a potentially powerful weapon in his old corps, led for the time by Maj. Gen. Benjamin F. Cheatham. It held the east side of the Atlanta City Line, fronting the Union Army of the Tennessee. If it attacked at the right time and with coordination between its three divisions (and between the brigades within each division), the corps could have dealt a devastating blow to McPherson's army as it was desperately trying to contend with Hardee's flank attacks.

But this corps was not a finely tuned weapon like Hardee's command. Created for Hood in March 1864, the new leader had misgivings about its quality. "My Corps is composed of all the untried troops of this army," Hood told an acquaintance. "So if I don't do as well as may be expected, I wish my friends to know, what troops I command." Hood failed to shape the corps into an effective unit. It remained a collection of individual brigades loosely commanded by a man who had risen above his level of ability. Hood's inveterate carping behind the scenes had helped undermine Johnston's stock with the authorities at Richmond, and that catapulted him into Johnston's place on July 18. Cheatham, a good division leader suddenly thrust into a much more complicated command level, had so far not proven that he was up to its demands. Moreover, many replacements had occurred within the corps since the start of the campaign, not just at the top. Of the three divisions, two now were led by new men;

of the dozen brigades, six also had new commanders. Many of these men, like Cheatham, were only recently elevated to levels of responsibility that they had scant experience to fill.[1]

Hood had to decide when and how to use this uncertain weapon in furtherance of his tactical plan. He left his headquarters at the Leyden House on Peach Tree Street at about 2 P.M. and established a command post on a rise of ground east of the city near Oakland Cemetery, just behind Cheatham's line. After sending a staff officer to check on Hardee's progress, Hood deemed the time appropriate and at 3:15 P.M. ordered Cheatham forward. He also ordered the artillery to open fire and continue until the infantry had moved forward. At about 4 P.M., Hood retired to the railroad depot in the center of town and awaited the results.[2]

As often happened with Hood, he gave mixed signals about what he wanted his men to do. In his report of the battle, written seven months later, the general asserted that he meant for Cheatham's move to be a diversion.[3] That made no sense within his original plan or in relation to what was actually happening on the ground with Hardee. At this crisis point, the only thing that did make sense was for Cheatham to conduct a heavy and determined assault from the west as Hardee was struggling with the Federals from the south, and that is most likely what Hood actually wanted on July 22. The assertion in his report probably was an effort to mitigate the impact of the army's overall failure in the battle, minimizing the intent and therefore maximizing the temporary success that Cheatham's men achieved.

The corps covered almost the entire front of McPherson's position. Stevenson's Division was on the right, fronting the Seventeenth Corps, while Hindman's Division, now led by Brig. Gen. John C. Brown, held the center, straddling the Georgia Railroad, and Clayton's Division occupied the left.[4]

Maj. Gen. Carter L. Stevenson's role in this advance is shrouded by the complete absence of official reports from his division. But circumstantial evidence indicates that his command moved part way toward the Union line and then failed to press home anything that could be considered a real attack. Historian Albert Castel concludes that the division did not even push the Union skirmishers back to their main line. Gary Ecelbarger goes further and asserts that a real attack took place, but he bases this only on the fact that troop strength in the division declined by thirty-six men between July 20 and July 31. Even if all those men were taken out of the ranks by combat, that would indicate a skirmish rather than a real battle. There is only one personal account by a member of Stevenson's Division that comments on the events of July 22. Robert M. Magill of the 39th Georgia in Brig. Gen. Alfred Cumming's brigade flatly stated that he saw no action that day. The best conclusion is that Stevenson made a show of advancing but failed to follow through. There is no clear and reliable documentation from the Federal side that he made any impression on the Union position.[5]

From the very beginning, then, one-third of Cheatham's strength was neutralized by timid divisional leadership, but the same was not true of Brown's command in the center. A former brigade leader in Stevenson's Division, Brown took over Hindman's Division sometime between June 30 and July 10 after Maj. Gen. Thomas C. Hindman was relieved due to illness—at least that was the official reason. In reality, Hindman had not been a success as a division leader, and many of his subordinates were dissatisfied with him. Brown proved only marginally better in the role, but he could rely on good brigade commanders. His division now occupied the center of Cheatham's line and aimed at one of the weakest parts of the Union position.[6]

When the troops left the Atlanta City Line and formed east of the works, Brown placed the brigade of Brig. Gen. Arthur M. Manigault on the left of his first line, with its right flank resting at the Georgia Railroad. Deas's Brigade, now led by Col. John G. Coltart, took post to the right of Manigault's Brigade and south of the track. Brown's second line consisted of Tucker's Brigade, now commanded by Col. Jacob Sharp, behind Manigault, and Walthall's Brigade, now led by Col. Samuel Benton, behind Coltart. Manigault remembered Brown's instructions for the advance, which were "to move on until we found the enemy, and then to attack and drive him out of his works, which we were to hold until further orders."[7]

The Federals opposite Brown's advancing troops were alert to trouble but ill prepared to fend off a vigorous assault..The sound of musketry from the start of Hardee's attack on McPherson's left produced "huge volumes of powder-smoke" rising above the treetops to the south. "We are going to have a fight here," said Brig. Gen. Morgan L. Smith, commander of the Second Division, Fifteenth Corps, which was positioned astride the Georgia Railroad. "They are raising the devil on our left, and we'll catch it here soon!" When word of McPherson's death arrived, Logan took command of the Army of the Tennessee and Morgan L. Smith took charge of the Fifteenth Corps. That elevated Brig. Gen. Joseph A. J. Lightburn from the brigade level to command of the Second Division.[8]

Not long after this shift of responsibilities, Lt. Samuel Edge, a Union signal officer perched 100 feet above the ground in a tall pine tree near the railroad, watched Brown's men assembling east of the Atlanta City Line. When informed of this development, Morgan L. Smith replied, "I am ready for them."[9]

The Federals were not as ready for battle as Smith pretended. The course of Hardee's attack thus far had weakened the Fifteenth Corps line. At about 2 P.M., after the start of Hardee's assault but well before the onset of Cheatham's, Smith received Logan's order to send help to Dodge. In response, he told Col. James S. Martin to dispatch the reserve regiments of his First Brigade, Second Division, namely Capt. John S. Windsor's 116th Illinois, Lt. Col. Frank S. Curtiss's 127th Illinois, and Lt. Col. Delos Van Deusen's 6th Missouri. Martin's only units remaining in the line of entrenchments were Capt. Francis H. Shaw's 55th Illinois and Lt. Col. Samuel R. Mott's 57th Ohio; Maj. William M. Mabry's 111th Illinois was stationed in front of the earthworks as a support to the brigade picket line. Martin, who had taken command of the First Brigade only the day before, personally took the three reinforcing regiments to Dodge's sector. That left Mott in charge of the thin brigade line, which extended south from the track of the Georgia Railroad, opposite the right wing of Brown's division and facing two Confederate brigades.[10]

Lightburn's Second Brigade, of which Col. Wells S. Jones barely took command before Brown's advance, held the line north of the railroad. Four companies of Lt. Col. John Wallace's 47th Ohio held the left near the track as Lt. Col. Robert Williams Jr. placed his 54th Ohio to Wallace's right. Maj. Charles Hipp's 37th Ohio then extended the line to the right, followed by Col. Theodore Jones's 30th Ohio. Capt. Francis De Gress's Battery H, 1st Illinois Light Artillery was posted to the right of Jones's command with, for the time, no infantry support to its right. Two other regiments completed the roster of the brigade. Wells S. Jones's own 53rd Ohio, now led by Lt. Col. Robert A. Fulton, was on the skirmish line but would return to the main line when the Confederates attacked and take place to the right of De Gress's battery. The last regiment in the brigade, Capt. George H. Scott's 83rd Indiana, was not available, having been sent off to guard hospitals and supply trains to the rear.[11]

Wells S. Jones's line was firm but threatened by an oversight on its left flank. The Georgia Railroad ran through a cut where it intersected the Fifteenth Corps line, and the Federals had neglected to properly secure it. The cut was from five to eighteen feet deep at various points, with the Decatur Road running twenty yards north of the track. Nothing had been done to blockade either the cut or the road. But two Napoleons of Lt. Samuel S. Smyth's Battery A, 1st Illinois Light Artillery were placed between the track and the Decatur Road, supported by Company K, 47th Ohio. Another section of Napoleons took position north of the Decatur Road, with three companies of the 47th in support to its right. The last section of Smyth's battery was on the skirmish line of Jones's brigade.[12]

Another landmark on the division line was the two-story George M. Troup Hurt House, located on the small ripple of ground through which the railroad cut. Built of brick 150 yards north of the track and facing south, it had been started at least by the summer of 1862 but was yet unfinished when the Battle of Atlanta engulfed the area. Hurt was the older brother of Augustus Hurt, whose house on Copenhill Sherman used as his headquarters. George was then serving somewhere in the Confederate army, according to local reports, and his family probably resided in Columbus, Georgia, leaving the house unoccupied.[13]

Another prominent structure lay in the area fronting the Union position. Located about 150 yards southwest of the Troup Hurt House, and closer to the railroad, it was known as the Widow Pope House to some but also as the White House because of its color. A two-story wooden-frame building, the house also had "a columned veranda with an upper porch-level enclosed by a railing," according to historian Wilbur G. Kurtz.[14]

But Troup Hurt's brick house remained the most prominent building in the area. Located fifteen feet behind the line of earthworks held by the 37th Ohio, Morgan L. Smith had used it as his headquarters before taking over Fifteenth Corps. John H. Puck of the 37th Ohio overheard a conversation between Smith and Charles Hipp while the former still controlled the division. Hipp suggested burning down both the Troup Hurt House and the White House and barricading the railroad cut. Smith refused, citing the need to use the buildings as hospitals and considering it a waste of effort to barricade the cut. Although Smith did not mention it, he probably knew that signal officers had established a station on the Troup Hurt House to observe Confederate movements. Moreover, at that time he might have believed the rumors that Hood was evacuating Atlanta that morning.[15]

The most famous artillery unit to take part in the battle was De Gress's Battery H, 1st Illinois Light Artillery, armed with four 20-pounder Parrott rifles, which took position at the extreme right of Lightburn's division line. De Gress occupied a slight rise of ground, the best spot for his guns in the area, but Wells S. Jones's brigade did not at the time have enough units to provide infantry support to his right. A gap of 800 yards separated the battery from the left flank of Woods's division on the southern slope of Copenhill. For most of that space, all that existed were the earthworks of the Confederate Outer Line, still facing east, without any Union troops in them. In fact, for at least 300 yards of that distance, there were no earthworks at all across a deep swale in the landscape. This unfortified section consisted of low and swampy ground; no one thought it was necessary to cover that space nor the rest of the undefended gap even with skirmishers. Only after the start of the Confederate attack did some infantry support appear to the right of De Gress's battery in the form of the 53rd Ohio, but that still left most of the land toward Copenhill unoccupied.[16]

Morgan L. Smith's division, now led by Lightburn, was not in the best shape to defend the center of the Fifteenth Corps position when Manigault's Brigade approached. The Rebel troops were well in hand and led by one of the better commanders in the Army of Tennessee. Col. James F. Pressley's 10th South Carolina held the right, just north of the Georgia Railroad, with Maj. James L. White's 19th South Carolina on its left, then Col. Julius C. B. Mitchell's 34th Alabama, and Col. Newton N. Davis's 24th Alabama on the left. Lt. Col. William L. Butler's 28th Alabama was on picket duty and did not participate in the attack.[17]

Manigault's command traversed a mixed landscape during its advance. For the most part, the space was "comparatively open; so that we could move along without difficulty," as the brigadier recalled. The undulations in the ground temporarily shielded the men from Union artillery fire, but that protection ended quickly as the line continued to advance. Passing through a belt of woods also concealed the brigade for a time. On the right, Manigault remembered, Pressley's 10th South Carolina passed across open fields skirting the railroad all along the way, while White's 19th South Carolina near the center encountered "rough ground, hills, narrow swamps, and thick forest." Manigault had to move across nearly 1,400 yards of Georgia countryside as the weather by midafternoon became "excessively warm," according to James A. Hall of the 24th Alabama. "I thought I would faint from heat & fatigue."[18]

Long before completing that approach, the Confederates encountered the Union skirmish line, located 500 yards from their starting point near the Outer Line "and in plain view of Atlanta," according to Wells S. Jones. He commanded the skirmishers for all of Lightburn's division, north and south of the Georgia Railroad, comprising the 53rd Ohio and six companies of the 47th Ohio on the skirmish line and the 111th Illinois plus one section of Battery A, 1st Illinois Light Artillery to support them. Lightburn instructed Jones to either fall back as soon as he saw the enemy approach or hold until forced back as he saw fit. Jones decided to stay and fight as long as possible.[19]

The Federals caught glimpses of Manigault's approach from quite a distance. "Look yonder; they are coming for us!" shouted a man in the 111th Illinois. "It looked like the whole rebel army was coming at once," remembered Alex Ralston of the same regiment. Maj. Thomas T. Taylor of the 47th Ohio, who was with the six companies on the skirmish line, was impressed. "What a grand sight, I was almost entranced by it. How well they moved, how perfectly and how grandly did the first line advance with the beautiful 'battle flags' waving in the breeze."[20]

The Union skirmishers could not hope to hold out long against an entire brigade. "On came the rebels with their well-known yell," reported Robert A. Fulton of the 53rd Ohio. As soon as the Confederates closed, the Federals fired one volley before falling back to the skirmish reserve. Here they held out for a while longer until Manigault's line began to flank them. Wells S. Jones shouted an order to retire to the main line, and the two guns escaped. The 111th Illinois, however, broke up in the withdrawal, giving the impression to some that the men lost their nerve and left the 53rd Ohio to fend for itself. The Ohioans retired with more order, rallied near the White House, then entered the main Union position and soon took post on the right of Jones's brigade line, supporting the right of De Gress's battery. Excited skirmishers yelled warnings to their comrades as they jumped the parapet. "Here they come, boys, four and five lines deep! They are right on us."[21]

No one expected the skirmish line and its supports to hold back Manigault's Brigade, but would the main Federal line be able to maintain its position? Forewarned and ready, the answer apparently was in the affirmative. They were aided by some degree of choppiness in the Confederate advance. Manigault recalled that he "had several times to check the movement of the line, as it got in advance somewhat of the brigade on our right." On reaching a hollow that ran nearly parallel to and 250 yards from the main Union line, he halted his command to dress the ranks. When he was about to resume the advance, a message arrived from division leader Brown to wait so that Coltart's regiments, to the right, could come even with him. This compelled Manigault to wait another five minutes, with Union artillery fire "annoying us much." When it seemed that Coltart had come up, he pushed his men forward once more.[22]

Manigault never forgot the sight that greeted him as the Rebel line emerged from the hollow. "There stood the enemy in their breastworks," their flags were "fluttering lazily in the breeze. I saw and noticed all this only for a moment, and thought it looked very pretty, but in the next instant the whole scene was shut out, everything enveloped in smoke." The Rebel line "staggered and reeled for a moment" with the impact of the first volley, but then it continued forward. The ground was largely open, and the intensity of fire from the Union line increased as the Confederates closed in. They soon slowed their pace, and "large gaps were visible here and there. The line had lost its regularity, warbling like the movements of a serpent, and things looked ugly." Jacob H. Sharp's brigade managed to keep pace about 100 yards to the rear of Manigault's halting line, and that tended to encourage the men. Only "small portions of two regiments" failed to press on despite the urgings of their officers, although Manigault did not identify the hesitant pair of units.[23]

But this first Rebel strike at the main Union line failed. Some Confederates managed to get close to the works, others stalled 50 yards away, and still others halted their progress much farther back. Numerous Federal reports confirm that Manigault's Brigade was stopped after about thirty minutes of heavy firing. Manigault retired a bit and stabilized his brigade line so that it ran just west of the White House. The situation settled into a stalemate, with both sides continuing to fire heavily at each other. Fifteen men of the 37th Ohio had earlier knocked loopholes through the west wall of the brick Troup Hurt House and now sniped at the stationary line of Rebels about 150 yards away.[24]

The right wing of Brown's command, advancing south of the railroad, fared little better. Coltart veered his brigade south during the course of the advance, "owing to buildings, impassable fences, and slight curves" in the railroad. The left most regiment, Col. George D. Johnston's 25th Alabama, started the advance with its left flank only twenty paces south of the track, but that small gap widened to 150 yards by the time the brigade reached the reserve post of the Union skirmish line. At this point, Coltart captured the position, but Johnston's left wing suffered a great deal because of the gap—Union fire enfiladed the regimental line in addition to the frontal fire received from the picket reserve. After absorbing prisoners, Coltart's command continued advancing to a point 400 yards short of the main Union line and then halted.[25]

At this point, Brown decided to fill the widening gap between his left wing north of the railroad and his right wing south of it by moving his reserve unit, Samuel Benton's brigade, into the space. Lt. Col. William C. Clifton's 39th Alabama of Coltart's command had been detached and placed on the left end of Benton's line from the start of the advance. Moving only 100 yards behind Coltart, Benton now moved forward while keeping his left flank snug against the railroad. The right wing of his brigade moved through the ranks of Coltart's brigade as Benton's men became the first Confederate line south of the track.[26]

Benton pushed his men forward into the teeth of increasingly heavy fire. His brigade consisted of five Mississippi regiments but was understrength. Col. Robert P. McKelvaine commanded the consolidated 24th and 27th Mississippi, but his unit was detached from the brigade and served on the skirmish line all day. That left only Col. William F. Brantly's consolidated 29th and 30th Mississippi and Capt. T. S. Hubbard's 34th Mississippi available to Benton. These two units, along with the 39th Alabama, confronted the 55th Illinois and 57th Ohio, the remaining two regiments of Martin's brigade south of the railroad temporarily under Samuel R. Mott. Those two Union regiments delivered enough firepower to stop the Confederates when they were about 40 yards from the works. Benton's men fell to the ground for protection. After ten minutes, he ordered them to retire, and they fell back 400 yards from their high tide. At some point in this action, Benton was wounded when a shell fragment slammed into his chest and a ball plunged into his foot, leading to amputation of the limb. Brantley now took command of the brigade. Benton died of his injuries six days later at a hospital in Griffin, Georgia.[27]

Just to the south, Coltart advanced his brigade immediately after Benton's repulse. It confronted the two regiments of Reuben Williams's Union brigade remaining in line, Lt. Col. James Goodnow's 12th Indiana on the right and Lt. Col. Owen Stuart's 90th Illinois on the left. Williams had earlier sent Lt. Col. Albert Heath's 100th Indiana to duty in Marietta and, at the start of the battle, had shifted Capt. Ira J. Bloomfield's 26th Illinois south in the line to help Walcutt. The Indianans opened "a terrible fire" when Coltart's men were but "a short distance" from the Union works and stopped the Confederates. A static firefight erupted and lasted for the next forty-five minutes, after which Coltart retired into some woods 200 yards from the Union line. As the firing died down, it seemed as if the fight had ended.[28]

Because Coltart outnumbered Williams, the right end of his line overlapped the Union left. That had allowed about a hundred Confederates to get into an empty section of earthworks, but fortunately for the Federals, "they didn't seem to know what to do," as Williams put it. After Coltart's repulse, Williams led two companies of the 90th Illinois to the occupied spot and called on the Rebels to give up, which they did without any trouble. During the fighting, Williams had roamed along his line and noticed an unusual incident. Several Alabama Unionists had joined the 12th Indiana the winter before when the regiment stayed at Scottsboro, and Williams had allowed one of them to bring a slave servant with him. During the repulse of Coltart, the servant handed his master cartridges so the man could fire faster.[29]

After the repulse of Brown's men both north and south of the railroad, the fight settled into a stalemate with the Confederates lodged a few hundred yards in front of the Union earthworks. Despite its weak lines, the Federal position held firm. North of the tracks, some Confederates sought a way to use the White House to their advantage. The 10th South Carolina's left flank and the 19th South Carolina's right flank met there, and the building seemed ready for use as a sharpshooter's post. Col. James F. Pressley and Lt. Col. C. Irvine Walker of the 10th South Carolina stood at the foot of the staircase leading to the front door, Walker pointed out that the upper porch would offer a good view of the Union line. They investigated and then ordered a group of sharpshooters to occupy the porch and harass the Federals. Pressley asked James L. White to send some of his 19th South Carolina men to assist in the action. "They shot right down into the enemy's

Soldiers of the 19th S.C. firing from
the upper porch of the white house
during the Battle of Atlanta —
July 22d, 1864

Confederates Firing from White House. This two-story wooden-frame build-
ing, also known as the Widow Pope House, had a porch on the second level and
was located 150 yards southwest of the George M. Troup Hurt House and the
Union line. After its initial repulse, Manigault's Brigade rallied in line with the
White House, and members of the 19th South Carolina entered it and climbed
up to the porch to shoot at the Federals to the east. Artist-historian Wilbur G.
Kurtz painted this image. From Wilbur G. Kurtz, "The Broken Line and the
DeGress Battery," *Atlanta Constitution*, February 8, 1931.

lines," Walker remembered. Other Confederates occupied the interior of
the house and fired through the windows.[30]

This sharpshooting had an unintended effect. Federal artillerists, especially those manning the two sections of Battery A, 1st Illinois Light Artillery at and near the railroad cut, now targeted the house. The rapid firing
of these four Napoleons produced a good deal of powder smoke that soon
blanketed the area around the cut, and the Confederates eventually took
advantage of that cover. Meanwhile, Brown had two artillery units, Capt.
James P. Douglas's Texas Battery and Capt. Staunton H. Dent's Alabama
Battery, placed in the woods 400 yards from the Union line. But Douglas and
Dent do not seem to have made an impression on the Federals with their
fire.[31]

Three of Brown's brigades had tried and failed; it was now up to the
fourth, Sharp's Mississippians, to make an effort to crack the Union line.

Sharp had kept about 200 yards behind Manigault in Brown's advance, marching "through the woods & over the hills," as Jesse L. Henderson of the 41st Mississippi put it. Soon after Manigault fell back from his high tide, Sharp's troops caught up with the stalled brigade and moved through its ranks. Now they were Brown's front line. Sharp pushed his men forward until they caught sight of the Federals, "raised a yell and charged them."[32]

Sharp succeeded only because some of his men discovered the Achilles heel of the Union position—the improperly defended railroad cut. Not only was it unblocked and too lightly manned but also the approach to it now was shrouded with smoke. This allowed a large group of Mississippians to move through the cut only a few feet from Union artillerists and supporting infantry and crack open the Fifteenth Corps line. Wells S. Jones thought this pivotal event took place no more than forty minutes after the start of the fight and at a time when the Federals assumed they had already won by repulsing the initial assaults on both sides of the track. Sharp's line also approached the front of Jones's brigade so that, as Capt. Henry S. Schmidt of the 37th Ohio put it, "in less than a minuet the Rebs were thick."[33]

Soon, the Union line began to unravel. First to fall were the two sections of Battery A, 1st Illinois Light Artillery at the railroad cut and the Decatur Road. Supporting infantrymen from the 47th Ohio who stayed and fought were killed, wounded, or captured, while those who fled early enough saved themselves. The Confederates captured the four Napoleons, and the battery also lost thirty-two men killed, wounded, and captured along with fifty-five horses. Battery commander Samuel S. Smyth was captured but survived the war, but Lt. Theodore W. Raub was mortally wounded.[34]

C. Irvine Walker, lieutenant colonel of the 19th South Carolina, insisted that his men were the ones who overran the position of Battery A. He failed to mention Sharp's command, although his men would have had to move through its ranks if they played the leading role in capturing the position. Walker only admitted that some other regiments of Manigault's Brigade helped his South Carolinians secure the prize. We are hampered in straightening out this contention by a shortage of accounts rising from Sharp's command. There are no reports, only one diary, and two collections of letters for the entire brigade relating to this battle. This shortage severely mutes our understanding of its role at this point in the engagement. The most fair conclusion is that Manigault advanced right behind Sharp and helped the Mississippians collapse the Union line north of the railroad.[35]

The 47th Ohio was the first of Wells S. Jones's regiments to suffer from the breakthrough. Everyone was surprised to see crowds of Confederates emerge from the pall of smoke around the railroad cut and begin to move into the rear areas. The Federals held their line as long as possible as a "fierce

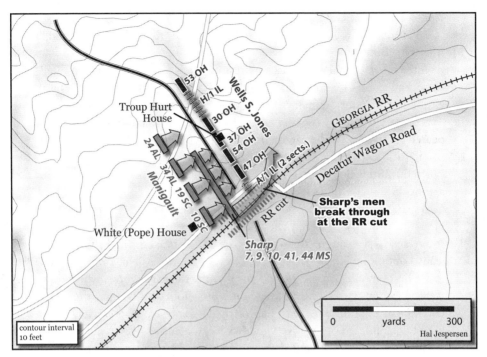

Manigault and Sharp Attack

struggle and hand-to-hand conflict" took place around the colors. Over-whelmed, the 47th fell back, losing its commander John Wallace, who was captured while "bravely laboring to form a new line." Retiring to the rear, Thomas Taylor heard a voice calling for the troops to stop and assumed it was a Union officer. When he stepped toward the man, Taylor realized it was a Confederate officer. "Halt! We'll treat you like men," the Rebel yelled. "Hell, stranger, this is no place for me to halt," Taylor responded as he dashed into the bushes and got away.[36]

The next regiment to feel the crunch was the 54th Ohio. The men saw a stream of Confederates emerging from the smoke-enshrouded area of the railroad cut. Regimental commander Robert Williams refused his line to face south, just behind the Troup Hurt House, but it did no good. The Confederates began to pass around the new position of his left flank, and Williams was compelled to fall back to the east when the enemy were little more than fifteen yards away.[37]

Anyone in the 54th Ohio who tried to stay got swallowed up by the ad-vancing tide. Capt. Edward B. Moore urged some of his men to "stand and fight to the last minute, which we did, and were thereby taken prisner [sic]." They were in for rough treatment. While the captives were moving to the

Confederate rear, Union artillery fire badly injured two of them. "We also had a number of men wounded by the enemy after they had surrendered," Moore recorded in his diary.[38]

After the 54th Ohio fell back, the rest of Wells S. Jones's line continued to peel away unit by unit. Next was the 37th Ohio and then the 30th Ohio, although the latter "remained some time" in order to give De Gress the opportunity to move his battery out of danger. But when Rebel troops appeared to the rear of the regiment, it was not possible to stay. "We looked round [to] behold they was upon our back yelling for us to surrender," recalled Edward E. Schweitzer of Company I. Then the 30th Ohio fell back "in a giffie."[39]

A group of fifteen sharpshooters on the upper floor of the Troup Hurt House was nearly trapped. They could see toward the west but not the south and were caught unaware by the Rebel breakthrough. One man leaned out of a window to get a view toward the railroad and was stunned to see his comrades on the ground abandoning the earthworks, which now were filling up with Confederates, some of whom also were at the front entrance of the house. At least half of the Union sharpshooters, including John Puck, jumped out of five windows located in the second story of the house's east wall. Puck landed on some knapsacks his comrades had piled up that morning. Sprawling as he landed, he managed to get up and run east as Confederates turned the corner of the house and shouted at him to stop. Of course Puck paid no attention to them and escaped.[40]

Manigault testified to the stubbornness of the Federals who, even though badly outflanked, stood and fought as long as reason warranted such bravery. In places, he lost many men in close-quarters, even hand-to-hand combat, but within a few minutes his troops had cleared most of the Union earthworks held by Wells S. Jones's brigade. How much credit is due Sharp's Mississippians in this process is unclear. Some of Manigault's men claimed they did it all, while others grudgingly admitted that Sharp's command played a role in it as well.[41]

But George S. Lea of the 7th Mississippi testified to the important role of Sharp's men in clearing out the Union earthworks. "The Yanks were very obstinate in leaving their work they remained in their ditches till we were in six feet of them some surrendered some run and some fought till they were Killed," Lea told his father. "I was right among them shooting[.] I have often heard of a hand to hand fight but this time I witnessed it. It was the closest quarters I ever was in."[42]

As the tide of battle rolled northward, it engulfed Battery H, 1st Illinois Light Artillery. Described as "a very brave and capable officer & A high

Capture of De Gress's Battery. While Col. Jacob H. Sharp's men initially broke the Fifteenth Corps line where the earthworks crossed the Georgia Railroad, elements of Manigault's and Col. Abda Johnson's brigades also participated in rolling up the Union position north of the track. Capt. Francis De Gress tried hard to maintain his Battery H, 1st Illinois Light Artillery just north of the George M. Troup Hurt House. He pointed the two 20-pounder Parrotts of his left section to the south and fired at very short distance until the position was nearly overwhelmed. De Gress and most of his men escaped, but they left behind all of their pieces and equipment. This image, while not accurate in detail, expresses the drama of the action around this storied battery. From Joseph M. Brown, *The Mountain Campaigns of Georgia; or, War Scenes on the W. and A.* (Buffalo, New York: Art-Printing Works of Matthews, Northrup, 1890), 69.

minded Chivalrous gentleman," De Gress tried to maintain the battery's position north of the Troup Hurt House and to the right of the 30th Ohio as long as possible. The fate of his command became one of the most prominent aspects of the Battle of Atlanta. Just before the breakthrough at the railroad cut, De Gress had been firing canister to the left oblique from his four 20-pounder Parrotts. Then it became obvious that something had gone terribly wrong on the left because Union infantry began to peel away from the works, one regiment after another. Col. Theodore Jones of the 30th Ohio ran to the artillery captain and urged him, in De Gress's words, "to save my Guns as everything on his left had given away and he had no support at all." Still, Jones's men held on a few minutes longer until the Confederates began to move into the rear area. Then the infantrymen evacuated the works, leaving De Gress unsupported on the left.[43]

Even at this nearly hopeless stage of the struggle, De Gress continued to hold on. He ordered the left section of two pieces to face south. Because the battery was located on the north side of a rise of ground, he was unable to see the advancing Rebels until they were only twenty yards away. Once they appeared, he opened on them with case shot, the fuzes cut for one second, because he had run out of canister. But this failed to stop the Confederates.[44]

By now, the only infantry support left to him, the 53rd Ohio positioned to his right, began to give way too. It became "somewhat confused and mixed up," according to Robert A. Fulton. That condition was understandable considering the circumstances, but the 53rd managed to fall back. For a time, De Gress stood alone, ordering the two south-facing pieces spiked. His men did so using ordinary nails, the only suitable items readily available. Then he abandoned those two pieces and fell back to the right section, which by now had faced south as well. The gun crews fired until advancing Confederates were fifteen yards away. Soon, De Gress ordered those pieces to be spiked, too, a task completed by Sgt. Peter S. Wyman.[45]

Even at this desperate stage of the contest, De Gress hoped to extricate his guns. But the Confederates had already moved between the pieces and the area where his limbers were parked. A quick attempt to use prolonges, long ropes with which gun crews could manually pull their pieces, came to naught because the Parrotts were too heavy and his men "much worn out." By now, De Gress had gone well beyond the call of duty, and his men had to scamper. Those who escaped did so by the skin of their teeth, while others were taken prisoner.[46]

The Confederates who overran Battery H, 1st Illinois Light Artillery were a jumbled mix of Manigault's and Sharp's commands. It is impossible to differentiate in this case, and by default, whatever distinction was attached to the capture has to be shared by both brigades.

The men of both brigades also shared credit for collapsing the infantry regiments in Wells S. Jones's battle line, but the Federals exacted a price in blood for this achievement. Col. James F. Pressley of the 10th South Carolina was wounded in the shoulder from close distance after mounting the Union parapet, "shot so close that the powder burnt his clothes," observed C. Irvine Walker, who took command of the regiment. Pressley survived the wound but never again served in the field.[47]

In falling back from the works, Wells S. Jones tried to steady his men and bounce back quickly. He attempted to reform in a bit of "low ground, about 400 yards from the works" but succeeded in rallying only "a few men." Since most of his troops were still moving east, Jones decided to reform the brigade in the old line of earthworks abandoned early that morning. He and his regimental commanders freely admitted that the fall back was done in confusion and disorder. The enlisted men also admitted that they ran "to save ourselves," leaving their knapsacks and "everything else" piled on the ground behind the earthworks they had abandoned.[48]

There was no need to feel embarrassed by such action; veteran troops knew better than to stand in a hopeless encounter, and they had every intention of reforming at what they considered an appropriate spot. That location was their former earthwork line several hundred yards east of the one they had given up, the position they held only that morning before moving forward to occupy the evacuated Outer Line. Here the trench offered a firm line beyond which it would have been shameful to run. Wells S. Jones had no trouble stopping and reforming his men there, aided by the efforts of Morgan L. Smith, Lightburn, and their respective staff members. The men were soon ready to attempt a restoration of their broken line.[49]

While Sharp and Manigault succeeded in pushing Wells S. Jones out of position north of the Georgia Railroad, Confederate forces made progress south of the track as well. Martin's brigade of Lightburn's division had only two regiments south of the railroad, the 55th Illinois and 57th Ohio. Those two units had repelled the first Rebel advance south of the track but were astonished when Sharp cracked the Union line at the cut. Samuel R. Mott, who temporarily commanded both regiments in the absence of brigade leader Martin, ordered the 55th Illinois to change front to the right and fire on a group of 500 Confederates who opposed his right flank.[50]

At this point, additional Confederate manpower came into play near the crucial sector where the Georgia Railroad sliced through the Union line. Sharp's and Manigault's brigades had thus far been responsible for success, but they were supported by part of Stovall's Brigade, now commanded by Col. Abda Johnson, of Clayton's Division, which now arrived on the scene.

Maj. Gen. Henry D. Clayton's troops had taken a position to the left of Brown's command in the Atlanta City Line before Cheatham began his attack. When word arrived for the men to move forward and form just east of the works, Clayton moved them to the right until his division straddled the railroad some distance behind Brown's command. Clayton arrayed his men in two lines, with Johnson's brigade on the right and Baker's Brigade (led by Col. John H. Higley) on the left in the first line. Holtzclaw's Brigade, now led by Col. Bushrod Jones, constituted the right wing of the second line, while the brigade of Brig. Gen. Randall L. Gibson composed the left wing.[51]

Clayton instructed Johnson, whose brigade was in the best place to reach the critical area of the fight, to advance with the sun to his back, "attack the enemy, [and] drive him, if possible, beyond the position recently held by our troops." Johnson had every intention of following those instructions, but he "knew nothing of the ground over which I was to move, nor of the position of the enemy or how other troops were to move or when attack." He deployed Capt. Joseph M. Storey's 43rd Georgia as skirmishers and moved forward. Soon, the brigade came upon the former Union skirmish line, with a few Federal dead scattered about the ground, and right after that began to receive fire from the Napoleons of Battery A, 1st Illinois Light Artillery at the railroad cut, just before Sharp's men broke open the Union line.[52]

While closing in, Capt. L. P. Thomas's 42nd Georgia, the left regiment of Johnson's line, marched north of the railroad with its right flank resting at the track. Lt. Col. John M. Brown's 1st Georgia State Line was to its right, just south of the track. These two regiments entered the zone of heaviest fire. Brown, the brother of Governor Joseph E. Brown, was shot in the thigh close to the Union line, and Capt. Albert Howell took charge of the regiment. John M. Brown died in Milledgeville on July 25.[53]

Johnson's line hit the Union position a bit skewed. Its left regiments closed in first, while the right regiments were thirty paces behind, but the Confederate line swung round until the right wing also closed in. Maj. Mark S. Nall's 41st Georgia, on the extreme right, was "temporarily repulsed," and Union resistance in the center was "determined and obstinate" for "a few minutes," as Johnson put it. There were no supporting troops to his right so the Federals of Harrow's division enfiladed his brigade with their fire for the last 100 yards of the Confederate advance.[54]

Nevertheless, the full weight of Johnson's command fell on Mott's 55th Illinois and 57th Ohio at about the same time that many of Sharp's men began to exploit their breakthrough at the railroad cut and move into the rear area of the two Union regiments. Mott ordered a retreat. The historians of the 55th Illinois indicated there was no time for Capt. Francis H. Shaw to execute the change of front to face north that Mott had earlier ordered. They also asserted that the 57th Ohio fell back quickly but that the 55th retired in an orderly, company-by-company fashion. Yet other men in the 55th Illinois indicated they, too, fell back in a free-for-all manner, at least in Companies E and G, which were positioned nearest the railroad. The fact that the regiment lost its flag while evacuating the works also supports the idea of a hurried and disorderly retreat.[55]

But some Federals doggedly resisted, holding out in the trench even as their comrades fell back. Sgt. B. J. McGinnis of Company C, 40th Georgia "killed two of the enemy with a spade, picked up in his trenches," reported Johnson. "One of the killed had just inflicted a severe bayonet wound in a man of his regiment."[56]

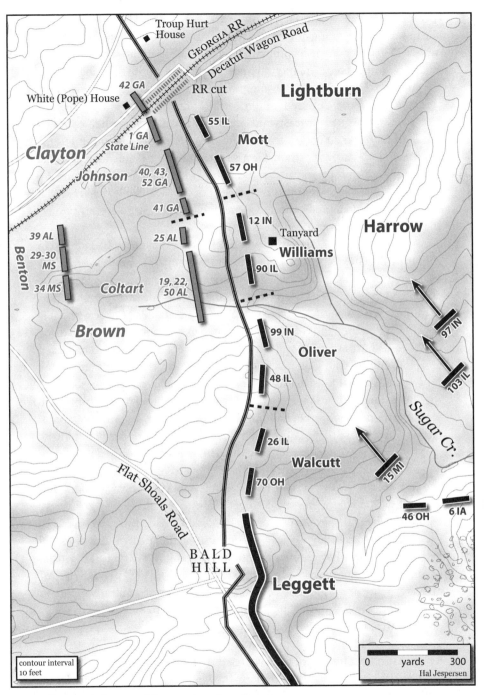

Johnson, Coltart, and Benton Attack

Mott, like Wells S. Jones north of the track, attempted to rally his men in the low ground running north to south a relatively short distance east of the works. Dense underbrush combined with confusion in the ranks, however, made this impossible. The men streamed farther east until reaching the line of works abandoned in the morning, where they quickly reassembled.[57]

Once inside the captured Union fortifications, a handful of Johnson's Confederates pushed on eastward "some distance" before they could be recalled. Rather than continuing the advance at this time, Johnson felt the need to consolidate his position. He assumed that more Confederates would come forward to support him on the right, "then I intended to resume an advance which I supposed was only suspended." Meanwhile, his men sent prisoners to the rear and collected abandoned weapons and accoutrements that lay "scattered over the ground."[58]

Veterans of the 42nd Georgia would later claim that they had a hand in capturing De Gress's battery. In fact, a strident controversy developed thirty years later over that issue, which led to an investigation by Robert L. Rodgers, historian of Atlanta Camp No. 154, United Confederate Veterans. After consulting several survivors of Johnson's and Manigault's brigades, Rodgers concluded that the 42nd Georgia participated in the capture. There is strong evidence to buttress his conclusion. In 1885, L. P. Thomas, who had been a captain in the 42nd Georgia, told artist Theodore R. Davis that he saw De Gress stand to the last at the battery position. "One young man, so young that he seemed but a boy," as Davis recalled the conversation in his own words, "stood by lanyard in hand until we were almost among the guns, in fact he was so brave that our men called out 'don't shoot; don't shoot him.'"[59]

Not long after Confederates from three brigades had captured De Gress's battery, the Federals tried a second, quick effort to recover the ground they had lost. North of the railroad, Wells S. Jones pushed his brigade forward, and at least part of it managed to get close to the captured earthworks before Confederate fire drove it back. Thomas Taylor took command of the 47th Ohio, according to his own account of the affair, and was joined by fragments of other regiments until he had around 250 men. They fixed bayonets and counterattacked as part of Jones's effort. A "hail storm of fire" greeted the troops a short distance from their works. With no support to right or left, Taylor fell back, but his regiment began to break up into wings on the retreat due to dense undergrowth.[60]

Reforming in more open ground, Taylor's men mounted another attempt. This time, the major took charge of the left wing while Capt. Joseph L. Pinkerton commanded the right. By now, the regiment had drifted considerably to the left so that Taylor was south of the Georgia Railroad and Pinkerton north of it. Both wings advanced to a point about fifty yards short of the captured earthworks before Confederate fire once again forced them to retire.[61]

Morale in Wells S. Jones's command understandably became depressed by this time. The men were "mortified that we had lost all we had gained in the morning," wrote John K. Duke of the 53rd Ohio. Division commander Lightburn also was deeply distressed by the turn of events. He "said we had disgraced ourselves," recalled Taylor. "I told him 'that was enough of that! I would show him whether we had.'" The major was angry and hastened to reorganize his battered regiment for a third counterstrike. "I had no idea that I had such determination," he later told his wife, "such stubbornness or strength. I was almost frantic, yet perfectly sane." But it would take fresh troops, which were on their way, to increase the chances that this third attempt might succeed.[62]

Jones's brigade had been driven from the works in a manner that bordered on the shameful, as far as many of the Union troops were concerned. But they had nothing to reproach themselves about because the Confederates had broken their line at an admittedly weak point and exploited that advantage. Tactical circumstances rather than cowardice accounted for the Union failure.

Because Lightburn's division fell back from its position north and south of the Georgia Railroad, Union troops south of this sector had to do likewise. At first, William Harrow was determined to stay and fight. But when Rebel troops began to appear in the rear areas of his division, he knew it was time to pull back. His division line was very thin at any rate; each of his three brigades had but two regiments in the west-facing line, with the rest still scattered to the east after having dealt with the threat from James A. Smith's Confederate brigade. Even if he had tried to hold fast, Harrow may have been driven from his works.[63]

Col. Reuben Williams, whose First Brigade held the right of Harrow's position immediately to the left of Mott's two regiments, had already sent off his lone reserve regiment (the 26th Illinois) to the concentration at the rear. Now he had only the 12th Indiana on the right and the 90th Illinois on the left to hold his brigade sector. "To my utter astonishment," as Williams put it, he saw Mott's troops falling back out of the earthworks. When Williams then saw Johnson's Confederate troops appear, he ordered the 12th Indiana to fire right oblique at them. That failed to stop the Rebels. Johnson's men gathered near the railroad and began "pouring in a terrible fire," so Williams ordered his two regiments to evacuate their works.[64]

Williams tried to take up a position between the west-facing line and the earthworks he had evacuated that morning. But along the way, a tanyard located "a few rods" to rear of the line offered some utility as a rallying point. Williams instructed the 90th Illinois to form behind its large building and wait for the 12th Indiana to join it. But then rounds from Union artillery firing from Copenhill on Confederate targets near the railroad cut began to sail into the tanyard area too. "The shelling of our own troops aided the enemy considerably," Williams later admitted, yet it happened to be an accident of war that was "at times . . . difficult to avoid."[65]

In this case, the friendly fire helped convince Williams to mount a quick counterattack to regain the west-facing line. His men managed to reoccupy their works because, until then, no Confederates had moved forward to hold them. But within minutes, Coltart's men appeared to the front, and Williams ordered everyone out once again. This time he moved his troops all the way to the line abandoned that morning and reformed both regiments.[66]

Soon after Williams abandoned his works, Col. John M. Oliver's Third Brigade came into play. It lay to the left of Williams's position, in the center of Harrow's division line, and also had only two regiments available to hold its sector. When Cheatham's Confederates appeared, Oliver shifted the 99th Indiana and 48th Illinois from the rear areas, where they had been available to repel James A. Smith's Texans, back to the west-facing line. The 99th Indiana took post on the right, with the 48th to its left. When Williams fell back, Col. Alexander Fowler covered Oliver's right flank by deploying skirmishers from his 99th Indiana. That only served as a temporary measure, however, before Oliver ordered both regiments to retire. He also recalled the 15th Michigan, which had held behind breastworks hastily constructed right after the repulse of Smith's Texans, to the west-facing line. But the regiment failed to arrive in time to support the 99th Indiana and 48th Illinois. Oliver also instructed the 70th Ohio to fall back. Yet this regiment, along with the 26th Illinois, was not even in his sector anymore. Sent much earlier to support Walcutt, that brigade leader had placed both units in his sector to the left of Oliver's.[67]

At this point Harrow intervened. Riding along his divisional line, he discovered Oliver's fall back and halted it. As his 70th Ohio began to move out, Maj. William B. Brown saw the division leader and sent Capt. James F. Summers to ask him for orders. Harrow immediately told Summers to get the regiment back into the earthworks. The Ohioans complied with loud cheering that encouraged everyone who heard it. The division leader then rode on to meet Oliver, who informed him of Williams's fall back. Harrow issued orders for both brigades to retake their former positions as soon as possible.[68]

All three brigade sectors—Williams's, Oliver's, and Walcutt's—were still contested even though two of them had been evacuated by Union troops. The left-most sector, just north of Leggett's Seventeenth Corps division, was Walcutt's responsibility, and thanks to Harrow, it was still held by two regiments. Ironically, neither of them belonged to Walcutt's brigade. He had shifted all of his men to the rear to block James A. Smith's Brigade and still held them at that location. Later, Oliver loaned him the 70th Ohio and Williams sent him the 26th Illinois, but Walcutt really did not need either regiment, so he sent both to hold his sector of the west-facing line. Then when Cheatham attacked, Walcutt sent his own 97th Indiana and 103rd Illinois from the blocking position his brigade had established in front of Smith's Confederates in order to support Williams's sector. He kept the 6th Iowa and 46th Ohio at the blocking position to the rear of the line for the remainder of the battle.[69]

While the 97th Indiana and 103rd Illinois moved toward Williams's sector, the 26th Illinois and 70th Ohio in Walcutt's sector helped contain the Confederates for a time. Capt. Ira J. Bloomfield directed his 26th Illinois, detached from Williams's brigade, to refuse the right two companies and fire at Coltart's men, who had compelled the 48th Illinois to fall back. After it returned to the trench, Brown's 70th Ohio did the same thing, refusing its right flank to deliver fire at those Rebels. The combined firing helped prevent the Confederates from causing trouble in the Union rear areas until help could arrive.[70]

Walcutt played a limited but significant role in reacting to the Confederate breakthrough by sending the two regiments from his blocking position. Lt. Col. Aden G. Cavins moved the 97th Indiana with the 103rd Illinois for more than a quarter of a mile at the double-quick. They met the two regiments of Oliver's brigade that had just evacuated their works and were falling back. Realizing the greater urgency of shoring up Oliver's sector, Cavins and Maj. Asias Willison of the 103rd Illinois decided to change their mission and assist Oliver instead of continuing to Williams's portion of the line. For his part, Col. Lucien Greathouse decided to turn his 48th Illinois around and go back in with the 97th Indiana and 103rd Illinois, while Fowler's 99th Indiana continued to fall back in obedience to Oliver's instructions.[71]

The 97th Indiana and 48th Illinois managed to get into the Union trench but were quickly faced with Coltart's men surging close to the parapet. Heavy firing erupted in which Greathouse was killed. Barely twenty-two years old, the colonel was shot through the right breast and died quickly. This shocked the Federals, and the 48th Illinois began to give way; likely its right flank was turned as well because the regiment had no support to the north. "The rebels swarmed across the works on our right," Cavins informed his wife, but the 97th Indiana stubbornly held on. Lt. William H. Sherfy, who had recovered enough from being knocked off his horse when McPherson was fired upon earlier that afternoon, rode to see how his old regiment was faring and got caught up in this battle. Cavins had asked him to take charge of the right wing just before the regiment entered the works, and now the lieutenant struggled to deal with the lack of support to the right. Sherfy reported that the regiment had to fall back, too, but Cavins made it clear in his detailed account that it stayed and fought. At worst, it is possible that part of the right wing fell back under tremendous pressure while most of the regiment remained in the trench.[72]

According to Cavins, the 97th Indiana put up a vigorous defense to meet an equally vigorous attack. In his front, many Confederates, including a colonel, a major, and a captain, fell within fifteen feet of the Union parapet. Still, his right flank nearly crumbled. Confederate troops "swarmed in so thick and fast that they captured five of Co. A," while two men of that company escaped by jumping on the west side of the works and running away. Sgt. Salathiel Thompson of Company A "saved himself by "jerking his gun from a rebel" after the Confederate had disarmed him. "It was really safe on our front, for we had kept them at bay" there. A caisson exploded 50 yards away, but Cavins did not notice it because of the dreadful noise created by the heavy musketry on his line. Finally, Coltart's men fell back 150 yards from his front, relieving the pressure.[73]

Cavins's regiment played an important role in stopping the spread of the Confederate breakthrough. Under great pressure, it held its position and repelled part of Coltart's brigade, serving as the shoulder of the Union position south of the breakthrough. Willison's 103rd Illinois played no role in this deadly struggle. The major managed to get his men into a stretch of empty trench to the left of the 97th Indiana but was not attacked in front. He gave no indication that he was aware of Cavins's struggle, reporting that Union troops seemed to be evacuating the trench, so he pulled his Illinois men out, too, and waited for orders. Willison also noted that the Confederates failed to occupy the trench he had just abandoned.[74]

Harrow's division had partially peeled away, right to left, in a similar way that Wells S. Jones's brigade had peeled from left to right north of the railroad. But that process south of the track was stopped by Harrow, Cavins, Bloomfield, and Brown. Thus, it is curious that a well-documented incident took place between Leggett and Walcutt. Leggett noticed trouble to the north and became concerned about his ability to hold Bald Hill, threatened as he was by fierce Confederate attacks coming from the south. He rode up to Walcutt's position for a consultation. According to Leggett's postwar writings, an order arrived for the brigade commander to fall back from the west-facing Fifteenth Corps line. Leggett argued vehemently against Walcutt obeying the order, explaining that he might not be able to hold the important hill without support to his right. Walcutt fully understood and assured Leggett he would not fail him.[75]

The problem with this interesting story is that Harrow never issued any orders for Walcutt to fall back. The division leader exerted all his influence to maintain the line, even stopping Oliver from pulling back all his regiments. There is no evidence to support the idea that Harrow wanted Walcutt to retire. Moreover, the brigade leader did not even have any of his own regiments in line. He merely instructed the 70th Ohio and 26th Illinois to hold their positions without even being aware that the 70th Ohio was acting under orders from other officers, including Harrow. Walcutt remained at the blocking position the entire time and was detached from immediate knowledge of the flow of events along the west-facing line. Harrow was more important in preserving what was left of that line and in moving troops to restore the lost portion than was Walcutt, even though contemporaries and historians have not given him credit for doing so.[76]

In the middle of all this the artillery assigned to Harrow's division had to scramble to save itself. Capt. Josiah H. Burton had sent each section of his Battery F, 1st Illinois Light Artillery to different spots before Cheatham attacked. He had also, under instructions from Capt. Henry H. Griffiths, Harrow's artillery chief, sent his caissons to the rear of Lightburn's division for better cover. The three sections, consisting entirely of Napoleons, retired in time, but the caissons fell victim to the sudden fall back of Wells S. Jones's brigade. Before the drivers could fairly get started, Confederate troops grabbed the bridles of the lead horses and stopped them. The Federals jumped off and ran for the nearby woods, escaping capture, but all six caissons fell into Rebel hands. Included with them was all the camp equipment, cooking utensils, and personal baggage of the battery personnel. Nevertheless, Burton pulled his guns back to safer positions and, as soon as he was certain the Confederates occupied Williams's and Oliver's sectors of the earthworks, opened fire on the trench line.[77]

Lt. William H. Gay's 1st Iowa Battery faced three of its 10-pounder Parrotts to the right and fired canister when the Confederates forced Williams to abandon his position. This failed to stop the Confederate breakthrough. Griffiths ordered the pieces to retire, and the 48th Illinois of Oliver's brigade helped. More than 100 men of the regiment "rushed out in front of the battery and opened fire, which for the moment checked them, and enabled us to get away." Gay quickly pulled away all but one of his pieces because the Confederates had shot three horses of this last gun. The crew cut these dead and injured animals from their harness and managed to retrieve the piece just before the Rebels closed in. Gay worried about his caissons and wagons parked 200 yards east of the battery position, but the men in charge of them were alert and moved out of danger in time.[78]

Behind Harrow's sector of the Union line there existed "a densely packed mass of ammunition, luggage, supply and hospital wagons, ambulances, etc.," which represented the most immediate link in the logistical chain supporting Sherman's army group. When Harrow's regiments began to retire from their position, drivers became alarmed and scurried to move their wagons east. The resulting traffic jam was memorable. Everyone "struggled for positions in the line of retreat," recalled Chaplain M. D. Gage of the 12th Indiana.[79]

The same was true of Lightburn's division trains farther to the north. George Frederick Renner, his chief quartermaster, reported to his sister that the sudden collapse of Wells S. Jones's line caught his personnel by surprise. By the time they started the wagons east, the Confederates were seventy-five yards away. "The bullets flew around as thick as hail and one hit my saddle mule in the foot," he wrote.[80]

With the fall back of Williams's and most of Oliver's men, most of Coltart's command moved forward to occupy the abandoned section of the Union earthworks. Sharp's breakthrough at the railroad cut and Johnson's capture of the works held by Mott's two regiments had compelled Williams and then most of Oliver to retire, but Coltart was unable to expand the Confederate breakthrough farther south.[81]

While these events transpired south of the Georgia Railroad, two more brigades of Clayton's Division contributed to operations north of the track. Bushrod Jones led Holtzclaw's Brigade on the right wing of Clayton's second line, 400 yards behind Abda Johnson's command. He received the same instructions given to the other brigade leaders, which were to advance with the sun to his back and "to continue the attack, prolonging the left" of Johnson's regiments if the latter managed to break through the Union position. The brigade was relatively small, with only 678 men on duty that afternoon. Maj. Shep Ruffin's 38th Alabama held the right, with Lt. Col. Thomas H. Herndon's 36th Alabama next, then Lt. Col. Peter F. Hunley's 18th Alabama and Colonel Jones's consolidated 32nd and 58th Alabama, now led by Capt. John Alfred Avirett Jr., holding the left.[82]

After starting the advance, Bushrod Jones encountered so much timber and underbrush that he soon lost sight of Johnson's troops but continued moving forward, using the Georgia Railroad as his guide. Before long he came within sight of the Union earthworks and the White House north of the railroad. By this time, Johnson had occupied the trenches, so Jones halted his men in the open about 100 yards from the captured earthworks, still south of the railroad, and tried to figure out what to do with them.[83]

Both Manigault and Sharp rode to him and offered some advice. They pointed out that no Confederate troops were positioned to their left, that the Federals still held Copenhill and seemed to be moving about as if to counterattack, and that it would be helpful if Jones extended Rebel control of the Union line and offered support to the left of their commands. They also suggested that Jones change the front of his brigade to face north and march forward to reach the desired location. The colonel gave the order, swinging his short line backward on the left by using his right regiment, Ruffin's 38th Alabama, as the pivot. Then he moved the line north across the track and up to a point near the Troup Hurt House, where he halted once again. Here the men came under heavy Union artillery fire directed at the captured De Gress battery, so Jones told them to lie down for protection. His Alabamians endured fifteen minutes of this fire while Jones scouted out the unknown terrain to see exactly how and where to place his regiments.[84]

Jones instructed Ruffin on where he decided to put the 38th Alabama in the captured works but told him to wait until he had given instructions to the other regimental leaders before moving. Even so, before he reached the left two regiments, he noticed that the 38th Alabama was on the move north without his orders. He later found out that Manigault had been anxious for Jones to shift more quickly into position and had told Ruffin to get going. Manigault also spoke with Herndon of the 36th Alabama, telling him "there was more danger in remaining in that position than in going forward." Initially, Herndon hesitated to obey a brigade leader other than his own, but when Ruffin moved the 38th Alabama forward, he felt compelled to do likewise. The two regiments marched quickly under artillery fire for 200 yards, performing a half wheel to the right, before reaching the relative safety of the Union works. Seeing this, Jones told Hunley of the 18th Alabama and Avirett of the consolidated 32nd and 58th Alabama to do the same. These units had more difficult ground to traverse, which slowed and deflected their progress. By this stage in events, Union efforts to mount a counterattack and restore their line came into play. These events will be detailed in the next chapter, but for now, the result was that the 18th Alabama and the 32nd and 58th Alabama never made it into the captured Federal works. They failed to connect with the 36th Alabama and 38th Alabama, which were now lodged in the Union trench.[85]

Bushrod Jones thus managed to insert only two of his regiments into line, extending Confederate occupation of the Fifteenth Corps position only incrementally and failing to adequately protect the left flank. In fact, a gap existed between the right of Ruffin's 38th Alabama and the left of Manigault's Brigade. Half of Jones's command was still in transit through the woods when the Federals returned to the area in force.[86]

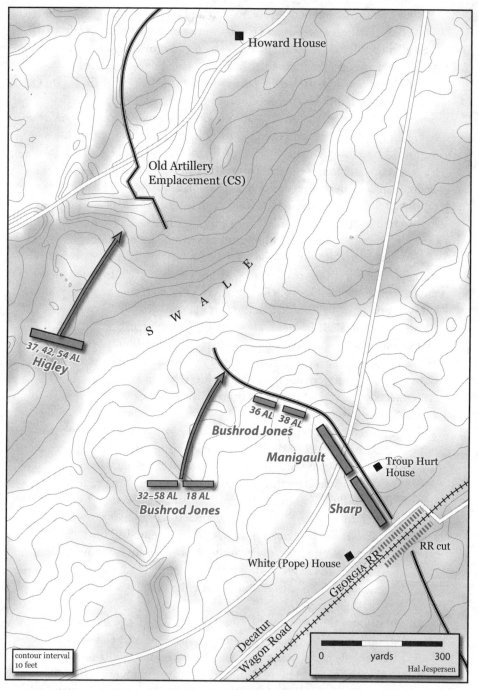

Howard House

Old Artillery
Emplacement (CS)

S W A L E

37, 42, 54 AL
Higley

36 AL 38 AL

Bushrod Jones

Manigault

32–58 AL   18 AL
Bushrod Jones

Sharp

Troup Hurt
House

White (Pope) House

GEORGIA RR

RR cut

Decatur
Wagon Road

contour interval
10 feet

0   yards   300

Hal Jespersen

Confederate Positions at End of Attack, North of Railroad

The other brigade of Clayton's Division that attempted to expand the Confederate occupation of the Fifteenth Corps line was Baker's Brigade, commanded by Col. John H. Higley. While Bushrod Jones managed to get only two of his four regimental organizations into line, Higley failed to get any of his men into it, even though his brigade constituted the left wing of Clayton's first line and was entirely north of the railroad. Higley led only three regiments, Lt. Col. Alexander A. Greene's 37th Alabama, Capt. Robert K. Wells's 42nd Alabama, and Lt. Col. John A. Minter's 54th Alabama. His own regiment, the 40th Alabama, was under command of Maj. Ezekiah Slocum Gulley but had been detached to perform picket duty and was not available.[87]

As Higley moved his three regiments forward along the north side of the railroad, he lost sight of Abda Johnson's troops to his right. Reports of the Unionists "moving on our left flank," portending a counterattack from the direction of Copenhill, led Clayton to order a change of direction for Higley. At a point about 800 yards from the start, Higley adjusted his brigade line until it angled at about thirty degrees, or roughly northeastward, compared to his original north–south line. He then moved forward toward the area north of where Bushrod Jones would eventually land up, aiming at a Union counterattack that had not yet been located. It was a blind advance into an uncertain situation for half a mile and consumed a good deal of time. But the change of direction did open up the ground for Bushrod Jones to move his own brigade from south to north of the railroad without running into Higley's formation.[88]

Higley failed to extend Confederate control of the Fifteenth Corps position before the Union counterattack took place. Meanwhile, Gulley's 40th Alabama spent the entire battle on picket duty under the orders of the divisional officer of the day, Col. Leon Von Zinken of the 20th Louisiana. That regiment was part of Gibson's Brigade, also of Clayton's Division. Gibson's Louisiana troops failed to become engaged in the Battle of July 22. Soon after the start of the division's advance, Clayton noticed that Manigault's Brigade had been repulsed from its first attempt to capture the Union line. He detached Gibson to support Manigault, after which everyone seems to have forgotten the Louisiana unit. There are no reports emanating from Gibson's Brigade, but the few surviving personal accounts of its members confirm that it remained idle all afternoon.[89]

One other concentration of troops was available to help Cheatham in his attack, but the corps leader had no control over it. Gov. Joseph E. Brown had called out the Georgia Militia early in June and placed Maj. Gen. Gustavus W. Smith in command, relieving Maj. Gen. Henry C. Wayne, who reverted to his usual position as adjutant and inspector general in the state government. Smith soon had two brigades of three regiments each plus a battalion of artillery, totaling a little more than 3,000 men. The quality of that force was well below average for the Confederate-sponsored regiments in the Army of Tennessee, but it was at least a small addition of manpower. The militia played a marginal role in operations on the north bank of the Chattahoochee River in late June and early July before crossing south and going into reserve.[90]

On July 22, with 2,000 men on duty, Smith's command held a section of the Atlanta City Line south of the Georgia Railroad. No one issued him any orders when Cheatham began to advance, so Smith took it upon himself to join in. "I closed the intervals in my line, formed the line of battle in the trenches, and moved the militia forward over the parapet more than a mile." He aimed at Bald Hill, south of the railroad, where Union artillery had already been punishing his men as they worked on strengthening their stretch of the City Line. Smith called a halt when the militiamen were 400 yards short of the Union works and awaited developments. Capt. Ruel W. Anderson's Georgia Battery, with four Napoleons, took post in the center of Smith's infantry line in an open field. Lumsden's Alabama Battery, which remained in the City Line, offered support by firing over the heads of the militiamen from a distance.[91]

Smith held there for several hours without seeing an opportunity for an assault. He was unaware that Brown and Clayton had broken the Fifteenth Corps line and could tell from the sound of battle that Hardee was not making much progress. Any further advance, he reasoned, would be un-supported and doomed to fail with high casualties. Nevertheless, the militiamen were subject to artillery fire and took losses. "We was ordered out of the diches to go and help our boys whip the yankes," wrote James W. Watkins to his wife. "We went and was hilt as reserves and did not go in the reglar ingagement though we was in a heap of danger we was under fire all the time the bullets whis all about there." Finally, an order arrived from Hood's headquarters to fall back to the Atlanta City Line.[92]

The two brigades of Georgia Militia were not the only formations avail-able to the Confederates that failed to become significantly engaged in the fighting that afternoon. Another was Gibson's Brigade farther north. If one counts Stevenson's Division, which conducted a show of advancing, that adds four more brigades to the total. These seven brigades were ill used in a serious struggle to take advantage of Hardee's flanking attacks. Even within the two divisions that broke the Fifteenth Corps line, neither Brown nor Clayton managed to get all of their men into action in an effective manner. Of their eight brigades, five managed to lodge inside the captured Union trenches for a relatively short time: Manigault's, Sharp's, Johnson's, most of

Coltart's, and half of Bushrod Jones's commands. Three and a half brigades never touched the Federal earthworks: Benton's, Gibson's, Higley's, and half of Bushrod Jones's formations. The quality of troop handling was very uneven among Cheatham's division and brigade leaders, and it severely limited the Rebels' ability to exploit success.

What is even more startling was an order arising from division commander John C. Brown to evacuate the captured Union works. It surprised Manigault, the only brigade leader to record the directive. He reluctantly obeyed and moved back about 250 yards to the point where his brigade had stopped to reform during its initial advance. Very soon after that, another order arrived to go back, and Manigault made haste to obey, settling his command for the second time in the captured works. Only one regimental leader in the brigade, Capt. Elijah W. Horne of the 19th South Carolina, mentioned this temporary fall back. No one in the other regiments referred to this retreat, and it is possible only part of Manigault's command fell back at all.[93]

Still, the whole incident is bizarre. Why did Brown issue the order, and why did only two Confederate officers confirm that it existed? Albert Castel assumes that some sort of miscommunication led to the fallback order and that this mistake was corrected immediately. One is tempted to discount the entire story, but Manigault and Horne were reliable witnesses. In fact, the 19th South Carolina in this process lost its commander, Maj. James L. White, who was severely wounded while returning to the trenches, leading Horne to take charge of the regiment. At the very least, the incident calls Brown's competency as a division commander into question.[94]

Actually, it cannot be said that the Confederate success thus far had come about because of good command and control. The key to the breaking of the Fifteenth Corps line had been the action of some Mississippi troops of Sharp's command in seizing the opportunity to move through the undefended railroad cut under cover of cannon smoke. That was the action of noncommissioned officers and company and regimental officers, not brigade, division, or corps commanders. Cheatham played no personal role of any kind in the fight along the Georgia Railroad. Stevenson did little, Brown came close to ruining his command's success with his strange order to retire from the captured works, and Clayton tried to help by redirecting Higley's advance in an effort to defend Confederate control of the Union line. Hood's only role was to order Cheatham to advance. The corps essentially stumbled into this tactical success by the actions of a handful of its low-ranking men rather than by the actions of anyone in high command. Moreover, literally no one told the troops who now occupied the Union position what they should do next.

Federal command and control was only a bit better in this third phase of the Battle of Atlanta. Morgan L. Smith made a serious mistake in taking the railroad cut so lightly as a weak element in his division line. No Federal officer can be blamed for the resulting failure to hold the Fifteenth Corps position once the Confederate breakthrough occurred, but the strength of Union efforts thereafter rested on stern decisions by a handful of men. North of the railroad, the resolve to reform and counterattack by Wells S. Jones was a key element in confining the damage. South of the railroad, effective decisions by Harrow, Williams, Oliver, and Walcutt were equally important. As with the fighting along Sugar Creek and south of Bald Hill, the Federals eventually managed to maintain more effective control of events than did their opponents, and that counted for much in determining the outcome of the battle on July 22.

It is remarkable that, after Manigault overcame the dire effects of Brown's odd order to retreat from the captured Union line, the Confederates settled into the nearly one-mile-long hole they had punched in the Fifteenth Corps position without any guidance as to their next move. Manigault shifted his brigade northward to make room for Sharp. The latter held the works from the railroad north, and the former continued the occupation up to the beginning of the dogleg section. Manigault's right flank, therefore, rested fifty yards north of the Troup Hurt House. Union batteries on Copenhill plastered the area, forcing C. Irvine Walker to place his 10th South Carolina on Manigault's far right to the east side of the Union works, where it could secure some degree of shelter due to the slight rise of ground just to the north where De Gress's battery had been posted. Many Confederates noticed how much the Federals had renovated the position, which had initially been constructed by the Rebels, by moving the parapet and the slight abatis from the east to the west side of the trench.[95]

Eight Union artillery pieces, four belonging to De Gress's Battery H, 1st Illinois Light Artillery and four of Smyth's Battery A, 1st Illinois Light Artillery, were in Confederate hands. Walker examined De Gress's 20-pounder Parrotts, but there was no conveniently located break in the Union works through which to pull them toward Atlanta. His men had no tools available to construct a ramp across the trench or to cut through the parapet. But Smyth's Napoleons were near the unbarricaded railroad cut and Decatur Road, so Walker arranged for troops to pull them through. This work had to be done by hand because the battery horses were either killed or scattered. Confederate sources indicate that a total of six captured artillery pieces were taken away; if so, most of them belonged to Smyth's battery.[96]

Watching all this was Lt. Theodore W. Raub of Battery A. Shot in the abdomen, he was slowly dying while holding part of his bowels in his left hand, his sword in the other. Capt. Starke H. Oliver of the 24th Alabama noticed Raub leaning against a tree, "gazing sadly on the scene around him, and apparently in abstracted thought." Without realizing Raub was mortally wounded, Oliver called on him to surrender, a call that "startled and surprised" the Federal officer. Oliver then arranged for his men to make Raub comfortable, but the lieutenant died a few minutes later.[97]

Raub's sad end epitomized the breaking of the Fifteenth Corps line on July 22. On no other battlefield of the war had the men of these Union formations been driven from a prepared line of defense. This dramatic turn of events elicited a degree of shame, blame, and anger among many Federals. They emphasized the disorderly retreat of Lightburn's two brigades, something that Lightburn himself expressed on the field to Thomas Taylor. Sherman used the phrase "some disorder" when reporting the battle to Henry W. Halleck, and Dodge wrote that Lightburn's command "became partially panic-stricken" when the enemy broke through at the railroad cut.[98]

There was some justification for all these characterizations of the Federal failure to hold the line, but such setbacks occurred to nearly all infantry commands at one point or another during the course of the war. The important question was could the Fifteenth Corps troops bounce back and restore their line quickly? The answer to that question would play a large role in determining the outcome of the bloody fighting on July 22.

9

Federal Resurgence

The dramatic break of the Fifteenth Corps line that began at the cut along the Georgia Railroad and extended north and south was clearly visible from Copenhill. Sherman's attention had been drawn elsewhere until Brig. Gen. Charles R. Woods, commander of the First Division, Fifteenth Corps, personally told him about signs of trouble to the south. At first, Sherman "was incredulous, and sent him back to be sure," but Willard Warner, his assistant inspector general, confirmed the report just before Woods returned to assert the same thing.[1]

Sherman wasted no time in reacting to the distressing news. He ordered Woods to adjust his division line, first to protect the flank and then to mount a counterattack to reclaim the lost segment of earthworks. Meanwhile, he instructed the artillery at and around Copenhill to reposition and open fire on the captured segment to impede Confederate reinforcements from filling the works. Schofield's Twenty-Third Corps was available as well, and Sherman gave instructions for it to be ready for action. Suddenly, all resources on and near Copenhill were mobilized in reaction to the startling development.[2]

Woods concentrated on adjusting his division line not only to repel a Confederate attack on his current left flank (if one was on the way) but also to orient his two brigades for a counterstrike to the south. "I threw back my left," he reported, maintaining his right flank on top of Copenhill near the Howard House.

Col. James A. Williamson's Second Brigade was on the right, continuing to anchor the division's flank near the house, while the left wing, Col. Milo Smith's First Brigade, evacuated the earthworks and retired swinging back to face entirely south. The two formations made a line extending east from near the Howard House and waited a few minutes to see if the enemy was approaching. Williamson and Smith kept their skirmish lines in place well in front of the earthworks to shield the now-vacant trenches.[3]

Meanwhile, Woods's artillery sprang into action. Earlier that morning, his artillery chief, Maj. Clemens Landgraeber, had placed two 3-Inch Ordnance Rifles of Battery F, 2nd Missouri Light Artillery plus two Napoleons and two 20-pounder Parrott guns of the 4th Ohio Battery in an earthwork in front of the Howard House. Now he pulled those six pieces away and placed them in position to fire spherical case at the Confederates holding the Fifteenth Corps line. Woods told Landgraeber to kill the horses belonging to De Gress's battery to prevent the Confederates from taking the captured pieces away. De Gress's location was 1,000 yards away, well within effective range of explosive ordnance, and Landgraeber was convinced his fire played a big role in saving De Gress's cannon.[4]

Sherman called on Schofield to bring all his available artillery into play and later reported that twenty pieces showed up from the two Twenty-Third Corps divisions. He personally pointed out positions for the batteries as they arrived and told them where to aim their rounds. These pieces added their weight to Landgraeber's guns in pounding the area occupied by De Gress's battery. "We shot down the horses," reported George W. Nash of Capt. Byron D. Paddock's Battery F, 1st Michigan Light Artillery. Some of Schofield's artillery obtained an enfilade fire on the Confederate infantry holding the captured works. "We could see fragments of men hats coats & c. flying in the air twenty feet height," wrote an amazed soldier in the 107th Illinois as he watched the effects of the fire.[5]

Schofield also adjusted his infantry positions in accordance with Woods's new alignment. Brig. Gen. Milo S. Hascall's Second Division, Twenty-Third Corps joined Woods's right at Copenhill with his left flank. He moved his reserve brigade, commanded by Col. William E. Hobson, to better protect the area around the Howard House as Woods redirected his attention to the south.[6]

While all this adjusting of infantry positions and the opening of artillery fire took place, Maj. Gen. Oliver O. Howard, commander of the Fourth Corps to Schofield's right, came riding onto Copenhill to see how the battle was developing. He saw the flurry of activity and soon learned the reason for it. Sherman and Schofield sat their horses in the middle of all this, calmly directing operations. Howard later contended that De Gress was here, too, "exhibiting much feeling and complaining of his loss," but the captain himself never indicated in his reports of the battle that he went to see Sherman. Regardless, the artillery was "blazing away with a terrific roar, making volumes of smoke," Howard recalled. He took his place next to the two generals, began scanning the terrain to the south with his field glasses, and saw the awful truth; Confederate troops and their flags could plainly be seen inside the Union earthworks.[7]

Capt. Charles Dana Miller of Company C, 76th Ohio just now came to Copenhill with a detail of men assigned to cut trees in front of Woods's line. "We found everybody excited there," he recalled. "A dreadful uncertainty and alarm was depicted on the faces of officers." Lt. Col. William E. Strong, who had by now finished the sad duty of recovering McPherson's remains, whispered to Miller that his chief was dead and "our army was being outflanked and driven back, but it must be kept a secrete [sic] from the men," he warned.[8]

The scene of this disaster to the Fifteenth Corps was very visible from Copenhill but only a bit less so from the vantage point of Bald Hill. There Maj. Gen. Frank P. Blair could not avoid noticing what had happened to Lightburn and Harrow. His first thought was that his own Seventeenth Corps, barely holding on to Bald Hill and the slim line of works extending south of it, would soon break and collapse too.[9]

In addition to managing affairs on Copenhill, Sherman sent word to Maj. Gen. John A. Logan that the Fifteenth Corps line had to be restored as soon as possible. This was a point Logan needed no urging to attend, but Sherman's message was not the first to reach him concerning this turn of events. Before any word of the break arrived, Logan rode to see how things fared with Maj. Gen. Grenville Dodge's corps. Along the way, he gave a good dressing down to a teamster who was driving his wagon in a panicked way to the rear. Soon after reaching Dodge, Logan was giving him instructions when Capt. Horatio N. Wheeler of Logan's staff rode up and told him of the break in the Fifteenth Corps line. Dodge always misremembered this moment, believing that Logan rode to him to get help to restore the line. "He came to me as we were in the habit of doing" when one command needed assistance, forgetting that by now Logan was in charge of the Army of the Tennessee and his superior rather than just another corps commander.[10]

C. P. Helmkamp of the 12th Illinois later claimed to be near enough to the assembled group to overhear what Logan said after Wheeler delivered his message. "Gen. Dodge, I want one of your best brigades as quick as God Almighty will let you." Dodge's answer was, "All right, General," and then he turned to August Mersy, who was part of the group, and told him, "Col. Mersy, take your brigade." The mission could not be in better hands.

Dodge assigned Capt. Edward Jonas, one of his aides-de-camp, to escort Mersy to the spot since Jonas was familiar with the route. Dodge also told the captain to inform whoever was in charge in that sector that he wanted Mersy returned to the Sixteenth Corps position as soon as possible. Before leaving, Logan told Dodge to call on the Twenty-Third Corps if he needed assistance; Brig. Gen. Jacob Cox's division was not far away and ready to respond.[11]

As Mersy's brigade moved out, word spread through the ranks that a crisis had developed with the Fifteenth Corps. "The day was excessively hot and the command was already much fatigued," wrote Lt. Col. Henry Van Sellar, commander of the 12th Illinois, "but the need was known." His regiment led Mersy's column on the two-mile march. The brigade moved at the double-quick for 200 yards, then slowed down to a "fast walk" for 100 yards before resuming the double-quick. Despite this effort to avoid straggling, "a good many dropped out" along the way.[12]

Mersy's column headed north until reaching the Georgia Railroad and then turned west. Although some sources insist that Logan accompanied the troops, Jonas emphatically denied this in a postwar letter. The aide rode beside Mersy at the head of the column, merely acting as a guide.[13]

Pushing on, Mersy's brigade came upon Lightburn's Fifteenth Corps troops. By this time, they had tried and failed to mount a quick counter-charge to reclaim their works and were understandably depressed in spirit. Whether they were "demoralized," as W. E. McCreary of the 81st Ohio put it, is questionable, but they obviously were in need of assistance. Just after passing through their line, Mersy's command began to receive Confederate artillery fire, and several men in the 81st Ohio were killed or injured.[14]

Mersy now turned the head of his column north and began to cross the railroad, intending to form line just north of the track. The brigade was still crossing when Mersy went down; his beloved horse Billy was killed, and he himself suffered a bullet wound in the leg. The German-born colonel was more distraught over the fate of his horse than about his own injury. "Oh! my poor Billy," he moaned, "my poor Billy." Lt. Col. Robert N. Adams of the 81st Ohio now took control of the brigade.[15]

Adams superintended the deployment of the regiments into line, with Van Sellar's 12th Illinois forming the left, its left flank resting at the railroad. Adams's own 81st Ohio, now led by Maj. Frank Evans, passed by the rear of Van Sellar's regiment and took position in the center of the brigade line, while Capt. William S. Boyd's 66th Illinois formed on the right. Some men of the Fifteenth Corps and a few artillerists dispossessed of their guns accompanied the 81st Ohio.[16]

As soon as the brigade line formed, Adams gave the order to advance.

The three regiments climbed "a strong board fence," realigned, and then moved forward with a purpose, cheering along the way. They received what Adams described as "a moderate fire" of small arms from the Confederates holding Lightburn's works, but according to Charles Wright, it mostly flew over their heads. The brigade crossed a ravine, and on the climb up the western side, Adams ordered a charge at fast speed. The Rebels were unnerved by the sight of these three regiments surging toward them with confidence. After the war, Confederate division commander John C. Brown happened to meet Dodge and offered an explanation for this turn of events. He asserted that Union artillery had fired so heavily on the area of the break in Lightburn's position that "it was impossible to force his men forward." His troops had tended to huddle in the works without further purpose. Arthur Manigault admitted in his memoirs that a dread feeling of isolation had settled on his mind during the time his brigade occupied the Federal works because there seemed to be no direction as to further efforts, no orders to follow up his success in breaking the Union line. The Confederates could rebuff the uncoordinated efforts by Lightburn to quickly restore the line, but not this charge by Mersy's brigade.[17]

The counterattack succeeded faster and better than one could have expected. As most of the Rebels fled west, Adams's men rescued a number of Federals from the 37th Ohio and 47th Ohio who had not yet been sent to Atlanta. They also captured about fifty Confederates in the works, many of them firing until subdued. The rest of Sharp's command and Manigault's Brigade pulled away with alacrity. Manigault bitterly resented the collapse of all that had been accomplished only a short time before. "Had proper use been made" of Rebel resources, "had a competent commander been present," he wrote, a third of Sherman's army group might have been smashed. While not naming anyone particularly, he blamed officers above the brigade level for this failure, obviously referring to Brown and Maj. Gen. Benjamin F. Cheatham.[18]

The most prominent feature of the counterattack as far as Mersy's men were concerned was reclaiming the guns of De Gress's Battery H, 1st Illinois Light Artillery. When the brigade hit the Union works, the battery was opposite the right wing of the 66th Illinois and close to the 81st Ohio. "It was a horrible sight to see the men and horses all lying together in a heap," wrote an anonymous soldier of the Ohio command. Veterans of both regiments would argue forever as to which unit deserved credit for reclaiming the battered guns. Reportedly, the first man to reach them was Mason R. Blizzard of Company I, 81st Ohio, but veterans of Companies G and K, 66th Illinois convincingly argued that they were the ones who spearheaded the recapture of the pieces. To a degree, both regiments deserve some credit.[19]

De Gress was on the scene, "bare headed and bristling with pluck as the Battery was recouped," wrote artist Theodore R. Davis. Other witnesses reported that the artillery officer "wept like a child" at the sight of the dead gunners and horses. "I want to thank you and your brigade for what you have done," he told Robert N. Adams before going to work. De Gress had several of his men with him, and the small group of artillerists put one gun back into action.[20]

About a dozen infantrymen from the 66th Illinois and 81st Ohio put another piece into action after pulling out the ordinary nails used to spike the vent. They successfully fired three rounds before Joe Schun of the 81st Ohio had a bright idea. He had observed how Sixteenth Corps batteries had used double canister and wanted to try it. "Feed 'em—give 'em double rations," he yelled while shoving a second 20-pounder percussion shell on top of the first. When Captain Boyd pulled the lanyard, the piece exploded, sending fragments whizzing through the air but not seriously hurting anyone. A fragment weighing up to 100 pounds landed a hundred yards away, and the gun's carriage was shattered. De Gress had noticed a flaw in the reinforcing band while trying to adjust that piece so as to fire at targets on Kennesaw Mountain on June 25 and had been careful not to stress it since.[21]

After this, the infantrymen realized it was better to let De Gress handle the artillery, and he recruited several infantrymen from both regiments to help his men serve the first piece they put back into action. The soldiers carried ammunition and even rammed it home under De Gress's supervision. Later, he managed to unspike a third piece. Nevertheless, the battery was in shambles as a military unit, even though three-fourths of the Parrotts were operable. De Gress could not have moved them because twenty-nine of his horses had been killed on the spot and another ten horses had been taken away by the Confederates, who had also cut the harness left behind. The enemy also had taken away his ambulance and two limbers. De Gress had lost two men killed, six wounded, and nine missing.[22]

South of the battery location, the left flank of the 12th Illinois came in along the north edge of the railroad track. The regiment settled into the recaptured Union line and nabbed 80 Confederate prisoners along the sector from the railroad to the Troup Hurt House. Adams noticed about 50 others cowering within the trench ready to give up and arranged for them to do so. He was struck by the sight of a Black man among them, the personal servant of some Rebel. Boyd reported that his 66th Illinois captured a total of 210 prisoners on July 22 but did not differentiate between those taken earlier in the day at Sugar Creek and those captured at the restoration of the Fifteenth Corps line. But an officer of the 81st Ohio indicated that his regiment took 29 prisoners in this attack compared to 226 taken in the unit's first fight earlier that afternoon. It is possible that Mersy's brigade took in 190 prisoners while restoring Lightburn's position.[23]

Very soon after Adams's success, Edward Jonas tried to find a responsible officer and tell him that Dodge wanted the brigade returned to the Sixteenth Corps sector as soon as possible. He could not locate Logan but found Brig. Gen. Morgan L. Smith, temporary commander of the Fifteenth Corps. "Say to Gen. Dodge that his Brigade has done nobly and shall have full credit in my official report," Smith told him while he retained the brigade for a while until everything had been settled in the area.[24]

But Smith failed to fulfill his promise, not even submitting a report of the battle. His assistant adjutant general, who wrote a report covering the Second Division, Fifteenth Corps during the entire campaign, barely acknowledged that Dodge's men had been involved in the recapture of the line. Capt. Gordon Lofland merely mentioned that, "with the assistance" of a Sixteenth Corps brigade, Lightburn's troops had restored their own position. He did not even identify the assisting command. This was a shameful way to cover up the fact that Lightburn's men were incapable of recapturing their line without assistance from Dodge. Mersy's men deserved much better.[25]

Very soon after the Sixteenth Corps troops broke the Confederate hold on the Fifteenth Corps line, Woods's division came into the picture. Woods led 2,033 men, 1,063 in Milo Smith's First Brigade and 970 in Williamson's Second Brigade. From their starting point at and east of Copenhill, they had to cross the low and swampy ground of the intervening swale. Williamson, on the right, could strike the Confederate left flank with his right wing, while Smith, on the left, needed to swing round to confront the Rebels head on. Woods had waited a short time to see if the Confederates mounted an attempt to expand their breakthrough by attacking Copenhill from the south. When that did not happen, he ordered the division to advance.[26]

Williamson had Lt. Col. Samuel D. Nichols's 4th Iowa on the right of his first line and Col. David Carskaddon's 9th Iowa on the left, while Col. George A. Stone's 25th Iowa held the second line. The formation descended the southern slope of Copenhill and negotiated the low area. Here a ravine with stagnant water stood in the way, its sides engulfed in brush, brambles, and fallen timber. This caused some delay in Williamson's movement, forcing him to pause on the southern side of the swale to reform his lines. Williamson claimed that all this was done "in the shortest possible time in which a work of this kind could be done."[27]

Exactly when Williamson hit the Confederates became a matter of opinion. Some men claimed it was nearly simultaneous with Mersy's strike, but more likely it occurred a few minutes later. Williamson approached from

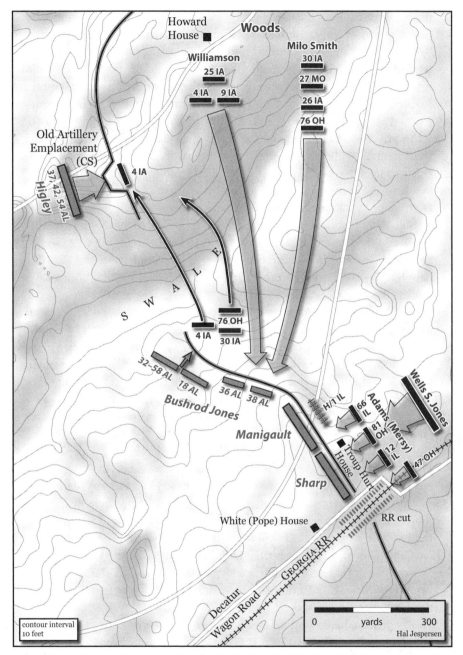

Woods

Howard
House

Williamson

25 IA

4 IA   9 IA

Milo Smith

30 IA

27 MO

26 IA

76 OH

Old Artillery
Emplacement
(CS)

37, 42, 54 AL
Higley

4 IA

S   W   A   L   E

76 OH

4 IA

30 IA

32–58 AL

18 AL

36 AL   38 AL

Bushrod Jones

Manigault

Sharp

White (Pope) House

Wells S. Jones

H/1 IL

66 IL

Adams (Mersy)

81 OH

Troup Hurt House

12 IL

47 OH

RR cut

Decatur

Wagon Road

Georgia RR

contour interval
10 feet

0   yards   300

Hal Jespersen

Union Counterattack North of Railroad

the north rather than the east. His regiments hit the 36th Alabama and 38th Alabama of Col. Bushrod Jones's command, located north of Manigault's Brigade in the dogleg of the Union trench line. Unsupported and outnumbered by this fresh Union formation, the Alabamians fled after offering scant resistance. The Federals not only reclaimed the dogleg but also moved south to the location of De Gress's battery, giving rise to claims that Woods's command was responsible for recapturing those guns. From Williamson down to his privates, brigade members tried to take responsibility for saving the most famous artillery unit engaged in the battle, but that honor belongs solely to the troops of Mersy's brigade. Sixteenth Corps men reported that Williamson's command arrived at the battery site anywhere from five to twenty minutes after they retook the guns.[28]

Milo Smith's brigade also negotiated the ravine at the bottom of the swale and then swung right to close on the target. According to most accounts, the brigade was arrayed in a column of regiments, with Col. William B. Woods (Charles's brother) and the 76th Ohio in front, followed by Lt. Col. Thomas G. Ferreby's 26th Iowa, then Maj. Dennis O'Connor's 27th Missouri, and Lt. Col. Aurelius Roberts's 30th Iowa in rear. The left flank of Manigault's Brigade, located north of De Gress's battery site, and possibly the 36th Alabama and 38th Alabama in the dogleg, opened fire when Smith was 100 yards away. The brigade's advance slowed, and the four regimental lines merged into one mass of Federals who fired back and continued to surge forward. The fight did not last long. As Williamson pressed ahead to the right, what was left of the Confederate position north of the railroad collapsed.[29]

All advantages had suddenly shifted to the Federals. Maj. Gen. Henry D. Clayton, riding along the rear of the Confederate line, saw what was happening and issued orders for not only Bushrod Jones but also Manigault to evacuate the trench and reform 100 yards to the west. Where Brig. Gen. John C. Brown was at this time is unknown. Bushrod Jones pulled out when the Federals were only thirty paces from his position. "The regiment acted well until almost cut off," reported Lt. John C. Dumas of the 38th Alabama, "when it became necessary for each man to take care of himself or be captured." Maj. Shep. Ruffin, commander of the 38th Alabama, "was shot down" during the fall back.[30]

The 36th Alabama waited until Federal troops were twenty paces from its works and then "left in disorder." The left wing of Bushrod Jones's command, the 18th Alabama and the consolidated 32nd and 58th Alabama, never made it into the captured Union works before Woods's attack and were not involved in the furtive defense of those trenches. Jones lost many Union prisoners, letting them go as his Alabamians escaped.[31]

Members of Milo Smith's brigade also laid some claim to liberating De Gress's cannon. Men of the 76th Ohio entered the recaptured works and then worked their way south to the battery site. Capt. Charles Dana Miller of Company C recalled that the Troup Hurt House "was badly riddled" by artillery fire. He found some Union prisoners still held by their guards inside the shattered building and quickly reversed their status. William Royal Oake of the 26th Iowa found Confederates robbing wounded Union men inside the house and took them prisoners. The desire to grab material goods seems to have been widespread among the Confederates. Crosby Johnson of the 76th Ohio found a dead Rebel with three Union knapsacks strapped on his body. "He wanted all the plunder he could get, and got too much of it," Johnson mused.[32]

The infusion of reinforcements turned the tide in the struggle for the earthworks north of the Georgia Railroad. Mersy's brigade played the leading role after its hard fight with Walker's Division earlier that afternoon, while Woods's command came from Copenhill fresh and ready for action. The restoration of the Union line occurred so fast in part because the Confederates had done little to consolidate much less expand their position. Neither Brown nor Clayton offered any guidance in shoring up their gains or in pushing their troops forward to exploit their limited success. While Sharp and Manigault had their brigades well in hand, Bushrod Jones had only the right wing of his brigade in the works. A significant gap still existed between his right and Manigault, and no Rebel troops manned the works to the left because Jones's left wing was unable to reach that position before the blue storm hit. Mersy's command punched a big hole in the Confederate position from the east while Woods cleaned out the rest from the north. "It would not be fair to say that we could have succeeded without Woods's coöperation," Robert N. Adams wrote after the war, "nor is it fair for them to say that they could have succeeded without ours."[33]

The discomfited units of Lightburn's division contributed in a marginal way to the restoration of their line. They had been chased out of the earthworks and had mounted quick attempts to retake them that utterly failed, but this was not through any lack of effort. Morgan L. Smith had been near the railroad cut when Sharp's Rebels initially broke through and exerted desperate energy in trying to correct the failure of his old division. Logan also did what he could to superintend the countermovement. He met Mersy's brigade just as it was forming for its charge and saw that Morgan L. Smith and Lightburn were in the area reforming their own troops. By this stage of the battle, Logan had been "riding furiously from one part of the field to another," as one observer phrased it, "covered with dust and perspiration." The combined efforts of Logan, Morgan L. Smith, and Lightburn brought some degree of order to the Second Division, Fifteenth Corps, and it was ready for another try by the time Adams pushed Mersy's brigade forward on its brilliantly successful charge.[34]

Logan asserted that Lightburn's men advanced simultaneously with Mersy and Woods, but that is not a convincing argument.[35] All three forces coming together in the same small area would have created chaos, and there is no evidence of chaotic conditions emerging from the reports and personal accounts that describe these movements. There is no doubt that Mersy's brigade led the way, that Woods came in a few minutes later, and that Lightburn's command, at best, followed through behind and to the left of Mersy's men.

Maj. Thomas T. Taylor directed one small element of Lightburn's division in trying to help Mersy's brigade retake the works. He admitted in his report that "it was impossible to preserve organizations intact in such a rapid advance, and regiments were completely intermixed and mingled." In addition to Taylor, the only officers left on duty with the 47th Ohio were two captains and two lieutenants. This hardly could be the type of formation that would have led a successful countercharge, ejecting enemy troops who held a trench. In fact, Taylor admitted that his men reached a point much farther than fifty yards short of the occupied Union trench and a bit south of the Georgia Railroad when they stopped and fell to the ground to avoid "the sheet of bullets which swept over" them fired by Col. Abda Johnson's troops to their left front. Afterward, Taylor tried to urge the men forward without success. It was only when he personally exposed himself by running forward alone did they get up and follow their major.[36]

Then Taylor came up to another line of Union troops that had stalled a short distance from the occupied works, and his men ground to another halt. This was yet a third Federal formation brought in from elsewhere to help restore the Fifteenth Corps line, but they were men who knew the position well. Col James S. Martin had personally led three regiments of his First Brigade, Second Division, Fifteenth Corps from their sector south of the railroad to help Dodge soon after the battle started. The 116th Illinois, 127th Illinois, and 6th Missouri had hardly reached the Sixteenth Corps area when word arrived to go back to their former position. The message came with a strong sense of urgency. In fact, Capt. Thomas Sewell of Company G, 127th Illinois recalled that Logan himself gave them a short talk before the new commander of the Army of the Tennessee had left Dodge. "'Boys!' he said, 'Your guns have all been captured. McPherson has been killed!' and with a terrible oath, 'These guns must be retaken. Let your battle cry be McPherson and revenge!'" Sewell felt that the moment had come "when we must sacrifice everything for our country."[37]

Martin moved his men as fast as they could go without utterly exhausting them in the process. When they reached the embattled area, survivors of Battery A, 1st Illinois Light Artillery begged them with tears in their eyes to retake their guns at the railroad cut. They also joined with Col. Samuel R. Mott, who was in charge of the brigade sector just to the battery's south when the Confederates broke through and had evacuated the 55th Illinois and 57th Ohio from the works. Mott now was reorganizing his two regiments in preparation for a counterstrike when Martin came up. The men of the 116th Illinois, 127th Illinois, and 6th Missouri did not stop to remove their knapsacks or to properly align with the 57th Ohio and 55th Illinois. They simply moved through the scattered formation of the two regiments and yelled for their comrades to follow them.[38]

Martin led with the 127th Illinois on his right, the 116th Illinois in the center, and the 6th Missouri on the left. Mott followed with the 57th Ohio on the right and the 55th Illinois on the left in a second line to the rear. The going was not easy. Johnson's Confederates offered stiff resistance, and the three leading regiments stalled well short of the captured works. Martin used the word "repulsed" to describe what happened, but it would be more accurate to say that the three regiments halted and held their position. Thomas Sewell told his men "to 'hug' the ground" to avoid the worst of the heavy fire coming from the trenches. They waited only "a few minutes" before Taylor's 47th Ohio appeared, approaching from the rear. Sewell then instructed his troops that "as soon as the column comes up to us raise up quickly, with a yell, and charge with them."[39]

In the center of Martin's line, the 116th Illinois lay fifty yards short of the captured works. A Confederate officer carried his regimental flag out of the trench and tried to organize an attack on the stalled Union line. Capt. John S. Windsor asked Lt. Samuel R. Riggs if he could capture that Rebel color before the enemy formed, and Riggs sallied forth with some men of his Company E. They indeed fulfilled their charge, taking in the flag as well as several Confederates.[40]

When Taylor's 47th Ohio, on the far left of Col. Wells S. Jones's brigade, approached Martin's stalled troops, his right was north of the Georgia Railroad and his left south of it. Taylor pushed his troops forward, the signal for the 127th Illinois to resume its advance as well. Everything now fell into place; the 116th Illinois and 6th Missouri also caught up the spirit and moved forward, followed by Mott's two regiments. Taylor's Ohioans captured seventeen Confederates as Johnson's command evacuated the earthworks and the rest of Wells S. Jones's brigade followed through behind Mersy's command, also claiming prisoners. Members of the 54th Ohio found seventy-four dead Confederates along their old regimental sector. Capt. Carl Moritz

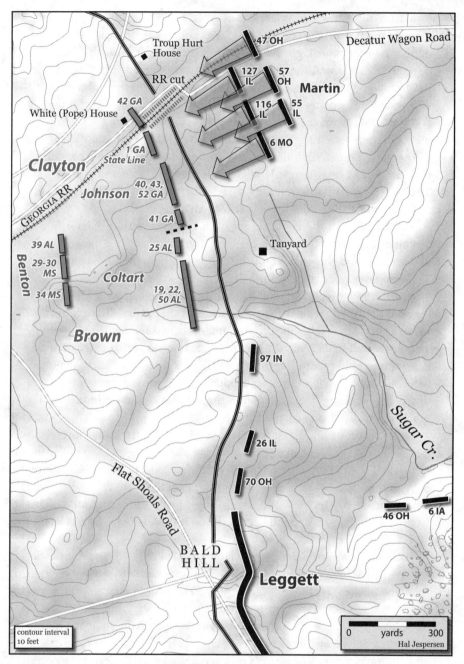

Union Counterattack South of Railroad

Decatur Wagon Road

Troup Hurt House

47 OH

RR cut

127 IL

57 OH

Martin

White (Pope) House

42 GA

116 IL

55 IL

Clayton

1 GA State Line

6 MO

GEORGIA RR

Johnson

40, 43, 52 GA

41 GA

Tanyard

39 AL

25 AL

Benton

29-30 MS

Coltart

34 MS

19, 22, 50 AL

Brown

97 IN

26 IL

Sugar Cr.

70 OH

Flat Shoals Road

46 OH

6 IA

BALD HILL

Leggett

contour interval
10 feet

0   yards   300

Hal Jespersen

estimated that his 37th Ohio settled back into its sector of the line an hour after having been driven out of it.[41]

Abda Johnson believed his Georgia brigade held the captured Union works south of the railroad for half an hour before the Federals counterattacked. In pulling his men away to the west, he encountered Gibson's Brigade of Clayton's Division advancing toward the east. Johnson naturally assumed that Brig. Gen. Randall L. Gibson had orders to help him in an effort to once again drive the Federals out of the earthworks. The colonel stopped and reformed his command while giving thought as to how the two brigades could coordinate their move forward. The appearance of Gibson's fresh formation inspired Johnson, who was "satisfied that together we could again carry the works and hold them." But he was soon deflated when Gibson, without warning, fell back west, forcing Johnson to do the same. Because so many of his men were exhausted and "disposed to rest by the way," Johnson personally remained on the field to make sure as many of them as possible were helped away.[42]

The only Confederates yet to be accounted for were those of Coltart's regiments south of Johnson's position. Brig. Gen. William Harrow's Federal troops were responsible for restoring this part of the Fifteenth Corps line. Logan was active in getting Harrow in gear, sending Maj. John R. Hotaling of his staff to order the division leader to restore his old position. Harrow really needed no such order, for he had been quite active ever since the Confederates broke the Union line. He ordered Col. Reuben Williams to retake the First Brigade position "at all hazards," giving similar orders to Col. John M. Oliver about the Third Brigade.[43]

The Second Brigade sector, controlled by Brig. Gen. Charles C. Walcutt, already was firmly held by three regiments that did not even belong to his brigade. Well before the Confederates had broken the line, Walcutt had moved his entire brigade out of this sector to establish a blocking position that stopped the advance of James A. Smith's Brigade east of the Union line. Later, receiving the 26th Illinois of Williams's brigade and the 70th Ohio of Oliver's brigade as support but not needing them, he redirected both regiments into his abandoned sector. When Cheatham attacked and the Union line north of his sector broke, these two regiments held firm and stopped the further deterioration of the Federal position. At the same time, Walcutt sent his 103rd Illinois and 97th Indiana from his blocking position to help Oliver hold the line just north of his own sector. The 97th Indiana managed to get into an unoccupied part of the trench and hold on firmly, even though the 103rd Illinois could not secure a position for itself.[44]

These three regiments—the 97th Indiana, 26th Illinois, and 70th Ohio—continued to hold their positions and block Confederate expansion of the breach. Along with a movement by the rest of Oliver's and Williams's brigades, the restoration of the entire line south of Martin's brigade appears to have been relatively easy. Coltart observed the movement of Union troops and gave an order for his brigade to evacuate the works and retreat westward. Williams confirmed that his command reoccupied their trench "without opposition." Harrow's artillery chief credited a twenty-minute bombardment of the Confederates occupying the works for the fact that the infantry recaptured the position "without firing a shot."[45]

Soon after the 103rd Illinois filed into the newly recaptured trenches, Charles W. Wills found evidence of an incident mentioned earlier. Abda Johnson later reported that Sgt. B. J. McGinnis of Company C, 40th Georgia had "killed two of the enemy with a spade, picked up in his trenches," because one of them "had just inflicted a severe bayonet wound on a man of his regiment." Wills discovered a Union soldier wounded in the thigh who told him that a Confederate had killed another Federal with a spade near his location. Wills also found another man badly wounded and suffering three cuts in his face inflicted by a spade. This man reported that a Confederate officer had demanded his surrender but the soldier shot him instead and "ran his bayonet through" another Rebel. Yet a third Confederate shot this stubborn Yankee, and the Rebel he had just bayoneted "used the spade on him." This second spade victim still lived.[46]

By the time Williams and Oliver reclaimed their former place in the Union line, all Confederates had been ejected from the break in the Fifteenth Corps position. But one final incident of this counterattack still had to play out. It had begun a short while before Mersy initiated the Federal recovery of the line and was yet another illustration of how ineffectually the Confederates had tried to consolidate and expand their hold on the position. Col. John H. Higley, commander of Baker's Brigade, had been moving three regiments eastward on the left of Clayton's first line during the initial Rebel advance until he lost contact with Abda Johnson to the right. Then Clayton, noticing Union activity at Copenhill, instructed Higley to adjust his line of approach and head northeast. Higley diverted his men in that direction but failed to reach the unoccupied Union line north of the dogleg where Bushrod Jones had planted two regiments of his own brigade. Woods's counterattack drove the Confederates out of the captured works before Higley could reach Jones's position.[47]

Unaware that Higley's three regiments were approaching, James A. Williamson worked to consolidate his Union brigade's hold of the recaptured earthworks. As part of this effort, he noticed an old Confederate battery emplacement located on the northern side of the swale and not too far from

Copenhill. Williamson sent Lt. Col. Samuel D. Nichols's 4th Iowa to occupy the position.[48]

Nichols had barely planted his men in the little fort when Higley's three regiments appeared in the area, leading to a small but fierce engagement. The earthwork was still in good repair, according to Willis H. Booth of Company I, 4th Iowa. It was located a bit west of the natural crest, with a parapet as high as a man's shoulder. Although "overgrown with grass and weeds," it could hold at least 100 men. Nichols filled the emplacement to capacity and lined up other troops just behind it as support.[49]

Higley brought Lt. Col. Alexander A. Greene's 37th Alabama, Capt. Robert K. Wells's 42nd Alabama, and Lt. Col. John A. Minter's 54th Alabama directly toward the 4th Iowa. The Confederates stopped fifty yards from the earthwork and opened fire. They continued to move forward slowly while reloading and firing until planting themselves fifteen steps from the Federals inside. A heavy exchange of gunfire continued for the next thirty minutes.[50]

The Confederates could see the heads of their enemy poking above the parapet of the little work. "The fire on our side was very spirited while that of the enemy was weak and wild," reported Wells, commander of the 42nd Alabama, with "most of the bullets passing high in the air." Because there was no abatis, Wells thought that an order by Higley to charge the work would have been successful, but the Confederates never tried this tactic. Federal accounts also portray the fight as spirited but insist the Confederates got the worst of it. Division leader Charles Woods may have exaggerated when he wrote of the "great slaughter" among the enemy, although Confederate regimental commander Alexander A. Greene was killed in the fight.[51]

At least part of Milo Smith's brigade became involved in this little fight. Smith noticed the action and assumed the Confederates were making a concerted effort to capture his brigade's former position north of the swale. He sent the 30th Iowa and 76th Ohio back to secure the position. While there is no indication that the former regiment became engaged, William B. Woods's 76th Ohio took a small part in the fight. The Confederates fired a volley at the Ohio unit as it moved rapidly northward, and the Federals stopped to return the fire. After that, Woods pushed his men on the double-quick up the lower slope of Copenhill and filled part of the earthworks near the position of the 4th Iowa.[52]

During the fight, Higley hesitated to push his command forward. He did not explain why, but the sight of two more regiments heading rapidly toward the area was the most likely cause. Higley had no support to his right or left, and he might have become aware by this time that the Confederates had been driven out of the Fifteenth Corps position to the south. Rather than try to break the 4th Iowa, Higley ordered his three regiments to fall back.[53]

The Federal resurgence was complete, the captured works fully reoccupied. "The whole was executed in superb style," Sherman told Halleck of the counterattacks that had restored the Fifteenth Corps line. The key to their success was bringing in fresh troops from other parts of the battlefield to spearhead the recovery of the position. Mersy's brigade, after already playing a key role in routing Walker's Division, conducted the first and most important of three countermoves in the Federal response. Woods's division conducted the second one and Martin's three regiments the third. The units that had been driven out of the earthworks, with the exception of Taylor's 47th Ohio, merely followed up as support for these three counterstrokes. It is possible that the Federals lost a total of about 500 men killed and wounded, plus another 500 captured, in their fight with Cheatham's divisions along the Georgia Railroad.[54]

The Confederates were dealt a dismal setback by these Union counterattacks. It had been about one hour from the moment that Sharp's men broke through the Fifteenth Corps line at the railroad cut until the last Rebel evacuated the captured trench and fell back toward Atlanta.[55] But some looked upon the fight positively. Manigault contended it was "one of the most spirited and dashing contests that the brigade ever fought." The cost in blood was high. Manigault reported losses of 400 men among the 1,400 engaged and believed the entire division lost a total of 1,000 troops. A man in the 7th Mississippi stated that Sharp's command lost 212 men. Among Coltart's regiments, the 25th Alabama lost 113 men out of 273 engaged, or 41.3 percent of its total. Reported losses in Clayton's Division tended to be lower. Bushrod Jones was unevenly engaged; his left wing hardly came under fire, while his right wing was in the path of Woods's division. Overall, his brigade lost 18.8 percent of its 678 men. But for the 38th Alabama, one of the two regiments most heavily involved, 41.6 percent of the 108 men engaged fell that afternoon.[56]

Confederate accounts avoid any serious analysis of the attack, its temporary success, and its ultimate failure. Clayton noted blandly in his memoirs that his division "was withdrawn from the fight," and Hood reported that Cheatham's men "had to abandon" the captured works "in consequence of the enfilade fire brought to bear" on them.[57]

Hood's hope that his old corps might support the further progress of Hardee proved utterly false. The fight for the Fifteenth Corps line had no appreciable influence on the tremendous struggle still raging south of Bald Hill. This was a fundamental failure of Hood's overall plan for July 22, a failure to properly coordinate the movements of his disparate forces, which isolated the combats taking place that day into separate but related fights. The fact that Mersy's brigade could march to the railroad and spearhead the recovery of the lost Fifteenth Corps line highlights both the early breakdown of the Bate-Walker attack at Sugar Creek and the lateness of Cheatham's assault. Even so, the sorry level of command and control exhibited by corps, division, and many brigade commanders along the Georgia Railroad contributed greatly to the Federal ability to recover the lost earthworks. Along the railroad as well as south of Bald Hill and along Sugar Creek, some Confederate units performed well, while many merely stumbled through the battle. In all three areas, Federal commanders managed to exert an appreciably higher level of control over their units to good effect. On the army and army-group level, Hood merely gave an order to assault and then took himself out of the picture. In contrast, Sherman watched from the vantage point of Copenhill and acted effectively to set in motion heavy artillery fire and a powerful division-level attack to retrieve a temporary setback.

The Battle of July 22 was not yet over. The bitter fighting south of Bald Hill continued to rage into the evening and early night, even though both sides in that struggle, which really represented the heart of the entire battle, were nearing a point of exhaustion. But the outcome of this main event of the day was still uncertain.

IO

Struggle for Bald Hill

By about 5 P.M., when the Federals completed the restoration of the Fifteenth Corps line, the fighting south of Bald Hill was reaching a crisis point. For the past five hours, Cleburne's Division and Maney's brigades had struggled forward in clearly defined stages, one after the other. First Govan's Brigade smashed the far left of Giles A. Smith's line. Then Maney's command failed to make a dent in the rest of that line. Then James A. Smith's Brigade wandered into the rear areas of the Seventeenth Corps position and was bluntly stopped by the Fifteenth Corps troops of Harrow's division. Then Lowrey's Brigade attacked from the east, aiming directly at Bald Hill and the area south of it, only to be repulsed. In the end, despite Govan's limited success, Cleburne and Maney had failed to crack open Blair's position.

But Hardee managed to bring in new troops to help them. Maney's Brigade, now led by Col. Francis M. Walker, initially detached to help Bate's Division attack Dodge, did not engage in that fight before receiving orders to return to its parent division. Hardee also ordered Mercer's Brigade, now led by Col. William Barkuloo, which belonged to William H. T. Walker's Division, to move to the left after failing in its attack on Dodge's position. These two formations spearheaded a renewal of Confederate attacks on the Seventeenth Corps at about 5 P.M. that ushered in another phase of heavy fighting for possession of the area south of Bald Hill.

Dodge estimated that Walker's brigade left his area of the battlefield between three and four o'clock that afternoon. Not yet under fire, these Tennesseans had done nothing but march around on that "excessively hot" afternoon and arrived at Cleburne's area worn out. After forming line, they had an opportunity to rest a few minutes. Francis M. Walker positioned his command west of Flat Shoals Road and just north of the far end of the Union line, which the 16th Iowa had held at the start of the battle.[1]

Barkuloo brought his brigade from the Sugar Creek area soon afterward. He then formed line to Francis M. Walker's right, resting the right flank of his own formation at Flat Shoals Road. A newcomer to this area, one of Cleburne's staff officers told Barkuloo a glowing story of how the division had already captured 2,000 Federals and several pieces of artillery. Barkuloo later stated that the officer also told him that Cleburne had no immediate need of assistance from his brigade, a strange claim considering the reality of how the battle had gone thus far in this sector. Because Cleburne seemed to have "no use for us," Barkuloo decided to excuse himself from field command. "Being but recently from a sick bed, and exhausted by the fatigues of the day, I here turned over" the brigade command to Lt. Col. Morgan Rawls of the 54th Georgia, "and reported to the brigade hospital." This represented the third change of commanders for Mercer's Brigade that afternoon.[2]

Soon after, Brig. Gen. Mark P. Lowrey came back into the picture. After his first attack, during which his brigade "had been shot to pieces," he searched for a better avenue of approach to the Federal position and thought he found one in the open ground that fronted the Seventeenth Corps line of works. When he suggested this to Cleburne, the division leader gave him the green light to try. In a move that negated the staff officer's report that Cleburne had no use for Barkuloo's command, the division commander also told Lowrey to attack in conjunction with Barkuloo. When Lowrey moved his brigade to Flat Shoals Road, however, he found Walker's and Barkuloo's commands already there. Frustrated that Maney had discovered this avenue of approach and formed on ground that he wished to use, Lowrey initially hesitated. He knew that Maney outranked him and respected his fellow general too much to argue with him. The only thing to do was to form his brigade to Barkuloo's right, extending the Confederate line east of Flat Shoals Road. But Lowrey could not refrain from criticizing Maney in his postwar writings, claiming that the division leader's "tardy movements" unnecessarily delayed the attack.[3]

Lowrey tried to inspire Barkuloo's men, who by now were under Rawls, to their upmost endeavors. "Genl Lowrey then came galloping up to us," wrote Lt. Hamilton Branch of the 54th Georgia, "and told us that we now had the yanks where we wanted them, and that now we would charge them and not leave one to tell a tale." Moreover, "says he, I know that you are just the boys to do it."[4]

In a sense, Lowrey was right. As it turned out, Walker's and Rawls's men had to play the principal role in the next wave of deadly combat because they occupied the key approach to the battered Union position, one that Lowrey had hoped to use with his own men. Walker had a longer march and would have to wheel his brigade to the right, but he also had no unusual impediments blocking the way to Bald Hill. Rawls had a shorter march, but his brigade would gradually shift to the right until its right wing crossed the line of Union earthworks on the way north. Lowrey, to the east of the road, had to deal with many obstacles during his advance, chief of which was the refused Union trench line that the 16th Iowa had held early in the battle and the detritus of combat left behind in a wide area around it. What was left of Govan's Brigade and James A. Smith's Brigade, now led by Lt. Col. Robert B. Young, to Lowrey's right had their own problems of exhaustion and disorganization to sort out, but both battered units would later participate in the fighting. Lowrey, Govan, and Young, however, could not support Walker and Rawls in driving out the remaining Union forces south of Bald Hill.

When ready, Walker began to advance across the ground west of the Seventeenth Corps line. He had about 750 yards to cover, and the landscape, according to Capt. James Iredell Hall of Company C, 9th Tennessee, was an "old field" with "deep furrows and ridges" typical of a cornfield. There were also "a few old trees and stumps scattered about." Some dead and wounded Confederates, victims of Maney's first advance in this area, still lay on the ground. The brigade moved well, and as it began to wheel halfway through the advance, also began to receive fire from the Bald Hill area. "Many of our men were shot down," Hall reported. The incoming fire intensified with each step the Tennesseans took up the long slope. "As I looked down the line," he wrote, "I could see men dropping by the scores."[5]

Hall soon joined them. A bullet slammed into his right thigh, creating a wound serious enough for him to leave the field but not so bad that he could not do so on his own power. But on his way to the rear, a second bullet tore into his left thigh, and he fell stunned between two corn ridges. Immobilized and caught under fire, Hall remained there until darkness offered an opportunity to be rescued. "I remember that the crash of bullets against an old tree which stood near me was as continuous as the ringing of a bell," he wrote.[6]

Francis M. Walker's men kept moving until they lodged very close to the Union earthworks on top and along the north and south slopes of Bald Hill. Leggett's Federals held firm behind their parapet as the Confederates ground to a halt. T. J. Walker of Company C carried the 9th Tennessee's

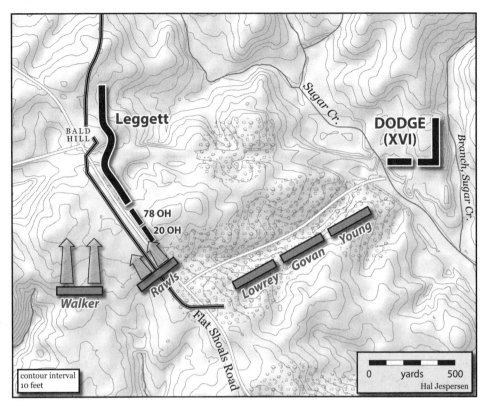

Walker and Rawls Attack

flag several paces ahead of the regiment without knowing it. Only when the Federals called out to him to surrender did the smoke lift a bit and the color bearer noticed "to my horror there was not a confederate soldier to be seen." He and two other men who had kept pace with him quickly retired to their line and saved the flag.[7]

Brigade members took what cover they could find on the bare slope, mostly crop ridges and undulations of the ground, as the Federals continued to fire heavily at short distance. Many more Confederates were hit, especially among the officers. Lt. C. H. Ridley of the 1st Tennessee had been convinced a few days before that he would fall in his next battle and was killed at this point in the engagement. Sam R. Watkins of the same regiment was hit in the heel and ankle and sought shelter among many other wounded men in the low spots of the ground. He watched in horror was an artillery round decapitated a man, "spattering his brains all over my face and bosom," and a horse "was literally ripped open" by another round.[8]

Brigade leader Francis M. Walker also went down. Described as "a modest, sincere christian [*sic*] gentleman, a kind, affectionate husband and father," he had practiced law in Chattanooga before the war and had served as a captain and colonel in the 19th Tennessee before replacing Maney in charge of the brigade. Permanent promotion was in the works for him, and a commission as brigadier general arrived the next day, July 23. But it came too late for Walker to savor the moment, for he died during the fighting at Bald Hill.[9]

Walker's brigade, in its first and only attack that day, had not actually driven any significant number of Federal troops from their position but had played an important supporting role for other Confederate troops. By occupying the attention of many Union soldiers on the top and slopes of Bald Hill, it prevented them from helping other Federals in the path of Rawls's regiments. Moving up along the line of earthworks toward Bald Hill, Rawls's men used the cover of those works to help them push Leggett's troops from that embattled Seventeenth Corps line and back upon the growing concentration of Federals on and near Bald Hill. In short, Rawls's Georgians played the main role in capturing the rest of Federal-held ground south of the hill.

Regiments of Lt. Col. Greenberry F. Wiles's brigade of Leggett's division held the position Rawls attacked. The 78th Ohio faced west in the trench, its right near the top of Bald Hill, while the 20th Ohio stood to its left. The latter regiment would bear the brunt of Rawls's advance, its left flank unprotected except by the traverses that jutted back from the parapet. But the Confederates could take advantage of similar traverses during their advance toward the embattled regiment.[10]

At the beginning, Rawls's troops advanced "in splendid order" but then veered right, crossing the Union earthworks at an angle and forcing the men to jump or crawl over and across parapet and trench. These works south of the 20th Ohio position were empty, but when the Georgians came close to the Federals, firing erupted. The Confederates made good use of the Union earthworks as cover, advancing up the trench and taking shelter behind traverses. Lt. Edmund E. Nutt of the 20th Ohio recalled seeing one attacker pop up from behind cover and fire at his men. A Rebel flag appeared not twenty feet from the left flank of the regiment, and hand-to-hand fighting occurred.[11]

When a group of Confederates began to rummage through a pile of knapsacks left behind by the Federals, it triggered something very basic. "Boys, they are rifling our knapsacks," called out one Ohioan. "Let us go for them all at once." A group impulsively moved south along the trench and captured a number of surprised Confederates, rescuing a few Union prisoners as well. No shots were fired by either side as these two groups of antagonists scuffled since they would likely hit their own men. The result was a small Union victory as the Federal group returned to their regiment's embattled position.[12]

The 20th Ohio continued to hold for a while in the earthworks, but it was running low on ammunition. Several boxes were located in the woods to the rear, so volunteers were called for, and two men agreed to get them. Both managed to retrieve one box each, and spare cartridges from the dead and wounded provided yet another supply.[13]

But the regiment could hardly hope to hold on very long. Soon Rawls's men came, "literally walking over our left companies," as Nutt put it, "pushing them back along the line about one-third the length of the regiment." The 20th men held for a time, but their situation was desperate. Francis M. Walker's Confederates had come wheeling in from the west, forcing away some 20th Ohio troops who had taken position west of the earthworks to fire on Rawls's extreme left. Walker's men also applied pressure on the front of the 20th Ohio and 78th Ohio alike.[14]

Hand-to-hand combat erupted where Union and Confederate came close to each other in the trench line. A man of Company B, 20th Ohio grabbed a Rebel soldier "by the hair of the head" and captured him, wrote Lt. Henry O. Dwight, the adjutant of the regiment. Union officers joined the fray and cut down at least three Confederates with their swords. Struggles for the possession of flags resulted in bayonet wounds, with one Federal grabbing a Rebel color and tearing it up on the spot as battle rage engulfed him.[15]

Under tremendous pressure from the south and confronted by more Confederates on the west, the 20th and 78th Ohio were compelled to give way. The 20th did so by leaving behind a group of thirty men who were closest to Rawls's command to fight a rearguard action as the rest of the unit pulled away to the north. That group then slowly fell back, about fifteen of them holding and firing while the rest moved north a few yards and established a position to open fire and cover the retreat of their comrades. In this fashion (a maneuver well represented in the tactical manual of the day), they made their way along the shortest possible route to safety, up the open slope toward the little fort on top of Bald Hill. This path, however, took them away from their parent regiment, which had gone farther east. Nutt estimated that the group of thirty suffered 50-percent losses on the way, and the survivors crawled into the fort through one of the artillery embrasures.[16]

By this time, the 78th Ohio had already fallen back under pressure applied by the right wing of Francis M. Walker's command. Confederate troops got close enough to grab Capt. William W. McCarty of Company E and three of his men before the rest fell back twenty paces and rallied under cover of the battle smoke. Then someone yelled, "Load quick as we go back to the rebels," and there was a blue surge forward. "We barely had time to ram home our cartridges and cap our guns as we advanced," recalled J. L. Brown of Company E, "and in the thick smoke came face to face with the rebels again. We gave them a volley that sent them back. . . . They were completely surprised." The group then continued falling back, but Company E lost twenty-one of thirty men in its effort to stop Walker.[17]

Force's brigade of Leggett's division, now led by Col. George E. Bryant, was primarily responsible for holding Bald Hill, and some of its regiments got caught up in the forced evacuation of the south slope. The 30th Illinois, located to the right of the 78th Ohio, suffered from a few well-placed Confederate artillery rounds that not only brought down men but also nearly created a panic in the ranks. When the 78th Ohio evacuated its position, the 30th had to follow suit, and a struggle took place for possession of its regimental flag. Color bearer Henry McDonald, who had earlier saved the colors in hand-to-hand fighting with Lowrey's Brigade, now was killed, and J. C. Leird of Company A, 27th Tennessee picked up the fallen banner. The regiment managed to disengage and fell back to the east slope of Bald Hill.[18]

Most of Bryant's regiments remained firmly on top of and along the north slope of Bald Hill, delivering heavy fire at Francis M. Walker's and Rawls's commands. In front of the 16th Wisconsin, which faced west, Walker's men had stalled at a point fifty paces from the Union parapet. A small earthwork, constructed earlier by members of the 16th for the purpose of delivering flank fire on enemy troops approaching from the west, had since been abandoned. It now became the focus of bitter firing. A number of Rebels took cover on the west side of the work and planted three flags on its parapet. For hours to come, both sides concentrated rifle fire from and on this spot until well past the onset of darkness. The flags fell three or four times but were always hoisted again. Charles M. Smith of the 16th Wisconsin fired 120 rounds altogether on July 22, most of them in this final, awful phase of the battle. Bryant did not exaggerate too much when he reported that his men were "literally piling the enemy's dead in heaps in front of the works."[19]

There were more Federal units in the vicinity of the Walker-Rawls attack, but we know very little of their movements during the action. Will M. McLain reported that his 32nd Ohio, part of Potts's brigade, fired away at Confederates who occupied abandoned Union earthworks for some time before receiving word that Hall's Iowa brigade had fallen back to the north, compelling the 32nd to do likewise one company at a time. McLain's comrades retired about 100 yards to the east side of Bald Hill.[20]

Fortunately for the Federals, the end result of all this adjusting unit placements under fire was a solid position on and east of Bald Hill. The fifteen 20th Ohio men who had fought their way into the little fort on top of the hill found it already crowded to overflowing with Union troops. When Nutt looked back over the south slope, he could plainly see Rawls's men "coming up the hill toward the fort in irregular order. They were dropping here and there . . . but on they came like cattle facing a storm, and in a few minutes they were masters of the situation outside." In response, the Federals organized themselves inside the little fort. Men were assigned to watch each embrasure and repel any Confederates who might try to enter. Others reloaded muskets for the better shooters, who in turn stationed themselves along the parapet. It was too dangerous to lift one's head above the earthen bank, so the shooters just aimed the rifle randomly over the parapet and pulled the trigger. This method at least prevented the Confederates from trying to make a rush toward the fort. As Nutt described it, the Federals systematized their method of holding the hill and established a stalemate with the enemy.[21]

About the time that Rawls's brigade finished clearing the southern slope of Federals, the unit lost its latest commander. Rawls was wounded and gave Lt. Col. Cincinnatus S. Guyton of the 57th Georgia command of the brigade. Quickly taking stock of the situation, Guyton found that the unit was in a state of confusion. Regiments intermingled with each other and even with some of the regiments on the right end of Walker's line, which had wrapped around to meld with his left wing. Guyton's men lodged for shelter within the abandoned earthworks about thirty paces from the new Federal position, trading shots with the Yankees.[22]

Guyton, nevertheless, ordered the brigade to continue advancing, but nothing happened. "The men could be induced to go no farther," he frankly reported. Guyton blamed it primarily on the disorganized state of the regiments, noting that officers found it impossible to reform their companies and regiments "under so close and deadly fire."[23]

Francis M. Walker and Rawls had, nevertheless, achieved something that Cleburne's Division had suffered heavily in failing to do. They had rolled up the Seventeenth Corps line after the initial success achieved by Govan's attack on Hall that started the battle here several hours earlier. There is no evidence that the rest of Maney's brigades participated in this final phase of the battle, and Cleburne's Division failed to contribute directly to Walker and Rawls during their advance.

This was a significant Confederate achievement, but ironically, it compelled the Federals to attempt something that Dodge had wanted them to do ever since the start of the battle—form a new west–east line in order to connect the Seventeenth Corps with his Sixteenth Corps troops. The best hope for staving off disaster was to establish a refused line from Bald Hill directly east and hope to reach Wangelin's position as well as Dodge's placement to form a united front against further Confederate assaults from the south. Union officers from Blair on down busily engaged in that process from the start of the Walker-Rawls attack, knitting the new line together haphazardly and under duress. But they succeeded in time.

Leggett tried to control events as far as possible while his left wing was being driven from the area south of Bald Hill. Seventeenth Corps signal officers had a station on the hill that could communicate by flag waving with a station at Blair's headquarters. Lt. Cornelius Conard and Lt. Clifford Stickney worked the Bald Hill station, while Blair's chief signal officer, Lt. James R. Dunlap, manned the headquarters station. Sometime before 4:30 P.M., before the Walker-Rawls attack, Leggett sent a message to Blair requesting a fresh brigade for a counterassault to recover all of the ground lost south of Bald Hill. Blair forwarded that message to Sherman and promised to recover "all that I have lost and drive the enemy easily." But nothing was done concerning this request before Walker and Rawls advanced.[24]

Later, after the start of this latest Confederate attack, Giles A. Smith sent a message to Blair. Signal officer Stickney flagged most of it himself, "for greater speed and accuracy," rather than rely on the trained enlisted men who were part of his team. Rebel bullets cut the bushes around him. The station was only a few feet east of the earthworks, a bit down the northern slope of the hill, and Walker's Confederates could easily see him from their stalled position fifty paces west. Some Federal stragglers got in Stickney's way, and he purposely hit them over the head with the staff of his signal flag as he waved the message to Dunlap. He also flagged another message from Leggett reporting to Blair that he had lost the area south of Bald Hill. Meanwhile, several members of the signal detachment were hit at the Conard-Stickney station.[25]

By this time, Giles A. Smith's division had been thoroughly cleared from its position south of Bald Hill. The Confederates had "doubled it back upon mine," as Leggett put it. Both divisions were "thoroughly intermingled," making for a difficult but not unmanageable situation.[26] Leggett, Blair, and their staff members made sense out of this confusion. Hall's brigade had received fire from Rawls's command and quickly moved north, losing men along the way, as the regiments formed eastward from Bald Hill. Potts's brigade also filed into this new position. Logan fully understood the work; he urged Blair to form a long refused line as quickly as possible and hold on to Bald Hill at any cost.[27]

Some of the Federals did not like the idea of falling back in the face of the enemy. When Battery H, 1st Michigan Light Artillery began to retire,

Richard S. Tuthill entreated William S. Williams, Leggett's artillery chief, "For God's sake, Captain, let us stop falling back and fight!" But Williams waited until the guns were in line before calling a halt on the open eastern slope of Bald Hill. As some men set up their six 3-inch Rodmans, others ran a short distance to the rear to dismantle a fence and bring the rails forward to create a breastwork. It provided "a very fair protection for men lying on their bellies."[28]

As Wiles's brigade fell back, its units found places in the developing line. The 68th Ohio also gathered fence rails to make a breastwork. Maj. John T. Rainey, who now led the 78th Ohio, misunderstood where his regiment was supposed to go and marched past the left flank of the 68th Ohio. Capt. Gilbert D. Munson of Company B, who had already directed Lt. Col. George E. Welles where to place his 68th Ohio, now ran to Rainey and stopped him. "Here is where Leggett orders you," he said, and the major retraced his steps to find the right place. Many 78th Ohio men also ran back to the rail fence and started to construct their own breastwork.[29]

Although patched together, the refused Union line running east from Bald Hill firmed up quickly. Bryant's brigade and Malloy's brigade of Leggett's division held firmly from the fort on the hill toward the north. The 11th Iowa, separated from the rest of Hall's brigade, held the top of the hill and extended a bit east, with the 14th Wisconsin and fifteen men of the 20th Ohio helping them in the little fort on the hill. Three regiments of Wiles's brigade, the 68th Ohio, 78th Ohio, and 20th Ohio, were next in line. Then the 13th Iowa and 15th Iowa of Hall's brigade continued the position eastward. Potts's brigade acted as a reserve to these half-dozen regiments facing south. Two artillery units, Cooper's Battery D, 1st Illinois Light Artillery and Elliott's Battery H, 1st Michigan Light Artillery, were on the right of the position.[30]

This new line bypassed Walcutt's command, which still maintained its holding position that had stopped the first advance by James A. Smith's Brigade. Walcutt was located too far north to become part of this last Union effort, but the developing position that stretched east from Bald Hill came into contact with Wangelin's brigade, which had been posted all alone in the gap between the Seventeenth and Sixteenth Corps since about 2 or 2:30 that afternoon. The brigade had not played an active role in the fighting thus far, but Blair was responsible for bringing it closer to the action. He rode to consult with Wangelin about 5 P.M., instructing him to close up on Giles A. Smith's division and to take orders from Smith. The colonel proceeded to do so, keeping his skirmish line in place to give the appearance of Union strength while moving his main line south and to the right through thick woods and underbrush. This took some time. By then, the Federals were

East Slope of Bald Hill. Taken on June 24, 1929, by a photographer of the *Atlanta Journal*, this image shows the irregular landscape of the battlefield a little more than thirty years before the construction of Interstate 20 virtually obliterated Bald Hill in the early 1960s. Wilbur G. Kurtz Sr. Visual Arts Collection, Atlanta History Center, ahc0197v-504.

forming their new refused line east from Bald Hill, and Wangelin came into contact with it, extending the position another brigade length. Unfortunately, the gap between Wangelin and Dodge's troops still existed, but it was now no more than 200 or 300 yards wide.[31]

Dodge tried but could not close that gap. He instructed Brig. Gen. John Fuller to pull the lone brigade still under his divisional control back toward the refused Seventeenth Corps line. Fuller first removed his wounded from the battlefield where his men had helped repel W. H. T. Walker's Division. Sweeny's division remained in place because it occupied the key ground in the area, a position that had played such a large role in repelling both Bate and Walker. In effect, all Dodge could do was adjust Fuller's line to extend toward Wangelin; it proved impossible to go any farther. As Fuller's men constructed breastworks, Dodge had to live with the gap for the rest of the evening and night.[32]

Fortunately for the Federals, the Confederate line did not extend far enough to front that ominous gap. The last attacks of the Battle of July 22 were delivered by only two brigades, Govan's and James A. Smith's (now commanded by Lt. Col. Robert B. Young), late that evening. Lowrey's

Brigade, originally to Govan's left, failed to keep pace with the march of events, having to negotiate the cluttered battlefield of Govan's first fight with Hall's brigade. Some of Rawls's troops cited Lowrey's failure to keep pace with their advance as a reason for the stalling of their own attack.[33]

As Francis M. Walker and Rawls had conducted their assault, Govan put his battered brigade back into shape and soon was ready to move forward. He had the advantage of marching to the east of the Union line of earthworks, well clear of the debris of battle. His men were still exhausted from their bitter fight earlier that afternoon, so they moved through the woods slowly until reaching the cleared area covering the southern and eastern slopes of Bald Hill. Govan's skirmish line, under Col. George F. Baucum of the 8th Arkansas, cleared most of this area and reportedly captured 200 Federals who could not get away, although Baucum was severely wounded in the process. By this time, Rawls had stalled, and the new Union position was firming up. Govan took in the situation and ordered his small command to alter direction to the left, aiming more directly at Bald Hill.[34]

Govan's Brigade hit Lt. Col. John C. Abercrombie's 11th Iowa of Hall's brigade and the 78th Ohio and 20th Ohio of Wiles's brigade in a bloody collision. Part of the 11th Iowa's Company A, under Capt. John W. Anderson, held the little fort with support from the 14th Wisconsin of Bryant's brigade. Anderson also had the help of those fifteen men of the 20th Ohio who had retreated into the work when their parent regiment moved off to the east. That fort was now the key to the Union position—to lose it "would have been disaster to us," as Abercrombie put it.[35]

When Govan's troops came near, the Iowans opened up a heavy fire. Anderson "was a host in himself," remembered W. L. Wade. Standing in the little fort, Anderson became conspicuous for "encouraging the men, loading guns, pointing out officers, and occasionally doing some rapid shooting himself." Signal officer Clifford Stickney now had to abandon his station because it was too exposed. With little else to do, he busied himself helping in any way he could. When a call for more cartridges went up, Stickney volunteered to bring a box of 1,000 rounds from the rear, exposing himself to fire while carrying the heavy load into the fort, stepping over the bodies of the fallen on the way. The harried troops cheered him; before his arrival, they had been forced to scavenge rounds from the cartridge boxes of those who had been killed and wounded. B. L. Wade was among those who distributed the cartridges Stickney delivered, calling the signal officer "a brave man." Stickney experienced the heat of battle while in the fort. "The rapid hissings of the minie bullets were interspersed with the sharp sounds made by their striking trees boards logs," he wrote, but the worst sound was the distinctive thud when a bullet hit human flesh.[36]

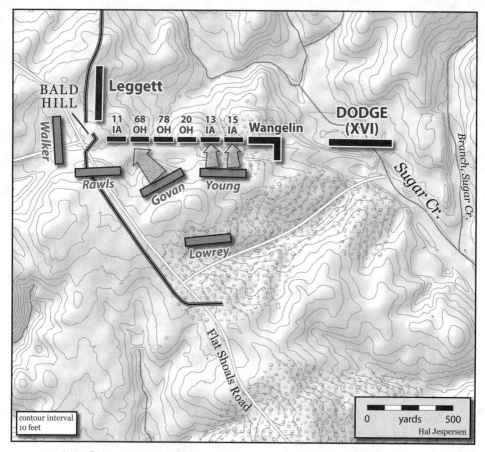

Final Confederate Attack

Govan's assault came to a halt twenty-five yards short of the Union position as the Confederates plopped to the ground. The fierce firing continued unabated. Some of the Confederate troops found "a small embankment" three feet high and seventy feet long only about twenty yards southeast of the little fort. Here they took cover, raised a regimental flag, and returned fire. This probably was a traverse of the west-facing Seventeenth Corps line. It mimicked a similar situation that had already developed north of the fort, where some of Walker's Confederates had taken refuge before a small work located fifty paces in front of the 16th Wisconsin. In both of these instances, the Confederates could not advance or retreat without getting shot. When Stickney saw the Rebel flag flying behind the seventy-foot-long embankment, he grabbed a musket and aimed "at a small piece of a man exposed near" the colors. He never knew whether his shot hit him.[37]

As the left end of Govan's line ground to a halt near the little fort, the center confronted the 78th Ohio. Rainey's Federals were lying "flat on the ground" as the Confederates approached. They fired a volley at short distance (twenty yards according to W. S. Ayres of Company A) and then stood up to reload. Both sides poured in fire, and some Rebels surged forward to engage in hand-to-hand combat with the Ohioans. Two of Govan's men tried to take the regimental flag, but color bearer Sgt. Russell Bethel of Company C knocked one down with his fist. Then Bethel was shot in the shoulder, and the Confederates began to drag him and the flag away. At that point, Capt. John Orr of Company H jumped forward and used his sword freely on the enemy until help arrived to save both Bethel and the flag. Sgt. James R. Earick of Company E took control of the colors for the remainder of this bitter fight.[38]

The 20th Ohio also played a role in this last Confederate attack. Whether it was confronted by Govan's command is unclear, but the regiment at least delivered withering fire obliquely at the Confederates. As cartridges ran low, it was necessary for volunteers to go for more. The grit displayed translated into odd circumstances. Capt. Harrison Wilson noticed Albert Hine of Company F "kneeling on one knee with his elbow resting on the other knee, and aiming his gun ready cocked at the enemy." But Hine did not fire. When Wilson asked him why, he realized that Hine was dead and his body had frozen in this firing position. "The brave boy should have a monument with a soldier kneeling in that attitude," Wilson concluded.[39]

All along the Union line, any Federals able to fire did so, and the field became enshrouded in powder smoke. It had the "appearance of a dense fog," recalled Richard S. Tuthill of Battery H, 1st Michigan Light Artillery. "The smell of gunpowder was everywhere," and Tuthill constantly heard the "unearthly yell" of the Confederates even if he could not see them. It seemed as if "the tidal wave of war" had come intimately close to the Federals as they desperately held on to their last line.[40]

To the right of Govan, the last Confederate formation moved north. James A. Smith's Brigade, now led by Young, had started the battle small like Govan's and had lost quite a few men since then. It now aimed at the 13th Iowa and 15th Iowa of Hall's brigade, the Texans becoming engaged as they drew within short reach of Union muskets. Reports are sketchy, but it is clear that at least parts of the brigade fought heavily. Lt. Thomas L. Flynt estimated that half of the consolidated 6th Texas Infantry and 15th Texas Cavalry (dismounted) "reached the enemy's works, where they fought with bayonets and clubbed muskets," but were "compelled to fall back." Flynt admitted that the Iowans fought stubbornly. The 7th Texas Infantry, 5th Confederate, and consolidated 17th and 18th Texas Cavalry (dismounted) also became engaged.[41]

Hosea Garrett Jr. of the 10th Texas Infantry noted that the brigade charged "pretty much over the same ground" it had covered in its first advance early in the battle. But it did not advance as far north this time because the new line stretching from Bald Hill was located farther south than Walcutt's blocking position. "I suppose I got in 10 paces of their works with the colors of the 10th Texas Regt. but could not stay there," Garrett informed his uncle. He found not over half a dozen comrades nearby. "The men were badly scattered and many exhausted from the loss of sleep and warm weather and long marching."[42]

Young's command endured a heavy crossfire, and at least part of it was delivered by Wangelin's brigade, which was not fronted by enemy troops. Giles A. Smith instructed Wangelin to swing his left around so as to threaten the exposed right flank of Young's formation. Wangelin did so "as far as he could without endangering his own left. The movement gave the enemy a decided check."[43]

The Texans fell back, as much from what Aaron A. Cox of the 5th Confederate called "the inadequacy and exhaustion of our forces" as to anything else. A. G. Anderson of the 7th Texas Infantry was wounded in the arm late in the charge and made his way to the rear. He stumbled upon a small pond at the edge of some timber where James A. Smith, who commanded the Texas brigade at the start of the day, was nursing his battle wound. The brigadier told his surgeon to place Anderson on his horse for a trip to the field hospital, where Smith told the attendants to take care of the soldier after they had treated him. Anderson's arm was later amputated, but he survived the war.[44]

In this last phase of the battle for control of Bald Hill, both sides exerted a rather impressive degree of command and control over their units. Confederate leaders performed better in this phase than in any previous one, organizing a two-brigade assault that finally cleared the Federals from south of the hill. Another two-brigade effort made a vigorous attempt to crack the new Union line stretching east from Bald Hill. That both efforts stalled was not due to bad leadership. On the Union side, much credit needs to be accorded a wide range of regimental, brigade, and division leaders, even Blair on the corps level, for patching together the formation that finally stopped all Confederate efforts to roll up the Army of the Tennessee.

The Battle of July 22 was essentially over, except for continued exchanges of firing on and near Bald Hill that lasted well past darkness. Several Federal observers asserted that the last attacks by Walker, Rawls, Govan, and Young were the worst of the battle. "In this part of the day our troops showed their true soldierly qualities," wrote Leggett. "They stood like rocks of adamant."

The fighting lasted until dusk, which occurred at 7:50 P.M., making for nearly eight hours of bitter fighting on this part of the battlefield. Although battered and driven from all the ground originally occupied by Giles A. Smith's division and part of Leggett's division, the Federals had held on to Bald Hill, the key to their position, and had saved Sherman's left flank.[45]

II

Decatur and the Rest of July 22

The great battle fought at Sugar Creek and along the earthwork line at Bald Hill and the Georgia Railroad overshadowed a much smaller fight at Decatur on the afternoon of July 22. Although marginal, it was an important struggle; at stake were 1,600 Union army wagons loaded with supplies of all kinds for Logan's men. The Federals were caught by surprise and barely had enough manpower to have a chance of protecting them. Only through skillful use of the few regiments and batteries available, and a great deal of tough fighting by Union troops, could the wagons be saved.

The Army of the Tennessee did not have all of its trains at Decatur. The wagons were parceled out across a wide area to the rear of the embattled earthwork line all the way to Decatur, but the concentration at the town represented a huge proportion of those available to Sherman's left wing. More were parked to the rear of their respective corps and in some cases had barely gotten away, under fire, when the Confederates attacked Blair and Morgan L. Smith.[1]

Col. John W. Sprague was in charge of Decatur that day, but he had only three regiments of his Second Brigade, Fourth Division, Left Wing, Sixteenth Corps: Col. John J. Cladek's 35th New Jersey, Lt. Col. Charles E. Brown's 63rd Ohio, and Col. Milton Montgomery's 25th Wisconsin. Col. Wager Swayne's 43rd Ohio, also of the Second Brigade, was guarding more trains farther north at Roswell. A section of Battery C, 1st Michigan Light Artillery, under Lt. Henry Shier, was available, and Sprague had the cooperation of some elements of Brig. Gen. Kenner Garrard's cavalry division. That mounted unit had left Decatur for its raid toward Covington on July 21, which led to Sprague's assignment to the town. Garrard had left behind two sections of the Chicago Board of Trade Battery, under the command of Lt. Trumbull D. Griffin and Lt. Henry Bennett, comprising four 10-pounder Parrotts. The 1,600 wagons were parked about a mile north of Decatur, and Sprague positioned his troops in various places about the town.[2]

No one had any inkling of trouble when the sun reached zenith and ushered in the afternoon of July 22. At that time, just before the fight began for Dodge and Blair, Maj. Gen. Joseph Wheeler reported to Lt. Gen. William J. Hardee that he had just received word of a large Union mounted force heading toward Covington. Hardee told him not to pursue but to continue advancing his own cavalry force toward Decatur, believing "the attack about to be made would cause the raiders to return." Hardee was wrong on that score but right to ignore the relatively insignificant consequences of Garrard's destruction of the Georgia Railroad, a line that already had been denied to the Confederates by Sherman.[3]

Because of an almost complete lack of reports and personal accounts by the Confederates, it is difficult to determine how many men Wheeler used in his attack on Decatur. He employed most of the five brigades in the Cavalry Corps, Army of Tennessee, although two or three units from each brigade are not listed in Edwin L. Drake's book on Wheeler's operations as participating in the battle. It is quite possible those units were performing picket duty at the time.[4]

But Drake lists at least one regiment, the 56th Alabama Cavalry of Ferguson's Brigade, Jackson's Division as participating in the battle. Maj. Gen. William H. Jackson's command was not part of Wheeler's Cavalry Corps but attached to Lt. Gen. Alexander P. Stewart's Army of Mississippi, which at the time was cooperating with the Army of Tennessee (and soon would be incorporated into it as Stewart's Corps). Brig. Gen. Samuel W. Ferguson after the war wrote an unpublished memoir in which, although poorly written and sometimes confusing, he discussed taking part in the Battle of Decatur but failed to give any details beyond those of a personal nature.[5]

Along with the bulk of Wheeler's five brigades we must add at least part of Ferguson's Brigade and some artillery, although the sources are completely unclear as to how many guns and which batteries they belonged to. As far as numbers are concerned, historians have estimated Wheeler's strength as 1,500 men. With Sprague fielding 900 troops, the Confederates outnumbered him by a considerable degree.[6]

Wheeler reported that he personally reconnoitered the area south of Decatur after Hardee told him to ignore Garrard's raid. He concluded that the town was held by a division of infantry rather than by Union cavalry, as Hardee had assumed. He also reported that the Federals were "strongly intrenched," which was not at all the case. When Wheeler sent a message reporting these conclusions to Hardee, the corps leader returned an order to attack as soon as possible. Wheeler dismounted his men and began to advance at 1 P.M.[7]

Far from being entrenched in a strong position, Sprague's command was spread out and unaware of any danger. On the evening of July 21, upon establishing his position at Decatur, Sprague put pickets one mile from town on the roads to the east and south to cooperate with some pickets Garrard had left behind. The brigade commander had also dispatched six companies of infantry, two from each of his three regiments, to support the picket line. These were Companies D and G of the 25th Wisconsin, Companies D and I of the 35th New Jersey, and two companies from the 63rd Ohio. Sprague positioned the rest of his units inside town between the courthouse and the railroad.[8]

By 1 P.M., reports of enemy activity reached Sprague, and he organized a reconnaissance in force to find out what was going on. Initially, he did not think the situation was serious, "nothing more than a few cavalry," as Lt. Trumbull D. Griffin recalled of a conversation he had with Sprague. The brigade leader sent out Companies A, D, F, and G of the 63rd Ohio and Companies B, E, F, and I of the 25th Wisconsin. Milton Montgomery of the latter regiment led the eight companies forward, deploying two of them as skirmishers, until the command encountered Confederates half a mile south of town. Wheeler's dismounted cavalrymen had already driven the pickets half a mile toward Decatur and were obviously "in strong force," as Lt. Col. Jeremiah Rusk of the 25th Wisconsin put it.[9]

The first phase of the battle for Decatur took place there, half a mile south of town, with the Federal line badly outnumbered. The Confederates opened fire from the timber 400 yards from the Union position, and a static firefight unfolded, with Wheeler taking in the situation and planning how to deal with Montgomery's small command. The Federal line ran along the north bank of a branch of Flat Shoals Creek and faced southwest, with its left flank resting on the Fayetteville Road. Pressure on it increased. Cpl. William J. Harris of Company C, color bearer of the 63rd Ohio, was killed. Pvt. Alonzo J. Shuman of Company D grabbed the flag, "waved it above his head, and called upon the men to stand by him for he would die before our banner should fall into rebel hands," wrote Maj. John W. Fouts.[10]

The Federals could not hope to stay there long. It soon became apparent

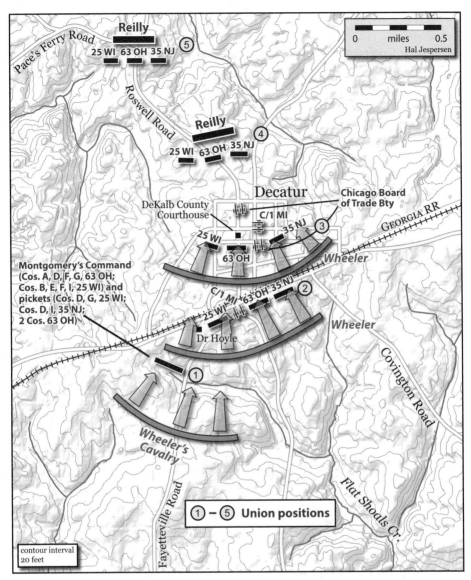

Battle of Decatur, July 22

that Wheeler intended to use his superior numbers to flank the Union position while keeping up a galling fire of small arms and artillery along its front. The primary Rebel move was around Montgomery's left flank, but reports indicate Confederate troops also were working around the right. Sprague was close enough to have an influence on events. When he realized the enemy turning movements would succeed, he directed Montgomery to retire by sliding left and to the rear so as to better come back into Decatur.[11]

The Confederates moved forward as soon as they saw the start of this fall back, and the Unionists were harried the entire way. Montgomery became a casualty in the process. At least part of his command had to cross a swamp and ditch, in which the colonel's horse got mired down, and Montgomery abandoned him. As he did he took two pistols from the saddle holsters and fired at the enemy, receiving a bullet in the arm that broke it between the wrist and elbow. Montgomery was then captured, and Rusk took command of the reconnaissance force. More Federals fell captive while struggling through this swamp, and their organization began to break up, with squads and individuals trying to make their way back to town. Companies D and I, 35th New Jersey, part of the original picket support, was particularly hard hit. The Confederates captured most of both companies, with only nine men escaping.[12]

As Wheeler put it, these Federals "were overthrown" when his men pushed forward, nabbing prisoners. But it was not easy for the Confederates to move through the tangled vegetation. Ferguson tried to ride through a "thick woods of black oak" even though his brigade was advancing dismounted. "I rode into a hornets nest, my horse dashed off, almost scraping me off through the thickets, my hat was knocked off." Ferguson was badly stung on the neck and head. He managed to regain control of the horse but had become lost in the woods. Only by catching glimpses of the sun could he navigate back to his command, where a trooper waited for him, faithfully holding his hat.[13]

Sprague halted the retiring Federals on a rise of ground just south of Decatur along which the Georgia Railroad slanted from northeast to southwest. Shier's section of Battery C, 1st Michigan Light Artillery, two 10-pounder Parrotts, had advanced to this spot and were supported by Companies C, H, and K of the 25th Wisconsin. Two companies of the 63rd Ohio also were positioned on the right near Doctor Hoyle's house south of the railroad track.[14]

Now the second phase of the fight for Decatur ensued. Wheeler's command moved forward and confronted the Federals. It soon became obvious that they held a stronger position than the previous one. Still, Wheeler felt that the Union right wing was in a weaker position than the left, so he began to move troops in an effort to turn its right flank and "bear obliquely" on it, maintaining the rest of his dismounted line to front the Unionists there in an effort to keep them busy. After positioning his flanking force, Wheeler ordered a simultaneous advance by all parts of the Confederate line. Part of his command was "most exposed" to Union fire and began to waver, but

Decatur. Taken at the intersection of McDonough Street and College Avenue from the location of the second Union position during the Battle of Decatur on July 22, the view looks north toward the site of the DeKalb County Courthouse in the center of town. The Georgia Railroad ran along the ridge that College Avenue now occupies. Wheeler's dismounted cavalrymen attacked the second Union position from the south, from behind the photographer, pushing the infantry and artillery of Col. John W. Sprague's brigade back toward their third position at the courthouse (near the building in the distance). Photograph by Earl J. Hess.

officers restored order. At some part of the line, Ferguson's horse was shot as he urged his men forward. One Rebel trooper, Robert Anderson Mc-Clellan of the 7th Alabama Cavalry, described the Federal fire as "a perfect rolling Storm of riflery."[15]

Confederate pressure became very heavy on the flanks. Cladek's 35th New Jersey, holding the left, became "hotly engaged." The 63rd Ohio to his right was driven north across the track, exposing Cladek's right flank as Rebel troops also began to turn his left. His men had stopped the Confederates in their front, but there was too much danger in continuing to hold on, so Cladek ordered a withdrawal. His men fell back about fifty yards and took another stand. "Knowing that it depended upon my regiment to cover the left of the brigade," Cladek was determined to buy as much time as possible in this new position. He sent Capt. John B. Sine's Company E to cover his left flank.[16]

But Cladek was not able to hold very long. The 63rd Ohio once again was pressed back, with the exception of some men of Capt. Frank T. Gilmore's Company A who remained close to Cladek's right flank. On the left, Sine's company was heavily pressed and had to "fall back step by step, . . . contesting sharply with the enemy for every foot of ground lost." Whether by orders of their officers or by spontaneous enthusiasm, the New Jersey men "cheered lustily" as they fell back. This tended to make the advancing Confederates a bit more cautious as they followed up the withdrawal. "The officers and men of my regiment showed no signs of giving up the contest without making the enemy pay dearly," wrote Cladek.[17]

Sprague formed the third Union position of the day in Decatur, centered on the DeKalb County Courthouse. A stout masonry building, it served as a readymade blockhouse to anchor the desperate Federals. The six companies of the 63rd Ohio that had been out on picket and reconnaissance duty rejoined the remaining four and took position immediately south of the courthouse as the 25th Wisconsin aligned to its right and the 35th New Jersey to its left.[18]

The third and final phase of the Battle of Decatur took place there. Sprague believed he had a good chance to hold out indefinitely in this position. While some Fifteenth Corps wagons had been parked in town when the battle started, their drivers had already moved them out and to the north by the time the Federals retired to the courthouse. But Sprague knew that two trains belonging to the Sixteenth and Seventeenth Corps were on their way down from Roswell with supplies and were expected to reach Decatur very soon. This added yet another worry to his already long list of concerns as the afternoon wore on under relentless Confederate pressure.[19]

Federal artillery provided an important element in Sprague's defense of the town. Henry Shier maneuvered the two Parrotts of his section, Battery C, 1st Michigan Light Artillery, with skill in the open areas around the courthouse. He posted them a bit to the left of the position held by Henry Bennett's section of the Chicago Board of Trade Battery near the jail and fired at Confederates attempting to turn the Union left flank. When he saw that Rebel skirmishers were extending farther to the left and rear, he moved his pieces fifty yards back to get a better fire at them. "We caused them to fall back for a short time," Shier reported. Then he noticed Confederates trying to turn the Union right flank and moved his section "farther to the right." His fire from this position stopped the Rebels from reaching the main road leading north of town, Sprague's line of retreat. Then Shier fell back about 150 yards to a point where he could better protect Union control of this road, from which he fired canister to keep the enemy at bay. One company of the 25th Wisconsin moved north to support the guns. Shier provided absolutely essential fire support for the Federal troops. His keen

DeKalb County Courthouse, Decatur, Georgia. Taken as the Civil War building was being torn down in 1898, this photograph shows the second courthouse, which had replaced the original structure that had burned in 1842. This stoutly constructed building faced east and served as the center of the Union third line during the Battle of Decatur on July 22. Wilbur G. Kurtz Sr. Visual Arts Collection, Atlanta History Center, ahc01974v-178.

eye, noticing trouble where it developed, and his ability to move about and stop Confederate advances saved Sprague's position.[20]

Trumbull Griffin's two sections of the Chicago Board of Trade Battery also proved of extreme value to the Union defense. At the start of the third phase of the battle, Griffin left Bennett's section near the jail and placed the other section north of the courthouse in case Bennett had to fall back. Bennett held his own for now, silencing a Confederate battery with "a few well-directed shots." From his post north of the courthouse, Griffin noticed Confederate troops nearly reaching the road linking Decatur with Atlanta. Firing one piece, he managed to stop them.[21]

As pressure mounted all along the front, the Federals became ever more hard pressed to hold their position. Bennett's section was forced to fall back but "became entangled in a heap of old iron and was in danger of being captured," reported Major Fouts of the 63rd Ohio. Company H of his regiment supported the guns to the right and Company G to their left. Fixing bayonets, both companies charged behind Lt. Col. Charles E. Brown and drove the startled Confederates away. This allowed Bennett the time to untangle his carriages and retreat in safety as Brown led the two companies back to the Union line.[22]

The Federals by now were only barely able to hold their ground at the courthouse. Sprague was worried about Confederate efforts to flank his right and also worried about the Sixteenth and Seventeenth Corps trains approaching Decatur from the north. He made a decision to give up the town altogether in order to secure the arriving trains by making another stand just north of Decatur. Sprague had to abandon three wagons of the Fifteenth Corps train that had remained parked in town because the teamsters had ridden off with the mules.[23]

The fight at the third Union position, around the courthouse, had lasted two hours, but Sprague's men gave way just before the Confederates were about to turn both flanks. The Federals reformed on a slight ridge just north of Decatur. Here they received their first reinforcements of the day, as Brig. Gen. James W. Reilly's First Brigade of Brig. Gen. Jacob D. Cox's Third Division, Twenty-Third Corps arrived on the scene. But some troops of Company H, 25th Wisconsin, earlier ordered into the courthouse to sharp shoot through its windows, still remained in town. Philip Roesch, who was among the number, recalled that his comrades barely fired for five minutes before the Union position was evacuated. They found out just in time to run out the back door as Confederates were entering the front and yelling for them to surrender.[24]

Chaplain Thomas Harwood of the 25th Wisconsin had been busy helping the surgeons with wounded men since the beginning of the battle and now witnessed the culmination of the fighting in Decatur. Fifteen to twenty ambulances had managed to bring wounded Unionists from both the first and second phase of combat into town, where the rear rooms of the courthouse were converted into a hospital. When an officer sent him to deliver a message, Harwood was near a house when a Confederate shell plunged through its roof. Two women came running out and asked the chaplain what they should do. He advised them to seek refuge in the courthouse, and they ran to it. What became of them when the Confederates captured the building is not known, but they probably left when the Federals scampered away.[25]

Other civilians were equally confused about what to do as the fighting engulfed their town. A refugee family named Henderson, from Dalton, Georgia, was living in the Banks George Hotel, where they sought shelter in the basement. Another family named Willard took refuge in the cellar of a store until a Confederate cavalryman entered and informed the frightened people that Wheeler had taken possession of the town.[26]

Outside on the streets of Decatur, Ferguson contended that his men had to take the place "house by house," a statement that may have contained a grain of truth. Historians of the Chicago Board of Trade Battery later contended that "the rebels came over fences and around buildings" in their advance toward the guns. But what happened was not a bitter urban battle. The Federals gave way in good order and formed again on the slight ridge north of town for their last stand. They left behind a good deal of material and personal equipment that Wheeler's men eagerly scooped up. "I am now heavily ladened with blankets, oil cloth, serving tricks, letters of all descriptions, besides a ream of paper which I have since lost," wrote Robert Anderson McClellan of the 7th Alabama Cavalry. In fact, it is quite possible that scavenging the battlefield became a preoccupation with enough Confederates to hinder Wheeler's ability to follow up his hard-won success.[27]

Confederate artillery continued to pound the new Union position north of town. Charles E. Brown, commander of the 63rd Ohio, was severely wounded by this fire. Griffin's and Shier's artillery supported Sprague's infantry at what was probably the strongest Union position of the day. The Confederates did not approach much less attack them.[28]

While Sprague waited to see what the enemy would do, the Sixteenth and Seventeenth Corps trains approached from the north. They had started from Roswell early that morning, escorted by nine companies of the 43rd Ohio, five companies of the 9th Illinois Mounted Infantry from Sweeny's division, and a section of Battery C, 1st Michigan Light Artillery, all under Col. Wager Swayne. One company of the 43rd had been left at Roswell to protect Fuller's division train as the other 400 wagons rumbled south. Only when the van of this column neared Decatur did Swayne learn of the heavy battle raging for possession of the town. He stopped the wagons immediately and soon after received Sprague's order to head the train toward the rear of Schofield's Twenty-Third Corps for safety. The Sixteenth Corps train, which was in the lead, immediately did so as did the Seventeenth Corps train to its rear, each taking separate roads a mile apart.[29]

As the wagons headed west, Swayne positioned his troops at the point where they had left the Roswell Road in case the Confederates advanced north of town. He sent Maj. John H. Kuhn's five companies of the 9th Illinois Mounted Infantry to report to Sprague. The embattled brigade leader sent Kuhn west along the Atlanta and Decatur Road to clear it of Confederates, who by now had not only crossed that road but the Georgia Railroad too. When it became apparent that there was no immediate danger of a Rebel advance north of Decatur, Swayne moved his infantry force west a quarter of a mile behind the wagons to protect their move to safety.[30]

With the precious trains secure, Sprague fell back from his position on the slight ridge just north of Decatur, selecting the junction of the Roswell Road and Pace's Ferry Road one mile from town as a good place to establish a defensive position. His men "threw up some rude but strong defenses" and advanced a skirmish line far enough so the men could see Decatur. But the Confederates failed to come out and make an appearance.[31]

Wheeler had intended to continue the fight north of town but was stopped by an urgent message from Hardee. In fact, no less than three of the corps commander's staff members arrived "in rapid succession" with the same message, to "re-enforce General Hardee as quickly as possible." With an order such as this, Wheeler immediately called off further action and prepared to mount his men and ride to the west. Ironically, by the time he arrived in Hardee's sector, the fighting there had ground to a halt with the coming of darkness, and the cavalry could do nothing to help their infantry comrades.[32]

Having started about 1 P.M., the fight at Decatur lasted about four hours. Sprague lost 254 of the 900 men engaged, a casualty ratio of 28.2 percent. He received high praise for handling his badly outnumbered command. "We were, no doubt, saved a serious disaster by his cool judgment and excellent dispositions," Dodge concluded. On July 30, 1864, Sprague was promoted to brigadier general and eventually received the Medal of Honor for his conduct at Decatur. The medal was awarded after the war, reaching his home on January 18, 1894, a little more than three weeks after he had passed away on December 24.[33]

Wheeler never reported his losses, but estimates place them as anywhere from 100 to 400 men. D. F. Fields of Company H, 11th Mississippi Cavalry in Ferguson's Brigade recalled a particularly gruesome casualty. A comrade was hit in the head, taking away the front part of his skull, "but it did not break the membrane around the brain." While another man tried to get an ambulance, Fields waited with the fatally wounded Mississippian. "I had to hold his hands to keep him from tearing out his brains. It was a sickening sight."[34]

The Confederates gathered what they could from the battlefield before the order to return toward Hardee's command arrived. Mostly, this consisted of camp equipage, stores, hospital supplies, and some artillery accoutrements. Wheeler claimed to have captured a 12-pounder fieldpiece, three flags, and more than 200 prisoners, but there is absolutely no support for any of this in Union sources on the battle. Also, Confederate reports that Sprague commanded a division of Federals, was well dug in, and inflicted as few as seventy casualties on Wheeler were flights of Southern fancy.[35]

The surprising thing arising from the bitter fight at Decatur is that

Wheeler failed to deliver a crushing defeat on the Federals. He greatly outnumbered his opponent, opposing Sprague's three infantry regiments and six guns with five brigades of cavalry and more than one battery. Yet the Federals prevented the worst possible result, the loss of their large trains, even if they had to evacuate the town. The result was largely due to two factors—Federal astute handling of their limited resources and Wheeler's obsession with fighting his enemy dismounted. A strong proponent of dismounted cavalry action (he had written a tactical manual that emphasized it the year before), Wheeler became fixated on approaching Sprague's three improvised positions from the front while extending his wings enough to threaten the Union flanks. This was good infantry tactics, but Wheeler seems to have forgotten that his men had horses. Why he did not send most of them riding around either Union flank and gaining their rear quickly is difficult to understand, but that oversight played a big role in saving Sprague's embattled command.

Of course, stiff fighting by Union infantrymen contributed greatly to Sprague's success. The work of his few artillery crews also played a large role in the Federal victory. All elements of Sprague's command from top to bottom worked effectively to pull off an essential success that afternoon. In contrast, Wheeler's tactical victory was meager and bore little fruit.

In fact, striking directly at Decatur turned out to be a poor use of the Confederate cavalry arm, and Hood was entirely responsible for that miscue. For some reason, he was determined that Hardee's turning movement reach Decatur. The town was five miles east of the Union line, and there was no earthly reason for the flanking force to march that far behind McPherson's position, especially when the Confederates knew essentially nothing about what the Federals were doing there. Hardee managed to get approval for most of his turning force to forget Decatur, but he felt compelled to send Wheeler's cavalry there to mollify Hood. As it turned out, the Federals did have precious assets at the town, protected by a force barely large enough to meet Wheeler. But the Confederate cavalry commander played into Sprague's hands by fixating on dismounted combat, and the result was entirely in favor of the Unionists.

Instead of striking at Decatur, Hardee could have directed the cavalry to run freely around the Union rear areas. That would have simulated what Wheeler had done during the Stones River Campaign of late December 1862, when he led a brigade of mounted troops in a circular ride around the Union army and destroyed several hundred supply wagons. The Union trains parked to the rear of the Army of the Tennessee were inadequately protected against a force that on July 22 amounted to five brigades of experienced Confederate cavalrymen. The potential result is chilling to contemplate. In this way, poor handling of resources by the Confederates greatly benefited their Union adversaries, saving them much grief.

While Rebel mistakes played a significant role in the outcome of events on July 22, the Federals could not solely rely on that factor. They also needed to handle their units smartly. Sherman was ultimately responsible for managing Union resources during the battle, and he played his hand carefully. Remaining at Copenhill where he could personally see and hear much that was going on, and where everyone knew he would be so they could send messages to him, Sherman largely kept his hands off the Army of the Tennessee. He fully trusted McPherson and then Logan to handle his old command. The only time he even lightly interfered was to send a message that Logan should restore the Fifteenth Corps line as soon as possible. Otherwise, he watched rather than directed the actions of his favorite army.[36]

While Sherman kept his hands off the Army of the Tennessee, he did want to know what was going on. Sherman sent one of his inspectors general, Lt. Col. Willard Warner, on such a mission early in the engagement, before Blair's troops were driven from the area south of Bald Hill. "Warner, you have been over all that ground to-day," he told him. "Go quickly, and see how matters stand, and report to me." Warner did as instructed, speaking briefly with Dodge, Blair, and Leggett. He found that all three were confident of success. "We have had a d—d hard fight," Blair told Warner, "but we whipped them, and can do it again if they come back at us." Such brave comments were meant to impart a sense that all was well, but they also gave Sherman an imperfect understanding of the true nature of events on his left flank.[37]

Sherman was very active in supporting the Army of the Tennessee. He was well positioned to give directions to Woods's division in dealing with the break in the Fifteenth Corps line and fully directed Schofield in arranging Twenty-Third Corps units to support Logan's right flank on and around Copenhill. He even personally directed artillery placement and firing. Sherman admitted that he worried more about what was happening at Decatur, once the firing there could be heard at his command post, than about what was taking place along the Army of the Tennessee line. He initiated movements to support Sprague even as he urged Thomas to seek out any opportunities to push the Army of the Cumberland forward to draw Confederate attention from the Federal left wing.[38]

To help Sprague at Decatur, Sherman instructed Schofield to send an infantry brigade to protect the trains parked near Pea Vine Creek and to act as a reserve. Schofield relayed this instruction to Jacob D. Cox, commander of his Third Division, who sent James W. Reilly's brigade. Reilly moved to the south bank of Pea Vine Creek and sent the 8th Tennessee and 16th Kentucky farther east "to a point near the Pace's Ferry and Decatur road to protect" Sprague's rear area.[39]

According to Cox, Sprague requested assistance, and Reilly moved his entire brigade forward to meet him at the fourth Union position on the slight ridge just north of town. The Confederates did not press this line, so Sprague and Reilly fell back to the fifth position at the junction of Pace's Ferry Road and Roswell Road. It is curious that neither Sprague nor any of his men even mentioned the Twenty-Third Corps troops, but Cox was one of the most careful chroniclers of military action to be found in the Union army, and his report has to be taken seriously. Apparently, inter-army jealousy prevented the Sixteenth Corps troops from giving credit to Schofield's men. "No enemy was met by any part of brigade," Reilly reported of his movements that day.[40]

Schofield fully understood his role as providing support for the Army of the Tennessee and fulfilled Sherman's instruction "to hold as large a force in reserve as possible" in case the Confederates overwhelmed Logan's command. He left his skirmish line in place but pulled most of his corps out of the trenches and rearranged the units for easier movement to threatened places. To protect the Atlanta and Decatur Road and the Georgia Railroad, he sent Cox with two more brigades from his division to a point about one and a half miles west of Decatur as indicated by Logan. Cox led Col. Richard F. Barter's First Brigade, First Division (temporarily attached to Cox's Third Division) and Col. Daniel Cameron's Second Brigade, Third Division to their assigned positions. He took along the 15th Indiana Battery for further support. These troops constructed breastworks to secure their post. Barter was aligned north of the road, Cameron south of it, and the battery in the center of the east-facing Union line. Logan had also indicated that Cox should help Dodge if called for, and at 5:30 P.M., Dodge did request aid, receiving Barter's brigade. Cox's position was three-quarters of a mile from Dodge's, so Barter's men had only a short distance to march but never came under enemy fire that day.[41]

While Cox moved his Third Division units to support distant parts of the army, Brig. Gen. Milo Hascall moved part of his Second Division to firm up the Union line at Copenhill. When Woods swung his First Division, Fifteenth Corps back to prepare for the counterattack that helped restore the broken line near the Georgia Railroad, the movement created a gap between Logan's army and Schofield's formation. Hascall moved his reserve brigade, led by Col. William E. Hobson, to cover that gap. That placed Hobson partially in support of the many batteries bombarding the target area farther south. Hascall's other two brigades, led by Col. Silas A. Strickland

and Brig. Gen. Joseph A. Cooper, held the Twenty-Third Corps sector of the main Union position facing west. They were pounded by Confederate artillery fire all afternoon and suffered more losses than Cox's units, which were positioned closer to the fighting.[42]

Sherman barely attempted to influence the action of the rest of his army group that day. Sometime before 4 P.M., according to his reckoning, he sent a message to Thomas and Schofield to advance if they saw a chance of gaining a lodgment in the Confederate-held Atlanta City Line. Neither officer thought that was possible, reporting that the works on their front were fully manned.[43]

But after news of the break in the Fifteenth Corps line at the Georgia Railroad settled in, Schofield proposed a major counterattack to cut off Hardee's Corps from the rest of Hood's army. Exactly where and how to conduct it was unclear, but there was no opportunity to work out the details because Sherman immediately refused to authorize it. Not only did it seem complicated and risky but also, according to Oliver O. Howard, who was privy to the conversation, Sherman wished not to interfere with his old command. "Let the Army of the Tennessee fight it out, this time," he said. In later years, Howard confessed that "my judgment would have leaned to Schofield's suggestion at this crisis, for it seemed the opportune moment to strike a decisive blow. Still, if it had failed of absolute success, it were better not to have undertaken it."[44]

When writing his memoirs, published thirty-three years later, Schofield continued to believe his suggestion was the right course of action. He then envisioned leading a part of Thomas's command and his own in a counterstrike against Hardee's Corps "with the hope of cutting it off from Atlanta." Schofield rejected Sherman's wish to let the Army of the Tennessee fight it out. "He does that army injustice," the Twenty-Third Corps commander wrote. "My impression was, and is, that they would have been very glad of assistance, and that timely help would have increased the fraternal feeling between the armies, instead of creating unworthy jealousy."[45]

Sherman opted for the most conservative course of action that afternoon rather than risk the uncertainties of a major counterstrike. He was motivated in part by a desire to allow his old army to shine, but that was a fatuous motive at best. The Army of the Tennessee was literally fighting for its life, and Schofield was correct to think in terms of not only helping it but also taking advantage of the fact that one-third of Hood's army was detached from the rest of it. A major attack west of the Union earthworks would have exposed the Federals to Rebel artillery fire but had a good chance of flanking Hardee's left and turning it decisively. A safer line of attack would have been to the east, turning Hardee's right flank, although that would not have separated his Confederates from Atlanta. It would have taken time to organize such an effort, and the day already was well advanced by the time Schofield proposed the idea, but Sherman's caution led him to lose what could have been a stunning reversal of Confederate fortunes that day.

As it was, the rest of Sherman's army group merely waited in their trenches as news of the desperate fighting on the left filtered along the line. At 1:15 P.M., word of the battle reached Howard's Fourth Corps headquarters, located northeast of Atlanta in the sector between Schofield and the rest of Thomas's Army of the Cumberland. At 2:10 P.M., Brig. Gen. John M. Corse, one of Sherman's inspectors general, stopped by Howard's headquarters on his way to see Thomas. He gave Howard the bad news that the Confederates had turned McPherson's left, that McPherson was dead, and that Howard should prepare to move his troops to the left if called on to do so. By 4:45 P.M., rumors stated that Schofield's left had been assaulted. "It appears that the enemy is rolling his attack down toward our position," concluded Lt. Col. Joseph S. Fullerton, Howard's assistant adjutant general. A half hour later, all troops were put into the trenches and told to be ready for action at any minute. A reserve brigade relieved the right-most brigade of Schofield's corps, which had moved to the left, and Howard placed pickets well to the rear of his line to detect any Confederate flanking movement. By the end of the day, the Fourth Corps was strung out from near Copenhill to the Atlanta and Buck Head Road north of the city with no reserves.[46]

The rest of Thomas's line was unable to mount an aggressive move. Maj. Gen. Joseph Hooker's Twentieth Corps occupied the line from the Atlanta and Buck Head Road to the Western and Atlantic Railroad two and a half miles northwest of Atlanta. From there, Maj. Gen. John M. Palmer's Fourteenth Corps extended the line west to Proctor's Creek northwest of the city. Thomas's command had moved forward early that morning when the Federals realized their opponents had abandoned the Peach Tree Creek Line. But rumors that Hood had abandoned Atlanta soon proved untrue, and the Unionists dug a new line of works that they would occupy for more than a month. The Atlanta City Line opposite was filled with Rebels throughout July 22.[47]

The sound of Logan's desperate battle on the far left could be heard all along the Union and Confederate lines around Atlanta. Like their Federal counterparts, the men of Stewart's Army of Mississippi, the only part of Hood's command unengaged in the battle, stood ready to respond to any orders. Some of them prepared to conduct an attack across the narrow space of ground separating them from the Unionists but no such orders arrived. "We took no part except as interested listeners," recalled J. P. Cannon of the 27th Alabama.[48]

July 22 was a day of intense fear and anxiety for the citizens of Atlanta. The night before, prompted by the sight of Hardee's Corps marching south out of the city, a general idea that Hood intended to abandon the town spread like wildfire. The march had been accompanied by widespread looting of stores and empty houses by Confederate soldiers. Then the sound of intense combat wafted over the city beginning about noon, and it seemed as if Hood intended to fight for Atlanta after all. The anxiety of having Yankee soldiers walk the streets was soon replaced by the terror of a nearby battle. Union prisoners and wounded Confederates began to stream into town, and no one knew what the outcome of this desperate fight would be.[49]

For some families, the stress of war added to personal grief. Fifteen-year-old Augusta Smith Clayton passed away of typhoid on the morning of July 22, and the family decided it was best to hurry the funeral arrangements. "But amid the terror and demoralization through the town, the difficulty was in getting something done," recalled Sarah Clayton. Someone managed to obtain a casket, and a service was held in the family home that afternoon as the sound of battle could be heard. Oakland Cemetery was too near the fighting to even think of trying to carry the casket out there, so Augusta was buried in the garden and removed to Oakland Cemetery many years later.[50]

It had been a terrible day for everyone involved in the Battle of July 22, both in uniform and out. By the time most of the fighting sputtered to a close at dusk, the Confederates had accomplished far more in hurting Sherman's army group than they had ever done previously (or would ever do again) in the Atlanta Campaign. But still, it had not been enough to achieve Hood's ambitious hopes for the flank attack. Although severely battered, having given up considerable ground and lost heavily in manpower and artillery, the Army of the Tennessee was intact and in a good defensive position. Sherman's left flank was saved, even though it had been a very close call and his most trusted subordinate had been killed. In the process, Hardee's Corps had fought itself to a frazzle and could not be expected to immediately carry on the struggle at such an intense level anytime soon. Cheatham's command had expended an enormous amount of manpower and energy on a limited victory, the results of which had quickly been lost.

The Federals were busy throughout the night adjusting their troop positions and preparing for whatever might come at dawn. After consulting with Sherman, Logan made a tour of his battered army to make "the best disposition I could of the troops." He found "one division of the Seventeenth Corps somewhat despondent, but think they will hold their position; have sent them three fresh regiments to support them in holding the hill that I think is the key point to my whole position." Whether Logan here referred to Leggett's or Giles A. Smith's division is unknown, but one could be forgiven a bit of despondency after what the latter, especially, had endured on July 22.[51]

Hugo Wangelin's small brigade, anchoring the left end of the Union line extending eastward from Bald Hill, adjusted its position at dusk. Wangelin ordered his left-most regiment to conduct a left back wheel to the rear to create a refused line facing east. Then he placed his reserve regiment, the 29th Missouri, 150 yards from the left flank of that refused line, also facing east. He posted a new skirmish line not only fronting his main line and the newly refused left flank but also connecting with the older skirmish line he had left at his first position that afternoon when joining his brigade with the Seventeenth Corps new line from Bald Hill. Wangelin had heard that his original skirmishers had by this time connected with those of Dodge's Sixteenth Corps. Although the Federals did not yet have a continuous battle line here, they at least had a combination of battle line and skirmish line all the way from Bald Hill to Dodge's position at Sugar Creek.[52]

At 12:30 A.M., Giles A. Smith instructed Wangelin to dig in. Brigade quartermasters distributed twenty-four spades and collected a few axes, and at 1 A.M. the Missourians went to work. They cut down the "small trees in front for abatis" and dug a rudimentary trench. These fieldworks went a long way toward securing their position. But for Maj. Abraham J. Seay of the 32nd Missouri, it was still an anxious night. He was well aware that the Union line was not continuous. "We were secure only in the weakness of the enemy and another assault expected at daylight."[53]

Sometime that night, Logan issued his second official order (the first announced his accession to command of the army earlier that day). With Sherman's consent, he wanted to shift Barter's and Cameron's brigades of Cox's division from their position one and half miles west of Decatur to replace Woods's two brigades in the west-facing line from Copenhill south. Then he would shift Woods to cover the rear areas of the Army of the Tennessee. Schofield had requested this rearrangement so as to consolidate Cox's command and move it back to the main Union line. Reilly's brigade was to remain for now at its present position at the Pace's Ferry Road and Roswell Road. Logan also cautioned his subordinates to construct earthworks wherever they were positioned and be under arms by 3:30 A.M. "prepared for any emergency." All positions were to "be held at all hazards, especially" Bald Hill.[54]

While all this was playing out, Dodge joined Logan and Blair at 10 P.M. to talk over the situation. The three met "under an oak tree" near the Georgia Railroad. Logan and Blair believed they needed fresh troops from either Schofield or Thomas to relieve exhausted Seventeenth Corps men. Sidestepping his responsibility, Logan told Dodge to bring this idea to Sherman's attention instead of doing it himself. Dodge later regretted that he agreed to do so. Riding to meet Sherman, the corps commander dutifully explained Logan's request and was embarrassed by the response. "Dodge, you whipped them today didn't you?" He was compelled to admit it. "Can't you do it again tomorrow?" Checkmated, the corps commander could only answer, "Yes, sir." He then left, vowing never to let himself be caught in such a situation again.[55]

This interesting story says a great deal about Sherman's attitude toward the terrible fighting on July 22. His desire to allow the Army of the Tennessee to shine was misplaced; he seems not to have fully realized how very close his favorite troops had come to utter disaster and was unwilling even to send fresh units to relieve them after their deadly fight for survival. He essentially shamed Dodge, a loyal and trusting subordinate, into never asking for relief troops again.

Sherman's attitude ran counter to a general practice within the higher commands of his army group that encouraged cooperation without stint between corps and between field armies. For that matter, his rebuff of Dodge's request for help was unusual even within the context of his own command experience prior to July 22. Sherman had never before been so stingy about holding back assistance to any part of his command during a deadly battle. It is not easy to understand or explain this unusual notion, except perhaps to blame it on the anger he felt at McPherson's death. The sudden loss of his friend and most trusted subordinate may have kicked in an unreasonably stubborn streak in his personality, compelling McPherson's army to fight for its survival on its own resources as a form of revenge for his death.

It is unfortunate that Sherman allowed emotions to cloud his judgment, for Blair's men genuinely needed help if the fighting should resume the next morning. Still, Logan was able to provide some relief for them without Sherman's assistance. Bald Hill had been the key to the Union position all day and now was hemmed in on the west and south by Confederate troops lodged only a few yards from the small fort that crowned its top. Firing continued for several hours after dusk, with some Federals reloading muskets for their comrades who were better shots. Those loaders became so exhausted with deepening nightfall that some fell asleep while ramming home charges.[56]

In consultation with Blair and Dodge, before the latter went off on his regrettable mission to Sherman, Logan managed to obtain aid for Bald Hill. Leggett came to join the group and also asked for some relief. When Logan told him everyone was exhausted, Leggett "declared that he was not willing to be responsible for the holding of Bald Hill with his worn-out troops."

Logan then asked Dodge, whose men had done little fighting since the first round of combat in early afternoon, and he was willing to oblige. Turning to William H. Chamberlin, his assistant commissary of musters, the Sixteenth Corps leader told him to send men from Mersy's brigade.[57]

Ironically, that command was the only part of the Left Wing, Sixteenth Corps that had conducted heavy fighting in the late afternoon, when it played the key role in reclaiming the broken Fifteenth Corps line. But, disregarding Dodge's wish that the brigade be returned to his sector as soon as possible, Morgan L. Smith still held Mersy's brigade (now led by Lt. Col. Robert N. Adams) as a reserve for the Fifteenth Corps, and thus it was readily available. Only two regiments were needed, considering the small space on top of Bald Hill, so the 12th Illinois and 81st Ohio were detached from the reserve line and placed under Leggett's temporary command.[58]

The two regiments received their orders at midnight and marched about a mile south to Bald Hill. At 1:30 A.M. Lt. Col. Henry Van Sellar ordered the 12th Illinois into the small fort to relieve the Seventeenth Corps troops. They found Confederates still lodged only ten to twenty paces away and commenced skirmishing with them. When the 81st Ohio entered the fort, they crawled in on their hands and knees to avoid the worst of the Rebel fire. "It was a fearful place to enter in the dark," commented Adams. After the 12th Illinois and 81st Ohio relieved them, the fragments of Seventeenth Corps regiments that left the small fort searched for their parent units in the dark.[59]

The firing at Bald Hill continued until at least 3 A.M., although Blair noted that it became less vicious and accurate with time. For many hours, all that could be seen were muzzle flashes from both sides of the battlefield. After a day of fierce fighting, the little fort on Bald Hill had been severely degraded, part of its parapet had been "shot away, razed to the ground" by artillery fire, as Gilbert Munson put it. Anyone passing by those eroded spots became easy targets even in the dark since the night sky was a bit lighter than the ground. Officers avoided sending their men near those exposed places, but the 12th Illinois still lost five men in ninety minutes of firing.[60]

The tactical circumstances that prevailed at the end of the fighting that day meant that there would be little rest for anyone after dusk. For most of that frightful night, hundreds of Confederate troops remained lodged close to the Union position, and firing continued at short distance. The Rebels controlled virtually all of the ground that had been the scene of combat, and a bright moon shone on the battlefield. "The pale faces of the dead men seen beneath the mellow rays of the moon gave the scene a ghastly and unearthly appearance," wrote Thomas J. Key. In places the dead lay so thick one could hardly walk without stepping on them. In the Sixteenth Corps sector, the opposing lines were not close, and no combat had taken place for hours. It was far easier for the opposing pickets to arrange an informal truce there to allow both sides to bring in wounded and begin to bury some of the dead that night.[61]

On other parts of the far-flung battlefield, similar collecting of wounded took place as circumstances allowed. Blair noted that the Confederates arrayed south and east of Bald Hill could be seen gathering their injured comrades during the night. On the Fifteenth Corps sector, the Federals controlled the battlefield around the railroad cut and thus could bring in many of their own as well as Confederate wounded. About 150 injured men were taken up as half a dozen surgeons worked feverishly throughout the night to care for them. An exhausted Reuben Williams tried to rest at midnight even though he could hear the cries and moans of the wounded nearby. "I fell asleep in spite of the horrors of a night I have remembered ever since," he wrote after the war, admitting that the experience "haunts me to this day."[62]

The Confederates did more than just gather their dead and wounded. While he had a chance, Wheeler examined the captured Seventeenth Corps earthworks south of Bald Hill, expressing surprise at how deep the trench seemed to be. Rank-and-file Rebels could not resist plundering the battlefield of anything useful. "We seen knapsak's piled up as high as a house," recalled Charles A. Leuschner of the 6th Texas Infantry, and "all of our boy's taken all the clothing they wanted; & the rest we destroyed." Leuschner thought almost all his comrades had three or four "daguerotype's from the yankey's." Food and clothing became the most prized booty from the battlefield. "I enjoyed a feast of Yankee coffee, crackers and ham taken from a dead Federal's haversack," boasted William Stephen Ray of the 154th Tennessee. Confederate officers made sure their men gathered military equipment such as small arms, artillery rounds, and ammunition wagons.[63]

For the Federals, it was a night of furtive efforts to catch some sleep, a process made more difficult by the continued firing. Exhaustion came to the rescue for many, as it did with Reuben Williams, but it had been a very hot day, and many suffered from the effects of having become overheated. Most Federal soldiers had lost their knapsacks and the small comforts their personal possessions brought them in the field. But they at least could console themselves with the realization that they had survived the worst day of their war experience.[64]

Near Decatur, well to the east of this frightful battlefield, the Federals wondered what was happening in town and moved forward during the night to find out. Before 8:45 P.M., James W. Reilly personally led a reconnaissance from his Twenty-Third Corps brigade and reported that Wheeler's men had evacuated the town. Chaplain Harwood of the 25th Wisconsin accompanied Sprague's ambulances as they rumbled into Decatur at 11 P.M. He was touched to see women who sympathized with the Confederacy taking care of wounded Unionists in their homes and in the town's hotels. "Ladies, I am glad to see you here caring for our poor boys," he told them. "What do you take us to be, sir?" they answered with a touch of indignation. The Wisconsin chaplain thought it "a scene of kindness and merit."[65]

There was little rest for any combatant during the long night of July 22–23. Hardee spent the entire night working on how to adjust his corps line. When dusk descended, his left flank was facing north and "rested at right angles to and within a short distance of where his right had faced east the evening before," as Cleburne's staff officer Irving A. Buck put it. In addition, that left flank was lodged within a few yards of the Federal works on Bald Hill, and the rest of his line stretched east at longer distances from the Union position. Hardee rode to Hood's headquarters at 9 P.M. to consult, then returned to his command and talked with Cleburne, his right-hand man in the corps. The two "appeared to be in hesitancy whether to give up the ground that we had gained in the battle," according to artilleryman Thomas J. Key.[66]

Daniel C. Govan played a role in the decision-making process. At 2 A.M. he told Hardee that it would not be safe for his men to remain so close to the Union line, so the corps leader decided to pull his entire command back from its close contact with the Federals. He gave general instructions to Govan and Mark P. Lowrey about where to establish the new line and assigned them to mark it more precisely. The two brigade leaders called on Captain Key to help them, and the group did the best they could in the dark. Hardee's command would fall back a relatively short distance to the refused end of the prebattle Seventeenth Corps line of earthworks that Govan had captured at the start of the engagement. The new Confederate line extended west to east, facing north, along the southern edge of the bloody battlefield.[67]

The exhausted Confederates pulled back in stages and utilized captured Union tools to dig in. Govan's men converted the Federal refused line for their own use, but the rest of Hardee's command had no earthworks to convert—they had to dig in from scratch. Lowrey's Brigade then extended the line to Govan's right. Mercer's Brigade, now led by Lt. Col. Cincinnatus S. Guyton, began pulling away from its dangerously close position near the Federals at 3 A.M. and did not complete the move until two hours later, taking position to the right of Lowrey. James A. Smith's Brigade, now led by Lt. Col. Robert B. Young, took post to the rear as a reserve. Maney's command broke its close contact with the Federals on and near Bald Hill, after having fired at them well into the night, and fell back to align left of Govan.

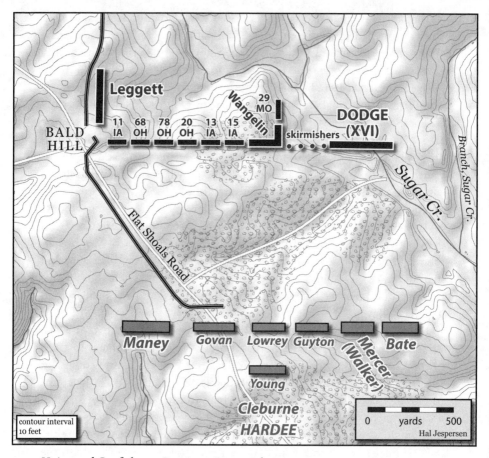

Union and Confederate Positions, Dawn, July 23

The Confederates established a picket line as soon as they took up this new position, but Key found it impossible to finish works for his artillery pieces before dawn lit up the battlefield.[68]

Bate's Division and the rest of W. H. T. Walker's Division, the latter now led by Brig. Gen. Hugh Mercer, also fell back to near this new position. Bate's men retired "a few hundred yards & lay their all night," as a member of the 7th Florida put it. Gist's Brigade, now led by Col. James McCullough, did roughly the same thing. Staff officer B. Benjamin Smith asked Mercer what McCullough should do. "His words were significant of his fitness to command. 'Sir,' he said, 'You must do the best you can.'" So Smith advised McCullough to place 900 of the 1,100 brigade members on the skirmish line to bluff the Federals. The remaining 200 men would form a line, half of them behind the left wing of the skirmish line and the rest behind the right wing to act as a reserve. There would be no main battle line. McCullough did so, resulting in one of the "most anxious" nights of the war for Smith.[69]

Hampered by physical, mental, and emotional exhaustion, the Confederates had slowly adjusted their posture on the battlefield during the course of this long night. After Govan, Lowrey, and Key had performed the initial task of deciding where the new position should be located, work on the second task (moving back to it) and the third task (fortifying the new line) proceeded simultaneously. None of the Confederate units managed to finish their fieldworks that night, but they at least had started the process. Both sides established picket lines in the dark, which wound up being no more than 200 to 300 yards apart. Eventually, by about 3 a.m. or so, silence finally fell upon a battlefield that had known nothing but noise, blood, and death since the previous noon.[70]

12

Aftermath

As dawn approached on July 23, the Federals half expected the worst. "At break of day everybody was straining their eyes to see where the Johnnies were," recalled Granville B. McDonald of the 30th Illinois, "and wondering if there was another days fighting in store for us." It soon became apparent that there would be no dawn assault—the battlefield remained quiet but was still cluttered with the human aftermath of battle. "They lay in every position over the ground," described signal officer Clifford Stickney of the Confederate dead. Close to the Union works on Bald Hill, the bodies lay in piles and in many cases already were beginning to blacken. "The ground was literally carpeted with their dead," marveled Frank P. Blair.[1]

What made the battlefield such an unusual sight was the comparatively small space of ground on which the most intense fighting occurred, which produced, with short-distance musketry, an unusually visible number of victims. John K. Duke of the 53rd Ohio estimated that 900 dead and wounded lay "within a radius of several acres," while Alonzo Miller of the 12th Wisconsin could stand at one place on the parapet and count 50 dead Confederates close by. Observers found piles of up to 10 bodies but assumed the Confederates had begun to collect them in preparation for burial during the night and then changed their minds when called on to retire. Many men counted up to 100 bodies lying in front of their regimental sector. In places where short Federal parapets provided some shelter, the slaughter was even greater because too many Confederates tried to take cover behind them and were hit by the dozens. Houses in front of the Fifteenth Corps line were filled with wounded, and the dead lay in windrows behind them. When David Allan Jr. of the 29th Missouri counted a dead Rebel every ten or twelve paces, he concluded it was "the bloodiest field I have ever seen."[2]

Surgeon A. W. Reese of Wangelin's brigade was appalled by the sights of the battlefield. "Some had fallen forward and laid flat upon their faces, with their white hands clutched full of dust. Some seemed to have sunk down dead at once, and remained in a sort of 'doubled-up' posture—others lay stretched out upon their sides with faces turned to the ground." Those who lay on their backs had "white and bloodless hands, with fingers, spread apart, thrown wildly up into the air above them, and their glassy, open eyes staring with their *expressionless balls*, straight up toward the pitiless sky." Those shot through the head lay "in a ghastly puddle of their own brains which had oozed from their shattered skulls."[3]

Reese also took in many details of the death scene that spoke to the personal lives of slain Confederates. They wore "coarse, gray jeans—coat, pants, and cap alike—the coat a short jacket—single breasted—cut with stand-up collar—the collar and cuffs of the coats being of *blue cloth*." They wore shoes that also were "coarse and broken, and, for the most of them, made out of *untanned leather*. Many of them had shoes on their feet but no socks." He found one large man lying with a Bible next to him that also had been cut by a bullet. An envelope made of coarse brown paper with a Jefferson Davis ten-cent postage stamp on it and a copy of *Litany of the Episcopal Church of the Confederate States of America* also lay near the body.[4]

Civilians also came out to see the sights of this terrible battlefield. Young Sara Huff, only eight years old, accompanied her mother and a number of other curious citizens. She forever remembered that "the ground looked as though it had been plowed up and it was literally red with blood."[5]

From privates to civilians to the highest-ranking Federal officers, many people came out of their protective earthworks and houses to look at this unusual sight. Sherman and Logan rode to Bald Hill at 10 A.M. and were greeted by "the wildest enthusiasm" from the men holding the line. Lt. Col. Willard Warner accompanied the generals and was appalled by the sight of the dead covering the western and southern slopes of this embattled hill. It was a view "never to be forgotten by those who saw it."[6]

Sherman was at Bald Hill when a small group of Confederates approached the Federals from the direction of Atlanta with a flag of truce at 10 A.M. The men delivered a request from Hood for a cease-fire for the purpose of recovering the wounded and burying the dead. Lt. Col. Andrew

J. Alexander, Blair's assistant adjutant general, went out to meet the flag party several hundred yards west of the Union line. He sent the request on to Blair, who forwarded it to Logan. Sherman was immediately consulted, and he authorized Logan to grant a short truce only on the battlefield, as operations continued along the rest of the Union line.[7]

Logan told Blair to send two officers out to negotiate the details with the Confederate party. Because Capt. Gilbert D. Munson of the 78th Ohio was Leggett's picket officer of the day, he was sent along with Lt. Archibald W. Stewart, one of Leggett's aides-de-camp. The most difficult part of the negotiations was setting a line in no-man's land marking how far toward the Union position the Confederates would be allowed to move. They wanted the line set as close to the Federal trench as possible, probably to provide an opportunity to spy on the works, Munson thought. "Some hot words passed, but finally a point further back than they desired was selected." While waiting for these negotiations to conclude, one of the Rebel officers also asked permission to roam the battlefield freely, ostensibly to look for a lost relative. Alexander did not trust him and denied permission, telling him the Federals were strengthening their defenses. The Rebel said with a smile that his comrades "had seen enough of them [the works] the day before." Later, Alexander found that this man really wanted to search for the body of Maj. Gen. William H. T. Walker, not knowing that it had always been in Confederate hands.[8]

Dodge related a similar story from the Sugar Creek battlefield. When he noticed that one of his staff officers had set the boundary line too close to the Union position, he criticized him for it. Maj. Gen. Patrick Cleburne happened to be near and assumed responsibility for it. Cleburne also assured Dodge that he "need not worry because they had seen all of our intrenchments they wanted to the day before."[9]

The other detail to be worked out was the length of the burial truce. Many sources indicate it was only for one hour, but others assert it lasted longer. William F. Graham of the 53rd Illinois precisely timed it as one hour and forty minutes.[10]

Given the short time, everyone had to work quickly. Burial parties were organized on both sides, with orders to roam across the ground up to the line selected in the negotiations. Musicians were used and men were detailed from the line with shovels. In the Sixteenth Corps sector, all Union dead had been carried into the line the previous evening, but Federals there buried Confederate dead within their zone. Altogether, Dodge reported that his men interred 422 Confederates on the Sugar Creek battlefield.[11]

In the area of Bald Hill, where the Federals had no opportunity to collect their dead the evening before, the ground was littered with a number of Union bodies. Details collected and lay them in rows on top of the hill. Comrades found Joseph Fears of Company F, 30th Illinois with eighteen bullet holes perforating his body. Wherever possible, the Unionists tried to give their comrades a decent burial. Members of Fuller's command interred their dead wrapped in blankets at "a clump of pines," while others erected makeshift headboards to mark the resting place of known victims. These headboards usually were fashioned of wood taken from hardtack and ammunition boxes. While the name and unit was scratched on one side, words like "Pilot Bread" and "Watervliet Arsenal" were stamped on the other side. Officers received more attention and care, with coffins hastily made of whatever wood was available. Two artificers of the 1st Iowa Battery made such a coffin for Col. Lucien Greathouse of the 48th Illinois.[12]

On the Confederate side, men were often singled out as scouts to look for the dead of their own regiment and ensure a proper burial. But the Confederates did not take much care to bury Union dead within their zone. According to Charles A. Leuschner of the 6th Texas Infantry, they threw "the dead yankeys' in their own made fortification & covered them up. We buried our dead, each one in a separate grave." Another Texan, Capt. Samuel T. Foster, wrote that "we cook and eat, talk and laugh with the enemy's dead lying all about us as though they were so many logs." The Federals did not treat Confederate dead with such callous disrespect.[13]

To some extent, the Confederates had already buried their dead the previous evening. Four men of the 45th Alabama in Lowrey's Brigade had gone in search of two comrades after dark on July 22. They managed to find their bodies and buried them, using bayonets and tin pans, after wrapping them "in their worn out blankets," according to Thomas J. Wilson. "Not over half a dozen words said in all this," he later recalled.[14]

According to Federal accounts, the total number of dead buried on July 23 was staggering. Logan reported that Blair's Seventeenth Corps either buried or delivered to the Confederates the bodies of about 2,000 Rebels, half of them from Leggett's part of the battlefield. Blair noted that this number actually came from only one-third of that sector; the Confederates controlled the other two-thirds of Leggett's and all of Giles A. Smith's former positions. On the Fifteenth Corps sector, at least 400 were buried, and (as mentioned) Dodge carefully noted that 422 were buried in the Sixteenth Corps sector of the battlefield. By the next day, Logan estimated the total number of Confederates buried by Union details reached 3,220; word of this number spread rapidly throughout the ranks of Sherman's army group.[15]

These numbers were reported authoritatively by high-ranking Union officers and deserve to be taken seriously, even if one is wise to take them also with some hesitation. They amount, as many Federals noted, to a total

Confederate loss approaching 10,000 men on July 22, a number that has been significantly downgraded by modern historians (as discussed later).

The short duration of the burial truce prevented the Confederates from finding and interring all their dead. Burial details were sent out again on July 24, at least by the Federals, to continue the process. Union pickets discovered "several bodies" and many horse carcasses that day. "The stench was sometimes almost unendurable," noted Cpl. Charles E. Smith of the 32nd Ohio. With the hot sun doing its worst on the remains, the smell of death simply grew more pervasive with each passing day, lasting until at least July 27. In fact, according to James Bell, a fifteen-year-old Atlanta resident, a handful of Confederates "only partially buried in a fence corner, remained visible for months afterward."[16]

Accounting for enemy casualties was an important feature of every postbattle phase of Civil War combat, but claiming credit for the capture of enemy flags also was important. Logan proudly reported that Army of the Tennessee troops had taken eighteen Confederate colors on July 22; Dodge's men accounted for eight of them. While soldiers then liked to use the word "captured" to describe how they obtained enemy colors, very often it was inaccurate. As Maj. Matthew G. Hamill honestly put it, his 2nd Iowans merely picked up an abandoned Confederate flag from the battlefield, and many of the eighteen colors Logan reported in Federal possession two days later were obtained that way. Blair's Seventeenth Corps claimed seven Rebel flags, with Fifteenth Corps troops accounting for the remaining three.[17]

In addition to the human debris of battle and abandoned flags, the field was littered with thousands of pieces of military equipment and personal belongings. Muskets, both usable and broken, mixed with canteens, cartridge boxes, bayonets, blankets, and articles of clothing. It took some time to clear up all this material, but when it was completed, the Federals had picked up 5,000 small arms. Lt. Col. Edwin A. Bowen sent details from his 52nd Illinois to recover 147 muskets, nearly all of them good Enfield rifles, and turned them in to his brigade ordnance officer, who found room for a total of 600 small arms. On the Fifteenth Corps sector, Wells S. Jones's brigade also collected 600 muskets. Dodge's men picked up 1,300 rifles and Leggett's division more than 800. There were nearly as many sets of accoutrements as there were abandoned rifles. Lt. Col. Michael W. Manning's 64th Illinois piled these items to be hauled away the next day by details.[18]

For the resource-starved Confederates, collecting abandoned equipment was vitally important. As far as possible, they did so on the night of July 22 while still holding most of the battlefield. Four days later, Hood issued orders asserting the importance of reclaiming everything possible from any future battlefield and setting up a procedure for doing it efficiently.[19]

Soldiers often lost their haversacks, knapsacks, and personal items under the stress of combat. On July 22, that tendency was accentuated by the fighting retreat of the Federals, many of whom deposited their haversacks and knapsacks in piles at the start of the battle and then had to abandon the area under fire. The Confederates found a treasure trove of personal items belonging to their opponents, eagerly rifling through those piles for food and other items such as "boots hats . . . watches [and] knives." Lt. Col. C. Irvine Walker of the 10th South Carolina wrote a letter home on "nice paper" found in a Federal knapsack. Capt. James P. Douglas of Douglas's Texas Battery was proud of the silver pencil and gold pen, "good shirts, a fine pair of pants," cravats, and socks taken from the baggage of a captured Union battery, "such as cannot be had in the Confederacy." He also used a memorandum book and a horse taken from the battlefield. All of this was actually given to him by his men, who had scavenged the material and the animal. At least one brigade band lost all of its musical instruments during the battle, which must have been quite a prize for the Confederates.[20]

The loss of equipment was bad enough, but the loss of personal items hit the Federals harder. Scrounging Confederates found many letters and diaries when they searched Union knapsacks on the battlefield. Some read what they hoped to learn about Union soldiers—that they were tired of the war. Capt. Peter Marchant of the 47th Tennessee focused on a few letters in which relatives of Federal soldiers urged them not to reenlist and to vote for "a pease candidate" in the coming November general election. "It is to be hoped that the people of the north has sean inuf to convince them that the south is not to be whipt without a grater sacrefise than they are willing to make," Marchant told his wife.[21]

Most Confederates adopted a more personal than political focus when evaluating what they found in the piles of knapsacks left behind by the Federals. Photographs of loved ones were especially prized. "Lord, but I should like to kill the one that has that picture," John Brobst of the 25th Wisconsin told his wife, Mary, about a photograph of her he had lost in the fighting at Decatur. "I could kill him with a good heart and clear conscience." For Brobst, knowing that another man possessed the photograph of his beloved wife was intolerable. Incredibly, he had an opportunity to settle this troubling score five months later when a Confederate deserter showed up and befriended him. At first Brobst merely saw this as an interesting chance to get to know the enemy. The two hit it off, and the deserter, Pvt. James Brown of Company E, 6th Tennessee Cavalry, spent a couple of days exchanging battle stories with him. When their conversation shifted to women, Brown said he had photographs of Northern girls taken from the field of July 22 at Decatur and showed them to Brobst. The Wisconsin man was stunned to see his wife and three sisters. At first Brown did not believe him, but when Brobst minutely described his knapsack, the Confederate had to admit it was true. Brown gave the photograph back to its owner. Brobst was pleased that Brown had taken good care of it and told the Confederate that Mary had wished she could find whoever took her image so she could "show him what a northern girl could do." Brown "laughed and wants me to tell you that he sends his best respects and that he has carried you in his coat pocket five months and you were docile and gentle as a lamb, never found a word of fault."[22]

Brobst's story is highly unusual; normally, the scavenging of personal items from the battlefield was a simple equation of loss on one side and gain on the other. But this simple equation was a two-way street—some Federals were able to secure Confederate material as well. Thomas D. Christie of the 1st Minnesota Battery received part of a handkerchief, stamps, and a letter that someone had taken from a dead Confederate officer.[23]

But the loss of personal items was far heavier for the Federals than for their opponents. Lt. John J. Safely of the 13th Iowa lost virtually everything in the confused fighting. "Blankets, all the canned fruit, dried fruit and butter you sent me—that is, what we had left, which was considerable—all our cooking utensils and food; killed my horse and stole my blouse; left me after a terrible hot days work, to Sleep on the damp ground in my Shirt Sleeves."[24]

Those men who lost their belongings were luckier, of course, than those who had been killed, wounded, or taken prisoner in the terrible fighting of July 22. High-level officers were responsible for establishing how many men that entailed. Logan reported two days later that his Army of the Tennessee had suffered 3,521 casualties and the loss of ten artillery pieces. That number did not include Sprague's brigade at Decatur, which brought the total Union casualties to 3,722, according to Logan's report of September 1864 and broken down as 430 killed, 1,559 wounded, and 1,733 missing. The Fifteenth Corps accounted for 1,067 of the total number of casualties, while the Left Wing, Sixteenth Corps lost 854 and the Seventeenth Corps 1,801 men. The number of missing, and the percentage of total casualties they represented, was higher than for any other battle of the Atlanta Campaign because of the tactical circumstances of the engagement. The total Federal loss on July 22 represented 14.8 percent of the 25,000 men engaged.[25]

McPherson was the highest-ranking casualty, and word of his death spread rapidly along the Union line from left to right on July 22. Many men could not believe the reports, but they were confirmed the next day, creating a great deal of gloom. Many men, including Dodge, stated that McPherson's loss was the only thing marring an otherwise sterling day of martial accomplishment by the Federals. Inaccurate reports that Giles A. Smith was killed, that Hardee was wounded and captured, and that Hood was mortally wounded also circulated.[26]

Just as he increased the number of men lost with the passage of a little time, Logan also increased the number of Federal guns lost. By September, he learned of additional pieces missing and reported that his army had lost a total of twelve guns on July 22. Four belonged to the Fifteenth Corps, six to the Sixteenth Corps, and two to the Seventeenth Corps. Confederate sources claimed more than that number. Lt. Col. Robert B. Young, who commanded James A. Smith's Brigade by the end of the fighting, assigned several men to count the number of captured pieces and concluded that a total of fifteen had been taken. It is difficult to reconcile all these conflicting reports with corroborative evidence. James P. Douglas reported taking four captured pieces off the field, while Capt. Thomas J. Key secured three. It is not known who, if anyone, took away the rest, but reports are firm that six Union pieces were recaptured on the Fifteenth Corps line.[27]

Based largely on the numbers of Confederate dead they buried on July 23, Federal officers tended to estimate total Rebel losses during the battle at anywhere from 7,000 to 10,000 men. Rumors tended to place these as high as 20,000. Blair believed that the Rebels lost three men for everyone who fell in the ranks of the Seventeenth Corps. He also guessed that the Rebels on his front suffered a higher proportion of killed compared to wounded and captured since they attacked several times over the same ground. Because of this, those wounded in previous assaults were subject to being hit again in subsequent attacks and to die from multiple injuries.[28]

When the Confederates reported their own losses, the numbers varied widely. Gen. Braxton Bragg, former commander of the Army of Tennessee and current military advisor to Jefferson Davis, placed the casualties for both the Battle of Peach Tree Creek on July 20 and that of July 22 at only 3,000 men, an impossibly low figure. Hardee reported on July 24 that his corps alone lost 3,299 troops on July 22. Irving A. Buck, a trustworthy member of Cleburne's staff, placed the division losses as 1,500 out of 3,500 men engaged on July 22, which amounts to a loss ratio of 42.8 percent. No estimates of losses among Cheatham's men (Hood's Corps) surfaced, but informal reports circulated among the Confederates that the Army of Tennessee's total casualties on July 22 amounted to anywhere from 5,000 to 10,000 men.[29]

It has been easy for historians to accept Union casualty figures because they were compiled authoritatively. But the Confederate army did not operate so efficiently, and it has been more difficult to settle on a reasonable conclusion. Bruce Catton accepted the 10,000 figure in 1956, while Albert Castel rejected it in 1992. "But again a close examination of Confederate sources and an application of what might be termed the laws of probability suggest a substantially lower figure" than the 8,000 often bandied about by Federal participants. Castel settled on 5,500 out of 35,000 engaged as a good estimate, assigning 2,000 as Cheatham's loss and 150 as Wheeler's casualty figure. Richard McMurry accepted Castel's conclusion in 2000. Gary Ecelbarger set the Confederate losses at between 5,700 and 6,300 out of between 27,000 and 30,000 engaged, or about 20 percent.[30]

One could conclude that the average estimate among historians falls at about 6,000 Rebel losses on July 22, but that figure could be too conservative. Ecelbarger noted evidence that the Confederates underreported their losses. When James Fowler, a veteran of the 30th Iowa, visited Atlanta in 1905, he talked with Col. Robert J. Henderson of the 42nd Georgia, who told him he had a hand in burying the dead of July 22. Henderson also stated that total Rebel casualties amounted to 6,381 killed and 10,386 wounded on July 22. When Fowler asked him why Confederate authorities had not publicized those figures, Henderson replied "that they were afraid to give the correct account for fear their men would give up." Of course, it is wise to take this report with a grain of salt, but it may represent at least a germ of truth. While it is doubtful that Hood's total losses amounted to more than 16,767 men, there is reason to believe that the Confederates were loath to publicly report an authoritative figure.[31]

Making a judgment based on available evidence, one can conclude that Hood suffered at least 5,549 losses on July 22. That includes the authoritative figure of 3,299 casualties in Hardee's Corps, the estimated 2,000 in Cheatham's command, and the estimated 250 lost by Wheeler.

Whatever the exact numbers, there is no doubt that the losses of July 22 seared the souls of Confederate survivors. "Many of the noblest, and most gallant spirits in the Army of Tenn, have been cut off," wrote John Henry Marsh, a staff member of Strahl's Brigade. Losses in Hardee's Corps were severe. Among field officers it was "unparalleled and irreparable," complained Thomas B. Roy. "It aggregated over sixty field and acting field officers in the corps; and thirty general field and acting field officers in Cleburne's division alone." Buck noted that Cleburne's Division "was never the same after this sad day."[32]

Both armies were burdened with thousands of wounded men following the battle. Surgeon John Moore reported that Army of the Tennessee hospitals admitted 2,060 wounded Federals and 500 injured Confederate prisoners by 10 P.M. on July 22. Medical personnel worked feverishly to tend them.

In Woods's First Division, Fifteenth Corps, eight surgeons and six assistant surgeons dressed wounds and operated on patients during the night and all the next day, stopping at midnight of July 23–24. This was typical of all other surgeons in Logan's army in the aftermath of this terrible fight. These surgeons mostly had to deal with the effect of small-arms fire. Of 401 wounded treated in Fifteenth Corps hospitals, 90 percent of them had been hit by musketry and only 9.2 percent by artillery fire.[33]

An added burden was the need to move field hospitals as the fighting neared. Surgeon Moore reported that many of them came under fire during the afternoon and evening of July 22. Some hospitals moved that day to escape artillery fire, while others shifted on July 23 and for several days after. "I went with the first load," noted James M. Thurston, a hospital worker in Dodge's command, "and have been very busy unloading the men as they come up and getting them properly placed in the tents."[34]

The Federals had a well-established pipeline for the wounded, with quick treatment in a field hospital and transfer to the rear as soon as the man was ready. In a fairly typical story, George W. Modil of the 20th Ohio was wounded in the stomach on July 22 and treated in the army's general field hospital that day. On July 23, he was moved to the Third Division, Seventeenth Corps hospital three miles east of Atlanta. That hospital was moved three miles to the northwest two days later, and Modil was transferred to Marietta by July 30, arriving in the North a month later.[35]

High-ranking officers received much more personal attention. Brig. Gen. Walter Q. Gresham had been shot in the leg below the knee on the evening of July 20 and had been quickly transported north. His wife, Matilda, met him at Nashville. The attending surgeon advised against treatment in a hospital due to the danger of contracting gangrene, so Gresham was hosted by the family of R. P. Mann in New Albany, Indiana. He stayed for a month in a tent pitched in the family yard, attended by a surgeon from the hospital in town. After that, his wife found a vacant house in which to reside, but Gresham did not improve much for ten months. The main reason for his slow progress was that the bone had been shattered by the bullet, a condition that most doctors believed called for amputation. But Gresham firmly resisted losing his leg. Matilda's patient care was the key to his very slow recovery. "It was a year in bed," she recalled, "most of the time on the flat of the back, three months more before he was on crutches, and five years before he could dispense with those crutches." Gresham returned to his law practice after the war and became postmaster general in the Chester A. Arthur administration. But he came to regret his stubborn insistence on saving the leg. John S. Bosworth, a veteran of the 15th Iowa, met Gresham one day, and the former general confessed of his doctors, "they knew more about it than I did, for, if the thing had been cut off, I would not have suffered half so much as I do now."[36]

Brig. Gen. Manning F. Force was another high-ranking officer given every advantage in dealing with his wound. He had tried to help his assistant adjutant general, Capt. James Bryant Walker, when the captain was hit in the thigh above the knee but was shot in the face while tending him. Lt. Samuel K. Adams, Force's aide-de-camp, accompanied the general on his journey north. Adams assured Force's family and friends that the general's eyesight and speech were unimpaired. Walker's wound was more serious; surgeons recommended amputation but thought he had a chance without it. The wound continued to bleed for several days, but Walker improved enough to offer hope of eventual recovery. In contrast, Force recovered relatively quickly. He spent some time at Judge Walker's residence in Cincinnati, where the judge's widow took care of him, before going to Washington, D.C., to be with his father. Force improved enough to go to a restaurant to celebrate the fall of Atlanta in September. "What a bore it is to have missed the actual capture of Atlanta," he told a friend.[37]

Force's recovery was marvelous considering the circumstances—a bullet literally traversed his oral cavity from one cheek to the other without damaging anything except the two cheeks. He was back in the field by October 1864 sporting what one of Sherman's staff officers called "an enviable scar." But the long-term effects of wounds exacted a hidden price. Force found it more difficult to move his jaw afterward and had reduced sensation on the left side of his face. By the 1890s, the wound caused "disturbed speech and twitching of the muscles of the face and neck." The sense of feeling in his arms, hands, and upper back dulled, and he gradually lost muscular control in these areas. While Force's personal physician blamed all this on his war wound, other doctors disagreed. The general died in 1899. His assistant adjutant general, Captain Walker, had died much earlier, in the winter of 1874–1875, due to the effects of his leg wound on July 22, according to Force.[38]

Those Federals, whether of high or low ranks, who remained in Union hands had a good chance to receive proper medical care. But many Unionists were wounded and fell into Confederate hands. More than one of them was compelled to lie for many hours on the battlefield before receiving attention from the Rebels. Alfred Rolf of the 32nd Ohio was hit in the head and lay all day and night before the enemy took him in, stealing his knapsack in the process. Confederate cavalryman William L. Trask, a courier for Hardee, helped bring in "twenty horribly mangled Yankees" who had suffered for forty-eight hours after being wounded. They were "without assistance, their wounds were fly blown and their condition was terrible. We carried them to our hospital."[39]

The Confederates also had a well-developed medical-care system that began with treatment as soon after injury as possible. For most of the wounded, that meant the initial care took place either in a field hospital or in Atlanta, since the city was so close to the July 22 battlefield. From there, transport to one of many hospitals established in towns along the rail lines south of Atlanta was the key to long-term care. For example, William F. Glaze of the 24th South Carolina in Gist's Brigade was shot through both legs. An ambulance transported him to Atlanta, and he was moved to Macon by train. After eight weeks in the hospital, a board of surgeons granted him a furlough for sixty days to go home. There he received extensions of his furlough until the war ended.[40]

For those not lucky enough to go on sick furlough, the hospitals became repositories of pain, anxiety, and oftentimes hopeless struggles for life. Kate Cumming, a civilian nurse in Newnan, Georgia, recorded many such cases of men with bullets so near the spine that they were paralyzed, men with holes in their skulls and brain matter oozing out, and men shot through the lungs so that blood ran out in streams with nearly every breath. Comrades who visited hospitals often were brought to tears at the sight of their friends' condition.[41]

But there also were stories of hope and resilience. Capt. James Iredell Hall of the 9th Tennessee did not believe the surgeons when they told him the bullet that entered his thigh near the femoral artery probably would kill him. He had been wounded at Perryville in October 1862 and knew he had a good chance to survive. Hall wisely carried lint, bandages, and castile soap, and as an officer, he was given his choice of hospital attendant to clean the wound regularly to avoid gangrene. On the morning of July 23, the field hospital was moved closer to Cobb's Mill as Hardee's Corps fell back from its temporary position of the night before. The next day, Hall was transported to Atlanta, where he boarded a train for Macon.[42]

Enlisted men had fewer advantages than officers in dealing with the sometimes troublesome hospital system. Carroll Henderson Clark of the 16th Tennessee was wounded in the arm but able to make his way to the rear. On the way, he stopped at a branch to bathe his arm, and in the process, someone stole his canteen. At the field hospital, a surgeon dressed the arm and gave him a drink of whiskey. After transport to Ocmulgee Hospital in Macon, hospital gangrene developed; "matter collected below the wound & my arm hands & fingers were terribly swollen." The surgeon recommended amputation, but Clark refused and was allowed to take his chances.

He escaped from the hospital by taking advantage of an offer previously given by a Mr. Leek of Dalton who had refugeed to Dawson, Georgia. Leek had promised to help him if ever he needed it and now took Clark into his home, where he was tended by a civilian physician named Roushenburg. Through a course of morphine to dull the intense pain and waiting for the proper time, Roushenburg lanced the arm to relieve the swelling, and "it began to heal at once." Clark recovered in time to return to his regiment before the end of the year.[43]

Clark's case was not unusual. Many Confederate wounded were farmed out to civilian families after an initial time of hospital care, either by the wounded man initiating the move to a civilian home, as in Clark's case, or by efforts of the hospital staff. Capt. Alfred Tyler Fielder of the 12th Tennessee, wounded in the thigh, was transported to Griffin, Georgia, two days later. M. G. Dobbins, who lived one mile outside town, offered to take him home. The surgeon approved, and Fielder found himself in the hands of a good family in a nice house. His wound improved much more rapidly in these surroundings, with the family applying home remedies such as slippery elm poultices to bring relief from the pain and swelling. After a good deal of healing, Fielder returned to the hospital system and was furloughed home by late September.[44]

Whether anyone survived his battle injury depended not only on the level of care but also the nature of the wound itself. Contrary to popular assumptions, the majority of wounds in any given engagement tended to be relatively light and far more easily survived than serious injuries, no matter how poor the care. Of 396 men who were wounded on July 22 and were treated in Fifteenth Corps hospitals, 330 (83.3 percent) needed only simple dressings. Only 28 (7.1 percent) endured amputation, and 38 required other kinds of surgical procedures. On the Confederate side, of eight wounded in Company C, 7th Mississippi, six were slight. As with the Fifteenth Corps statistics, amputation was not by any means a common treatment for injuries among the Confederates. Of twenty-two wounded men mentioned by Surgeon James Madison Brannock of the 5th Tennessee, only one required amputation. That man represented less than 5 percent of the injuries.[45]

This is not meant to minimize the suffering caused by a variety of battlefield injuries, for there seemed to be a deep well of grief attending every battle for those who were hit but survived. Even wounds not requiring extreme measures such as amputation could be bloody and life threatening. Brannock found time on July 26 to write his wife. "We have scarcely eaten or slept until last night, & have worked in blood until it is absolutely sickening. Indeed for four days I have not washed my face & combed my hair until this morning." Moreover, the mortally wounded man who became aware of his pending fate suffered a trauma all his own. Lt. Samuel McKittrick of the 16th South Carolina told J. J. McKinney that he was willing to die, but he wanted McKinney to tell his wife that he "hated to leave his poor helpless family." Nevertheless, McKinney told Mrs. McKittrick that her husband wanted her "to reconcile it as best you could and prepare to meet him in Heaven."[46]

A number of Confederate wounded fell into Union hands. Although they received good medical care, they suffered from the anxiety and depression that often accompanied capture in battle. According to one of Sherman's staff officers, the number amounted to 1,017 injured captives. "I never saw such badly wounded men as these rebels we have in our hospital," commented James M. Thurston, a Sixteenth Corps hospital attendant. "They make more fuss, twice over, than our men. They don't seem to have the 'vim' that our men generally do, to keep up under intense pain."[47]

Of course, those Confederates fell into Union hands because they had been too badly injured to remove themselves and naturally were suffering more than most of the other wounded. According to accounts, a large proportion of these men soon died. One of these captives who were less seriously injured turned out to be a woman dressed as a man, according to Joseph A. Saunier of the 47th Ohio. She lost a leg due to her battlefield wound.[48]

The Federals scooped up a relatively large number of able-bodied prisoners during the Battle of July 22, although exactly how many is not entirely clear. Unofficial reports range from 1,200 to 1,800, numbers that seem to be reasonable. Fifteenth Corps troops took in at least 481 prisoners, and Blair's Seventeenth Corps captured 500. Sixteenth Corps sources disagree on the number taken; Dodge reported 351 prisoners exclusive of the number Adams's brigade captured during the restoration of the Fifteenth Corps line. But other officers reported that Sweeny's division alone took in 660 prisoners, while Fuller's single brigade garnered 200 captives. Part of the problem of accountability is that there was a tendency to shuttle the prisoners to the rear as fast as possible, and no one could take an accurate count. It is highly probable that the total of Confederates taken prisoner on July 22 reached 2,800 men, but we do not know if those wounded and captured were included in that total. After all, such men did not go to the rear as prisoners but were treated as patients in the field hospitals. If they were not included, then the total would amount to 3,800 prisoners.[49]

The Federals established a system to handle these captives. They were sent to the rear and gathered into a group. On the morning of July 23, Union troops escorted them to Decatur, where other troops escorted them on a march to Marietta. There they boarded cars for further transport north. By July 26, trainloads of prisoners were reaching Chattanooga, packed forty men to a boxcar. Some were able to trick or knock out their guards and jump out of the moving cars along the way, but most of the enlisted men wound up at Camp Chase, Ohio, by early August. Although several captives complained of food shortages and poor sleeping arrangements, others found the living quite comfortable. Many were sent to Richmond early in March 1865 for exchange, but the fall of the Confederate capital curtailed that process, and none of the Confederates captured on July 22 ever resumed duty in the field. Officers were separated from the enlisted men and wound up at Johnson's Island, Ohio, where they sat out the rest of the war in prison.[50]

Logan reported 1,733 men missing after the Battle of July 22, and Daniel C. Govan believed his brigade alone captured about 700 of them in the first round of fighting on the Seventeenth Corps line. But he also admitted that not all of those reported captives were moved into the prisoner-care system because the brigade was under orders from Cleburne not to stop and secure spoils or prisoners but to keep moving forward. As a result, Govan sent the captives to the rear without guards. "I doubt not many escaped through the woods."[51]

Nevertheless, most of the Federals who were captured wound up in the Confederate prisoner system and faced a grueling experience. Many of them were escorted off the battlefield by Confederate soldiers. "Squads of prisoners coming in," wrote a member of Cheatham's escort at 6:30 P.M. Artilleryman Key obtained a diary from one prisoner. Robert J. Campbell of the 3rd Iowa had made entries in it until July 21, but Key used it from July 22 on to record his own experiences.[52]

In fact, taking things from prisoners was a very common thing to do during the Civil War. Humiliating prisoners in public rituals to buoy up popular morale also was common, and treating them as unworthy of care was yet another. Federal prisoners experienced all of these mistreatments as they journeyed through the Rebel prisoner system.

Lt. George W. Bailey of the 6th Missouri served as an aide-de-camp for Brig. Gen. Morgan L. Smith. He was captured when Cheatham's men broke the Fifteenth Corps line. Escorted west to Atlanta, he was impressed by the carpet of Confederate bodies covering the ground for more than 100 yards in front of the Union earthworks. This was a testament not only to the heavy fire Smith's men delivered but also to the close proximity of small-arms fire that took place during the Civil War. On entering Atlanta, a Confederate dragged a captured Union flag in the dust to excite the watching citizens. "Women taunted us with, 'Ah! Boys, you've got into Atlanta at last, haven't you?' Everybody seemed crazed with delight." Poor people were "sneering with scorn or pale with hatred," while upper-class men and women stood with "compressed lips, and eyes scintillating with expressions of hatred." After being enrolled by the provost marshal, the officers were separated from the enlisted men, and both groups began their journey south. The sidewalks once again filled with citizens to see them off, and Bailey could detect "ignorance, prejudice, indifference, joy, and contempt" on hundreds of faces as he passed.[53]

Orderly Sgt. Edwin R. Mason of the 13th Iowa had his watch stolen soon after capture, but he appealed to a Confederate colonel who forced the man to return it. Pvt. John A. Melcher of the 37th Ohio was not so lucky. A Confederate lieutenant "plundered me of everything I possessed," he recalled. Escorted to Atlanta, Melcher saw Hood, who stopped the prisoners and pumped them for information on the Union lines. Passing Confederate units contained men who cursed the captive soldiers and others who looked at them with pity. Some guards tried to prevent friendly citizens from offering water to the prisoners, even turning over water pails, and kept the men moving through the dust and heat of the day without mercy. A handful of captives managed to escape before reaching Atlanta.[54]

The prisoners marched to East Point, where they were herded into a small mule corral. Those who had not been enrolled at Atlanta were now processed and marched in large groups farther south. The 54th Virginia, detached from Brig. Gen. Alexander W. Reynolds's brigade of Maj. Gen. Carter L. Stevenson's division, escorted the prisoners south. As far as James Miller Wysor of Company F, 54th Virginia was concerned, it was a welcome assignment. "We had a very nice time," he told his father, "anything . . . was preferable to the front where for 90 days not a day had passed in which we had not heard the boom of the cannon." The assembled prisoners and guards marched to Griffin, where they boarded railroad cars to continue the journey to Macon. From there, the enlisted prisoners traveled to Andersonville. Wysor knew full well how awful conditions were in this worst military prison of the war, telling his father that 50–100 inmates died every day. But when his regiment returned to duty at Atlanta, he was happy that the ten-day trip had been so pleasant, "almost as good as a furlough while it lasted."[55]

But for the Federals Wysor deposited at Andersonville, their private hell had just begun. Some 30,000 prisoners from across the war zone were assembled there in a stockade with no shelter—the men had to dig holes into the ground for sleeping arrangements. Their only source of water was a small stream running through the enclosure that guards also used upstream from the stockade. It already was polluted and unhealthy. Living conditions inside the prison were inhuman. John B. Shafter of the 13th Iowa went from weighing 185 pounds to 79 pounds in a few weeks. Food shortages, rampant diseases stemming from the impossibility of keeping clean, and harassment by guards amounted to an experience worse than combat.[56]

For many captives of July 22, deliverance was soon at hand. Sherman initiated efforts for a prisoner exchange with Hood on September 9, soon after the fall of Atlanta. He proposed giving up the twenty-eight officers and 782 enlisted Confederate prisoners he held in the city, adding to that number ninety-three officers and 907 prisoners held at Chattanooga, in exchange for all the Union prisoners from his army group. The total of 1,810 Confederate prisoners would cover at least those Federals taken on July 22. By that time, Govan was in Union hands, captured at the Battle of Jonesboro on September 1, and Sherman was willing to add him to the mix. Hood agreed, and Rough and Ready was fixed as the point of exchange.[57]

It was all quickly arranged. Sherman sent a provost marshal from each of his three field armies along with 200 guards and the prisoners. They took position on one side of a large open field outside town, while the Confederates similarly assembled on the other side. Sherman insisted that only recent captives be exchanged, as men taken early in the campaign would be too weak by now to constitute an equivalent for the recent captives he offered. Some prisoners who left Andersonville expecting release were deeply disappointed. When three miles short of Rough and Ready, Confederate guards stopped to do a final count and discovered they had too many men, so they sent a number back to prison.[58]

At Rough and Ready, the prisoners endured another weeding process. Union provost marshals asked each man when he had been captured and refused to allow those who did not fall into the date range Sherman had mandated. Lt. Col. James Wilson, provost marshal of the Army of the Tennessee, was heartbroken to tell them they could not be accepted. The rejected men "sobbed like children. I was quite unmanned by their grief," he later wrote. But Wilson asserted that most of those rejected managed to escape that night, either through the negligence or connivance of their Confederate guards, and returned to Union lines. When Hood protested to Sherman about this, the Union general said it was the duty of all prisoners to escape.[59]

Willard Warner, Sherman's assistant inspector general, was in charge of the proceedings at Rough and Ready. He delivered a total of 128 officers, 225 noncommissioned officers, and 979 privates on September 19, 22, 28, and 30. That amounted to the equivalent of 2,045 privates, according to the Dix-Hill Cartel of 1862. For these, he received 146 officers, 212 noncommissioned officers, and 770 privates in blue, equivalent to 2,047 privates according to the cartel. Most of the Federals were among "the last captured" and thus included those taken on July 22. It took more than two months for the paperwork to be completed, but the men were officially declared exchanged by early December.[60]

The 1,128 Federal prisoners officially repatriated, plus the estimated 150 who managed to escape from Confederate guards at Rough and Ready, were the lucky ones. They included most of the 16th Iowa's enlisted men who had been captured by Govan's Brigade in the first round of fighting along the Seventeenth Corps line but not its officers. Sgt. Maj. Oliver Anson was pleased to rejoin his shattered regiment but appalled by the conditions he only briefly experienced at Andersonville. They were "shocking in the extreme," he reported immediately after release. "It is killing the men faster than the Army," mostly through diarrhea and scurvy. Emanuel Howard of the 43rd Ohio, who had been detailed to Battery F, 2nd U.S. Artillery, believed he would have died in Andersonville if not exchanged.[61]

James H. Bradd, commissary sergeant of the 13th Iowa, would have agreed with Howard. He struggled with the terrible conditions at Andersonville. "It is merely a Question of time in here whether we live or Die," he scribbled in his diary on August 18. "Some will Hold out longer than others; but all are a going Down."[62]

Col. Robert K. Scott, commander of a brigade in Leggett's division, was the highest-ranking captive to be exchanged. He had managed to escape on July 27 but was recaptured on August 5. Scott was repatriated and returned to Federal lines on September 28. "He says the Confederacy is a shell," wrote M. F. Force, "no white men are at home, except detailed men." It was reported that even some Confederate guards seemed to be eager to escape to Union lines.[63]

Those men exchanged in September were extremely fortunate. Many other prisoners remained to rot in prison or risk the dangers of escape. For some, successful efforts to break out of confinement were followed by harrowing treks through the Confederate countryside in what often turned out to be vain efforts to reach Union lines. Lucky ones managed to escape and reach their own army, helped by the fact that captured officers were often shifted about from prison to prison, giving them enhanced opportunities to find a guard willing to take a bribe or landing up near the Atlantic coast, where they could escape to the beach and signal Union blockading vessels.[64]

For most, finding their way back to Union lines proved the most difficult part of escaping from prison. George W. Bailey got away from the guards pretty early in his trip south from Atlanta, but then he barely survived a long and dangerous effort to reach Union lines. He was helped greatly by friendly slaves and a handful of white Unionists. The latter even dressed him in women's clothes and pretended he was their sister "Betsy" so he could scout out avenues of escape. Eventually, however, Bailey was caught by Confederate sympathizers, one of whom wanted to murder him in cold blood. That man forced him deep into the woods near Decatur, but Bailey realized his intention and ducked at the last minute. The bullet severely injured his arm, but in the darkness, he managed to escape, eventually winding up in Union lines by early November.[65]

While prisoners dealt with their fate in various ways, survivors of the battle began the long process of communicating with a wide array of men and women connected with them. At the higher levels, commanders informed their governments of the event, and at the personal level, men who made it through the ordeal assured their loved ones they were still alive. Waves of communication of all kinds came from both armies beginning on July 23 and continued for a long while, radiating out to every corner of the disrupted nation.

John Bell Hood's first dispatch to Richmond was penned at 10:30 P.M., July 22, and contained overly optimistic reports of success. He failed to mention that the Union position held under great duress and asserted that his men had captured more prisoners, artillery, and flags than was true. The next day he reduced the number of guns captured but increased the number of flags taken. By February 1865, when he finally penned his official report of the Atlanta Campaign, Hood listed more accurate numbers of captures, but he never admitted that his men failed in the primary purpose of their attack.[66]

Hood can be forgiven somewhat for waffling on the number of guns and flags captured because it normally took time for statistics like that to be worked out. For the larger national community, filled with civilians whose relatives were involved in the fight, waiting for accurate reports was frustrating. They endured rumors that were "very confused and unsatisfactory" for many days after the battle, relying heavily on hearsay and newspaper reports. Maj. Gen. Howell Cobb at Macon knew that Hood's men had achieved some level of success, but he also knew that unless they drove the Federals "to the other side of the Chattahoochee," it would not be decisive in saving Atlanta.[67]

In Virginia, everyone assumed the most optimistic view of Hood's initial report, believing a great victory had been accomplished. Gen. Robert E. Lee hoped it would lead to a Federal retreat and the opening of wide areas of the West to Confederate foraging as a way to relieve a crushing food shortage in the Army of Northern Virginia. Newspapers and personal comments in Virginia exaggerated the number of prisoners and guns captured even beyond Hood's overstated claims. The same was true of many newspapers and civilians in the West as well. Hood's initial report generated an inflated public perception of the battle's results, and it would take time to slowly deflate that bubble. Some civilians, like agriculturist Edmund Ruffin, carefully sifted through the reports and kept a level head about what had been accomplished, but many others were only too eager to believe the best.[68]

Hood knew full well that his army had achieved only a limited success on July 22. By mid-September, soon after he lost Atlanta, he blamed Hardee not only for that limited victory but also for the abject failures at Peach Tree Creek on July 20 and at Jonesboro on August 31–September 1. This was an astonishing effort to whitewash his own record by blaming someone who did not deserve it. The two officers had never liked each other ever since the upstart Hood had been elevated to corps command in the Army of Tennessee in March 1864, but making Hardee a scapegoat was a sordid expression of Hood's low character. "Hardee failed to entirely turn the enemy's left as directed," he asserted in his official report. Hood wanted him out of the Army of Tennessee, something Hardee had been trying to accomplish himself for some time. Soon after Atlanta's fall, the best corps leader in the Army of Tennessee was transferred to a district command in Savannah.[69]

In his report, Hood had to reconcile his criticism of Hardee with his continued efforts to portray the army's July 22 attack as having enjoyed at least some success. He contradicted himself by asserting that Hardee's effort stopped Sherman's movement toward the last rail line leading into Atlanta from the south. Hardee was flabbergasted when he read Hood's report of his failings and wrote a strong defense of himself. But that defense was penned on April 5, 1865, only days before the war ground to an end in utter Confederate defeat.[70]

Hood had been a controversial figure ever since his elevation to command the army, and the failure of his first two attacks on Sherman intensified that controversy. There is evidence that the general keenly felt his failure and the public condemnation heaped on him by many people. He had requested Lt. Gen. Stephen D. Lee's transfer to the Army of Tennessee to replace Cheatham as permanent commander of his old corps, soon renamed Lee's Corps. Lee arrived on July 26 and initially met Hardee. When Lee asked him if the men liked Hood, Hardee said no, admitting that he did not like him either. Asked why, he said Hood was a liar. Then Lee met Hood in his headquarters tent in the backyard of the Windsor Smith House on Whitehall Street. He noticed an opened Bible on the table and commented on it. "Yes, I must find consolation somewhere," Hood told him, "my men have lost confidence in me; my corps commanders are insubordinate." Moreover, the newspapers "were saying he was butchering his men," as Lee later recalled the conversation.[71]

But some participants of the battle and distant observers of events supported Hood. Gustavus W. Smith, the Georgia Militia commander, was a strong advocate of the general and accepted his blaming of Hardee for the poor results at Peach Tree Creek, July 22, and Jonesboro. Other men liked Hood's aggressiveness but were worried that the Army of Tennessee could not sustain such heavy casualties.[72]

There were a number of commentators who strove to see anything positive in the outcome of the battle without supporting or criticizing Hood. They emphasized the shock inflicted on the Federals by the surprise flank attack, the moral victory achieved by the near catastrophe suffered by the Army of the Tennessee, and the number of guns, flags, and prisoners taken. In fact, Hardee called July 22 "the only decided success achieved by the army at Atlanta."[73]

But other commentators saw nothing to brag about in the battle. "We lost a great many men for mity little gain," wrote Thomas Warrick of the 34th Alabama. Lt. Hugh Black of Company A, 6th Florida in Finley's Brigade lost all hope in the cause. He deliberately got drunk on July 23 as a ploy to support his intention to resign from the army. "I am the boy that don't intend to fight and I am not by myself," he told a friend. Black was convinced the Confederacy was doomed, and he detested its military authorities. Other soldiers were convinced that Hood was ruining the Army of Tennessee. "If we lose this army we will be in a bad fix to carry on the war much longer," thought militiaman William J. Dickey. Anyone who took solace in Hood's argument that the battle stopped Sherman's effort to cut his last rail line into Atlanta found that comfort shattered to pieces when the Federals moved to the west side of the city on July 27 in a continued effort to reach the track.[74]

Hood made his situation worse by trying to pin blame not only on Hardee but also on Gen. Joseph E. Johnston, turning in equally shabby efforts in both cases to pretend he had nothing to do with his army's failures. Hood argued that Johnston had wrecked the fighting spirit of the troops by constant retreats from the start of the campaign, losing 20,000 men in the process and leaving a wounded army in Hood's hands. He failed to admit that as a corps commander, he had been responsible for urging Johnston to retreat on more than one occasion and that he had written long letters to influential men in Richmond that were highly critical of his superior officer's leadership, quietly undermining his commander's credibility. Some newspapers even took up Hood's line of attack on Johnston.[75]

But Hood reserved his most serious attacks on Hardee and Johnston for his memoirs, which were published shortly after he and many members of his family died of yellow fever in 1879. According to this book, Hardee pouted because Hood had been named as Johnston's successor, and Hardee lacked aggressive spirit when attacking Union earthworks. He also lashed into Johnston in his memoirs, devoting more attention to that general than to his own memories. He could not pin the defeat of July 22 on Johnston but excoriated him for what he perceived as the general decline of fighting spirit in the rank and file of the army prior to the battle.[76]

The fight between Hood, Hardee, and Johnston was never settled, but it is obvious that many factors came to play a role in the outcome of July 22. The long flank march fatigued the troops greatly, and the dense vegetation on the battlefield posed a serious obstacle to unit coordination. The Confederates brought artillery with them but were unable to use it effectively when and where it counted. For many commentators, a simplistic explanation was enough. They believed that if W. H. T. Walker had not been killed, his division would have routed the Federals. Others more accurately pinpointed a dire lack of coordination on all levels of command in the Army of Tennessee, with brigades advancing out of synchronization with others in the same division. This was, in fact, a long-term problem in the Army of Tennessee that never was solved. A handful of high-ranking officers came in for severe criticism, among them Maj. Gen. William B. Bate, who was probably the least popular and least trusted division commander in the army.[77]

While Confederate opinion on the results of July 22 were divided immediately after the battle, by the time the war ground to an end, no one could look back on those events except to condemn the assault as an utter failure. While Rebel soldiers were largely critical of Hood, or at least wary of him, right after he succeeded Johnston in command, they uniformly condemned his generalship after the war. They hated his tendency to blame other officers for his own failures. Lot D. Young of the 4th Kentucky (C.S.) was not only disappointed by Hood's botched plans for the attack but also found them "really disgusting." It had been "the most ill-conceived and unsatisfactory executed plan of battle of the whole war in which I participated." Those plans involved "a lack of understanding and cooperation of movement, coupled with almost insurmountable obstacles that might have been avoided." Many others also "turned away sick at heart," according to artilleryman Philip Daingerfield Stephenson, as time gave them an opportunity to view July 22 from a long perspective.[78]

In contrast, the Federals reported and evaluated the results of July 22 from a positive, celebratory point of view, except for mourning the loss of a beloved army commander. Sherman penned his first report to Washington at 10:30 A.M. of July 23, soon after the Confederates started negotiations for the burial truce. It was a full and accurate account in contrast to Hood's communications with the Richmond authorities. But reports emanating from the army group into the outside world spread erroneous information. Flooding into Chattanooga were rumors that Atlanta had fallen into Union hands, only to be completely refuted by the next round of grapevine intelligence.[79]

Newspapers reflected this swirl of unsubstantiated reports, for several days printing what they received even though it put readers through a rollercoaster ride of emotions. When soldiers complained of bad newspaper coverage, they often were irritated that some reporters gave more credit to units other than their own. Sixteenth Corps men often thought their comrades in the Fifteenth and Seventeenth Corps received too much praise in the press. One would assume that at least the *New York Herald* had some accurate reports because James P. Snell of the 52nd Illinois, a clerk on Brig. Gen. Thomas W. Sweeny's division staff, had just agreed to write articles for it a week before the engagement. He sent three pieces to the paper before the Battle of July 22, covering the left wing of Sherman's army group, while David P. Conyngham, a civilian correspondent who had earlier served as a volunteer aide-de-camp for Brig. Gen. Thomas G. Meagher in Virginia, covered the right wing for the *Herald*. Snell had an expense account to cover cost of postage and sent a piece to the editor, James Gordon Bennett, on July 23 describing the fight of the day before.[80]

Efforts to make sense of the Battle of July 22 were rife in the Union army. It was, everyone agreed, a desperate and fierce engagement. "These fellows fight like Devils & Indians combined," wrote Sherman to his wife, "and it calls for all my cunning & Strength." He felt great satisfaction in beating Johnston and pushing all the way to Atlanta, but "Hood is a new man and a fighter and must be watched Closer, as he is reckless of the lives of his Men." Many Federals recognized the new, aggressive policy inaugurated by Hood with two offensive actions on July 20 and 22, and they expected more of the same for the foreseeable future. With Johnston's removal, gone were expectations that Atlanta would fall into Union hands anytime soon.[81]

Sixteenth Corps men, from Dodge down to the lowest private, were convinced they had saved the Army of the Tennessee. It had been the first open-field fight they had engaged in since the fall of 1862, and they gloried in their ability to stand firmly (as in the case of Sweeny's division) and maneuver under duress (as in the case of Fuller's division) to achieve a stunning victory over a numerically superior enemy.[82]

Seventeenth Corps men could be forgiven if they believed they, not the Sixteenth Corps, had saved the Army of the Tennessee. Their officers lavished praise on the troops for resiliency in repelling attacks from any direction on the afternoon of July 22. "They fought to whip," asserted Col. George E. Bryant, who succeeded Manning F. Force in command of one of

Leggett's brigades. Fifteenth Corps officers also heaped praise on their men. William Harrow thought he had seen "the most distinguished exhibition of courage" in his three years of war service on July 22.[83]

The only exception to this string of praise was, in a slight way, within the Second Division, Fifteenth Corps, commanded at the start of the battle by Morgan L. Smith and led through most of it by Brig. Gen. Joseph A. J. Lightburn. This was Sherman's old division from his Shiloh days, and it fell back after the Confederates wormed their way through the improperly defended area around the railroad cut. "I regret to say that the command did not behave as on former occasions," reported Lightburn, "as it seemed that when the column of the enemy broke through one regiment, the whole command became panic-stricken and fell back in disorder." He admitted that there were "unfavorable" circumstances that led to this event and that the men resisted as long as they could. But when a line was broken as decisively as this one, there was little the troops could do except retire, regroup, and counterattack, which is exactly what they proceeded to do.[84]

As with the previous battle at Peach Tree Creek on July 20 and the subsequent fight at Ezra Church on July 28, many Federals believed their opponents had been fortified with whiskey just before conducting their attacks. This seemed to be the only way to explain the fierce nature of Confederate efforts that day, blaming them on "their drunken phrenzy." But there is no evidence to support the notion that Rebel soldiers quaffed whiskey or any other kind of liquor that day.[85]

But there is evidence that a failure to grasp the emotional challenge of battle among some of Hood's men limited their success on July 22. Brig. Gen. John C. Brown admitted that it was impossible to urge his men to leave the relative safety of the captured Fifteenth Corps works to continue the offensive. Moreover, Capt. Alfred Tyler Fielder of Company B, 12th Tennessee in Col. Michael Magevney's brigade of Maney's division, quietly admitted in his diary that some of the men failed the test of battle. "Several of our boys acted badly and played out of the fight and in hopes they will do so no more I will not expose them by inserting their names here."[86] Fielder's comments represent a common theme in Civil War history— recognizing a failure in battle spirit but refusing to bring individual cases out in the open. Civil War commanders in both armies had a strong tendency to do this while at the same time they tried to openly praise and encourage good behavior on the battlefield as a way to inspire the less-enthusiastic men to higher levels of performance.

The Federals went much further than the Confederates in efforts to encourage bravery through public recognition. Blair led the way by creating a board of officers to decide which men in his corps deserved a Seventeenth

Corps Medal of Honor. Commanders of each regiment, battery, and detachment of more than 100 men were instructed to nominate one officer and two men of each regiment (or one man of each battery and detachment) for consideration. They were to describe in detail why they nominated each person. The recommendations came pouring in soon after the instruction was issued on July 25, and by August 28, the board had deliberated and published its findings. Two tiers of awards, a gold medal and a silver medal, were issued in general orders along with details of the individual's actions that justified the award. All of the actions involved saving unit flags or personally leading dangerous local counterattacks. Among the recipients were Chaplain Russell B. Bennett of the 32nd Ohio, Lt. Edmund E. Nutt of the 20th Ohio, color bearer Sgt. Russell Bethel of the 78th Ohio, Lt. David W. Poak of the 30th Illinois, Lt. Col. John M. Hedrick of the 15th Iowa, and Sgt. Maj. John G. Safely of the 11th Iowa. All told, thirteen men received medals, representing six out of twenty-four regiments and eight batteries in the Seventeenth Corps. The legend "Atlanta, July 22" was inscribed on each medal.[87]

On July 29, Sherman submitted a list of seven colonels for promotion to brigadier general based on their performance during the fight. Among them was William W. Belknap of the 15th Iowa. The next day, he learned that Abraham Lincoln had already approved Belknap's promotion. This jumped him ahead of three other colonels in Hall's brigade, and he immediately took command of the unit. "I was of course well satisfied," he informed a friend, but William Hall was not at all happy. Born in Canada of American parents, Hall had attended Oberlin College, the Western Military Institute of Kentucky, and Harvard Law School before practicing law in Davenport, Iowa. He was noted as a brave and skillful tactician but was small in stature and sickly, irritable, and not well liked by his subordinates. Hall possessed "large self-esteem, and prides himself in doing things his own way," remembered Capt. A. A. Stuart of the 17th Iowa in the Fifteenth Corps, while showing "great indignity, if he thinks his services underrated." Not surprisingly, Hall resigned in a huff over his demotion, and Belknap gloated. "Hall had commanded the Brigade so long that he deemed he had a life estate in the office," he told an acquaintance. The other officers who had been passed over "behaved more sensibly" and did not complain. On August 2, officers of the 15th Iowa presented Belknap with a sword, saddle, holster, and spurs to honor his elevation while the band of Potts's brigade serenaded him.[88]

Blair probably had a role to play in Belknap's unusual promotion; he certainly had everything to do with honoring Pvt. George J. Reynolds of the 15th Iowa. On July 26, Blair publicized Reynolds's role in trying to help the mortally wounded McPherson in the general's dying moments and in

William W. Belknap. He was "a brawny, red-bearded giant," according to Capt. William H. Chamberlin, commissary of musters on Dodge's staff, in his article "Hood's Second Sortie." Belknap certainly was brave, but he also was ruthlessly ambitious. Based on his personal capture of Col. Harris D. Lampley of the 45th Alabama, he was quickly promoted to brigadier general and replaced the long-time commander of his brigade, even though at least two officers were senior to him in rank. Belknap later connived against General in Chief William T. Sherman, who had enthusiastically supported his Civil War–era promotion, when he served as secretary of war in the Ulysses S. Grant administration. He also instigated a number of questionable and fraudulent schemes, one of which, the Trader Post Scandal, led to his resignation and impeachment by the House of Representatives. Library of Congress, LC-DG-cwpb-06120 playing a key role in the recovery of his body. Reynolds became the first recipient of the Seventeenth Corps Medal of Honor (gold). Officers organized an award ceremony that very day, transporting Reynolds in an ambulance to the parade ground where the 15th Iowa was waiting. "I gave him the medal in the presence of the Regiment," wrote Belknap, "and the boy was so modest & simple in his ideas that he did not know why this distinction should be conferred on him or why he was thought to have done more than his duty." Reynolds nevertheless came to take a deep and lasting pride in the award for the rest of his life, which he spent as a farmer in Missouri. The award received widespread publicity in the newspapers, including a write-up in *Harper's Weekly*.[89]

Reynolds's fame angered Pvt. George Sherland of the 64th Illinois, who had helped him initiate efforts for the recovery of McPherson's body. Lt. Col. Michael W. Manning credited Sherland more than Reynolds in the recovery, but that was an exaggeration. Sherland was a latecomer to the scene, only joining Reynolds after the Iowa man had assured him there was no danger, and at best did no more than did Reynolds in the effort. Yet Sherland remained bitter at not receiving public recognition. He wrote a short book about his war experiences, which was published in 1865. "Although I have been entirely wronged of the credit due me" in the McPherson incident, he claimed to be satisfied "that I performed my duty, and only wish that I could have done more under the deeply tragic circumstances of his death."[90]

Doling out rewards was scant compensation for the devastating effect of heavy combat during the afternoon of July 22, felt both emotionally and administratively. Emotionally, many men of Giles A. Smith's division were stunned by the fierce and repeated assaults delivered by Hardee's Corps. It took two days for Lt. John J. Safely of the 13th Iowa to report that he and his comrades had "fully recovered from the Shock sustained on the 22d," and they were once again ready for anything to come. On the Confederate side, some men seemed to be more shocked by losing Johnston and receiving Hood as their commander than they were upset by the fighting on July 22.[91]

Capt. Francis De Gress was not only emotionally traumatized by the devastation inflicted on his Battery H, 1st Illinois Light Artillery but also faced a daunting task in trying to restore its field effectiveness. Sherman recalled that De Gress appealed directly to himself, tears in his eyes, "lamenting the loss of his favorite guns." When the captain asked him for help in obtaining a full resupply of all lost equipment, the army-group commander told him "he must beg and borrow of others till" it was possible to do so. De Gress was fully capable of doing that. He had only two serviceable guns after the battle and managed to restore a third by hand-drilling the spike out of the vent on July 23. The fourth piece had burst when inexperienced infantrymen fired it after the restoration of the Fifteenth Corps line. Battery A, 1st Illinois Light Artillery had only two pieces and one caisson left, so De Gress obtained permission to use its remaining horses and harnesses.[92]

On July 23, a new commander was brought in to take charge of Battery A, 1st Illinois Light Artillery. Lt. George Echte, who transferred from Battery F, 2nd Missouri Light Artillery, managed to obtain two more pieces from the 1st Iowa Battery along with the horses and harnesses. He also got thirty-three men detailed from infantry regiments in Martin's brigade, Lightburn's division, and managed to get the battery in "fighting trim" by July 24.[93]

Dodge also reshuffled personnel and equipment from one devastated battery in the Sixteenth Corps to another after the engagement. Battery F, 2nd U.S. Artillery had lost all its guns, many of its men, and much of its equipment when Govan's right wing overran it early in the battle. The remaining personnel were sent to reinforce the 14th Ohio Battery and Battery H, 1st Missouri Light Artillery. The ordnance property was given to Battery C, 1st Michigan Light Artillery or sent to the ordnance department at Marietta. Four horses also went to the 14th Ohio Battery, while four more, all that were left, were given to Fuller's division headquarters.[94]

Seventeenth Corps units were among the most seriously affected by the heavy fighting of July 22. Several days afterward, Belknap issued a circular ordering his regimental commanders to submit requisitions for "Clothing, Camp and Garrison Equip required" for the upcoming month of August. This was not only because the Iowa units had lost most of this type of equipment in the fighting but also because their troop strengths were much lower now than before July 22. Returned prisoners began to trickle in by September 22 thanks to Sherman's exchange program with Hood, but it took quite some time to rebuild the 16th Iowa, which had suffered more than any other regiment in the brigade. The returned regimental captives were desperately in need of new clothing, proper food, and some medical care. The officers were not exchanged, however, and the 16th Iowa remained woefully short of qualified leadership. Eight of its companies were commanded by noncommissioned officers, and a captain continued to lead the regiment.[95]

To a greater or lesser extent, similar problems were felt by all of the regiments in Belknap's brigade. He was promised more than 1,000 draftees, but these men came dribbling in from the North in squads throughout the fall of 1864. Nearly half of the draftees had failed to report for duty by the time the brigade set out on Sherman's March to the Sea. The Iowans also suffered a small but persistent problem with finding enough guns to arm everyone in the ranks. A total of 8.6 percent of the men in the brigade had no muskets. Belknap tried to get some of the reported 1,500 guns recovered from the battlefield of Griswoldville on November 22, 1864, to fill out his needs. His brigade was lacking only 100 weapons by that time.[96]

As Belknap's command demonstrated, the process of dealing with the aftermath of July 22 could be a long, drawn-out affair lasting for months. In a wider arena than mere army administration, that process was far more complicated than rebuilding units; it also involved dealing with emotional trauma, horrible bodily injuries, and the effects of battlefield death on the families of the slain. What had taken place immediately after the guns fell silent was only the beginning of how the fighting of July 22 resonated throughout America.

I3

Moving Out, July 23–28

From their perspective, the Confederates' attack on July 22 blunted Sherman's apparent effort to reach the Macon and Western Railroad, the last supply line leading into Atlanta. They could not know that Sherman never intended to hit that line by moving to the east of the city. He had already accomplished his immediate goal before noon of July 22, which was to tear up the Georgia Railroad leading into Atlanta from the east, and already was planning to move the Army of the Tennessee from his far left to his far right in an effort to reach the Macon and Western Railroad by marching west of Atlanta. The attack on July 22 did make him pause for several days. If Hood intended to continue his assault the next day, Sherman was ready to stand and fight. If not, Logan's battered army needed time to recover before undertaking what the Federal commander aptly called a "delicate movement."[1]

The first order of business was to see if the Rebels meant to continue fighting, a question all Federals were eager to answer. Sherman informed Thomas at 2 A.M. of July 23 that he should be ready to conduct a heavy demonstration on the Federal right if action resumed on the left. Rank-and-file Federals lay on their arms for some sleep until dawn and were relieved when silence rather than the sounds of combat greeted them as the sun rose. For some, the relief came in stages over time. Mifflin Jennings of the 11th Iowa was happy every morning from July 23 to July 25 that the enemy remained quiet.[2]

In planning to shift Logan's army to the right, Sherman pondered how to use his available cavalry. Maj. Gen. Lovell H. Rousseau had led a force of 2,500 mounted men from Middle Tennessee into central Alabama, destroying thirty miles of the West Point and Montgomery Railroad at and near Opelika, Alabama, on July 17–19. He then rode to Marietta, Georgia, by July 22. Sherman believed that rail line, which fed into the Macon and Western Railroad, would be out of commission for a month. On July 23, Brig. Gen. Kenner Garrard's cavalry division returned from its raid toward Covington after having destroyed ten miles of track and several bridges on the Georgia Railroad fifty miles east of Atlanta. Sherman considered that line "sufficiently crippled." With Garrard back and Rousseau's contingent now available, Sherman planned a large mounted raid on the Macon and Western Railroad to coincide with his upcoming shift of Logan to the west of Atlanta.[3]

But moving the Army of the Tennessee depended a good deal on what the enemy was doing on the Union left flank. Hardee actually fell back some more on July 23. After the terrible fighting of the previous day had ended, the Confederates disengaged during the night and retired about 1,000 yards to establish a new position, the center of which was anchored on the refused Seventeenth Corps line that Govan's Brigade had captured from Hall's brigade in the first round of fighting. Here Hardee's men remained until the morning of July 23, when they began to arrange a new line still farther from the Federals. For some units, it was a fall back of two miles from the refused Seventeenth Corps line. Jacob D. Cox aptly described this withdrawal as a half wheel to the rear by Hardee's Corps, bringing it into position along the irregular ridge that separated the watershed of Sugar Creek from Entrenchment Creek. The corps now faced toward the northeast. Hardee's left flank was "in practical connection with the salient of the Atlanta fortifications," according to Cox, but Thomas B. Mackall of Hood's staff thought there was a "large interval" between those two points. Still, Hardee was "intrenched in a tenable position," as Cox put it, with his picket and skirmish lines also dug in for protection. From here, he could block any Federal move south toward the Macon and Western Railroad by a route east of Atlanta.[4]

Hood wisely tried to cover all possible Union moves. Just in case Sherman tried to extend the Federal right flank west of Atlanta, he ordered Hardee to send Bate's Division over to the left flank of the Confederate line. Bate marched through Atlanta on the night of July 23–24 and took position to the left of Alexander P. Stewart's left flank.[5]

Wheeler's cavalry had joined Hardee near the end of the fighting on July 22 but had not been engaged in the effort to roll up the Union infantry line. On July 23, the mounted men were torn in their responsibilities.

Wheeler received permission to send off part of his command in a belated effort to chase Garrard. He had discovered this Union cavalry raid toward Covington just before attacking Sprague at Decatur early on the afternoon of July 22, but Hardee had told him to continue with the battle plan. Now Wheeler's horsemen set out on an ultimately vain attempt to prevent the Federal cavalry from wrecking the Georgia Railroad. After detaching a few regiments to protect Hardee's left and right flanks, the cavalry rode forty miles from noon to midnight of July 23 only to learn that Garrard had safely returned to the Federal line. The exhausted troopers made their way back to take position on Hardee's right.[6]

Meanwhile, the Federals busied themselves with adjusting troop positions and shoring up their defensive arrangements. In order to have his own men cover the rear areas of the Army of the Tennessee, Logan arranged for Twenty-Third Corps units to change places with Charles R. Woods's division in the main line from the Howard House southward. Woods relieved Schofield's men who were temporarily holding positions between that line and Decatur. Then he filled in the gap between Wangelin's brigade and Dodge's Sixteenth Corps troops. Jacob D. Cox reassembled his Twenty-Third Corps division to fill the sector vacated by Woods on the main Union line facing west. Mersy's brigade, now led by Robert N. Adams, remained on that main line and distributed its regiments to reinforce weak sectors for the time being. John W. Sprague's brigade moved a mile south and reoccupied Decatur on the morning of July 23. His men collected the killed and wounded left on the field and took up a position just west of town near the abandoned Confederate conscript camp.[7]

The most common activity among Federal units was to fortify their positions. Everyone became busy with spade and pick on July 23 to strengthen the line. It was not only an operational imperative but also an emotional reaction to the shock of battle the day before. Sherman issued orders for all units to construct works of sufficient strength to resist another attack. The greatest effort took place on the far left of the Union formation, where the hastily assembled line stretching east from Bald Hill was in dire need of strengthening. The men needed no urging; they readily understood how important fieldworks had become and worked for the next three days until they had "immense breastworks in every possible direction, works within works," recorded William F. Graham of the 53rd Illinois, "and it will be hard for the enemy to harm us much within them." Even on the main line facing west, work continued on the defenses. Cox's infantrymen placed wooden obstructions in front of the line vacated by Woods's division as his artillerists dug emplacements for their guns.[8]

Sherman was pleased. "All have covered their fronts with parapets so that

Union Earthworks along Flat Shoals Road. Exposed by George N. Barnard in late May 1866, this is one of three photographs depicting extensive Union earthworks on the July 22 battlefield. In these images, one sees not so much the earthworks as they existed during the battle but their appearance after the Federals had constructed and rearranged them July 23–26 before moving out of the area. Barnard failed to note exactly where these works were located, but this photograph probably was taken along Flat Shoals Road. Standing in front of the Union line, one can see a cleared area on the other side of the works that appears as a light-colored patch at the center of the left edge. This patch is most likely the road. Head logs still grace the top of the parapet, and one can see the outer end of an artillery embrasure. These substantial and well-connected trenches and parapets were made by troops who had learned an important lesson from the Confederate surprise attack of July 22—it paid to be ready for anything. George N. Barnard, *Photographic Views of Sherman's Campaign* (New York: Dover, 1977), plate 36.

the enemy will not attempt a sally," he wrote to Logan at 8 P.M. that night. "The question now is, What next?" It was not really a question of what to do now but when to start doing it. Sherman wanted to wait for a couple of days to allow all of Garrard's cavalry to return from the Covington raid. Until then, he kept his men busy. Sherman instructed Dodge to send out heavy skirmish lines toward Wheeler's cavalry in his front. He wanted Woods's men to more thoroughly destroy the Georgia Railroad, heating and twisting rails. Leaving behind a heavy skirmish line to cover the sector of the works stretching east from Bald Hill, Woods was to move the rest of his men into

Union Earthworks at Bald Hill. Barnard's second image of Federal defenses also was exposed in late May 1866. It is a more expansive view than the earlier one, and the lay of the land suggests Bald Hill. The view probably is from the northern side of the hill looking toward the northwest. The head logs are gone, indicating that local landowners had begun extracting wood from the defenses, the first step in rehabilitating the ground for peaceful purposes. George N. Barnard, *Photographic Views of Sherman's Campaign* (New York: Dover, 1977), plate 37.

Decatur on July 24, not only to wreck the track but also to give the impression of Union offensive moves in that quarter.[9]

On July 24, Logan consulted with Sherman about his logistical support. Army of the Tennessee wagon trains had been based at Roswell ever since McPherson crossed the Chattahoochee River, but Logan had no cavalry to escort them to the front lines and too few infantrymen to detach large numbers for such duty. He suggested bringing all the army's trains forward at once so they could be protected just behind the lines.[10]

Sherman took this as an opportunity to inform Logan of his larger plans. He wanted the logistical arrangement to remain in place because the Army of the Tennessee would be starting the move to the right flank very soon, and he did not want it bogged down by protecting large wagon trains. Logan could route the wagons by way of other Chattahoochee crossings to reach the troops as they shifted, and he should detach an entire division to protect them if necessary. Sherman still had to work out the details of the shift, and in the meantime, he encouraged his subordinate to "act with confidence.

Another View of Union Earthworks at Bald Hill. Barnard's third image also covers the Federal entrenchments at Bald Hill in late May 1866, but from a different perspective. He again stood in front of the works to capture the image, and one or two artillery embrasures are barely visible to left and right. These earthworks would not stand the test of time, as suburban development gradually covered the hill and the rest of the battlefield within a few decades. NARA 524946, 111-B-536.

Know that the enemy cannot budge you from your present ground, and act offensively to show him that you dare him to the encounter."[11]

One of the tasks Sherman faced was recommending a permanent commander for the Army of the Tennessee to succeed McPherson. On July 24, he consulted with Maj. Gen. George H. Thomas, commander of the Army of the Cumberland and his second in command of the army group, and told him he was satisfied with naming Logan. But Sherman was surprised at Thomas's response. His subordinate had developed a sour attitude toward Logan in the early months of 1864, just before the onset of the campaign, when Logan complained to Sherman that Thomas's subordinates did not cooperate with Army of the Tennessee personnel in logistical arrangements. The railroad system was within the boundaries of the Department of the Cumberland and thus controlled by Thomas's people, who often did not recognize orders for transportation issued by the visiting Army of the Tennessee. Rather than inform Thomas, the department commander, who was unaware of this, Logan unwisely complained to Sherman. Thomas was embarrassed and felt insulted; he explained the situation to Logan and rectified the problem but continued to harbor ill feelings in private.[12]

Now, on July 24, Thomas frankly told Sherman that he could not accept Logan as his equal and even threatened to resign his position when Sherman did not immediately validate his feelings. Sherman reluctantly agreed, and Thomas then recommended Maj. Gen. Oliver Otis Howard, commander of the Fourth Corps, to succeed McPherson. Later that day, while reconnoitering with Howard, Sherman asked him if he would welcome promotion to command the Army of the Tennessee. The answer was yes, and Sherman wrote to Washington to that effect before the end of the day. He awaited confirmation before making any of this public.[13]

Meanwhile, Logan continued under the assumption that he would be the permanent commander of McPherson's army. His concern about logistics and detaching troops to protect rear areas was echoed by Blair and Dodge. After the bloodletting of July 22, all three commanders worried about shrinking troop strength. Blair had left the largest Seventeenth Corps division at Vicksburg for occupation duties, taking 10,000 men to Georgia in May and early June 1864. He had been compelled to detach a brigade and two batteries, amounting to 1,200 men, to garrison Allatoona on arrival and lost 3,000 troops killed, wounded, and sick thus far in the grueling campaign. After receiving some returned men, he could count on no more than 6,000 effective troops in the two divisions under his charge. Dodge still had not retrieved Sprague's brigade and noted to army-group headquarters that two other of his brigades were on detached duty at Rome, Georgia, and at Decatur, Alabama. Two mounted regiments also were detached along with three regiments of Black infantry. Attrition due to casualties, sickness, and detachment had reduced his available troop strength in the Left Wing, Sixteenth Corps from 12,500 men to only 6,000 by July 24.[14]

Sherman could do little about these problems in his favorite army. Detachments were absolutely necessary for the protection of support services in the rear areas, and there were no experienced troops available elsewhere to serve as reinforcements. The Army of the Tennessee would have to muddle through while performing the most important and dangerous elements in Sherman's operational plan.

For the time, Logan's troops busied themselves with many tasks. Details went out to retrieve pieces of artillery equipment that skirmishers reported were abandoned between the lines, sometimes firing at Confederate skirmishers in the process. Other troops escorted prisoners to Marietta or continued perfecting their earthworks. Woods's division marched to Decatur as instructed to create a diversion for Confederate attention and then returned, tearing up track along the way. Sprague deployed his brigade along the railroad to help in this work of destruction. Signal officers reestablished some of the signal stations they had been forced to abandon on July 22 and sent up colored rockets after dusk to experiment with an unusual method of communicating with each other. Both Union and Confederate soldiers noticed and enjoyed the show. The Confederates even gave out loud cheers to show their appreciation.[15]

Hood also was busy with work, although his plan did not call for risky moves for the foreseeable future. The Confederates intended to wait and see what Sherman would do before setting any offensive plans. Meanwhile, the new commander of the Army of Tennessee began a process of weeding out unwanted staff officers. His chief of staff, Brig. Gen. William W. Mackall, was a close friend and supporter of Johnston. Hood had to put up with him thus far due to the press of events but now had a chance to relieve him. Gen. Braxton Bragg visited Atlanta for consultations, and his presence on July 24 must have emboldened Hood to act. There was no love lost between Mackall and Bragg, and when the former reached Hood's headquarters on the afternoon of July 24, he refused to accept Bragg's hand in greeting. As Mackall's nephew, Thomas B. Mackall (who was his uncle's aide-de-camp) noted, within a half hour the chief of staff was handed orders relieving him of his position at his own request. Hood named his artillery chief, Brig. Gen. Francis A. Shoup, as his new chief of staff.[16]

The severe losses of July 22 intensified the Army of Tennessee's persistent manpower shortages. Hood tried to compensate by issuing an order recalling all men previously detailed as clerks who could be spared. "The interests of the public service require this in the present emergency." He also called on Georgia governor Joseph E. Brown for any state troops that could be furnished. "Please send me men with muskets as fast as possible," he implored. Meanwhile, rank-and-file Confederates, along with their officers, continued to work on the city's defenses.[17]

Sherman began to set plans for shifting the Army of the Tennessee to the right on July 25. He instructed Logan to move his army trains to a safe position behind Thomas's line and plan to pull the troops out of their earthworks early on the morning of July 27 for the move westward. At that same time, Sherman planned to launch a large cavalry raid on the Macon and Western Railroad. That evening, he also informed Grant of events to date, telling him that Hood had attacked twice now and "both times got more than he bargained for." The pending move against the last Confederate supply line promised results, but Sherman began to feel that he would prefer Hood to fight it out near Atlanta rather than to fall back farther toward Macon as Johnston would most likely have done if he still commanded the Army of Tennessee.[18]

For most Federals, July 25 flowed along much as the previous day had passed. The air was filled with smoke from the burning railroad ties along the Georgia Railroad, and an apprehension that the enemy might assault again continued to plague many units. The men were called into line to be ready only to realize that no attack seemed in the offing. August Mersy, nursing his wound from July 22, began traveling north that day. Logan busied himself with unit placements. Garrard's cavalry division took post north and east of Decatur, connecting with Sprague's left flank to screen the extreme left end of the Union position. Later that day, Logan pulled Sprague out of line and positioned him as the army's only reserve, forcing Garrard to close up and cover the sector vacated by the infantry.[19]

On the Confederate side, Hood took measures to shore up his men's fighting spirit. In a general order, he lectured them that "experience has proved to you that safety in time of battle consists in getting into close quarters with your enemy. Guns and colors are the only unerring indications of victory." He also warned them that allowing Sherman to continue flanking Atlanta would result in the fall of the city. "Your recent brilliant success proves the ability to prevent it. You have but to will it, and God will grant us the victory your commander and your country expect." Yet on the same day, he issued another general order calling on all division commanders to create a provost guard of sixty men "to prevent straggling."[20]

The effect of the fighting on July 22 led to a drastic decision concerning Walker's Division. That unit had lost its commander early in the fight, and each of its three brigades had lost their leaders in rapid order soon after Walker's fall. The current division commander, Brig. Gen. Hugh W. Mercer, was not up to his responsibilities. Both Hood and Hardee preferred to break up the division, and Bragg authorized it. What was left of the three brigades was distributed to other divisions in Hardee's Corps. Mercer's Brigade went to Cleburne's Division, Gist's to Cheatham's Division, and Stevens's to Bate's Division. Bragg instructed Mercer to go to Savannah and report to the Adjutant General's Office in Richmond for assignment. He left on July 26. B. Benjamin Smith, one of Gist's staff members, was convinced the breakup was primarily implemented to avoid giving Mercer permanent command of the division.[21]

Sherman also had to deal with a number of personnel issues in the aftermath of July 22. The first one had nothing to do with the battle but had been brewing for some time since the onset of the campaign. On July 25, he received notification from the Adjutant General's Office in Washington, D.C., that Peter J. Osterhaus had been promoted to major general of volunteers. A reliable officer, Osterhaus was currently on sick leave, with Charles R. Woods filling in for him at the head of the First Division, Fifteenth Corps.

This came only a few days after Sherman had been notified that Alvin P. Hovey, former commander of First Division, Twenty-Third Corps, had been breveted major general of volunteers.[22]

Both appointments set off an angry letter by Sherman, one of his famous intemperate missives. He objected to the appointments because they had been offered to officers not currently on duty. That gave, in his view, the wrong message. Both men "left us in the midst of bullets to go to the rear in search of personal advancement. If the rear be the post of honor, then we had better all change front on Washington." Of course, this was not only rash but unfair. Sherman forgot for the moment that Osterhaus had left on July 15 because of illness.[23]

He remembered, however, that Hovey had left because of frustrated ambition. Hovey had done well at division command during the Vicksburg Campaign but then lobbied shamefully for promotion to major general for months afterward. Having raised ten infantry and ten cavalry regiments in Indiana during the early months of 1864, he took the infantry units to the field and formed them as the First Division of Schofield's corps. Hovey, however, did very poorly at Resaca and then petulantly pushed for the addition of his ten cavalry regiments to be joined to his division, a request that Sherman obviously could not approve. Hovey then offered his resignation and left the field. Lincoln felt bad about this situation, as he genuinely intended to promote him, but for the time could only offer a brevet as major general, which mollified Hovey enough to keep him in backwater assignments for the rest of the war.[24]

After seeing Sherman's letter, Lincoln responded with assurances that the general had misunderstood the motives behind these appointments. Osterhaus had been elevated mostly due to his sterling record and partly to his German nativity. The timing of the appointment had been unfortunate, perhaps, but the promotion was deserved. The Washington authorities did not approve of Hovey's petulant actions, but they did not wish to insult an officer with such a generally good record. Timing here also was unfortunate, but the appointment was justified. Lincoln assured Sherman that the authorities fully understood the need to reward men for merit on the battlefield. The letter satisfied Sherman; he had copies of it distributed to army, corps, and division leaders for their information.[25]

At the same time, Grant was informed of this riffle and of Sherman's recommendation that Howard replace McPherson as head of the Department and Army of the Tennessee. Although Howard was not his own first choice, the general in chief deferred to Sherman's judgment on the matter. "No one can tell so well as one immediately in command the disposition that should be made of the material on hand," he wrote. As for Osterhaus,

Grant admitted the German had "proved himself a good soldier," but he did regret that the promotion was announced while he was away from the army. Moreover, Sherman had thus far "conducted his campaign with great skill and success" and deserved to have his personnel recommendations approved.[26]

Thomas W. Sweeny offered his superiors far more trouble than Hovey and Osterhaus combined, and the trigger to his sordid story was the fighting on July 22. The Irishman had lost his right arm at the Battle of Churubusco during the Mexican War as a volunteer and received a commission in the regular army at that war's end. Sweeny had been wounded at Wilson's Creek and again at Shiloh, where he commanded a brigade. Perhaps these repeated battlefield injuries warped his attitude, for he became a combative colleague who unnecessarily made enemies. Among them was Grenville M. Dodge, who had to deal with Sweeny's insistence on minor points of army protocol ever since the fall of 1862. Their relationship worsened under the strain of the Atlanta Campaign. On July 8, Dodge wrote a complaint that Sweeny had placed a battery in an exposed position improperly supported by infantry and that he had to do something about it personally. Sweeny denied there was any need for Dodge's intervention and resented the corps leader's assertion that such circumstances had occurred many times.[27]

Sweeny also did not hesitate to violate orders when it suited his purpose. The War Department had forbidden officers from utilizing ambulances for their personal use in April 1864, but Sweeny paid no attention to that order. On July 10, as the Federals were moving about in response to Johnston's falling back across the Chattahoochee, Maj. Norman Gay, medical director of the Left Wing, Sixteenth Corps, tried to separate Sweeny from an ambulance the division leader had been using for his personal needs. Sweeny became angry, mercilessly cursed Gay, tried to force him into a duel, and threatened to kill him if he ever saw him again. Brigade leader Elliott W. Rice had to intervene to prevent bloodshed. Then Sweeny wrote to McPherson's headquarters, the adjutant general of the U.S. Army, and to Sherman's staff to inquire if it was permissible for Gay to order the ambulance away from his headquarters without prior notice. McPherson allowed Dodge to answer his inquiry by stating on July 12 that Sweeny had no right to use the ambulance. Sherman also replied to Sweeny's inquiry on July 24. "I cannot be called on to decide such questions," he wrote, but he followed up with a blunt statement that medical directors have every right to control all ambulances without the permission of division commanders. The Adjutant General's Office replied much later, on August 4, by stating that ambulances should be used for the benefit of the sick and wounded, not for the convenience of officers.[28]

The accumulation of bad blood between Dodge and Sweeny exploded on July 25 because of the Battle of Atlanta. John W. Fuller was at Dodge's headquarters complaining about Sweeny when the object of his complaint dropped by. The three conversed about the battle until the division commander started to claim that Fuller's brigade broke and ran under pressure. That was, at best, only a half-truth. The brigade was being flanked by Gist's Brigade and had to retire quickly, coming apart along the way, but recovered when Fuller personally intervened to restore order. He tried to explain this, but Sweeny refused to give him or his men any credit. When Dodge tried to reason with him, Sweeny turned on his superior and said anyone who denied it was a liar. Exactly who struck the first blow is not entirely clear, but at this point the argument erupted into a physical fight among the three. Dodge ordered Sweeny placed under arrest.[29]

Sherman was upset at this development and urged Dodge to treat Sweeny with circumspection due to his long and reliable service in the field. But Dodge had not only the right but also the responsibility to relieve Sweeny and file charges against him after creating a fistfight with his superior officer. Sweeny was ordered to Nashville, as Elliott Rice assumed temporary command of the Second Division, to be replaced as the permanent commander by Brig. Gen. John M. Corse, one of three inspectors general on Sherman's staff, on July 26.[30]

Dodge asserted after the war that Sweeny's entire division "was up in arms against him and after the battle they made a universal complaint." There was at least some truth to that assertion. When Logan's headquarters found out about the arrest, Lt. Col. William T. Clark, assistant adjutant general of the Army of the Tennessee, promised Dodge, "I will see that the 'Dog' is placed where he can do no more harm." Dodge believed that Clark also reflected McPherson's opinion of Sweeny. While awaiting trial, Sweeny privately wrote to friends that Dodge had a vendetta against him and that his men had saved Fuller's brigade from annihilation on July 22. The latter statement was completely false, and if the former statement was true, it was only because of Sweeny's aggressive and irresponsible actions.[31]

Dodge forwarded charges on July 28, but it was not until December 3 that a court-martial could be assembled in Louisville. In the testimony, some witnesses claimed that Dodge hit Sweeny first, on the cheek with an open palm, and that Sweeny hit with a closed fist, causing Dodge's nose to bleed. Others claimed that Sweeny and Fuller wrestled and Dodge stayed out of it. But there is no doubt that the two division leaders struggled after Sweeny swung at Fuller first and no doubt that Sweeny bitterly cursed Dodge and challenged him to a duel. There is also no doubt that the entire fracas was started by Sweeny's intemperate and thoroughly disrespectful attitude toward both of the other officers. His own artillery chief, Capt. Frederick Welker, testified that Sweeny wanted him to fire on Fuller's men when they were retreating, but of course, Welker refused this astonishing order.[32]

In his "Statement in Defense," Sweeny indirectly revealed the true source of his troublesome character. He wrote emotionally about how insulted he felt that Dodge slapped him with an open palm instead of delivering a "round solid blow . . . straight out from the shoulder." That would have represented respect for "the resistance it anticipates, but to be contemptuously slapped, with the open hand, in the face, is the most provoking, the most humiliating act which one man may do to another." He also noted that his right arm was gone because of Churubusco, his left arm had been injured at Shiloh, and a bullet remained imbedded in his thigh. It appears that the true source of his trouble was the accumulated assaults on his body and his self-concept of manliness. Sweeny demanded constant assurances of respect to shore up his shaky self-image and magnified every perceived slight to a point where it became a major point of bitter controversy, justifying his readiness to lie and strike out physically.[33]

Perhaps it was because Sherman had suffered when accused of insanity in the fall of 1861, charges that nearly ruined his army career, that he was so sensitive to Sweeny's case. The court actually found Sweeny not guilty on December 24, apparently because the members believed that Dodge had struck the first blow. Howard, now in charge of the Army of the Tennessee, reluctantly certified the court's findings but made it clear that he had no intention of giving Sweeny another assignment. The former division commander languished for months despite meeting Sherman in May 1865 and being treated "very kindly."[34]

Dodge was happy that he was able to separate Sweeny from his command, which had been the least he hoped to achieve from this unfortunate affair. Two days after the scuffle at his headquarters, the Army of the Tennessee received a surprise when Howard was announced as McPherson's permanent replacement. No one anticipated that Logan would be bypassed, especially by an officer from outside the army. They had no misgivings about Howard personally, for he had done well as Fourth Corps commander, but it seemed hard for many to accept that an Army of the Tennessee man could not permanently lead Grant's and Sherman's old command.

It was not until 10 P.M. of July 26 that Sherman received confirmation of Howard's appointment from Washington, and he decided to make the change the next day, after the Army of the Tennessee had set out on its shift to the Union right flank. By that time, all had been readied for the move. Schofield would be in charge of protecting the left flank of the army group with his Twenty-Third Corps after the Army of the Tennessee left its position. To that end, Logan's troops had dug a new refused line of earthworks stretching east from Copenhill. This new line gave up most of the July 22 battlefield to the Confederates, if they chose to occupy it. Schofield had an additional idea, to connect the new refused line with an empty Confederate line of earthworks running north–south and facing east that was located to the east of Copenhill. This empty line had been temporarily occupied by the Federals on July 21. Schofield wanted to refurbish a long stretch of it so that the new refused line would complete a three-sided formation facing west, south, and east. Within this near enclosure, he could park his wagon trains and locate his field hospitals for protection. The nearly fatal flank attack of July 22 had made an impression on the Federals.[35]

Logan superintended the pullout of units early on the morning of July 27 and began moving them north and west behind Schofield's and Thomas's line. But he received the shock of his life when Sherman told him that Howard would take over command of the army. Logan could not forgive his superior for this until very late in his life, holding a deep and bitter grudge against Sherman for decades. He also found it difficult to work with Howard even though the latter had done nothing to wrong him. In fact, Howard went out of his way to consider Logan's feelings, giving him full credit every time it was due. Most officers and members of the rank and file in the Army of the Tennessee were surprised but willing to give Howard a chance.[36]

The new commander had a splendid opportunity only the next day. His career had barely survived the results of Stonewall Jackson's flank attack at Chancellorsville, where his Eleventh Corps, Army of the Potomac had been stunned by an assault that played a large role in the Union defeat. Howard was determined never to let that happen again. He carefully planned the Army of the Tennessee's march to the west side of Atlanta so that all units would be prepared for action immediately if caught on the move. Once there, Howard positioned Logan's Fifteenth Corps in a long refused line to protect Sherman's right flank.[37]

At noon on July 28, the Confederates suddenly attacked Logan's line. Hood had not intended this to happen. His plan to deal with Sherman's new move was to use his old corps, now known as Lee's Corps under the command of Lt. Gen. Stephen D. Lee, to block further Union progress short of the Lick Skillet Road, while Lt. Gen. Alexander P. Stewart's former Army of Mississippi, now incorporated into the Army of Tennessee structure as Stewart's Corps, would launch an attack on the Union rear areas the next day. But Lee panicked when Logan's skirmishers reached the Lick Skillet Road, and he ordered his entire command into action. The attacks were poorly coordinated and went in with little information about the Union position, but they were fiercely pressed and came surprisingly close in some instances to local success. Logan's men fought with the same skill, determination, and resilience as they had on July 22 and repelled every assault. The Battle of Ezra Church, named after a meetinghouse on the field, resulted in 3,000 Confederate losses but only 632 Union casualties.[38]

Howard deserved full credit for skillfully handling the army to take into account the real possibility of another enemy attack. The fight at Ezra Church sealed the men's faith in Howard's ability to lead the army, and Sherman was gratified as well. Howard effectively led the Army of the Tennessee for the rest of the war, longer than Sherman and McPherson had commanded it. In some ways, he was a better commander than McPherson. Given his care in protecting the army from a flank attack on July 27–28, it is difficult to imagine Howard would have allowed the left flank to have been unguarded so long on July 21–22 as McPherson had done.[39]

In addition to creating a bitter feeling for Logan, Howard's promotion angered Maj. Gen. Joseph Hooker, commander of the Twentieth Corps in the Army of the Cumberland. His commission predated Howard's, and he had been Howard's superior as commander of the Army of the Potomac at Chancellorsville. Hooker was incensed at not being tapped as McPherson's replacement, believing his rank and experience justified it. But he had no real idea how much he was disliked not only by Sherman but by Thomas as well. Possessing an ego that knew no bounds, abrasive, and nursing an inflated self-image, Hooker unwittingly played into the hands of his superiors by offering to resign his position on July 27. Both Thomas and Sherman approved it before he could change his mind, and a thorn in their side was out of the campaign. Hooker nurtured a lifelong hatred of Sherman, even writing long letters to friends in the U.S. government trying to undermine public confidence in his leadership, but it had no effect. Hooker also hated Howard for the rest of his life but failed to bring him down despite his bitter efforts to do so.[40]

Within a week after the bloody battle of July 22, Sherman had managed to deal with three personnel problems among his division and army commanders, gotten rid of a troublesome subordinate, managed a difficult shift from left to right, and rejoiced in the success of a splendid defensive victory over his enemy. It had been a busy week, indeed, and one that promoted his operational plan against Atlanta by a long stride.

For Hood, the week had brought nothing but additional trouble. The Federal move from left to right had proven that whatever benefit the Battle of July 22 had brought the Confederates in terms of stopping Sherman's flanking moves had been temporary at best. His careful plan to deal a similar blow west of Atlanta had unraveled because of Lee's impetuous attack on the afternoon of July 28. In three battles, fought on July 20, 22, and 28, the Army of Tennessee had lost at least 11,000 men to achieve nothing of real value to justify the loss of life. In the first ten days of his tenure as commander of the army, Hood had largely failed those members of the rank and file who had given him a chance to prove himself.[41]

The Battle of Atlanta on July 22 had been the biggest, most spectacular engagement of the campaign. But it did not decisively determine who would win or lose the struggle for Atlanta. The campaign continued with only a brief pause. Each phase of the operation, every battle fought within it, to a greater or lesser degree influenced the outcome. But none of those phases or battles were the key to opening the gates of the city until the last phase in late August and the last battle at Jonesboro allowed Federal troops to walk the streets of Atlanta on September 2, 1864.

14

Battlefield, Commemoration, and Memory

When the Army of the Tennessee evacuated its position on the far left of the Union line on the morning of July 27, it took the flow of events in the Atlanta Campaign away from the battlefield of July 22. From that point in time, the field became an object of curiosity for some and for many others a sacred ground of contested memory and commemoration. Others forgot what happened there, but the survivors and their loved ones could never put it out of their minds. Veterans of the 31st Illinois chose July 22 as their annual meeting date after the war because, as Lt. Edmund E. Nutt of the 20th Ohio phrased it, that "was the most memorable day of the war" for many men who survived it.[1]

Curiosity mixed with sadness impelled visitors to seek the battleground as soon as the Federals evacuated the area. A number of Confederate generals toured the field on July 27 and were impressed by the Union earthworks, mostly constructed since the battle, which "were like rat holes in a curve and were thrown up on all sides," wrote Capt. Thomas J. Key. He found a Northern newspaper that confirmed McPherson's death. Other curious Confederates discovered that their enemy had buried some Rebel dead in a trench so imperfectly that they could recognize the individuals before reinterring them. In some areas, legs and arms were sticking out of the shallow graves, green flies swarmed over the field, and many horse carcasses still littered the ground.[2]

By early August, Schofield also shifted his Army of the Ohio (Twenty-Third Corps) from the Union left to the right, leaving Maj. Gen. David S. Stanley's Fourth Corps to hold the left at Copenhill. Stanley extended his picket line south of the Georgia Railroad and onto a part of the battle-field of July 22. By August 19, he moved his main line south of the railroad to divert Confederate attention from Sherman's efforts to extend his right flank west of Atlanta. After the fall of the city, Federal forces established semipermanent camps near Decatur to rest, giving them easy access to the battlefield. "Houses burned, fences destroyed, trees scarred with bullet marks, and everything now as silent as the grave," as Lt. Russell M. Tuttle of the 107th New York described it. Graves, in fact, seemed to be the most prominent feature of the battlefield, scattered individually or collected in a trench. Intricate earthworks dug after the engagement were the next most prominent sight. Men who survived the battle now sought souvenirs. Capt. Charles Dana Miller of the 76th Ohio cut saplings to make two canes, one of which he gave to a Sanitary Fair to be sold to raise money for the war effort, while the other became a gift to his father. Bald Hill, the epicenter of Seventeenth Corps fighting, was covered with earthworks and graves and thus was "much changed" when a recovered Manning F. Force looked at it on November 14 just before the start of the March to the Sea.[3]

In fact, as they moved along the road to Decatur, many Federals passed right through the battlefield of July 22 as they began marching to Savannah. Sherman and his staff stopped at Copenhill on the way and took a last look at the ground. The general could spot the wooded area where McPherson was killed, he noted the pall of smoke rising from the burned buildings in Atlanta, and was touched when members of the passing Fourteenth Corps began to sing a spirited song. Decatur was nearly empty of inhabitants, its buildings badly battered and worn by occupation and combat.[4]

The battlefield became an object of recovery, commemoration, and memory after Sherman's forces left Atlanta. The first priority after the war was to remove the hasty burials to permanent cemeteries. The ex-Confederates had to rely on private means to do this. T. R. Bell of Atlanta helped a Mississippi man named A. R. Raymond recover the body of Raymond's son, who had been killed in the 41st Mississippi of Tucker's (Sharp's) Brigade. It was removed to a civilian cemetery in the city. In contrast, Federal dead were removed by the U.S. Army and reburied in a national cemetery at Marietta.[5]

With time and improvement in the local economy, development affected the battlefield. By the 1880s, it already was encroaching on the ground. Veterans of the 15th Iowa reported that building lots 50 by 150 feet in size were selling for $500 each. Houses sprouted on the very spot where some veterans had fought and suffered, and it did not make them happy to see them. They had difficulty locating key positions they had held and felt disoriented when visiting the field. The earthworks were steadily disappearing, and the veterans knew it would only be a matter of time before they were all gone forever. The area that included the battlefield became the target of large-scale development by the late 1880s, when Inman Park was laid out as Atlanta's first electric-streetcar suburb.[6]

Bald Hill, the epicenter of Seventeenth Corps fighting, became known to Union veterans as Leggett's Hill after the war. Mortimer D. Leggett wanted to purchase the hill and negotiated a deal with its current owner, James Brown. In fact, there were three men in the Atlanta area named James Brown, so this one was called "Spanish Jim" to differentiate him from "Black Strap Jim" and "Little Jim." Unfortunately, Leggett died before money changed hands, and his widow backed out of the deal. As a result, when Spanish Jim died in 1893, Fred Koch purchased Leggett's Hill and built a three-story brick home on its top at 282 Moreland Ave. Koch was willing to guide at least some of the many Union veterans who flocked to this historic site and show them where the earthworks were still intact, but that did not last long. The remnants gradually disappeared, and more houses were constructed until Leggett's Hill was covered with development. The veterans erected a sign and the city set up a marker to remind visitors of the historic spot as the "old breastworks" gradually wore away in the backyards of numerous houses. As a final insult, the hill was virtually obliterated when Interstate 20 was constructed over it in the early 1960s.[7]

Historic buildings on the battlefield also did not fare well. The White House, also called the Pope House, the white frame structure a short distance in front of the Fifteenth Corps line that was used by the Confederates as a sharpshooting post, was burned on the night of July 22. The Troup Hurt House, near the site of De Gress's battery, burned on the evening of July 27, 1864, probably set afire by the Confederates. Although the Federals had evacuated the area early that morning, the Rebels might have worried they would soon return.[8]

The Howard House on Copenhill survived a bit longer than the two near the Georgia Railroad. A signal station was established on its roof and maintained until the fall of Atlanta in early September 1864. Soon after, the structure was torn down to construct huts in the semipermanent camps the Federals constructed around the city. After the war, Maj. Gen. John B. Gordon of the Army of Northern Virginia built a home near the site of the Howard House. Beginning in 1890, building lots all over Copenhill were sold as part of a massive development copying Inman Park farther south. One of the houses near the top of the hill was occupied from 1916 to 1918 by Wilbur G. Kurtz, the Illinois-born illustrator and engraver who became the most famous authority on Atlanta's Civil War history by the 1930s. The A. L. Waldo House at the corner of Cleburne Avenue and Copenhill Avenue marked the site of the old Howard House. In the 1960s, long after the allure of Copenhill and Inman Park had faded, many houses in both areas were razed to make way for the planned interstate bypass of Atlanta now called Interstate 485. But public resistance forced planners to move the beltway farther east, and by 1986, Copenhill was chosen as the site of the Jimmy Carter Presidential Library. In 1992, Freedom Parkway linked the library with the older expressway system of Interstate 75 running through the center of Atlanta. Thus, a key site of the Battle of July 22 was converted into a center that not only houses the historic resources of Carter's presidency but also fosters international understanding, peace, and health care.[9]

In the Sugar Creek area, Terry's Mill apparently was burned by Twenty-Third Corps skirmishers sometime between July 27 and August 1, but the millpond remained intact for some time after the war. The railroad cut that doomed the Fifteenth Corps line, however, had disappeared by the 1930s.[10]

Visual representations of the battlefield appeared in the form of photographs and paintings. George N. Barnard, a civilian photographer under government contract, left his base at Nashville on September 11, 1864, and traveled to newly occupied Atlanta. He exposed at least four images of McPherson's death site, by then including a board nailed to a tree to indicate the significance of the spot. These images were reproduced in a woodcut engraving that appeared in *Harper's Weekly* on February 18, 1865, and prints of them were sold by the E. and H. T. Anthony Company of New York City early in 1865. Barnard returned to Atlanta early in November 1864 and late in May 1866 to expose more views of the general's death site. This time he tried to make it appear more "natural" by arranging animal bones and foliage and painted out the inscription on the board. Barnard also exposed in May 1866 three images of Union earthworks on the battlefield. He did not indicate exactly where those works were located, but one of the photographs appears to represent part of the Union line along Flat Shoals Road and the other two were probably exposed on Bald Hill.[11]

Three paintings of the Battle of Atlanta were executed by talented artists during the later nineteenth century. James E. Taylor, a native of Cincinnati and graduate of the University of Notre Dame, had served in the 10th New York during the first half of the war before devoting himself full time to documenting the conflict through his art. *Frank Leslie's Illustrated Newspaper* published sixty-one of his sketches, all of them depicting the eastern campaigns. But Taylor worked with John W. Fuller after the war to produce two paintings of Sixteenth Corps action on July 22. One of them highlights

Maj. Gen. Grenville M. Dodge's role in the battle, while the other focuses on Fuller. Taylor worked closely with Fuller on the latter scene, which depicts the general rallying the 27th Ohio at the key moment of his battle with Gist's Brigade and includes Col. Mendel Churchill and other officers encouraging the troops. The originals of both paintings have disappeared, but prints remain to preserve Taylor's work.[12]

The third painting of the battle is the largest and most famous. It was part of a general interest in huge panoramic paintings of battles that swept the country in the later nineteenth century. German-born William Wehner established the American Panorama Company in Milwaukee in 1883, recruited artists from Europe, and began in 1885 a cyclorama of the Union attack up Missionary Ridge during the Battle of Chattanooga. Wehner also initiated plans for a cyclorama of the Battle of July 22, taking his team to Atlanta in the summer of 1885. They thoroughly studied the landscape, erecting a forty-foot tower near the Georgia Railroad to gain a higher perspective, and made sketches and oil paintings of the terrain.[13]

Wehner employed the services of Theodore R. Davis, a staff artist for *Harper's Weekly* during the war who was an eyewitness of the battle. Born in 1841, Davis had studied art before the conflict and extensively covered the fighting in both the East and the West by accompanying the armies and exposing himself to enemy fire. He submitted a total of 252 drawings, many of which were converted into woodcut illustrations in *Harper's Weekly*. Davis traveled to Atlanta with his field notes and wartime sketchbook to minutely examine the terrain in 1885. He had already done similar work for Wehner on the battlefield of Missionary Ridge, but the Atlanta field held a special place in his memory. He scoured the terrain and, despite the encroachment of suburban development, was able to locate all of its historic spots with the aid of his records and the helpful suggestions of ex-Confederate officers living in the area. The Germans, on the other hand, needed interpreters to communicate with the local inhabitants.[14]

On his return, Davis contacted Reuben Williams to ask what color horse the brigade leader rode on July 22. When Williams also referred to the tannery building behind his line, Davis replied that half a dozen officers told him there was no such structure. It took "a full month of correspondence" for Williams to convince the artist that such a building existed.[15]

Back at the Milwaukee studio by the end of 1885, the Wehner team began working on the Atlanta painting in January 1886. They accumulated specimens of uniforms, weapons, and equipment and studied reports and maps supplied by the War Department. The seventeen artists represented specialists in landscape painting, as well as animal and equipment depiction, and worked together to produce an artwork 400 feet long and 50 feet tall.

When the two ends were connected, the whole formed a circular view of the precise moment when Mersy's brigade was about to pounce on the Confederates to start the recovery of the Fifteenth Corps line. The viewer had to enter through an underpass to emerge in the center of the circle. Backed by extensive research into every nuance of the scene, *The Battle of Atlanta*, better known as the Atlanta Cyclorama, is minutely accurate.[16]

Wehner had spent $40,000 to make this massive painting by the end of 1886 and could only recoup his expenses if the public was willing to pay admission to see it. That involved moving the cyclorama around, no small matter considering it weighed 18,000 pounds and required a special building. Therefore the painting traveled to five different cities during the next five years until reaching Atlanta itself. Then it shifted from one building to another in that city before reaching its final home in 2019. This long journey began when Wehner transported the cyclorama to Detroit for its premiere on February 26, 1887. By some it was called "Logan's Great Battle," apparently in an effort to boost the Illinois Democrat's chances for a presidential nomination in 1888, but that proved a futile hope. There is not even any evidence that Logan saw the cyclorama, although an image of him riding furiously across the battlefield is a prominent part of it.[17]

Soon, the cyclorama continued its long journey. Wehner moved it next to Minneapolis and, by May 29, 1888, to Indianapolis, where it was housed in a newly constructed circular building. Initial public interest soon waned, and financial difficulties set in. During August 1890, a receiver was appointed to manage the financially troubled painting, which resulted in a public auction. The Miller estate, which owned the property on which the building was located in Indianapolis, purchased the cyclorama for only $6,060 on October 4, 1890. Then Paul Atkinson of Madison, Georgia, owner of Wehner's Missionary Ridge cyclorama, bought the Atlanta painting in March 1891. He moved it to Chattanooga and exhibited both paintings there, drawing in $27,000 within eighteen months. Atkinson then separated the two, sending Missionary Ridge first to Atlanta and then to Nashville. He shifted the July 22 cyclorama to Atlanta in 1892, where it has remained ever since. The Missionary Ridge cyclorama was destroyed by a tornado soon after it arrived at Nashville, leaving July 22 as the only surviving work of Wehner's company.[18]

But the Atlanta Cyclorama's troubles were only beginning. Financial difficulties plagued its history, and Atkinson sold the painting to H. H. Harrison of Florida, who planned to show it at the World's Columbian Exposition in Chicago in 1893. But the exposition management insisted on a new brick building to house it, and Harrison could not afford one. The cyclorama, therefore, remained in a structure on Atlanta's Edgewood Avenue near the battlefield, where on January 18–19, 1893, an unusual eight-inch snowstorm broke the roof and seriously damaged the painting. Meanwhile, rent and taxes piled up until the cyclorama was sold at public auction, once again, on August 1, 1893. This time, Ernest Woodruff purchased it for $1,100 and soon sold it to Atlanta businessmen George V. Gress and Charles Northen for $4,000. Atlanta city officials now became involved in the history of the cyclorama, constructing a building for it at Grant Park in the southeastern part of the city. Gress and Northen continued to own the painting, however, working out a deal with the city for the use of the building. They netted $12,000 in four and a half years, although ticket prices were no more than ten cents. Gress and Northen donated their proceeds to charity and offered to deed the cyclorama to the city if officials agreed to repair the building and refurbish the painting. That was done in the summer of 1898.[19]

But maintaining the building as well as the painting continued to be major problems. When the wooden structure in Grant Park again needed refurbishment, the city decided to construct a new building of marble not far away. They shifted the cyclorama to its new marble home in 1921. The city also moved the Civil War locomotive *Texas* to the new building. This had been the engine used by William H. Fuller to chase down the *General*, which had been hijacked by a group of Union soldiers disguised as civilians in the spring of 1862. Their objective had been to tear up the Western and Atlantic Railroad between Atlanta and Chattanooga. Fuller had hounded them so closely that they were unable to do much damage, and most of the Federals were captured. Wilbur G. Kurtz had married Fuller's daughter in 1911.[20]

The July 22 cyclorama never failed to impress an audience; the only problem lay in getting enough visitors interested in seeing it over the long term. While Civil War soldiers still lived, they represented a hefty proportion of the audience. The painting depicts many real players in the battle, from Sherman and Logan down to obscure staff officers. Its depiction of unit placements, the flow of action, and the landscape is nearly impeccable. When Reuben Williams saw the cyclorama in Indianapolis, he called it "a very correct picture of the battle." But after it moved to Atlanta, the interpretive stance dramatically changed. Granville McDonald of the 30th Illinois viewed it there in 1895 and hated the pro-South slant of the explanatory text given to visitors. It deliberately gave the troop strength of Sherman's entire army group as if all of the men in the three field armies had been engaged in the battle, even though only one of them actually opposed Hood's attack. When James Cooper Nisbet mentioned the cyclorama in his memoirs, he incorrectly wrote that it depicted the Confederate capture of De Gress's battery rather than the Union recapture of the guns. It was inevitable that the painting would become involved in the ambiguous nature of sectional reconciliation after the war.[21]

The contested nature of the cyclorama continued even as further restoration work took place. The city applied to the Civil Works Administration, a New Deal agency designed to employ out-of-work Americans, to enhance the display. The Public Works of Art Project of the CWA agreed to take on the job, hiring artists from 1934 to 1936. Until then, the area at the foot of the cyclorama had remained flat, with a few objects scattered about. It was now proposed to grace it so as to blend in with the painting and install 128 plaster models of human figures. The artists also wanted to blast tree stumps with dynamite to simulate battle damage. With the addition of "exploded shells, fragments of rails and cross-ties, . . . simulated grass and a great deal of Georgia clay," the foreground assumed its modern character. The workers also repaired a few tears and other minor damage to the painting. Sculptors Joseph Victor Llorens and Wies Snell were in charge of the project, and Kurtz contributed to the team's efforts.[22]

Atlanta was in some ways the epicenter of the Lost Cause mythology that extolled Southern virtue, apologized for slavery, and posited Confederate soldiers as American patriots. No single document better exemplified the unreality of Lost Cause tenets than Margaret Mitchell's novel *Gone with the Wind*, which was made into a movie released in 1939 with a major premiere in Atlanta; Kurtz served as a technical advisor for the film. The hoopla also involved celebration of the cyclorama, even though the painting depicted a Confederate defeat and had been created by a group of German artists headquartered in a Northern city.[23]

Lost Cause myths continued to buttress the Southern slant accorded the cyclorama until desegregation began to unravel racial suppression in the ex-Confederate states. The tide slowly began to turn. Atlanta's first Black mayor, Maynard Jackson, pushed efforts to repair the cyclorama in 1979, pointing out that it celebrated a victory for the Federal government and its antislavery efforts during the Civil War. Another Black mayor, Kasim Reed, signed the painting over to the Atlanta History Center in 2014. The center raised $35 million to create a new building for the painting and carefully planned its presentation to the public as an effort to destroy the false claims of the archaic Lost Cause mythology. A grand opening of the refurbished cyclorama in its new and permanent home, with an accurate presentation of the Civil War history surrounding it, took place on February 22, 2019. This fit into national trends; all across the South, efforts to take down or remove Lost Cause symbols such as monuments to Confederate generals and the placement of the Stars and Bars on state flags finally reached a turning point in the contentious summer of 2020. We can finally hope that true history is replacing racist myths in Civil War memory.[24]

Despite the leading role played by the cyclorama in relation to the Battle of Atlanta and contested perceptions of the Civil War among modern audiences, the death of James B. McPherson was far more prominent in the minds of the Civil War generation. The general had been so widely admired, mostly for his genial personality and competent administrative leadership, that his sudden death on July 22 shocked everyone and created a wellspring of intense interest that never diminished until his contemporaries followed him in death.

The fascination began immediately. Widespread rumors that McPherson had unnecessarily exposed himself led Sherman to spread the word that it was not so. His favorite subordinate had been doing his duty, as all responsible officers had to do. The problem was the heavily vegetated landscape of the battle, which hid dangers until they were too close to be avoided.[25]

McPherson's body began a long journey home soon after its recovery from the battlefield. Sherman sent it north to Clyde, Ohio, under the supervision of three of his personal staff officers, Maj. Lot S. Willard, Capt. George R. Steele, and Capt. David H. Gile. Taken to Marietta, where it was dressed and placed in a casket, the body was then moved by rail, reaching Nashville by the morning of July 25. There McPherson's brother Russell, who had been working for government military railroads at Memphis. joined the group. He helped bury his brother in the family plot at Clyde on July 29.[26]

In a bizarre stroke of irony, a trainload of Confederate prisoners captured during the Battle of July 22 stopped briefly in Clyde on its way to the prison for enemy officers at Johnson's Island on July 29. Among the number was Capt. Richard Beard, one of whose men had fired the shot that mortally wounded McPherson. When Beard saw the flag flying at half-mast, he asked a Federal soldier what it meant. McPherson had been buried that day, he was told, "the 'damned Rebels had murdered'" him. Along with Beard was his friend, Capt. William A. Brown, who had taken McPherson's hat at the death site and ironically was wearing it in the railroad car. Brown continued to use it throughout his stay at Johnson's Island. Both men were released in May 1865 a few weeks after the war ended.[27]

Sherman remained scarred by the death of his friend for the rest of his life. "I lost my Right bower in McPherson," he told his wife. Sherman also assumed McPherson would rise to the top levels of command if anything happened to either himself or Grant. "General McPherson fell in battle, booted and spurred, as the gallant knight and gentleman should wish." Schofield recalled that Sherman bitterly said that "the whole of the Confederacy could not atone for the sacrifice of one such life." Sherman also publicly commented that Hood would never have graduated from West Point if not for McPherson's tolerance of his errant behavior and his willingness to help the younger cadet catch up with his studies. Hood was deeply hurt when he heard about this comment. He once told former Union colonel Lionel A. Sheldon, who happened to travel with him on a train from New Orleans to Louisville, that it was an unkind comment. "He said he was a wild Kentucky boy and liked to be out nights," recalled Sheldon, and counted on McPherson's kindness to make up for it. Hood also "spoke affectionately of McPherson."[28]

Grant also felt the pain of McPherson's loss. When the slain commander's grandmother, eighty-seven-year-old Lydia Slocum, heard that the general in chief "wept like a child" at the news, she was moved to write a long letter to him. Grant replied, assuring her that "to know him was but to love him." Sentiments of respect and love were echoed by all of McPherson's colleagues, including Howard, Blair, Logan, Dodge, and Schofield. Staff members mourned as if he had been their father. "An hundred times an hour the memory of poor Mc flashes over my brain, & only with severe effort can I refrain the scalding tears," wrote Capt. Lewis M. Dayton, one of Sherman's aides-de-camp. Capt. Andrew Hickenlooper, McPherson's artillery chief, called him "my *best friend . . . a perfect man*," whose death created a void in his life that could never be filled. Such feelings penetrated deeply into the officer corps. "I knew & loved him well. He was my best friend in the Army," wrote William W. Belknap to his fiancée. The story of McPherson's doffing his hat courteously just before trying to escape struck a chord and was often repeated.[29]

The effect of McPherson's death on his family was even more devastating. Lydia Slocum fought against the gloom that settled on her mind. She found some solace in a laudatory article about her grandson written by B. Randolph Keim and published in the *United Service Magazine* of October 1864. Brother Russell traveled to Atlanta soon after the fall of the city in a vain effort to track down McPherson's personal effects. He picked a few wildflowers and evergreen sprigs from the death site. The general's horse, which had escaped the Confederate fire that killed McPherson, had been retrieved by the Federals and shipped to Clyde. McPherson's younger brother Billy was responsible for taking care of it. But on March 22, 1871, the horse suddenly kicked Billy as the young man was currying it, and he died the next day. The horse was later given to other family members and died of old age. Lydia Slocum passed away in 1876 at age ninety-nine.[30]

But the person most deeply affected by McPherson's death was his fiancée, Emily Hoffman. They had postponed their marriage because of Sherman's need to have McPherson available for preparations concerning the Atlanta Campaign. Brig. Gen. William F. Barry, Sherman's artillery chief, asked Capt. John C. Van Duzer, an assistant superintendent of the U.S.

Military Telegraph traveling with the army group, to inform the Hoffman family of the bad news on July 23. It so shocked Emily that the young lady shut herself in a darkened room, refusing to speak to anyone, for several weeks. She eventually allowed a sister to read to her from the Bible. Sherman wrote a long consolatory letter to Emily, but it did not seem to help much. A year later, she gave up her seclusion but lived a short, bitter life after that, never marrying.[31]

Such intense shock and grief, felt throughout many layers of McPherson's society, produced a long struggle to properly commemorate his life and death. In July 1865, Blair initiated efforts to raise money from among Seventeenth Corps veterans to erect a monument to McPherson at Clyde, Ohio. He wanted it to be "a soldier's offering to a soldier's memory" and expected the rank and file to contribute generously. Logan, who then commanded what was left of the Army of the Tennessee, strongly supported the drive, which soon became the responsibility of a new organization called the Society of the Army of the Tennessee. Despite strong support, it took many years for the society to marshal enough funds.[32]

Meanwhile, efforts to monumentalize McPherson's death site took place. Orlando M. Poe, Sherman's chief engineer, spent much time scouring the battlefield of July 22 in November 1875 to gather information for an official map of this part of the Atlanta Campaign. He found that much of the wooded areas already were being cleared and new houses were dotting the field. Poe's letters to Sherman about his work led the general to recommend that McPherson's death site be purchased and marked before it disappeared. On receiving approval from the War Department, officials bought the plot from Spanish Jim Brown and erected a fence made of musket barrels surrounding a 32-pounder artillery tube standing upright with a shell on top. Maj. John R. McGuinness acted as chief agent to arrange everything, which included finding the trees that someone had blazed in 1864 to mark the exact spot of McPherson's fall. He also secured enough property to construct a road from the site out to Flat Shoals Road to be called McPherson Avenue. All this was done by July 1877. The Society of the Army of the Tennessee owned the monument as well as the twelve square feet of ground that surrounded it.[33]

But the monument soon became a target for avaricious tourists. When former Union artillerist Henry J. Hunt visited the McPherson death site in May 1880, he was appalled at the vandalism that had already taken place. Forty-eight arrowheads, seventeen gun barrels, and two flowers on the corner posts of the fence had been broken off. Hunt made arrangements to effect repairs at government expense, but when he returned to the site in July, he found that even more damage had been done. Locals told him that relic hunters were the problem, but the grounds had been preserved in a natural state, appropriate for the purpose, Hunt thought. He recommended that the elaborate fence be removed to take away the temptation to destroy it.[34]

Nevertheless, the fence remained and continued to be broken and carried away in pieces by tourists, who even began to chip away at the granite base supporting the artillery tube. Sometime before 1896, the government completely changed the monument, albeit along similar lines to the original. The base was replaced and a different artillery tube without a shell on its top was put on it. The elaborate fence was replaced by a simple one of two iron rails held up by concrete posts. Relic hunters eventually disappeared, and the newly streamlined monument has since stood the test of time.[35]

Meanwhile, a struggle was slowly developing for the right to honor McPherson through outdoor sculpture. In November 1865, only four months after Blair and Logan began collecting money for a monument at Clyde, another group of officers began a fundraising effort for a McPherson monument to be erected at West Point. That group suggested that the Clyde group pool its resources with them, but the offer was flatly rejected. Yet another monument drive sprang up in 1865 to erect an equestrian statue of McPherson in Washington, D.C. To make matters even more complicated, army officials appointed William B. Hazen, Mortimer D. Leggett, and Andrew Hickenlooper, the exact three men who managed the Clyde statue drive sponsored by the Society of the Army of the Tennessee, to manage this Washington statue effort as well. In fact, the society became the sponsor of both monuments. The three veterans worked quietly for ten years, and as their efforts reached a stage when it became necessary to publicize them, many veterans were naturally confused. They had supported the Clyde statue, not this Washington statue, with their contributions. Moreover, the Clyde project continued to languish. A base for it was installed, but as yet no statue was available. Meanwhile, Hickenlooper devoted most of his efforts to the Washington statue as a labor of love for his former chief and shortchanged attention on the Clyde project.[36]

In June 1876, a bizarre incident occurred when two strangers came to Clyde from Washington. They hired several local men and began to tear apart the base of the long-awaited statue that had not yet been erected over McPherson's grave. The trustees of the cemetery stopped them and demanded an explanation. The two men claimed they knew nothing about the Clyde monument drive or that $1,500 had already been spent on building the base. Their objective was to disinter McPherson's remains and remove them to Washington. It turned out, surprisingly, that McPherson's mother had authorized the removal and that Pres. Ulysses S. Grant had given the

McPherson Monument. Initially erected in 1877 at the site of Maj. Gen. James B. McPherson's death, the monument consisted of a fence made of musket barrels surrounding a 32-pounder artillery tube standing upright with a shell on top. Vandals immediately began to break off parts of the monument as souvenirs, and by 1896, the government rebuilt it in its present form. Once isolated in the countryside, the site is now a part of suburban Atlanta. Photograph by Earl J. Hess.

orders. Clyde officials put a stop to it and also tried the pair in a local court to recover the estimated $300 in damage inflicted on the base.[37]

It would take some time to complete the Clyde monument, but meanwhile national attention was focused on the equestrian statue to be erected in Washington. The Society of the Army of the Tennessee held its tenth annual meeting in the national capital on October 18–19, 1876, in part to dedicate the bronze equestrian statue at McPherson Square three blocks from the White House. Louis Rebisso, an Italian-born sculptor who had fled to the United States after supporting Giuseppe Mazzini's failed effort to form a united republic in Italy, had created the statue. President Grant had ordered all government departments to close at noon on October 18 to allow employees to attend the unveiling and arranged to have the Marine Corps Band play at the ceremonies. While Sherman presided over the event, Logan gave a two-hour oration telling the story of McPherson's life. That evening, the society held a meeting in Lincoln Hall at which Logan and Grant made short speeches.[38]

The Society of the Army of the Tennessee had contributed most of the funds for the Washington monument, but it continued to plow ahead with its plans for the Clyde monument at the same time. Rebisso also made the

Clyde statue, this one at the Cincinnati Art Foundry. For this monument, he portrayed McPherson standing rather than riding. It was unveiled on July 22, 1881, with former Pres. Rutherford B. Hayes presiding. Members of many Grand Army of the Republic posts, National Guard units, and local militia organizations participated in the ceremonies. The massive event drew a crowd of 20,000 people, including McPherson's mother and sisters. Among the speakers were several survivors of the Battle of Atlanta, including Manning F. Force, William E. Strong, Mortimer D. Leggett, and William W. Belknap. Sherman also gave a long speech about his friend before he formally unveiled the statue.[39]

As a result of all these efforts, three permanent monuments honor McPherson to this day, erected after much time and money on the part of his friends in the army and the government. At the same time, key players in McPherson's fate and in the Battle of Atlanta struggled to erect a monument of words to give what they believed was a correct version of events for posterity. Richard Beard survived captivity and settled in Murfreesboro, Tennessee as a lawyer after the war. Northern grief over McPherson's death boiled up until many people began spreading the rumor that the general had been murdered on the battlefield. Beard felt compelled to tell his side of the story and began with an article in the *Nashville Union and American* in 1875: "The circumstances under which General McPherson met his death were perfectly justifiable. He had every opportunity on earth to surrender and refused to do so, but preferred to take the chances of flight." Beard wrote several other articles and gave interviews to protect his reputation, living well past 1920 into ripe old age.[40]

On the Federal side, Strong, who masterminded the recovery of McPherson's remains from the battlefield, became the unofficial historian of the tragic death. By 1876, he solicited information from Logan and Sherman and began writing articles. The latter endorsed Strong's account as the best available, urging him to make sure everyone realized that McPherson had not unwisely exposed himself to danger by riding along the little road to reach the Seventeenth Corps that fateful day. Belknap also conducted research into McPherson's death and solicited information from his former enemies in 1878. On reading a report supplied by Daniel C. Govan, Belknap "again fought over that battle in imagination. It was a terrific fight, perhaps the most severe of the war."[41]

The Confederates had no one of McPherson's stature to eulogize. Their highest-ranking casualty, William H. T. Walker, was a relatively minor figure in the Southern pantheon of generals. Georgia born and West Point educated, he had been wounded during the Second Seminole War as well as the Mexican War but saw little field service in the Civil War. Poor health contributed to this, but luck more than anything consigned Walker to largely inactive areas. He had commanded Georgia state troops for a while in 1862 and had risen to the rank of major general in the Confederate service. Walker commanded the Reserve Corps, Army of Tennessee at Chickamauga but was killed before entering what would have been his most important Civil War battle on July 22.[42]

To the extent that Southerners thought about Walker, they were impressed by his vigorous Confederate sympathies and his desire to close with the enemy. On the other hand, he had an abrasive, touchy personality. Octavius Cohen Myers recognized the dual nature of this man but was nevertheless devoted to him. Walker had courted Myers's sister long before the war. "I became very much attached to him," Myers remembered, even though his sister rejected Walker and instead married Goode Bryan, who later became a brigadier general in the Army of Northern Virginia. "Whilst he had a great many faults at the same time he possessed many virtues." Myers served as Walker's assistant adjutant general when the general commanded Georgia state troops.[43]

After Walker's death near the northern end of Terry's Mill Pond, his body was transported by rail to Augusta via a roundabout way through Macon because the Federals had cut the Georgia Railroad. His funeral took place on July 24. Thirty-eight years later, ready for a slain hero to emerge, Confederate eulogizers latched on to Walker. Julius L. Brown organized an effort to raise funds for the erection of a monument at his death site "in exact duplicate of the one to McPherson," as he put it. An Atlanta attorney, Julius was the brother of wartime governor Joseph E. Brown and of Lt. Col. John M. Brown, who had been mortally wounded on July 22. Julius worked swiftly; the landowner, a Confederate veteran, donated the site, and Brown arranged for a right of way to build a road to the spot. He organized a dedication ceremony for July 22, 1902. Joseph B. Cumming, Walker's assistant adjutant general, gave the major commemoration speech. After the dedication, Brown continued his overall plan by raising private funds and obtaining a Civil War cannon tube from the U.S. government.[44]

But by the 1930s, Wilbur G. Kurtz had uncovered evidence that the Walker monument had been misplaced. J. W. McWilliams, a veteran of the 42nd Georgia and longtime Atlanta resident, told him that he understood it had been deliberately put short of the exact spot because of the difficulty of moving the artillery tube and the granite for its base over the swampy ground that had existed since the drainage of the millpond. On further examining the case, Kurtz became convinced that McWilliams was right. Since 1902, Glenwood Avenue had been built west to east, passing what had been the northern extent of the pond, and offered ready access to the spot. He concluded that Walker had fallen "a few feet N. E. of where Glenwood Ave-nue crosses Sugar Creek" and two-tenths of a mile east of the monument.[45]

Kurtz began an effort to move the monument in 1931, working with the city planning commission. The new site was dedicated on May 21, 1937, with Kurtz giving the major speech. The older monument was moved intact, but a new tablet, unveiled by a Georgia Tech student who was a great-grandson of the general, was installed. The Brown family was involved still; Charles M. Brown, the nephew of Julius and executor of his uncle's estate, had to give permission for the move.[46]

This story of dueling monuments was a lopsided one. Walker garnered limited interest even among Southerners compared to the avalanche of interest generated by McPherson among Northerners. But he was all the Lost Cause people could muster from this battle that, after all, was a Confederate defeat. For many decades, the Lost Cause had ridden on the fame of the Atlanta Cyclorama until very recent times.

Capt. Francis De Gress and his Battery H, 1st Illinois Light Artillery gained a lesser but significant profile of public interest after the war. This started with one of those tactical arguments that often arose among veterans, generated by their limited knowledge of the larger flow of events in any given battle. The argument was expressed in a number of letters to the editor of the *National Tribune*, a newspaper based in Washington, D.C., that was aimed at Union veterans. By the early 1880s, many letters discussed the question concerning which units recaptured De Gress's battery in the counterattacks that restored the Fifteenth Corps line. Veterans of the Fifteenth Corps insisted they alone accomplished that feat without any help from others, while Sixteenth Corps people pointed out the involvement of Mersy's brigade. Most of these veterans were writing before the 1891 publication of volume thirty-eight, part three of *The War of the Rebellion: A Compilation of the Official Records of the Union and Confederate Armies*, which contained reports that clearly spelled out who did and did not recapture the guns. But the arguments continued even after 1891, as most of these veterans based their letters on faulty memory rather than research. The arguments spilled out into published soldier memoirs and even regimental histories.[47]

There can be little doubt that this flood of public arguments influenced the Wehner group when it formulated its plan for the Atlanta Cyclorama in 1885. The recapture of De Gress's battery became the centerpiece of this magnificent painting. Moreover, De Gress himself became an object of commemoration for some people. Born in Cologne, Germany, in 1841, his family came to the United States eleven years later. The battery commander was featured by *Harper's Weekly* with a portrait and a short, adulatory piece about his role in the Battle of Atlanta on September 3, 1864. He was breveted

Walker Monument. This memorial marks the death site of the highest-ranking Confederate casualty of the Battle of July 22, Maj. Gen. William H. T. Walker. It was erected by the driving energy of lawyer Julius L. Brown, brother of Georgia's wartime governor, Joseph E. Brown, and of Lt. Col John M. Brown, who had been mortally wounded on July 22. The monument was dedicated in 1902, but thirty years later Wilbur G. Kurtz concluded it was not properly located. He spearheaded an effort to move the monument two-tenths of a mile east to its present location in 1937. Photograph by Earl J. Hess.

major near the war's end and soon moved permanently to Mexico, where he formed a company with a colleague that sold weapons and ordnance supplies, changing their products to peaceful items after the internal troubles of that country settled down. De Gress married and raised a family but died of blood poisoning near Mexico City in early 1883.[48]

Artist Theodore R. Davis had been greatly impressed by De Gress during the battle and always remembered him "bare headed and bristling with pluck as the Battery was recouped." While roaming the battlefield for days in the fall of 1885, Davis often felt De Gress's spirit was near him. He felt compelled to tell Mrs. De Gress of Wehner's plans to feature the recapture as the centerpiece of the cyclorama. "I have experienced a genuine pleasure in placing my old friend where others could see how true a soldier he was," Davis told her.[49]

De Gress's battery became an object of tactical argument among Confederate veterans as well, although on a smaller scale than among their Union counterparts. Controversy erupted in 1896 over which unit had captured Battery H, 1st Illinois Light Artillery, with some veterans insisting it had been the 42nd Georgia of Stovall's (Johnson's) Brigade. The question was hotly debated among attendees at the United Confederate Veterans' reunion in Atlanta two years later and prompted an official investigation by Robert L. Rodgers, the historian of Atlanta Camp No. 154. Rodgers conducted research and solicited testimony from survivors of the battle, producing a fairly accurate report of the events surrounding its capture. He concluded that the 42nd Georgia did participate in the capture but was unable to decide to what extent it was responsible for taking the guns. The truth was that the capture of De Gress's battery was a joint effort by elements of three brigades, and the exact sequence of events was indeed difficult to pinpoint. In this way, the taking of the guns seemed to mimic their recovery by the Federals. Elements of three brigades were involved in the restoration of the Fifteenth Corps, but in this case, it is easier to see that Mersy's men got to the guns first.[50]

Both Union and Confederate veterans centered much of their July 22 memories on the four fieldpieces of De Gress's battery. The pages of the *National Tribune* became filled with letter after letter about the topic. A total of 205 letters appeared in the newspaper concerning various aspects of the Battle of Atlanta. Of that number, McPherson's death was the subject of 40, while the recapture of De Gress's battery appeared in 30. The rest, 135, covered various aspects of the battle, including the Dodge-Sweeny controversy, the fight for Bald Hill on July 21, and the Battle of Decatur on July 22.

But cooperation coexisted with controversy in memories of the battle. By the early 1880s, when arguments over De Gress's battery surfaced, Govan felt a desire to return the flag of the 16th Iowa his brigade had captured early in the engagement. He contacted Belknap, who invited him to bring it to the Iowa Brigade reunion at Cedar Rapids on September 26, 1883. What happened was a ritual of reconciliation. Govan handed over the colors, and Belknap then waved it as the attendees raised a raucous cheer. Govan spoke and was followed by Addison Sanders, the regiment's commander during the battle who had survived captivity. Even Walter Q. Gresham spoke to the enthusiastic crowd.[51]

The flag of the 3rd Iowa of Benjamin F. Potts's brigade also found its way back to Iowa. It had wound up in the possession of Maj. Gen. Patrick Cleburne, but he gave it as a souvenir to Laura J. Massengale, who visited Atlanta while the Confederates still held the city; Cleburne was a friend of her family. Laura preserved the colors in a cedar chest, where it lay undisturbed until her brother, H. F. Massengale, who had been a Confederate staff member, happened to discover it. He contacted officials in Iowa and arranged to have it sent by express delivery in 1883.[52]

The flag of the 30th Illinois had a bloody history. Color bearer Henry McDonald had defended it with a cavalry carbine early in the battle but lost both it and his life later in the day when J. C. Leird of the 27th Tennessee overpowered him and bore off the banner. It had been sent up the chain of command to Hardee, whose daughter found it in his effects after the general passed away in 1873. She kept it for many decades until sending the flag to Leird in 1910. The aged veteran retained it only one year before initiating contacts with a Confederate veteran post in Chicago and the local Grand Army of the Republic posts. This effort eventually landed the colors in the hands of Illinois state officials. Veterans of the 30th Illinois offered a resolution of thanks to Leird. Granville McDonald, brother of the slain color bearer, drafted the resolution but was careful, when referring to Leird's capture of the colors not to mention that the Confederate had killed his brother in order to take it.[53]

The need to remember and commemorate continued in its most intense form as long as the generation that fought the war lived. But it waned considerably after that, lasting far longer in the Atlanta area than in most other regions of the former Confederacy. Robert G. Stephens, a grandson of Confederate vice president Alexander Stephens, was born at Atlanta in 1913 and became a prominent lawyer in the city. He grew up in an atmosphere suffused with the Rebel past, but in the wake of World War II, it began to noticeably dim. "The 22nd of July used to be heralded in the papers and articles written calling attention to the anniversary occurrence," he wrote to a friend on July 23, 1948, "but this last time I looked in vain for some mention of the day." He recalled as a boy exploring the remnants of the Atlanta City

Line and could tell anyone in 1948 exactly where development had destroyed and built over those earthworks. Stephens long maintained a personal ritual of visiting the fortification remnants and then spending the rest of the day at the cyclorama every July 22. As time went by, he found no one who was interested in joining him.

> I fear the old war has been eclipsed by the two World Wars and the threatened 3rd World War and will never be of the interest it used to be. We will just have to realize we are the rear guard of an old defeated civilization and stand attention with the romance of the past on our left and the unknown of eternity on our right and dip our colors in salute to the March of Time.[54]

By the early twenty-first century, about all that was left of the Battle of July 22 was the Atlanta Cyclorama, preserved in its new setting and with the best restoration possible for a very long time to come. The battlefield has all been covered over with housing and commercial development, all the earthworks involved in it long since gone. A great deal of information that ranges from the accurate to the absurd can be found on the internet, the most impressive means of mass communication ever developed. While the cyclorama is a magnificent piece of American culture, the Battle of July 22 deserves more than it has received in the way of battlefield preservation and reliable treatment by buffs and historians alike.

Conclusion

The feeling was general among Union and Confederate survivors of July 22 that the engagement that day represented something unusual in the Atlanta Campaign and, in a larger sense, their entire war experience. "We had a fight her[e] that was a little a head [*sic*] of anything I ever saw," concluded J. T. Downs, one of Lt. Gen. William J. Hardee's soldiers. Irving Buck always contended that July 22 was "the most severe, fatal and hard-fought" day in the history of Cleburne's Division. Some Federal commentators were effusive in assessing the event. It was "the most serious, threatening, and hotly contested" battle of the campaign, wrote Capt. Henry Stone of Maj. Gen. George H. Thomas's staff. Sherman devoted more space to July 22 than to any other battle in his official report of the drive toward Atlanta, and historians such as Albert Castel agree that this day's combat represented "the largest and bloodiest battle of the campaign."[1]

Even so, Maj. Gen. Grenville M. Dodge always contended that the Federal accomplishments on July 22 were muted by the tragedy of Maj. Gen. James B. McPherson's death. The shock produced by the loss of their favored commander led Union veterans to fail in properly evaluating the significance of their victory outside Atlanta, according to Dodge.[2]

The passage of time as well as the Civil War generation offers us the opportunity to evaluate the significance of July 22 in its widest perspective. The key features of the battle that impressed so many men that day need to be discussed, followed by measured judgments of what the participants in both armies did and did not accomplish. The resonance of that engagement—its effect on the outcome of the Atlanta Campaign and on the war—also need to be discussed.

The key features of the Battle of Atlanta started with one of the most complete tactical surprises suffered by any field army, North or South, during the Civil War. The left flank of the Union Army of the Tennessee was completely turned in what was the best tactical move ever conducted by the Confederate Army of Tennessee. That flanking movement was at least as difficult if not more so than the more famous flank march conducted by Lt. Gen. Thomas J. "Stonewall" Jackson at Chancellorsville on May 2, 1863. It was longer than Jackson's flanking march but conducted throughout a grueling night of hard marching. Yet it placed Hardee's Corps as completely on the opponent's flank as had Jackson's move.[3]

The primary cause for this Federal surprise was the lack of cavalry screening on the left flank. Brig. Gen. Kenner Garrard's mounted division should have provided it, but Sherman sent the troopers off to tear up the Georgia Railroad farther east. Even so, why did the infantry of McPherson's army fail to better screen that exposed flank? To the men who paid the price for this lack of vigilance, there were decades of muted criticism about the issue. They contended that it was a worse surprise even than the great one the same army had endured at Shiloh on April 6, 1862, because, according to W. L. Wade of the 11th Iowa, at Shiloh they confronted the surprise attack frontally instead of on their flank and rear. The survivors never blamed McPherson for this because of their love for the slain commander, but they tended to blame Sherman, sometimes including some of his unnamed subordinates. Veterans of the 30th Illinois quietly noted after the war that they had been left out in an exposed position to be sacrificed for some reason. "Sherman with all his cavalry, scouts and pickets, should have known where his enemy was," argued B. F. Boring.[4]

Sherman rightly deserves part of the blame for the surprise assault unleashed on his favorite army. It had been his decision to strip it of its only cavalry support. But Castel has rightly fixed part of the blame on McPherson as well. While praising him for sending Dodge's command into the exact spot where it could repel the moves of Bate's and Walker's Divisions, and just in time too, Castel also criticizes McPherson for not sending Dodge toward his exposed left flank much earlier. It is astonishing that the commander of the Army of the Tennessee left his flank exposed all day of July 21 and all morning of July 22. This was not the first or only laxness displayed by McPherson during the campaign, all of them supporting Castel's conclusion that this affable young man, who possessed real administrative talent, had risen above his level of skill when it came to battlefield management of such a large command.[5]

Fortunately for the Federals, the advantage gained by their opponents in achieving a surprise on the left flank did not result in a catastrophic defeat. Hardee failed to drive either the Left Wing, Sixteenth Corps or the Seventeenth Corps as readily or as fully as Jackson had driven the Eleventh Corps at Chancellorsville. The most important reason for this failure was, of course, the fortuitous placement of Dodge's men directly in the path of the two divisions that had the best chance of attacking the Federal rear areas as well as on the best defensive ground in the area. This, combined with stout resistance by Dodge's officers and men, stymied much of Hardee's attack. "Upon what a slight chance, then, hung the fate of Sherman's army that day," mused William H. Chamberlin, Dodge's commissary of musters, after the war. Dodge's stand "put an entirely different phase on the battle" compared to what likely would have happened if his troops had not done their job so well.[6]

Two primary causes account for Hardee's limited success. First, his corps attacked on a broad front, encountering rugged landscape obstacles in the form of Terry's Mill Pond and numerous thickets and swampy areas that diverted brigades and divisions and hindered their progress. This contributed to a persistent problem all Civil War armies had to deal with, which constituted the second major reason for Confederate failure on July 22—the difficulties inherent in coordinating the movement of large units on the battlefield.

The Army of Tennessee probably was the least successful of all the major field armies of the war in coordinating its units during an attack. For the most part, it could achieve coordination on the brigade level, although even on July 22 one can see Confederate brigades splinter, as one or two regiments became separated from the rest. But the Army of Tennessee had real and persistent problems in coordinating movements on the division level. In fact, other than perhaps the large assault at Franklin the following November, one cannot find a good example of it coordinating the movement of an entire corps on any other battlefield of the war. Terrain obstacles, heat, and physical exhaustion greatly intensified the systemic problems in unit coordination in Hood's army on July 22. If Hardee's division and brigade leaders had been able to better control their units and more closely cooperate with their neighbors, the Federals would have been in far worse trouble, and Hood might have achieved the stunning battlefield victory he so desperately needed.[7]

Of course, some of the failure to coordinate arose from poor divisional leadership coupled with bad luck. Hardee's right consisted of a division led by Maj. Gen. William Bate, one of the weakest division leaders in the army, and next to him, Maj. Gen. William H. T. Walker was among the first to fall at the start of the fight on the Sixteenth Corps sector. These two divisions had the best opportunity of any Confederate units that day. They confronted only three Union brigades, but Dodge made full use of his major advantage, which was the strongest natural position on the battlefield, and his men fought with pluck and confidence.

Cleburne's Division, the best in Hood's army, also held the most enviable record of coordinating its brigades across battlefields cluttered by natural obstacles, as it did at Stones River on December 31, 1862. But even Maj. Gen. Patrick R. Cleburne could not coordinate the attacks of his brigades on July 22. They went in almost independently of each other, nullifying most of their advantages in gaining the flank and rear of the embattled Seventeenth Corps. The only apparent explanation for this breakdown of coordination in a division that usually excelled in united action is exhaustion. Part of Cleburne's command endured an absolutely grueling experience under Union artillery fire the day before, and no one in the division had any sleep all night of July 21–22.

It is not easy to understand the operations of Cheatham's Division, led by Brig. Gen. George E. Maney, on July 22 due to an appalling lack of battlefield reports by commanders and personal accounts by the rank and file. Judging from available evidence, Maney poorly handled his resources. Only two of his brigades became heavily engaged. If any others also contributed in significant ways, we do not have any evidence of it.

Even so, Hardee's Corps performed better than Hood's Corps, led by Maj. Gen. Benjamin F. Cheatham, on July 22. It is ironic that Cheatham's command actually broke the Fifteenth Corps line, something that had never happened to that storied Federal unit, which Sherman had created and commanded for many months. Ironic, too, because Cheatham's attack was a lumbering, poorly coordinated affair that succeeded in a limited way despite, rather than because, of the way it was conducted. An entire division led by Maj. Gen. Carter L. Stevenson contributed not a bit to the effort. In Hindman's Division, led by Brig. Gen. John C. Brown, two brigades were primarily responsible for breaking the line, a third helped that effort by extending the break southward, while the fourth failed in its only attack on the Federals. In Clayton's Division, one brigade was placed in reserve and never engaged, while parts of the other three helped extend the break. Out of twelve brigades in the corps, only six actively participated in punching that hole in the Union line.

All three division leaders were mediocre at best. There is no evidence, for example, that Brown played a role in the success of his division. Brig. Gen.

Arthur M. Manigault and Col. Jacob H. Sharp were primarily responsible for breaking the Union line without any aid from Brown. For that matter, if it had not been for some of Sharp's troops discovering the unfortified railroad cut, the break probably would never have happened. The failures of Brig. Gen. Morgan L. Smith and Brig. Gen. Joseph A. J. Lightburn to recognize the railroad cut as a serious weak link in the Fifteenth Corps line played into Confederate fortunes that day.

Cheatham himself was out of his element as a corps commander, far better suited and more experienced at the division level than his division leaders. It should also be pointed out that the corps, created just before the onset of the Atlanta Campaign for Hood to command, had not been molded into an effective fighting unit as Hardee had done for his own command. Hood was not up to corps leadership, having been a superb brigade and division commander but with no experience at dealing with the greatly enhanced challenges of corps command, and he never improved much during the course of the campaign. In short, Cheatham may have done better on July 22 if Hood had left him a better corps to command. As it was, Brown's and Maj. Gen. Henry D. Clayton's men exhausted their stock as soon as they chased away the Federals and settled into the captured Union earthworks. No one provided any leadership to take the next step, and as a result, all they could do was wait for the inevitable Union counterattack, which they had no means to repel.

Reports of lack of coordination within Cheatham's command quickly found their way to army headquarters. They generally credited Brown's men with breaking the Fifteenth Corps position but blamed Clayton's command for not properly supporting that success. These reports were at least partially correct, although they failed to note that it was not solely Clayton's fault. Cheatham himself aligned his divisions in a confusing manner that only increased Clayton's difficulties.[8]

As a result of this persistent, systemic problem of coordinating units in the Army of Tennessee, a campaign-changing battlefield victory eluded the Confederates. Maj. Gen. Frank P. Blair Jr. was keenly aware of this point. His Seventeenth Corps had been outflanked, assailed on three sides, and yet stood its ground for a long while, eventually giving up much of its line but surviving the terrible contest. "If the enemy had concerted his attacks from front, flank, and rear, so as to strike my line at the same moment with his different lines of battle, it would have been extremely difficult, if not impossible, to hold our ground, but this was not done."[9]

The Confederates also performed poorly in the area of combined-arms operations. This concept, involving the coordinated use of infantry, artillery, and cavalry, rarely had a good showing in the history of the Army of Tennessee. Its use of artillery in other battles was at best moderately successful but was conspicuously absent on July 22. There is no easy explanation for this lack of success at using the long arm of Civil War armies, yet it was apparent to Rebel artillerists and modern-day historians alike. "It was not an artillery fight," Philip Daingerfield Stephenson of the 5th Company, Washington Artillery declared in his memoirs. "It was an infantry fight (on our side) pure and simple. I doubt if a battery on our side had a chance to do any special service." The Federals more ably used their big guns than their opponents. Larry Daniel estimates Sherman's forces brought eighty-six pieces from thirty-six batteries into action, but the reports are so sketchy on the Rebel side that it is very difficult even to estimate how many Confederate gun detachments actually fired a shot on July 22.[10]

Neither Hood nor Hardee even tried to use their available cavalry in close cooperation with their infantry forces, and, of course, the Federals committed the same error. The Battle of July 22 was, on both sides, largely an infantry fight. It displayed even less combined-arms coordination than was typical of most Civil War engagements.

Although it is a trope of popular Civil War historiography to proclaim that all soldiers were heroes, the truth is quite different. No matter how conspicuously any Union or Confederate unit performed under fire, every one of them contained at least some men who failed the test of combat. The question is how far did battle spirit infuse a unit and to what degree did it suffer from a weakening of will to face danger. The Army of Tennessee always had a more checkered history in this regard than any other field army of the war, and its behavior on July 22 was no exception. Many units made little more than a show of advancing toward the Federals and then failed to close in for intense combat. All of Stevenson's Division, for example, fell into this category. Recognizing this fact of military life is not meant to level charges of cowardice on anyone, but it is important to acknowledge human limitations. Much of the failure to engage when ordered can be attributed to exhaustion (which most men in the Army of Tennessee were suffering to an unusually high degree on July 22) and to other factors beyond their control.

The most prominent cause of a failure to engage on July 22 was straggling. "A fight was not expected and the men broke down from loss of sleep and hard work," wrote Van Buren Oldham of the 9th Tennessee, who missed the battle because he could not keep up with the regiment. Based on this comment, Albert Castel has estimated that one-third of Hardee's troops failed to come under fire at all that day due to a widespread problem of straggling. The combination of hard service for several days before the engagement, the all-night flank march during which no one got any useful rest, and the heat of the day all contributed to this problem.[11]

We could know much more about problems like straggling if the Confederates had kept better records of their experiences on July 22. During the entire Atlanta Campaign, the Army of Tennessee failed to maintain good official reports, and this nagging problem was especially pronounced for the Battle of July 22. There are none at all for Stevenson's Division, and very few for any others. Even some of the reports that do exist are short, vague, and almost useless in terms of illuminating such issues as the rate and distance of infantry firing, the number of men engaged, the losses, and especially the timing of important events.

Some commanders bemoaned this problem and sought reasons to explain it. "Owing to the fact that every regimental commander in the brigade but one was either killed, wounded, or replaced, and the commands devolving on inexperienced officers, their reports are meager and imperfect," wrote Brig. Gen. James A. Smith of his regimental commanders. Smith did not have the time to send these reports back for revision because he needed to make his own brigade-level report and, of course, had many other things to do as well. Reporting on a past engagement was far less important than moving on with a fluid and often fast-developing set of circumstances. The Atlanta Campaign did not stop for anyone.[12]

Regardless of all these problems associated with unit coordination, physical exhaustion, and lax accountability, Hood ultimately must shoulder most of the blame for the failure of his second effort to save Atlanta. Castel has correctly concluded that "the fundamental reason for Hood's failure on July 22 is that he tried to do too much with too little in too short a time."[13]

Hood could not correct the shortage of troops and resources, but he had control over the timing and the goals assigned to the troops under his command. He simply expected too much of them. Many of the Confederates did not start on the flank march until very late on July 21, and thus fatigue became a major factor in their performance. Any force that loses one-third of its manpower to straggling is in dire straits if expected to go into heavy combat without a chance to rest.

Of course one could argue that Hood felt he had no time to give the men this rest for fear of losing the opportunity to strike while McPherson's flank was still in the air. As it turned out, if Hardee's march had been conducted with fresh troops starting early, they could have hit the Federals at dawn instead of at noon. The difference of six hours was all important; the rear areas of McPherson's army were fully exposed at dawn, but Dodge's three brigades had moved into a perfect position to protect those areas by noon. But the proper question is whether the Confederates had the opportunity to conduct the flank march quickly enough to strike at dawn, and the obvious answer is no.

There were alternatives plans open to Hood, but the new army commander failed to explore them. As Castel has noted, the general could have opted for a much shorter movement, having Bate and Walker attack the south side of Bald Hill while the rest of Hardee's Corps replaced the ineffectual division of Stevenson and attacked from the west. Or, as I have mentioned in my study of the battle at Peach Tree Creek, Hood could have canceled his assault against Thomas's Army of the Cumberland on July 20 and marshaled his resources for a better-planned strike against McPherson. Even if he hit the Army of the Tennessee after the left flank was secured, he could have gone in with fresher troops and a different line of march to envelope the Union left. But Hood seems to have approached his job with one-dimensional thinking and a bulldog tenacity that refused to brook delay. His approach "could be used as a classic example of a commander's not making sufficient allowance for the factors of time, distance, fatigue, and what is called the 'friction of battle,'" as Castel puts it.[14]

There was another option not considered by Hood, which was to attack not the left flank, but the center of the Union position outside Atlanta. According to available evidence, the Confederates knew that a gap stretching a mile and half existed northeast of the city between Sherman's left wing and his right wing. It actually was located in the middle of Howard's Fourth Corps, separating two of his divisions in the left wing from the third one in the right wing. Thomas was in charge of the right wing, which consisted entirely of troops from his Army of the Cumberland. That gap to the northeast of Atlanta existed at least until the morning of July 22. Hood never mentioned it, but Maj. Gen. Joseph Wheeler contended after the war that everyone at Army of Tennessee headquarters knew of is existence. A successful attack through that gap would have separated the two halves of Sherman's host, whereas a successful flank attack on McPherson would have merely crunched the Federal forces back upon themselves, concentrating rather than dispersing or separating them. Wheeler also guessed that Hood assumed the gap would soon be filled; that was the only way to explain why the Rebel commander did not try to exploit it.[15]

Hood was no scholar, either at West Point or as a professional military officer, and thus he failed to write a thorough report of his tenure as commander of the Army of Tennessee. His memoirs also fail to cover all aspects of his command problems. As a result, we have too little detailed information about his thinking process as he approached the daunting operational and tactical situation that confronted him at Atlanta. Instead, what we have from Hood, in both his report and his memoirs, is a sordid attempt to shift the blame for his failure onto Hardee. Virtually all commentators and historians who have looked into this issue agree that Hood was unjustified in his criticism of the corps leader.[16]

Hood liked to model his actions as army commander on those of his hero, Gen. Robert E. Lee. His flank march aped that of Jackson at Chancellorsville. But Hood ignored another important lesson from Lee. When things went wrong, as they did at Gettysburg, Lee accepted full responsibility for the result rather than set up a scapegoat to deflect blame. Hood not only failed as a commander but also failed to conduct himself with dignity and integrity as a man and fellow officer. He had been promoted well above his competence level and was struggling to find firm ground in these early days as the head of the Army of Tennessee. It was not at all easy for him to do so, but that was no reason to smear the reputation of subordinates who were more competent than he to fill his position.

Although they won the Battle of July 22, the Federals were not entirely free of fault. They set up their near-disaster by allowing themselves to be totally surprised by the Confederate onslaught. Sherman was too obsessed with wrecking railroads; he should not have stripped McPherson of the only cavalry available to the Army of the Tennessee. But one can also criticize Garrard. Even before Sherman sent him off toward Covington, he seems to have mainly planted his fine horsemen in and around Decatur, with a thin screen of pickets a distance away, instead of conducting aggressive patrols into the area south and southeast of the town to properly screen McPherson's left flank. The Federals needed to have notice of Hardee's flank march as early as possible, and it is ironically possible that, even if Garrard had not been sent off toward Covington, he might not have provided that essential information. His horsemen could help protect the rear of the Army of the Tennessee while stationed at Decatur but could not warn McPherson of all danger just by staying there.

The other major problem concerning Federal actions on July 22 is the inaction of Thomas and to a lesser degree Maj. Gen. John M. Schofield. While the Army of the Tennessee was fighting for its life, the Army of the Cumberland did nothing. The Army of the Ohio (Twenty-Third Corps) was active in a defensive, supporting way. But the question of using Thomas and Schofield to conduct an attack on the enemy came up that afternoon. Sherman decisively nipped it in the bud by arguing that Maj. Gen. John A. Logan's men would feel "jealous" if help was sent to them.[17]

There is literally no evidence coming from Logan's troops to support the idea that they would have resented receiving aid. We know that Logan, Blair, and Dodge were eager for help, and the last of them went to ask Sherman for it on the night of July 22 only to be rebuffed by the army-group commander.

As a result, upward of 50,000 Federal soldiers remained idle that afternoon because of what historian Thomas Robson Hay calls a "reprehensible sentiment" on Sherman's part. Castel deems it "sheer nonsense" and points out that it was Sherman rather than the men who would have felt jealous if his favorite field army needed help in its life-and-death struggle. But Castel errs in asserting that Thomas could have broken through the Atlanta defenses if he had mounted a major attack that afternoon. Such a result might have been possible, but all indications point to a bloody failure, despite the disparity of numbers. The Atlanta City Line was not as poorly constructed as Castel believes; Lt. Gen. Alexander P. Stewart's command would have had a good chance to repel any assault.[18]

But there was a real possibility inherent in Schofield's and Howard's idea to use Army of the Ohio and Army of the Cumberland troops in mounting a counterattack to separate Hardee from Atlanta. There was room to do so even though the Federal columns would have been harassed by Rebel artillery fire from the Atlanta City Line. Hardee's left flank was vulnerable, and such a Union move could at least have neutralized his final attack on the new Union line stretching east from Bald Hill. It could even have inflicted serious damage on Hardee's Corps, turning the tables decisively against the Confederates.

Sending off Garrard's cavalry and refusing to mount an effort to more effectively support Logan's embattled command were not the only missteps Sherman committed during the Atlanta Campaign. No one can be expected to be perfect. Fortunately for the Union cause, Sherman made many more correct decisions than false ones during the operations against the Gate City, and his subordinates as well as the rank and file of his army group more than compensated for the occasional mistake enacted at headquarters.

The Army of the Tennessee was a superb military organization, honed to a fine point by years of campaign and combat experience. Most of its regimental, brigade, division, and corps commanders, as well as the majority of its rank and file, were resilient, determined soldiers with a high level of self-confidence. They were "skilled veterans who were always ready to fight, were not alarmed by flank or rear attacks, and met their assailants with heroic valor," as Sherman put it after the war.[19]

July 22 ranks alongside April 6 at Shiloh as one of the most trying days of the war for these men, and in both cases, they met the challenge brilliantly. What took place east of Atlanta was "a terrific battle," as Maj. Gen. Oliver O. Howard expressed it, "the most distinctly marked of any day during this remarkable campaign." Even though it occurred five days before Howard took command of the army, he saw much of the action from Copenhill. "I have a picture of that fight on the wall of my office," he wrote many decades later, "and always look at it with wonder and interest."[20]

The thing that intrigued Howard most was the same thing that Granville McDonald of the 30th Illinois wanted to understand. "But the greatest wonder of all, is, why Hood did not crush us in the first attack," given all the tactical advantages Hardee had gained with his flank march. McDonald knew the answer to that question. "We did not know what it was to be licked by the Johnnies, and it was the dogged, stubborn, individual fighting on the part of every man that saved the day."[21]

McDonald asserted that "very few commands were given" by officers on July 22, that the rank and file knew their jobs and proceeded to do them without much direction from their superiors. Capt. Harrison Wilson of Company F, 20th Ohio recalled seeing Brig. Gen. Giles A. Smith during a hot part of the battle. The division commander had earlier exposed himself to fire in order to inspire courage in his subordinates but by this time had learned the value of taking cover. Wilson saw him crouching in a trench to escape the worst of it. When he asked Smith what to do, feeling that the situation was almost overwhelming, the division leader reassured him. "We're all Major Generals now," he told Wilson, acknowledging that there was relatively little higher-level commanders could do in such a situation.[22]

Although thoroughly surprised, the Army of the Tennessee reacted quickly and well to the Confederate attacks. Stout, resilient fighting was the key, but in many other ways, the army performed magnificently, too. The transition in command from McPherson to Logan was conducted quickly and smoothly. The latter used McPherson's staff officers and immediately took charge, inspiring troops and issuing orders when necessary. A high level of cooperation between units had long characterized the operations of the army, and that also played a role on July 22. The Fifteenth Corps sent regiments early in the battle to help the Sixteenth Corps, and Dodge in turn sent a brigade to help the Fifteenth Corps commanders reclaim their broken line. Although the Seventeenth Corps eventually became jumbled together and confused, Blair's men did not panic, run away, or allow themselves to be reduced to a rabble incapable of fighting back. There is no evidence of an unusual level of straggling or combat failure among Union regiments.

It can be said that both sides operated near the edge of their capabilities on July 22, but the Confederates were far closer to that extremity than the Federals and thus more vulnerable to failure. Hardee was separated from the rest of Hood's army and operated with a command experiencing unusual fatigue. Its only advantage was a successful flank march followed by a surprise attack. Its ability to launch assaults was limited by inherent systemic weaknesses, the worst of which, lack of coordination between units, played a huge role in the outcome of the battle that day.

The Federals employed their strengths to compensate for and overcome the Confederates' advantages. Their tradition of cooperation between units, the confidence felt by their rank and file, the fact that the course of the battle allowed them to concentrate their manpower rather than disperse it, and the tough fighting ability of the common soldier all played significant roles in deciding who won and who lost the Battle of Atlanta.

It is also instructive to set the Battle of July 22 within its military context. That context comprised the tactical, operational, and strategic levels. Thus far we have mostly discussed the tactical level, which consists of handling resources on the battlefield. The operational level consists of how opposing commanders handled their resources during the campaign, and the strategic level consists of the role played by the campaign and its battles on the larger political-military goals of the opposing governments.

In addition to all that has already been said about the tactical level, one can point out that this was the level wherein both sides were more on a level playing field than on either the operational or strategic levels. This means that both Union and Confederate armies used the same tactical system of formations and maneuvers, what could be termed the primary level of tactics. They may have used these formations and maneuvers with varying levels of proficiency, but the systems were exactly the same. The landscape helped protect the Confederates as they neared the end of their fatiguing flank march by screening their approach, yet it also inhibited their ability to maintain unit cohesion when they launched their attacks. In general, the terrain favored the Federals more than the Confederates, especially when considering Dodge's strong position and the Seventeenth Corps use of Bald Hill.[23]

Both sides also used the same type of weapon, a modern rifle musket with a potential distance of up to 500 yards, which had generally replaced the older smoothbore musket with an effective distance of no more than 100 yards. But the evidence is overwhelming that on July 22, as in all other Civil War battles, most combatants preferred to fire at short distance consistent with that of the smoothbore rather than at distances consistent with the potential of the rifle. When staff officer George W. Bailey was captured and led west along the Decatur Road from the ruptured Fifteenth Corps line, he noticed that the overwhelming majority of Confederate dead and wounded were scattered within 100 yards of the Union earthworks. Despite the new weaponry, Civil War combat remained close-distance combat, as it had been ever since the musket had been developed during the seventeenth century.[24]

While both sides may have operated on a level playing field as far as primary tactics were concerned, they were not by any means symmetrical on the operational level. The Federals possessed many important advantages during the Atlanta Campaign. Sherman developed exactly the right operational policy for his advance into Georgia. He generally avoided ruinous frontal attacks on strong Confederate positions, employing only limited numbers when he did try them at Resaca, New Hope Church, Pickett's Mill, and Kennesaw Mountain. Although many men on both sides yearned for a general engagement, a climactic battle that would settle the winner of the campaign one way or the other, Sherman consistently avoided all make-or-break moments unless he could find one in which he had all the advantages of winning. His policy demanded patience and care, and despite moments in which his frustration mounted, Sherman managed to maintain that patient and careful approach throughout the campaign.

Once across the Chattahoochee River, Sherman needed patience and care even more than he had north of that dividing line in his drive through northwest Georgia. The defenses of Atlanta were far too strong for a frontal attack; striking at Confederate supply lines was the only feasible option. Sherman thus conducted movements against the city's rail lines in a manner that minimized the risks involved in them. This required time, but he could afford to take that time as long as he could continue to supply his huge army group deep in Confederate territory. His supply line stretched more than 350 miles to Louisville at the start of the campaign, but Sherman had already arranged for thousands of garrison troops, the stockpiling of supplies at many depots along the way, and the deployment of a couple of thousand railroad-construction men to repair breaks in that line of track, exposed as it was to inevitable attacks by guerrillas and detached Confederate cavalrymen.[25]

Sherman's juggernaut was able to penetrate northwest Georgia that summer not only because he had more men than the Confederates but also, and even more importantly, because he possessed many more war making resources than his opponent. And critically, he knew very well how to manage those resources, which consisted of material, manpower, and logistical capabilities that the Confederate government could never hope to match.

Advantages like these may have been difficult to appreciate when a desperate battle erupted as it did on the afternoon of July 22, but in at least one way it is possible to clearly see them. As William E. Strong observed, even if the Army of the Tennessee had been defeated that day, Sherman had many more troops available near the scene of action. Schofield, Thomas, and their commands were ready for defensive action and could easily have put a stop to Hardee's progress.[26]

Mere numbers mean little if a commander cannot supply them while operating in the field, so we should not make the mistake of assuming that the Federals' big battalions were the main reason they won the Battle of July 22 or the Atlanta Campaign. The twin abilities to gather large forces *and to keep them supplied through logistical power* were required to bring numerical superiority to the tactical level. Those abilities are components of the operational art of war making.

One would have assumed that the Confederates possessed many advantages on the operational level as well during the campaign. They acted on the defensive, operated during the early part of the campaign in mountainous country, and had three major rivers to use as defensive barriers. Their supply line to Atlanta was short and absolutely free from guerrilla threats, so the Army of Tennessee was well fed during the campaign and suffered no serious shortage of material. The men loved Gen. Joseph E. Johnston and were ready to do anything he asked of them.

Yet the Confederates utterly failed to utilize all of these advantages. They failed to put together an operational plan for the campaign that had a real hope of countering Sherman's plan. Johnston bears most of the blame for this failure. Throughout his tenure, he possessed only a vague conception of operations, essentially doing little more than taking up strong defensive positions and waiting for something to happen. Now and then he tentatively planned a limited counteroffensive, as at Resaca and along the New Hope Church–Pickett's Mill–Dallas Line, but never committed himself to a vigorous attack. He failed to use the three major rivers as strong defensive barriers, usually allowing Federal forces to cross them with little opposition. And he was too ready to give up strong positions for relatively slight reasons. Although Johnston deserves high marks for taking care of his men and for his administrative ability, he failed as an operational manager and a tactical leader.

With each developing phase of the campaign, the Confederates lost one advantage after another until, by the time Hood replaced Johnston on July 18, the odds were more seriously stacked against them than ever. Their backs were against the wall around Atlanta, and Sherman's command was across the Chattahoochee River and snipping away at their lifelines. Moreover, Hood was no more capable of developing an operational plan to deal with the threat than Johnston. His only advantage over his predecessor was a fierce willingness to try offensive action, and the result was the bloodletting at Peach Tree Creek on July 20 and the even heavier battle on July 22. By this stage of the campaign, Sherman had a very good chance of withstanding anything his opponent threw at him. That does not mean that Union success was inevitable, it only means that the chances of success were tilted in the Federals' favor. Hardee's and Cheatham's men had a lot to overcome if they hoped to win the campaign for Atlanta by attacking McPherson on July 22.

On the strategic level, historians are divided on whether the Battle of Atlanta played a major role in determining the outcome of the campaign and of the war. On one end of the spectrum is Richard McMurry, who concludes that the engagement "had no significant result."[27] On the other end is Gary Ecelbarger, who believes the Battle of July 22 held the potential to change the course of American history. The "complete destruction of a major field army" was possible that day, in his view. "The Army of the Tennessee was on the verge of collapse and annihilation. The consequence of that potential Union disaster could ultimately affect the most important presidential election in United States history." By not only surviving but actually defeating Hood's army, the Federals "caused the death of Dixie," according to Ecelbarger. The Battle of July 22 "was the most important military effort that assured the end of the Confederate States of America."[28]

As indicated in the preface of this book, I do not support Ecelbarger's assessment of the strategic significance of July 22. Nor do I support McMurry's contention. The terrible bloodletting of that day had significance, but not of the inflated type posited by Ecelbarger or the deflated type proposed by McMurry.

"All campaigns have a turning point . . . where the tide turned inevitably in the direction of one side over another," Ecelbarger writes.[29] I also do not agree with that assertion. Long and complicated campaigns like that leading to Atlanta's fall rarely have a single moment in which the outcome is decided on a single day. More usually they have many points at which the flow of events incrementally shift toward one side or the other. It is impossible, in my view, to identify a single battle as the turning point of the Atlanta Campaign. Moreover, little-noticed trends or events, such as the steady application of logistical power to sustain a force in the field, usually have as much influence on who wins a campaign as obvious events such as battles. Union success in every engagement tended toward a Union success in the campaign, but on none of the many battlefields of the drive toward Atlanta can one see anything like a clear, decisive shift toward that end. The Confederates achieved surprise when they attacked Thomas's Army of the Cumberland at Peach Tree Creek on July 20 at a time when two Union divisions were not even in a proper position for defense. Yet the Federals reacted well and repelled those attacks. Peach Tree Creek seems to fulfill Ecelbarger's slim requirements for decisive battle as well as July 22, yet he does not identify it as the turning point of the campaign.

Simply because an attack held the potential to cripple one of the three Union field armies under Sherman's command and then failed to do so does not constitute a strong argument for decisive strategic effect. The outcome of July 22 simply meant that the campaign once again settled down into a state of temporary stasis. McMurry's argument that nothing changed is closer to the truth than Ecelbarger's assertion of dramatic change. It is true that the Army of Tennessee lost much of whatever offensive power it possessed in the bloodletting around Sugar Creek, Bald Hill, and the Georgia Railroad, but even here Ecelbarger exaggerates the effect. "The Battle of Atlanta wrecked the Confederate Army of Tennessee through and through," he writes, which would have been a huge surprise to the Federals who barely stopped that army's attacks at Ezra Church on July 28 and its ferocious assault against the Fourth and Twenty-Third Corps at Franklin on November 30, 1864.[30]

Relying on dramatic and simplistic assessments does not do justice to the men who fought and suffered on July 22. Their battle did not determine the outcome of the campaign or of the presidential election of 1864. Students of the conflict ought to assess their actions in a balanced and convincing manner.

In the larger strategic sense, the Atlanta Campaign represented a continuation of the long Union drive along the railroads that linked Louisville with Nashville, Chattanooga, and Atlanta. This drive began in a consistent way with the Stones River Campaign of late 1862. It certainly was one of the longest continuous drives of the war, and its outcome has always been associated with boosting Lincoln's chances of reelection in the fall of 1864. The capture of Atlanta denied the Confederates a manufacturing city and a transportation hub, but it did not represent an unusually decisive moment in the strategic course of the Civil War any more than did the fall of Nashville, New Orleans, or Memphis. Like those cities, the fall of Atlanta represented another significant increment in the movement toward eventual Union victory in the conflict.

The only way to argue that Sherman's capture of Atlanta represented something unique in that string of incremental advances from late 1862 to late 1864 was its possible effect on the presidential election. Historians have largely assumed that Sherman handed Lincoln a vital political advantage, disproving Democratic assertions that the administration's handling of the war was a bloody failure and giving rise to a threatening upsurge of voters who were ready for negotiated compromise with the Confederacy. The primary basis for this historical view of the campaign rests on the comments of key Union politicians and government administrators, many of whom believed the Republicans would lose the presidency if some general failed to deliver an important battlefield victory. The fall of Atlanta on September 2 represented the most important of several such victories and thus assumes center place in the argument that Lincoln's reelection was assured by Union military success.[31]

Even if one accepted the idea that the Battle of July 22 was the decisive moment in delivering Atlanta into Sherman's hands, one should question the old assumption that the fall of the city was the decisive factor in Lincoln's reelection, which in turn was the decisive factor in destroying the Confederacy. The argument that Atlanta's fall led to Lincoln's second term, after all, is based entirely on the feelings and thoughts of a handful of leading Republicans; were those feelings and thoughts truly reflective of the political reality? In the absence of opinion polls, one can only guess, but it would be helpful if some political historian would explore whether we are correct to make such an assumption. Political campaigns are as complex as military campaigns, and thus any simplistic assessment of them tends to be unconvincing. It may turn out that Sherman genuinely deserves credit for keeping Lincoln in the White House, but it could just as well be argued otherwise after deeper reflection on the issue.

To sum up, I see no grounds for arguing that the Battle of July 22 played a large role in determining the outcome of the Civil War. It played only an incremental role in determining the outcome of the Atlanta Campaign. But that does not mean it was unimportant. The Federals certainly did nullify the most dangerous Confederate threat to Sherman's push for Atlanta by repelling Hardee and Cheatham that day in order to keep the drive through northwest Georgia on track. The Battle of Atlanta also was one of the most impressive days of combat not only in the Civil War but also in all of American military history. It is a case study of combat morale, tactical resilience, and the operational art. The human drama of combat rose to prominent heights on July 22 outside Atlanta. The battle also became one of the most commemorated of the Civil War, with monuments to its slain heroes North and South and a magnificent cycloramic painting, the survival of which has been almost miraculous.

Ultimately, the Battle of Atlanta proved not only the fighting strength but also the destiny of the Army of the Tennessee, the field force created by Grant, loved by Sherman, and led to the day of his death by McPherson. Col. Theophilus Lyle Dickey, a cavalry officer who had served under Grant during the first half of the war, once wrote to his former commander about a prominent memory he retained of service in that army. It related to a comment made by John A. Rawlins, Grant's trusted chief of staff. "I will never forget Rawlins' old toast of the 'Army of the Tennessee'—that it was, 'wedded to victory.'"[32] At Shiloh and on July 22, the rank and file of that army proved the validity of Rawlins's comment.

Battle of Bald Hill, July 21
ARMY OF THE TENNESSEE: MAJ. GEN. JAMES B. MCPHERSON

Fifteenth Corps: Maj. Gen. John A. Logan
FOURTH DIVISION: Brig. Gen. William Harrow
Third Brigade: Col. John M. Oliver
48th Illinois: Col. Lucien Greathouse

Seventeenth Corps: Maj. Gen. Frank P. Blair Jr.
THIRD DIVISION: Brig. Gen. Mortimer D. Leggett
First Brigade: Brig. Gen. Manning F. Force
20th Illinois: Lt. Col. Daniel Bradley
30th Illinois: Col. Warren Shedd
31st Illinois: Lt. Col. Robert N. Pearson
12th Wisconsin: Col. George E. Bryant
16th Wisconsin: Col. Cassius Fairchild

Second Brigade: Col. Robert K. Scott
20th Ohio: Lt. Col. John C. Fry
68th Ohio: Lt. Col. George E. Welles
78th Ohio: Lt. Col. Greenberry F. Wiles

Third Brigade: Col. Adam G. Malloy
17th Wisconsin: Lt. Col. Thomas McMahon
Worden's Battalion (detachments of 81st Illinois, 95th Illinois, and 14th Wisconsin): Maj. Asa Worden

Artillery: Capt. William S. Williams
Battery D, 1st Illinois Light Artillery: Capt. Edgar H. Cooper
Battery H, 1st Michigan Light Artillery: Capt. Marcus D. Elliott
3rd Ohio Battery: Lt. John Sullivan

FOURTH DIVISION: Brig. Gen. Giles A. Smith
First Brigade: Col. Benjamin F. Potts

53rd Illinois: Lt. Col. John W. McClanahan
23rd Indiana: Lt. Col. William P. Davis
53rd Indiana: Lt. Col. William Jones
3rd Iowa (3 companies): Capt. Pleasant T. Mathes
32nd Ohio: Capt. William M. Morris

Third Brigade: Col. John Shane
11th Iowa: Lt. Col. John C. Abercrombie
13th Iowa: Maj. William A. Walker
15th Iowa: Col. William W. Belknap
16th Iowa: Lt. Col. Addison H. Sanders

Artillery: Capt. Edward Spear Jr.
Battery F, 2nd Illinois Light Artillery: Capt. Walter H. Powell
1st Minnesota Battery: Capt. William Z. Clayton
15th Ohio Battery: Lt. James Burdick

ARMY OF TENNESSEE: GEN. JOHN B. HOOD

Hardee's Corps: Lt. Gen. William J. Hardee
CLEBURNE'S DIVISION: Maj. Gen. Patrick R. Cleburne
Smith's Brigade: Brig. Gen. James A. Smith
6th Texas Infantry and 15th Texas Cavalry (dismounted) Consolidated:
Capt. Rhoads Fisher (w), Capt. M. M. Houston
7th Texas Infantry: Capt. T. B. Camp
10th Texas Infantry: Col. Roger Q. Mills
17th and 18th Texas Cavalry (dismounted) Consolidated:
Capt. George D. Manion
24th and 25th Texas Cavalry (dismounted) Consolidated: Lt. Col.
William L. Neyland (w), Maj. William A. Taylor

Wheeler's Cavalry Corps: Maj. Gen. Joseph Wheeler
MARTIN'S DIVISION: Maj. Gen. William T. Martin
Allen's Brigade: Brig. Gen. William W. Allen
1st Alabama Cavalry: Lt. Col. D. T. Blakey
3rd Alabama Cavalry: Col. James Hagan
4th Alabama Cavalry: Col. Alfred A. Russell
7th Alabama Cavalry: Capt. George Mason
12th Alabama Battalion Cavalry: Capt. Warren S. Reese
51st Alabama Cavalry: Col. M. L. Kirkpatrick

Iverson's Brigade: Brig. Gen. Alfred Iverson
 1st Georgia Cavalry: Lt. Col. James H. Strickland
 2nd Georgia Cavalry: Maj. James W. Mayo
 3rd Georgia Cavalry: Col. Robert Thompson
 4th Georgia Cavalry: Maj. Augustus R. Stewart
 6th Georgia Cavalry: Col. John R. Hart

ARMY OF MISSISSIPPI: LT. GEN. ALEXANDER P. STEWART

JACKSON'S DIVISION: Brig. Gen. William H. Jackson
 Ferguson's Brigade: Brig. Gen. Samuel W. Ferguson
  2nd Alabama Cavalry: Lt. Col. John N. Carpenter
  56th Alabama Cavalry: Col. William Boyles
  12th Mississippi Battalion Cavalry: Col. William M. Inge
  Miller's Mississippi Regiment Cavalry (9th Mississippi Cavalry):
   Col. Horace H. Miller
  Perrin's Mississippi Regiment Cavalry (11th Mississippi Cavalry):
   Col. Robert O. Perrin
  Scout Company, Mississippi Cavalry: Capt. Thomas C. Flournoy

Battle of Atlanta, July 22
ARMY OF THE TENNESSEE: MAJ. GEN. JAMES B. MCPHERSON (k),
MAJ. GEN. JOHN A. LOGAN

Fifteenth Corps: Maj. Gen. John A. Logan, Brig. Gen Morgan L. Smith
FIRST DIVISION: Brig. Gen. Charles R. Woods
 First Brigade: Col. Milo Smith
  26th Iowa: Lt. Col. Thomas G. Ferreby
  30th Iowa: Lt. Col. Aurelius Roberts
  27th Missouri: Maj. Dennis O'Connor
  76th Ohio: Col. William B. Woods

 Second Brigade: Col. James A. Williamson
  4th Iowa: Lt. Col. Samuel D. Nichols (w), Capt. Randolph Sry
  9th Iowa: Col. David Carskaddon
  25th Iowa: Col. George A. Stone
  31st Iowa: Col. William Smyth

 Third Brigade: Col. Hugo Wangelin
  3rd Missouri: Col. Theodore Meumann
  12th Missouri: Lt. Col. Jacob Kaercher

17th Missouri: Maj. Francis Romer
29th Missouri: Maj. Philip H. Murphy
31st Missouri: Lt. Col. Samuel P. Simpson
32nd Missouri: Maj. Abraham J. Seay

Artillery: Maj. Clemens Landgraeber
Battery F, 2nd Missouri Light Artillery: Capt. Louis Voelkner
4th Ohio Battery: Capt. George Froehlich

SECOND DIVISION: Brig. Gen. Morgan L. Smith,
Brig. Gen. Joseph A. J. Lightburn
First Brigade: Col. James S. Martin
55th Illinois: Capt. Francis H. Shaw
111th Illinois: Maj. William M. Mabry (w)
116th Illinois: Capt. John S. Windsor
127th Illinois: Lt. Col. Frank S. Curtiss
6th Missouri: Lt. Col. Delos Van Deusen
57th Ohio: Lt. Col. Samuel R. Mott

Second Brigade: Brig. Gen. Joseph J. A. Lightburn, Col. Wells S. Jones
83rd Indiana: Capt. George H. Scott
30th Ohio: Col. Theodore Jones
37th Ohio: Maj. Charles Hipp
47th Ohio: Lt. Col. John Wallace (c), Maj. Thomas T. Taylor
53rd Ohio: Col. Wells S. Jones, Lt. Col. Robert A. Fulton
54th Ohio: Lt. Col. Robert Williams Jr.

Artillery: Capt. Francis De Gress
Battery A, 1st Illinois Light Artillery: Lt. Samuel S. Smyth (c)
Battery H, 1st Illinois Light Artillery: Capt. Francis De Gress

FOURTH DIVISION: Brig. Gen. William Harrow
First Brigade: Col. Reuben Williams
26th Illinois: Capt. Ira J. Bloomfield
90th Illinois: Lt. Col. Owen Stuart
12th Indiana: Lt. Col. James Goodnow
100th Indiana: Lt. Col. Albert Heath

Second Brigade: Brig. Gen. Charles C. Walcutt
103rd Illinois: Maj. Asias Willison

97th Indiana: Lt. Col. Aden G. Cavins
6th Iowa: Maj. Thomas J. Ennis
46th Ohio: Capt. Joshua W. Heath (k), Capt. Isaac N. Alexander

Third Brigade: Col. John M. Oliver
48th Illinois: Col. Lucien Greathouse (k), Maj. Edward Adams
99th Indiana: Col. Alexander Fowler
15th Michigan: Lt. Col. Frederick S. Hutchinson
70th Ohio: Maj. William B. Brown

Artillery: Capt. Henry H. Griffiths
Battery F, 1st Illinois Light Artillery: Capt. Josiah H. Burton
1st Iowa Battery: Lt. William H. Gay

Left Wing, Sixteenth Corps: Maj. Gen. Grenville M. Dodge
SECOND DIVISION: Brig. Gen. Thomas W. Sweeny
First Brigade: Brig. Gen. Elliott W. Rice
52nd Illinois: Lt. Col. Edwin A. Bowen
66th Indiana: Lt. Col. Roger Martin
2nd Iowa: Lt. Col. Noel B. Howard (w), Maj. Matthew G. Hamill
7th Iowa: Lt. Col. James C. Parrott

Second Brigade: Col. August Mersy (w), Lt. Col. Robert N. Adams
12th Illinois: Lt. Col. Henry Van Sellar
66th Illinois: Capt. William S. Boyd
81st Ohio: Lt. Col. Robert N. Adams, Maj. Frank Evans

Artillery: Capt. Frederick Welker
Battery H, 1st Missouri Light Artillery: Lt. Andrew T. Blodgett

FOURTH DIVISION: Brig. Gen. John W. Fuller
First Brigade: Col. John Morrill (w), Lt. Col. Henry T. McDowell
64th Illinois: Lt. Col. Michael W. Manning
18th Missouri: Lt. Col. Charles S. Sheldon
27th Ohio: Lt. Col. Mendal Churchill
39th Ohio: Lt. Col. Henry T. McDowell, Maj. John S. Jenkins

Artillery: Capt. George Robinson
14th Ohio Battery: Lt. Seth M. Laird
Battery F, 2nd U.S. Artillery: Lt. Albert M. Murray (c)

Seventeenth Corps: Maj. Gen. Frank P. Blair Jr.

THIRD DIVISION: Brig. Gen. Mortimer D. Leggett

First Brigade: Brig. Gen. Manning F. Force (w), Col. George E. Bryant
20th Illinois: Lt. Col. Daniel Bradley
30th Illinois: Col. Warren Shedd (c), Lt. Col. William C. Rhoads
31st Illinois: Lt. Col. Robert N. Pearson
12th Wisconsin: Col. George E. Bryant, Lt. Col. James K. Proudfit
16th Wisconsin: Col. Cassius Fairchild

Second Brigade: Col. Robert K. Scott (c), Lt. Col. Greenberry F. Wiles
20th Ohio: Lt. Col. John C. Fry (w), Maj. Francis M. Shaklee
68th Ohio: Lt. Col. George E. Welles (w)
78th Ohio: Lt. Col. Greenberry F. Wiles, Maj. John T. Rainey

Third Brigade: Col. Adam G. Malloy
17th Wisconsin: Lt. Col. Thomas McMahon
Worden's Battalion (detachments of 81st Illinois, 95th Illinois, and
14th Wisconsin): Maj. Asa Worden

Artillery: Capt. William S. Williams
Battery D, 1st Illinois Light Artillery: Capt. Edgar H. Cooper
Battery H, 1st Michigan Light Artillery: Capt. Marcus D. Elliott
3rd Ohio Battery: Lt. John Sullivan

FOURTH DIVISION: Brig. Gen. Giles A. Smith

First Brigade: Col. Benjamin F. Potts
53rd Illinois: Lt. Col. John W. McClanahan
23rd Indiana: Lt. Col. William P. Davis
53rd Indiana: Lt. Col. William Jones (mw), Maj. Warner L. Vestal (w),
Capt. George H. Beers
3rd Iowa (3 companies): Capt. Pleasant T. Mathes (mw),
Lt. Lewis T. Linnell
32nd Ohio: Capt. William M. Morris

Third Brigade: Col. William Hall
11th Iowa: Lt. Col. John C. Abercrombie
13th Iowa: Col. John Shane
15th Iowa: Col. William W. Belknap
16th Iowa: Lt. Col. Addison H. Sanders (c), Capt. Crandall W. Williams

Artillery: Capt. Edward Spear Jr.
    Battery F, 2nd Illinois Light Artillery: Capt. Walter H. Powell (c)
    1st Minnesota Battery: Capt. William Z. Clayton
    15th Ohio Battery: Lt. James Burdick

ARMY OF THE OHIO (TWENTY-THIRD CORPS): MAJ. GEN. JOHN M. SCHOFIELD

SECOND DIVISION: Brig. Gen. Milo S. Hascall
Artillery: Capt. Joseph C. Shields
    22nd Indiana Battery: Lt. Edward W. Nicholson
    Battery F, 1st Michigan Light Artillery: Capt. Byron D. Paddock
    19th Ohio Battery: Capt. Joseph C. Shields

THIRD DIVISION: Brig. Gen. Jacob D. Cox
Artillery: Maj. Henry W. Wells
    15th Indiana Battery: Capt. Alonzo D. Harvey
    23rd Indiana Battery: Lt. Luther S. Houghton
    Battery D, 1st Ohio Light Artillery: Capt. Giles J. Cockerill

ARMY OF TENNESSEE: GEN. JOHN B. HOOD

Hardee's Corps: Lt. Gen. William J. Hardee
BATE'S DIVISION: Maj. Gen. William B. Bate
Finley's Brigade: Brig. Gen. Jesse J. Finley
    1st Florida Cavalry (dismounted) and 3rd Florida Infantry Consolidated:
        Capt. Matthew H. Strain
    1st and 4th Florida Consolidated: Lt. Col. Edward Badger
    6th Florida: Lt. Col. Daniel L. Kenan
    7th Florida: Lt. Col. Robert Bullock

Lewis's Brigade (Orphan Brigade): Brig. Gen. Joseph H. Lewis
    2nd Kentucky: Col. James W. Moss
    4th Kentucky: Lt. Col. Thomas W. Thompson
    5th Kentucky: Lt. Col. Hiram Hawkins
    6th Kentucky: Col. Martin H. Cofer
    9th Kentucky: Col. John W. Caldwell

Tyler's Brigade: Brig. Gen. Thomas B. Smith
    37th Georgia: Col. Joseph T. Smith
    15th and 37th Tennessee Consolidated: Lt. Col. R. Dudley Frayser

20th Tennessee: Lt. Col. William M. Shy
30th Tennessee: Lt. Col. James J. Turner
4th Georgia Battalion Sharpshooters: Maj. Theodore D. Caswell

CHEATHAM'S DIVISION: Brig. Gen. George E. Maney
Maney's Brigade: Col. Francis M. Walker (k)
1st and 27th Tennessee Consolidated: Lt. Col. John L. House
4th Tennessee (Confederate): Lt. Col. Oliver A. Bradshaw
6th and 9th Tennessee Consolidated: Col. George C. Porter
19th Tennessee: Maj. James G. Deaderick
50th Tennessee: Col. Stephen H. Colms

Strahl's Brigade: Brig. Gen. Otho F. Strahl (w)
4th and 5th Tennessee Consolidated: Maj. Henry Hampton
24th Tennessee: Col. John A. Wilson (w)
31st Tennessee: Lt. Col. Fountain E. P. Stafford
33rd Tennessee: Lt. Col. Henry C. McNeill
41st Tennessee: Lt. Col. James D. Tillman

Vaughan's Brigade: Col. Michael Magevney Jr.
11th Tennessee: Col. George W. Gordon
12th and 47th Tennessee Consolidated: Col. William M. Watkins
13th and 154th Tennessee Consolidated: Lt. Col. John M. Dawson (w),
    Maj. William J. Crook
29th Tennessee: Col. Horace Rice

Wright's Brigade: Col. John C. Carter
8th Tennessee: Col. John H. Anderson
16th Tennessee: Capt. Benjamin Randals
28th Tennessee: Lt. Col. David C. Crook
38th Tennessee: Lt. Col. Andrew D. Gwynne
51st and 52nd Tennessee Consolidated: Lt. Col. John W. Estes

CLEBURNE'S DIVISION: Maj. Gen. Patrick R. Cleburne
Govan's Brigade: Brig. Gen. Daniel C. Govan
1st and 15th Arkansas Consolidated: Col. J. W. Colquitt (w),
    Capt. Felix G. Lusk
2nd and 24th Arkansas Consolidated: Col. E. Warfield (w)
5th and 13th Arkansas Consolidated: Col. John E. Murray (w)
6th and 7th Arkansas Consolidated: Col. Samuel G. Smith (w)

8th and 19th Arkansas Consolidated: Col. George F. Baucum
3rd Confederate: Capt. M. H. Dixon

Lowrey's Brigade: Brig. Gen. Mark P. Lowrey
  16th Alabama: Lt. Col. Frederick A. Ashford
  33rd Alabama: Lt. Col. R. F. Crittenden
  45th Alabama: Col. Harris D. Lampley (w, c), Lt. Col. Robert H.
    Abercrombie
  3rd Mississippi Battalion: Lt. Col. J. D. Williams
  5th Mississippi: Lt. Col. John B. Herring
  8th Mississippi: Col. John C. Wilkinson
  32nd Mississippi: Col. W. H. H. Tison

Smith's Brigade: Brig. Gen. James A. Smith (w), Col. Roger Q. Mills (w),
Lt. Col. Robert B. Young
  5th Confederate: Maj. Richard Person (c), Capt. Aaron Cox
  6th Texas Infantry and 15th Texas Cavalry (dismounted) Consolidated:
    Capt. S. E. Rice (k or c), Lt. Thomas L. Flynt
  7th Texas: Capt. J. William Brown
  10th Texas: Col. Roger Q. Mills, Lt. Col. Robert B. Young,
    Capt. John A. Formwalt
  17th and 18th Texas Cavalry (dismounted) Consolidated:
    Capt. George D. Manion
  24th and 25th Texas Cavalry (dismounted) Consolidated:
    Maj. William A. Taylor

WALKER'S DIVISION: Maj. Gen. William H. T. Walker (k),
Brig. Gen. Hugh W. Mercer
  Gist's Brigade: Brig. Gen. States R. Gist (w), Col. James McCullough
    8th Georgia Battalion: Col. Zachariah L. Watters
    46th Georgia: Maj. Samuel J. C. Dunlop
    16th South Carolina: Col. James McCullough
    24th South Carolina: Col. Ellison Capers

  Mercer's Brigade: Brig. Gen. Hugh W. Mercer, Col. Charles H. Olmstead (w),
  Col. William Barkuloo (sick), Lt. Col. Morgan Rawls (w),
  Lt. Col. Cincinnatus S. Guyton
    1st Georgia (Volunteer): Col. Charles H. Olmstead
    54th Georgia: Lt. Col. Morgan Rawls
    57th Georgia: Col. William Barkuloo; Lt. Col. Cincinnatus S. Guyton
    63rd Georgia: Maj. Joseph V. H. Allen

Stevens's Brigade: Col. George A. Smith (w)
    1st Georgia (Confederate): Col. George A. Smith
    25th Georgia: Col. William J. Winn
    29th Georgia: Capt. J. W. Turner
    30th Georgia: Lt. Col. James S. Boynton
    66th Georgia: Col. James Cooper Nisbet (c)
    1st Georgia Battalion Sharpshooters: Maj. Arthur Shaaff

ARTILLERY: Col. Melancthon Smith
  Cobb's Battalion: Maj. Robert H. Cobb
    Gracey's Kentucky Battery: Lt. R. B. Matthews
    Mebane's Tennessee Battery: Lt. J. W. Phillips
    5th Company, Washington Artillery: Capt. Cuthbert H. Slocomb

  Hotchkiss's Battalion: Maj. T. R. Hotchkiss
    Goldthwaite's Alabama Battery: Capt. Richard W. Goldthwaite
    Key's Arkansas Battery: Capt. Thomas J. Key
    Swett's Mississippi Battery: Lt. H. Shannon

  Hoxton's Battalion: Maj. Llewellyn Hoxton
    Perry's Florida Battery: Capt. Thomas J. Perry
    Phelan's Alabama Battery: Lt. Nathaniel Venable
    Turner's Mississippi Battery: Capt. William B. Turner

  Martin's Battalion: Maj. Robert Martin
    Bledsoe's Missouri Battery: Capt. Hiram M. Bledsoe
    Ferguson's South Carolina Battery: Lt. John A. Alston
    Howell's Georgia Battery: Capt. Evan P. Howell

Hood's Corps: Maj. Gen. Benjamin F. Cheatham
CLAYTON'S DIVISION: Maj. Gen. Henry D. Clayton
  Baker's Brigade: Col. John H. Higley
    37th Alabama: Lt. Col. Alexander A. Greene (k)
    40th Alabama: Maj. Ezekiah Slocum Gulley
    42nd Alabama: Capt. Robert K. Wells
    54th Alabama: Lt. Col. John A. Minter

  Gibson's Brigade: Brig. Gen. Randall L. Gibson
    1st Louisiana (Regulars): Capt. W. H. Sparks
    13th Louisiana: Lt. Col. Francis L. Campbell
    16th and 25th Louisiana Consolidated: Lt. Col. Robert H. Lindsay

19th Louisiana: Col. Richard W. Turner

20th Louisiana: Col. Leon Von Zinken

4th Louisiana Battalion: Maj. Duncan Buie

Austin's Louisiana Battalion Sharpshooters: Maj. John E. Austin

Holtzclaw's Brigade: Col. Bushrod Jones

18th Alabama: Lt. Col. Peter Forney Hunley

32nd and 58th Alabama Consolidated: Capt. John Alfred Avirett Jr.

36th Alabama: Lt. Col. Thomas H. Herndon

38th Alabama: Maj. Shep. Ruffin (w, c)

Stovall's Brigade: Col. Abda Johnson

1st Georgia State Line: Lt. Col. Joseph M. Brown (mw),
   Capt. Albert Howell

40th Georgia: Capt. John F. Groover

41st Georgia: Maj. Mark S. Nall

42nd Georgia: Capt. L. P. Thomas

43rd Georgia: Capt. Joseph M. Storey

52nd Georgia: Capt. Rufus R. Asbury

HINDMAN'S DIVISION: Brig. Gen. John C. Brown

Dea's Brigade: Col. John G. Coltart

19th Alabama: Lt. Col. George R. Kimbrough

22nd Alabama: Col. Benjamin R. Hart

25th Alabama: Col. George D. Johnston

39th Alabama: Lt. Col. William C. Clifton (w),
   Capt. Thomas J. Brannon

50th Alabama: Capt. George W. Arnold

17th Alabama Battalion Sharpshooters: Capt. James F. Nabers

Manigault's Brigade: Brig. Gen. Arthur M. Manigault

24th Alabama: Col. Newton N. Davis

28th Alabama: Lt. Col. William L. Butler

34th Alabama: Col. Julius C. B. Mitchell

10th South Carolina: Col. James F. Pressley (w),
   Lt. Col. C. Irvine Walker

19th South Carolina: Maj. James L. White (w), Capt. Elijah W. Horne

Tucker's Brigade: Col. Jacob H. Sharp

7th Mississippi: Col. William H. Bishop

9th Mississippi: Lt. Col. Benjamin F. Johns

10th Mississippi: Lt. Col. George B. Myers
41st Mississippi: Col. J. Byrd Williams
44th Mississippi: Lt. Col. R. G. Kelsey
9th Mississippi Battalion Sharpshooters: Maj. William C. Richards

Walthall's Brigade: Col. Samuel Benton (mw), Col. William F. Brantly
24th and 27th Mississippi Consolidated: Col. Robert P. McKelvaine
29th and 30th Mississippi Consolidated: Col. William F. Brantly
34th Mississippi: Capt. T. S. Hubbard

STEVENSON'S DIVISION: Maj. Gen. Carter L. Stevenson
Brown's Brigade: Col. Joseph B. Palmer
3rd Tennessee: Lt. Col. Calvin J. Clack
18th Tennessee: Lt. Col. William R. Butler
23rd and 45th Tennessee Battalion Consolidated: Col. Anderson Searcy
26th Tennessee: Col. Richard M. Saffell
32nd Tennessee: Capt. Thomas D. Deavenport

Cumming's Brigade: Brig. Gen. Alfred Cumming
2nd Georgia State Troops: Col. James Wilson
34th Georgia: Maj. John M. Jackson
36th Georgia: Maj. Charles E. Broyles
39th Georgia: Capt. J. W. Cureton
56th Georgia: Col. E. P. Watkins

Pettus's Brigade: Brig. Gen. Edmund W. Pettus
20th Alabama: Col. James M. Dedman
23rd Alabama: Lt. Col. Joseph B. Bibb
30th Alabama: Col. Charles M. Shelley
31st Alabama: Capt. J. J. Nix
46th Alabama: Capt. George E. Brewer

Reynolds's Brigade: Brig. Gen. Alexander W. Reynolds
58th North Carolina: Capt. Alfred T. Stewart
60th North Carolina: Col. Washington M. Hardy
54th Virginia: Lt. Col. John J. Wade
63rd Virginia: Capt. David O. Rush

ARTILLERY: Col. Robert F. Beckham
Courtney's Battalion: Maj. Alfred R. Courtney
Dent's Alabama Battery: Capt. Staunton H. Dent

Douglas's Texas Battery: Capt. James P. Douglas
Garrity's Alabama Battery: Lt. Philip Bond

Eldridge's Battalion: Maj. J. Wesley Eldridge
Eufaula Alabama Battery: Capt. McDonald Oliver
Fenner's Louisiana Battery: Capt. Charles E. Fenner
Stanford's Mississippi Battery: Lt. James S. McCall

Johnston's Battalion: Maj. John W. Johnston
Van Den Corput's Georgia Battery: Lt. William S. Hoge
Marshall's Tennessee Battery: Capt. Lucius G. Marshall
Rowan's Georgia Battery: Capt. John B. Rowan

GEORGIA MILITIA: MAJ. GEN. GUSTAVUS W. SMITH

Two Brigades, Three Regiments Each

Artillery
Anderson's Georgia Battery: Capt. Ruel W. Anderson
Lumsden's Alabama Battery: Capt. Charles L. Lumsden

Battle of Decatur, July 22

ARMY OF THE CUMBERLAND: MAJ. GEN. GEORGE H. THOMAS

Cavalry Corps: Brig. Gen. Washington L. Elliott
SECOND DIVISION: Brig. Gen. Kenner Garrard
Chicago Board of Trade Battery (two sections): Lt. Trumbull D. Griffin
and Lt. Henry Bennett

ARMY OF THE OHIO (TWENTY-THIRD CORPS):
MAJ. GEN. JOHN M. SCHOFIELD

THIRD DIVISION: Brig. Gen. Jacob D. Cox
First Brigade: Brig. Gen. James W. Reilly
112th Illinois: Lt. Col. Emery S. Bond
16th Kentucky: Capt. Jacob Miller
100th Ohio: Col. Patrick S. Slevin
104th Ohio: Col. Oscar W. Sterl
8th Tennessee: Col. Felix A. Reeve

ARMY OF THE TENNESSEE: MAJ. GEN. JAMES B. MCPHERSON (k),
MAJ. GEN. JOHN A. LOGAN

Left Wing, Sixteenth Corps: Maj. Gen. Grenville M. Dodge
SECOND DIVISION: Brig. Gen. Thomas W. Sweeny
Second Brigade: Col. August Mersy (w), Col. Robert N. Adams
9th Illinois Mounted Infantry (five companies): Maj. John H. Kuhn

FOURTH DIVISION: Brig. Gen. John W. Fuller
Second Brigade: Col. John W. Sprague
35th New Jersey: Col. John J. Cladek
43rd Ohio: Col. Wager Swayne
63rd Ohio: Lt. Col. Charles E. Brown (w), Maj. John W. Fouts
25th Wisconsin: Col. Milton Montgomery (w, c),
Lt. Col. Jeremiah M. Rusk

Artillery
Battery C, 1st Michigan Light Artillery (one section): Lt. Henry Shier

ARMY OF TENNESSEE: GEN. JOHN B. HOOD

Wheeler's Cavalry Corps: Maj. Gen. Joseph Wheeler
MARTIN'S DIVISION: Maj. Gen. William T. Martin
Allen's Brigade: Brig. Gen. William W. Allen
1st Alabama Cavalry: Lt. Col. D. T. Blakey
3rd Alabama Cavalry: Col. James Hagan
4th Alabama Cavalry: Col. Alfred A. Russell
7th Alabama Cavalry: Capt. George Mason
51st Alabama Cavalry: Col. M. L. Kirkpatrick
(12th Alabama Cavalry Battalion, Capt. Warren S. Reese,
detached and not engaged)

Iverson's Brigade: Brig. Gen. Alfred Iverson
2nd Georgia Cavalry: Maj. James W. Mayo
4th Georgia Cavalry: Maj. Augustus R. Stewart
6th Georgia Cavalry: Col. John R. Hart
(1st Georgia Cavalry, Lt. Col. James H. Strickland, and 3rd Georgia
Cavalry, Col. Robert Thompson, detached and not engaged)

KELLY'S DIVISION: Brig. Gen. John H. Kelly
Anderson's Brigade: Col. Robert H. Anderson
8th Confederate Cavalry: Lt. Col. John S. Prather

10th Confederate Cavalry: Capt. W. J. Vason
(3rd Confederate Cavalry, Lt. Col. John McCaskill; 12th Confederate
Cavalry, Capt. Charles H. Conner; and 5th Georgia Cavalry,
Lt. Col. Edward Bird, detached and not engaged)

Dibrell's Brigade: Col. George G. Dibrell
8th Tennessee Cavalry: Capt. Jefferson Leftwich
9th Tennessee Cavalry: Capt. James M. Reynolds
11th Tennessee Cavalry: Col. Daniel W. Holman
(4th Tennessee Cavalry, Col. William S. McLemore, and 10th
Tennessee Cavalry, Maj. John Minor, detached and not engaged)

Williams's Brigade: Brig. Gen. John S. Williams
1st Kentucky Cavalry: Col. J. R. Butler
2nd Kentucky Cavalry: Maj. Thomas W. Lewis
9th Kentucky Cavalry: Col. William C. P. Breckinridge
(2nd Kentucky Cavalry Battalion, Capt. John B. Dortch; Allison's
Tennessee Squadron Cavalry, Capt. J. S. Reese; and Hamilton's
Tennessee Cavalry Battalion, Maj. Joseph Shaw,
detached and not engaged)

Artillery: Lt. Col. Felix H. Robertson
Ferrell's Georgia Battery (one section): Lt. Nathan Davis
Huggins's Tennessee Battery: Lt. Nat. Baxter
Ramsey's Tennessee Battery: Lt. D. Breck. Ramsey
White's Tennessee Battery: Lt. Arthur Pue Jr.
Wiggins's Arkansas Battery: Lt. J. Wylie Calloway

ARMY OF MISSISSIPPI: LT. GEN. ALEXANDER P. STEWART

JACKSON'S DIVISION: Brig. Gen. William H. Jackson
Ferguson's Brigade: Brig. Gen. Samuel W. Ferguson
2nd Alabama Cavalry: Lt. Col. John N. Carpenter
56th Alabama Cavalry: Col. William Boyles
12th Mississippi Cavalry Battalion: Col. William M. Inge
Miller's Mississippi Regiment of Cavalry (9th Mississippi Cavalry):
Col. Horace H. Miller
Perrin's Mississippi Regiment of Cavalry (11th Mississippi Cavalry):
Col. Robert O. Perrin
Scout Company, Mississippi Cavalry: Capt. Thomas C. Flournoy

Abbreviations

ADAH	Alabama Department of Archives and History, Montgomery
AHC	Atlanta History Center, Atlanta, Georgia
ALPL	Abraham Lincoln Presidential Library, Springfield, Illinois
CHM	Chicago History Museum, Chicago, Illinois
CMC	Cincinnati Museum Center, Cincinnati, Ohio
CWM	College of William and Mary, Special Collections, Williamsburg, Virginia
DU	Duke University, Rubenstein Rare Book and Manuscript Library, Durham, North Carolina
EU	Emory University, Manuscripts, Archives, and Rare Books Library, Atlanta, Georgia
FHS	Filson Historical Society, Louisville, Kentucky
GHS	Georgia Historical Society, Savannah
GLIAH	Gilder Lehrman Institute of American History, New-York Historical Society, New York
HL	Huntington Library, San Marino, California
HSP	Historical Society of Pennsylvania, Philadelphia
ISL	Indiana State Library, Indianapolis
IU	Indiana University, Manuscripts Department, Lilly Library, Bloomington
KHS	Kentucky Historical Society, Frankfort
LC	Library of Congress, Manuscripts Division, Washington, D.C.
LMU	Lincoln Memorial University, Abraham Lincoln Library and Museum, Harrogate, Tennessee
LSU	Louisiana State University, Louisiana and Lower Mississippi Valley Collection, Baton Rouge
MAHS	Massachusetts Historical Society, Boston
MDAH	Mississippi Department of Archives and History, Jackson
MHM	Missouri History Museum, Saint Louis
MNHS	Minnesota Historical Society, Saint Paul
MOC	Museum of the Confederacy, Richmond, Virginia
MSU	Mississippi State University, Special Collections, Starkville
MU	Miami University, Special Collections, Oxford, Ohio
NARA	National Archives and Records Administration, Washington, D.C.
NC	Navarro College, Pearce Civil War Collection, Corsicana, Texas
NL	Newberry Library, Chicago, Illinois

N-YHS	New-York Historical Society, New York
NYSL	New York State Library, Albany
OHS	Ohio Historical Society, Archives/Library, Columbus
OCHM	Old Court House Museum, Vicksburg, Mississippi
OR	*The War of the Rebellion: A Compilation of the Official Records of the Union and Confederate Armies*, 70 vols. in 128 pts. (Washington: Government Printing Office, 1880–1901; all citations to series 1 unless otherwise indicated)
PU	Princeton University, Rare Books and Special Collections, Princeton, New Jersey
RBHPC	Rutherford B. Hayes Presidential Center, Fremont, Ohio
SAF	State Archives of Florida, Tallahassee
SCHS	South Carolina Historical Society, Charleston
SHSI	State Historical Society of Iowa, Des Moines
SHSM-RCC	State Historical Society of Missouri, Research Center Columbia
SOR	*Supplement to the Official Records of the Union and Confederate Armies*, 100 vols. (Wilmington, NC: Broadfoot, 1993–2000)
SU	Syracuse University, Special Collections Research Center, Syracuse, New York
TC	The Citadel, Archives and Museum, Charleston, South Carolina
TSLA	Tennessee State Library and Archives, Nashville
TLCHS	Toledo–Lucas County Historical Society, Toledo, Ohio
UA	University of Alabama, W. Stanley Hoole Special Collections Library, Tuscaloosa
UAF	University of Arkansas, Special Collections, Fayetteville
UCSB	University of California, Special Collections, Santa Barbara
UGA	University of Georgia, Hargrett Rare Book and Manuscript Library, Athens
UI	University of Iowa, Special Collections, Iowa City
UM	University of Mississippi, Archives and Special Collections, Oxford
UNC	University of North Carolina, Southern History Collection, Chapel Hill
UND	University of Notre Dame, Special Collections, South Bend, Indiana
UO	University of Oklahoma, Western History Collections, Norman
USAMHI	U.S. Army Military History Institute, Carlisle, Pennsylvania
USM	University of Southern Mississippi, Archives, Hattiesburg
USMA	U.S. Military Academy, Special Collections and Archives Division, West Point, New York
UTC	University of Tennessee, Special Collections, Chattanooga
UTK	University of Tennessee, Special Collections, Knoxville
UTM	University of Tennessee, Special Collections, Martin
UW	University of Washington, Special Collections, Seattle

UWYO	University of Wyoming, American Heritage Center, Laramie
VHS	Virginia Historical Society, Richmond
VNMP	Vicksburg National Military Park, Vicksburg, Mississippi
WHS	Wisconsin Historical Society, Madison
WLC-UM	University of Michigan, William L. Clements Library, Ann Arbor
WRHS	Western Reserve Historical Society, Cleveland, Ohio

Preface

1. Ingersoll, *Iowa and the Rebellion*, 261.

2. Logan, *Volunteer Soldier*, 689.

3. Ecelbarger, *Day Dixie Died*, 232.

4. Cate, *Two Soldiers*, 99; *OR*, 38(3):50, 170–171, 699; *OR*, ser. 2, 8:359; Howell to wife, July 28, 1864, Evan P. Howell Letters, AHC; Davis, *Requiem for a Lost City*, 116; William W. Belknap to Aaron, August 5, 1864, Belknap Family Papers, N-YHS; Dwight, "Battle of July 22"; Hawkins, "5th Ky. Infantry C.S.A.," 61, Hiram Hawkins Papers, KHS; Fleming, *Band of Brothers*, 76.

5. Sherman, *Memoirs*, 2:81; Boynton, *Sherman's Historical Raid*, 119; Logan, *Volunteer Soldier*, 689.

6. Kurtz, *Atlanta Cyclorama*, 7; McMurry, *Atlanta*, 155; Castel, *Decision in the West*, 410; Bonds, *War like the Thunderbolt*, 170.

1. Atlanta Is in Sight

1. For good general histories of the Atlanta Campaign, see Castel, *Decision in the West*, and McMurry, *Atlanta*.

2. For a discussion of terrain and topography in the campaign, see Hess, *Fighting for Atlanta*, 5–6.

3. For the Kennesaw phase of the campaign, see Hess, *Kennesaw Mountain*.

4. For a discussion of the significance of crossing the Chattahoochee River, see Hess, *Peach Tree Creek*, 8–11.

5. Hess, *Fighting for Atlanta*, 143–150.

6. *OR*, 38(5):66.

7. Gresham, *Life of Walter Quintin Gresham*, 1:301.

8. Whaley, *Forgotten Hero*, 21, 95, 110–111, 114, 119, 121; Keim, "Life and Character of Major-General James B. McPherson," 369.

9. Whaley, *Forgotten Hero*, 138, 141–142; Keim, "Life and Character of Major-General James B. McPherson," 375–376.

10. Kirk, *History of the Fifteenth Pennsylvania Volunteer Cavalry*, 720.

11. McPherson to mother, April 4, 1864, McPherson Papers, TLCHS.

12. Hickenlooper, "Reminiscences of General Andrew Hickenlooper," 48, *Civil War Times Illustrated* Collection, USAMHI.

13. McPherson to My Dear Friend, July 12, 1864, James Birdseye McPherson Papers, USMA.

14. *OR*, 38(5):68, 76–77.

15. *OR*, 38(2):515–516, 38(5):873.

16. *OR*, 38(2):516, 38(5):89, 92.

17. *OR*, 38(2):804, 38(5):75–76, 100.

18. *OR*, 38(1):200–201.

19. *OR*, 38(3):383, 431, 506, 38(5):93, 100; "General G. M. Dodge's Account of Part taken by *Sixteenth Army Corps*, in movement on *Resaca*, attack of 4th of July, and *Battle* of *Atlanta*," November 30, 1875, William T. Sherman Papers, LC; "Historical Memoranda of the 52nd Regiment Illinois Infantry Volunteers," Edwin A. Bowen Papers, HL; Dodge, "Stories of Sherman"

20. Connelly, *Autumn of Glory*, 397–398.

21. *OR*, 38(5):879.

22. Cox, *Atlanta*, 144–145; Hess, *Peach Tree Creek*, 10–11.

23. *OR*, 38(2):767, 38(5):108, 127–128.

24. *OR*, 38(3):66, 100, 210; Jacobs diary, July 15–16, 1864, Wayne Johnson Jacobs Diaries and Lists, LSU.

25. *OR*, 38(2):912–913, 38(3):38, 553, 38(5):117, 135, 144–145; Boughton to mother, July 15, 1864, Clement Abner Boughton Papers, WLC-UM; Frank P. Blair to wife, July 18, 1864, Breckinridge Long Papers, LC.

26. Bonner, *Journal of a Milledgeville Girl*, 50; Garrett, "Civilian Life in Atlanta," 30; Walker to Mary, July 12, 1864, W. H. T. Walker Papers, DU; Walker to daughter, July 15, 1864, ibid.; Lovell diary, July 16, 1864, Mansfield Lovell Papers, HL.

27. *OR*, 38(5):108, 125, 132.

28. *OR*, 38(5):142–143.

29. *OR*, 38(3):66, 81, 38(5):123, 128–129, 146–147.

30. *OR*, 38(5):167.

31. *OR*, 38(3):498; "Historical Memoranda of the 52nd Regiment Illinois Infantry Volunteers," Edwin A. Bowen Papers, HL; Schweitzer diary, July 15, 1864, Edward E. Schweitzer Papers, HL; Clarke, "With Sherman in Georgia," 363; *OR*, 38(5):155.

32. *OR*, 38(5):114, 150; Simpson and Berlin, *Sherman's Civil War*, 669.

2. From Roswell to Bald Hill, July 17–20

1. *OR*, 38(3):101, 280, 318, 350, 38(5):157–158, 165–166; Wills, *Army Life*, 281.

2. Saunier, *Forty-Seventh Regiment Ohio*, 272; 38(5):149; Clarke, "With Sherman in Georgia," 363.

3. *OR*, 38(3):383, 486; 38(5):165.

4. *OR*, 38(3):553, 579; 38(5):158; Modil Diary, July 17, 1864, George W. Modil Papers, MDAH; Sylvester Daniels Diary, July 17, 1864, Theophilus M. Magaw Papers, HL.

5. *OR*, 38(5):165.

6. *OR*, 38(2):571, 686, 38(5):163–164.

7. *OR*, 38(1):155–156.

8. *OR*, 38(3):951, 38(5):166.

9. *OR*, 38(5):882–883.

10. *OR*, 38(3):717, 38(5):885; Lovell Diary, July 17, 1864, Mansfield Lovell Papers, HL; Daniel, *Conquered*, 297.

11. *OR*, 38(5):885.

12. Hess, *Peach Tree Creek*, 23–27.

13. *OR*, 38(5):170.

14. *OR*, 38(3):38, 101, 38(5):168, 175.

15. *OR*, 38(2):808, 813, 38(5):176, 177, 52(1):569; Moore Diary, July 18, 1864, Edward B. Moore Diary and Correspondence, UWYO.

16. *OR*, 38(5):170, 176.

17. *OR*, 38(3):383, 579, 38(5):176, 52(1):569.

18. *OR*, 38(1):156, 38(2):571, 686.

19. Thomas B. Mackall Journal, July 18, 1864 (McMurry transcript), Joseph E. Johnston Papers, CWM; *OR*, 38(5):888–889.

20. *OR*, 38(3):717; Walker to Mary, July 18, 1864, W. H. T. Walker Papers, DU.

21. Lovell Diary, July 18, 1864, Mansfield Lovell Papers, HL.

22. Sherman, *Memoirs*, 2:72; Blair to J. E. Austin, February 1875, in Hood, *Advance and Retreat*, 190.

23. Sherman, *Memoirs*, 2:72; *OR*, 38(5):178–179.

24. *OR*, 38(5):158, 169–170.

25. *OR*, 38(5):179–180.

26. *OR*, 38(2):516, 38(5):183; Notebook, 64–65, 69, Folder 3, Box 78, Wilbur G. Kurtz Sr. Papers, AHC; Gallup to wife, July 18 (continued July 19), 1864, George W. Gallup Papers, FHS; James P. Snell Diary, July 19, 1864, ALPL; Kurtz, "Augustus F. Hurt House." Theodore Davis's sketch of the Chapman Powell House appeared in *Harper's Weekly*, August 27, 1864, 557.

27. *OR*, 38(2):516, 560, 571, 616, 673; E. S. to editor, July 19, 1864, *New York Daily Tribune*, July 28, 1864.

28. *OR*, 38(2):686.

29. *OR*, 38(5):181–182.

30. *OR*, 38(2):561, 38(3):383–384, 486; Typo, "From the 14th Ohio Battery"; *SOR*, pt. 2, 12:587; "Historical Memoranda of the 52nd Regiment Illinois Infantry Volunteers," Edwin A. Bowen Papers, HL; Edwin Witherby Brown, "Under a Poncho with Grant and Sherman," 94, MU; Schweitzer Diary, July 15, 1864, Edward E. Schweitzer Papers, HL; Gallup Diary, July 19, 1864, George W. Gallup Papers, FHS.

31. *OR*, 38(3):198, 298; Jacobs Diary, July 19, 1864, Wayne Johnson Jacobs Diaries and Lists, LSU; Schweitzer Diary, July 19, 1864, Edward E. Schweitzer Papers, HL.

32. Modil Diary, July 19, 1864, George W. Modil Papers, MDAH; Smith, "Civil War Diaries of Mifflin Jennings," July 19, 1864, Iowa in the Civil War website; Sylvester Daniels Diary, July 19, 1864, Theophilus M. Magaw Papers, HL.

33. *OR*, 38(2):808, 842.

34. Evans, "Fight for the Wagons," 21; Seay Diary, July 19, 1864, Abraham J. Seay Collection, UO; William E. Titze Diary, July 19, 1864, ALPL; Wills, *Army Life*, 283; Thurston Diary, July 19, 1864, James M. Thurston Papers, MAHS.

35. Thoburn, *My Experiences*, 105; Miller to wife, father, children, July 22, 1864, Marshall Mortimer Miller Papers, LC; "Historical Memoranda of the 52nd

Regiment Illinois Infantry Volunteers," Edwin A. Bowen Papers, HL; Schweitzer Diary, July 15, 1864, Edward E. Schweitzer Papers, HL; William E. Titze Diary, July 19, 1864, ALPL; Diary, July 19, 1864, James M. Thurston Papers, MAHS; Wright, *Corporal's Story*, 125; James P. Snell Diary, July 19, 1864, ALPL.

36. *OR*, 38(1):156; Hess, *Peach Tree Creek*, 39–42, 44–50.

37. Lovell Diary, July 19, 1864, Mansfield Lovell Papers, HL; Thomas B. Mackall Journal, July 19, 1864 (McMurry transcript), Joseph E. Johnston Papers, CWM; *OR*, 28(5):893; Davis, *Texas Brigadier*, 273.

38. *OR*, 38(3):951–952; Dodson, *Wheeler and His Cavalry*, 206–207; Gibbons, *Recollections*, 7.

39. Moore Diary, July 19, 1864, Edward B. Moore Diary and Correspondence, UWYO.

40. Sherman, *Memoirs*, 2:72; *OR*, 38(5):185.

41. *OR*, 38(5):186, 193, 195.

42. *OR*, 38(5):194.

43. *OR*, 38(3):101–102, 210, 228, 265, 358, 38(5):205; Clarke, "With Sherman in Georgia," 363; *SOR*, pt. 1, 7:48.

44. *OR*, 38(3):384, 431, 524; James P. Snell Diary, July 20, 1864, ALPL.

45. *OR*, 38(3):553, 579, 590; Sylvester Daniels Diary, July 20, 1864, Theophilus M. Magaw Papers, HL; Smith, "Civil War Diaries of Mifflin Jennings," July 20, 1864, Iowa in the Civil War website; William F. Graham Diary, July 20, 1864, DU; Modil Diary, July 20, 1864, George W. Modil Papers, MDAH; [Rood], *Story of the Service of Company E*, 305.

46. *OR*, 38(3):590; Calhoun, *Gilded Age Cato*, 8, 18, 26–27, 31–33.

47. William F. Graham Diary, July 20, 1864, ALPL; *OR*, 38(3):39, 543; Bosworth, "Battle of Atlanta," in *Under Both Flags*, 162; Cryder and Miller, *View from the Ranks*, 415; Gresham, *Life of Walter Quintin Gresham*, 1:306; Welsh, *Medical Histories of Union Generals*, 141; Calhoun, *Gilded Age Cato*, 34; Kurtz, "Walter Q. Gresham at Atlanta."

48. Gresham, *Life of Walter Quintin Gresham*, 1:307; *OR*, 38(3):543.

49. Modil Diary, July 20, 1864, George W. Modil Papers, MDAH; [Rood], *Story of the Service of Company E*, 305; Special Orders No. 178, Headquarters, Seventeenth Corps, July 20, 1864, M. F. Force Papers, UW; William F. Graham Diary, July 20, 1864, ALPL.

50. *OR*, 38(3):543, 580, 38(5):208; Alexander, "Battle of Atlanta."

51. William E. Titze Diary, July 20, 1864, ALPL; *OR*, 52(1):569.

52. *OR*, 38(2):516, 686–687.

53. *OR*, 38(2):842, 38(5):208–209.

54. Hess, *Peach Tree Creek*, 36–37.

55. Hess, *Peach Tree Creek*, 57.

56. Hess, *Peach Tree Creek*, 181.

57. Hess, *Peach Tree Creek*, 72–73, 80–177.

58. Hess, *Peach Tree Creek*, 185–186, 247; *OR*, 38(5):195–198, 208; Gallup to wife, July 20, 1864, George W. Gallup Papers, FHS.

59. Hess, *Peach Tree Creek*, 74; *OR*, 38(3):952, 970, 38(5):895–897.

60. Hess, *Peach Tree Creek*, 98–99.

61. *OR*, 38(3):748–749, 751–752; *SOR*, pt. 1, 7:72; Brown, *One of Cleburne's Command*, 108; Nichols and Abbott, "Reminiscences of Confederate Service by Wiley A. Washburn," 70; McCaffrey, *Only a Private*, 68; Gibbons, *Recollections*, 7–8.

62. *OR*, 38(2):904–909, 38(5):897.

63. *OR*, 38(5):208–210.

3. Battle of Bald Hill, July 21

1. *OR*, 38(5):218–219.

2. William H. Lynch Diaries, July 21, 1864, SHSM-RCC; James B. David Diary, July 21, 1864, UTK; Seay Diary, July 21, 1864, Abraham J. Seay Collection, UO; *OR*, 38(3):455, 544; Bosworth, "Battle of Atlanta," *Blue and Gray*, 237; Bradford, "Fighting Not All Done by the 12th and 16th Wisconsin Regiments"; Hammond, "Charge at Atlanta"; Kurtz, "What James Bell Told Me about the Siege of Atlanta," July 15, 1935, 5–6, Folder 14, Box 87, Wilbur G. Kurtz Sr. Papers, AHC.

3. *OR*, 38(3):952, 38(5):219; Castel, *Decision in the West*, 383; Ecelbarger, *Day Dixie Died*, 36.

4. Munson, "Battle of Atlanta," 214–215; M. D. Leggett, "Battle of Atlanta," May 6, 1886; *OR*, 38(3):571; [Rood], *Story of the Service of Company E*, 306–308. Maj. Asa Worden's battalion consisted of detachments from the 72nd Illinois, 95th Illinois, and 14th Wisconsin. These men had been delayed in returning from their veteran furlough early in 1864 because of snowstorms. By the time they were ready to return to the field, their regiments had already left as part of the Red River Campaign, so they were sent to Georgia and attached to the Third Brigade, Third Division, Seventeenth Corps. Goodwin, "In Atlanta's Front."

5. *OR*, 38(3):733, 746, 952; Buck, *Cleburne and His Command*, 232–233.

6. McCaffrey, *Only a Private*, 68–69.

7. Munson, "Battle of Atlanta," 215; Alexander, "Battle of Atlanta."

8. [Rood], *Story of the Service of Company E*, 309.

9. [Rood], *Story of the Service of Company E*, 309–310; Morris, Hartwell, and Kuykendall, *History 31st Regiment Illinois*, 103; Hammond, "Charge at Atlanta"; McDonald, *30th Illinois*, 73; James P. Snell Diary, July 21, 1864, ALPL; A. E. Kinney to Mrs. Boughton, July 26, 1864, Clement Abner Boughton Papers, WLC-UM.

10. Munson, "Battle of Atlanta," 216; Wray, "Battle of Bald (or Leggett's) Hill"; Hammond, "Charge at Atlanta"; Styple, *Writing and Fighting*, 279; Walker, "In Front of Atlanta."

11. *OR*, 38(3):952; Hammond, "Charge at Atlanta"; A. E. Kinney to Mrs. Boughton, July 26, 1864, Clement Abner Boughton Papers, WLC-UM; Munson, "Battle of Atlanta," 216.

12. Gibbons, *Recollections*, 8; *OR*, 38(3):952.

13. *OR*, 38(3):580–581; William F. Graham Diary, July 21, 1864, DU; Throne, "History of Company D," 62.

14. *OR*, 38(3):601; John J. Safely to Mary McEwen, July 23, August 14, 1864, John

J. Safely Letters, McEwen Family Papers, MHM; Cryder and Miller, *View from the Ranks*, 416–417.

15. *OR*, 38(3):746, 752–753; Brown, *One of Cleburne's Command*, 109.

16. Munson, "Battle of Atlanta," 217; *SOR*, pt. 2, 75:714; Cate, *Two Soldiers*, 93.

17. *OR*, 38(3):564, 753, 38(5):219.

18. *OR*, 38(3):342, 348; William Odell to nephew, August 3, 1864, Jonathan Blair Papers, ALPL.

19. Barlow, "Personal Reminiscences," 118; Leggett, "Battle of Atlanta," May 6, 1886; *OR*, 38(3):20, 544; William E. Strong, "The Death of Major General James B. McPherson, July 22nd 1864," August 25, 1876, William T. Sherman Papers, LC.

20. *OR*, 38(3):550, 571; *SOR*, pt. 2, 75:714; A. E. Kinney to Mrs. Boughton, July 26, 1864, Clement Abner Boughton Papers, WLC-UM.

21. *OR*, 38(3):734, 746.

22. *OR*, 38(3):746, 748–749; Spurlin, *Civil War Diary of Charles A. Leuschner*, 44; Nichols and Abbott, "Reminiscences of Confederate Service by Wiley A. Washburn," 70; Brown, *One of Cleburne's Command*, 108–109.

23. Buck, *Cleburne and His Command*, 234; W. W. Royall account, n.d., in Yeary, *Reminiscences of the Boys in Gray*, 656.

24. William W. Belknap to De Gress, May 6, 1877, Francis De Gress Papers, AHC: *OR*, 38(3):265, 363, 366–367.

25. *OR*, 38(5):898; E. B. Wade to Cleburne, July 21, 1864, Letter Book, Irving Buck Papers, MOC; Franklin, *Civil War Diaries of Capt. Alfred Tyler Fielder*, 189; Van Buren Oldham Diary, July 21, 1864, UTM; Rennolds Diary, July 21, 1864, Edwin Hansford Rennolds Sr. Papers, UTK.

26. Bradford, "Fighting Not All Done by the 12th and 16th Wisconsin Regiments"; Leggett, "Battle of Atlanta," May 6, 1886.

27. Adams, "Battle and Capture of Atlanta," 148; McDonald, *30th Illinois*, 74; Munson, "Battle of Atlanta," 219; Morris, Hartwell, Kuykendall, *History 31st Regiment Illinois*, 104.

28. Bradford, "Fighting Not All Done by the 12th and 16th Wisconsin Regiments."

29. Bradford, "Fighting Not All Done by the 12th and 16th Wisconsin Regiments"; Marcus D. Elliott account, n.d., in *Portrait Biographical Album*, 819–820.

30. Cox, *Atlanta*, 174; *OR*, 38(1):72–73.

31. *OR*, 38(2):813, 38(5):221; Evans, "Fight for the Wagons," 17.

32. *OR*, 38(3):20, 38(5):220.

33. *OR*, 38(3):20, 564; Leggett, "Battle of Atlanta," May 6, 1886.

34. *OR*, 38(3):544, 608.

35. *OR*, 38(3):474, 506, 524.

36. *OR*, 38(3):474–475; Dodge, "Battle of Atlanta," 39–40; "Personal Biography of Major General Grenville Mellen Dodge, 1831–1870," 1:240, Grenville Mellen Dodge Papers, SHSI; Fuller, "Terrible Day."

37. *OR*, 38(2):572, 643, 38(3):102, 407; Michael Houck Diary, July 21, 1864, UTK; James P. Snell Diary, July 21, 1864, ALPL; Edington reminiscences, n.d., Thomas

Doak Edington Papers, UTK; Nugen to father and sister, July 21, 1864, William H. Nugen Letters, DU.

38. *OR*, 38(3):631.

39. Hess, *Peach Tree Creek*, 219–221; Davis, *Texas Brigadier*, 308.

40. *OR*, 38(3):699; T. B. Roy to Cheatham, October 15, 1881, notes attached to copy of Roy, "General Hardee and the Military Operations around Atlanta," in Benjamin F. Cheatham Papers, TSLA.

41. *OR*, 38(3):631, 38(5):899.

42. Roy, "General Hardee," 356; Castel, *Decision in the West*, 388; Kurtz, "Death of Major General W. H. T. Walker," 176; Bonds, *War like the Thunderbolt*, 128–129; Ecelbarger, *Day Dixie Died*, 55, 58, 63.

43. Circular, Headquarters, Stewart's Corps, July 21, 1864, Featherston Order Book, Winfield Scott Featherston Collection, UM; Tower, *Carolinian Goes to War*, 225.

44. Hughes, *Civil War Memoir of Philip Daingerfield Stephenson*, 216; Young, *Reminiscences*, 90; Cabaniss, *Civil War Journal and Letters of Serg. Washington Ives*, 69.

45. Speech, July 22, 1902, in Joseph B. Cumming Recollections, 47, UNC; Joslyn, *Charlotte's Boys*, 270–271.

46. T. B. Roy to Cleburne, July 21, 1864, 7:30 P.M. and 11 P.M., Letter Book, Irving Buck Papers, MOC; Roy, "General Hardee," 358–359.

47. McCaffrey, *Only a Private*, 70; *OR*, 38(3):737.

48. *OR*, 38(3):734; Spurlin, *Civil War Diary of Charles A. Leuschner*, 44; *SOR*, pt. 1, 7:72; Brown, *One of Cleburne's Command*, 110–111.

49. *OR*, 38(5):900.

50. Cate, *Two Soldiers*, 93–94.

51. *OR*, 38(3):952; T. B. Roy to Wheeler, February 27, 1880, Box 127, Joseph Wheeler Family Papers, ADAH; T. B. Roy to Govan, March 8, 1880, Daniel Chevilette Govan Papers, UNC.

52. *OR*, 38(5):900; Thomas B. Mackall Journal, July 21, 1864 (McMurry transcript), Joseph E. Johnston Papers, CWM.

53. Hafendorfer, *Civil War Journal of William L. Trask*, 170; Venet, *Sam Richards's Civil War Diary*, 228; Kurtz, "What James Bell Told Me about the Siege of Atlanta," July 15, 1935, 7, Folder 14, Box 87, Wilbur G. Kurtz Sr. Papers, AHC; "From the Army of Tennessee," special correspondence of the *Savannah Republican*, in *Daily Confederate* (Raleigh), July 30, 1864; Willis Perry Burt Diary, July 21–22, 1864, Laura Burt Brantley Collection, GHS.

54. Dyer, *Secret Yankees*, 8, 69, 322–326.

55. Leggett, "Battle of Atlanta," May 6, 1886; *OR*, 38(5):220 (copy of which can be found in M. F. Force Papers, UW); Morris, Hartwell, Kuykendall, *History 31st Regiment Illinois*, 104.

56. *OR*, 38(5):210–212, 222.

4. Morning, July 22

1. Alexander, "Battle of Atlanta."

2. McPherson quoted in Alexander, "Battle of Atlanta."

3. Willard Warner to editor of *Tribune*, April 8, 1876, newspaper clipping, James Birdseye McPherson Papers, USMA; Strong, "Death of General James B. McPherson," 317.

4. *OR*, 38(1):72, 38(3):224, 231; Leggett, "Battle of Atlanta," May 6, 1886; Bakhaus, "Logan at Atlanta."

5. Leggett, "Battle of Atlanta," May 6, 1886; Ecelbarger, *Day Dixie Died*, 253n; Arbuckle, *Civil War Experiences*, 69; James P. David Diary, July 22, 1864, UTK; William H. Lynch Diaries, July 22, 1864, SHSM-RCC.

6. Frank P. Blair to J. E. Austin, February 1875, in Hood, *Advance and Retreat*, 188; *OR*, 38(3):544–545.

7. Gresham, *Life of Walter Quintin Gresham*, 1:308; *OR*, 38(3):139, 147, 156.

8. *OR*, 38(3):188, 228, 287, 363; Vance, *Report of the Adjutant General*, 5:312; Nugen to father and sister, July 22, 1864, William H. Nugen Letters, DU.

9. William F. Graham Diary, July 22, 1864, ALPL; Foster Diary, July 22, 1864, Brigham Foster Papers, USAMHI; Nutt, "Fight at Atlanta."

10. Munson, "Battle of Atlanta," 220–221; *OR*, 38(3):254, 355; Ralston, "De Grasse's Battery."

11. *OR*, 38(3):369, 384; "Personal Biography of Major General Grenville Mellen Dodge, 1831–1870," 1:245, Grenville Mellen Dodge Papers, SHSI.

12. "General G. M. Dodge's Account of Part taken by *Sixteenth Army Corps*, in movement on *Resaca*, attack of 4th of July, and *Battle* of *Atlanta*," November 30, 1875, William T. Sherman Papers, LC; Chamberlin, "Recollections," 279; "Personal Biography of Major General Grenville Mellen Dodge, 1831–1870," 1:242, Grenville Mellen Dodge Papers, SHSI.

13. "Personal Biography of Major General Grenville Mellen Dodge, 1831–1870," 1:241–242, Grenville Mellen Dodge Papers, SHSI; *OR*, 38(3):369, 418, 453–454; James P. Snell Diary, July 22, 1864, ALPL.

14. *OR*, 38(3):418, 425–426; Wright, *Corporal's Story*, 126; "Historical Memoranda of the 52nd Regiment Illinois Infantry Volunteers," Edwin A. Bowen Papers, HL.

15. *OR*, 38(2):572, 608, 38(3):229–230; Tracie, *Annals of the Nineteenth Ohio Battery*, 359–361.

16. Stone, "Atlanta Campaign," 444; Cook Diary, July 22, 1864, Albert M. Cook Papers, SU.

17. Strong, "Death of General James B. McPherson," 319.

18. Willard Warner to editor of *Tribune*, April 8, 1876, newspaper clipping, James Birdseye McPherson Papers, USMA; Leggett, "Battle of Atlanta," May 6, 1886.

19. Castel, *Decision in the West*, 393; Davis, *Requiem for a Lost City*, 115–116; Dyer, *Secret Yankees*, 179–180; Kurtz, "Augustus F. Hurt House."

20. *OR*, 38(1):72.

21. Strong, "Death of General James B. McPherson," 320.

22. Sherman, *Memoirs*, 2:75–76.

23. Sherman, *Memoirs*, 2:76.

24. William E. Strong, "The Death of Major General James B. McPherson, July 22nd 1864," August 25, 1876, William T. Sherman Papers, LC.

25. *OR*, 38(3):223.

26. Fuller, "Terrible Day"; Sherman, *Memoirs*, 2:78–79; Cox, *Atlanta*, 166–167; Munson, "Battle of Atlanta," 220.

27. Fout, *Dark Days*, 385; Dwight, "Battle of July 22."

28. Neal to Ma, July 23, 1864, Andrew Jackson Neal Letters, EU.

29. *OR*, 38(3):102, 116, 223.

30. Strong, "The Death of Major General James B. McPherson, July 22nd 1864," August 25, 1876, William T. Sherman Papers, LC.

31. Strong, "Death of Major General James B. McPherson, July 22nd 1864."

32. Brown, *To the Manner Born*, 263–264; Kurtz, "Death of Major General W. H. T. Walker," 176; Thompson, *Orphan Brigade*, 261; Durham, *Blues in Gray*, 223; William McLeod Civil War Pocket Diary, July 22, 1864, SAF; George Anderson Mercer Diary, July 22, 1864, UNC. For a photo of William Cobb, see Wilbur G. Kurtz Sr. Visual Arts Collection, AHC. Kurtz had taken photos of Cobb's house on January 13, 1935, and noted that vandals burned it in the fall of 1965.

33. Kurtz, "Death of Major General W. H. T. Walker," 177.

34. Castel, *Decision in the West*, 391; Fleming, *Band of Brothers*, 76.

35. Castel, *Decision in the West*, 608n; Roy, "General Hardee," 359.

36. *OR*, 38(3):900–901, 953.

37. Roy, "General Hardee," 354–355, 359–360, 365.

38. Castel, *Decision in the West*, 389; *SOR*, pt. 1, 7:80; Thompson, *Orphan Brigade*, 261.

39. *OR*, 38(3):737; McCaffrey, *Only a Private*, 70.

40. Howard, "Struggle for Atlanta," 316; Aten, *Eighty-Fifth Regiment, Illinois Volunteer Infantry*, 209.

41. Adams, "Battle and Capture of Atlanta," 155; Dodge, "Battle of Atlanta," 41; Ecelbarger, *Day Dixie Died*, 109, 214.

42. Semmes to wife, July 22, 1864, Benedict Joseph Semmes Papers, UNC.

5. Dodge Stops Bate and Walker

1. Thompson, *Orphan Brigade*, 261–262; Hughes, *Civil War Memoir of Philip Daingerfield Stephenson*, 217.

2. William McLeod Civil War Pocket Diary, July 22, 1864, SAF.

3. Thompson, *Orphan Brigade*, 262.

4. Hughes, *Civil War Memoir of Philip Daingerfield Stephenson*, 217.

5. Thompson, *Orphan Brigade*, 262–263.

6. Young, *Reminiscences*, 91.

7. McMurray, *Twentieth Tennessee Regiment Volunteer Infantry*, 320–321.

8. Kurtz, "Death of Major General W. H. T. Walker," 178; "Memo of Data from J. W. McWilliams—June 30, 1930," 9, 11, Folder 11, Box 49, Wilbur G. Kurtz Sr. Papers, AHC; transcript of *Southern Confederacy*, August 6, 1861, Folder 3, Box

78, ibid.; Notes on Kurtz to Joseph B. Cumming, May 26, 1951, 3, Folder 12, Box 90, ibid.; Kurtz, "Major-General W. H. T. Walker."

9. Thompson, *Orphan Brigade*, 261; Hughes, *Civil War Memoir of Philip Daingerfield Stephenson*, 217–220.

10. "Personal Biography of Major General Grenville Mellen Dodge, 1831–1870," 1:242, 246, Grenville Mellen Dodge Papers, SHSI; Dodge, "Battle of Atlanta"; Chamberlin, "Hood's Second Sortie," 326.

11. "Personal Biography of Major General Grenville Mellen Dodge, 1831–1870," 1:242, 245, Grenville Mellen Dodge Papers, SHSI.

12. Adams, "Battle and Capture of Atlanta," 150; Morgan, *Through American and Irish Wars*, 8, 10–11; Sweeny to William B. Bodge, July 30, 1864, Thomas William Sweeny Papers, HL.

13. *OR*, 38(3):450, 456; Vance, *Report of the Adjutant General*, 4:424.

14. *OR*, 38(3):418; Donaldson, "Sweeny's Fighters"; Ackley to wife, July 24, 1864, Charles Thomas Ackley Civil War Letters, UI.

15. *OR*, 38(3):418, 467, 469, 536; Dodge, *Personal Recollections*, 215; Wright, *Corporal's Story*, 127–128. Wilbur Kurtz placed the position of Laird's 14th Ohio Battery as "just south of where Clay street joins Fair" on a 1930 map of Atlanta. See Kurtz, "McPherson's Last Ride."

16. *OR*, 38(3):490, 503; Churchill to wife, July 23, 1864, Mendal C. Churchill Papers, UWYO; Fuller, "Terrible Day."

17. *OR*, 38(3):371; "Personal Biography of Major General Grenville Mellen Dodge, 1831–1870," 1:245, Grenville Mellen Dodge Papers, SHSI; Thompson, *Orphan Brigade*, 263; Ecelbarger, *Day Dixie Died*, 76, 85.

18. Hawkins, "5th Ky. Infantry C.S.A.," 61, Hiram Hawkins Papers, KHS.

19. Kirwan, *Johnny Green*, 148–149.

20. *OR*, 38(3):418.

21. Donaldson, "Sweeny's Fighters"; *OR*, 38(3):418–419, 442, 469; Hawkins, "5th Ky. Infantry C.S.A.," 61, Hiram Hawkins Papers, KHS.

22. *OR*, 38(3):372, 538; H. E. Haynes to editor, August 4, 1864, *Western Reserve Chronicle* (Warren, OH), August 17, 1864; Smith, *Fuller's Ohio Brigade*, 169.

23. Hawkins, "5th Ky. Infantry C.S.A.," 61, Hiram Hawkins Papers, KHS; Donaldson, "Sweeny's Fighters."

24. Grainger, *Four Years*, 19; Thompson, *Orphan Brigade*, 263.

25. Ackley to wife, July 24, 1864, Charles Thomas Ackley Civil War Letters, UI; *OR*, 38(3):438.

26. *OR*, 38(3):419, 438; "Historical Memoranda of the 52nd Regiment Illinois Infantry Volunteers," Edwin A. Bowen Papers, HL.

27. "Historical Memoranda of the 52nd Regiment Illinois Infantry."

28. William McLeod Civil War Pocket Diary, July 22, 1864, SAF.

29. Ecelbarger, *Day Dixie Died*, 83, 256–257n.

30. Ecelbarger, *Day Dixie Died*, 83.

31. Davis, *Orphan Brigade*, 230; Ecelbarger, *Day Dixie Died*, 76–77, 79, 80, 82. Gary Ecelbarger asserts that Finley attacked Rice's right, aiming at the position of

Laird's 14th Ohio Battery, but the only sources he cites to support this assertion come from the Union side and from members of Lewis's Kentucky Brigade. The Federals did not identify their attackers, and Ecelbarger admits that the Kentuckians did not mention Finley's Brigade either, so it is difficult to understand why he believes Finley was able to attack at all. He did not consult McLeod's diary, which states that his unit did nothing that day. Ecelbarger also cites the letters of an officer in Finley's Brigade, but that man only mentioned that Finley's troop strength had declined a lot over the general period of the Battle of July 22, not that the brigade was engaged in any fighting that day. Moreover, there is a matter of brigade frontages. It is clear that Lewis's right flank ended in front of the 2nd Iowa and that Confederate troops approached Rice's right wing as well. The normal frontage of Lewis's Brigade would have brought his left wing opposite Laird's guns, leaving no room for Finley's troops there. Ecelbarger artificially extends the right end of Rice's line by placing the 7th Iowa between the 66th Indiana and the 2nd Iowa after it shifted to the right instead of it replacing the 66th Indiana, as is clearly stated in the official reports and in a diary of a 7th Iowa man that Ecelbarger did not consult. Moreover, there is a matter of timing. Finley advanced from Fayetteville Road to Lewis's left, which meant that Terry's Mill Pond lay directly in the path of his march. He had to fall behind Lewis to sidestep that huge obstacle, resulting in much shifting to the right, which McLeod's diary amply documents, and delaying his march a great deal. There was no possibility he could have attacked the Federals at the same time as Lewis. In short, I can find no evidence that Finley attacked at all or that he lost 300 men on July 22.

32. "Memo of Data from J. W. McWilliams—June 30, 1930," 3–5, Folder 11, Box 49, Wilbur G. Kurtz Sr. Papers, AHC; Ecelbarger, *Day Dixie Died*, 85; B. Benjamin Smith to Capers, April 3, 1880, Ellison Capers Papers, TC.

33. B. Benjamin Smith to Capers, April 3, 1880.

34. Speech, July 22, 1902, in Joseph B. Cumming Recollections, 48, UNC.

35. Speech, July 22, 1902, in Cumming Recollections, 47–48; "Sketch of Lieut [Gen] W. J. Hardee," 31, Hardee Family Papers, ADAH.

36. "Memo of Data from J. W. McWilliams—June 30, 1930," 3–5, Folder 11, Box 49, Wilbur G. Kurtz Sr. Papers, AHC; speech, July 22, 1902, in Joseph B. Cumming Recollections, 48–49, UNC.

37. Haldeman, "Other Versions"; Brown, *To the Manner Born*, 266; Kurtz, "Major-General W. H. T. Walker"; Kurtz, "Death of Major General W. H. T. Walker," 179; "Memo of Data from J. W. McWilliams—June 30, 1930," 6, Folder 11 Box 49, Wilbur G. Kurtz Sr. Papers, AHC; Notes on Kurtz to Joseph B. Cumming, May 26, 1951, 3, Folder 12, Box 90, ibid. Kurtz indicates that the site of Walker's death is where modern Glenwood Avenue crosses Sugar Creek.

38. Rountree, "Letters," 290; J. H. Steinmyer to Capers, March 16, 1880, Ellison Capers Papers, DU; Smith, *Fuller's Ohio Brigade*, 169; Kurtz, "Major-General W. H. T. Walker"; Brown, *To the Manner Born*, 271–275; Ecelbarger, *Day Dixie Died*, 97; Castel, *Decision in the West*, 395; "The Death of Maj. Gen. W. H. T. Walker in the Battle of Atlanta, July 22, 1864," January 31, 1955, 14, Folder 12, Box 90, Wilbur

G. Kurtz Sr. Papers, AHC. Walker's biographer, Russell K. Brown, and Albert Castel, author of the standard history of the Atlanta Campaign, fully accept Turner's version, but Gary Ecelbarger, who did not consult Kurtz's findings, accepts the story that Walker was killed with Gist's Brigade.

39. Ecelbarger, *Day Dixie Died*, 85.

40. "Personal Biography of Major General Grenville Mellen Dodge, 1831–1870," 1:250, Grenville Mellen Dodge Papers, SHSI.

41. Chamberlin, "Recollections," 280; Compton, "Second Division," 118; Ackley to wife, July 24, 1864, Charles Thomas Ackley Civil War Letters, UI.

42. Sweeny to William B. Bodge, July 30, 1864, Thomas William Sweeny Papers, HL.

43. Wright, *Corporal's Story*, 128–129; *OR*, 38(3):454, 463, 469–470.

44. *OR*, 38(3):451, 464; Wright, *Corporal's Story*, 130–131, 135.

45. Brown, *"Our Connection,"* 113. *OR*, 38(3):475, 500. Although colorful and detailed, Nisbet's memoirs are also unreliable. He writes as if he commanded the brigade in the attack even though never explicitly stating that he had ever been informed of Smith's wounding. See Nisbet, *4 Years*, 212.

46. *OR*, 38(3):502; Nisbet, *4 Years*, 212–216.

47. Angus McDermid quoted in Brown, *"Our Connection,"* 116; Mitchell to Nettie, July 23, 1864, Robert Goodwin Mitchell Papers, UGA.

48. B. Benjamin Smith to Capers, April 3, 1880, Ellison Capers Papers, TC; *OR*, 38(3):476; Fuller, "Terrible Day."

49. *OR*, 38(3):504.

50. *OR*, 38(3):500; Churchill to wife, July 23, 1864, Mendal C. Churchill Papers, UWYO; Fuller, "Terrible Day."

51. Fuller, "Terrible Day."

52. Churchill to wife, July 23, 1864, Mendal C. Churchill Papers, UWYO; *OR*, 38(3):476; Fuller, "Terrible Day."

53. *OR*, 38(3):492.

54. "Personal Biography of Major General Grenville Mellen Dodge, 1831–1870," 1:245, Grenville Mellen Dodge Papers, SHSI; Russell, "Where McPherson Fell."

55. Sheldon, *Personal Recollections*, n.p.; *OR*, 38(3):494, 496; Ben Sweet quoted in Anders, *Eighteenth Missouri*, 236; B. Benjamin Smith to Capers, April 3, 1880, Ellison Capers Papers, TC.

56. Correspondent of *Columbia Carolinian*, August 8, 1864, in *Charleston Mercury*, August 20, 1864; Welsh, *Medical Histories of Confederate Generals*, 81; Cisco, *States Rights Gist*, 128; *OR*, 38(3):476; Dodge, "Letter to General Raum," 56; Sheldon, *Personal Recollections*, n.p.; Fuller, "Terrible Day."

57. Fuller, "Terrible Day"; *OR*, 38(3):476–478, 492; *SOR*, pt. 2, 12:588; Russell, "Where McPherson Fell."

58. George Anderson Mercer Diary, July 22, 1864, UNC; B. Benjamin Smith to Capers, April 3, 1880, Ellison Capers Papers, TC.

59. Hawes, "Memoirs of Charles H. Olmstead," pt. 10, 44–46; Durham, *Blues in Gray*, 225. Olmstead obviously suffered a concussion because he could reme-

mber little of what happened to him for two or three weeks following his head injury.

60. *OR*, 38(3):758–759.

61. *OR*, 38(3):759; Joslyn, *Charlotte's Boys*, 271; George Anderson Mercer Diary, July 22, 1864, UNC.

62. "Personal Biography of Major General Grenville Mellen Dodge, 1831–1870," 1:245, Grenville Mellen Dodge Papers, SHSI.

63. Chamberlin, "Recollections," 280; *OR*, 38(3):24; Chamberlin, "Hood's Second Sortie," 326–328; "Military History of Capt. Thomas Sewell, Co. G, 127th Ill. Vol. Inf. during the War of the Rebellion 1861 to 1865," Thomas Sewell Papers, DU.

64. Thompson, *Orphan Brigade*, 263; Fleming, *Band of Brothers*, 76; Dodge, "Battle of Atlanta."

65. *OR*, 38(1):73–74, 38(3):536; "General G. M. Dodge's Account of Part taken by *Sixteenth Army Corps*, in movement on *Resaca*, attack of 4th of July, and *Battle* of *Atlanta*," November 30, 1875, William T. Sherman Papers, LC; Sweeny to William B. Bodge, July 30, 1864, Thomas William Sweeny Papers, HL.

66. Ecelbarger, *Day Dixie Died*, 103, 212; *OR*, 38(3):456; Vance, *Report of the Adjutant General*, 4:424; Thurston Diary, July 22, 1864, James M. Thurston Papers, MHS.

6. McPherson's Last Ride

1. William E. Strong, "The Death of Major General James B. McPherson, July 22nd 1864," August 25, 1876, William T. Sherman Papers, LC.

2. Strong, "Death of General James B. McPherson," 322–323; A. J. Thompson to Sherman, July 22, 1878, William T. Sherman Papers, LC; "Gen. McPherson's Death," *New York Times*, August 15, 1881; *OR*, 38(3):81–82; Wade, "Signal Service"; Allen, "Death of Gen. McPherson."

3. "General G. M. Dodge's Account of Part taken by *Sixteenth Army Corps*, in movement on *Resaca*, attack of 4th of July, and *Battle* of *Atlanta*," November 30, 1875, William T. Sherman Papers, LC; William E. Strong, "The Death of Major General James B. McPherson, July 22nd 1864," August 25, 1876, ibid.; William E. Strong to Cynthia McPherson, August 21, 1864, quoted in Whaley, *Forgotten Hero*, 172–173; Strong, "Death of General James B. McPherson," 324; Sherman to Howard, July 27, 1864, quoted in "Autobiographical Sketch of William E. Strong at the Age of 42," CHM. Wilbur G. Kurtz places McPherson's observation point on the hill occupied by Murphy Junior High School in 1930. That institution's name was changed to Alonzo A. Crim Open High School in 1988 and is located at 256 Clifton N.E. See Kurtz, "McPherson's Last Ride."

4. Strong, "Death of General James B. McPherson," 324–325; *OR*, 38(3): 22–23.

5. Leggett, "Battle of Atlanta," May 6, 1886; Thompson, "McPherson's Death"; A. J. Thompson to Sherman, July 22, 1878, William T. Sherman Papers, LC.

6. *OR*, 38(5):246; William E. Strong to editor, *Chicago Daily Tribune*, August 5, 1864, in *Weekly Ottumwa (IA) Courier*, August 25, 1864; Keckler, "Some Recollections."

7. *OR*, 38(3):394–395; William H. Sherfy to editor, July 8, n.d., *Indianapolis Journal* clipping, James Birdseye McPherson Papers, USMA.

8. Bosworth, "Day That McPherson Fell"; Frank P. Blair to J. E. Austin, February 1875, in Hood, *Advance and Retreat*, 188; "Gen. McPherson's Death," *New York Times*, August 15, 1881.

9. "Gen. McPherson's Death," *New York Times*, August 15, 1881; Thompson, "McPherson's Death"; A. J. Thompson to William W. Belknap, October 25, 1878, quoted in Bosworth, "McPherson's Death."

10. Richard Beard questionnaire, 1920, in Elliott and Moxley, *Tennessee Civil War Veterans Questionnaires*, 1:298–299; Beard to Mrs. George A. Justice, October 8, 1925, quoted in "Comrades in War," 87.

11. Beard to Mrs. George A. Justice, October 8, 1925, quoted in "Comrades in War," 87; Beard quoted in "Incidents of Gen. McPherson's Death," 118–119; Beard, "McPherson's Fate"; Beard to Palmer, n.d., in Palmer, "Gen. McPherson's Death"; A. J. Thompson to Sherman, July 22, 1878, William T. Sherman Papers, LC.

12. Beard and Robert F. Coleman quoted in "Incidents of Gen. McPherson's Death," 118–119; Beard to Palmer, n.d., in Palmer, "Gen. McPherson's Death"; Beard, "McPherson's Fate"; Sherman, *Memoirs*, 2:78; Welsh, *Medical Histories of Union Generals*, 219.

13. Thompson, "McPherson's Death"; A. J. Thompson to William W. Belknap, October 25, 1878, quoted in Bosworth, "McPherson's Death"; Thompson quoted in William E. Strong, "The Death of Major General James B. McPherson, July 22nd 1864," August 25, 1876, William T. Sherman Papers, LC.

14. A. J. Thompson to Sherman, July 22, 1878, William T. Sherman Papers, LC.

15. Beard to Palmer, n.d., in Palmer, "Gen. McPherson's Death"; Beard to Mrs. George A. Justice, October 8, 1925, quoted in "Comrades in War," 87; Beard quoted in "Incidents of Gen. McPherson's Death," 118–119. For the rest of his long life, Beard believed that the man who fell near McPherson had been a staff officer, either an adjutant, inspector, or signal officer. But there is no doubt that it was orderly Thompson. When asked about it, Thompson later said that he was still a bit stunned by his fall from the horse but believed it was possible he had told Beard of McPherson's identity. See "Gen. McPherson's Death," *New York Times*, August 15, 1881. For unreliable accounts by Confederates who claimed to have seen McPherson's body right after the shooting, see James H. Mathis account in Yeary, *Reminiscences of the Boys in Gray*, 474; and McNeill, "Death of Gen. McPherson."

16. William B. Cullen statement concerning Robert F. Coleman's statement to him and Richard Beard's reply to Cullen, all quoted in "Incidents of Gen. McPherson's Death," 118–119; Beard to Palmer, n.d., in Palmer, "Gen. McPherson's Death"; Beard, "McPherson's Fate"; William E. Strong, "The Death of Major General James B. McPherson, July 22nd 1864," August 25, 1876, William T. Sherman Papers, LC; *Army and Navy Journal*, August 6, 1864, 819. Rumors circulated that the Confederates found a canteen filled with whiskey on McPherson's saddle and consumed it on the spot. That was impossible because the horse had run away without a single Confederate touching its saddle. See Truman, "Memoirs," www.cedarcroft.com/cw/memoir/index.html.

17. Loop, "Sounding the Alarm"; Leggett, "Battle of Atlanta," May 13, 1886;

Strong, "Death of General James B. McPherson," 334–335; *OR*, 38(3):747; Buck, *Cleburne and His Command*, 239. Strong was convinced that the man captured at McPherson's death site was Scott, but there is no doubt that it was orderly Thompson.

18. Allen, "Death of Gen. McPherson"; William H. Sherfy to editor, July 8, n.d., *Indianapolis Journal* clipping, James Birdseye McPherson Papers, USMA; *OR*, 38(3):394–395; Fish, "'Uncle Billy's' Praise."

19. Strong, "Death of General James B. McPherson," 339; William H. Sherfy to editor, July 8, n.d., *Indianapolis Journal* clipping, James Birdseye McPherson Papers, USMA. Gary Ecelbarger believes McPherson was shot at or before 1:45 P.M. For this and other estimates, see Ecelbarger, *Day Dixie Died*, 260n; *OR*, 38(1):23, 38(3):122, 370, 38(5):234; William E. Strong to editor, *Chicago Daily Tribune*, August 5, 1864, in *Weekly Ottumwa (IA) Courier*, August 25, 1864; William W. Belknap to Govan, September 2, 1878, Daniel Chevilette Govan Papers, UNC; and William E. Strong, "The Death of Major General James B. McPherson, July 22nd 1864," August 25, 1876, William T. Sherman Papers, LC.

20. Allen, "Death of Gen. McPherson"; William E. Strong, "The Death of Major General James B. McPherson, July 22nd 1864," August 25, 1876, William T. Sherman Papers, LC; Keim, "Life and Character of Major-General James B. McPherson," 378; Barton, "McPherson's Death"; Yates, "Something Further as to the Death of McPherson."

21. H. S. Halbert article, Philadelphia *Times,* included in *Minneapolis Tribune* clipping, n.d., James Birdseye McPherson Papers, USMA; H. S. Halbert testimony related by John Moore in Yeary, *Reminiscences of the Boys in Gray*, 532–533; Tracie, *Annals of the Nineteenth Ohio Battery*, 365n; Buck, *Cleburne and His Command*, 243n; Brown, *One of Cleburne's Command*, 111–112; Lossing, *Pictorial Field Book*, 3:385n; Worsham, *Old Nineteenth Tennessee*, 128.

22. "Incidents of Gen. McPherson's Death," 118; Frazer, "Fifth Confederate," 151.

23. Strong, "Death of General James B. McPherson," 338; "Gen. McPherson's Death," *New York Times*, August 15, 1881; Thompson, "McPherson's Death."

24. Reynolds, "Gen. McPherson's Death."

25. William E. Strong, "The Death of Major General James B. McPherson, July 22nd 1864," August 25, 1876, William T. Sherman Papers, LC.

26. Reynolds, "Gen. McPherson's Death." Sherland, who spelled his name "Sharland" when writing his 1865 book, claimed that McPherson was still alive and even asked for his hat after he arrived at the scene. There is no reason to support this assertion. Sharland, *Knapsack Notes*, 66. George Reynolds, an unassuming and honest man, is a more reliable witness to these events.

27. Strong, "Death of General James B. McPherson," 326; *OR*, 38(3):165; Allan to Jim, July 25, 1864, David Allan Jr. Letters, MHM; A. W. Reese, "Personal Recollections of the Late Civil War in the United States," 1870, 516–517, 519, SHSM-RCC; William Charles Pfeffer Diary, July 22, 1864, MHM; Seay Diary, July 22, 1864, Abraham J. Seay Collection, UO.

28. *OR*, 38(3):165, 546; William E. Strong, "The Death of Major General James B. McPherson, July 22nd 1864," August 25, 1876, William T. Sherman Papers, LC; Albert Hiffman reminiscences, n.d., Hiffman Family Papers, MHM; Allan to Jim, July 25, 1864, David Allan Jr. Letters, MHM; A. W. Reese, "Personal Recollections of the Late Civil War in the United States," 1870, 521–524, SHSM-RCC. Wilbur G. Kurtz believed Wangelin's position was on the western slope of a knoll on which Murphy Junior High School stood in 1930. See Kurtz, "McPherson's Last Ride."

29. William E. Strong, "The Death of Major General James B. McPherson, July 22nd 1864," August 25, 1876, William T. Sherman Papers, LC; Strong, "Death of General James B. McPherson," 326–327.

30. Keim, "Life and Character of Major-General James B. McPherson," 378; Strong, "Death of General James B. McPherson," 327–328; William E. Strong, "The Death of Major General James B. McPherson, July 22nd 1864," August 25, 1876, William T. Sherman Papers, LC; Reynolds, "Gen. McPherson's Death"; Brown, "Gen. McPherson's Death"; James H. Mathis account in Yeary, *Reminiscences of the Boys in Gray*, 474; McNeill, "Death of Gen. McPherson"; McNeill, "Recovery of McPherson's Body."

31. *OR*, 38(1):73; Strong, "Death of General James B. McPherson," 334; Dyer, *Secret Yankees*, 180; Sherman, *Memoirs*, 2:77–78; Simpson and Berlin, *Sherman's Civil War*, 683; Coverdale to James W. Denver, July 23, 1864, Robert Todd Coverdale Letter, GLIAH.

32. Sherman, *Memoirs*, 2:78; Simpson and Berlin, *Sherman's Civil War*, 683; Strong, "Death of General James B. McPherson," 334.

33. Fuller, "Terrible Day"; Fuller to Sherman, July 1, 1878, William T. Sherman Papers, LC; William E. Strong, "The Death of Major General James B. McPherson, July 22nd 1864," August 25, 1876, ibid.; Sherman, *Memoirs*, 2:78; *SOR*, pt. 2, 12:587; *OR*, 38(3):492. Pvt. Frederick Sonner of Company F, 64th Illinois was credited with capturing the man who had McPherson's papers. He gave them to Lt. Ward Knickerbocker, who passed them up the chain of command. See Ward Knickerbocker to Sherman, May 27, 1875, William T. Sherman Papers, LC.

34. William E. Strong to editor, *Chicago Daily Tribune*, August 5, 1864, in *Weekly Ottumwa (IA) Courier*, August 25, 1864; Sharland, *Knapsack Notes*, 66. William H. Sherfy stated that McPherson's field glass had been borrowed from his signal officer, Ocran Howard, who eventually recovered it after the battle. George Sharland refers to it as a "marine glass." See ibid.; and William H. Sherfy to editor, July 8, n.d., *Indianapolis Journal* clipping, James Birdseye McPherson Papers, USMA.

35. Sherman, *Memoirs*, 2:76–77; *OR*, 38(5):522; Ray, "Gen. McPherson's Death"; Arthur O. Granger, "The 'Fifteenth' at General Joe Johnston's Surrender," in Kirk, *Fifteenth Pennsylvania Volunteer Cavalry*, 590; copy of Sherman to W. C. Church, July 25, 1876, William T. Sherman Papers, LC; *OR*, 38(3):546.

36. *OR*, 38(3):24, 102, 116, 179; Connelly, *Seventieth Ohio*, 92; William E. Strong, "The Death of Major General James B. McPherson, July 22nd 1864," August 25, 1876, William T. Sherman Papers, LC.

37. Dodge, *Personal Recollections*, 154–155, 216; *OR*, 38(3):370.

38. Hood, *Advance and Retreat*, 182.

7. Desperate Struggle South of Bald Hill

1. Buck, *Cleburne and His Command*, 235; Ecelbarger, *Day Dixie Died*, 120; Roy, "General Hardee," 360; T. B. Roy to Wheeler, February 27, 1880, Box 127, Joseph Wheeler Family Papers, ADAH.

2. *OR*, 38(3):740.

3. *OR*, 38(3):737–738; T. B. Roy to Govan, March 8, 1880, Daniel Chevilette Govan Papers, UNC; Nichols and Abbott, "Reminiscences of Confederate Service by Wiley A. Washburn," 70–71.

4. *OR*, 38(3):576, 594, 610–611.

5. *OR*, 38(3):738; Cate, *Two Soldiers*, 94; G. A. Williams letter, March 14, 1880, in Roy, "General Hardee," 364. In 1930 remnants of the Union refused line were still visible along the streets and through the yards of houses in this part of Atlanta. Wilbur G. Kurtz traced them in the area where Flat Shoals Road, Moreland Avenue, and McPherson Avenue near each other. The line also traversed the home lot where J. W. McWilliams, a veteran of the battle in Stovall's Brigade, then lived. See "Memo of Data from J. W. McWilliams—June 30, 1930," 11, Folder 11, Box 49, Wilbur G. Kurtz Sr. Papers, AHC.

6. William W. Belknap to Govan, September 2, 1878, Daniel Chevilette Govan Papers, UNC; Stuart, *Iowa Colonels and Regiments*, 308.

7. *OR*, 38(3):600, 608; Stuart, *Iowa Colonels and Regiments*, 309.

8. *OR*, 38(3):608–609; Stuart, *Iowa Colonels and Regiments*, 309.

9. *OR*, 38(3):609, 738.

10. *OR*, 38(3):967; Cate, *Two Soldiers*, 94.

11. *OR*, 38(3):594, 600, 602, 610.

12. *OR*, 38(3):609.

13. *OR*, 38(3):609.

14. *OR*, 38(3):738.

15. *OR*, 38(3):371, 477, 539; Fehrenbaker, "Capture of the Regular Battery"; Poe to wife, July 25, 1864, Orlando Metcalfe Poe Papers, LC; Howard, "Murray's Battery"; Brackett, "Capture of Murray's Battery."

16. Cate, *Two Soldiers*, 95; Sniff, "Capture of the 16th Iowa."

17. *OR*, 38(3):581, 588.

18. *OR*, 38(3):588; Kurtz, "Walter Q. Gresham at Atlanta"; "5,000 Killed in Battle of Atlanta"; Hedley, *Marching through Georgia*, 294, 297. Hedley related a different version of the story. Jones had employed the young Lincoln as a clerk in his store at Gentryville, Indiana, but refused his request for a pair of boots to be paid out of his wages. When Lincoln was elected president, Jones wrote him requesting a postmaster position, but Lincoln refused him.

19. *OR*, 38(3):581–582, 606; William W. Belknap to Govan, September 2, 1878, Daniel Chevilette Govan Papers, UNC.

20. *OR*, 38(3):599–600; Hubbart, *Iowa Soldier Writes Home*, 52; Strang, "Crocker's Iowa Brigade."

21. *OR*, 38(3):609, 738.

22. *OR*, 38(3):609.

23. *OR*, 38(3):609–610.

24. Sanders, "Gen. Sanders' Sword."

25. *OR*, 38(3):594, 608, 738; *SOR*, pt. 1, 7:67, pt. 2, 20:283.

26. [Rood], *Company "A,"* 16.

27. *OR*, 38(3):58, 576.

28. *OR*, 38(3):610.

29. Smith, "Civil War Diary," 151; *OR*, 38(3):610.

30. *OR*, 38(3):738; Cate, *Two Soldiers*, 95–96.

31. *OR*, 38(3):738–740; Ecelbarger, *Day Dixie Died*, 113.

32. *OR*, 38(3):739–740; Ecelbarger, *Day Dixie Died*, 115.

33. Throne, "History of Company D," 63–64; *OR*, 38(3):595, 610–611; Cander, "Before Atlanta."

34. *Fifteenth Iowa*, 373–374.

35. Ecelbarger, *Day Dixie Died*, 120–121.

36. *OR*, 38(3):582, 588, 594, 602.

37. Stuart, *Iowa Colonels and Regiments*, 301–302; *Proceedings of Crocker's Iowa Brigade*, 9:250–251; *OR*, 38(3):582, 594, 602.

38. Will M. McLain letter, August 8, 1864, in Post, *Soldiers' Letters*, 401–402; *OR*, 38(3):582.

39. *OR*, 38(3):558, 584, 589; Hord, "Atlanta Experience."

40. Will M. McLain letter, August 8, 1864, in Post, *Soldiers' Letters*, 404–405.

41. *OR*, 38(3):558, 589.

42. "Autobiography," 30, Edwin Hansford Rennolds Sr. Papers, UTK.

43. John Henry Marsh to Quintard, July 26, 1864, Charles Todd Quintard Papers, DU; Henry Hampton to Quintard, July 25, 1864, ibid.; Henry D. Hogan to John T. Moore, June 23, 1922, in Elliott and Moxley, *Tennessee Civil War Veterans*, 5:2219.

44. Rennolds Diary, July 22, 1864, Edwin Hansford Rennolds Sr. Papers, UTK; "Autobiography," 30, ibid.; John Henry Marsh to Quintard, July 26, 1864, Charles Todd Quintard Papers, DU.

45. Franklin, *Civil War Diaries of Capt. Alfred Tyler Fielder*, 189.

46. Marchant to wife, August 2, 1864, Peter Marchant Civil War Correspondence, AHC; Franklin, *Civil War Diaries of Capt. Alfred Tyler Fielder*, 189; Bishop, "Twenty-Ninth Tennessee Infantry," 437; Ecelbarger, *Day Dixie Died*, 125.

47. *OR*, 38(3):747, 753; Ecelbarger, *Day Dixie Died*, 126.

48. Brown, *One of Cleburne's Command*, 111; *OR*, 38(3):748, 751, 753.

49. *OR*, 38(3):747, 749–750, 753.

50. *OR*, 38(3):280, 298, 319.

51. *OR*, 38(3):338; Wright, *Sixth Iowa*, 304–305.

52. *OR*, 38(3):342.

53. *OR*, 38(3):747, 751, 753.

54. *OR*, 38(3):753.

55. *OR*, 38(3):747, 750, 753–754.

56. *OR*, 38(3):342; Case, "15th Mich. at Atlanta."

57. *OR*, 38(3):353, 751–752; Case, "15th Mich. at Atlanta"; "Return of a Confederate Flag," 302; McCaffrey, *Band of Heroes*, 120.

58. Beard letter in Palmer, "Gen. McPherson's Death"; Doyle, "Gen. McPherson's Death"; McCaffrey, *Only a Private*, 71; B. M. Thompson account in Yeary, *Reminiscences of a Soldier of the Orphan Brigade*, 746; *OR*, 38(3):730–731, 750.

59. Lucas, *New History of the 99th Indiana*, 104, 106–107.

60. *SOR*, pt. 1, 7:49; *OR*, 38(3):58–59, 361.

61. *OR*, 38(3):353.

62. Ecelbarger, *Day Dixie Died*, 131.

63. *OR*, 38(3):731.

64. *OR*, 38(3):731.

65. *OR*, 38(3):731.

66. *OR*, 38(3):731.

67. *OR*, 38(3):732.

68. *OR*, 38(3):547, 582, 748; Ecelbarger, *Day Dixie Died*, 133–134, 146; Cate, *Two Soldiers*, 96–97.

69. Ecelbarger, *Day Dixie Died*, 137–138, 140–142.

70. *OR*, 38(3):606; *History of the Fifteenth Regiment, Iowa Veteran Volunteer Infantry*, 371.

71. Belknap, "Obedience and Courage," 167–168.

72. Hedley, *Marching through Georgia*, 152–153, 157–158.

73. W. W. Belknap to Aaron, August 5, 1864, Belknap Family Papers, N-YHS; *History of the Fifteenth Regiment, Iowa Veteran Volunteer Infantry*, 371–372.

74. Cards, H. D. Lampley Service Record, 45th Alabama, M311, RG109, NARA; Jordan, "Forty Days," 140, 146; Walker, "In Front of Atlanta"; Brown to Fannie, July 27, 1864, Edward Norphlet Brown Letters, ADAH.

75. Buck, *Cleburne and His Command*, 240; Irving A. Buck to W. W. Belknap, 1881, and Logan Crawford account, in *History of the Fifteenth Regiment, Iowa Veteran Volunteer Infantry*, 350, 372; Castel, *Decision in the West*, 403.

76. Alexander, "Battle of Atlanta."

77. Bosworth, "Battle of Atlanta," 237.

78. *OR*, 38(3):582–583.

79. *OR*, 38(3):606.

80. *OR*, 38(3):602.

81. John J. Safely to Mary McEwen, July 23, 31, 1864, McEwen Family Papers, MHM.

82. Strang, "Crocker's Iowa Brigade"; *OR*, 38(3):600.

83. *OR*, 38(3):600; John J. Safely to Mary McEwen, July 23, 1864, McEwen Family Papers, MHM.

84. Loop, "Sounding the Alarm."

85. *OR*, 38(3):564; Alexander, "Battle of Atlanta"; Samuel K. Adams to John Kebler, July 23, 1864, M. F. Force Papers, UW.

86. Bradford, "Fighting Not All Done by the 12th and 16th Wisconsin Regiments"; *OR*, 38(3):565; Wilson Reminiscences, 8, Harrison Wilson Civil War Collection, UCSB; Samuel K. Adams to Peter Force, July 23, 27, 1864, M. F. Force Papers, UW; Manning F. Force to Sherman, August 31, 1875, William T. Sherman Papers, LC; Welsh, *Medical Histories of Union Generals*, 117.

87. Bradford, "Fighting Not All Done by the 12th and 16th Wisconsin Regiments"; McDonald, *30th Illinois*, 76–78; *OR*, 38(3):556.

88. Morris, Hartwell, and Kuykendall, *31st Regiment*, 106–108; *OR*, 38(3):557.

89. *OR*, 38(3):558.

90. Styple, *Writing and Fighting*, 279.

91. Wood, "20th Ohio at Atlanta"; Loop, "Sounding the Alarm"; Leggett, "Battle of Atlanta," May 6, 1886; Nutt, "Fight at Atlanta."

92. *OR*, 38(3):575.

93. *OR*, 38(3):285, 319.

94. *OR*, 38(3):294, 319, 354.

95. A. W. Reese, "Personal Recollections of the Late Civil War in the United States," 1870, 520–521, 526–527, 529, SHSM-RCC.

96. *History of the Fifteenth Regiment, Iowa Veteran Volunteer Infantry*, 338; Lowrey to Calhoun Benham, September 30, 1867, in Mark Perrin Lowrey Autobiographical Essay, 6, USM; Brown to Fannie, July 27, 1864, Edward Norphlet Brown Letters, ADAH; Ecelbarger, *Day Dixie Died*, 145; *OR*, 38(3):606, 732; C. C. McDowell to sister, July 23, 1864, Sam Whigham Papers, ADAH; William W. Belknap to Govan, September 2, 1878, Daniel Chevilette Govan Papers, UNC; extract of Belknap address, September 28, 1881, in *Proceedings of Crocker's Iowa Brigade*, 244; Bosworth, "Day That McPherson Fell."

97. *OR*, 38(3):25, 583, 732.

98. Ecelbarger, *Day Dixie Died*, 147.

99. Blair to Gresham, August 20, 1864, in Gresham, *Life of Walter Quintin Gresham*, 1:308; *OR*, 38(1):73.

8. Breaking the Fifteenth Corps Line

1. Hess, *Peach Tree Creek*, 20–30, 73–75; Hood to James Chesnut, March 7, 1864, John Bell Hood Letters, GLIAH.

2. Castel, *Decision in the West*, 389, 395; Davis, *Texas Brigadier*, 325; Thomas B. Mackall Journal, July 22, 1864 (McMurry transcript), Joseph E. Johnston Papers, CWM. An interesting case study of the variance in reported timing of events in a Civil War battle can be had in trying to ascertain when Cheatham started his advance. I have found a total of twenty-one reports as follows: Eight indicate 3 P.M., six assert 4 P.M., and five note the time as 3:30. One report each opted for 1:30 and 2 P.M.

3. *OR*, 38(3):631.

4. Castel, *Decision in the West*, 405.

5. Castel, *Decision in the West*, 405; Ecelbarger, *Day Dixie Died*, 264n; Phillips, *Personal Reminiscences of a Confederate Soldier Boy*, 53. Gary Ecelbarger asserts that Stevenson arrayed his units in two lines with two brigades in each, but he provides no source to support that assertion. It appears as if he based his argument that Stevenson made a real attack, in part, on Brig. Gen. William Harrow's report that his line was vigorously attacked. But I believe Harrow was referring to the first contact he had with Brown's division, not Stevenson's. See Ecelbarger, *Day Dixie Died*, 154; and OR, 38(3):280.

6. Hess, *Kennesaw Mountain*, 38, 46.

7. Tower, *Carolinian Goes to War*, 226; Walker, *Rolls and Historical Sketch*, 113–114.

8. Bailey, *Private Chapter*, 2.

9. OR, 38(3):81; Lossing, *Pictorial Field Book*, 3:386–387.

10. OR, 38(3):180, 195, 235; *Story of the Fifty-Fifth Regiment Illinois*, 337–338.

11. OR, 38(3):210, 237, 250–251, 254.

12. Fowler and Miller, *Thirtieth Iowa*, 60; Schweitzer Diary, July 22, 1864, Edward E. Schweitzer Papers, HL; OR, 38(3):246; SOR, pt. 1, 7:49. Smyth's battery had just undergone reorganization on July 12, as men with unexpired terms of enlistment in Battery A and Battery B, 1st Illinois Light Artillery were consolidated. The new organization continued to be known as Battery A. See Kimbell, *Battery "A,"* 86; and Lewis F. Lake Reminiscences, 5, ALPL.

13. Kurtz, "At the Troup Hurt House"; *Report of Robert L. Rodgers*, 20; Castel, *Decision in the West*, 393.

14. Kurtz, "At the Troup Hurt House"; Ecelbarger, *Day Dixie Died*, 159.

15. John H. Puck address, *Ninth Reunion of the 37th Regiment O.V.V.I.*, 49; Fish, "'Uncle Billy's' Praise."

16. Evans, "Report of the Battle of Atlanta," 29; OR, 38(3):265.

17. OR, 38(3):787.

18. Tower, *Carolinian Goes to War*, 226; OR, 38(3):787; Hall to father, July 24, 1864, James A. Hall Letters, Walter King Hoover Collection, TSLA.

19. OR, 38(3):223, 235.

20. Ralston, "De Grasse's Battery"; Castel, *Tom Taylor's Civil War*, 146.

21. Castel, *Tom Taylor's Civil War*, 146; OR, 38(3):223, 254; Ralston, "De Grasse's Battery"; Duke, *Fifty-Third Regiment Ohio Volunteer Infantry*, 148; Bailey, *Private Chapter*, 3.

22. Tower, *Carolinian Goes to War*, 226–227; OR, 38(3):787.

23. Tower, *Carolinian Goes to War*, 227; White and Runion, *Great Things*, 132.

24. OR, 38(3):217, 224, 246, 250–251, 257, 260; John H. Puck address, *Ninth Reunion of the 37th Regiment O.V.V.I.*, 49.

25. OR, 38(3):778–779.

26. OR, 38(3):779.

27. OR, 38(3):779; Ecelbarger, *Day Dixie Died*, 161, 163; R. A. Jarman, "The History of Company K, 27th Mississippi Infantry, and Its First and Last Muster Rolls," MDAH; *Story of the Fifty-Fifth Regiment Illinois*, 338; Willie J. Honnoll to Annie Honnoll, August 4, 1864, Honnoll Family Papers, EU; Warner, *Generals in Gray*, 27.

28. *OR*, 38(3):285, 304; Hogan, *Reub Williams's Memories*, 182; Ecelbarger, *Day Dixie Died*, 169.

29. Hogan, *Reub Williams's Memories*, 181–182.

30. C. Irvine Walker to Rodgers, December 1, 1896, in *Report of Robert L. Rodgers*, 8; Tower, *Carolinian Goes to War*, 261n; Walker, *Rolls and Historical Sketch*, 114; White and Runion, *Great Things*, 132; *OR*, 38(3):787.

31. *OR*, 38(3):189; Douglas, *Douglas's Texas Battery*, 115–116.

32. Jesse L. Henderson Civil War Diary, July 22, 1864, UM; Marshall to Jane, July 28, 1864, John H. Marshall Letters, MSU.

33. *OR*, 38(3):228; Henry S. Schmidt to Kate, July 25, 1864, Schmidt Family Papers, FHS.

34. *OR*, 38(3):246, 262; Castel, *Tom Taylor's Civil War*, 147; Kimbell, *Battery "A,"* 87.

35. White and Runion, *Great Things*, 132–133; *OR*, 38(3):787; Tower, *Carolinian Goes to War*, 261n.

36. Castel, *Tom Taylor's Civil War*, 147–148; *OR*, 38(3):246. Another man of the 47th Ohio also witnessed the incident of the Confederate officer calling on Taylor to give up. See Bakhaus, "Logan at Atlanta."

37. *OR*, 38(3):257–258, 260.

38. Moore Diary, July 22, 1864, Edward B. Moore Diary and Correspondence, UWYO; *OR*, 38(3):258.

39. *OR*, 38(3):210; Schweitzer Diary, July 22, 1864, Edward E. Schweitzer Papers, HL.

40. John H. Puck address, *Ninth Reunion of the 37th Regiment O.V.V.I.*, 50–51.

41. Tower, *Carolinian Goes to War*, 227; C. Irvine Walker sketch, in *Report of Robert L. Rodgers*, 24; Hall to father, July 24, 1864, James A. Hall Letters, Walter King Hoover Collection, TSLA.

42. Lea to father, July 25, 1864, in Robert J. Cull, comp., "The Civil War Letters of George S. Lea, 1861–1864," MDAH.

43. L. B. Mitchell to William Rigby, September 14, 1901, Battery H, 1st Illinois Light Artillery Folder, VNMP; Evans, "Report of the Battle of Atlanta," 29.

44. Evans, "Report of the Battle of Atlanta," 29.

45. Evans, "Report of the Battle of Atlanta," 29; *OR*, 38(3):251, 254.

46. Evans, "Report of the Battle of Atlanta," 29–30.

47. White and Runion, *Great Things*, 132–133; Tower, *Carolinian Goes to War*, 227.

48. *OR*, 38(3):224, 228, 251; Jacobs Diary, July 22, 1864, Wayne Johnson Jacobs Diaries and Lists, LSU.

49. *OR*, 38(3):179–180; Crummel, "De Grasse's Battery."

50. *OR*, 38(3):217.

51. *OR*, 38(3):819; *SOR*, pt. 1, 7:121.

52. *SOR*, pt. 1, 7:127–128; Kurtz, "Broken Line and the De Gress Battery."

53. L. P. Thomas to Rodgers, n.d., and Rodgers letter, September 1898, in *Report of Robert L. Rodgers*, 15, 18, 47; Bragg, *Joe Brown's Army*, 89–91; *SOR*, pt. 1, 7:128.

54. *SOR*, pt. 1, 7:127, 129.

55. *OR*, 38(3):217; *Story of the Fifty-Fifth Regiment Illinois*, 339, 342; Myers, "Atlanta."

56. *SOR*, pt. 1, 7:129.

57. *OR*, 38(3):217.

58. *SOR*, pt. 1, 7:128.

59. Clement A. Evans to Bishop, August 8, 1898, Ellison Capers Papers, TC; *Report of Robert L. Rodgers*, 5–6; Theodore R. Davis to Mrs. De Gress, November 30, [1885], Francis De Gress Papers, AHC; Davis, "War Artist at Vicksburg," 99.

60. *OR*, 38(3):210, 224, 246–247, 254; Castel, *Tom Taylor's Civil War*, 148.

61. Castel, *Tom Taylor's Civil War*, 148; *OR*, 38(3):246–247.

62. Duke, *Fifty-Third Regiment Ohio Volunteer Infantry*, 149; Castel, *Tom Taylor's Civil War*, 149.

63. *OR*, 38(3):280–281.

64. *OR*, 38(3):285, 287; Hazzard Diary, July 22, 1864, Lemuel H. Hazzard Papers, HL.

65. Hogan, *Reub Williams's Memories*, 183; *OR*, 38(3):304.

66. *OR*, 38(3):285, 304, 779–780. According to the commander of the 90th Illinois, only that regiment's right wing conducted the return movement to temporarily reoccupy the abandoned earthworks before falling back again. See *OR*, 38(3):298–299.

67. *OR*, 38(3):342; Lucas, *New History of the 99th Indiana Infantry*, 108.

68. *OR*, 38(3):342, 355.

69. *OR*, 38(3):319.

70. *OR*, 38(3):294, 355–356; Bloomfield, "Colonel Bloomfield's Recollections."

71. *War Letters of Aden G. Cavins*, 89.

72. *War Letters of Aden G. Cavins*, 89; *OR*, 38(3):117, 281, 395; William Odell to nephew, August 3, 1864, Jonathan Blair Papers, ALPL.

73. *War Letters of Aden G. Cavins*, 89–90.

74. *OR*, 38(3):327.

75. Leggett, "Battle of Atlanta," May 13, 1886.

76. *OR*, 38(3):319.

77. *OR*, 38(3):58, 363–364.

78. *OR*, 38(3):58, 368; Black, *Soldier's Recollections*, 84.

79. Gage, "Battle of Atlanta."

80. George Frederick Renner to sister, August 1, 1864, Treutler Family Papers, MHM.

81. *OR*, 38(3):779–780.

82. *SOR*, pt. 1, 7:118–119, 121.

83. *SOR*, pt. 1, 7:118–119, 121.

84. *SOR*, pt. 1, 7:119, 121.

85. *SOR*, pt. 1, 7:119–123.

86. *SOR*, pt. 1, 7:122.

87. *SOR*, pt. 1, 7:126.

88. *SOR*, pt. 1, 7:126, 131; *OR*, 38(3):819.

89. *SOR*, pt. 1, 7:130; *OR*, 38(3):819; Ross to Mary, July 24, 1864, Emmett Ross Papers, MSU.

90. *OR*, 38(3):969–970; Smith, "Georgia Militia," 331–332.

91. *OR*, 38(3):970–971; Smith, "Georgia Militia," 334–335; Little and Maxwell, *History of Lumsden's Battery*, 47; Ecelbarger, *Day Dixie Died*, 147.

92. Smith, "Georgia Militia," 334; Watkins to wife, July 24, 1864, James W. Watkins Papers, EU.

93. Tower, *Carolinian Goes to War*, 228; *OR*, 38(3):787–788.

94. *OR*, 38(3):787–788; Castel, *Decision in the West*, 407.

95. Walker, *Rolls and Historical Sketch of the Tenth Regiment*, 115; Walker to Rodgers, December 1, 1896, in *Report of Robert L. Rodgers*, 10; Tower, *Carolinian Goes to War*, 227–228.

96. Tower, *Carolinian Goes to War*, 228, 261–262n; White and Runion, *Great Things*, 133; Hall to father, July 24, 1864, James A. Hall Letters, Walter King Hoover Collection, TSLA.

97. Tower, *Carolinian Goes to War*, 230.

98. *OR*, 38(1):74; Dodge, "Battle of Atlanta," 47.

9. Federal Resurgence

1. Sherman, *Memoirs*, 2:81; Willard Warner to editor of *Tribune*, April 8, 1876, newspaper clipping, James Birdseye McPherson Papers, USMA.

2. *OR*, 38(1):74.

3. *OR*, 38(3):139, 147, 156.

4. *OR*, 38(3):116, 174.

5. Schofield, *Forty-Six Years*, 147; Sherman, *Memoirs*, 2:81; Schofield to Sherman, March 10, 1880, William T. Sherman Papers, LC; *Military Record of Battery D*, 130; Nash to Erastus Winters, January 3, 1911, George W. Nash Letter, FHS; John A. Morlan to parents, July 23, 1864, Folder 27, Box 1, Antebellum and Civil War Collection, AHC; *OR*, 38(2):687.

6. *OR*, 38(2):517, 572.

7. Howard, "Battles about Atlanta," 394; Howard, "Struggle for Atlanta," 317; Evans, "Report of the Battle of Atlanta," 29–30; *OR*, 38(3):265.

8. Bennett and Tillery, *Struggle for the Life of the Republic*, 186.

9. Blair to J. E. Austin, February 1875, in Hood, *Advance and Retreat*, 189.

10. *OR*, 38(1):74; Chamberlin, "Recollections of the Battle of Atlanta," 281–282; *OR*, 38(3):26, 372; Dodge, *Personal Recollections*, 154–155.

11. Helmkamp, "Before Atlanta"; Edward Jonas to Dodge, May 7, 1892, in "Personal Biography of Major General Grenville Mellen Dodge, 1831–1870," 1:248, Grenville Mellen Dodge Papers, SHSI; *OR*, 38(3):371.

12. *OR*, 38(3):454–455; Wright, *Corporal's Story*, 132. The timing of Mersy's start was estimated by contemporaries as anywhere from 2 to 6 P.M. See *OR*, 38(3):454, 462; and James P. Snell Diary, July 22, 1864, ALPL.

13. Edward Jonas to Dodge, May 7, 1892, in "Personal Biography of Major General Grenville Mellen Dodge, 1831–1870," 1:248, Grenville Mellen Dodge Papers, SHSI; Chamberlin, "Hood's Second Sortie," 330; Wright, *Corporal's Story*, 132.

14. W. E. McCreary to Edward Jonas, July 1884, in "Personal Biography of Major

General Grenville Mellen Dodge, 1831–1870," 1:249, Grenville Mellen Dodge Papers, SHSI.

15. Edward Jonas to Dodge, May 7, 1892, in "Personal Biography of Major General Grenville Mellen Dodge, 1831–1870," 1:248, Grenville Mellen Dodge Papers, SHSI; Adams, "Battle and Capture of Atlanta," 156; "General G. M. Dodge's Account of Part taken by *Sixteenth Army Corps*, in movement on *Resaca*, attack of 4th of July, and *Battle* of *Atlanta*," November 30, 1875, William T. Sherman Papers, LC. For more attempts to reconstruct what Mersy said when his horse was shot, see "Who Recaptured the De Gress Battery"; James P. Snell Diary, July 22, 1864, ALPL; and Shelley, "Battle of July 22."

16. *OR*, 38(3):464; "Capture of the De Gress Battery."

17. Robert N. Adams letter, quoted in Chamberlin, "Hood's Second Sortie," 330; Wright, *Corporal's Story*, 133; Dodge, "Battle of Atlanta," 47; Tower, *Carolinian Goes to War*, 228.

18. "Who Recaptured the De Gress Battery"; Robert N. Adams letter, quoted in Chamberlin, "Hood's Second Sortie," 330; Jesse L. Henderson Civil War Diary, July 22, 1864, UM; Isaac Gaillard Foster Diary, July 22, 1864, James Foster and Family Correspondence, LSU; Tower, *Carolinian Goes to War*, 228–229; *OR*, 38(3):788.

19. "Capture of the De Gress Battery"; "Who Recaptured the De Gress Battery"; Wright, *Corporal's Story*, 133; and Shelley, "Battle of July 22."

20. Theodore R. Davis to Mrs. De Gress, November 30, [1885], Francis De Gress Papers, AHC; Evans, "Report of the Battle of Atlanta," 29; Adams, "Battle and Capture of Atlanta," 157.

21. "Capture of the De Gress Battery"; "Who Recaptured the De Gress Battery"; W. E. McCreary to Edward Jonas, July 1884, in "Personal Biography of Major General Grenville Mellen Dodge, 1831–1870," 1:249, Grenville Mellen Dodge Papers, SHSI; Childress, "Before Atlanta"; Evans, "Report of the Battle of Atlanta," 30; *OR*, 38(3):265.

22. Naylor, "To the Editor National Tribune"; Evans, "Report of the Battle of Atlanta," 29–30.

23. Wright, *Corporal's Story*, 133–134; *OR*, 38(3):262, 408, 454, 459, 462; Adams, "Battle and Capture of Atlanta," 157.

24. Edward Jonas to Dodge, May 7, 1892, in "Personal Biography of Major General Grenville Mellen Dodge, 1831–1870," 1:248, Grenville Mellen Dodge Papers, SHSI.

25. *OR*, 38(3):189.

26. *OR*, 38(3):139, 156; Stuart, *Iowa Colonels and Regiments*, 211.

27. *OR*, 38(3):157; Stuart, *Iowa Colonels and Regiments*, 211.

28. Dodge to Sherman, November 19, 1865, in "Personal Biography of Major General Grenville Mellen Dodge, 1831–1870," 1:248, Grenville Mellen Dodge Papers, SHSI; James Thomas to Friend, July 23, 1864, Robert T. Jones Papers, UTK; *OR*, 38(3):157; "Atlanta Campaign"; McCunniff, "De Gress's Battery"; "Who Recaptured the De Gress Battery"; "Capture of the De Gress Battery."

29. Allen, *On the Skirmish Line*, 230; William G. Baugh to parents, July 25, 1864,

William G. Baugh Letters, Union Miscellany, EU; Bennett and Tillery, *Struggle for the Life of the Republic*, 186–188, 231–232; Johnson, "Battle of Atlanta"; Fowler and Miller, *Thirtieth Iowa Infantry*, 60.

30. *OR*, 38(3):819; *SOR*, pt. 1, 7:122–124.

31. *SOR*, pt. 1, 7:119–120, 122.

32. Bennett and Tillery, *Struggle for the Life of the Republic*, 188, 232; Allen, *On the Skirmish Line*, 232; Johnson, "Battle of Atlanta." Several men claimed that De Gress accompanied Milo Smith's brigade during its advance, which seems to support the notion that the artillery captain had gone to implore Sherman for help at Copenhill. See Bennett and Tillery, *Struggle for the Life of the Republic*, 187–188; and Allen, *On the Skirmish Line*, 232. But the weight of evidence (De Gress himself never reported that he went to Copenhill) supports the conclusion that he remained in the area east of the break in the Fifteenth Corps line until Mersy's brigade arrived and then went in with those Sixteenth Corps troops.

33. Robert N. Adams letter, quoted in Chamberlin, "Hood's Second Sortie," 330.

34. *OR*, 38(3):26, 117; A. W. Reese, "Personal Recollections of the Late Civil War in the United States," 1870, 525, SHSM-RCC.

35. *OR*, 38(3):26.

36. *OR*, 38(3):247; Castel, *Tom Taylor's Civil War*, 148–149.

37. Castel, *Tom Taylor's Civil War*, 149; *OR*, 38(3):195; "Military History of Capt. Thomas Sewell, Co. G, 127th Ill. Vol. Inf. during the War of the Rebellion 1861 to 1865," Thomas Sewell Papers, DU; Chamberlin, "Hood's Second Sortie," 329.

38. "Military History of Capt. Thomas Sewell, Co. G, 127th Ill. Vol. Inf."; *OR*, 38(3):217; Coleman to sister, July 29, 1864, Thomas M. Coleman Letter, AHC.

39. *OR*, 38(3):195; "Military History of Capt. Thomas Sewell, Co. G, 127th Ill. Vol. Inf."; *Story of the Fifty-Fifth Regiment Illinois Volunteer Infantry*, 339–340; "War Diary of Thaddeus H. Capron," 388.

40. *OR*, 38(5):244–245.

41. Castel, *Tom Taylor's Civil War*, 149; *OR*, 38(3):189, 241, 247, 251, 260.

42. *SOR*, pt. 1, 7:127–128.

43. *OR*, 38(3):26, 285.

44. *OR*, 38(3):294, 327, 355–356.

45. *OR*, 38(3):288, 361, 779.

46. Wills, *Army Life*, 285–286; *SOR*, pt. 1, 7:129.

47. *SOR*, pt. 1, 7:126, 131; *OR*, 38(3):819.

48. *OR*, 38(3):147, 157; Bennett and Tillery, *Struggle for the Life of the Republic*, 187, Baugh to parents, July 25, 1864, William G. Baugh Letters, Union Miscellany, EU.

49. *OR*, 38(3):140, 157; Booth, "Battle of Atlanta."

50. *SOR*, pt. 1, 7:131–132; Booth, "Battle of Atlanta."

51. *SOR*, pt. 1, 7:124–126, 131; Booth, "Battle of Atlanta"; *OR*, 38(3):140.

52. *OR*, 38(3):147, 157; Bennett and Tillery, *Struggle for the Life of the Republic*, 187, Baugh to parents, July 25, 1864, William G. Baugh Letters, Union Miscellany, EU.

53. *SOR*, pt. 1, 7:125, 132.

54. *OR*, 38(1):74; Ecelbarger, *Day Dixie Died*, 190.

55. Crummel, "De Grasse's Battery."

56. Tower, *Carolinian Goes to War*, 229–230; Lea to father, July 25, 1864, in Robert J. Cull, comp., "The Civil War Letters of George S. Lea, 1861–1864," MDAH; *OR*, 38(3):778; *SOR*, pt. 1, 7:120, 123.

57. Narrative, Henry De Lamar Clayton Sr. Papers, UA; *OR*, 38(3):631.

10. Struggle for Bald Hill

1. Dodge, "Battle of Atlanta"; Fleming, *Band of Brothers*, 76.

2. George Anderson Mercer Diary, July 22, 1864, UNC; *OR*, 38(3):759.

3. Lowrey to Calhoun Benham, September 30, 1867, in Mark Perrin Lowrey Autobiographical Essay, 6, USM; Lowrey, "Autobiography," 372.

4. Joslyn, *Charlotte's Boys*, 271.

5. Fleming, *Band of Brothers*, 76–77.

6. Fleming, *Band of Brothers*, 77–78.

7. T. J. Walker Reminiscences, 20–21, UTK.

8. William Mebane Pollard questionnaire, in Elliott and Moxley, *Tennessee Civil War Veterans*, 4:1744; Watkins, "Co. Aytch," 184.

9. *Chattanooga Daily Rebel*, July 25, 1864; Losson, *Tennessee's Forgotten Warriors*, 183.

10. Nutt, "Fight at Atlanta."

11. Nutt, "Fight at Atlanta"; Joslyn, *Charlotte's Boys*, 271; Durham, *Blues in Gray*, 225.

12. Nutt, "Fight at Atlanta."

13. Nutt, "Fight at Atlanta."

14. Nutt, "Fight at Atlanta."

15. Dwight, "Battle of July 22."

16. Nutt, "Fight at Atlanta."

17. Brown, "78th Ohio in Close Quarters."

18. Bradford, "Fighting Not All Done by the 12th and 16th Wisconsin"; Morris, Hartwell, and Kuykendall, *History 31st Regiment Illinois*, 107; McDonald, *30th Illinois*, 77–78, 82.

19. Allen to Mary, August 5, 1864, Edward W. Allen Papers, UNC; Styple, *Writing and Fighting*, 279; Smith to father, July 26, 1864, Charles M. Smith Papers, WHS; *OR*, 38(3):572.

20. Will M. McLain letter, August 8, 1864, in Post, *Soldiers' Letters*, 402–403.

21. Nutt, "Fight at Atlanta."

22. Joslyn, *Charlotte's Boys*, 271; *OR*, 38(3):754.

23. *OR*, 38(3):754.

24. *OR*, 38(3):81, 38(5):219; Stickney to Rose, August 5, 1864, Clifford Stickney Collection, CHM.

25. Stickney to Rose, August 5, 1864, Clifford Stickney Collection, CHM; *OR*, 38(3):560–561.

26. Leggett, "Battle of Atlanta," May 13, 1886.

27. *OR*, 38(3):25, 547, 565, 583, 594; Wade, "Bald Knob"; Alexander, "Battle of Atlanta."

28. Tuthill, "Artilleryman's Recollections," 302–304.

29. Munson, "Battle of Atlanta," 226.

30. Ecelbarger, *Day Dixie Died*, 192.

31. *OR*, 38(3):165; Blair to Gresham, August 20, 1864, in Gresham, *Life of Walter Quintin Gresham*, 1:309.

32. *OR*, 38(3):370, 426, 477, 490, 502; Fuller, "Terrible Day."

33. Durham, *Blues in Gray*, 225.

34. *OR*, 38(3):739–740; Mumford H. Dixon Diary, July 22, 1864, EU; Ecelbarger, *Day Dixie Died*, 198.

35. *OR*, 38(3):594–595, 600.

36. Wade, "Bald Knob"; Stickney to Rose, August 5, 1864, Clifford Stickney Collection, CHM.

37. *OR*, 38(3):740; Stickney to Rose, August 5, 1864, Clifford Stickney Collection, CHM; Cander, "Before Atlanta."

38. Ayres, "78th Ohio at Bald Hill"; Speer, "Battle of Bald Hill"; Stickney to Rose, August 5, 1864, Clifford Stickney Collection, CHM; *OR*, 38(3):556–557.

39. *OR*, 38(3):557–558; Wilson Reminiscences, 8–9, Harrison Wilson Civil War Collection, UCSB.

40. Tuthill, "Artilleryman's Recollections," 305; Loop, "Sounding the Alarm."

41. *OR*, 38(3):731, 749, 752; Tuthill, "Artilleryman's Recollections," 304–305.

42. Garrett to uncle, August 1, 1864, Hosea Garrett Jr. Civil War Letters, AHC.

43. *OR*, 38(3):583, 731, 752.

44. *OR*, 38(3):731; A. G. Anderson account, in Yeary, *Reminiscences of the Boys in Gray*, 19.

45. *OR*, 38(3):117, 565, 583; Leggett, "Battle of Atlanta," May 13, 1886; Dodge, "Letter to General Raum," 58; Ecelbarger, *Day Dixie Died*, 205.

11. Decatur and the Rest of July 22

1. Cox, *Atlanta*, 167; Tracie, *Annals of the Nineteenth Ohio Battery*, 362.

2. *OR*, 38(3):39, 506–507; *OR*, 38(2):854; Brittin, "Who Saved the Trains at Decatur?"; Evans, "Fight for the Wagons," 19.

3. *OR*, 38(3):953.

4. Drake, *Chronological Summary of Battles and Engagements*, 98.

5. Drake, *Chronological Summary of Battles and Engagements*, 98; Samuel Wragg Ferguson Memoirs, SCHS.

6. Bonds, *War like the Thunderbolt*, 160; Evans, "Fight for the Wagons," 19, 21.

7. *OR*, 38(3):952.

8. *OR*, 38(3):506, 511, 521, 52(1):108.

9. *OR*, 38(3):506, 516, 521, 52(1):108–109.

10. *OR*, 38(3):516–517. The Civil War–era Fayetteville Road is approximated by the modern Oakview Avenue, and the location of this first phase of the fighting at Decatur is approximately where Oakhurst Park is situated.

11. *OR*, 38(3):506, 521.

12. *OR*, 38(3):506, 511, 516, 521.

13. *OR*, 38(3):952; Samuel Wragg Ferguson Memoirs, SCHS.

14. *OR*, 38(3):506, 521; Brittin, "Who Saved the Trains at Decatur?" The site of the second phase at Decatur, the fight along the Georgia Railroad half a mile south of town, is now covered by the modern town. The railroad track is gone, but College Avenue runs along its approximate course. The Union position was about where McDonough Street intersects College Avenue.

15. *OR*, 38(3):952–953; Wheeler quoted in Roy, "General Hardee," 366; Samuel Wragg Ferguson Memoirs, SCHS; McClellan to father, July 26, 1864, Robert Anderson McClellan Papers, DU.

16. *OR*, 38(3):510–511.

17. *OR*, 38(3):511.

18. *OR*, 38(3):517; Thurston Diary, July 20, 1864, James M. Thurston Papers, MHS.

19. *OR*, 38(3):506.

20. *OR*, 38(3):537.

21. *OR*, 52(1):109.

22. *OR*, 38(3):517; Jackson, *Colonel's Diary*, 140–141; Philip Roesch Memorandum, 17–18, OCHM.

23. *OR*, 38(3):506; *OR*, 38(1):74.

24. *OR*, 38(3):517, 519; *OR*, 38(2):687, 705; Philip Roesch Memorandum, 18, OCHM.

25. Harwood, "Fight at Decatur," 236–237.

26. Levi Willard to Milton A. Candler, August 31, 1882, Confederate Miscellany Collection, Series 1, EU.

27. Samuel Wragg Ferguson Memoir, SCHS; *Historical Sketch of the Chicago Board of Trade Battery*, 28; McClellan to father, July 26, 1864, Robert Anderson McClellan Papers, DU.

28. *OR*, 38(3):517, 537, 52(1):109.

29. *OR*, 38(3):507, 513, 515; William E. Titze Diary, July 22, 1864, ALPL.

30. *OR*, 38(3):506–507, 513.

31. *OR*, 38(3):507, 524. The current location of Sprague's last position a mile north of Decatur is the modern junction of Clairmont and North Decatur Streets. See Evans, "Fight for the Wagons," 21.

32. *OR*, 38(3):953.

33. *OR*, 38(3):371, 507; Evans, "Fight for the Wagons," 21–22; Ecelbarger, *Day Dixie Died*, 102.

34. Ecelbarger, *Day Dixie Died*, 102; D. F. Fields account, in Yeary, *Reminiscences of the Boys in Gray*, 223–224.

35. *OR*, 38(3):953; F. Halsey Wigfall to Mama, July 31, 1864, Louis Trezevant Wigfall Family Papers, LC; Cash and Howorth, *My Dear Nellie*, 190; Drake, *Chronological Summary of Battles and Engagements*, 98; Dodson, *Wheeler and His Cavalry*, 210–211.

36. *OR*, 38(1):74.

37. Willard Warner to editor of *Tribune*, April 8, 1876, newspaper clipping, James Birdseye McPherson Papers, USMA.

38. Sherman, *Memoirs*, 2:76; *OR*, 38(1):73.

39. *OR*, 38(2):516, 687, 705; Cox, *Atlanta*, 171; Blazer Diary, July 23, 1864, Tilghham Blazer Collection, UTK.

40. *OR*, 38(2):687, 705.

41. *OR*, 38(1):73; John M. Schofield to Sherman, March 10, 1880, William T. Sherman Papers, LC; Schofield, *Forty-Six Years*, 146–147; *OR*, 38(2):516–517, 687, 38(5):230; Cox, *Atlanta*, 171; Fout, *Dark Days*, 379.

42. *OR*, 38(2):617, 643, 648; Edington Reminiscences, Thomas Doak Edington Papers, UTK; Michael Houck Diary, July 22, 1864, UTK.

43. Sherman, *Memoirs*, 2:80.

44. Howard, "Battles about Atlanta," 395; Schofield, *Forty-Six Years*, 147; Howard, "In Memoriam," 440.

45. Schofield, *Forty-Six Years*, 148.

46. *OR*, 38(1):157, 908–909, 38(5):227; Longacre and Haas, *To Battle*, 202; Gates, *Rough Side of War*, 247.

47. Douglas Hapeman Diaries, July 22, 1864, ALPL; Foering Diary, July 22, 1864, John D. Foering Diary/Papers, HSP.

48. *OR*, 38(3):872; French, *Two Wars*, 219; Cannon, *Inside of Rebeldom*, 239.

49. "What James Bell Told Me about the Siege of Atlanta," July 15, 1935, 7, Folder 14, Box 87, Wilbur G. Kurtz Sr. Papers, AHC; Venet, *Sam Richards's Civil War Diary*, 228.

50. Davis, *Requiem for a Lost City*, 125–126.

51. *OR*, 38(5):232.

52. *OR*, 38(3):165.

53. *OR*, 38(3):165–166; Seay Diary, July 23, 1864, Abraham J. Seay Collection, UO.

54. *OR*, 38(5):231, 233–234.

55. Dodge, *Personal Recollections*, 155–156.

56. Nutt, "Fight at Atlanta."

57. Chamberlin, "Recollections," 284.

58. *OR*, 38(3):451, 454.

59. *OR*, 38(3):454; Adams, "Battle and Capture of Atlanta," 158; Nutt, "Fight at Atlanta."

60. Frank P. Blair to Gresham, August 20, 1864, in Gresham, *Life of Walter Quintin Gresham*, 1:309; Munson, "Battle of Atlanta," 228–229; *OR*, 38(3):454–456.

61. Cate, *Two Soldiers*, 99; Hubbart, *Iowa Soldier Writes Home*, 52; Fuller, "Terrible Day."

62. Frank P. Blair to Gresham, August 20, 1864, in Gresham, *Life of Walter Quintin Gresham*, 1:309; Hogan, *Reub Williams's Memories*, 185.

63. Roy, "General Hardee," 360; Spurlin, *Civil War Diary of Charles A. Leuschner*, 44; Cate, *Two Soldiers*, 98–99; George Anderson Mercer Diary, July 22, 1864, UNC; William Stephen Ray Memoir, 36, UAF.

64. William H. Odell to nephew, August 3, 1864, Jonathan Blair Papers, ALPL; "Military History of Capt. Thomas Sewell, Co. G, 127th Ill. Vol. Inf. during the War of the Rebellion 1861 to 1865," Thomas Sewell Papers, DU.

65. *OR*, 38(5):230–231; Harwood, "Fight at Decatur," 237–238.

66. Buck, *Cleburne and His Command*, 241; Thomas B. Mackall Journal, July 22, 1864 (McMurry transcript), Joseph E. Johnston Papers, CWM; Cate, *Two Soldiers*, 98.

67. Cate, *Two Soldiers*, 98–99; *OR*, 38(3):740.

68. Cate, *Two Soldiers*, 99; *OR*, 38(3):740, 754; Joslyn, *Charlotte's Boys*, 272; Alexander, "Battle of Atlanta."

69. William McLeod Civil War Pocket Diary, July 22, 1864, SAF; B. Benjamin Smith to Capers, April 3, 1880, Ellison Capers Papers, TC.

70. Cate, *Two Soldiers*, 99; Durham, *Blues in Gray*, 225; Joslyn, *Charlotte's Boys*, 272; McDonald, *30th Illinois*, 82, 88; *OR*, 38(3):454, 583; Record of Events, 12th Wisconsin, *SOR*, pt. 2, 75:715.

12. Aftermath

1. McDonald, *30th Illinois*, 82; Stickney to Rose, August 5, 1864, Clifford Stickney Collection, CHM; Allen to Mary, August 5, 1864, Edward W. Allen Papers, UNC; Baugh to parents, July 25, 1864, William G. Baugh Letters, EU; A. E. Kinney to Mrs. Boughton, July 26, 1864, Clement Abner Boughton Papers, WLC-UM; Frank P. Blair to Gresham, August 20, 1864, in Gresham, *Life of Walter Quintin Gresham*, 1:309.

2. Duke, *Fifty-Third Regiment Ohio*, 149; Miller to Father and the rest, July 24, 1864, Alonzo Miller Papers, WHS; Allan to Jim, July 25, 1864, David Allan Jr. Letters, MHM; James Thomas to friend, July 23, 1864, Robert T. Jones Papers, UTK; Alexander, "Battle of Atlanta"; Smith to father, July 26, 1864, Charles M. Smith Papers, WHS; Abernethy, *Private Elisha Stockwell*, 92–93; Cander, "Before Atlanta"; *OR*, 38(3):235, 354; Morris, Hartwell, and Kuykendall, *History 31st Regiment Illinois*, 112; Styple, *Writing and Fighting*, 279; Vance, *Report of the Adjutant General of the State of Illinois*, 6:147; *Story of the Fifty-Fifth Regiment Illinois*, 344; McDonald, *30th Illinois*, 83; Castel, "War Album of Henry Dwight, Pt. 4," 36.

3. A. W. Reese, "Personal Recollections of the Late Civil War in the United States," 1870, 532, SHSM-RCC.

4. Reese, "Personal Recollections," 532–533.

5. Huff, "My 80 Years in Atlanta," 15, http://www.arteryatl.org/uploads/1/2/5/0/125073152/my80yearsinatlanta_all.pdf.

6. Munson, "Battle of Atlanta," 229; Willard Warner to editor of *Tribune*, April 8, 1876, newspaper clipping, James Birdseye McPherson Papers, USMA.

7. Albert Hiffman Reminiscences, Hiffman Family Papers, MHM; Cate, *Two Soldiers*, 99; Alexander, "Battle of Atlanta"; *OR*, 38(5):248.

8. Alexander, "Battle of Atlanta"; Munson, "Battle of Atlanta," 229.

9. "Personal Biography of Major General Grenville Mellen Dodge, 1831–1870," 1:255, Grenville Mellen Dodge Papers, SHSI.

10. Albert Hiffman Reminiscences, Hiffman Family Papers, MHM; Williamson, *Third Battalion Mississippi Infantry*, 227; William F. Graham Diary, July 23, 1864, ALPL.

11. Black, "Marching with Sherman," 324; *OR*, 38(3):371, 502; Frederick E. Pimper to friend, July 25, 1864, Frederick E. Pimper Letters, Pimper Manuscripts, IU; Dodge Diary, July 23, 1864, Grenville Mellen Dodge Papers, SHSI.

12. McDonald, *30th Illinois*, 83–84; Smith, *Fuller's Ohio Brigade*, 173; Hight, *Fifty-Eighth Regiment Indiana*, 413; Martin, *"Out and Forward,"* 37–38; Black, *Soldier's Recollections*, 83.

13. T. J. Walker Reminiscences, 21, UTK; Spurlin, *Civil War Diary of Charles A. Leuschner*, 44; Brown, *One of Cleburne's Command*, 115.

14. Thomas J. Wilson account, in Yeary, *Reminiscences of the Boys in Gray*, 809.

15. *OR*, 38(3):21; "Personal Biography of Major General Grenville Mellen Dodge, 1831–1870," 1:255, Grenville Mellen Dodge Papers, SHSI; Coverdale to James W. Denver, July 23, 1864, Robert Todd Coverdale Letter, GLIAH; Clarke, "With Sherman in Georgia," 364; Hart to Mary, July 26, 1864, Albert Gaillard Hart Papers, WRHS; Roberts to father, July 28, 1864, John H. Roberts Civil War Letters, WHS; *OR*, 38(3):118, 548, 566.

16. Black, "Marching with Sherman," 324; Cryder and Miller, *View from the Ranks*, 420; Hafendorfer, *Civil War Journal of William L. Trask*, 171; Throne, "History of Company D," 64; Robert W. Burt to editors, July 29, 1864, in *Newark True American*, August 19, 1864; *Story of the Fifty-Fifth Regiment Illinois*, 344; Cash and Howorth, *My Dear Nellie*, 193; *OR*, 38(3):419; "What James Bell Told Me about the Siege of Atlanta," July 15, 1935, 7, Folder 14, Box 87, Wilbur G. Kurtz Sr. Papers, AHC.

17. *OR*, 38(3):21, 371, 442; Frank P. Blair to Gresham, August 20, 1864, in Gresham, *Life of Walter Quintin Gresham*, 1:310.

18. A. W. Reese, "Personal Recollections of the Late Civil War in the United States," 1870, 531, SHSM-RCC; *OR*, 38(3):21, 224, 371, 419, 427, 492, 566.

19. *OR*, 38(5):912; Rennolds Diary, July 28, 1864, Edwin Hansford Rennolds Sr. Papers, UTK; Cate, *Two Soldiers*, 98–99.

20. Stickney to Rose, August 5, 1864, Clifford Stickney Collection, CHM; Francis to sister, July 31, 1864, Owen Francis Letter, Box 1, Miscellaneous Manuscripts and Papers, LMU; McDonald, *30th Illinois*, 85; White and Runion, *Great Things*, 133; Brown, *One of Cleburne's Command*, 115; George Pomutz to Mortimer D. Leggett, October 28, 1864, M. F. Force Papers, UW; Douglas, *Douglas's Texas Battery*, 116, 118, 120.

21. Lea to father, July 25, 1864, in Robert J. Cull, comp., "The Civil War Letters of George S. Lea, 1861–1864," MDAH; Marchant to wife, August 2, 1864, Peter Marchant Civil War Correspondence, AHC.

22. Roth, *Well Mary*, 91–92, 107–108.

23. Smith, *Brother of Mine*, 243; William W. Belknap to Aaron, August 5, 1864, Belknap Family Papers, N-YHS.

24. John J. Safely to Mary McEwen, July 31, 1864, McEwen Family Papers, MHM.

25. *OR*, 38(3):21, 28; Stone, "Atlanta Campaign," 446.

26. Philip R. Ward Diary, July 22–23, 1864, Charles S. Harris Collection, UTC; George A. Cooley Civil War Diary, July 23, 1864, WHS; Realf to Laura B. Merritt and Marian M. Cramer, July 23, 1864, Richard Realf Letters and Poems, NL; Patrick and Willey, *Fighting for Liberty*, 233; *OR*, 38(3):387; Bloomfield to sister, July 24, 1864, A. S. Bloomfield Civil War Letter, OHS.

27. *OR*, 38(3):28; Robert B. Young to James A. Smith, August 3, 1864, "Records Cleburnes Div Hardees Corps A of Tenn," chap. 2, no. 265, RG 109, NARA; Douglas, *Douglas's Texas Battery*, 116; Cate, *Two Soldiers*, 99; Thomas B. Mackall Journal, July 23, 1864 (McMurry transcript), Joseph E. Johnston Papers, CWM.

28. *OR*, 38(3):21, 548, 38(5):240; Poe to wife, July 25, 1864, Orlando Metcalfe Poe Papers, LC; Hart to Mary, July 26, 1864, Albert Gaillard Hart Papers, WRHS; Coverdale to James W. Denver, July 23, 1864, Robert Todd Coverdale Letter, GLIAH; Donaldson to father, July 29, 1864, William R. Donaldson Papers, MHM; Stone, "Atlanta Campaign," 447; Frank P. Blair to wife, August 3, 1864, Breckinridge Long Papers, LC.

29. *OR*, 52(2):714; Roy, "General Hardee," 367; *SOR*, pt. 1, 7:80; Taylor Beatty Diaries, July 23, 1864, UNC; Epperly to My most dear Companion, August 2, 1864, Christian M. Epperly Letter, GLIAH.

30. Catton, "Battle of Atlanta," 264; Castel, *Decision in the West*, 412; McMurry, *Atlanta*, 155; Ecelbarger, *Day Dixie Died*, 212–214; Brown, *To the Manner Born*, 278.

31. Ecelbarger, *Day Dixie Died*, 213; Fowler and Miller, *Thirtieth Iowa*, 61.

32. John Henry Marsh to Quintard, July 26, 1864, Charles Todd Quintard Papers, DU; Roy, "General Hardee," 367; "Sketch of Lieut [Gen.] W. J. Hardee," 30, Hardee Family Papers, ADAH; Buck, *Cleburne and His Command*, 243; Irving A. Buck to William W. Belknap, August 30, 1883, in *History of the Fifteenth Regiment*, 352.

33. *OR*, 38(3):54; Thurston Diary, July 23, 1864, James M. Thurston Papers, MHS; A. W. Reese, "Personal Recollections of the Late Civil War in the United States," 1870, 542, SHSM-RCC; "Atlanta, July 22nd Wounds," ser. 1, Folder 453, U.S. Sanitary Commission Records, NYPL.

34. *OR*, 38(3):54; Alfred Bolton Diary, July 21–22, 26, 1864, WHS; Thurston Diary, July 23, 1864, James M. Thurston Papers, MHS.

35. Edwin Witherby Brown, "Under a Poncho with Grant and Sherman," 95, MU; Modil Diary, July 22–23, 25, 29–30, 1864, George W. Modil Papers, MDAH. For more individual case studies of Federal wounded, see John W. Griffith Diaries, July 20–22, 25, 1864, OHS; *Medical and Surgical History*, 8:372, 9:214, 293, 347; and Stuart, *Iowa Colonels and Regiments*, 302. For interesting details on the Union field-hospital system, see John M. Woodworth, "Inspection Report of the Field Hospital, 15th A. C. at Marietta Ga., Aug. 9th, 1864," ser. 1, Folder 16, U.S. Sanitary Commission Records, NYPL.

36. Gresham, *Life of Walter Quintin Gresham*, 1:302, 305–306, 312; Calhoun, *Gilded Age Cato*, 34–35; Welsh, *Medical Histories of Union Generals*, 141; Bosworth, "Battle of Atlanta," 236.

37. Samuel K. Adams to John Kebler, July 23, 1864, and to Peter Force, July 27, 1864, M. F. Force Papers, UW; W. E. Soule to Peter Force, July 30, 31, 1864, ibid.; Mortimer D. Leggett to Manning F. Force, August 10, 1864, ibid.; Manning F. Force to Peter Force, August 15, 1864, ibid.; Manning F. Force to Mrs. Perkins, September 13, 1864, ibid.; Manning F. Force to John Kebler, September 14, 1864, ibid.

38. Howe, *Marching with Sherman*, 230; Welsh, *Medical Histories of Union Generals*, 117; Manning F. Force to Sherman, August 31, 1875, William T. Sherman Papers, LC.

39. *OR*, 38(3):584; Rolf to father and mother, August 7, 1864, Alfred Rolf Letters, AHC; Hafendorfer, *Civil War Journal of William L. Trask*, 171.

40. Lovell Diary, July 23, 1864, Mansfield Lovell Papers, HL; Sidney Dell to Mr. Enecks, July 23, 1864, William R. Enecks Papers, DU; Kinloch Falconer to Stout, July 24, 1864, Samuel Hollingsworth Stout Papers, EU; Whitehead to Irene Cowan, July 25, 1864, Dr. P. F. Whitehead Letters, USM; Bradford Nichol, "Civil War Memoir, 1901," 96–97, TSLA; Mewborn Memoir, 34–35, 38, Joshua W. Mewborn Papers, USAHMI; William F. Glaze account, in Yeary, *Reminiscences of the Boys in Gray*, 272. For an excellent study of the Army of Tennessee hospital system, see Schroeder-Lein, *Confederate Hospitals on the Move*.

41. Harwell, *Kate*, 212–213; John Henry Marsh to Quintard, July 26, 1864, Charles Todd Quintard Papers, DU.

42. Fleming, *Band of Brothers*, 78, 80–81, 83; Worsham, *Old Nineteenth Tennessee*, 129–130.

43. C. W. Clark Jr., "My Grandfather's Diary of the War," UTK.

44. Franklin, *Civil War Diaries of Capt. Alfred Tyler Fielder*, 190, 192, 194–196.

45. "Atlanta, July 22nd Wounds," ser. 1, Folder 453, U.S. Sanitary Commission Records, NYPL; Lea to father, July 25, 1864, in Robert J. Cull, comp., "The Civil War Letters of George S. Lea, 1861–1864," MDAH; "List of Killed & Wounded of 12th and 47th Tenn Regts Vaughans Brig Cheatham's Div H.C A.T, Battle of Decatur July 22d 1864," James Madison Brannock Papers, VHS.

46. Brannock to wife, July 26, 1864, James Madison Brannock Papers, VHS; J. J. McKinney to Mrs. McKittrick, July 25, 1864, Samuel McKittrick Letters, TC.

47. *OR*, 38(5):249; Thurston Diary, July 23, 1864, James M. Thurston Papers, MHS.

48. *OR*, 38(3):288, 305; Thurston Diary, August 1, 1864; Saunier, *Forty-Seventh Regiment Ohio*, 295.

49. Coverdale to James W. Denver, July 23, 1864, Robert Todd Coverdale Letter, GLIAH; Hart to Mary, July 26, 1864, Albert Gaillard Hart Papers, WRHS; *OR*, 38(3):118, 371, 408, 477, 548.

50. "Military History of Capt. Thomas Sewell, Co. G, 127th Ill. Vol. Inf. during the War of the Rebellion 1861 to 1865," Thomas Sewell Papers, DU; Julius E. Thomas Civil War Diary, July 26, 1864, UTK; W. W. Royall account, in Yeary, *Reminiscences of the Boys in Gray*, 656–657; Wiley, *Confederate Letters of John W. Hagan*,

53–54; Gibbons, *Recollections*, 10–29; McCaffrey, *Only a Private*, 73–88; Nisbet, *4 Years on the Firing Line*, 216–237.

51. *OR*, 38(3):28, 740.

52. W. B. Corbitt Diary, July 22, 1864, EU; Cate, *Two Soldiers*, 258.

53. Bailey, *Private Chapter*, 7–8, 11–13.

54. Edwin R. Mason account, in [Rood], *Company "A,"* 16; John A. Melcher, "Eight Months a Prisoner in Andersonville," in *Ninth Reunion of the 37th Regiment O.V.V.I.*, 83–84; Lewis F. Lake Reminiscences, 10, ALPL; McDonald, *30th Illinois*, 85.

55. Meyer, "Atlanta to Andersonville"; Alvah Stone Skilton Diary, July 24, 1864, Skilton-Davis-Heyman Family Papers, RBHPC; Moore Diary, July 26–August 1, 1864, Edward B. Moore Diary and Correspondence, UWYO; Bradd Diary, July 23, 1864, James H. Bradd Papers, USAMHI; Smith, "Civil War Diary," 151; Lewis F. Lake Reminiscences, 10–11, ALPL; Epperly to My most dear Companion, August 2, 1864, Christian M. Epperly Letter, GLIAH; Wysor to father, August 7, 1864, James Miller Wysor Letters, VHS.

56. John B. Shafer account, in [Rood], *Company "A,"* 20–23.

57. *OR*, ser. 2, 7:791–792.

58. "Gen. James Wilson," 492–493; Meyer, "Atlanta to Andersonville."

59. "Gen. James Wilson," 493, 495; Winther, *With Sherman*, 127–128.

60. *OR*, ser. 2, 7:908, 1178.

61. Winther, *With Sherman*, 128; *SOR*, pt. 1, 7:67–68; Howard, "Murray's Battery."

62. Bradd Diary, August 18, 1864, James H. Bradd Papers, USAMHI.

63. G. C. Morton to Captain, August 24, [1864]: Force to John Kebler, October 20, 1864, M. F. Force Papers, UW; Smith, "Civil War Diary," 153; Alvah Stone Skilton Diary, August 5, 1864, Skilton-Davis-Heyman Family Papers, RBHPC; Loop, "Sounding the Alarm."

64. Alvah Stone Skilton Diary, August 11, 1864 to April 15, 1865, Skilton-Davis-Heyman Family Papers, RBHPC; Smith, "Civil War Diary," 162–169; Edwin R. Mason account in [Rood], *Company "A,"* 18–20.

65. Bailey, *Private Chapter*, 138, 238, 245–253.

66. *OR*, 38(3):631, 38(5):631, 900, 903.

67. Phillips, *Correspondence of Robert Toombs, Alexander H. Stephens, and Howell Cobb*, 2:648–649.

68. *OR*, 38(5):903; *SOR*, pt. 1, 7:344; Wiley, *Norfolk Blues*, 135; Smythe to wife, July 24, 1864, D. L. Smythe Letters, TSLA; *Charleston Mercury*, July 29, 1864; Bonner, *Journal of a Milledgeville Girl*, 50–51; Scarborough, *Diary of Edmund Ruffin*, 3:509–510, 514.

69. *OR*, 38(3):631, 39(2):832.

70. *OR*, 38(3):631, 699.

71. "Some Unofficial Glimpses of General John B. Hood," August 28, 1950, 9–10, Folder 2, Box 49, Wilbur G. Kurtz Sr. Papers, AHC; "What James Bell Told Me about the Siege of Atlanta," July 15, 1935, Folder 14, Box 87, ibid.

72. *OR*, 38(3):971; Cash and Howorth, *My Dear Nellie*, 190; William Hawkins to sister, July 23, 1864, Elijah T. D. Hawkins Papers, DU; Jim Huffman, comp., "Pre– & Civil War Letters of Lt. Col. Columbus Sykes 16th [*sic*] Regiment, Mississippi

Infantry," 76, MDAH; Sykes to wife, July 26, 1864, William E. Sykes Papers, MSU; Jones and Martin, *Gentle Rebel*, 62; Champion to wife, July 23, 1864, Sidney S. Champion Papers, DU; Semmes to wife, July 25, 1864, Benedict Joseph Semmes Papers, UNC; Whitehead to Irene Cowan, July 24, 1864, Dr. P. F. Whitehead Letters, USM.

73. *Charleston Mercury*, July 29, August 20, 1864; *Daily Confederate* (Raleigh), July 30, 1864; William J. Hardee to wife, n.d., Hardee Family Papers, ADAH; *OR*, 38(3):699, 38(5):908; F. Halsey Wigfall to Mama, July 31, 1864, Louis Trezevant Wigfall Family Papers, LC; White and Runion, *Great Things*, 134; Thomas L. Clayton to wife, July 28, 1864, Clayton Family Papers, UNC; Marchant to wife, August 2, 1864, Peter Marchant Civil War Correspondence, AHC; E. D. Willett Diary, July 22, 1864, ADAH; Brannock to wife, July 26, 1864, James Madison Brannock Papers, VHS; Ross to Mary, July 24, 1864, Emmett Ross Papers, MSU; Neal to Ma, July 23, 1864, Andrew Jackson Neal Papers, EU.

74. Warrick to wife, July 31, 1864, Thomas Warrick Papers, ADAH; Frano, *Letters of Captain Hugh Black*, 67–68; Wynne and Taylor, *This War So Horrible*, 106; Dickey to Anna, July 25, 1864, William J. Dickey Papers, UGA; Scarborough, *Diary of Edmund Ruffin*, 3:516.

75. Hess, *Peach Tree Creek*, 12–16; Joseph E. Johnston to Wigfall, February 28, 1865, Louis Trezevant Wigfall Papers, UTA.

76. Hood, *Advance and Retreat*, 130–135, 183, 186, 251.

77. *SOR*, pt. 1, 7:80; Hughes, *Civil War Memoir of Philip Daingerfield Stephenson*, 220–221; Daniel, *Cannoneers in Gray*, 160; Smith, *Palmetto Boy*, 100; Garrett to Uncle Hosea, August 1, 1864, Hosea Garrett Jr. Civil War Letters, AHC; B. Benjamin Smith to Capers, April 3, 1880, Ellison Capers Papers, TC; Hawkins, "5th Ky. Infantry C.S.A.," 62, Hiram Hawkins Papers, KHS; Buck, *Cleburne and His Command*, 241–243.

78. Young, *Reminiscences*, 90–91; Hughes, *Civil War Memoir of Philip Daingerfield Stephenson*, 223.

79. *OR*, 38(5):234; Gates, *Rough Side*, 247; Longacre and Haas, *To Battle*, 202; James Thomas to friend, July 23, 1864, Robert T. Jones Papers, UTK; Newell to Kate, July 24, 1864, William McCulloch Newell Papers, NC; Alpheus C. Williams Diary, July 22, 1864, MHM; George Rolfe Diaries, July 22–23, 1864, NYSL.

80. *Louisville Daily Journal*, July 25, 1864; James P. Snell Diary, July 15, 20–21, 23, 1864, ALPL; Churchill to wife, August 4, 1864, Mendal C. Churchill Papers, UWYO; Thomas D. Christie to Sandy, July 30, 1864, Christie Family Letters, MinnHS.

81. John J. Safely to Mary, July 24, 1864, McEwen Family Papers, MHM; Simpson and Berlin, *Sherman's Civil War*, 671, 676; Poe to wife, July 24, 1864, Orlando Metcalfe Poe Papers, LC; Moore to Mary, July 25, 1864, John Moore Letters, GLIAH.

82. *OR*, 38(3):385; Barto to father, sister, mother, brother, July 24, 1864, Alphonso Barto Letters, ALPL; James P. Snell Diary, July 22, 1864, ALPL; Churchill to wife, July 23, 1864, Mendal C. Churchill Papers, UWYO.

83. *OR*, 38(3):27–28, 548, 572, 583, 595; Samuel K. Adams to John Kebler, July 23, 1864, M. F. Force Papers, UW; "General G. M. Dodge's Account of Part taken by *Sixteenth Army Corps*, in movement on *Resaca*, attack of 4th of July, and *Battle of Atlanta*," November 30, 1875, William T. Sherman Papers, LC; *OR*, 52(1):571.

84. *OR*, 38(3):180, 454, 588.

85. Hess, *Peach Tree Creek*, 217; Hess, *Ezra Church*, 170; Mulligan, *Badger Boy*, 112; Watkins to Sarah, July 26, 1864, John Watkins Papers, UTK; Cobb to friends, July 28, 1864, Thomas Cobb Letter, GLIAH; Griffin to wife, July 30, 1864, Daniel F. Griffin Papers, ISL; Richard W. Burt to editors, July 29, 1864, *Newark True American*, August 19, 1864.

86. Franklin, *Civil War Diaries of Capt. Alfred Tyler Fielder*, 190.

87. *OR*, 38(3):556–558, 586, 597–598, 612; William W. Belknap to assistant adjutant general, 4th Division, August 13, 1864, 17th Army Corps Letters Sent (entry 6363), vol. 20/79, pt. 2, RG 393, NARA; Anderson, ed., *"Dear Sister Sadie,"* 203.

88. Sherman, *Memoirs*, 2:95; William W. Belknap to Aaron, August 5, 1864, Belknap Family Papers, N-YHS; Stuart, *Iowa Colonels and Regiments*, 237, 241–242; Belknap to Clara B. Wolcott, August 6, 1864, William Worth Belknap Papers, PU; *History of the Fifteenth Regiment*, 385–386.

89. *OR*, 38(3):556; "Gen. McPherson's Death"; *Keokuk (IA) Daily Gate City*, August 8, 1864; *Harper's Weekly*, August 20, 1864, 531; Foster Diary, August 1, 1864, Brigham Foster Papers, USAMHI; Belknap to Clara B. Wolcott, August 6, 1864, William Worth Belknap Papers, PU.

90. *OR*, 38(3):492; Sharland, *Knapsack Notes*, 66. Sharland's name was spelled consistently in the rosters and in Manning's report as "Sherland"; it is not known why the private's name was spelled "Sharland" in his book.

91. John J. Safely to Mary F. McEwen, July 24, 1864, McEwen Family Papers, MHM; Hall to father, July 24, 1864, James A. Hall Letters, Walter King Hoover Collection, TSLA.

92. Sherman, *Memoirs*, 2:81; Evans, "Report of the Battle of Atlanta," 30; *OR*, 38(3):265.

93. *OR*, 38(3):262–263; Kimbell, *Battery "A,"* 87–88.

94. *OR*, 38(3):538, 539.

95. Circular, Headquarters, 3rd Brigade, 4th Division, 17th Corps, July 29, 1864, 17th Army Corps Letters Sent (entry 6363), vol. 20/79, pt. 2, RG 393, NARA; John C. Abercrombie to assistant adjutant general, 4th Division, September 22, 1864, ibid.; John C. Abercrombie to James Wilson, September 22, 1864, ibid.; John C. Abercrombie to assistant adjutant general, Department and Army of the Tennessee, September 24, 1864, ibid.

96. William W. Belknap to assistant adjutant general, 4th Division, November 8, 14, 26, 1864, 17th Army Corps Letters Sent (entry 6363), vol. 20/79, pt. 2, RG 393, NARA; William W. Belknap to assistant adjutant general, Department and Army of the Tennessee, March 28, 1865, ibid.

13. Moving Out, July 23–28

1. *OR*, 38(5):66.

2. *OR*, 38(5):235; William F. Graham Diary, July 23, 1864, ALPL; Smith, "Civil War Diaries of Mifflin Jennings," July 23–25, 1864, Iowa in the Civil War website.

3. *OR*, 38(1):75, 38(2):846, 904–909, 38(5):237.

4. Durham, *Blues in Gray*, 225; Cox, *Atlanta*, 174; Thomas B. Mackall Journal, July 18, 1864 (McMurry transcript), Joseph E. Johnston Papers, CWM; William McLeod Civil War Pocket Diary, July 23, 1864, SAF; George Anderson Mercer Diary, July 23, 1864, UNC; Rennolds autobiography, 31, Edwin Hansford Rennolds Sr. Papers, UTK.

5. William McLeod Civil War Pocket Diary, July 24, 1864, SAF.

6. *OR*, 38(3):953, 38(5):905–906.

7. *OR*, 38(2):688, 38(3):29, 140, 148, 157, 385, 464, 520, 524, 590; James Thomas to Friend, July 23, 1864, Robert T. Jones Papers, UTK; Palmer Diary, July 23, 1864, David James Palmer Papers, UI.

8. *OR*, 38(3):66, 38(5):232–233, 237; Allen to parents, July 25, 1864, Edward W. Allen Papers, UNC; Levi H. Nickel Diary, July 23–25, 1864, WHS; Sylvester Daniels Diary, July 23, 1864, Theophilus M. Magaw Papers, HL; Jacobs Diary, July 23, 1864, Wayne Johnson Jacobs Diaries and Lists, LSU; William F. Graham Diary, July 23, 1864, ALPL; Watkins Diary, July 23–24, 1864, John Watkins Papers, UTK.

9. *OR*, 38(5):237–240.

10. *OR*, 38(5):242.

11. *OR*, 38(5):242–243.

12. *OR*, 32(3):521–522.

13. *OR*, 38(5):240–241; Sherman, *Memoirs*, 2:85; Hess, *Ezra Church*, 14–17.

14. *OR*, 38(5):242–244.

15. Cryder and Miller, *View from the Ranks*, 420; *OR*, 38(3):140, 166, 237, 385; Sylvester Daniels Diary, July 24, 1864, Theophilus M. Magaw Papers, HL; Connelly, *Seventieth Ohio*, 96; Cate, *Two Soldiers*, 100.

16. Thomas B. Mackall Journal, July 24, 1864 (McMurry transcript), Joseph E. Johnston Papers, CWM; *OR*, 38(5):907.

17. *OR*, 38(3):734, 38(5):906, 908; Cate, *Two Soldiers*, 99; Rennolds Diary, July 24–25, 1864, Edwin Hansford Rennolds Sr. Papers, UTK.

18. *OR*, 38(5):247, 255.

19. William F. Graham Diary, July 25, 1864, ALPL; Allen to parents, July 25, 1864, Edward W. Allen Papers, UNC; Sylvester Daniels Diary, July 25, 1864, Theophilus M. Magaw Papers, HL; "Historical Memoranda of the 52nd Regiment Illinois Infantry Volunteers," Edwin A. Bowen Papers, HL; George Lemon Childress Diary, July 25, 1864, ALPL; *OR*, 38(3):385, 38(5):252.

20. *OR*, 38(5):909.

21. *OR*, 38(5):907, 52(2):713; George Anderson Mercer Diary, July 25–26, 1864, UNC; B. Benjamin Smith to Capers, April 3, 1880, Ellison Capers Papers, TC.

22. *OR*, 38(5):247; Hess, "Alvin P. Hovey," 35–40.

23. *OR*, 38(5):247; Townsend, *Yankee Warhorse*, 158–163.

24. Hess, "Alvin P. Hovey," 43–49.

25. *OR*, 38(5):259–260, 271.

26. *OR*, 38(5):260.

27. Morgan, *Through American and Irish Wars*, 1–60; Anders, "Fisticuffs at Headquarters," 9–10; Sweeny to Dodge, July 11, 1864, Thomas William Sweeny Papers, HL.

28. "Historical Memoranda of the 52nd Regiment Illinois Infantry Volunteers," Edwin A. Bowen Papers, HL; Sweeny to Clark, July 11, 1864, and Dodge endorsement, July 12, 1864, Thomas William Sweeny Papers, HL; Sweeny to Dayton, July 16, 1864, and Sherman endorsement, July 24, 1864, ibid.; Sweeny to adjutant general of the Army, July 26, 1864, and E. D. Townsend endorsement, August 4, 1864, ibid.; court records, Court-Martial Case Files, Thomas W. Sweeny, File LL-2995, RG 153, NARA.

29. "Personal Biography of Major General Grenville Mellen Dodge, 1831–1870," 1:251, Grenville Mellen Dodge Papers, SHSI; Frederick Welker statement, n.d., Thomas William Sweeny Papers, HL.

30. *OR*, 38(3):385, 38(5):252–253, 270.

31. "Personal Biography of Major General Grenville Mellen Dodge, 1831–1870," 1:251, 253, Grenville Mellen Dodge Papers, SHSI; Sweeny to William B. Bodge, July 30, 1864, Thomas William Sweeny Papers, HL.

32. Transcript and Special Orders No. 227, Headquarters, Department and Army of the Tennessee, October 7, 1864, Court-Martial Case Files, Thomas W. Sweeny, File LL-2995, RG 153, NARA.

33. "Statement in Defense," Court-Martial Case Files, Thomas W. Sweeny, File LL-2995, RG 153, NARA.

34. Transcript and Oliver O. Howard endorsement, Court-Martial Case Files, Thomas W. Sweeny, File LL-2995, RG153, NARA; Anders, "Fisticuffs at Headquarters," 14; Sweeny to daughter, May 26, 1865, Thomas William Sweeny Papers, HL.

35. *OR*, 38(5):261; Hess, *Ezra Church*, 9, 24.

36. Hess, *Ezra Church*, 30–34.

37. Hess, *Ezra Church*, 14–16.

38. Hess, *Ezra Church*, 58–131.

39. Hess, *Ezra Church*, 164–167.

40. *OR*, 38(5):273, 45(2):110; Sherman, *Memoirs*, 2:86–87.

41. Castel, *Decision in the West*, 381, 411–412, 434.

14. Battlefield, Commemoration, and Memory

1. John J. Safely to Mary F. McEwen, August 22, 1864, McEwen Family Papers, MHM; Dawson, *Life and Services of Gen. John A. Logan*, 65–66; Nutt, "Fight at Atlanta."

2. Cate, *Two Soldiers*, 102; Van Buren Oldham Diary, July 27, 1864, UTM; Deupree, "Noxubee Squadron," 101–102.

3. Longacre and Haas, *To Battle*, 211; *OR*, 38(5): 602; *History of the Organization . . . of Battery M, First Regiment Illinois Light Artillery*, 243; Tappan, *Civil War Journal of Lt. Russell M. Tuttle*, 153; Maley to father and mother, September 13, 1864, Henry H. Maley Letters, UND; Edington reminiscences, Thomas Doak Edington Papers, UTK; Bennett and Tillery, *Struggle for the Life*, 214; Force Journal, November 14, 1864, M. F. Force Papers, UW.

4. Sherman, *Memoirs*, 2:178–179; Hight, *Fifty-Eighth Regiment of Indiana Volunteer Infantry*, 413–414; Howe, *Marching with Sherman*, 60.

5. T. R. Bell to A. H. Raymond, August 25, 1866, S. P. Raymond Letters, MSU.

6. *History of the Fifteenth Regiment*, 385n; McDonald, *30th Illinois*, 86; Wiesman, "Field of Atlanta"; Kurtz, "At the Troup Hurt House."

7. "Memo of Data from J. W. McWilliams—June 30, 1930," 1, 9, 12, Folder 11, Box 49, Wilbur G. Kurtz Sr. Papers, AHC; Kurtz, "What James Bell Told Me about the Siege of Atlanta," July 15, 1935, 6, Folder 14, Box 87, ibid.; Wiesman, "Field of Atlanta"; Kurtz, "At the Troup Hurt House"; Delany, "Leggett's Hill"; McCarley, "'Atlanta Is Ours,'" 58. Three photographs of the Fred Koch House on Leggett's Hill, taken March 25, 1927, and a photograph of the unveiling of a bronze marker at the Koch house, taken March 13, 1938, can be found in Wilbur G. Kurtz Sr. Visual Arts Collection, AHC.

8. Kurtz, "Broken Line and the DeGress Battery"; *OR*, 38(5):275; Kurtz, "At the Troup Hurt House."

9. Philip Sidney Post to Mollie S. Post, August 18, 1864, Confederate Miscellany Collection, ser. 1, EU; Kurtz, "Augustus F. Hurt House"; Frankenberry, "Visiting War Scenes." One can see Kurtz's photograph of the top of Copenhill, taken November 23, 1918, in Wilbur G. Kurtz Sr. Visual Arts Collection, AHC.

10. Kurtz, "At the Troup Hurt House"; Kurtz, "Augustus F. Hurt House"; "Statement by J. W. McWilliams as to What Case Turner Told Him about the Death of Major-General W. H. T. Walker, in the Battle of Atlanta, July 22d, 1864," 6, Folder 12, Box 90, Wilbur G. Kurtz Sr. Papers, AHC.

11. Davis, *George N. Barnard*, 77–80, 98, 100.

12. James E. Taylor to Miss E. Stem, December 13, [no year], and attached advertisement, Folder 137, Box 24, Western Reserve Manuscripts, WRHS.

13. Jamieson, "Cyclorama," 60–61; Kurtz, *Atlanta Cyclorama*, 25.

14. Kurtz, *Atlanta Cyclorama*, 26; Davis, "War Artist at Vicksburg," 7–8; Theodore R. Davis to Mrs. De Gress, November 30, [1885], Francis De Gress Papers, AHC.

15. Hogan, *Reub Williams's Memories*, 184–185.

16. *"Battle of Atlanta,"* 3; Jamieson, "Cyclorama," 62; Theodore R. Davis to Mrs. De Gress, November 30, [1885], Francis De Gress Papers, AHC.

17. Jamieson, "Cyclorama," 58; Kurtz, *Atlanta Cyclorama*, 24, 26. J. O. Cochran estimates the cost of the cyclorama as $37,500, while Gary Ecelbarger sets it at $43,000. Cochran, *Battle of Atlanta*, 13; Ecelbarger, *Day Dixie Died*, 272–273n.

18. Kurtz, *Atlanta Cyclorama*, 26; Jamieson, "Cyclorama," 67–69. A copy of the July 22 cyclorama had been made by Wehner at Milwaukee and exhibited for several years until E. W. McConnell purchased it and moved it to Baltimore in 1897. "It had been in damp storage for some years in Indianapolis and during its Baltimore Exhibition it fell to pieces and could not be repaired for further exhibition," recalled McConnell many years later. Jamieson, "Cyclorama," 66.

19. Kurtz, *Atlanta Cyclorama*, 26–28; Jamieson, "Cyclorama," 62, 68.

20. Jamieson, "Cyclorama," 74; Kurtz, *Atlanta Cyclorama*, 28.

21. Kurtz, *Atlanta Cyclorama*, 12, 14–23; Hogan, *Reub Williams's Memories*, 183; McDonald, *30th Illinois*, 86–87; Nisbet, *4 Years on the Firing Line*, 216.

22. Kurtz to R. L. McDougall, December 14, 1934, Wilbur G. Kurtz Sr. Papers, AHC; J. J. Haverty to George I. Simons, November 21, 1934, ibid.; Kurtz to J. Walter Coleman, December 4, 1948, ibid.; Jamieson, "Cyclorama," 74.

23. Cotter, "Victory for the Civil War 'Cyclorama.'"

24. Cotter, "Victory for the Civil War 'Cyclorama'"; Judt, "Atlanta's Civil War Monument," www.theatlantic.com/ideas/archive/2019/03/how-atlanta-cyclo rama-lost-its-confederate-overtone/584938/.

25. Simpson and Berlin, *Sherman's Civil War*, 672; Howe, *Marching with Sherman*, 54–55.

26. *OR*, 38(5):241; Ray, "Gen. McPherson's Death"; Whaley, *Forgotten Hero*, 165–167. Herman Melville wrote a poem to honor McPherson's death and burial entitled "A Dirge for McPherson, Killed in Front of Atlanta (July, 1864)." See Melville, *Battle-Pieces*, 124–125.

27. Beard, "McPherson's Fate"; Richard Beard to Mrs. George A. Justice, October 8, 1925, in "Comrades in War," 87.

28. Willard Warner to editor of *Tribune*, April 8, 1876, newspaper clipping, James Birdseye McPherson Papers, USMA; *OR*, 38(5):241, 39(2):203; Simpson and Berlin, *Sherman's Civil War*, 672; Garth interview with Sherman, December 30, 1886, *Cincinnati Enquirer*, December 31, 1886, in Dawson, *Life and Services of Gen. John A. Logan*, 519–520n; Schofield, *Forty-Six Years*, 146; "General William T. Sherman," 9, Lionel Allen Sheldon Collection, HL.

29. Whaley, *Forgotten Hero*, 171; Simon, *Papers of Ulysses S. Grant*, 11:397, 397–398n; *OR*, 38(3):28, 39–40, 372, 550; Schofield, *Forty-Six Years*, 137; Sword, "New Perspective on the Death of Gen. James B. McPherson," 38; Hickenlooper to Maria L. Smith, August 13, 1864, Andrew Hickenlooper Collection, CMC; Belknap to Clara B. Wolcott, August 6, 1864, William Worth Belknap Papers, PU; Baugh to mother, August 6, 1864, William G. Baugh Letters, Union Miscellany Collection, EU; Gilbert Thompson Journal, 303, LC; Cox, *Atlanta*, 169; Grant, "Boy's Experience at Vicksburg," 97.

30. Slocum to Lydia Mary Chase, December 20, 1864, Lydia Norton Russell Chase Slocum Letters, RBHPC; Whaley, *Forgotten Hero*, 175, 177–179.

31. Lord, "General Sherman," 102–104; Simpson and Berlin, *Sherman's Civil War*, 682; Whaley, *Forgotten Hero*, 169, 177.

32. *OR*, 49(2):1097; *McPherson Monument* flyer, Francis De Gress Papers, AHC.

33. Orlando M. Poe to Sherman, November 11, 24, 1875, William T. Sherman Papers, LC; John R. McGuinness to Sherman, June 8, 1877, ibid.; Philip Breitenbucher to John C. Black, November 4, 1901, in *Report of the Proceedings of the Society of the Army of the Tennessee*, 76; Kurtz, "McPherson's Last Ride."

34. Henry J. Hunt to Sherman, July 22, 23, 1880, William T. Sherman Papers, LC.

35. Wiesman, "Field of Atlanta"; Philip Breitenbucher to John C. Black, November 4, 1901, in *Report of the Proceedings of the Society of the Army of the Tennessee*, 76–80; Ecelbarger, *Day Dixie Died*, 273n; McPherson Monument, photograph by Mr. Sparks of the *Atlanta Journal*, taken June 24, 1929, Wilbur G. Kurtz Sr. Visual Arts Collection, AHC.

36. *McPherson Monument* flyer, Francis De Gress Papers, AHC; Sherman to Hazen, December 23, 1865, William T. Sherman Papers, LC; Ralph Buckland to Sherman, October 18, 1875, ibid.; Manning F. Force to Sherman, November 8, 1875, ibid.; Andrew Hickenlooper to Sherman, November 9, 1875, ibid.

37. Whaley, *Forgotten Hero*, 179–181; *New York Times*, June 9, 1876.

38. Whaley, *Forgotten Hero*, 180–181; Brown and Williams, *Diary of James A. Garfield*, 3:365, 367; Simon, *Papers of Ulysses S. Grant*, 27:337–338; Hedley, *Marching through Georgia*, 444.

39. Whaley, *Forgotten Hero*, 182–191.

40. Richard Beard questionnaire, 1920, in Elliott and Morley, *Tennessee Civil War Veterans*, 1:299; Beard, "McPherson's Fate"; Beard, "Incident of the Battle of Atlanta," 324–327.

41. Sherman to Logan, July 21, 1876, William T. Sherman Papers, LC; Sherman to W. C. Church, July 25, 1876, ibid.; William E. Strong, "The Death of Major General James B. McPherson, July 22nd 1864," August 25, 1876, ibid.; William W. Belknap to Govan, September 2, 1878, Daniel Chevilette Govan Papers, UNC.

42. Brown, *To the Manner Born*, 1–266.

43. Octavius Cohen Myers, "Personal Memoirs of the Civil War," 2–3, 25, GHS.

44. Brown, *To the Manner Born*, 282; Julius L. Brown to Clement A. Evans, April 12, 1902, Folder 12, Box 90, Wilbur G. Kurtz Sr. Papers, AHC; Kurtz to Joseph B. Cumming, May 26, 1951, ibid.; Kurtz, "Major-General W. H. T. Walker"; "Honor to Gen. W. H. T. Walker," 402–407.

45. "Statement by J. W. McWilliams as to What Case Turner Told Him about the Death of Major-General W. H. T. Walker, in the Battle of Atlanta, July 22d, 1864," 7, Folder 12, Box 90, Wilbur G. Kurtz Sr. Papers, AHC; "The Death of Maj. Gen. W. H. T. Walker in the Battle of Atlanta, July 22, 1864," 14, ibid.; "Memo of Data from J. W. McWilliams—June 30, 1930," 6, Folder 11, Box 49, ibid.

46. Minutes, City Planning Commission meeting, July 30, 1931, 3, Folder 12, Box 90, Wilbur G. Kurtz, Sr., Papers, AHC; Charles M. Brown to Mrs. Arthur McD. Wilson Jr., March 18, 1935, ibid.; Program, "Rededication of the Gen. W. H. T. Walker Monument and Unveiling of the Tablet," May 21, 1937, ibid.; clipping, "Memorial Group to Re-dedicate Walker Tablet," ibid.; Map FF 309, T4, October 1931, ibid.; photograph of Walker Monument, March 13, 1938, Wilbur G. Kurtz Sr. Visual Arts Collection, AHC.

47. Shadley, "Who Recaptured the De Gress Battery?"; Saunier, *Forty-Seventh Regiment Ohio Veteran Volunteer Infantry*, 285–286; Wright, *Corporal's Story*, 134n.

48. Clipping, *Harper's Weekly*, September 3, 1864, Francis De Gress Papers, AHC; clipping, *The Two Republics*, January 7, 1883, ibid.; Theodore R. Davis to Mrs. De Gress, November 30 [1885], ibid.

49. Theodore R. Davis to Mrs. De Gress, November 30 [1885], Francis De Gress Papers, AHC.

50. *Report of Robert L. Rodgers*, 5–6, 8–10.

51. Hedley, *Marching through Georgia*, 170–172.

52. Cate, *Two Soldiers*, 225–226.

53. McDonald, *30th Illinois*, 76–81. The colors of the 45th Alabama of Lowrey's Brigade, captured on the field, remained in the Iowa Capitol for many decades after the war. See Buck, *Cleburne and His Command*, 240.

54. Skinner and Skinner, *Death of a Confederate*, 256–258.

Conclusion

1. Downs to Mr. N. Dudley, July 25, 1864, J. T. Downs Letter, Confederate Miscellany Collection, ser. 1, EU; Irving A. Buck to William W. Belknap, 1881, in *History of the Fifteenth Regiment*, 351; Stone, "Atlanta Campaign," 447; McClintock Diary, July 22, 1864, James M. McClintock Papers, HL; Leggett, "Battle of Atlanta," May 6, 1886; *OR*, 38(1):72–75; Castel, *Decision in the West*, 411.

2. "Personal Biography of Major General Grenville Mellen Dodge, 1831–1870," 1:245, Grenville Mellen Dodge Papers, SHSI.

3. Sears, *Chancellorsville*, 274–300; Davis, *Texas Brigadier*, 337–343.

4. Cox, *Atlanta*, 174–175; Wade, "Bald Knob"; McDonald, *30th Illinois*, 87; Chamberlin, "Hood's Second Sortie," 328; Boring, "A Criticism."

5. Castel, *Decision in the West*, 411.

6. Chamberlin, "Hood's Second Sortie," 326.

7. Hess, *Civil War Infantry Tactics*, 176–201.

8. Thomas B. Mackall Journal, July 22, 1864 (McMurry transcript), Joseph E. Johnston Papers, CWM; Taylor Beatty Diaries, July 22, 1864, UNC.

9. *OR*, 38(3):546.

10. Hughes, *Civil War Memoir of Philip Daingerfield Stephenson*, 220–221; Daniel, *Cannoneers in Gray*, 160.

11. Van Buren Oldham Diary, July 24 1864, UTM; Castel, *Decision in the West*, 412.

12. *OR*, 38(3):746–747.

13. Castel, *Decision in the West*, 413.

14. Castel, *Decision in the West*, 413; Hess, *Peach Tree Creek*, 240–241.

15. Wheeler quoted in Roy, "General Hardee," 361; Hess, *Peach Tree Creek*, 180–181.

16. Cox, *Atlanta*, 176; Hay, "Atlanta Campaign," 1–4, 40, 42–43.

17. Sherman, *Memoirs*, 2:82.

18. Stone, "Atlanta Campaign," 447; Hay, "Atlanta Campaign," 42; Castel, *Decision in the West*, 414; Hess, *Fighting for Atlanta*, 158–161.

19. Sherman, "Grand Strategy," 253.

20. *OR*, 38(1):203, 38(3):39; "Personal Recollections: Strategy and Battles of Sherman & Johnston Illustrated in Active Campaigns," Folder 3, Box 5, Oliver Otis Howard Papers, LMU.

21. McDonald, *30th Illinois*, 87–88.

22. McDonald, *30th Illinois*, 88; Wilson reminiscences, 8, Harrison Wilson Civil War Collection, UCSB.

23. Hess, *Civil War Infantry Tactics*, 81–176; Chamberlin, "Recollections," 278–279.

24. Bailey, *Private Chapter*, 7–8.

25. Hess, *Civil War Supply and Strategy*, 139–175.

26. Strong, "Death of General James B. McPherson," 324.

27. McMurry, *Atlanta*, 155.

28. Ecelbarger, *Day Dixie Died*, 172, 225.

29. Ecelbarger, *Day Dixie Died*, 225.

30. Ecelbarger, *Day Dixie Died*, 215.

31. Waugh, *Reelecting Lincoln*, 295–303.

32. Simon, *Papers of Ulysses S. Grant*, 10:209.

BIBLIOGRAPHY

Archives

Abraham Lincoln Presidential Library, Springfield, Illinois
    Alphonso Barto Letters
    Jonathan Blair Papers
    George Lemon Childress Diary
    William F. Graham Diary
    Douglas Hapeman Diaries
    Lewis F. Lake Reminiscences
    James P. Snell Diary
    William C. Titze Diary

Alabama Department of Archives and History, Montgomery
    Edward Norphlet Brown Letters
    Hardee Family Papers
    C. C. McDowell Letters, Sam Whigham Papers
    Thomas Warrick Papers
    Joseph Wheeler Family Papers
    E. D. Willett Diary

Atlanta History Center, Atlanta, Georgia
    Thomas M. Coleman Letter
    Francis De Gress Papers
    Hosea Garrett Jr. Civil War Letters
    Evan P. Howell Letters
    Wilbur G. Kurtz Sr. Papers
    Wilbur G. Kurtz Sr. Visual Arts Collection
    Peter Marchant Civil War Correspondence
    J. A. Morlan Letter, Antebellum and Civil War Collection
    Alfred Rolf Letters

Chicago History Museum, Chicago, Illinois
    "Autobiographical Sketch of William E. Strong at the Age of 42"
    Clifford Stickney Collection

Cincinnati Museum Center, Cincinnati, Ohio
    Andrew Hickenlooper Collection

The Citadel, Archives and Museum, Charleston, South Carolina
    Ellison Capers Papers
    Samuel McKittrick Letters

College of William and Mary, Special Collections, Williamsburg, Virginia
    Joseph E. Johnston Papers

Duke University, Rubenstein Rare Book and Manuscript Library, Durham, North Carolina
    Ellison Capers Papers
    Sidney S. Champion Papers
    William R. Enecks Papers
    William F. Graham Diary
    William Hawkins Letter, Elijah T. D. Hawkins Papers
    John Henry Marsh Letter, Charles Todd Quintard Papers
    Robert Anderson McClellan Papers
    William H. Nugen Letters
    Charles Todd Quintard Papers
    Thomas Sewell Papers
    W. H. T. Walker Papers
Emory University, Manuscripts, Archives, and Rare Books Library, Atlanta, Georgia
    William G. Baugh Letters, Union Miscellany Collection
    W. B. Corbitt Diary, Confederate Miscellany Collection, Series 1
    Mumford H. Dixon Diary
    J. T. Downs Letter, Confederate Miscellany Collection, Series 1
    Honnoll Family Papers
    Andrew Jackson Neal Letters
    Philip Sidney Post Letter, Confederate Miscellany Collection, Series 1
    Samuel Hollingsworth Stout Papers
    James W. Watkins Papers
    Levi Willard Letter, Confederate Miscellany IIa Collection
Filson Historical Society, Louisville, Kentucky
    George W. Gallup Papers
    George W. Nash Letter
    Henry Schmidt Letters, Schmidt Family Papers
Georgia Historical Society, Savannah
    Willis Perry Burt Diary, Laura Burt Brantley Collection
    Octavius Cohen Myers, "Personal Memoirs of the Civil War"
Gilder Lehrman Institute of American History, New-York Historical Society, New York, New York
    Thomas Cobb Letter
    Robert Todd Coverdale Letter
    Christian M. Epperly Letter
    John Bell Hood Letters
    John Moore Letters
Historical Society of Pennsylvania, Philadelphia
    John D. Foering Diary / Papers
Huntington Library, San Marino, California
    Edwin A. Bowen Papers
    Lemuel H. Hazzard Papers

Mansfield Lovell Papers
Theophilus M. Magaw Papers
James M. McClintock Papers
Edward E. Schweitzer Papers
Lionel Allen Sheldon Collection
Thomas William Sweeny Papers
Indiana State Library, Indianapolis
Daniel F. Griffin Papers
Indiana University, Manuscripts Department, Lilly Library, Bloomington
Frederick E. Pimper Letters, Pimper Manuscripts
Kentucky Historical Society, Frankfort
Hiram Hawkins Papers
Library of Congress, Manuscripts Division, Washington, D.C.
Breckinridge Long Papers
Marshall Mortimer Miller Papers
Orlando Metcalfe Poe Papers
William T. Sherman Papers
Gilbert Thompson Journal
Louis Trezevant Wigfall Family Papers
Lincoln Memorial University, Abraham Lincoln Library and Museum,
    Harrogate, Tennessee
Owen Francis Letter, Miscellaneous Manuscripts and Papers
Oliver Otis Howard Papers
Louisiana State University, Louisiana and Lower Mississippi Valley
    Collection, Baton Rouge
Isaac Gaillard Foster Diary, James Foster and Family Correspondence
Wayne Johnson Jacobs Diaries and Lists
Massachusetts Historical Society, Boston
James M. Thurston Papers
Miami University, Special Collections, Oxford, Ohio
Edwin Witherby Brown, "Under a Poncho with Grant and Sherman"
Minnesota Historical Society, Saint Paul
Christie Family Letters
Mississippi Department of Archives and History, Jackson
Robert J. Cull, comp., "The Civil War Letters of George S. Lea,
    1861–1864"
Jim Huffman, comp., "Pre– & Civil War Letters of Lt. Col. Columbus
    Sykes 16th [sic] Regiment, Mississippi Infantry"
R. A. Jarman, "The History of Company K, 27th Mississippi Infantry, and
    Its First and Last Muster Rolls"
George W. Modil Papers
Mississippi State University, Special Collections, Starkville
John H. Marshall Letters
S. P. Raymond Letters

Emmett Ross Papers
William E. Sykes Papers
Missouri History Museum, Saint Louis
David Allan Jr. Letters
William R. Donaldson Papers
Hiffman Family Papers
William Charles Pfeffer Diary
George Frederick Renner Letter, Treutler Family Papers
John J. Safely Letters, McEwen Family Papers
Alpheus C. Williams Diary
Museum of the Confederacy, Richmond, Virginia
Irving Buck Papers
National Archives and Records Administration, Washington, D.C.
17th Army Corps Letters Sent, entry 6363, vol. 20/79, pt. 2, Records of
United States Continental Commands, Polyonymous Succession of
Commands, 1861–1870, RG 393
Court-Martial Case Files, Thomas W. Sweeny, File LL-2995, RG 153,
Records of the Office of the Judge Advocate General, Army, 1809–1894
H. D. Lampley Service Record, 45th Alabama, M311, Compiled Service
Records of Confederate Soldiers Who Served in Organizations from
the State of Alabama, RG 109
"Records Cleburnes Div Hardees Corps A of Tenn," chap. 2, no. 265, RG 109
Navarro College, Pearce Civil War Collection, Corsicana, Texas
William McCulloch Newell Papers
Newberry Library, Chicago, Illinois
Richard Realf Letters and Poems
New-York Historical Society, New York
Belknap Family Papers
New York Public Library, New York
U.S. Sanitary Commission Records
New York State Library, Albany
George Rolfe Diaries
Ohio Historical History, Archives/Library, Columbus
A. S. Bloomfield Civil War Letters
John W. Griffith Diaries
Old Court House Museum, Vicksburg, Mississippi
Philip Roesch Memorandum
Princeton University, Rare Books and Special Collections, Princeton,
New Jersey
William Worth Belknap Papers
Rutherford B. Hayes Presidential Center, Fremont, Ohio
Alvah Stone Skilton Diary, Skilton-Davis-Heyman Family Papers
Lydia Norton Russell Chase Slocum Letters

South Carolina Historical Society, Charleston
  Samuel Wragg Ferguson Memoirs
State Archives of Florida, Tallahassee
  William McLeod Civil War Pocket Diary
State Historical Society of Iowa, Des Moines
  Grenville Mellen Dodge Papers
State Historical Society of Missouri, Research Center Columbia
  William H. Lynch Diaries
  A. W. Reese, "Personal Recollections of the Late Civil War in the United
    States," 1870
Syracuse University, Special Collections Research Center, Syracuse, New York
  Albert M. Cook Papers
Tennessee State Library and Archives, Nashville
  Benjamin F. Cheatham Papers
  James A. Hall Letters, Walter King Hoover Collection
  Bradford Nichol, "Civil War Memoir, 1901"
  D. L. Smythe Letters, Civil War Collection
Toledo–Lucas County Historical Society, Toledo, Ohio
  McPherson Papers
U.S. Army Military History Institute, Carlisle, Pennsylvania
  James H. Bradd Papers
  Brigham Foster Papers
  Gordon Hickenlooper, ed., "The Reminiscences of General Andrew
    Hickenlooper, 1861–1865," *Civil War Times Illustrated* Collection
  Joshua W. Mewborn Papers
U.S. Military Academy, Special Collections and Archives Division, West Point,
    New York
  James Birdseye McPherson Papers
University of Alabama, W. Stanley Hoole Special Collections Library,
    Tuscaloosa
  Henry De Lamar Clayton Sr. Papers
University of Arkansas, Special Collections, Fayetteville
  William Stephen Ray Memoir
University of California, Special Collections, Santa Barbara
  Harrison Wilson Civil War Collection
University of Georgia, Hargrett Rare Book and Manuscript Library, Athens
  William J. Dickey Papers
  Robert Goodwin Mitchell Papers
University of Iowa, Special Collections, Iowa City
  Charles Thomas Ackley Civil War Letters
  David James Palmer Papers
University of Michigan, William L. Clements Library, Ann Arbor
  Clement Abner Boughton Papers

University of Mississippi, Archives and Special Collections, Oxford
    Winfield Scott Featherston Collection
    Jesse L. Henderson Civil War Diary
University of North Carolina, Southern History Collection, Chapel Hill
    Edward W. Allen Papers
    Taylor Beatty Diaries
    Clayton Family Papers
    Joseph B. Cumming Recollections
    Daniel Chevilette Govan Papers
    George Anderson Mercer Diary
    Benedict Joseph Semmes Papers
University of Notre Dame, Special Collections, South Bend, Indiana
    Henry H. Maley Letters
University of Oklahoma, Western History Collections, Norman
    Abraham J. Seay Collection
University of Southern Mississippi, Archives, Hattiesburg
    Mark Perrin Lowrey Autobiographical Essay
    Dr. P. F. Whitehead Letters
University of Tennessee, Special Collections, Chattanooga
    Philip R. Ward Diary, Charles S. Harris Collection
University of Tennessee, Special Collections, Knoxville
    Tilghman Blazer Collection
    C. W. Clark Jr., "My Grandfather's Diary of the War"
    James B. David Diary
    Thomas Doak Edington Papers
    Michael Houck Diary
    Robert T. Jones Papers
    Edwin Hansford Rennolds Sr. Papers
    Julius E. Thomas Civil War Diary
    T. J. Walker Reminiscences
    John Watkins Papers
University of Tennessee, Special Collections, Martin
    Van Buren Oldham Diary
University of Washington, Special Collections, Seattle
    M. F. Force Papers
University of Wyoming, American Heritage Center, Laramie
    Mendal C. Churchill Papers
    Edward B. Moore Diary and Correspondence
Vicksburg National Military Park, Vicksburg, Mississippi
    Battery H, 1st Illinois Light Artillery Folder
Virginia Historical Society, Richmond
    James Madison Brannock Papers
    James Miller Wysor Letters

Western Reserve Historical Society, Cleveland, Ohio
    Albert Gaillard Hart Papers
    James E. Taylor Letter, Western Reserve Manuscripts
Wisconsin Historical Society, Madison
    Charles A. Booth Journal
    George A. Cooley Civil War Diary
    Alonzo Miller Papers
    Levi H. Nickel Diary
    John H. Roberts Civil War Letters
    Charles M. Smith Papers

Newspapers

Army and Navy Journal
Charleston Mercury
Chattanooga Daily Rebel
Chicago Daily Tribune
Columbia Carolinian
Daily Confederate (Raleigh)
Harper's Weekly
Keokuk (IA) Daily Gate City
Louisville Daily Journal
Nashville Union and American
Newark (OH) True American
New York Daily Tribune
New York Times
Savannah Republican
Weekly Ottumwa (IA) Courier
Western Reserve Chronicle (Warren, OH)

Websites

Huff, Sara. "My 80 Years in Atlanta." (1937). http://www.arteryatl.org/uploads/1/2/5/0/125073152/my80yearsinatlanta_all.pdf.

Judt, Daniel. "Atlanta's Civil War Monument, Minus the Pro-Confederate Bunkum." *The Atlantic*, March 17, 2019. www.theatlantic.com/ideas/archive/2019/03/how-atlanta-cyclorama-lost-its-confederate-overtone/584938/.

Smith, Ron, trans. "The Civil War Diaries of Mifflin Jennings, 11th Iowa Infantry." Iowa in the Civil War. Last update April 4, 2009. http://iagenweb.org/civilwar/books/mifflinj.htm.

Truman, W. L. "Memoirs of the Civil War." www.cedarcroft.com/cw/memoir/index.html.

Articles and Books

Abernethy, Byron R., ed. *Private Elisha Stockwell, Jr., Sees the Civil War*. Norman: University of Oklahoma Press, 1958.

Adams, Robert N. "The Battle and Capture of Atlanta." In *Glimpses of the Nation's Struggle, Fourth Series: Papers Read before the Minnesota Commandery of the Military Order of the Loyal Legion of the United States, 1892–1897*, 144–163. Wilmington, NC: Broadfoot, 1992.

Alexander, Andrew J. "The Battle of Atlanta: Sherman's Whip-cracker on the March to the Sea." *Philadelphia Weekly Press*, June 8, 1887.

Allen, Stacy Dale, ed. *On the Skirmish Line behind a Friendly Tree: The Civil Memoirs of William Royal Oake, 26th Iowa Volunteers*. Helena, MT: Farcountry, 2006.

Allen, W. W. "Death of Gen. McPherson: A Circumstantial Account of the Tragedy of July 22, 1864." *National Tribune*, September 4, 1902.

Anders, Leslie. *The Eighteenth Missouri*. Indianapolis: Bobbs-Merrill, 1968.

———. "Fisticuffs at Headquarters: Sweeny vs. Dodge." *Civil War Times Illustrated* 15, no. 10 (February 1977): 8–15.

Anderson, Matthew, ed. *"Dear Sister Sadie": The Letters of David W. Poak, 30th Illinois Infantry, during the Civil War, also the Diary of Edward Grow and Letters of Henry M. McLain*. North Charleston, SC: CreateSpace, 2013.

Arbuckle, John C. *Civil War Experiences of a Foot-Soldier Who Marched with Sherman*. Columbus, OH, 1930.

Aten, Henry J. *History of the Eighty-Fifth Regiment, Illinois Volunteer Infantry*. Hiawatha, KS: Henry J. Aten, 1901.

"The Atlanta Campaign." *National Tribune*, December 15, 1887.

Ayres, W. S. "The 78th Ohio at Bald Hill." *National Tribune*, January 17, 1884.

Bailey, George W. *A Private Chapter of the War (1861–65)*. St. Louis: G. I. Jones, 1880.

Bakhaus, William. "Logan at Atlanta: How Narrowly He Escaped the Fate of Gen. McPherson." *National Tribune*, April 28, 1887.

Barlow, John W. "Personal Reminiscences of the War." In *War Papers: Being Papers Read before the Commandery of the State of Wisconsin, Military Order of the Loyal Legion of the United States*, 1: 106–119. Wilmington, NC: Broadfoot, 1993.

Barnard, George N. *Photographic Views of Sherman's Campaign*. New York: Dover, 1977.

Barton, R. H. "McPherson's Death." *National Tribune*, September 10, 1885.

"Battle of Atlanta": Cyclorama Building, Market St., bet. State House & Soldiers' Monument. Indianapolis: Sentinel Printing, [1888].

Bauer, K. Jack, ed. *Soldiering: The Civil War Diary of Rice C. Bull, 123rd New York Volunteer Infantry*. San Rafael, CA: Presidio, 1977.

Beard, Richard. "An Incident of the Battle of Atlanta, July 26 [*sic*], 1864." In *Battles and Sketches of the Army of Tennessee*, by Bromfield L. Ridley, 324–327. Mexico, MO: Missouri Printing, 1906.

———. "McPherson's Fate." *Nashville Union and American*, June 27, 1875.

Belknap, William W. "The Obedience and Courage of the Private Soldier." In *War Sketches and Incidents as Related By Companions of the Iowa Commandery, Military Order of the Loyal Legion of the United States*, 1:157–171. Wilmington, NC: Broadfoot, 1994.

Bennett, Stewart, and Barbara Tillery, eds. *The Struggle for the Life of the Republic:*

A Civil War Narrative by Brevet Major Charles Dana Miller, 76th Ohio Volunteer Infantry. Kent, OH: Kent State University Press, 2004.

Bishop, W. P. "Twenty-Ninth Tennessee Infantry." In *The Military Annals of Tennessee, Confederate*, edited by John Berrien Lindsley, 433–441. Spartanburg, SC: Reprint Company, 1974.

Black, Samuel. *A Soldier's Recollections of the Civil War*. Minco, OK: Minco Minstrel, 1912.

Black, Wilfred W., ed. "Marching with Sherman through Georgia and the Carolinas: Civil War Diary of Jesse L. Dozer." *Georgia Historical Quarterly* 52, no. 3 (September 1968): 308–331.

Bloomfield, Ira J. "Colonel Bloomfield's Recollections." *National Tribune*, September 13, 1883.

Bonds, Russell S. *War like the Thunderbolt: The Battle and Burning of Atlanta*. Yardley, PA: Westholme, 2009.

Bonner, James C., ed. *The Journal of a Milledgeville Girl, 1861–1867*. Athens: University of Georgia Press, 1964.

Booth, Willis H. "Battle of Atlanta." *National Tribune*, December 8, 1892.

Boring, B. F. "A Criticism: Comrade Boring Thinks Gen. Sherman Showed Bad Generalship When Fighting Hood." *National Tribune*, July 5, 1894.

Bosworth, John S. "The Battle of Atlanta." *Blue and Gray* 2, no. 3 (September 1893): 236–238.

———. "The Battle of Atlanta." In *Under Both Flags: A Panorama of the Great Civil War*, 162–164. Chicago: National Book Concern, 1896.

———. "The Day That McPherson Fell and Belknap Won His Stars." *National Tribune*, August 30, 1883.

———. "McPherson's Death." *National Tribune*, September 27, 1883.

Boynton, H. V. *Sherman's Historical Raid: The Memoirs in the Light of the Record*. Cincinnati: Wilstach, Baldwin, 1875.

Brackett, Albert G. "Capture of Murray's Battery at Atlanta." *National Tribune*, December 16, 1886.

Bradford, J. H. "The Fighting Not All Done by the 12th and 16th Wisconsin Regiments." *National Tribune*, November 15, 1883.

Bragg, William Harris. *Joe Brown's Army: The Georgia State Line, 1862–1865*. Macon, GA: Mercer University Press, 1987.

Brittin, D. S. "Who Saved the Trains at Decatur?" *National Tribune*, July 19, 1883.

Brown, Harry James, and Frederick D. Williams, eds. *The Diary of James A. Garfield*. 4 vols. Lansing: Michigan State University Press, 1973.

Brown, J. L. "The 78th Ohio in Close Quarters." *National Tribune*, February 21, 1884.

Brown, Joseph M. *The Mountain Campaigns of Georgia; or, War Scenes on the W. and A*. Buffalo, NY: Art-Printing Works of Matthews, Northrup, 1890.

Brown, Norman D., ed. *One of Cleburne's Command: The Civil War Reminiscences and Diary of Capt. Samuel T. Foster, Granbury's Texas Brigade, CSA*. Austin: University of Texas Press, 1980.

Brown, Russell K. *"Our Connection with Savannah": History of the First Battalion Georgia Sharpshooters, 1862–1865*. Macon, GA: Mercer University Press, 2004.

———. *To the Manner Born: The Life of General William H. T. Walker*. Athens: University of Georgia Press, 1994.

Brown, W. T. "Gen. McPherson's Death: A 30th Ill. Man Tells What He Knows about It." *National Tribune*, December 5, 1895.

Buck, Irving A. *Cleburne and His Command*. Jackson, TN: McCowat-Mercer, 1959.

Cabaniss, Jim R., ed. *Civil War Journal and Letters of Serg. Washington Ives, 4th Florida C.S.A.* N.p., 1987.

Calhoun, Charles W. *Gilded Age Cato: The Life of Walter Q. Gresham*. Lexington: University Press of Kentucky, 1988.

Cander, F. P. "Before Atlanta, and the Part That the Eleventh Iowa Played There." *National Tribune*, November 8, 1883.

Cannon, J. P. *Inside of Rebeldom: The Daily Life of a Private in the Confederate Army*. Washington, D.C.: National Tribune, 1900.

"Capture of the DeGress Battery—The Question Settled." *National Tribune*, July 19, 1883.

Case, Frederick B., Jr. "The 15th Mich. at Atlanta." *National Tribune*, February 17, 1887.

Cash, William M., and Lucy Somerville Howorth, eds. *My Dear Nellie: The Civil War Letters of William L. Nugent to Eleanor Smith Nugent*. Jackson: University Press of Mississippi, 1977.

Castel, Albert. *Decision in the West: The Atlanta Campaign of 1864*. Lawrence: University Press of Kansas, 1992.

———. *Tom Taylor's Civil War*. Lawrence: University Press of Kansas, 2000.

———. "The War Album of Henry Dwight, Pt. 4." *Civil War Times Illustrated* 19, no. 3 (June 1980): 32–37.

Cate, Wirt Armistead, ed. *Two Soldiers: The Campaign Diaries of Thomas J. Key, C.S.A., and Robert J. Campbell, U.S.A.* Chapel Hill: University of North Carolina Press, 1938.

Catton, Bruce. "The Battle of Atlanta." *Georgia Review* 10, no. 3 (Fall 1956): 256–264.

Chamberlin, W. H. "Hood's Second Sortie at Atlanta." In *Battles and Leaders of the Civil War*, edited by Robert Underwood Johnson and Clarence Clough Buel, 4:326–331. New York: Thomas Yoseloff, 1956.

———. "Recollections of the Battle of Atlanta." In *Sketches of War History, 1861–1865: Papers Prepared for the Commandery of the State of Ohio, Military Order of the Loyal Legion of the United States, 1903–1908*, 6: 276–286. Wilmington, NC: Broadfoot, 1992.

Childress, G. L. "Before Atlanta: The Recapture of DeGress's Battery and the Bursting of the Gun." *National Tribune*, August 18, 1887.

Cisco, Walter Brian. *States Rights Gist: A South Carolina General of the Civil War*. Shippensburg, PA: White Mane, 1991.

Clarke, John T. "With Sherman in Georgia." *Bulletin of the Missouri Historical Society* 8, no. 4 (July 1952): 356–370.

Cochran, J. O. *Battle of Atlanta: Story of the Cyclorama, Johnston-Sherman Campaign, and History of the Engine "Texas."* N.p., 1917.

Compton, James. "The Second Division of the 16th Army Corps, in the Atlanta Campaign." In *Glimpses of the Nation's Struggle, Fifth Series: Papers Read before the Minnesota Commandery of the Military Order of the Loyal Legion of the United States, 1897–1902,* 103–123. Wilmington, NC: Broadfoot, 1992.

"Comrades in War." *Confederate Veteran* 34 (1926): 87.

Connelly, Thomas Lawrence. *Autumn of Glory: The Army of Tennessee, 1862–1865.* Baton Rouge: Louisiana State University Press, 1971.

Connelly, Thomas W. *History of the Seventieth Ohio Regiment.* Cincinnati, OH: Peak Brothers, 1902.

Cotter, Holland. "A Victory for the Civil War 'Cyclorama.'" *New York Times,* February 22, 2019.

Cox, Jacob D. *Atlanta.* New York: Charles Scribner's Sons, 1882.

Crummel, A. B. "DeGrasse's Battery." *National Tribune,* September 10, 1885.

Cryder, George R., and Stanley R. Miller, comps. *A View from the Ranks: The Civil War Diaries of Charles E. Smith.* Delaware, OH: Delaware County Historical Society, 1999.

Daniel, Larry J. *Cannoneers in Gray: The Field Artillery of the Army of Tennessee, 1861–1865.* Tuscaloosa: University of Alabama Press, 1984.

———. *Conquered: Why the Army of Tennessee Failed.* Chapel Hill: University of North Carolina Press, 2019.

Davis, Keith F. *George N. Barnard: Photographer of Sherman's Campaign.* Kansas City, MO: Hallmark Cards, 1990.

Davis, Robert Scott, Jr., ed. *Requiem for a Lost City: A Memoir of Civil War Atlanta and the Old South.* Macon, GA: Mercer University Press, 1999.

Davis, Stephen. *Texas Brigadier to the Fall of Atlanta: John Bell Hood.* Macon, GA: Mercer University Press, 2019.

Davis, Theo R. "A War Artist at Vicksburg." *Blue and Gray* 2, no. 1 (July 1893): 7–9.

———. "A War Artist at Vicksburg." In *Under Both Flags: A Panorama of the Great Civil War,* 99–101. Chicago: National Book Concern, 1896.

Davis, William C. *The Orphan Brigade: The Kentucky Confederates Who Couldn't Go Home.* Garden City, NY: Doubleday, 1980.

Dawson, George Francis. *Life and Services of Gen. John A. Logan, as Soldier and Statesman.* Chicago: Bedford, Clarke, 1887.

Delany, Frank P. "Leggett's Hill: Where Iowa and Wisconsin Fought Cleburne's Hard Fighters." *National Tribune,* November 9, 1905.

Deupree, J. G. "The Noxubee Squadron of the First Mississippi Cavalry, C.S.A., 1861–1865." In *Publications of the Mississippi Historical Society,* Centenary Series, 2 (1918): 12–143.

Dodge, Grenville M. "Battle of Atlanta: The Terrible Struggle of July 22, 1864—Hood's Desperate Attempt to Turn Sherman's Left, and Drive Him Back from Atlanta." *National Tribune,* September 1, 1904.

———. "The Battle of Atlanta Fought July 22, 1864." In *The Battle of Atlanta and Other Campaigns, Addresses, Etc.*, 39–51. Denver, CO: Sage Books, 1965.

———. "Letter to General Raum." In *Battle of Atlanta and Other Campaigns*, 53–61.

———. *Personal Recollections of President Abraham Lincoln, General Ulysses S. Grant, and General William T. Sherman*. Denver, CO: Sage Books, 1965.

———. "Stories of Sherman: Gen. G. M. Dodge Entertains an Iowa Campfire with Unpublished Incidents of the War." *National Tribune*, June 12, 1902.

Dodson, W. C., ed. *Campaigns of Wheeler and His Cavalry, 1862–1865*. Atlanta, GA: Hudgins, 1899.

Donaldson, J. R. "Sweeny's Fighters: Plenty of Work for Them on July 22, 1864, at Atlanta." *National Tribune*, May 19, 1898.

Douglas, Lucia Rutherford, ed. *Douglas's Texas Battery, CSA*. Tyler, TX: Smith County Historical Society, 1966.

Doyle, Timothy W. "Gen. McPherson's Death." *National Tribune*, October 6, 1892.

Drake, Edwin L., ed. *Chronological Summary of Battles and Engagements of the Western Armies of the Confederate States, including Summary of Lt. Gen. Joseph Wheeler's Cavalry Engagements*. Nashville: Tavel, Eastman, & Howell, 1879.

Duke, John K. *History of the Fifty-Third Regiment Ohio Volunteer Infantry, during the War of the Rebellion, 1861 to 1865*. Portsmouth, OH: Blade Printing, 1900.

Durham, Roger S., ed. *The Blues in Gray: The Civil War Journal of William Daniel Dixon and the Republican Blues Daybook*. Knoxville: University of Tennessee Press, 2000.

Dwight, Henry O. "The Battle of July 22." *New York Times*. August 12, 1864.

Dyer, Thomas C. *Secret Yankees: The Union Circle in Confederate Atlanta*. Baltimore: Johns Hopkins University Press, 1999.

Ecelbarger, Gary. *Black Jack Logan: An Extraordinary Life in Peace & War*. Guilford, CT: Lyons, 2005.

———. *The Day Dixie Died: The Battle of Atlanta*. New York: St. Martin's, 2010.

Elliott, Colleen Morse, and Louise Armstrong Moxley, eds. *The Tennessee Civil War Veterans Questionnaires*. 5 vols. Easley, SC: Southern Historical, 1985.

Evans, David. "The Fight for the Wagons." *Civil War Times Illustrated* 26, no. 10 (February 1988): 16–22.

Evans, E. Chris, ed. "Report of the Battle of Atlanta by Capt. Francis DeGress Commanding Battery H, 1st Illinois Light Artillery." *Blue & Gray Magazine* 11, no. 4 (April 1994): 28–30.

Fehrenbaker, J. F. "Capture of the Regular Battery at Atlanta." *National Tribune*, November 28, 1886.

Fish, Charles H. "'Uncle Billy's' Praise: Signal Corps Invaluable in Many Ways on Sherman's Raid." *National Tribune*, February 6, 1896.

"5,000 Killed in Battle of Atlanta." *Atlanta Journal Magazine*, July 27, 1941.

Fleming, James R. *Band of Brothers: Company C, 9th Tennessee Infantry*. Shippensburg, PA: White Mane, 1996.

Fout, Frederick W. *The Dark Days of the Civil War, 1861 to 1865*. F. A. Wagenfuehr, 1904.

Fowler, James, and Miles M. Miller. *History of the Thirtieth Iowa Infantry Volunteers.* Mediapolis, IA: T. A. Merrill, 1908.

Frankenberry, A. D. "Visiting War Scenes: Reminiscences of a United State Signal Corps Man." Part 4. *National Tribune,* January 30, 1896.

Franklin, Ann York, comp. *The Civil War Diaries of Capt. Alfred Tyler Fielder, 12th Tennessee Regiment Infantry, Company B, 1861–1865.* Louisville, KY: Ann York Franklin, 1996.

Frano, Elizabeth Coldwell, ed. *Letters of Captain Hugh Black to His Family in Florida during the War between the States, 1862–1864.* Evansville, IN: Evansville Bindery, 1998.

Frazcr, C. W. "Fifth Confederate." In *The Military Annals of Tennessee, Confederate,* edited by John Berrien Lindsley, 146–153. Spartanburg, SC: Reprint Company, 1974.

French, Samuel G. *Two Wars: An Autobiography.* Nashville, TN: Confederate Veteran, 1901.

Fuller, John W. "A Terrible Day." *National Tribune,* April 16, 1885.

Gage, M. D. "The Battle of Atlanta: A Vivid Remembrance of That Stormful and Stressful July 22, 1864." *National Tribune,* August 5, 1909.

Garrett, Franklin M. "Civilian Life in Atlanta." *Civil War Times Illustrated* 3, no. 4 (July 1964): 30–33.

Gates, Arnold, ed. *The Rough Side of War: The Civil War Journal of Chesley A. Mosman.* Garden City, NY: Basin, 1987.

"Gen. James Wilson: Late Provost Marshal, Army of the Tennessee." *Iowa Historical Record* 3, no. 3 (July 1887): 481–496.

"Gen. McPherson's Death." *National Tribune,* October 1, 1881.

Gibbons, A. R. *The Recollections of an Old Confederate Soldier.* Shelbyville, MO, n.d.

Goodwin, B. F. "In Atlanta's Front: A Wisconsin Boy Details Some Experience of July 22." *National Tribune,* August 15, 1895.

Grainger, Gervis D. *Four Years with the Boys in Gray.* Franklin, KY: Favorite Office, 1902.

Grant, Frederick D. "A Boy's Experience at Vicksburg." In *Personal Recollections of the War of the Rebellion: Addresses Delivered before the Commandery of the State of New York, Military Order of the Loyal Legion of the United States,* 3rd ser., 86–100. Wilmington, NC: Broadfoot, 1992.

Gresham, Matilda. *Life of Walter Quintin Gresham, 1832–1895.* 2 vols. Chicago: Rand McNally, 1919.

Hafendorfer, Kenneth, ed. *Civil War Journal of William L. Trask: Confederate Sailor and Soldier.* Louisville, KY: KH, 2003.

Haldeman, J. B. "Other Versions." *National Tribune,* June 28, 1883.

Hammond, M. F. "Charge at Atlanta: A 16th Wis. Comrade Describes His Regiment's Part." *National Tribune,* June 30, 1898.

Hamrick, W. G. "The Sixteenth Corps at Atlanta." *National Tribune,* September 13, 1883.

Harwell, Richard Barksdale, ed. *Kate: The Journal of a Confederate Nurse*. Baton Rouge: Louisiana State University Press, 1959.

Harwood, Thomas. "The Fight at Decatur, July 22, 1864." In *The War of the 'Sixties*, compiled by E. R. Hutchins, 236–238. New York: Neale, 1912.

Hawes, Lilla Mills, ed. "The Memoirs of Charles H. Olmstead." Part 10. *Georgia Historical Quarterly* 45, no. 1 (March 1961): 42–56.

Hay, Thomas Robson. "The Atlanta Campaign." *Georgia Historical Quarterly* 7, no. 1 (March 1923): 18–43.

Hedley, F. Y. *Marching through Georgia*. Chicago: Donohue, Henneberry, 1890.

Helmkamp, C. P. "Before Atlanta." *National Tribune*, September 9, 1909.

Hess, Earl J. "Alvin P. Hovey and Abraham Lincoln's 'Broken Promises': The Politics of Promotion." *Indiana Magazine of History* 80, no. 1 (March 1984): 35–50.

———. *The Battle of Ezra Church and the Struggle for Atlanta*. Chapel Hill: University of North Carolina Press, 2015.

———. *The Battle of Peach Tree Creek: Hood's First Effort to Save Atlanta*. Chapel Hill: University of North Carolina Press, 2017.

———. *Civil War Infantry Tactics: Training, Combat, and Small-Unit Effectiveness*. Baton Rouge: Louisiana State University Press, 2015.

———. *Civil War Supply and Strategy: Feeding Men and Moving Armies*. Baton Rouge: Louisiana State University Press, 2020.

———. *Fighting for Atlanta: Tactics, Terrain, and Trenches in the Civil War*. Chapel Hill: University of North Carolina Press, 2018.

———. *Kennesaw Mountain: Sherman, Johnston, and the Atlanta Campaign*. Chapel Hill: University of North Carolina Press, 2013.

Hight, John J. *History of the Fifty-Eighth Regiment of Indiana Volunteer Infantry*. Princeton, IN: Press of the Clarion, 1895.

Historical Sketch of the Chicago Board of Trade Battery, Horse Artillery, Illinois Volunteers. Chicago: Henneberry, 1902.

History of the Fifteenth Regiment, Iowa Veteran Volunteer Infantry. Keokuk, IA: R. S. Ogden & Son, 1887.

History of the Organization, Marches, Campings, General Services, and Final Muster Out of Battery M, First Regiment Illinois Light Artillery. Princeton, IL: Mercer & Dean, 1892.

Hogan, Sally Coplen, ed. *General Reub Williams's Memories of Civil War Times*. Westminster, MD: Heritage Books, 2004.

"Honor to Gen. W. H. T. Walker." *Confederate Veteran* 10 (1902): 402–407.

Hood, J. B. *Advance and Retreat: Personal Experiences in the United States and Confederate States Armies*. New Orleans: Hood Orphan Memorial Fund, 1880.

Hord, L. D. "An Atlanta Experience: Recollections of a Rather Lively July Day in '64." *National Tribune*, January 19, 1899.

Howard, E. "Murray's Battery: Concerning its Capture in the Battle Before Atlanta." *National Tribune*, January 13, 1887.

Howard, O. O. "The Battles about Atlanta." *Atlantic Monthly* 38, no. 228 (October 1876): 385–399.

———. "In Memoriam—Lieutenant-General John M. Schofield, U.S.A." In *Personal Recollections of the War of the Rebellion: Addresses Delivered before the Commandery of the State of New York, Military Order of the Loyal Legion of the United States, Third Series*, 438–447. Wilmington, NC: Broadfoot, 1992.

———. "The Struggle for Atlanta." In *Battles and Leaders of the Civil War*, edited by Robert Underwood Johnson and Clarence Clough Buel, 4:293–325. New York: Thomas Yoseloff, 1956.

Howe, M. A. DeWolfe, ed. *Marching with Sherman: Passages from the Letters and Campaign Diaries of Henry Hitchcock, Major and Assistant Adjutant General of Volunteers, November 1864–May 1865*. Lincoln: University of Nebraska Press, 1995.

Hubbart, Phillip A., ed. *An Iowa Soldier Writes Home: The Civil War Letters of Union Private Daniel J. Parvin*. Durham, NC: Carolina Academic Press, 2011.

Hughes, Nathaniel Cheairs, Jr., ed. *The Civil War Memoir of Philip Daingerfield Stephenson, D. D.* Conway: University of Central Arkansas Press, 1995.

"Incidents of Gen. McPherson's Death." *Confederate Veteran* 11 (1903): 118–119.

Ingersoll, Lurton Dunham. *Iowa and the Rebellion*. Dubuque, IA: B. M. Harger, 1866.

Jackson, Oscar L. *The Colonel's Diary*. N.p., n.d.

Jamieson, Alma Hill. "The Cyclorama of the Battle of Atlanta." *Atlanta Historical Bulletin* 10 (July 1937): 58–75.

Johnson, Crosby. "The Battle of Atlanta." *National Tribune*, June 10, 1886.

Jones, Mary Miles, and Leslie Jones Martin, eds. *The Gentle Rebel: The Civil War Letters of 1st Lt. William Harvey Berryhill, Co. D, 43rd Regiment, Mississippi Volunteers*. Yazoo City, MS: Sassafras, 1982.

Jordan, Philip D., ed. "Forty Days with the Christian Commission: A Diary by William Salter." *Iowa Journal of History and Politics* 33, no. 2 (April 1935): 123–154.

Jordan, Weymouth T., ed. "Mathew Andrew Dunn Letters." *Journal of Mississippi History* 1, no. 2 (April 1939): 110–127.

Joslyn, Mauriel Phillips, ed. *Charlotte's Boys: Civil War Letters of the Branch Family of Savannah*. Berryville, VA: Rockbridge, 1996.

Keckler, George W. "Some Recollections: Interesting Episodes of the War Recalled by an Iowa Veteran." *National Tribune*, September 7, 1899.

Keim, B. Randolph. "The Life and Character of Major-General James B. McPherson." *United States Service Magazine* 2 (October 1864): 367–381.

Key, William. *The Battle of Atlanta and the Georgia Campaign*. New York: Twayne, 1958.

Kimbell, Charles B. *History of Battery "A," First Illinois Light Artillery Volunteers*. Chicago: Cushing Printing, 1899.

Kirk, Charles H., ed. *History of the Fifteenth Pennsylvania Volunteer Cavalry, Which Was Recruited and Known as the Anderson Cavalry in the Rebellion of 1861–1865*. Philadelphia, 1906.

Kirwan, A. D., ed. *Johnny Green of the Orphan Brigade: The Journal of a Confederate Soldier*. Lexington: University Press of Kentucky, 1956.

Kurtz, Wilbur G. *The Atlanta Cyclorama: The Story of the Famed Battle of Atlanta*. Atlanta: City of Atlanta, 1966.

———. "At the Troup Hurt House." *Atlanta Constitution*, January 25, 1931.

———. "The Augustus F. Hurt House." *Atlanta Constitution Magazine*, June 22, 1930.

———. "The Broken Line and the DeGress Battery." *Atlanta Constitution*, February 8, 1931.

———. "The Death of Major General W. H. T. Walker, July 22, 1864." *Civil War History* 6, no. 2 (June 1960): 174–179.

———. "Major-General W. H. T. Walker." *Atlanta Constitution*, July 27, 1930.

———. "McPherson's Last Ride." *Atlanta Constitution Magazine*, June 29, 1930.

———. "Walter Q. Gresham at Atlanta." *Atlanta Constitution*, August 24, 1930.

Leggett, M. D. "Battle of Atlanta." *National Tribune*, May 6, 1886.

———. "Battle of Atlanta." *National Tribune*, May 13, 1886.

Little, George, and James R. Maxwell. *A History of Lumsden's Battery, C.S.A.* Tuscaloosa, AL: R. E. Rhodes Chapter, United Daughters of the Confederacy, n.d.

Logan, John A. *The Volunteer Soldier of America*. Chicago: R. S. Peale, 1887.

Longacre, Glenn V., and John E. Haas, eds. *To Battle for God and the Right: The Civil War Letterbooks of Emerson Opdycke*. Urbana: University of Illinois Press, 2003.

Loop, M. B. "Sounding the Alarm: The 68th Ohio's Trying Time at the Battle of Atlanta." *National Tribune*, December 1, 1898.

Lord, Walter. "General Sherman and the Baltimore Belle." *American Heritage* 9, no. 3 (April 1958): 102–104.

Lossing, Benson J. *Pictorial Field Book of the Civil War: Journeys through the Battlefields in the Wake of Conflict*. 3 vols. Baltimore: Johns Hopkins University Press, 1997.

Losson, Christopher. *Tennessee's Forgotten Warriors: Frank Cheatham and His Confederate Division*. Knoxville: University of Tennessee Press, 1989.

Lowrey, M. P. "General M. P. Lowrey: An Autobiography." *Southern Historical Society Papers* 16 (1888): 365–376.

Lucas, D. R. *New History of the 99th Indiana Infantry*. Rockford, IL: Horner Printing, 1900.

Martin, William. *"Out and Forward"; or, Recollections of the War of 1861 to 1865*. Manhattan, KS: Art Craft Printers, 1941.

McCaffrey, James M. *This Band of Heroes: Granbury's Texas Brigade, C.S.A.* College Station: Texas A&M University Press, 1996.

———, ed. *Only a Private: A Texan Remembers the Civil War, The Memoirs of William J. Oliphant*. Houston, TX: Halcyon, 2004.

McCarley, J. Britt. "'Atlanta Is Ours and Fairly Won': A Driving Tour of the Atlanta Area's Principal Civil War Battlefields." *Atlanta Historical Journal* 28, no. 3 (Fall 1984): 7–98.

McCunniff, Thomas. "De Gress's Battery." *National Tribune*, February 2, 1888.

McDonald, Granville B. *A History of the 30th Illinois Volunteer Regiment of Infantry*. Salem, MS: Higginson Book, 1998.

McMurray, W. J. *History of the Twentieth Tennessee Regiment Volunteer Infantry, C.S.A.* Nashville: Publication Committee, 1904.

McMurry, Richard M. *Atlanta 1864.* Lincoln: University of Nebraska Press, 2000.

McNeill, C. D. "Death of Gen. McPherson: A Confederate Eye-Witness Tells of Events before Atlanta, July 22, 1864." *National Tribune*, June 5, 1902.

————. "Recovery of McPherson's Body." *National Tribune*, April 9, 1903.

The Medical and Surgical History of the Civil War. 12 vols. Wilmington, NC: Broadfoot, 1991.

Melville, Herman. *Battle-Pieces and Aspects of the War.* New York: Harper & Brothers, 1866.

Meyer, G. F. C. "Atlanta to Andersonville: From the Firing Line to the Place of Torture by Exposure and Hunger." *National Tribune*, April 21, 1904.

A Military Record of Battery D, First Ohio Veteran Volunteers Light Artillery. Oil City, PA: Derrick, 1908.

Morgan, Jack. *Through American and Irish Wars: The Life and Times of General Thomas W. Sweeny, 1820–1892.* Portland, OR: Irish Academic, 2006.

Morris, W. S., L. D. Hartwell, and J. B. Kuykendall. *History 31st Regiment Illinois Volunteers, Organized by John A. Logan.* Carbondale: Southern Illinois University Press, 1998.

Mulligan, William H., Jr., ed. *A Badger Boy in Blue: The Civil War Letters of Chauncey H. Cooke.* Detroit, MI: Wayne State University Press, 2007.

Munson, Gilbert D. "Battle of Atlanta." In *Sketches of War History, 1861–1865: Papers Prepared for the Ohio Commandery of the Military Order of the Loyal Legion of the United States, 1888–1890,* 3:212–230. Cincinnati: Robert Clarke, 1890.

Myers, J. H. "Atlanta." *National Tribune*, September 2, 1886.

Naylor, J. M. "To the Editor National Tribune." *National Tribune*, June 28, 1883.

Nichols, James L., and Frank Abbott, eds. "Reminiscences of Confederate Service by Wiley A. Washburn." *Arkansas Historical Quarterly* 35, no. 1 (Spring 1976): 47–90.

Ninth Reunion of the 37th Regiment O.V.V.I. Toledo, OH: Montgomery & Vrooman, 1890.

Nisbet, James Cooper. *4 Years on the Firing Line.* Jackson, TN: McCowat-Mercer, 1963.

Nutt, E. E. "Fight at Atlanta: Work of the Seventy-Eighth and Twentieth Ohio That Day." *National Tribune*, January 3, 1884.

Palmer, J. R. "Gen. McPherson's Death." *National Tribune*, July 28, 1892.

Patrick, Jeffrey L., and Robert J. Willey, eds. *Fighting for Liberty and Right: The Civil War Diary of William Bluffton Miller, First Sergeant, Company K, Seventy-Fifth Indiana Volunteer Infantry.* Knoxville: University of Tennessee Press, 2005.

Phillips, Brenda D., ed. *Personal Reminiscences of a Confederate Soldier Boy.* Milledgeville, GA: Boyd, 1993.

Phillips, Ulrich B., ed. *Correspondence of Robert Toombs, Alexander H. Stephens, and Howell Cobb: Annual Report of the American Historical Association for the Year 1911.* 2 vols. Washington: Government Printing Office, 1913.

Portrait Biographical Album of Oakland County, Michigan. Chicago: Chapman Brothers, 1891.

Post, Lydia Minturn, ed. *Soldiers' Letters from Camp, Battle-Field, and Prison*. New York: Bunce & Huntington, 1865.

Proceedings of Crocker's Iowa Brigade at the Eleventh Biennial Reunion. Vol. 9. Cedar Rapids, IA: Record, 1906.

Ralston, Alex. "De Grasse's Battery." *National Tribune*, August 27, 1885.

Ray, Joseph. "Gen. McPherson's Death." *National Tribune*, August 25, 1892.

Report of Robert L. Rodgers, Historian to Atlanta Camp No. 159, U.C.V., on the Capture of the DeGress Battery, and Battery A, 1st Ill. Light Artillery, in the Battle of Atlanta, July 22d, 1864, with Other Papers Bearing Thereon. N.p., n.d.

Report of the Proceedings of the Society of the Army of the Tennessee at the Thirty-Third Meeting Held at Indianapolis, Indiana, November 13–14, 1901. Cincinnati: F. W. Freeman, 1902.

"Return of a Confederate Flag." *Confederate Veteran* 22 (1914): 302.

Reynolds, George. "Gen. McPherson's Death." *National Tribune*, October 1, 1881.

[Rood, Henry H.]. *History of Company "A," Thirteenth Iowa Veteran Infantry, from September 12th, 1861, to July 21st, 1865*. Cedar Rapids, IA: Daily Republican, 1889.

[Rood, Hosea W.]. *Story of the Service of Company E, and of the Twelfth Wisconsin Regiment, Veteran Volunteer Infantry, in the War of the Rebellion*. Milwaukee, WI: Swain & Tate, 1893.

Roth, Margaret Brobst, ed. *Well Mary: Civil War Letters of a Wisconsin Volunteer*. Madison: University of Wisconsin Press 1960.

Rountree, Benjamin. "Letters from a Confederate Soldier." *Georgia Review* 18, no. 3 (Fall 1964): 267–297.

Roy, T. B. "General Hardee and the Military Operations around Atlanta." *Southern Historical Society Papers* 8 (1880): 337–387.

Russell, Robert. "Where McPherson Fell: The General Killed 'On the Road That Went Down through the Timber.'" *National Tribune*, December 5, 1895.

Sanders, Add H. "Gen. Sanders' Sword: Surrendered at Atlanta When the 16th Iowa Was Overwhelmed by Numbers, He Now Seeks to Recover It." *National Tribune*, January 10, 1901.

Sauers, Richard A. Comp. *The National Tribune Civil War Index: A Guide to the Weekly Newspaper Dedicated to Civil War Veterans, 1877–1943*. 3 vols. El Dorado Hills, CA: Savas Beatie, 2017, 2019.

Saunier, Joseph A., ed. *A History of the Forty-Seventh Regiment Ohio Veteran Volunteer Infantry*. Hillsboro, OH: Lyle Printing, [1903].

Scarborough, William Kauffman, ed. *The Diary of Edmund Ruffin*. 3 vols. Baton Rouge: Louisiana State University Press, 1972–1989.

Schofield, John M. *Forty-Six Years in the Army*. New York: Century, 1897.

Schroeder-Lein, Glenna R. *Confederate Hospitals on the Move: Samuel H. Stout and the Army of Tennessee*. Columbia: University of South Carolina Press, 1994.

Sears, Stephen W. *Chancellorsville*. Boston: Houghton Mifflin, 1996.

Shadley, L. "Who Recaptured the De Gress Battery?" *National Tribune*, June 14, 1883.

Sharland, George. *Knapsack Notes of Sherman's Campaign through the State of Georgia*. Springfield, IL: Johnson & Bradford, 1865.

Sheldon, Charles Sargeant. *Personal Recollections of the 18th Missouri Infantry in the War for the Union*. Unionville, MO: Stille & Lincoln, 1891.

Shelley, Thomas J. "The Battle of July 22 as Seen by an 81st Ohio Comrade." *National Tribune*, September 15, 1887.

Sherman, William T. "The Grand Strategy of the Last Year of the War." In *Battles and Leaders of the Civil War*, edited by Richard Underwood Johnson and Clarence Clough Buel, 4: 247–259. New York: Thomas Yoseloff, 1956.

———. *Memoirs*. 2 vols. New York: D. Appleton, 1875.

Simon, John Y., ed. *The Papers of Ulysses S. Grant*. 28 vols. Carbondale: Southern Illinois University Press, 1967–2005.

Simpson, Brooks D., and Jean V. Berlin, eds. *Sherman's Civil War: Selected Correspondence of William T. Sherman, 1860–1865*. Chapel Hill: University of North Carolina Press, 1999.

Skinner, Arthur N., and James L. Skinner, eds. *The Death of a Confederate: Selections from the Letters of the Archibald Smith Family of Roswell, Georgia, 1864–1956*. Athens: University of Georgia Press, 1996.

Smith, Bobbie Swearingen, ed. *A Palmetto Boy: Civil War–Era Diaries and Letters of James Adams Tillman*. Columbia: University of South Carolina Press, 2010.

Smith, Charles H. *The History of Fuller's Ohio Brigade, 1861–1865*. Cleveland, OH: A. J. Watt, 1909.

Smith, David M., ed. "The Civil War Diary of Colonel John Henry Smith." *Iowa Journal of History* 47, no. 2 (April 1949): 140–170.

Smith, Gustavus W. "The Georgia Militia about Atlanta." In *Battles and Leaders of the Civil War*, edited by Robert Underwood Johnson and Clarence Clough Buel, 4:331–335. New York: Thomas Yoseloff, 1956.

Smith, Hampton, ed. *Brother of Mine: The Civil War Letters of Thomas and William Christie*. St. Paul: Minnesota Historical Society Press, 2011.

Sniff, Amos. "The Capture of the 16th Iowa." *National Tribune*, March 27, 1884.

Speer, W. S. "Battle of Bald Hill: The 78th Ohio Was There, and Had a Lively Time." *National Tribune*, August 22, 1895.

Spurlin, Charles D., ed. *The Civil War Diary of Charles A. Leuschner*. Austin, TX: Eakin, 1992.

Stone, Henry. "The Atlanta Campaign." In *The Mississippi Valley, Tennessee, Georgia, Alabama, 1861–1864: Papers of the Military Historical Society of Massachusetts*, 8:341–492. Wilmington, NC: Broadfoot, 1989.

The Story of the Fifty-Fifth Regiment Illinois Volunteer Infantry in the Civil War, 1861–1865. Clinton, MA: W. J. Coulter, 1887.

Strang, John. "Crocker's Iowa Brigade: How It Fought in the Battle of Atlanta." *National Tribune*, February 24, 1887.

Strong, William E. "The Death of General James B. McPherson." In *Military Essays and Recollections: Papers Read before the Commandery of the State of Illinois, Military Order of the Loyal Legion of the United States*, 1:311–343. Wilmington, NC: Broadfoot, 1992.

Stuart, A. A. *Iowa Colonels and Regiments*. Des Moines, IA: Mills, 1865.

Styple, William B., ed. *Writing and Fighting the Civil War: Soldier Correspondence to the New York Sunday Mercury*. Kearny, NJ: Belle Grove, 2000.

Supplement to the Official Records of the Union and Confederate Armies. 100 vols. Wilmington, NC: Broadfoot, 1993–2000.

Sword, Wiley, ed. "A New Perspective on the Death of Gen. James B. McPherson at Atlanta." *Blue & Gray* 22, no. 5 (2005): 38–40.

Tappan, George, ed. *The Civil War Journal of Lt. Russell M. Tuttle, New York Volunteer Infantry*. Jefferson, NC: McFarland, 2006.

Thoburn, Lyle, ed. *My Experiences during the Civil War*. Cleveland, OH: Lyle Thoburn, 1963.

Thompson, A. J. "McPherson's Death." *National Tribune*, July 23, 1885.

Thompson, Ed Porter. *History of the Orphan Brigade*. Dayton, OH: Morningside, 1973.

Throne, Mildred, ed. "A History of Company D, Eleventh Iowa Infantry, 1861–1865." *Iowa Journal of History* 55, no. 1 (January 1957): 35–90.

Tower, R. Lockwood, ed. *A Carolinian Goes to War: The Civil War Narrative of Arthur Middleton Manigault, Brigadier General, C.S.A.* Columbia: University of South Carolina Press, 1983.

Townsend, Mary Bobbitt. *Yankee Warhorse: A Biography of Major General Peter Osterhaus*. Columbia: University of Missouri Press, 2010.

Tracie, Theodore C. *Annals of the Nineteenth Ohio Battery Volunteer Artillery*. Cleveland, OH: J. B. Savage, 1878.

Tuthill, Richard S. "An Artilleryman's Recollections of the Battle of Atlanta." In *Military Essays and Recollections: Papers Read Before the Commandery of the State of Illinois, Military Order of the Loyal Legion of the United States*, 1:299–309. Chicago: A. C. McClurg, 1891.

Typo. "From the 14th Ohio Battery." *Western Reserve Chronicle* (Warren, OH), August 24, 1864.

Vance, J. W., ed. *Report of the Adjutant General of the State of Illinois*. 8 vols. Springfield, IL: H. W. Rokker, 1886.

Venet, Wendy Hamand, ed. *Sam Richards's Civil War Diary: A Chronicle of the Atlanta Home Front*. Athens: University of Georgia Press, 2009.

Wade, B. R. "The Signal Service: A Sequel to Lieutenant Fish's Story—How McPherson Fell." *National Tribune*, September 13, 1883.

Wade, W. L. "Bald Knob." *National Tribune*, July 3, 1884.

Walker, C. I. *Rolls and Historical Sketch of the Tenth Regiment, So. Ca. Volunteers, in the Army of the Confederate States*. Charleston, SC: Walker, Evans, & Cogswell, 1881.

Walker, Henry J. "In Front of Atlanta." *National Tribune*, October 11, 1883.

"War Diary of Thaddeus H. Capron, 1861–1865." *Journal of the Illinois State Historical Society* 12 (1919–1920): 330–406.

War Letters of Aden G. Cavins Written to His Wife Matilda Livingston Cavins. Evansville, IN: Rosenthal-Kuebler, n.d.

Warner, Ezra J. *Generals in Gray: Lives of the Confederate Commanders.* Baton Rouge: Louisiana State University Press, 1959.

The War of the Rebellion: A Compilation of the Official Records of the Union and Confederate Armies. 70 vols. in 128 parts. Washington: Government Printing Office, 1880–1901.

Watkins, Sam R. *"Co. Aytch": A Side Show of the Big Show.* New York: Collier Books, 1962.

Waugh, John C. *Reelecting Lincoln: The Battle for the 1864 Presidency.* New York: Crown, 1997.

Welsh, Jack D. *Medical Histories of Confederate Generals.* Kent, OH: Kent State University Press, 1995.

———. *Medical Histories of Union Generals.* Kent, OH: Kent State University Press, 1996.

Whaley, Elizabeth J. *Forgotten Hero: General James B. McPherson, the Biography of a Civil War General.* New York: Exposition, 1955.

White, William Lee, and Charles Denny Runion, eds. *Great Things Are Expected of Us: The Letters of Colonel C. Irvine Walker, 10th South Carolina Infantry, C.S.A.* Knoxville: University of Tennessee Press, 2009.

"Who Recaptured the De Gress Battery in the Battle before Atlanta." *National Tribune,* June 28, 1883.

Wiesman, John T. "Field of Atlanta: Disgrace of a Monument to Gen. James B. McPherson." *National Tribune,* May 28, 1896.

Wiley, Bell Irvin, ed. *Confederate Letters of John W. Hagan.* Athens: University of Georgia Press, 1954.

Wiley, Kenneth, ed. *Norfolk Blues: The Civil War Diary of the Norfolk Light Artillery Blues.* Shippensburg, PA: Burd Street, 1997.

Williamson, David. *The Third Battalion Mississippi Infantry and the 45th Mississippi Regiment: A Civil War History.* Jefferson, NC: McFarland, 2004.

Wills, Charles W. *Army Life of an Illinois Soldier.* Washington: Globe Printing, 1906.

Winther, Oscar Osburn, ed. *With Sherman to the Sea: The Civil War Letters, Diaries, & Reminiscences of Theodore F. Upson.* New York: Kraus Reprint, 1969.

Wood, D. W. "The 20th Ohio at Atlanta." *National Tribune,* August 14, 1884.

Worsham, W. J. *The Old Nineteenth Tennessee Regiment, C.S.A.* Knoxville: Paragon Printing, 1902.

Wray, J. G. "Battle of Bald (or Leggett's) Hill, Atlanta, July 27, 1864." *Zanesville (OH) Daily Gazette.* April 6, 1912.

Wright, Charles. *A Corporal's Story: Experiences in the Ranks of Company C, 81st Ohio Vol. Infantry.* Philadelphia: James Beale, 1887.

Wright, Henry H. *A History of the Sixth Iowa Infantry.* Cedar Rapids, IA: Torch, 1923.

Wynne, Lewis N., and Robert A. Taylor, eds. *This War So Horrible: The Civil War Diary of Hiram Smith Williams*. Tuscaloosa: University of Alabama Press, 1993.

Yates, Thomas C. "Something Further as to the Death of McPherson." *National Tribune*, October 11, 1883.

Yeary, Mamie, comp. *Reminiscences of the Boys in Gray, 1861–1865*. Dallas: Smith-Lamar, 1912.

Young, L. D. *Reminiscences of a Soldier of the Orphan Brigade*. Louisville: Courier-Journal, n.d.

Bullock, Robert, 70
Burnes, Thomas H., 102
Burton, Josiah H., 47, 128, 165
Butler, William L., 147

Cadle, Cornelius, Jr., 134–135
Caldwell, John W., 76
Cameron, Daniel, 221, 225
Campbell, Robert J., 246
Cannon, J. P., 223
Carskaddon, David, 180
Carter, John C., 120, 129–130
Cassville, Battle of, 2
Castel, Albert, xvi, 134, 143, 171, 240,
    297–298, 302–304, 306, 344n38
Catton, Bruce, 240
Cavins, Aden G., 126, 163–164
Chamberlin, William H., 60, 72, 91,
    227, 299
Chancellorsville, Battle of, 68, 274–275,
    298–299
Chattahoochee River, 4, 6, 9–12, 14, 19,
    63, 250, 265, 309, 333n4
Cheatham, Benjamin F., 35, 51–52, 67,
    142–143, 171, 178, 187, 191, 224, 240,
    251, 269, 300–301, 310, 352n2
Chickamauga, Battle of, xiv, 291
Christie, Thomas D., 238
Churchill, Mendal, 83, 85–86, 281
civilians, 55–56, 64, 216, 224, 229, 233, 244,
    246–247
Civil Works Administration, 284
Cladek, John J., 208, 213–214
Clark, Carroll Henderson, 243–244
Clark, William T., 94, 107, 109, 128, 272
Clay, Green B., 32
Clayton, Augusta Smith, 224
Clayton, Henry D., 35, 157, 169, 171,
    182–183, 188, 190, 301
Clayton, Sarah, 224
Cleburne, Patrick R., 37, 40, 54, 68,
    78, 111–112, 124, 130–131, 140,
    192–193, 199, 234, 240, 246, 269,
    295, 297, 300
Clifton, William C., 149
Cobb, Howell, 250

Cobb, William, 65, 71
Cobb's Mill, 65, 67–68, 70, 81, 243
Cochran, J. O., 372n17
Cofer, Martin H., 76
Coleman, Robert F., 98, 102
Colquitt, J. W., 113
Coltart, John G., 144, 148–150, 162–164,
    166, 171, 187–188
Compton, Robert D., 102
Conard, Cornelius, 200
Confederate unit: 5th Infantry, 87, 98,
    102, 125–128, 205–206
Conyngham, David P., 254
Cooper, Edgar H., 48, 131
Cooper, Joseph A., 222
Cooper, Samuel, 19
Copenhill, 58, 60–63, 108, 141, 146, 162,
    169, 172, 174–176, 180, 188–189, 191,
    220–221, 274, 278–280, 306, 358n32,
    372n9
Corse, John M., 223, 272
Cowan, Henry H., 102
Cox, Aaron A., 128, 206
Cox, Jacob D., 17–18, 22, 25, 34, 48, 60,
    177, 216, 220–222, 225, 262
Crawford, Logan, 131
Crittenden, R. F., 129
Cross Keys, Georgia, 10, 16–17,
    21–22, 48
Crosswell, J. R., 123
Crowder, Lewis, 135
Cullen, William B., 102
Cumming, Alfred, 143
Cumming, Joseph B., 53, 79, 291
Cumming, Kate, 243
Curtiss, Frank S., 145

Dallas, Battle of, 4, 78
Daniel, Larry, 302
Davis, Jefferson, xi, 19–20, 22
Davis, Jefferson C., 28
Davis, Newton N., 147
Davis, Theodore R., 160, 179, 281, 294
Davis, William P., 121
Dawson, John M., 124
Dayton, Lewis M., 286

65, 78–81, 88, 92, 230, 234, 253, 269,
290–292, 300, 343n37, 344n38
Monument, 291–293
Wallace, John, 145, 153
Wangelin, Hugo, 105, 107, 109, 200–202,
206, 225, 263, 348n28
Warfield, E., 113
Warner, Willard, 57, 108, 220, 248
War of the Rebellion, 292
Warrick, Thomas, 252
Watkins, James W., 170
Watkins, Sam R., 195
Watkins, William M., 124
Wayne, Henry C., 169
Wehner, William, 281–282, 294, 372n18
Welker, Frederick, 273
Welles, George E., 101, 138, 201
Wells, Robert K., 169, 189
West Point and Montgomery
Railroad, 262
Wheeler, Horatio N., 176
Wheeler, Joseph, 10, 12, 29, 35–37, 40, 43,
51–52, 54, 65, 67, 209–212, 218–219,
228, 240, 262, 304
White, James L., 147, 150, 171
White, George W., 138
White House (Widow Pope House), 146,
149–150, 166, 279
Widow Akers, 68, 111
Widow Parker, 67–68
Widow Pope House (White House), 146,
149–150, 166, 279
Wiles, Greenberry F., 131, 138, 196, 201
Wilkinson, John C., 129
Willard, Lot S., 285
Williams, J. D., 129
Williams, John S., 10
Williams, Reuben, 139, 150, 161–162, 172,
187–188, 228, 281, 283

Williams, Robert, Jr., 145, 153
Williams, William S., 201
Williamson, James A., 175, 180, 182,
188–189
Wills, Charles W., 188
Wilson, Harrison, 205, 307
Wilson, James, 248
Wilson, John, 72
Wilson, John A., 123
Wilson, Thomas J., 235
Wilson's Creek, Battle of, 110, 271
Windsor, John S., 145, 185
Wisconsin units
2nd Infantry, 95
12th Infantry, 40, 44–45, 47–48, 131, 133,
137, 232
14th Infantry, 201, 203, 337n4
16th Infantry, 40, 43, 47, 131, 138, 198, 204
17th Infantry, 40, 138
25th Infantry, 208, 210, 212, 214, 216,
228, 237
Wood, Thomas J., 9, 28, 34–36
Woodruff, Ernest, 283
Woods, Charles R., 16–17, 30, 50, 58–59,
174–175, 180, 183–184, 188–189, 225,
241, 263–264, 267, 269
Woods, William B., 182, 189
Worden, Asa, 138, 337n4
Wright, Charles, 83, 178
Wright, Marcus J., 55
Wyman, Peter S., 156
Wysor, James Miller, 247

Yates, Thomas, 138
Yates, Thomas C., 102
Young, L. D., 70–71, 253
Young, Robert B., 127, 194, 202, 205–206,
229, 239